MAP OF THE

UNITED STATES

OF

AMERICA

NEW YORK.

PUBLISHED BY J.H. COLTON.

No. 86 Cedar St.

1850.

AmericanHeritage®
HISTORY OF THE
UNITED STATES

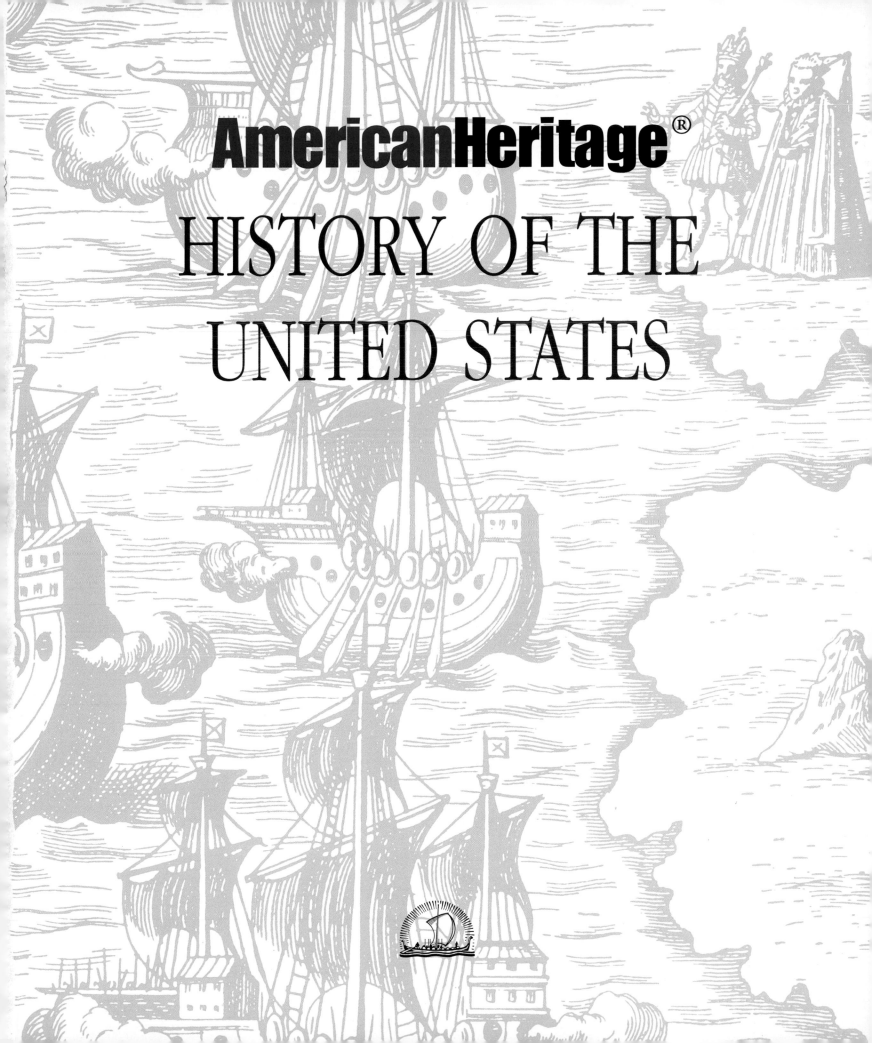

HISTORY
OF THE
UNITED
STATES

BY

DOUGLAS BRINKLEY

CAPTIONS BY JULIE M. FENSTER

VIKING

VIKING
Published by the Penguin Group
Penguin Putnam Inc., 375 Hudson Street,
New York, New York 10014, U.S.A.
Penguin Books Ltd, 27 Wrights Lane,
London W8 5TZ, England
Penguin Books Australia Ltd, Ringwood,
Victoria, Australia
Penguin Books Canada Ltd, 10 Alcorn Avenue,
Toronto, Ontario, Canada M4V 3B2
Penguin Books (N.Z.) Ltd, 182–190 Wairau Road,
Auckland 10, New Zealand
Penguin India, 210 Chiranjiv Tower,
43 Nehru Place, New Delhi, 11009 India

Penguin Books Ltd, Registered Offices:
Harmondsworth, Middlesex, England

First published in 1998 by Viking Penguin,
a member of Penguin Putnam Inc.

10 9 8 7 6 5 4 3 2 1

Copyright © 1998 Douglas Brinkley, American Heritage, a division of Forbes Inc.,
and Byron Preiss Visual Publications, Inc.

American Heritage is a registered trademark of Forbes Inc. Its use is pursuant
to a license agreement with Forbes Inc.

A Byron Preiss Book
Project Editor: Kathryn Huck
Design: Gilda Hannah
Picture Research: Valerie Cope, Katherine Miller, Karen Cissel
Line Editor: Ruth Ashby
Executive Editor: Michael Sagalyn
Computer Map Illustrations: Steven Jablonoski

LIBRARY OF CONGRESS CATALOGING IN PUBLICATION DATA
Brinkley, Douglas.
    American Heritage History of the United States / by Douglas Brinkley
    p.   cm.
    Includes bibliographical references and index.
    ISBN: 0-670-86966-X
    1. United States—History.I. Title.
    E178.B838   1998
    973—dc21   98-7337

This book is printed on acid-free paper.
∞
Printed in the United States of America
Set in ITC Garamond

For Steve and Moira Ambrose . . .
friends and mentors who have shown me the
beautiful backcountry of the American West and
the hidden hamlets of the Mississippi Delta.

Always the prairies, pastures, forests, vast cities, travelers, Kanada, the snows;
Always these compact lands tied at the hips with the belt
  stringing the huge oval lakes;
Always the West with strong native persons . . .
All sights, South, North, East—all deeds, promiscuously done at all times,
All characters, movements, growths . . .

—Walt Whitman, *Leaves of Grass*, 1891

CONTENTS

	Introduction	viii
CHAPTER 1	Setting the Stage	1
CHAPTER 2	The Emergence of England	25
CHAPTER 3	The Road to Independence	51
CHAPTER 4	A New Nation	79
CHAPTER 5	A More Perfect Union	103
CHAPTER 6	Growing Pains	127
CHAPTER 7	Cotton Versus Cloth	159
CHAPTER 8	The Split of the Union	183
CHAPTER 9	The Civil War	211
CHAPTER 10	Postbellum America	241
CHAPTER 11	The Rise of American Industry	263
CHAPTER 12	Beyond Manifest Destiny	293
CHAPTER 13	Imperialism and Reform	313
CHAPTER 14	The Great War	337
CHAPTER 15	The Jazz Age	365
CHAPTER 16	The Great Depression and the New Deal	395
CHAPTER 17	World War II	423
CHAPTER 18	The Cold War	463
CHAPTER 19	The New Frontier and the Great Society	497
CHAPTER 20	A Season of Discontent	531
CHAPTER 21	The Reagan Reformation	565
CHAPTER 22	The Millennial Nation	589
	Acknowledgments and Selected Bibliography	612
	Picture Credits	615
	Index	617

INTRODUCTION

Almost all of us have some dream power in our childhood but without encourage-
ment it leaves us and then we become bored and tired and ordinary. . . . We are
carefully coached in the most modern and efficient ways of making our bodies com-
fortable and we become so busy about getting ourselves all nicely placed that we are
apt to forget the dream spirit that is born in all of us. — Grant Wood (1921)

Since I was a boy growing up in Perrysburg, Ohio, a town of 8,000 named for Oliver Hazard Perry—the famous commodore who won the Battle of Lake Erie in the War of 1812, allowing the peaceful settlement of the Northwest Territory—the study of American history has been my passion. When I look back and try to understand how that infatuation sprang to life, a pattern of experiences appears. The earliest harks back to my elementary schoolteacher Ned Hoffman and his riveting stories about how our placid Maumee River community was part of the Black Swamp where in 1810 Amos Spafford, the first white settler in the area, had been forced to combat both horrendous lightning fires and deadly cholera.

Then, when I turned eight, a local boy made better than good: on July 20, 1969, astronaut Neil Armstrong of Wapakoneta, Ohio, became the first human being to set foot on the moon, disembarking from the *Eagle* landing module and proclaiming, "That's one small step for a man, one giant leap for mankind." At the time, the Vietnam War was a gruesome blur on the nightly news, but the *Apollo 11* moon mission was undaunted heroism of the first order. When the Neil Armstrong Air and Space Museum opened in 1972, I was one of the first in line to see the moon rock exhibit.

Soon I would enjoy a steady diet of high school field trips to such nearby sites as Thomas Edison's birthplace in Milan, Rutherford B. Hayes's Shady Grove estate in Fremont, and Sherwood Anderson's hometown of Clyde, which served as the model for my favorite book, *Winesburg, Ohio* (1919). The fact that only Virginia had produced more presidents than Ohio—eight to seven—contributed to my provincial pride. One summer at a Lucus County Fair gift stand I purchased a three-dollar portfolio containing framable sketches of the pantheon of Ohio-born presidents, Ulysses S. Grant being my favorite.

Occasionally our teachers would chaperone us across the state line to visit Johnny Appleseed's grave in Fort Wayne, Indiana, or Gerald Ford's hometown of Grand Rapids, Michigan. Without fail, these day trips filled me with a sense of the history that occurred in my own backyard. The War of 1812 had swirled around Perrysburg, where in 1813 General William Henry Harrison had built Fort Meigs and bravely held out against numerous British attacks through that spring and summer. The fort became known as the Gibraltar of the Northwest, and in 1840, when Harrison was running his log-cabin campaign for president, he revisited Fort Meigs. But the mother lode of all field trips was our annual school excursion to automotive pioneer

Henry Ford's Greenfield Village in Dearborn, Michigan, fifty miles away. In 1929 Ford had determined to create a unique museum where Americans could learn how their ancestors had lived and worked. The Village consists of more than eighty historical structures on an eighty-one-acre site. Most of the buildings were brought from other states and represent a variety of time periods. Some are the homes or workshops of famous thinkers and inventors such as Thomas Edison, Noah Webster, and George Washington Carver, but the majority had less famous residents. Although today, as a professional historian, I have to question the rationale behind moving a historical building from its original location to a theme park in Michigan, there is no denying that as a youth Greenfield Village excited me like no other place.

School was not the only source of my urge to become an American historian; there were also the family vacations during which my father, mother, sister, and I crisscrossed our nation in search of our past, present, and future. A blue Pontiac station wagon and a twenty-four-foot pale cream Coachman trailer became our "Buckeye Buggy," as we named it. We traditionally began planning our annual trip in late winter, and historical destinations such as Mt. Vernon or Hull-House were always part of the itinerary. There was something magical about deciding where our summer journey would take us—an overcast, cold winter evening became pregnant with the possibility of entering the very room where Robert E. Lee surrendered to Ulysses S. Grant at Appomattox Court House, Virginia, or of walking the very streets of Independence, Missouri, where the ghost of Harry Truman would be your companion. My father and I would sit at our kitchen table, a well-worn road atlas and a KOA Kampground guide open in front of us, and together plot our route in exact detail. He was Lewis and I was Clark as we made our careful preparations for that big July day when America's historical sites would open up before our very eyes.

Both of my parents were high school humanities teachers, so books and periodicals were everywhere in our home. Family favorites were the illustrated histories and magazines published by American Heritage, which blended the techniques of journalism with the discipline of history into works enjoyable either to read straight through or to browse at random. It was in Pulitzer Prize-winning historian Bruce Catton's *Civil War* volume that I first encountered the stark sepia daguerreotype photographs of Mathew Brady that had made of soldiers and saw the unfathomable squalor of Andersonville prison. These books had the same integrity of presentation that had become the hallmark of *American Heritage* magazine.

Given this teenage exposure to all things American Heritage, it came as a delightful shock when editor Richard Snow asked me in 1995 if I would write the history of the United States. My next reaction was hesitation: the notion of synthesizing 500 years of history into a single volume was almost too overwhelming to contemplate. But then I recalled what novelist Sinclair Lewis had said when he received the 1930 Nobel Prize for Literature: "Our American professors like their literature clear and cold and pure and very dead." Lewis had a point: it had seemed to me, too, that American history professors needed to make studying our nation's past more accessible—and less dreary. "Those concerned with popular education must realize that most people are not suscepti-

ble to any dry scholarship," historian James Thomas Flexner noted in *Random Harvest* (1998), a collection of gemlike essays. "However, a history book that is well written can reach and persuade a large audience."

It was the combination of how important American Heritage had been to me growing up and wanting to turn others on to our 500-year drama that persuaded me to write this Greenfield Village-like book. But saying yes and signing the contract were the easy parts. Obviously, the story of the United States is far too grand and sweeping to capture between two covers, or even a few hundred covers. In order to write American Heritage's first history of the United States I would thus have to make a choice of approach and many decisions about what to include and what would have to be excluded for space. It tormented me how much history would have to be left out.

Before a single word was written I had nightmares about receiving letters expressing disappointment: from the American Red Cross complaining that I never mentioned Clara Barton, from football fans denouncing me for leaving out the NFL, from urbane scholars scoffing that it's impossible to write about the Cold War without mentioning the Quemoy and Matsu crisis. But once I overcame those fears, writing this illustrated history—drawn largely from lecture notes I've used at the U.S. Naval Academy, Princeton University, Hofstra University, and the University of New Orleans—has been a rewarding challenge.

To appreciate *The American Heritage History of the United States* it is essential to understand that this book is *not,* and in no way pretends to be, a comprehensive history of our nation's origins and developments. As novelist Thomas Wolfe once noted, there are "a billion forms of America," and it's simply impossible to understand, much less explain, them all. It is, however, my intent to put U.S. economic and political history into a coherent perspective, less through a linear narrative than via a series of twenty-two essays divided as chapters. My main objective is to demonstrate that America's economic dynamism is the engine that drives our political, social, and civic lives—as Dutch historian and journalist Hendrick von Loon once observed, "The history of the world is the record of a man in quest of his daily bread and butter."

As an illustrated volume meant to pique the general reader's interest in U.S. history, this book is not aimed to please academic scholars or specialists. Instead, my approach draws from author Barbara Tuchman, who when asked what the role of the historian is replied: "To make it known." After all, the Library of Congress houses more than 30,000 volumes on the Civil War alone; my brief synthesis chapter here does not claim to add anything to the historiography on the subject. Rather, I hope this book supports Arthur Schlesinger, Jr.'s belief that history, by "putting crisis in perspective," supplies an antidote to "every generation's illusion that its own problems are uniquely oppressive."

The reader should be apprised of a few other considerations before starting this book. Given the space limitations, I was unable to properly address many significant issues, such as some points of Native American history. "Do you know who I am?" Sitting Bull asked a delegation of U.S. senators visiting the Standing Rock Sioux reservation in 1883. The answer, then as now, should be a resounding "yes"—but it is not adequately proclaimed in the narrative that follows. When Columbus landed in the New World in 1492 he found a highly developed society of approximately seventy-five million people speaking nearly 2,000 different languages. These indigenous people were hardly "backward"—they had built grand cities and monuments, developed sophisticated astronomical observatories, solar calendars, and healing medicines, and created exquisite works of art. Perhaps most important, these native inhabitants had what historian N. Scott Momaday has called "a spiritual comprehension of the universe." Instead of trying to squeeze in a few perfunctory paragraphs on the beauty and depth of Native American culture, I chose to focus on the Europeans' arrival in the New World, these adventurers' lust for riches, and the consequences of both. Readers looking for more about indigenous societies can find an in-depth examination in editor Alvin M. Josephy, Jr.'s *America in 1492: The World of the Indian Peoples Before the Arrival of Columbus* (1991), which offers accurate descriptions of what the Americas were like before the *Niña*, the *Pinta*, and the *Santa Maria*.

Finally, about the dust jacket. After careful consideration I selected Grant Wood's fantasy farmscape *Stone City*. Although most Americans know Wood—a native of Iowa—for his famous 1930 painting *American Gothic*, permanently housed at the Chicago Art Institute but regularly reproduced on everything from cornflake boxes to computer commercials, he was in fact a prolific student of the American Midwest. In his 1987 book *Grant Wood: A Study in American Art and Culture*, James M. Dennis provides a remarkable explication of *Stone City*—the bulbous trees, the modern bridge built over the Wapsipinicon River, the curlicuing roadways, descending sun, and toyland buildings in a churchless farm town. But whatever its technical merits and flaws, *Stone City*, a bucolic Midwestern dreamscape, triggers the history minded imagination in varied ways. Gazing at the painting makes me realize, for example, how different U.S. roads are from those in Europe. The highways of America ribbon into an endless horizon, where in Europe they typically end—or begin—in an enclosed communal space: a *piazza*, a *place*, an *agora*, a *forum*. The old adage that "All roads lead to Rome" applies in every great European capital; all roads converge upon the city. But the American pattern is different, as Manifest Destiny dictates—the grid disperses population centers outward, which is perhaps not surprising in a nation born of the pioneering frontier spirit.

And so Grant Wood's road still rolls on today, into the sleepy suburbs and their industrial parks, on into the abundant countryside, through Nebraska's wheat farms and Colorado's Rocky Mountains, to Promontory Point in Utah, where the transcontinental railroad's golden spike connected East to West, to the slot arcades of Reno and the domed capital in Sacramento, to Silicon Valley and on to the Hawaiian Islands, to our military bases in South Korea and throughout Western Europe. Wood's road did not begin in Iowa; it opened on the Atlantic coast when the first settlers hitched their wagons and started plowing westward. Now the American road spans the globe, and the vehicles of our progress keep driving on, forward toward the next horizon. It is my hope that this book will inspire the pioneers of tomorrow to take a moment from their rush onward to ponder the ways of our past, and to learn from them.

DOUGLAS BRINKLEY
New York City, August 20, 1998

CHAPTER 1

SETTING THE STAGE

"Your Highnesses have an Other World here, by which our holy faith can be so greatly advanced and from which such great wealth can be drawn." So wrote Christopher Columbus to the king and queen of Spain on October 18, 1498, after his third voyage across the ocean. Yet he didn't have any real idea of what he had found and what he had started—how could he have? Who could have imagined the vast lands that stretched thousands of miles beyond anything he had seen, the tens of millions of people living there, and the death and devastation he and his successors had already begun to bring upon them, and the future empires that would grow up on the lands they inhabited? Who, above all, could have imagined the new kind of civilization, the world's first experimental civilization, that centuries later would arise as the United States of America?

Columbus went to his grave in 1506 still boasting that he had discovered a new route to Asia; nonetheless, Columbus's tales of the strange lands he visited and the riches they held captivated Europeans, just as the tales of Marco Polo and the legendary explorer Prester John had captivated them centuries earlier. The human spirit had begun to stir in Western Europe in the late fif-

Englishmen plan an ocean voyage in this detail of the painting *The Cognoscenti* (Those who know), left, the work of an unknown Flemish artist, circa 1620. It is a portrait of the new science of exploration: the table holds an array of the latest in navigational instruments, nautical charts and maps, while the globe indicates that the men in the picture understood the world to be round. The nocturnal, above, was held up to the stars to determine time and latitude.

Henry VII sat for this portrait by artist Michael Sitium in 1505. He had seized the English crown in battle in August 1485, ending the Wars of the Roses, and Richard III's life, on a field called Bosworth. As king, Henry loved peace above all else, although money was a very close second. Henry VII encouraged commerce on every level and negotiated an agreement with Flanders that maintained the overseas market for English wool. Difficult and miserly he may have been, but he turned England's ambitions outward and prepared the country for a New World.

teenth century, and Europeans had begun to reach outward—down and around the coast of Africa, far to the distant East, and into the unknown Atlantic. After the long, dull stasis of the Dark and Middle Ages from the fifth through the fourteenth centuries, when religious philistinism held sway, and after the bubonic plague had wiped out nearly one-third the population of Europe between 1348 and 1350, people in every country, at every level of society, and in every realm of human endeavor were eager for change. This restlessness eventually spawned economic growth, a revival of the arts, and a passion for nation building. For a time, however, the mere suggestions of what later would be dubbed the commercial revolution, the Renaissance, and the Reformation disturbed Europe's intellectuals, divided the powerful Church, and agitated everyone from king to peasant with the threat of transforming the most basic ways life was lived. Many felt the winds of change, but few agreed as to their meaning. Some observers thought any change presaged the end of European civilization through invasions by groups such as the Turks, while others feared the growing anti-Church sentiments would lead to bloody conflicts that even the might of the pope could not quell.

Amid the confusion, a small handful of Europeans, particularly in port cities, saw more reason for hope than for fear. These early capitalists believed their continent's future depended on its commercial ties to other lands in every direction: Asia, Africa, and whatever lay beyond the known world. Such forward thinking was, however, a minority view. Most Europeans looked at the changing society as they had always regarded everything: as necessarily focused around the Mediterranean Sea that had been the center of Western civilization for all five thousand years of its existence.

At the time, it was hard to imagine political and social power developing anywhere else. After all, since the early medieval era eight centuries earlier, western Europe had been divided between the world's two mightiest entities—the nobility and the papacy—which had struggled for power with one another far more often than they had joined together against common foes. Victory usually had gone to Rome, but that began to change toward the end of the fifteenth century. The Church had been weakened by internal corruption and schisms, allowing kings across the Continent to seize power from local bishops and then to flout papal policies and directives. Throughout Europe, monarchs ruled over nation-states that were becoming ever more secular and their populations ever more worldly and less pious (not to mention ever more interested in the kingdoms on earth than in the promised one of heaven).

Nowhere was this transformation more apparent than in Britain, which had been ripped apart over the preceding two hundred years by court intrigues, troubles with Rome, a bloody Hundred Years' War with France, and a struggle for the throne between the houses of Lancaster and York known as the Wars of the Roses. It wasn't until 1485 that Britain's agony appeared to end with the coronation of Henry VII, who then spent ten years quashing coup attempts before Charles VIII of France gave him the support he needed to sustain his rule. At the time, the resulting rapprochement between Britain and France seemed the most important event of 1492.

After a period of political turmoil of its own, France was united and free

from foreign influence, which allowed Charles VIII to turn to his fondest project: the conquest of Italy, the epicenter of civilization since before the Christian era that had made Rome so dominant and, over the centuries, so domineering.

By the late fifteenth century, however, Italy comprised a patchwork of monarchies, republics, and factional papal states, none of which trusted any of the others. It was a disunion that seemed to augur well for the French and badly for the Italians. The particularly ineffectual papacy of Innocent VIII allowed the election of Rodrigo Borgia, who succeeded him in 1492 as Pope Alexander VI and devoted his reign to aggrandizing his notorious family, a decadent lot given to unsavory political machinations, sexual escapades, and the fairly indiscriminate use of poison rings. Italy, for so long the heart and soul of Europe, was insular, rudderless, and, as a consequence, threatened from all sides.

The greatest menace came from the East in the form of the Turks, who deemed the country a great prize. Sultan Bayezid II wanted to follow in the footsteps of his father, Mehmed II, who had conquered Constantinople and expanded the Ottoman Empire to the Balkans, Greece, and Bosnia—in the

Turks rush the gates of the city in the sixteenth-century painting by Jacopo Palma Giovane, *First Attack on Constantinople*, depicted above, which struck terror throughout Europe in 1453. With the expansion of the Ottoman Empire, the longstanding struggle between the Muslim and the Christian worlds seemed to balance on the fulcrum of the ancient capital. As the seat of the Orthodox Church, Constantinople (known today as Istanbul) had long been considered a European and thoroughly Christian city. However, Sultan Mehmed II, the Ottoman emperor, took the prize with the characteristic efficiency of his well-oiled war machine.

Hanseatic merchants ready their shipments for various branch officers in this fifteenth-century miniature painting. The Hanseatic League, as much a trade tradition as a formal agreement, bound cities in northern Europe from the 700s to the 1400s. In effect, it was something like a traffic code that allowed commerce to progress as smoothly as possible. Without mail service, overseas credit, or other tools of international trade, Hanseatic merchants routinely traveled with their wares over sea and sand and made their deals at dockside. The Hanseatic system worked: at a single fair in Bruges, Belgium, for example, shoppers could buy fruit from Spain, silk from Italy, olive oil from France, yew wood from Austria (for longbows), butter from Sweden, wax from Russia, cloth from Flanders, salt from Germany, and nearly anything else that Europe had to offer.

process cutting Western trade and other contacts with the Byzantine Empire that then dominated southeastern Europe. But Italy was eyed just as hungrily from the West by Spain's shrewd Kind Ferdinand II. Although in the mid-fifteenth century his nation was splintered by geography, religion, culture, and language—Catalan being spoken in the east and northeast, Castilian in the north and central regions, Arabic in the far south, and various Hebrew dialects across the entire Iberian Peninsula—the calculating king had plans. Ferdinand had assumed power in Aragon in 1479, but it was his strategic marriage to Queen Isabella of Castile, who had come to him for help, that united their two small nation-states into what would become Spain, a sovereign power strong enough to drive back incursions from Portugal, the Holy Roman Empire, and, in 1492, expel both the Moors (Muslims whose ancestors had invaded Spain in the eighth century) from Granada and the Jews from across the nascent nation.

That momentous year, 1492, thus marked any number of turning points for Europe. To observers of the time, it looked as though the future hinged on political maneuvers in northern Italy, from which either France or the Holy Roman Empire would likely emerge as the Continent's dominant power. Britain and Spain, both led by strong kings and graced with abundant access to the seas, seemed likely to prosper, but their distance from the supposed center of power made them unlikely to prevail. In 1492, Europe's heart remained in Rome, and its major arteries still wound along the Mediterranean Sea. Populations grew across western Europe, thus creating a need for trade routes over land as well as over the seas.

The economic boom in fifteenth-century Europe was paced by a sharp upturn in commerce growing out of the rise of population and migration. Local markets in more communities teemed with business and multiplied in both size and number. The most dramatic expansion occurred in the long crucial seaports where Europe made contact with the rest of the world, but cities throughout the Continent's interior also blossomed as overland trade was conducted over greater distances rarely traversed since the fall of the Roman Empire.

The inadequacy of fifteenth-century Europe's road systems quickly grew into a major problem as the volume of trade expanded along with the population. Most goods sent overland were toted by pack animals or in wheeled carts on rutted dirt paths. Aside from a few thoroughfares in Lombardy that were kept open year-round, most roads were unpaved, neglected, and impassable in poor weather. Even the marvelous road system that was perhaps the greatest legacy of the Roman Empire had fallen into near irretrievable disrepair during the Middle Ages, when most Europeans simply had no need of roads. During that timid era, the vast majority of people seldom ventured more than a few miles from the small hamlets in which they had been born, raised, and married, and where they lived and died, nestled among generations of their families and friends.

When the occasional need or longing for travel did arise, therefore, sea routes usually proved easier, faster, and a lot cheaper. For much of the fifteenth century, vessels from Genoa and Florence engaged in regular trade at ports throughout the Hanseatic League, a loose confederation of northern European cities principally along the coasts of the Baltic Sea. Although these sea routes covered longer distances, prices for shipping goods averaged less than one-fiftieth what land transport cost. In fact, the "round ships" used in Mediterranean trade, which could carry nearly eight hundred tons of cargo apiece, were not only faster but in most cases more reliable than the horse- and mule-drawn wagons and carriages that were their overland counterparts.

The round ships were also noticeably lucrative, so it wasn't long before the financial attractions of sea trading inspired technological innovations aimed at making it even more profitable. The fifteenth century witnessed great advances in shipbuilding techniques and the engineering of navigational equipment such as the compass and astrolabe, the precursor to the sextant. Accurate maps, called *portolani,* began to be produced in Spain and northern Italy and found their way across the Continent. These maps showed land forms, winds, currents, and tides, although not latitude nor longitude.

The high point of Marco Polo's trip to the Far East, which lasted almost a quarter century, was his meeting with Kublai Khan, the emperor of China, a scene re-created in the early fifteenth-century manuscript above. As Polo described the scene in the third person: "They [Polo and his companions] go off immediately to the chief palace where they find the great Khan with a very great company of barons. And they kneel before him with great reverence and humble themselves. . . . The great Khan makes them rise and stand upright on their feet and receives them with the greatest honor. . . ."

Ship captains, therefore, needed great skill in reading winds and tides if they hoped to sail out of sight of land for any length of time—not that many were so bold. Although men (and the occasional woman) of means could and did travel from place to place across Europe to study, conduct business, or pursue various pilgrimages, voyages beyond the Continent were rare.

But boundaries vex the human spirit, and, before long, visionaries and adventurers began looking for ways to broaden the world. These bold mariners ignored the daunting risks and opened the way to the forging not only of new nations but of a new civilization based on interdependence among states in every portion of the globe. It is little wonder that explorers' stories of discovery remain so enticing across the centuries.

In fact, it was the tales brought back from faraway lands by the first few individuals brave enough to have made the journeys that helped fuel the passion for unknown realms. Various popes, of course, had been sending emissaries to the Far East for hundreds of years; in the thirteenth century, one John of Plano Carpini had been dispatched to Asia as papal representative to the Mongol court of Genghis Khan at Karakorum in Central Asia and returned to write and speak widely of his experiences and discoveries. Another envoy sent by Louis IX of France, William de Rubruquis, traveled to the northwestern Himalayas, to Karakorum, and to other Eastern cities, then fascinated scholars with his writings on the Orient. But history depends as much upon who reads it as who writes it, and it was Marco Polo who best knew his audience and how to play to their interests.

Polo and some of his family had left Constantinople for China in 1260, and eleven years later he embarked on his monumental overland journey through Asia. It was not until 1298, while in a Genoese prison after being captured in a sea battle, that Polo dictated his epochal *Book of Ser Marco Polo, the Venetian, Concerning the Kingdoms and Marvels of the East*. Like Plano Carpini and William de Rubruquis, Polo wrote of the highly sophisticated societies he had encountered in the Orient, but, unlike them, he did not write for scholars. At a time when commerce was growing exponentially in both volume and importance, Marco Polo found a much larger readership among the trading classes, who took a hearty self-interest in his descriptions of "valuable and odorous woods, the gold and gems, and all manner of spices—pepper white as snow, and also the black kind, in great quantities." In fact, Polo took pains to point out just how vast an opportunity for trade China represented, a notion that had immense appeal for the small European merchant class who had been frustrated for years by the Continent's interminable political conflicts.

Suddenly a new world beckoned, and a commercially promising one at that. Why stop there? For several centuries Europeans had been hearing tales of Prester John, a Catholic priest who supposedly had once held dominion over a vast and rich land "to the East." Both William de Rubruquis and Marco Polo wrote of the mysterious kingdom, the latter making several references to its "storehouses of wealth." At first, it was thought that Prester John's realm must have been in Asia, but by the mid-fifteenth century most Europeans who took an interest in the matter believed this precursor of El Dorado had been located somewhere on the east coast of Africa.

Both opinions proved right, if not in the details. Asia and Africa each had a great deal to offer Europe, and contacts among the three continents had grown steadily during the preceding hundred years. By the beginning of the fifteenth century, European merchants were routinely sending ships to ports on the Mediterranean's eastern rim, where caravans were organized to traverse Asia Minor with cargoes destined for trading centers in India and China. These overland journeys were costly, but their rewards were potentially far greater. At a time when necessities such as rye, wheat, and barley sold for less than four Prussian marks a ton, and salt for six and olives for thirty, the rare Eastern spice saffron garnered more than 3,000 marks a ton, and the less exotic ginger 500. Even lowly pepper, a leading trade commodity, commanded considerably more than 300 marks a ton. These exorbitant prices resulted from the simple law of supply and demand, in this case the latter coming from wealthy Europeans who deemed Eastern condiments not only delicious but indicative of the social status of those who could afford them. As a consequence, trade grew more lucrative than ever: if an Italian merchant dispatched ten ships to the East and only one returned, his net profits could still exceed 5,000 percent.

At first, Italy's city-states enjoyed the lion's share of this remunerative Mediterranean trade. Before long, however, both Italy and Mediterranean commerce had fallen into decline. The friendly relations and active commerce Venice and Florence had maintained with the Byzantine Empire came to naught when the Ottoman Turks destroyed the empire in 1453. Pope Nicholas V called for a crusade to drive the invaders from Constantinople, but Rome's previously invincible military forces failed, as did a subsequent attempt to convert the Turks to Christianity. These events precipitated the falloff in Mediterranean commerce—and a consequent rise in the prices of Eastern goods, which made transporting them all the more profitable. The resulting vigorous interest in trade demanded that new routes and methods be found for obtaining products from the East.

Nicholas's failure to take Constantinople tolled the death knell for the Catholic Church's dominance in European affairs. After this proof of papal fallibility, Italy's city-states petered out, and the Continent's economic center began to shift from the Mediterranean to the eastern Atlantic, where nations favored with coasts to the north and west continued to gain commercial—and thus political—significance. A new age was dawning, even if it was apparently evident to only a few forward thinkers in an obscure corner of Europe.

Prince Henry the Navigator, shown below in an undated engraving, a younger son of King John of Portugal, had no real chance at becoming king. Nonetheless, in the early fifteenth century he was his country's most vigorous leader, demonstrating that sea power in the new age would be based not on how many ships a nation had but rather on how far they could sail. Henrique, as he is known more simply in Portugal, was not a navigator at all, except of court politics. He is credited with establishing a nautical library and map-making studio at his base in the village of Sagres (on the southwest tip of Portugal now known as Cape Saint Vincent) and also with pioneering the caravel ship. By the time of Henry's death in 1460, tiny Portugal was sending ships far longer distances than any other country.

Opening to the East

A small, poor seafaring nation that so far had not figured much in European affairs, Portugal was destined to assume importance, if briefly, by dint of its fortunate location on the southeastern edge of the Continent on the Iberian Peninsula between Spain and the Atlantic Ocean and just northwest of the Strait of Gibraltar, the narrowest gap separating Europe and Africa. What's more, while Britain and the Holy Roman Empire had occupied themselves with fighting over Italy and various lingering animosities, Portugal had remained at a distance that allowed for taking advantage of new opportunities, which a succession of strong leaders fully intended to do. A young nation in spirit as well as in fact, Portugal had not united into a sovereign state until the thirteenth century and did not become a European power until the late fourteenth century, when its King John I drove out the Castilians and formed an alliance with Britain against further Spanish meddling. Acknowledging defeat in 1411, Castile signed a peace treaty with King John that allowed the Portuguese monarch to concentrate on the seas. His successors Edward and Alfonso followed suit throughout the fifteenth century, slowly but surely adding to Portugal's financial, and thus political, power. But it was King John's third son and Kind Edward's younger brother, Prince Henry, who put Portugal on top of the map of Europe.

Henry the Navigator, as he came to be called, was a man of eclectic interests. As a devout Christian, he had striven to drive the Moors from Europe and then to hound them across North Africa. As a scion of the Portuguese royal family, he worked to advance the causes of his nation and its monarchy. As a would-be Renaissance man, he pursued knowledge for its own sake. As a shrewd businessman, he encouraged promising new trade efforts. And as a believer in a horoscope that forecast greatness for both himself and his country, Henry went out of his way to prove the prophecy true.

His father, King John, had read Marco Polo's book and had been captivated by the tales of Prester John. As a result, the king ordered the siege and capture of Ceuta, an important Moroccan port he intended to be Portugal's first step toward the East and its abundant wealth. So, in 1415, the twenty-one-year-old Prince Henry obeyed his father and took part in the conquest of Ceuta, where he was then ordered to remain as governor—and explorer. While taking stock of the region, Henry met scholars and traders from all over North Africa, which fueled a fascination with African affairs that soon eclipsed his interest in European matters. He dreamed of Portuguese ships sailing down the west coast of Africa to the kingdom of Prester John and of an alliance with fellow Christians to encircle the Muslim lands to the north and thereby win a continent for Portugal and the Church. Naturally, the enormous wealth to be gained from such an enterprise did not escape the prince's notice.

At first Henry found it hard to persuade Portuguese sailors to embark on the African voyages; in fact, it wasn't until 1434 that one Gil Eanes reached Cape Bojador in northwest Africa, the farthest south any European had ever traveled. Eanes found no gold and little worth trading for, but not everyone was deterred by his report. In 1441, Antão Gonçalves and Nuno Tristão captured twelve Africans from the Cape Bojador area, bound them in slavery, and brought them back to Portugal, thus beginning one of the most shameful episodes in the history of civilization: the African slave trade.

Sadly, money has often vanquished morality in human history, and the voyages went on, allowing Portugal to establish a string of trading posts along Africa's northwest coast from which to import gold, spices, and slaves.

The mid-sixteenth-century watercolor by Lizuarte de Abreu, above, depicts a fleet of Portuguese caravels. In the aftermath of Columbus's discovery, Spain forbade any other country from sailing westward, and even received a papal decree granting it sole possession of the Western Hemisphere (with the exception of the southern part of Brazil). The Portuguese looked southward to the route Prince Henry had been pointing to all his life. Thanks to Spain's barricade of the west, Portuguese ships like the ones in the picture discovered what Columbus's little fleet could not have: a sea route to the Far East.

Explorer Vasco da Gama, well rewarded for pioneering the sea route from Europe to India, is shown in an illustration from a seventeenth-century manuscript decked out in finery after he was made viceroy of India by the king of Portugal. Da Gama's journey around Africa in 1497 was not merely a matter of following the coast. In charting a course still admired (and used) by mariners, da Gama somehow calculated that in order to pass the Cape of Good Hope at the southern end of Africa, he would have to catch easterly trade winds by sailing more than a thousand miles west of Africa into the South Atlantic. As he predicted, he caught the wind that took his fleet into the Indian Ocean.

When Henry the Navigator died in 1460, others took up his work, pushing farther south and initiating trade with more and more African nations, all with the blessing of Portugal's succeeding monarchs. Then, in 1482, Diogo Cam discovered the Congo River, which he believed to be a sea route to the Indies—the fount of so many legends of gold and dreams of riches—loosely defined as China, Japan, the Spice Islands, and everything else between Thailand and India. If he was proved right and Portugal managed to gain control of the Congo, Cam knew that his nation could well become economic master not just of Europe but of the world.

Portugal designed a three-pronged drive to the East and executed it throughout the next decade. As Diogo Cam set sail up the Congo, King John II sent explorers across the Mediterranean and south along the African coast, all in search of the treasures of the Orient. In 1493, an expedition returning from India's Malabar Coast reached the eastern coast of Africa, where the wealth of the Ethiopian court dazzled the Portuguese visitors: here indeed was the fabled land of Prester John, even if he did turn out to be an Abyssinian chieftain.

It didn't matter. An expedition headed by Bartolomeu Dias reached the Cape of Good Hope in 1488 and sent word back to Lisbon that Portugal had discovered a new passage to the Indies. King John was not all that impressed; he remained convinced that the best current routes lay through the Mediterranean and that the most promising one for the future would be found in crossing the Congo. When King Manuel I took the throne in 1495, however, he turned to Dias's achievement to fulfill his hope of establishing relations with the nations of the Orient. In 1497, the new king launched an expedition south to the Indies headed by his newly minted ambassador Vasco da Gama, who was charged with formulating Portugal's "Oriental policy."

Da Gama's four small ships rounded the cape and then sailed north, hugging the coast to visit the ports and city-states along the way. In the process, the Portuguese captain encountered a number of African, Indian, and Muslim vessels, and in 1498 he picked up a Gujarati sailor sufficiently familiar with the Indian Ocean and Arabian Sea to lead him on to the seaport of Calicut in southwestern India. Da Gama sailed back to Lisbon after a stay of three months in ships laden with gems and rare spices. The voyage had been an unqualified success: da Gama's exploits not only opened a new route to the Indies but put Portugal at the forefront of commerce between Europe and Africa. In fact, when talk of a "new world" arose in European capitals toward the end of the fifteenth century, the phrase referred not to the Americas but to Africa, which looked more commercially promising. Unfortunately, the Portuguese also imported African Muslim prisoners of war back to the Iberian Peninsula; the custom of black slavery had started to grow in Europe.

Opening to the West

The lure of Africa's rich trading opportunities might well have satisfied the expansionist interests of the rest of Europe had it not been for other explorers who were as daring and ambitious as da Gama, yet devoted to different directions. Had Christopher Columbus not forayed westward, for example, it is conceivable that Spain and then France, Britain, and the Netherlands would have sent their ships south instead, in search of new lands to trade with and perhaps colonize. The scarcity of harbors on Africa's west coast presented some difficulties in establishing settlements there, but the rewards looked to be substantial. Africa was wealthier in gold than the Americas and it was far more familiar. Thus, the first European transatlantic crossings take on added significance. Coming when they did, Columbus's voyages helped turn at least some of Europe's attention away from Africa and toward the New World.

Although every American schoolchild may know that in 1492 Christopher Columbus sailed the ocean blue, details about the explorer's life remain spotty. A few facts are reasonably certain: he was an experienced sea captain who had been born in Genoa around 1451. By 1476 he was in Lisbon, whence he sailed down the African coast as far south as Guinea. He visited Iceland in 1477, when he likely heard tales of early Viking forays to the West, such as the one that led Leif Eriksson to what Eriksson called Vinland, which may have been part of North America. Columbus also probably heard the stories the British had told for centuries about St. Brendan's Land, which supposedly had been settled by Irish monks in the sixth century.

Still, the great question remained: Just how far west were these lands? Columbus sought counsel from two sources. One was the scientist and theologian Cardinal d'Ailly, who believed that the earth was round, that its land mass exceeded the volume of its oceans, and that the sea to the west was relatively small. The other source was the Florentine astronomer and cartographer Paolo dal Pozzo Toscanelli, who believed the Indies were just a short distance from Europe and with whom Columbus corresponded throughout the late 1470s. It proved not to matter that both were pretty much wrong.

In any case, once again commercial concerns determined the course of history. Recognizing that his Italian homeland had neither the interest nor the resources to undertake major expeditions into the unknown, in 1484 Columbus approached Portugal's King John II about funding a voyage all the way

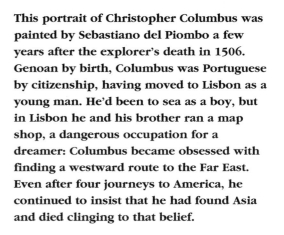

This portrait of Christopher Columbus was painted by Sebastiano del Piombo a few years after the explorer's death in 1506. Genoan by birth, Columbus was Portuguese by citizenship, having moved to Lisbon as a young man. He'd been to sea as a boy, but in Lisbon he and his brother ran a map shop, a dangerous occupation for a dreamer: Columbus became obsessed with finding a westward route to the Far East. Even after four journeys to America, he continued to insist that he had found Asia and died clinging to that belief.

west. The king, however, was both preoccupied with internal affairs and convinced that the East had more to offer than anything to be found in the West. Undaunted, Columbus immediately set out for Spain when he heard that Queen Isabella, envious of Portuguese trade, wanted to gain a foothold in Asia for her nation.

At the time, most Spaniards seemed more concerned with ejecting the Moors than with exploring unknown territories, but their queen nevertheless proved willing to support an expedition. She and Columbus forged an agreement whereby he was named admiral and was granted the right to invest one-eighth of any profits gained—with Isabella putting up one-fourth and the rest coming from Italian bankers. Queen Isabella also provided Columbus with three ships: the 60-ton *Niña,* the 55-ton *Pinta,* and the 120-ton *Santa Maria.* Today, many yachts larger than the *Niña* can be found docked in marinas on the Great Lakes, not to mention off the coasts—and not one owner would be so foolhardy as to take such a little boat beyond sight of land.

In consideration of the danger, in addition to giving him a percentage of any profits resulting from the voyage, Isabella also stipulated that Columbus receive the right to govern any islands or mainlands he might discover. Al-

The map below was drawn according to the writings of the Alexandrian astronomer Claudius Ptolemy, who lived in the second century A.D. Ptolemy's book *Geography* assembled all that was known about the world's features and peoples, and described how to draw a round world on a flat piece of paper. Ptolemy's methodology impressed even Leonardo da Vinci, who dismissed the work of most other scientists as sloppy. Christopher Columbus was also deeply influenced by *Geography* and the promise it held that, as he scrawled in the margin of his own edition, every ocean can be navigated.

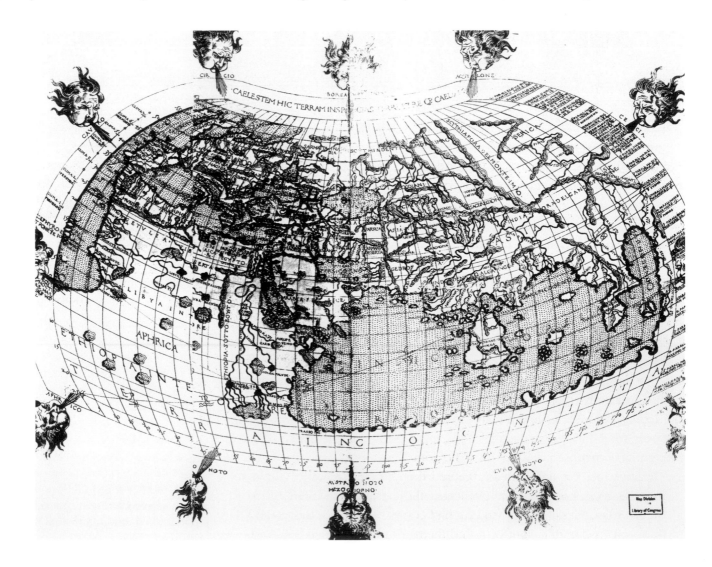

though the expedition was ostensibly undertaken in the name of trade on the supposition that a clear route to the commerce-rich Indies lay to the west, the provision regarding discoveries has led some historians to conclude that Columbus may have believed the legends of a spectacularly wealthy land somewhere west of the known world.

On August 3, 1492, Christopher Columbus and his crew of eighty-seven pushed off from Palos, Spain, in their three ships and headed for the Canary Islands, where they picked up the trade winds and started sailing west. It wasn't exactly a smooth journey. Along the way, Columbus felt obliged to doctor his captain's logs and to lie to his men about the distances they had traversed, hoping to keep them focused fearlessly on their goal. After all, most of the sailors were relatively uneducated, still convinced that the Earth was flat and that at some point they would simply fall off the end of it. As Columbus wrote on October 10, 1492, as reported in his journal of the first voyage:

> Here, the people could stand it no longer and complained of the long voyage; but the Admiral cheered them as best he could, holding out good hope of the advantages they would have. He added that it was useless to complain, he had come to [find] the Indies, and so had to continue it until he found them, with the help of Our Lord.

Edward Moran's 1892 painting *Debarcation of Columbus* shows the explorer and his crew loading onto a smaller boat in anticipation of setting foot on the newly discovered land. This moment occurred early in the morning of October 12, 1492, and the sight of the European sailors so scared the Native Americans on the island that they went into temporary hiding.

This undated woodcut celebrates the reign of Ferdinand and Isabella, the Spanish monarchs who made Columbus's voyages possible.

Two days later, on the morning of October 12, Columbus sighted the Bahamas and landed on Watling Island, which he named San Salvador. From there he sailed on to Cuba and then to Haiti, trading with the natives on each and even persuading some to take the voyage back to Europe with him. (Because he thought he had landed in the Indies, he called the native inhabitants Indians.) When Columbus returned to Spain in March 1493, his ships' logs, many of them falsified, created a wave of public interest. Queen Isabella learned of her explorer's exploits within a few weeks, even if the accounts were far from the truth. The admiral claimed to have reached China and Japan and to have found great wealth in them. Although he was clearly not only exaggerating but lying outright, people ate up his stories.

The Spaniards set about legalizing their claims in short order through negotiations with Portugal and Rome, and by May, Pope Alexander VI had granted Spain possession of all lands to the south and west not held by other Christians as of Christmas Day, 1492. Two years later Portugal accepted the Treaty of Tordesillas, a modified version of the papal contract under which a line of demarcation was set at the meridian 370 leagues west of the Cape Verde Islands. East of this meridian all discoveries belonged to Portugal; west of it, all discoveries belonged to Spain. In effect, this meant that Spain was granted the Americas while Portugal got all of Africa plus the tip of Brazil—which at the time looked like the better part of the bargain. Of course, this contract embraced only the Iberian parties interested; Britain and the Netherlands had yet to be heard from.

The Spanish Main

After Columbus's voyages, wealth from the New World began pouring into Spain. Throughout the early sixteenth century, more expeditions were launched and settlements established on the eastern coasts of Central America and South America, from whose natives gold was seized and sent back to Spain. The new breed of adventurers who led these expeditions came to be called conquistadores, soldiers of fortune to whom exploration and settlement came second to the quest for gold. During the next century, the Spanish conquistadores would plunder both Central America and South America and make incursions into North America in pursuit of the precious yellow metal and any other riches they could find.

Of course, some significant discoveries were made by explorers from countries other than Spain. The Italian navigator Amerigo Vespucci, for example, journeyed to the mouth of the Amazon in 1499 and later proved that South America was not part of Asia—for which he earned the considerable distinction of having the Americas named after him. Vespucci expressed his appreciation of what he had found in a 1503 letter to Lorenzo de' Medici:

> Those new regions [America] which we found and explored with the fleet . . . we may rightly call a New World . . . a continent more densely peopled and abounding in animals than our Europe or Asia or Africa; and, in addition, a climate milder than in any other region known to us.

Meanwhile, however, religious conflicts were wracking most of Europe. In 1517, the professor of divinity Martin Luther nailed his ninety-five theses to the door of the court church in Wittenberg, Germany, sparking questions about Church dogma that shook the very foundations of Christendom—including ways that would have important implications for the New World. None of this philosophical turmoil concerned the conquistadores, however, who went on exploring and plundering the strange lands they fanned out to from stations in the West Indies.

In 1513, Vasco Núñez de Balboa crossed the Isthmus of Panama and discovered the Pacific Ocean, committing atrocities upon many of the native populations he met along the way. Simultaneously, Juan Ponce de León sailed north to Florida, where he made the first Spanish landing in North America. That same decade Diego Velazquez completed Spain's conquest of Cuba, while still other Spaniards landed on the west coast of Central America. Some ventured north up both sides of the new continent. One expedition got as far as Virginia before returning to the Indies. These northward excursions likely would have progressed farther and farther had it not been for what Hernando Cortés discovered in Mexico in 1519: vast stores of gold, which he and his men seized by overrunning the Aztec Empire of Montezuma. One Indian observer of Cortés's first meeting with Montezuma's ambassadors reported that upon receiving the envoy's official gifts, "the Spaniards . . . picked up the gold and fingered it like monkeys. . . . Their bodies swelled with greed."

When Cortés arrived in Mexico, the Aztecs numbered some 5 million, many living in established cities of more than 100,000 people; in fact, an estimated 250,000 inhabited the capital of Tenochtitlán, making it twice the size of any European city of the time. These densely packed populations were supported by sophisticated drainage, irrigation, and canal systems. The European invaders were stupefied by the Aztecs' advanced architecture, science, and art. Because some of the structures resembled the pyramids of Egypt, the Spaniards concluded that the Mexican natives must have descended from Egyptians who had journeyed to the Americas centuries earlier. Whether this was in fact the case remains unknown.

Most surprising to Cortés was that the Aztecs seemed not at all shocked and in fact somewhat pleased to see him. This grew out of the culture's legend of the great bearded god Quetzalcoatl, whom they held to be one of the founders of civilization. According to Aztec belief, Quetzalcoatl had left Mexico. He did, however, promise to come back, and he prophesied that major events would occur upon his return. As a consequence, the Aztecs looked upon their Spanish visitors, with their superior weaponry and their utterly alien but magnificently useful horses, as minor deities, and at Cortés as Quetzalcoatl himself. It wasn't long before the conquistador, a shrewd diplomat and an astute judge of character, found a way to turn these beliefs to Spain's financial advantage, imprisoning Montezuma in his own capital and seizing gold and other valuables from the empire on the grounds that he himself was, after all, a god and thus entitled to take whatever he wanted. As Cortés wrote on July 10, 1519, in one of his first dispatches from Mexico to Spain's royal family:

Martin Luther is shown above at the age of fifty in a painting by Lucas Cranach the Elder, 1533. His deeply personal quarrel with the Catholic Church spread through Europe in the 1520s. Many people were no doubt drawn to Reformation views on salvation and other religious matters. However, Luther's break with the papacy and its powerful church also appealed to the nationalistic spirit of the sixteenth century, which encouraged countries as well as individuals to think for themselves.

yeqtla ti tetzavitl yn mal ques.

This Aztec illustration from the 1540s depicts the fighting on the steps of the Aztec temple (Teocalli) in Mexico City in 1520. As Cortés himself described the scene in a letter to the Spanish king, "Those [Aztecs] who remained on the terrace fought so valiantly, that we were more than three hours in completely dispatching them: and not one escaped. Your Sacred Majesty may believe that we captured this tower only because God had clipped their wings: because twenty of them were sufficient to resist the ascent of a thousand men."

It seems most credible that our Lord God had purposefully allowed these lands to be discovered . . . so that Your Majesties may be fruitful and deserving in His sight by causing these barbaric tribes to be enlightened and brought to the faith by Your hand.

In addition to destroying the brilliant Aztec civilization, Cortés's conquests in Mexico affected the course of world history by making an enormous economic impact on all of Europe. His expeditions turned Spain into the wealthiest nation on the Continent, which enabled its monarchs to finance the religious crusades of their choice. The success of Cortés's exploits also ensured that Spain's efforts in the New World would remain centered on the search for precious metals rather than on settlements; for the same reason, the Spanish forgot about the quest for a westward passage to the Orient. In other words, Spain opted to concentrate on Central America and South America, leaving both North America and the Orient to mariners from other European countries such as Britain, France, Portugal, and the Netherlands.

When Cortés returned to Spain to report his findings in North America to Charles V, among his recommendations was that a route to India be created by digging a canal across the Isthmus of Panama. The king considered the idea but finally rejected it by quoting Jesus in the Bible: "What God hath joined together let no man put asunder."

Before giving up entirely on North America, however, the Spaniards made a few more significant incursions. One began when the governor of Cuba sent Pánfilo de Narváez to Mexico to arrest Cortés for disobeying papal orders. Instead, Narváez was captured and imprisoned by Cortés's forces. Still, it turned out well for him: While in jail Narváez concocted the idea of conquering the northern part of the Aztec Empire just as Cortés had taken the east and south—and then he had an even more ambitious notion that he got to work on as soon as he was released and could return to Spain, where he obtained a patent for exploration and colonization. Thus armed, in 1528 Narváez landed in Florida and began his quest for the fabled city of Apalache, which legend held to be a fount of gold and riches. Plagued by disease, bad weather, and a shipwreck off the coast of Texas, Narváez pressed on as far west as the Gulf of California. In the end, nearly all his party were lost; only four men returned to Mexico in 1536, although those four were full of stories of vast prairies, gold-bedecked Indians, and cities brimming with wealth.

Before long, these tales reached Hernando de Soto, one of the toughest and most experienced of the Spanish conquistadores. Like Narváez, as soon as he obtained a patent to establish a colony in Florida, he organized an expedition, which arrived at Tampa Bay in 1539. De Soto eventually pressed north through the Carolinas to the Mississippi River in what is now Tennessee; his party also crossed into Arkansas and Oklahoma, then continued its journey by boat up the Arkansas River. De Soto died in 1542, but the expedition went on, with a few remnants of the original crew making it back to Mexico the following year.

Financial motives inspired another quest that resulted in further exploration of North America when Francisco de Coronado, governor of the Spanish province of New Galicia, set out in search of the mythical land of Cibola and its supposed seven cities of gold. Coronado and a party of 370 left Northwest Mexico in 1540 and headed into

Theodore de Bry's engraving illustrates the holocaust perpetrated by Spanish colonizers on a West Indian village that rejected Christianity. De Bry's artwork illustrated *America,* a series of eyewitness accounts of the New World he started publishing in 1590. One of the first, *A Very Short Report on the Devastation of the Indies,* had been written by a humanistic cleric named Bartolomé de Las Casas about twenty-five years after Columbus's discovery. De Las Casas had tried in vain to stop the cruelties that were common in the Spanish colonies; this picture is based on one of his descriptions. Later volumes in the series showed more pleasant, pastoral scenes of indigenous peoples, especially on the American mainland, but the engravings of Spanish atrocities riled Protestant reformers, who blamed the conquistadores' inhumanity on dogmatic Roman Catholic teachings about heathens.

In October 1992, when the United States celebrated the quincentennial of Christopher Columbus's first journey to the New World, a controversy erupted over whether the famed explorer should be honored for having "discovered" America or be denounced as a brutal conqueror whose exploits exterminated millions of native people. Approximately seventy-five million native Indians lived in the Americas in 1492. These Native Americans were divided among more than 300 distinct cultures and spoke more than 200 different languages. Although scholarly opinions about Columbus ran the entire critical gamut by 1992, one clear fact emerged: he was no longer a golden hero. As historian Howard Zinn noted, even Columbus's biggest booster, Samuel Eliot Morison, admitted in his 1942 Pulitzer Prize–winning biography, *Admiral of the Ocean Sea: A Life of Christopher Columbus,* "The cruel policy initiated by Columbus and pursued by his successors resulted in complete genocide."

Consensus was also reached on at least one other point: no matter the moral considerations, the primary objective of Columbus's journeys had been the acquisition of gold. As Columbus himself had written in his journal, "As soon as I arrived in the Indies, on the first island which I found, I took some of the natives by force in order that they might give me information of whatever there is in these parts"—that "whatever" being gold. His mission was to look for riches to bring back to Europe, and it was this economic impulse that led to the settling of the New World. The Sioux leader Sitting Bull summarized the exploits of Columbus and other European explorers—Cortés

in Mexico, Pizarro in Peru, and the English in Virginia—when he noted that "the love of possessions is a disease among them."

Beginning in 1492, therefore, two totally different but equally sophisticated and complex societies collided in the New World, each with its own distinct culture, heritage, and view of God. Unfortunately, the natives gained only misery from the exchange: While they taught the Europeans to grow corn and potatoes, the Indians were introduced to smallpox, measles, and other diseases against which they had no immunity—and which, combined with the Europeans' zeal for acquisition and superior military might, spelled disaster for the indigenous populations. "Native populations were massacred; Indian cities and towns destroyed and abandoned to the elements; religious structures defiled and looted; political and spiritual leaders slain; confederacies, chiefdoms, and other societies ripped apart; and disoriented, leaderless survivors enslaved or forced to flee and move in with other groups—or revert, as many of them did, to more primitive levels of existence, hunting or foraging again for wild foods in the wake of the collapse of their world," wrote historian Alvin M. Josephy, Jr., in *The Native Americans: An Illustrated History* (1993). As Josephy stated, some demographers estimate that by the seventeenth century more than fifty million indigenous people in North and South America had perished as a result of war, disease, and enslavement in what he deemed "history's greatest holocaust by far." The most virulent killer, spread by direct human contact, was smallpox, previously unknown among Native Americans. Its impact

was staggering: when Columbus landed on Hispaniola in 1492, more than three million people resided there; fifty years later only 500 natives remained. Even in the north, where smaller Indian populations encountered only a few European explorers, traders, and fishermen, diseases ravaged the countryside. "The final chapters of the story have yet to be written," Native American historian Vine Deloria, Jr., warned during the Columbus quincentennial. "Old prophecies relate that the white man will surely come to dominate the continent, but that his time in the sun will be the shortest of all the people who will dwell here. He has not, as yet, come to grips with the land on which he lives."

The map at right locates the more prominent tribes which inhabited North America before the advent of European settlement. Adapting to varied conditions across the continent, the Native Americans developed remarkable, highly independent cultures, from the Five Nations of Iroquois, who originated a democratic style of government, to the Apache tribe, who had no formal sense of citizenship and instead stressed individualism. It is estimated that in 1492, about 1.5 million Native Americans occupied what is now the United States—but no single tribe had more than about 15,000 people.

TRIBES
of
NORTH AMERICA

0   200   400   600

William Henry Powell painted *The Discovery of the Mississippi by de Soto, A.D. 1541,* for the rotunda of the U.S. Capitol, finishing the work in 1855. De Soto, looking splendid on horseback, is accompanied by his personal confessor (the man with the white beard) and met by chiefs holding the pipe of peace. By the time de Soto crossed the Mississippi, he had already spent two years traveling north from Florida looking for gold. His journey would end at the river the following year when he died of a fever and those few of his men who remained buried his body at sea with a formal Christian service.

the American Southwest, exploring Texas and New Mexico before turning east into Kansas. He never did find Cibola, and Coronado returned to Mexico in 1543, bitter at having wasted so much time and energy, yet full of information about the North American interior that would serve as the basic guide to that part of the world for the next two centuries.

Thanks to these and other conquistadores who braved the unknown in Peru, Venezuela, and elsewhere throughout Central America and South America, Spain became the dominant power in the New World just half a century after Columbus first stepped ashore in San Salvador. Although both the early explorers and the later conquistadores had been seeking wealth and power more than knowledge, without intending to they ushered in an age of the Atlantic that would last half a millennium. While most of Europe's monarchs busied themselves with Continental affairs and the Church pursued its endless religious wars, a new kind of civilization was evolving—and this one was led by soldiers, sailors, scientists, and, most important, merchants.

This map shows the principal voyages of Europeans to the American continent. The yellow line on the map traces the route that may have been taken by Leif Eriksson, the Viking who allegedly found America in about A.D. 1000. Columbus and the mariners who followed him kept more exact logs and so there is little conjecture about their progress, or lack of it: the line denoting Columbus's fourth and last voyage to America pauses at Jamaica, where he suffered a shipwreck and was marooned on the beach for eight months. There is valor in the very sweep of Sir Francis Drake's voyage around the world, though perhaps not in his frequent stops along the South American coast to raid Spanish settlements. Vasco da Gama's determined course in the South Atlantic was perhaps the bravest of all, due to his conviction that to get around the southern tip of Africa he would have to sail far from land and pick up a prevailing wind.

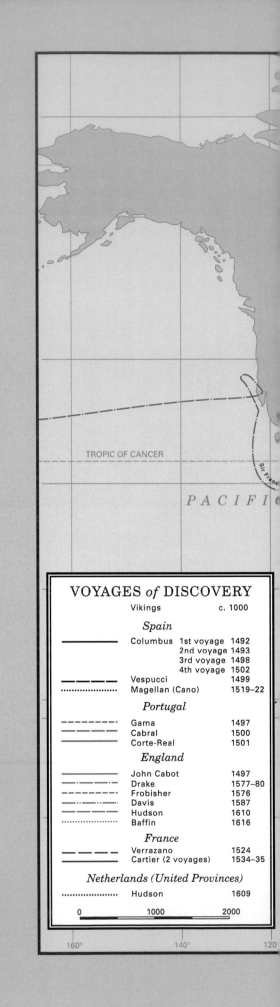

TROPIC OF CANCER

PACIFIC

VOYAGES *of* DISCOVERY

	Vikings	c. 1000
	Spain	
————	Columbus 1st voyage	1492
	2nd voyage	1493
	3rd voyage	1498
	4th voyage	1502
– – – –	Vespucci	1499
··············	Magellan (Cano)	1519–22
	Portugal	
- - - - - -	Gama	1497
— — — —	Cabral	1500
————	Corte-Real	1501
	England	
————	John Cabot	1497
—·—·—·	Drake	1577–80
- - - - -	Frobisher	1576
—··—··—	Davis	1587
— — — —	Hudson	1610
··············	Baffin	1616
	France	
— — — —	Verrazano	1524
————	Cartier (2 voyages)	1534–35
	Netherlands (United Provinces)	
··············	Hudson	1609

0	1000	2000

160°   140°   120

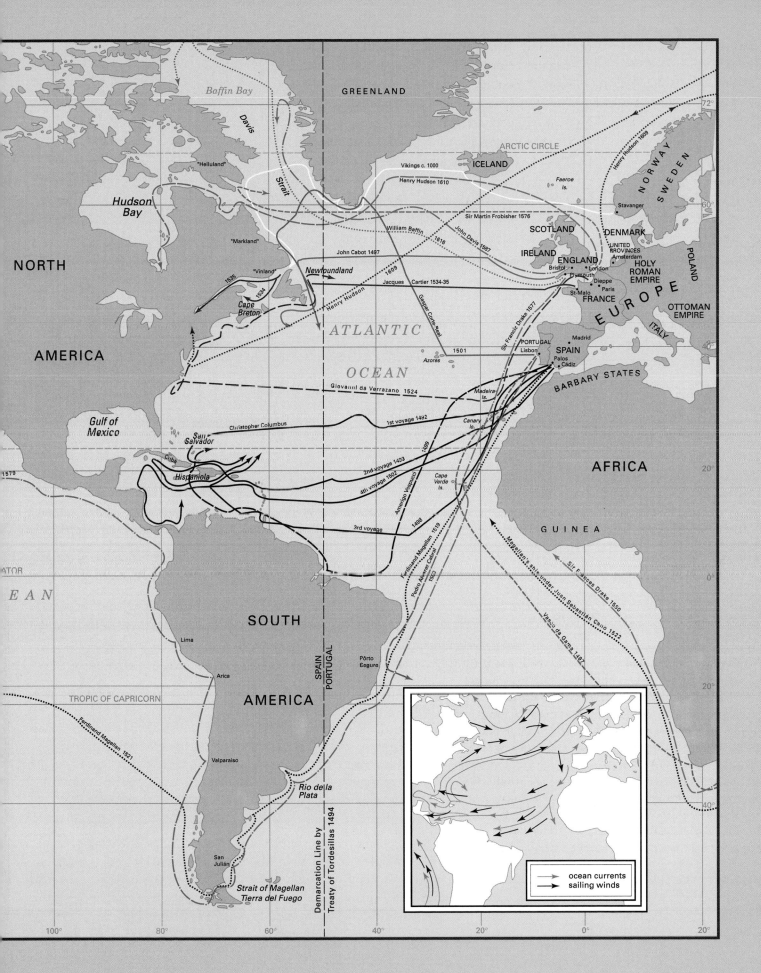

Baffin Bay

GREENLAND

Davis

Strait

Hudson
Bay

"Helluland"

ARCTIC CIRCLE

Vikings c. 1000   ICELAND

Henry Hudson 1610

72°

Henry Hudson 1609

N
O
R
W
A
Y

S
W
E
D
E
N

Faeroe
Is.

60°

Stavanger

Sir Martin Frobisher 1576

"Markland"

William Baffin

John Davis 1587

1616

SCOTLAND   DENMARK

NORTH

John Cabot 1497

IRELAND

UNITED
PROVINCES
Amsterdam

HOLY
ROMAN
EMPIRE

POLAND

1535   "Vinland"

Newfoundland

1609

ENGLAND
Bristol • London
Plymouth

Jacques Cartier 1534-35

Dieppe
• Paris

St-Malo

FRANCE

E
U
R
O
P
E

ITALY

OTTOMAN
EMPIRE

AMERICA

1534

Cape
Breton

Henry Hudson

Gaspar Corte-Real

ATLANTIC

Sir Francis Drake 1577

Madrid

40°

PORTUGAL
Lisbon

SPAIN

Palos
• Cádiz

1501

OCEAN

Azores

Giovanni da Verrazano 1524

BARBARY STATES

Madeira
Is.

Gulf of
Mexico

Christopher Columbus

1st voyage 1492

Canary
Is.

San
Salvador

AFRICA

20°

1579

Cuba

2nd voyage 1493

Amerigo Vespucci

1498

Hispaniola

4th voyage 1502

Cape
Verde
Is.

G U I N E A

3rd voyage

1498

1519

EAN

Ferdinand Magellan

Pedro Alvarez Cabral

1500

Magellan's ship under Juan Sebastián Cano 1522

Sir Frances Drake 1580

0°

SOUTH

Lima

Vasco de Gama 1497

Arica

SPAIN

PORTUGAL

Pôrto Seguro

20°

TROPIC OF CAPRICORN

AMERICA

Demarcation Line by
Treaty of Tordesillas 1494

Valparaiso

Rio de la
Plata

Ferdinand Magellan 1521

40°

San Julián

Strait of Magellan
Tierra del Fuego

100°   80°   60°   40°   20°   0°   20°

→ ocean currents

→ sailing winds

CHAPTER 2

THE EMERGENCE OF ENGLAND

Although Spain had a few decades' head start, by the 1570s Britain, France, and the Netherlands also had begun to take an interest in the New World. Of the three, France was the largest, strongest, and thus most likely to succeed. Even though not quite unified due to ongoing religious wars, most of the people living in French-owned territories considered themselves citizens of a nation that was among the powers of Europe. Second most promising was the Netherlands, despite having remained under Spanish control until 1579. For centuries Dutch mariners and, equally important, its bankers had been among the most skilled and respected on the Continent. That said, the Netherlands had some significant drawbacks: it was small, flood-prone, and threatened by its neighbors. Even so, it seemed better off than Britain, which was blessed with neither the natural resources of France nor the banking power of the Dutch. Worse, some Britons living abroad considered their monarchy illegitimate. The country's liabilities were daunting in-

The HMS Prince Royal and Other Shipping in an Estuary, **left, painted by Adam Willaerts in 1577, reflects the excitement of traveling to the New World. For a trading ship like the one in the picture, the round-trip journey to the East Indies would take about two years. The 1609 handbill, above, tried to entice Londoners to take a one-way voyage to America.**

Queen Elizabeth I's reign, from 1558 to 1603, marked the birth of the British Empire. A powerful monarch, she cultivated an unruly but effective generation of explorers: Francis Drake, John Norris, Richard Grenville, John Hawkins, and Walter Raleigh, among others, firmly established Britain as a maritime nation and power. By the end of her reign, England had earned considerable wealth on the high seas.

deed—but in time, some of them came to be seen as assets.

Early in the sixteenth century, while Spain explored and plundered two continents and France vied for power with the Holy Roman Empire over Italy and Central Europe, Britain began to mature politically and lay the foundations for economic growth. Since the end of the Wars of the Roses in 1485, the House of Tudor had reasserted royal prerogatives, but the government had continued to be run by—and divided among—independent ministries and a unified nobility operating through the House of Lords. To secure a divorce from his first wife and remarry, the lusty, sybaritic, and innovative King Henry VIII had taken full advantage of the Protestant Reformation and instituted radical new religious policies that antagonized Catholics and Protestants alike. The religious squabbling continued after Henry VIII died in 1547 and was succeeded by his frail nine-year-old son, Edward VI, whose death six years later set off a Protestant plot to secure the crown for one of their own. But Henry's elder daughter, the devoutly Catholic Mary, prevailed, became queen, and then married King Philip of Spain, further complicating the situation. Britain thus had been adrift for generations when Queen Mary I died in 1558. But that changed once the crown passed to her brilliant, fiery-haired Protestant younger sister Elizabeth, who had spent most of her twenty-five years observing court intrigues and gaining an education in shrewdness that fostered a magnificent forty-five-year reign that gave her name to the age.

Before Queen Elizabeth I ascended the throne, religious and dynastic turmoil had strangled Britain's economy. Unlike France and Spain, where strong and wealthy rulers had control over their country's business and commerce, Britain's merchants had organized themselves into trading companies that bid to pay the crown for the right to monopolies on foreign trade in various commodities. In addition to bestowing tremendous wealth on those so chartered, the arrangement provided the monarch with enough funds to rule without having to make political concessions to get appropriations from Parliament. Elizabeth I put a spin on this protocapitalist system that would make Britain the economic superpower not only of Europe but of the world.

From the beginning of her reign, Elizabeth maintained an extraordinarily

America came into existence as it did in part because of religious differences. Although economic incentives had inspired the discovery of the New World, spiritual ones shaped it; many colonists left Europe to escape persecution for their beliefs, which grew out of the Protestant Reformation that swept the Continent beginning in the early sixteenth century.

When Columbus made his famous first voyage to the New World in 1492, Europe was still Catholic and subject to the spiritual dictates of the pope. That unity started to splinter in 1517, when German theologian Martin Luther nailed his ninety-five theses to the door of the court church in Wittenberg. Luther decried the corruption of the Catholic Church and its mercenary practice of "indulgences"—expiations from sin in exchange for cash—and maintained that only faith in Christ and a direct relationship with God via the Bible could lead one to salvation. As he exhorted in 1529, in the Second Commandment of the Great Catechism, "What can only be taught by the rod and with blows will not lead to much good; they will not remain pious any longer than the rod is behind them."

The reform movement caught fire across Europe in several forms. One of the most popular, Calvinism, followed the severe preachings of French theologian John Calvin from his adopted city of Geneva. His philosophy of predestination held that at the beginning of time God had elected those who would attain salvation, which the chosen demonstrated by living according to a strict moral code that, if not quite logically, demanded faith in the redemptive powers of Christ's sacrifice. Calvinist doctrine informed the beliefs of French Huguenots, Scottish Presbyterians, the German and the Dutch Reformed churches, and some of Britain's Puritans.

In England the Reformation was spurred by King Henry VIII's need for an annulment of marriage in his quest for a viable male heir. Ironically, his fragile son Edward VI died six years into a tenuous reign, and it was Henry's daughter Elizabeth I who would preside over what was perhaps Britain's greatest era—a period that spelled the end of Catholic dominance in Europe. Because Henry VIII had married Elizabeth's mother, Anne Boleyn, after jury-rigging a papally unauthorized annulment of his first marriage, Catholics considered Elizabeth illegitimate and therefore not Catholic; so the Church of England turned Protestant. Its hierarchical structure remained essentially the same, but its rites and doctrines underwent radical changes: clergy were permitted to marry, saints lost their cult status, and the Latin catechism was translated and revised into the English Book of Common Prayer.

Still, not all the reformers were satisfied, particularly those who adhered to the Continent's Calvinist beliefs. These self-designated Puritans wanted to rid the Church of England of every scrap of Catholicism in favor of simplified rituals and an absolutist reading of the Bible rather than the Anglican prayer book. It was, of course, these very Puritans who founded some of the colonies that would become the United States.

John Calvin presides over the Council of Geneva of 1549 in P. A. Labouchere's painting. Calvin had been invited to turn the Swiss city into a living experiment for his form of Protantism. Music and bells, incense and perfume, artwork and icons were all discouraged, if not outlawed.

global view for the time. She displayed this broad-mindedness with characteristic imperiousness in dismissing a knight seeking pardon for having treated her rudely before she assumed the throne, asking him, "Do you not know that we are descended of the lion, whose nature is not to prey upon the mouse or any other such small vermin?"

At first Britain's private trading monopolies conducted single expeditions and then dissolved upon their completion, but by the mid-sixteenth century, a number of royally authorized companies were selling shares in various ongoing trade ventures. It helped that Britain was not entirely unfamiliar with the New World in which it had so far taken such scant official interest. In 1497, John Cabot had sailed west at the behest of King Henry VII, who sought a sea route through North America by which British ships could trade with the Orient. Cabot landed in Newfoundland and at Cape Breton Island in Nova Scotia, and his exploration of what is now northeastern Canada stripped some of the fearsomeness from the West, although not enough to inspire the British to turn away from their domestic problems for another century.

The tide finally turned in 1576, when the Cathay Company was formed and revived Britain's hope of finding a westward sea passage to the Orient. Here lay the crucial difference between Spain's early expeditions to the west and those of the British a few decades later. Whereas the conquistadores had braved the unknown in search of gold and glory for their sovereign, the merchants of Albion went looking for moneymaking opportunities for themselves and their investors. Despite this potent incentive, the first British forays amounted pretty much to nothing; both Martin Frobisher for the Cathay Company and then Sir Humphrey Gilbert failed to find a waterway to the Orient, and Gilbert didn't even make use of a patent of settlement he had taken pains to obtain from the queen.

Elizabeth I was herself persuaded to sponsor a few expeditions to North America by the famously gallant Sir Walter Raleigh. Whether or not he was actually so suave as to have flung his fine new cloak across a puddle for his queen to walk on, Raleigh knew how to catch the attention of the one Englishwoman he knew could fulfill his dreams of the New World: he told his queen in ardent terms of the westward continent's passage to the Orient, of the markets it could open, and of the stores of gold and natural resources it offered for the digging. Elizabeth had the means—and the grit—to turn Raleigh's vapory ambitions into realities.

Raleigh's expedition landed on the coast of what later would be called North Carolina in 1585, returning to London brimming with by then familiar accounts of America's riches. Shortly thereafter and with the queen's blessing, Raleigh made two additional attempts to establish a colony at Roanoke, Virginia—named for Elizabeth, the "Virgin Queen"— both meeting with disaster due as much to poor leadership as to underfunding and indifference from home. One of the men Raleigh had chosen to lead the first colony, Sir Richard Grenville, was perhaps apocryphally the sort of fellow given to chewing wineglasses and then swallowing the shards to prove that he could stand the sight of blood. The Roanoke colonists soon vanished, leaving only the word "Croatoan," the name of a nearby island, carved on a tree. But in addition to teaching his queen how not to colonize North America, Raleigh's exploits went far to whet British interest in the New World. And as trading enterprises continued to grow in size and strength with the crown's encouragement, it was only a matter of time before private resources and government cooperation came together to take advantage of the rich new continent.

Of course, other countries had the same idea, and by the late sixteenth century the North Atlantic powers with interests in the New World came to blows. The results shifted the course of history: Britain's newfound might could not be denied after 1588, when Queen Elizabeth's fleet destroyed the Spanish Armada and with it the Spanish Century. Just six years later France, under King Henry IV, became unified and powerful enough to make its presence felt in both the Old and New Worlds. Before long, Europe's nascent powers would clash on a global scale. Although not recognized at the time, the most important arena in that struggle would be the Atlantic Ocean and its opening to North America. The battle would last for two centuries.

The First British Settlements

Britain owed its upper hand as much to its established trading companies as to its formidable navy. As early as 1555, the Muscovy Company had a stake in the future of North America, while the Levant Company had a monopoly on trade with Turkey and the Barbary Company held a charter for North Africa. In 1588, Queen Elizabeth bestowed the rights to American trade on the Guinea Company. It was in 1600, however, when the East India Company—what would become the greatest joint stock company—was formed and was granted a fifteen-year monopoly on British trade with countries between the Cape of Good Hope at the southern tip of Africa and the Strait of Magellan between Tierra del Fuego and the South American mainland at Patagonia. By 1610 this lucrative route had enabled the East India Company to swell to nineteen facilities that shipped exotic spices and fabrics from the Orient to Britain.

Early on, the company put considerable effort into finding the elusive northwest passage to the Indies. None of these expeditions discovered either the passage or any gold, but they did report back that the North American coastline was suitable for agriculture and thus colonization. The explorers' failure to meet their original goals turned out to be the best thing that ever happened to Britain. In the absence of riches from either the soil or the Orient, the British decided to make the best of the situation and established settlements in North America—which in time proved far more profitable than all the gold and tea in China would have.

Unlike the Spanish, whose American colonies included few settlers other than the imperial officials sent to oversee trade operations, the British deliberately set out to populate the New World. In 1606, three years after he succeeded Elizabeth I, Britain's King James I granted North American settlement charters to two groups of merchants whose capitalistic tendencies would conceive a nation: the Virginia Company of London, which was granted license to the south, and the Virginia Company of Plymouth, which received the rights to exploit New England. A leader of the former, Sir Thomas Smythe, set to work immediately marshaling resources and trying to make sure that he had enough on hand to succeed before setting sail. Despite his conscientious efforts, Smythe's first attempt was understaffed, underfunded, and thus doomed to fail; the would-be settlers of "Jamestown," a mélange of unemployed laborers and skilled craftsmen, blanched at the unexpected obstacles they encountered. For starters, to deter surprise attacks from the Spanish the settlers picked a swampy, thickly forested inland site at the mouth of Virginia's James River that proved a breeding ground for malaria, typhoid, yellow fever, and dysentery. Moreover, the laborers, the craftsmen, and gentlemen who arrived at Jamestown in the spring of 1607 knew little about farming, and after a severe drought their failure to raise enough crops led to widespread starvation that drove some colonists to eat corpses, and at least one to cannibalize his wife. Dissension and disease ravaged the ill-prepared settlers. Given the dire situation, most of the settlers abandoned the idea of remaining in America and quickly shifted their focus to plundering the new continent before getting back to Britain, the sooner the better.

Undeterred, the London Company decided to continue the experiment and went on providing supplies to any colonists willing to make the voyage west. Then luck befell the remnants of Britain's first permanent settlement in North America: Captain John Smith arrived and took command. He put his intentions bluntly, asking, "Why should the brave Spanish soldier brag the sun never sets in the Spanish dominions, but ever shineth on one part or other we have conquered for our king?" A smooth diplomat as well as a

The eighteenth-century engraving at right shows a Virginia planter and clerk overseeing slaves loading tobacco into barrels for overseas shipment. Tobacco was America's first important export. It was so valuable that Walter Raleigh once bet Queen Elizabeth that he could weigh the smoke itself. First he weighed the tobacco leaves, then put them in his pipe, smoked them, and subtracted the weight of the ashes from the original weight of the leaves. The difference was the weight of the smoke, according to Raleigh.

forceful leader, Smith soon whipped the Jamestown colonists into obedient enthusiasm, negotiated fruitfully with the local natives—the Powhatan Confederacy, a group of thirty Algonkian tribes—and in time established several settlements. His success owed largely to an embrace of capitalism; rather than allowing everyone to draw from the common stores, he encouraged individuals to work harder by giving each his share in direct proportion to his production. By the summer of 1609, when 500 additional colonists arrived, Jamestown had grown into a community of small farmers living off the land and their trade with the natives. The settlement fell into decline only after Smith was succeeded by a series of incompetents.

Jamestown's struggles abated again in 1612, when Virginia found the cash crop it so desperately needed in tobacco, introduced by John Rolfe (who later married Pocahontas, the Indian maiden credited, by legend, with saving John Smith from execution on a false murder charge). By 1620 Virginia was exporting 40,000 pounds of cured leaves; the great tobacco boom had begun. Although the leafy plant kindled the economic powerhouse that would become the United States, it also led to a shameful blot on the history of civilization: plantation slavery. It turned out that tobacco cultivation was lucrative only with a lot of backbreaking work—and Virginia's nascent colony did not boast a large enough labor force to make it worthwhile. Thus was created an opening for capitalism at its ugliest, the lust for profit driving the greedy to disregard moral concerns. In 1619 a Dutch frigate landed in Jamestown and unloaded the first of many such cargoes: twenty black Africans captured to be put to work in the tobacco fields of the New World.

Like the Virginia Company of London, the Plymouth Company initially found colonization heavy going. Its first two ships had landed in Maine in 1607 and a settlement was established. When a supply ship visited the following spring, however, it found only a miserable handful of surviving settlers clamoring to be taken home to Europe.

For another decade, the Plymouth Company continued sending ships to explore the New England region, but no further attempts were made at colonization. Even after John Smith paid a visit in 1614 and presented glowing accounts of the region to potential settlers, there were no takers. By 1620, the company was in shambles, and its reorganization into the Council for New England dissolved fifteen years later. Smith's reports, however, did not go entirely unheeded. In fact, Plymouth Company representatives looking for colonists found an eager audience in a group of religious dissenters from East Anglia who called themselves "Pilgrims" and had relocated to the Netherlands to escape persecution for their beliefs. Most of the Pilgrims were in fact Protestant Separatists of humble backgrounds who had given up Anglican worship in the 1560s when they decided that the Church of England was simply too corrupt to be reformed. Although they had met secretly, the soon-to-be Pilgrims had been routinely fined, imprisoned, and even executed by the government, prompting their flight to Holland and its freedom of religion. They were dismayed, however, when their children began acting more Dutch than British, which made the parents more receptive to the idea of practicing their beliefs in a British colony. The London Company sealed the deal

Two famous figures of Jamestown: above, dashing John Smith was a natural leader who assured the success of the Virginia settlement, and Pocahontas, below, in a painting that was done during a visit to England in 1619, became its first heroine, allegedly saving Smith's life in 1608. Captain Smith was twenty-six years old when he arrived with the third group of settlers to establish a colony in Jamestown. He was the only one of the Europeans to take a sincere interest in the native culture. Pocahontas, the daughter of King Powhatan, was about ten years old when Smith arrived. Though just a youngster, she served as her father's ambassador to them.

Slavery is without question the most heinous fact of American history. How it came to be proves that capitalism can succeed as a social system only when it is conducted under a moral code that values humanity.

Such a code was sorely lacking anywhere in the 1600s. Many European nations engaged in the enslavement of Africans, virtually all of whom were brought to North America from the west coast of their continent. Some 125,000 blacks were captured and transported to the Portuguese islands off the African coast. By the early seventeenth century, however, Spain controlled the bulk of the slave trade and sent tens of thousands more Africans to its possessions in the West Indies. The Netherlands took over in the mid-seventeenth century and for a brief time became the main exporter of African slaves to the New World. The commerce came full circle when Portugal reclaimed Brazil from the Dutch in 1654 and then conquered the west African Congo in 1670 to regain control of the slave trade—which by that point had become far more profitable than digging for North American gold.

The American colonists had not failed to notice this financial bonanza. The first American ship to engage in the slave trade had sailed from Marblehead, Massachusetts, in 1637, heading a caravan of greed that would go on enslaving Africans for another two centuries. The monetary gains to be had were so extraordinary that few Americans paid any attention in 1673 when England granted the Royal Africa Company a monopoly on carrying slaves between Africa and English possessions; the colonists' grim trafficking continued unabated

and soon became the hypotenuse in a vicious triangle connecting New England, Africa, and the Caribbean islands. The system encompassed many variations on the same pattern. In one scenario, for example, ships from New England would voyage to Africa to trade rum for slaves, who would then be transported to the Caribbean and sold. Those profits would be used to buy molasses, which would be taken back to New England to be turned into rum. Although this triangular trade brought the Americas only a small portion of their slaves, it remains a blot on the history of New England.

Even though many of the Africans captured or bought from their own countrymen died in holding pens along the African coast, and even though slave ships routinely lost half of their human cargo to suffocation, disease, and brutality, profits from a single voyage often exceeded 100 percent—the best rate of return in commerce. If smallpox broke out on a ship, it was not uncommon for the captain to order his entire cargo of human beings, whether healthy or infected, to be tossed overboard. After all, whatever capital was lost on one voyage could easily be made up in profit on the next. Some of the captive Africans committed suicide rather than allow themselves to be sold into slavery, while others openly revolted, mostly without success.

As Virginia's tobacco plantations expanded throughout the eighteenth century, the colony's slave population grew and diversified apace. Many tobacco farmers had no slaves, and most owned fewer than ten; on small farms just one or two Africans were kept as hired hands and worked in the fields alongside their master. On large plantations, by contrast, most slaves toiled in gangs under white overseers, with a lucky few designated as house servants. In the northern colonies virtually all slaves worked as domestics.

No matter what form it took, the practice of slavery gave the lie to the notion of America as a land of opportunity for all. While it was true that the social stratification of Europe, where lords, merchants, yeomen, and peasants were kept in specific ranks, had become blurred in the early colonies, this relative egalitarianism was only for whites. The distinction between white Europeans and black Africans was by contrast razor-sharp and utterly insurmountable, making what seemed a paradise to many Europeans into a dungeon for Africans. This appalling dichotomy would haunt America and remain the nation's greatest social problem for centuries to come, even long after slavery was abolished.

The drawing opposite, How the Negro Slaves Work and Look for Gold in the Mines of the Region Called Varaguas, *is taken from the* Histoire Naturelle des Indes (Natural History of the Indies) *written in the late sixteenth century. The need for laborers in the Spanish colonies was insatiable and after native populations were depleted, Madrid encouraged the importation of Africans, a trade commodity that it could tax. In Francis Meynell's painting,* Slaves Below Deck of Albanez, *above, Africans endure the transatlantic voyage on a Spanish slave ship. Traders expected to find three to seven people to a* tonelada, *the unit of measure for such human cargo, which measured 100 cubic feet, or four feet by five feet by five feet.*

when it offered to send the Pilgrims to Virginia not as employees but as stockholders.

In the end storms blew them to Cape Cod and the Pilgrims' famed *Mayflower* arrived in 1620 not in Virginia but in Massachusetts, where the new settlers established a small town they named Plymouth after their point of departure from Britain. The *Mayflower* remained through the winter as a haven from the elements; nevertheless, by the time the ship left the following April, half of the colonists had died.

Those who survived carried on doggedly. The colony was replenished that autumn when another ship, the *Fortune,* dropped off thirty-five new settlers before carrying a cargo of American furs back to the Plymouth Company in Britain, only to be captured by the French before they reached England. Thanks to the region's abundance of furs and other valuable natural resources, the Pilgrims' settlements began to turn a small profit almost immediately. Plymouth succeeded where other colonies had failed in part because the Pilgrims established friendly relations with the region's Native Americans. Samoset and Squanto, two Indians who had learned English during an involuntary visit to Europe in 1615, not only arranged a treaty between the Pilgrims and the local Wampanoag tribe, but also introduced the settlers to native crops such as corn, leading to the familiar tale of the first Thanksgiving. Plymouth grew strong enough to remain independent until 1691, when the Pilgrims decided to annex themselves to the larger and more powerful Puritan settlements in Massachusetts.

British settlements continued to spread along America's east coast from 1603 to 1732. The most significant was established by the Puritans, a group of aggressively reform-minded gentlemen, merchants, and lawyers who arrived in Massachusetts in 1628. The Massachusetts Bay Company was formed in England the following year and a new batch of Puritans soon arrived in New England. The company's first governor, the smart, tough lawyer John Winthrop, betrayed visionary tendencies in 1630 by telling his compatriots, "We shall be as a city up on a hill. The eyes of all people are upon us." Unlike the Pilgrims, these Puritans insisted they were not abandoning the Church of England, just reorganizing a better society across the Atlantic to fight corruption by example. Given their worldly makeup, it is not surprising that despite their religious leanings, the Puritans won the royal charter to most of Massachusetts and New Hampshire.

Apart from that grant, the Puritans had little use for royalty, as they proved by revising their company's charter into a more or less democratic constitution for governing the colony. The charter had provided for the governor and his assistants to be elected annually by stockholders at a meeting of the General Court, but Winthrop broadened support for the new government by allowing every adult church member to vote, provided he was male. The General Court, composed of the governor, his assistants, and the voting freemen, passed laws, set up courts to impose them, levied taxes, and controlled military efforts. By 1634 each town in the Massachusetts Bay Colony elected representatives to the General Court, the first step in establishing what would become a bicameral legislature a decade later.

John Winthrop, above, was the founder of the Massachusetts Bay Colony, which established Boston as the preeminent American city of the seventeenth century. The seal of the colony, below, was made in 1672 and features a Native American who says, "Come Over and Help Us." A profit-making company, a political body, and a religious experiment, the Massachusetts Bay Colony was successful as all three.

Despite the aristocracy of their leaders, local self-governance characterized most of the ensuing British colonies founded through royal charters. With Lord Baltimore as proprietor, Maryland was settled in 1634 as a refuge for British Catholics, who now faced persecution at home. A group of nobles formed an expedition to settle the Carolinas to their tastes in 1663, while James, Duke of York, took responsibility for an area seized by the English from the Dutch in 1664 and named New York in honor of himself. That same year the duke gave two of his favorite minions, Lord John Berkeley and Sir George Carteret, five million acres of his grant, on which they founded New Jersey. Berkeley and Carteret proved true capitalists: their New Jersey offered settlers land, religious freedom, and a democratic assembly in exchange for a small annual fee.

One of the most unlikely colonial founders, William Penn, was a favorite of the king despite being a proselytizing Quaker. Stranger still, in 1681 Charles II, in payment of a debt owed to Penn's father granted him East Jersey, perhaps in an effort to put all the troublesomely egalitarian, pacifist Quakers in one place under a trusted leader. In 1682, the Duke of York and future James II gave Penn what is now the state of Delaware. What became Pennsylvania was a tremendous economic and social success, attracting some 21,000 skilled settlers by 1700, mostly hard-working Quakers but also Catholics, Lutherans, Baptists, Presbyterians, and a few Anglicans willing to go along with the Quaker belief that the Native Americans rightfully owned their lands in the regions, which made for enduring peace with their tribes. In addition, Penn's 1682 Frame of Government guaranteed freedom of reli-

New Amsterdam, pictured above in a mid-seventeenth-century print, was founded in 1624 as little more than a storehouse for the Dutch West India Company, but grew quickly after 1647, when Peter Stuyvesant became governor. Stuyvesant personally disliked foreigners, but when the company directors back in Amsterdam ordered him to increase the population, he found ways to attract immigrants from many different countries. By 1650, New Amsterdam was already more cosmopolitan than Boston, a much bigger city. Since the Dutch West India Company was actively involved in the slave trade, New Amsterdam had a large body of Africans, most of them enslaved, accounting for about a quarter of the total population.

FOLLOWING SPREAD: *The First Thanksgiving at Plymouth,* painted by Jennie A. Brownscombe in 1914, presents the legendary harvest feast as an idyllic, harmonious celebration of nature's bounty and God's grace.

Native Americans sign a treaty with William Penn, who is facing forward in the center of this undated painting by Edward Hicks. Penn purchased land from the Indians in order to establish his new colony of Pennsylvania, regardless of the fact that the King of England had already given him legal title to the lands. Penn's beneficent attitude went beyond either business or the law: in 1681, he wrote to the Indians from England, addressing the letter to "My Friends." In it he stated, "I have great love and regard towards you, and I desire to win and gain your love and friendship by a kind, just and peaceable life. . . ." Penn managed to do just that, and there was very little trouble between the native population and the settlers during his lifetime.

gion and civil liberties for all, and created a representative assembly as well as a system for providing good land to new arrivals. One of its tenets stated that "Any government is free to the people under it where the laws rule and the people are a party to the laws." Penn proved prescient, and was not just boasting a year later when he wrote, "Our Wilderness flourishes as a Garden."

And all the while, as its colonial empire spread up and down America's Atlantic coast, Britain faced strong competition from another European country with strong finances and a vigorous merchant class: the Dutch Republic.

Anglo-Dutch Rivalry

The Netherlands became a world power in the seventeenth century by establishing colonies in the Americas and, in concert with the Portuguese, opening Japan to European trade. The nation had been strong in commerce even before 1568, when the Dutch revolted against their Spanish occupiers; thanks to their country's fortunate location on the North Sea, Dutch fishing fleets had long sold their enormous catches throughout landlocked central and southern Europe. Once the Netherlands became independent of Spain in 1581, Dutch merchants cut into the Hanseatic League trade and brought their nation into the commercial life of the Mediterranean. Its mariners, widely called "sea-beggars," organized the Dutch East and West India Companies, the Amsterdam Stock Exchange, and the Bank of Amsterdam, a tripod forming the power base that would make the Netherlands great. And all the while the Dutch fought a series of wars with Britain and France, sometimes simultaneously, that cost the country far more in financial terms than in human ones. Holland's leaders hired entire armies of foreign mercenaries to fight for their nation's interests abroad, leaving the Dutch themselves to concentrate on business.

And concentrate they did. The Dutch East India Company, formed in 1602, was awarded a nineteen-year monopoly on Oriental trade that was renewed regularly. The company enjoyed the enthusiastic support of the Dutch government, which gave it the rights to establish colonies, maintain armed forces, and assume sovereign power when it was needed to conduct business. The Dutch East India Company thus became a power in and of itself, and before long built a strong presence in the spice trade by driving the Portuguese from Southeast Asia and the Indian Ocean and displacing the region's British traders. As a result of this dominance, for many years the company paid tremendous dividends that made it the best performer on the mighty Amsterdam Stock Exchange.

The success of the Dutch East India Company inspired others, not all so well organized, to get in on the act. In 1613, the New Netherlands Company was awarded a three-year monopoly on commerce in the Americas, but lost its charter when it failed to turn a profit. Eight years later the Dutch West India Company took over the New Netherlands Company's territory and more through a charter to conduct trade and establish colonies in the Americas and on the west coast of Africa below the Tropic of Cancer. The new company grew quickly and fanned out across the Western Hemisphere, establishing the small colony of New Amsterdam in the New York harbor as well as others farther up the Hudson River, in New Jersey, and in South America and the Caribbean. Although these settlements lacked the consequence of the Dutch East India Company's, they did allow Dutch shipping interests to cut deep into the trade of the British and French colonies.

The Netherlands got a further boost from Britain's internal troubles. Weakened by a civil war that had begun seven years earlier, in 1648 Britain's monarchy fell to the forces of antiroyalist Oliver Cromwell, who had King Charles I beheaded and whose Puritan Commonwealth government ruled until 1660, only two years after the death of Cromwell himself. They were not quiet years: Cromwell was forced to devote most of his attention to putting down royalist uprisings and attacks from Catholic nations.

In this painting by Robert Walker, below, Oliver Cromwell wears the red sash that symbolized his cause in the English Civil War. A Puritan with violently antipapist views, he is said to have been packing his household to emigrate to Massachusetts when Charles I's softhearted policies toward the Roman Catholic Church compelled him to stay—and fight. The urgent issues of the civil war that broke out in 1642 were mainly political, but Cromwell's rage was directed at Charles's religious vacillation, and proved unstoppable in the war and its aftermath. An ordinary Englishman in most respects, Cromwell emerged as a brilliant military leader. After his Parliamentary force defeated the Royalists, the king's fate rested in his hands. But Charles so mismanaged the subsequent negotiations that he was beheaded, a fate that once would have been as unthinkable as Mr. Oliver Cromwell, country squire, becoming dictator of England.

Six years before Cromwell's accession, the northernmost British colonies in America had united into the New England Confederation, which fulfilled its intention of halting Dutch expansion beyond New Amsterdam and the Hudson Valley. Once Britain became preoccupied with its civil war, however, the Dutch moved in to take over the fast-growing British markets in the Americas that it had long looked upon with more than benign interest. As the war disrupted British shipping and drove up the prices of British goods, the Dutch undersold their main competitors with impunity, successfully displacing them from several of their own colonial markets. Before long, Dutch hardware, beer, and dry goods far outsold British products in Virginia and New England. By 1643 Dutch currency was being used in the former, and it became common in other American colonies within a decade. The Dutch also took control of trade in Britain's sugar-producing islands in the Caribbean and replaced the British as financial agents in Barbados. By 1655, four out of every five ships engaged in trade with Africa and the Americas belonged to the Netherlands.

Cromwell set about trying to meet the Dutch challenge as soon as he took power. Puritan merchants had strong representation in the new Commonwealth government, and they meant to use it to drive the Dutch from the high seas. A sharp rise in shipbuilding after 1649 indicated the new temper of the times; another sign was passage of the mercantile-inspired Navigation Act of 1650, which prohibited any other nation from trading with Britain's American colonies. Legislation of similar intent would follow shortly as Cromwell moved to tighten London's control over its colonies.

A cagey leader, he tried to avoid antagonizing the Dutch unnecessarily. After all, like him they were Protestants and might make useful allies in his planned attack on Catholic Europe. After the Navigation Act had been passed, Cromwell went out of his way to placate Dutch merchants. Recognizing their strength, however, the Dutch rejected offers of closer political and military ties and insisted on free trade with North America and the Caribbean islands. Negotiations between Britain and the Netherlands stalled, and in 1651, anti-Dutch Puritans in Parliament passed a new Navigation Act that denied all foreigners the right to carry goods between Britain and other nations. The only trade with Britain the legislation permitted the Dutch was the transport of their own goods to ports in Britain, but, as already stipulated in the first Navigation Act, not to any of Britain's colonies. The new Navigation Act was tantamount to a declaration of trade war and sparked a real, if brief, naval war between Britain and the Netherlands in 1652–54. In alliance with the homeland, the New England Confederation planned an attack on the Dutch possessions to the south, but after losses in battle and at sea, and with its trade suffering, the Netherlands agreed to abide by Britain's Navigation Acts and to enter into a defensive alliance with Cromwell's Protestants. During treaty negotiations at the end of the war, Cromwell suggested a Protestant League in which the Netherlands would control trade in the East Indies, and Britain would have sway throughout the Americas except Brazil. Both members would share in the plunder of Africa. The Dutch rejected this suggestion as well.

As manufacturing and other industries blossomed in the colonies, how-

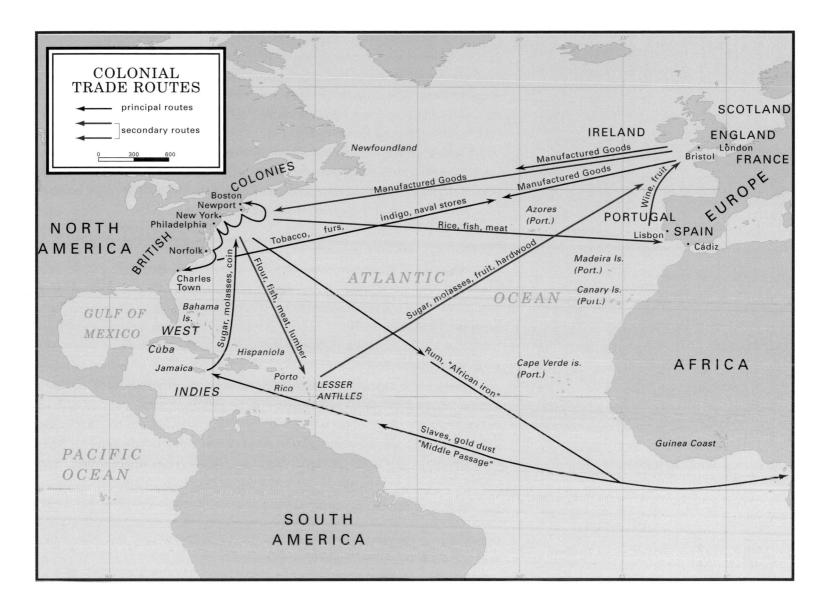

SCOTLAND

IRELAND   ENGLAND

ENGLAND   London

Newfoundland   Bristol   FRANCE

Manufactured Goods

COLONIES   Manufactured Goods

Boston   Manufactured Goods   Wine, fruit   EUROPE

Newport   indigo, naval stores   Azores   PORTUGAL   SPAIN

New York   (Port.)

Philadelphia   Rice, fish, meat

NORTH   Tobacco,   furs,   Lisbon   SPAIN

AMERICA   BRITISH   Cádiz

Norfolk

ATLANTIC   Madeira Is.

Charles   (Port.)

Town

GULF OF   Bahama   *OCEAN*   Canary Is.

MEXICO   Is.   (Port.)

WEST   Sugar, molasses, fruit, hardwood

Cuba   Flour, fish, meat, lumber   AFRICA

Jamaica   Hispaniola   Cape Verde is.

Sugar, molasses, coin   (Port.)

Porto   Rum, "African iron"

INDIES   Rico

LESSER

ANTILLES

PACIFIC   Slaves, gold dust   Guinea Coast

OCEAN   "Middle Passage"

SOUTH

AMERICA

ever, both colonial and British businessmen began to bridle at the legislative restrictions on their trade. Many began to voice their objections and continued to do so after the monarchy was restored in 1660. The most significant evidence of colonial disgruntlement, however, took place under the Commonwealth: Bacon's Rebellion in 1676 (which has been characterized as the first incidence of the common man's struggle against the nobility even though its leader, Nathaniel Bacon, was the spoiled son of a rich squire). The uprising grew out of the ongoing skirmishes between Indians and British colonists migrating west; when Governor William Berkeley of Virginia denied Bacon a commission to fight the Indians, the landowner assembled his frontier neighbors to massacre friendly as well as hostile native tribes and then to plunder the governor's plantation.

Trouble was brewing in Britain as well in the form of the Glorious Revolution of 1688, when Parliamentary leaders who had had enough of King James II's open Catholicism invited his Protestant daughter Mary and her husband, Dutch ruler William of Orange, to take joint command of the British throne. This bloodless change of monarchs was echoed in smaller revolu-

American colonies made the most of the limited range of products they could offer to world markets by tracing or joining triangular trade routes, as indicated on the above map (the ocean's trade-wind routes are not shown accurately).

John Locke, in a painting by Sir Godfrey Kneller, was the most important figure in English philosophy at the end of the seventeenth century. Trained as a doctor, he became a civil servant with a pronounced interest in intellectual discussions. One such discussion in 1670 ended in a disagreement, and his friends requested that he pursue the matter by writing a list of the objects for which the human mind is, and is not, best fitted. Locke was agreeable, presuming that his answer would take up an evening's leisure and one sheet of paper. In fact, it was twenty years before the publication of the first installment of his seminal four-volume work, *An Essay Concerning Human Understanding*.

tions in the colonies against royalist leaders. What's more, the overthrow of James II set a precedent for disposing of unwanted monarchs that British philosopher John Locke defended in 1690 in his *Two Treatises of Government,* which played a significant role in sparking the American Revolution. In addition to denying the divine right of kings, Locke set forth his contractual model of government, in which citizens would have the right to overthrow rulers who violated their natural rights to life, liberty, and property. As the pragmatic Locke wrote three years later in *Some Thoughts Concerning Education,* "Good and evil, reward and punishment, are the only motives to a rational creature: these are the spur and reins whereby all mankind are set on work and guided."

By this point, many American colonists had begun to take exception to Britain's suffocating control over their commerce. In 1699, Parliament made matters worse, forbidding the colonies to export wool, yarn, and cloth, then paper and iron as well. As a result, by 1700 the colonies were operating at a trade deficit substantial for the time, importing more in goods than they exported annually to the mother country—a figure that reached an average of $5 million by the 1760s.

The economic strangulation of the colonies intensified in 1733, when Britain imposed a duty of twelve cents per gallon on molasses imported from outside Britain or its settlements, a tariff aimed at putting an end to the colonies' trade with their non-British counterparts in the West Indies. Rather than comply, many colonists resorted to the increasingly popular alternative of smuggling, while some opted to defy the British government openly. The seeds of the American Revolution, sown generations earlier, had begun to sprout.

One of the most significant factors feeding the growing revolutionary fervor was the waning Dutch threat and with it one of the main motives for colonial loyalty to Britain and its military might. The Netherlands was falling victim to its own success as much as to its small size. Once leaders and merchants in other countries learned to imitate Dutch methods, they no longer had need of Dutch financial services, and the major banking center in Europe embarked on a slow decline. By the middle of the seventeenth century, the static Netherlands was overtaken as a power by Britain and France, which were already heading toward yet another major confrontation—this one on a global scale that would have deep repercussions for North America.

Britain's northern colonists were ever more flagrantly violating the Navigation Acts, trading with foreigners so openly that the mother country could not help but take notice. Neither Parliament nor the crown, however, opted to do anything about this disobedience. Because the settlements were so far away, and as the climate and soil of New England made it impossible to cultivate tobacco or any other really lucrative trade commodities, disciplining the wayward colonists would be more trouble that it was worth. At the time, agriculture-minded settlers found New England suitable only for small sustenance farms, which prompted the evolution of a local economy balanced among fishing, cattle, grain, lumber, and shipbuilding. As a result, the colonists' transgressions against the Navigation Acts took the form of surreptitious voyages carrying fish and lumber to the Mediterranean and probing for additional trading opportunities in Spanish America—as well as forays into the African slave trade and its lure of spectacular financial rewards.

As had been the case since the birth of American commerce, fishing formed the mainstay of New England's trade economy in the middle of the seventeenth century, earning more than exports of either fur or timber. The composition of the catch, however, was changing, and with it other industries. Early in the colonial period Boston and other seafaring ports had focused on cod and some two hundred other varieties of food fish aimed at the European market, particularly at Catholics who followed papal restrictions on eating meat. The need to preserve food fish for transport overseas led to the creation of other manufacturing enterprises such as salt works, the first of which had opened in 1621; because New England contained no salt mines, one of the region's strongest industries had grown up around boiling sea water to fulfill demand for the preservative.

But Atlantic salt manufacturing fell into decline in the second half of the seventeenth century, when shipbuilding and navigational advances enabled New England mariners to abandon food fishing for a far more lucrative, if dangerous, sea harvest: whales. Unfortunately for the whales, nearly every part of their massive carcasses could be used to make something human beings wanted, ensuring the giant mammal's commercial value even across occasional downturns in one industry or another. Although tallow from pigs and other animals fueled most candles and lamp oils, whale oil also could provide ever-needed illumination; whalebone proved ideal for a wealth of

Virgin timber flows like water from a colonial lumberyard, probably in New Hampshire in this undated etching below. By all accounts, New England white pines made the best ship masts in the world and, to officials in London, they were the most vital commodity the American colonies offered. In 1644, one felled tree measuring thirty-five inches in diameter was worth £115—three times the cost of a house in Boston.

The whaling industry was a huge business, as depicted in the undated watercolor above. Throughout the seventeenth century, whaling was limited to catches made right off the beaches where whales boldly swam. Once a whale was spotted, the fishermen set out in pursuit. Early in the eighteenth century, a Nantucket whaler discovered that the same methods could be used out on the open sea. Launching their pursuit boats from sloops or schooners many miles from shore, fishermen turned whaling into an industry that provided New England its most valuable export by far.

products, from corset stays to needles to piano keys; whale ambergris made for marvelous perfumes, and whale meat for quite a nice meal—for hundreds from just one catch. And Europeans were eager for every one of these by-products.

The first record of the capture of a sperm whale—the enormous "Moby Dick" variety rather than the smaller humpback and pilot whales that had launched the industry—off the New England coast dates to 1712 and belongs to one Captain Christopher Hussey of Nantucket. The take from that giant catch was so profitable that fishermen of all descriptions abandoned whatever they had been doing and rushed to hunt for whales off the shores of the New World; by the mid-eighteenth century some fifty whaling vessels plied the coastal waters as far as South America in pursuit of the enticing new quarry. Many men died in the dangerous enterprise, but far more whales did; in fact, the hunt was waged so relentlessly over the succeeding centuries that many of the most fascinating species were driven to extinction.

Whaling set off a boom in the New England economy that put its settlements on the economic map. In addition to the direct financial fruits, whaling contributed to the growth of other industries, including shipbuilding and forestry; the demand for large whaling vessels increased the demand for lumber and by-products such as pitch, tar, resin, and turpentine. In consequence, within a very brief time sawmills popped up on every swiftly moving stream in New England, using the water power to turn white pines into masts and other wood products for sale to shipyards and other construction concerns. Before long, Massachusetts was equipping the fleets of Britain as well as the Americas.

The Anglo-French Struggle for Empire

While Britain and the Netherlands were establishing colonies along North America's eastern seaboard from Maine to Georgia, France set about founding settlements in eastern Canada from which it could expand south into the Mississippi Valley. Relations among the three nations' colonists were tense and wary; clashes over fishing rights and the fur trade were not uncommon. It didn't help that the three home countries could not stop squabbling. When the Netherlands allied with Britain to fight France in Europe, for example, the conflict naturally spilled over into the colonies.

Europe's War of the League of Augsburg (1688–97)—an anti-French coalition created by Great Britain, Austria, Spain, Holland, Sweden, and many German principalities which sought to stem French expansion under Louis XIV—for instance, was echoed in King William's War in the colonies. Dutch and French forces clashed in Africa, and a small Dutch troop overran the French garrison in Pondicherry, India. In America, skirmishes broke out between British and French colonists and escalated into actual battles, leading Britain to dispatch a small task force to its northern settlements to help them fight the French, who were sending troops to Canada to mount an expedition to the south.

Although the American colonists considered themselves loyal Englishmen, they were also fighting for their own agendas. In 1690, for example, New Englanders took the French town of Port Royal in Nova Scotia, which just happened to be a vital center for the Canadian fishing fleet, not to mention the gateway to all of northeastern Canada. Quebec and Montreal, then the heart of Canadian power as well as commercial centers for the fur trade, were also prime targets for the British settlers. Nationalistic sentiment alone apparently was not reason enough to fight the French in the absence of any other, say, financial incentives; settlers in the colonies south of New York, which were not threatened by French incursions, paid little attention to the war and took no part in it.

The war in Europe ended in 1697 with the Treaty of Ryswick, under which France was obliged to recognize Queen Mary's Dutch husband, William of Orange, as king of England; abandon its claims to the Rhineland in central Europe; negotiate a favorable trade pact with the Netherlands, and allow the Dutch to install garrisons in the Spanish Netherlands as a bulwark against any future French attacks. For their part, the Dutch had to give Pondicherry back to the French, while Britain and France agreed to declare a status quo antebellum in their North American colonies, which required the return of Port Royal to the French colonists.

This did not sit well with the New Englanders. The treaty's provisions may have appeared reasonable to Europeans in the geopolitical sense, but to the British colonists in North America they looked awfully unfair. More important, London's apparent cavalier disregard for American concerns made many colonists realize that their mother country considered them mere ap-

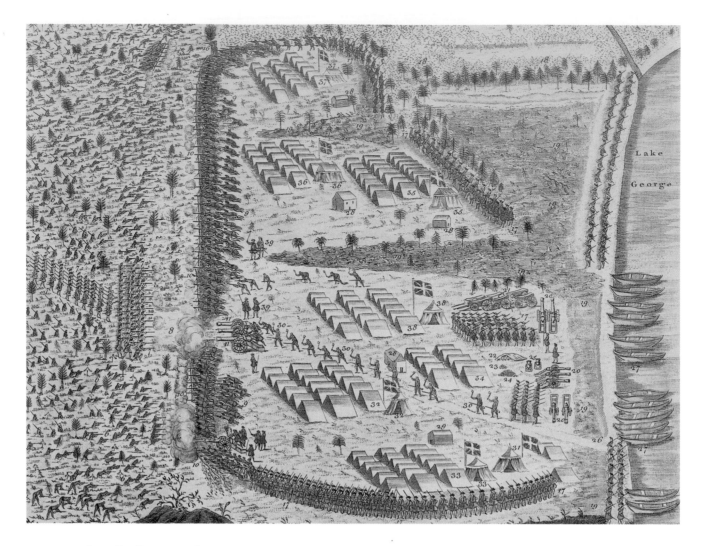

Camp George was constructed on the fly on New York's Lake George during the summer of 1755 by an American-Iroquois force advancing on French-Algonquin positions farther north. The American leader, William Johnson, was fast becoming one of New York's largest landowners; his Indian name was *War-rac-ji-ja-gey* (He-who-does-much-business). As this contemporary print shows, after the French made a surprise attack on Camp George on September 8, Johnson's cannon opened fire for the first time, obliterating the French regiment and scattering Algonquin troops unused to cannon fire. Johnson received a British baronetcy.

pendages to the empire rather than true Englishmen. Slights such as these helped stoke the fires beneath a simmering rebellion.

And they kept coming. In 1702, King James II's younger daughter, Anne, ascended the throne and immediately found herself at the head of a strong alliance that had declared war on France shortly before the death of her predecessor and brother-in-law William III in an effort to keep it from uniting with Spain into one dynasty. This War of the Spanish Succession, called Queen Anne's War in the colonies, lasted until 1714. In the end, although New England's attempts to capture the French fisheries had failed once again, under the terms of the Treaty of Utrecht that ended the war Britain obtained Nova Scotia. The New England colonists rejoiced, but their victory was short-lived; the French quickly developed Cape Breton Island, which became more important to North American trade than Nova Scotia had ever been. Once again the British colonists were frustrated.

Over the next generation, the French pushed rapidly down the Mississippi, making alliances with various Indian tribes along the way and occasionally coming into contact with British colonists moving westward. The encounters were tense but for the most part civil; it was not until the War of the Austrian Succession erupted in Europe in 1740 that North America's British and French settlers went at it again, this time in King George's War.

For the first time, all the British colonies felt the effects of a war imported from Europe. Southern forces invaded French holdings in Florida, while the ambitious New Englanders took the French citadel of Louisburg—and were so emboldened by that and other successes in Canada that they mounted an expedition to take Porto Bello all the way down in Panama.

King George's War came to a close in 1748 with the Treaty of Aix-la-Chapelle, which returned Louisburg and all the other territories the British colonists had captured to France, setting off vigorous protests in the American colonies. The settlers couldn't help but notice that the British had gained important French holdings in India in return for territorial concessions in the colonies. Again, while this deal may have made geopolitical sense, it didn't throw so much as a crumb to the colonists in reward for their valiant efforts. From Boston, the forced return of Louisburg, Cape Breton, and the Canadian fisheries the New Englanders had fought so long to win looked like proof of callous indifference to colonial interests on the part of the mother country.

Over the next six years, British settlers from Pennsylvania and Virginia began moving into the Ohio Valley, where increased contact intensified conflicts with the French; the same occurred in the Hudson River Valley, along the Maine frontier with Canada, and throughout the South. By 1754, the British colonies had become united in the desire to remove the French, who early that year had taken the fork of the Ohio River, where they built the formidable Fort Duquesne, near present-day Pittsburgh. The well-meaning but generally ineffectual Virginia governor, Robert Dinwiddie, sent three hundred troops to the area under the command of a twenty-one-year-old lieutenant colonel named George Washington. Hardly a precursor of things to come, Washington's mission—the first sally in what would become known in America as the French and Indian War—failed, and made the way look open to French domination of the region.

Shortly thereafter, the British government called a colonial meeting in Albany, New York, to develop plans for facing the French menace. It was there that Benjamin Franklin set forth his "Plan of Union" to bring all of Britain's American colonies together under a governor-general designated by King George II to rule in his name. Nothing immediately came of the idea, but it helped to spread the notion of colonial union.

The French and Indian War crossed the Atlantic in earnest in 1755, when General Edward Braddock arrived in Virginia to take command of the British forces in America. He was killed in his failed attempt to take Fort Duquesne, but even a defeat represented a significant shift in the international balance; for the first time, a war begun in America over American issues had spread overseas to Europe, where the conflict from 1756 to 1763 was known simply as the Seven Years' War. Early on, the French attained major victories in both India and America, where colonial distrust of British rule contributed to the setbacks; after all, some settlers maintained, there was little incentive to fight for new territories, as the British had a habit of signing peace treaties giving them back. As a result, most colonists responded to the call to arms only where they were directly threatened, such as in New York and New England;

Benjamin Franklin produced this famous 1754 placard calling for unity among the British colonies during the French and Indian War. It was later used in the American Revolution as a nationalistic symbol of the colonies' need to unite against Great Britain.

Colonel George Washington (center) of the Virginia Militia raises his hat to the British flag over Fort Duquesne in November 1758, as depicted in this nineteenth-century colored engraving, below. The fort was part of French defenses during the French and Indian War that stretched from Quebec City on the St. Lawrence River to New Orleans on the Mississippi. Determined to contain British colonization to the east, the French filled in strategic gaps as quickly as possible. The British were repelled from Fort Duquesne in 1755, but they attacked again in 1758. They gained the fort, by then renamed for British prime minister William Pitt, and broke the French chain of defense almost exactly in half.

there was scant participation in and little support for the effort elsewhere. This conduct convinced the British government that its American colonists were disloyal; for their part, the settlers lost some of their respect for Britain as a power when they saw the mother country's soldiers routinely defeated by seemingly inferior French forces.

The character of the war changed when William Pitt became prime minister in 1757. The worldly Pitt had a broader view of the British Empire than had his predecessors, and thus he concentrated Britain's military and naval efforts on America and India rather than Europe. The tide began to turn against the French: Britain's Robert Clive captured most of their possessions in India, while General James Wolfe took Quebec in a daring raid, although he was killed in the process. In 1760, Canada fell to Britain's General Jeffrey Amherst, while colonial forces under American commander Robert Rogers took Detroit and the other French territories in the Great Lakes region. France sued for peace in 1763, ending both America's French and Indian War and Europe's Seven Years' War with the Treaty of Paris. Under its terms Britain acquired all of France's American possessions except the West Indies and a few

other small islands. Nevertheless, the French and Indian War continued in the colonies as France's Indian allies in the Mississippi Valley went on fighting under the Ottawa tribe's Chief Pontiac. Even so, the British colonists assumed that the region would be opened for settlement once the French and Indian menaces were completely removed. Again the Americans had assumed incorrectly, and the Ohio Valley soon became a bone of contention between them and their mother country. Once Britain and its colonies had defeated the common foes that had drawn them together, their interests began to draw apart, creating a gap in which the sprouting revolution could thrive.

Up to this time most colonists had thought of themselves as British—in a new setting to be sure, but British all the same, with the religious, political, and moral beliefs of the old country. That identity had slowly changed over the previous two centuries as British settlers had turned into Americans. It was an inevitable evolution, in part because the colonists hardly comprised a representative cross section of British society—they were instead a group of hardscrabble adventurers who shared little but the daring to take a chance on an unknown world. But it was that bravery, combined with the adjustments all the settlers had to make to an unfamiliar new life in America, that transformed the British colonies into an entirely new branch of Western civilization. The character of this new society varied in some ways from colony to colony, of course. The New Englanders had faced and had to adapt to a different climate and conditions than the Virginians and Carolinians, for example, but over time, all the British settlers came to have more in common with one another than they did with their former countrymen. Although the new Americans continued to embrace a good deal of their British heritage, including its beliefs in limited government, common law, and free enterprise, they used these fundamental philosophies to build not just a new culture but a new nation.

This 1776 painting, *The Death of General Wolfe*, was so popular a subject that Benjamin West painted it four times. James Wolfe, a well-respected officer in the British Army, earned the ultimate assignment of the French and Indian War in 1759: the capture of Quebec. Wolfe executed an aggressive plan and was routing the enemy on the outskirts of Quebec when he was mortally wounded. He fell unconscious, but revived when he heard that the enemy was on the run. He issued orders to cut off the French retreat and then turned over and said, "Now, God be praised, I will die in peace."

CHAPTER 3

The Road to Independence

While economic and commercial concerns inspired the discovery of the New World and religious interests played a role in its colonization, political pragmatism turned America into a nation. In 1763, when all of Britain was celebrating its victory over the French, the American colonies from Boston to Charleston were as English— and as loyal to young King George III—as the counties from Newcastle to Bristol back home. Not only were the colonies' basic systems of government and courts of law modeled on those of Britain, but their people spoke the same language, read the same books as their countrymen across the Atlantic, and retained as many British customs as they could in their strange new land.

Naturally, that new land required adaptations that in time pulled the colonies away from the British mold. By the end of the Seven Years' War, Britain was a global power as well as an established commercial society; America, while civilizing rapidly, was still largely a wild and untamed place, and although the first settlers had found the mid-Atlantic region's climate and topography reasonably similar to what they were used to, those who migrated farther, whether to the north, south, or west, found that hardly the case. Moreover, the British back home had no idea what it was like to have to contend with Native American Indians, both friendly and hostile. Ulti-

In the nineteenth-century colored engraving at left, Patrick Henry shocks the Virginia House of Burgesses with a resolution asserting the colonies' right to independence in the face of the Stamp Act. Above, the propaganda of 1765 reached even the breakfast table.

mately, the colonists' pioneer experiences gave rise to a population with British roots but American trunks and branches, a pattern that would be repeated around the globe from the sixteenth through the nineteenth centuries as British citizens followed their flag and settled in unfamiliar lands to keep the British Empire expanding. Like America, in time the large colonies of Canada, Australia, and New Zealand would be developed and governed by people of British ancestry tempered by the conditions of the lands they had settled, a phenomenon also echoed in Britain's African, Caribbean, and Southeast Asian colonies. Of course, only Americans had a passionate enough commitment to liberty and equality to revolt and create a less hierarchical society.

The British character of the American colonies would fade as settlers' memories of the homeland dimmed over succeeding generations, but it was never erased, as was evident in the way the American Revolution was conducted. The wonder was not that the colonies rebelled, but that their revolution was so British through and through—and so successful as a result. The American colonists managed to unite and form a nation in large part because they were imbued with the same universally underestimated attribute that had long guided the mother countrymen they were fighting: the ability to compromise and reach solutions based on common sense rather than ideology.

Although many of the first Americans were well-read in philosophy even beyond John Locke's *Two Treatises of Government,* their colonies were hardly built on abstractions. The few early settlers who had attempted to found utopian communities based on the notions of one or another thinker failed quickly. The colonists who succeeded were those who had survived the physical and psychological impact of the ocean voyage and who had embraced the challenge of their new environment and had taken a pragmatic approach to meeting it. As a consequence, American intellectuals were more down-to-earth than their European counterparts, whose influence on governance was limited by their continent's rigid social hierarchy. While British philosophers were for the most part relegated to the vaporous groves of theology and academe, in America's nascent society any country lawyer with a few solid ideas (and a prosperous family background) stood a fair chance of becoming the leader of his community. Real power could be acquired easily in the colonies—but with it came a sense of responsibility as well as genuine accountability.

American intellectuals thus avoided advocating broad programs or sweeping reforms for the very good reason that their infant society allowed ideas to be put into practice—and thus to the test—nearly immediately, well before their origins had been forgotten. As a result, the colonies played little part in what came to be known as the Enlightenment of the eighteenth century, when a number of talented British and other European scientists and political philosophers produced myriad discoveries and thoughtful works, which were studied avidly by the colonies' philosophical politicians. The settlers' familiarity with England's latest thinking as well as its longstanding traditions afforded Americans an understanding of their soon-to-be adversary that was not reciprocated; the British knew little about the colonists, their problems, and their desires, and appeared to care even less.

The Rift Widens

King George III had assumed the British throne in 1760 at the age of twenty-two. Although industrious, dedicated to his country, and eager to establish his power, the king was both very young and not terribly bright, although he did know enough to turn control of most state matters over to the political professionals in Parliament such as his dearest friend, John Stuart, the Earl of Bute and Britain's prime minister. In 1763, to the king's dismay, Bute was forced to resign his office two months after he signed the geopolitically savvy but colonially insensitive Treaty of Paris that ended both the Seven Years' and the French and Indian wars. Stuart was replaced by Whig George Grenville, who had little taste for colonial projects, believing that the cost of maintaining them was more than the settlements were worth. Balance sheets forced him to concede that some of Britain's colonial efforts, particularly those in the West Indies, made substantial contributions to his nation's economic well-being—but that was not the case with the thirteen colonies on the North American mainland.

The northern American colonies provided the Indies with the foodstuffs that enabled the islands to produce as much sugar as they did, and some of the southern colonies grew tobacco, still North America's most profitable export to England, but these staples could be obtained from other sources and the tobacco trade had never been as important as the southerners liked to think. As Scottish economist Adam Smith noted in the late eighteenth century, "Our tobacco colonies send us home no such wealthy planters as we frequently see arrive from our sugar islands." The same sentiment was expressed less stiffly in *The West Indian,* a play popular during the 1765 London season, in which a servant at a reception for a West Indian plantation owner remarks, "He's very rich, and that's sufficient. They say he has rum and sugar enough belonging to him to make all the water in the Thames into punch." No plays were staged about Virginia plantation owners or Albany fur traders, neither of whom boasted either the numbers or the profits of the more experienced and better situated West Indian merchants. And if London playgoers were aware of the disparity, so was Lord Grenville, who was further irked by the self-importance of those colonial representatives he had encountered in London.

America's smugness and commercial mediocrity might have been overlooked had it not been for the colonists' brazen and repeated flouting of British laws. According to the crown, New England was not only supposed to provide the Indies with grain, fish, and other staples but also to trade them for sugar, molasses, and other products from the islands. The Americans car-

George III posed in his coronation robes for Scottish artist Allan Ramsay in 1767. He was determined to rule actively, as a "patriot king," but he proved unable to steer the country in one direction politically, and his reign produced five prime ministers in its first ten years. Anything but an internationalist, George III could neither understand the American colonies nor grasp the need to try; he knew only that he wanted to keep them subject to Britain.

George Grenville served as England's prime minister from 1763 to 1765. His favorite issue was fiscal responsibility, and he was expected to take a hard line when he assumed office: the annual tax burden for those in the mother country averaged eighteen pounds per person, while the average for colonists was eighteen shillings. (His tragedy, said wits of the day, was that he was the first prime minister to actually read the colonial dispatches.) Grenville decided to rectify the situation with the misguided Stamp Act.

Right, Chief Pontiac of the Ottawa League smokes a peace pipe with Major Robert Rogers of the British Army in 1760. At the end of the French and Indian War, the British tried to reassure Native Americans that they would prosper despite the removal of their longtime friends, the French. But the Indians learned to dislike the British, and Chief Pontiac gathered a great army of allied tribes against them. As Pontiac captured more and more British forts, George III conceded control over the lands west of the Appalachians to the indigenous Indians in the Proclamation of 1763. The map (opposite) shows the colonists' subsequent establishment of self-proclaimed "colonies," such as Transylvania and Vandalia, in the West.

ried out the first half of this plan by delivering the foodstuffs, but reneged on the second by insisting upon payment in cash that they could spend in the French-owned Caribbean islands on better and cheaper sugar and molasses to turn into rum, an important trading commodity.

Although their motives were financial rather than political, the merchants of New England were making a profit by benefiting Britain's enemies, and not just in a few instances. In 1763, the last year of the war with France, more than 95 percent of the molasses imported into Massachusetts came from the French islands. This was a flagrant violation of the Molasses Act the British Parliament had passed in 1733 to aid its own West Indian colonies by imposing a heavy duty on molasses imported from the French and Dutch islands. America's defiance of the law was hurting the islands, which put Grenville under pressure from Parliament's sugar lobby to enforce the Molasses Act and the trade-controlling Navigation Acts of more than a century earlier, as well as to pass additional legislation to help the sugar islands and punish the American smugglers.

The ingredients of rum were not the only points of contention between the mother country and its colonies. The North American settlements made for a major drain on the British exchequer by their very existence. England's brilliant victories in the European and colonial wars with France had left the nation near bankruptcy, with a debt of £130 million that siphoned off another £4.5 million in annual interest. Those sums made the £350,000 a year spent to maintain the North American garrison look relatively paltry, but the Americans had no intention of chipping in, especially once the French and Indian menaces had been removed and with them any need for England's military might.

In 1763 Grenville had no choice but to search for means of enforcing the Navigation Acts and getting the colonists to pay their share of the costs of the French war. The prime minister also had to deal with an ongoing menace

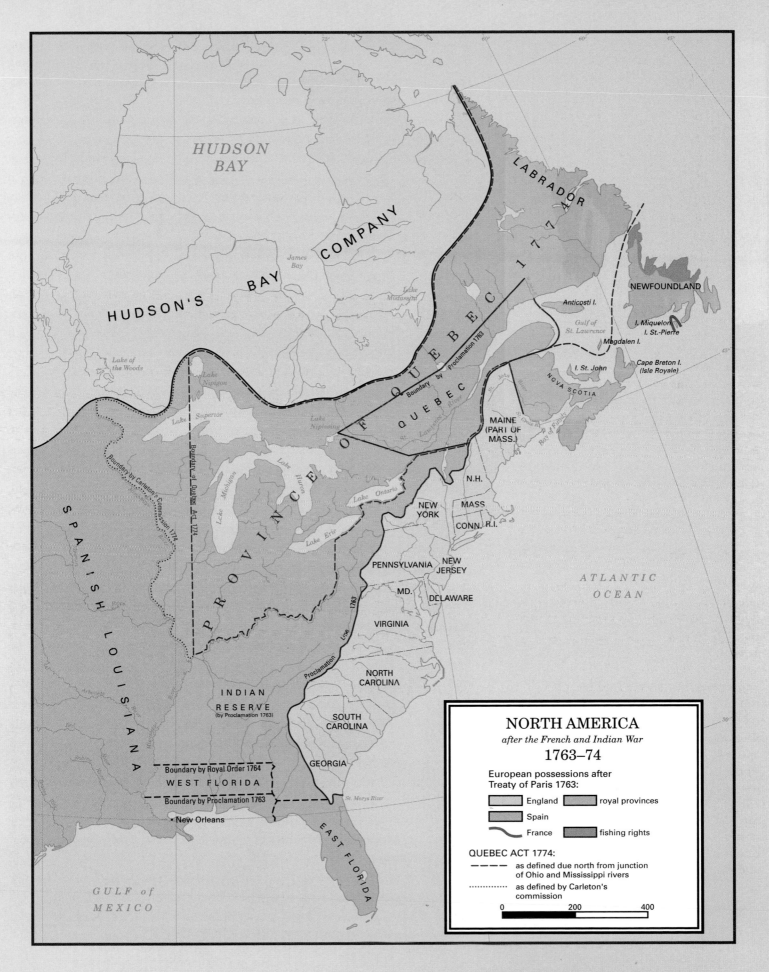

NORTH AMERICA
after the French and Indian War
1763–74

European possessions after
Treaty of Paris 1763:

England   royal provinces

Spain

France   fishing rights

QUEBEC ACT 1774:

— — — as defined due north from junction
of Ohio and Mississippi rivers

·············· as defined by Carleton's
commission

0   200   400

HUDSON BAY

James Bay

Lake Mistassini

HUDSON'S BAY COMPANY

LABRADOR 1774

NEWFOUNDLAND

Anticosti I.

Gulf of St. Lawrence

I. Miquelon
I. St.-Pierre

Magdalen I.

I. St. John

Cape Breton I.
(Isle Royale)

NOVA SCOTIA

Boundary by Proclamation 1763

PROVINCE OF QUEBEC

QUEBEC

St. Lawrence River

Lake of the Woods

Lake Nipigon

Boundary of Quebec Act 1774

Boundary by Carleton's Commission 1774

Lake Superior

Lake Nipissing

MAINE
(PART OF
MASS.)

Bay of Fundy

Lake Michigan

Lake Huron

N.H.

Lake Ontario

NEW YORK

MASS

CONN. R.I.

Lake Erie

SPANISH LOUISIANA

PENNSYLVANIA

NEW JERSEY

MD.

DELAWARE

Proclamation Line 1763

VIRGINIA

NORTH CAROLINA

INDIAN RESERVE
(by Proclamation 1763)

SOUTH CAROLINA

GEORGIA

Boundary by Royal Order 1764

WEST FLORIDA

Boundary by Proclamation 1763

St. Marys River

New Orleans

EAST FLORIDA

GULF of MEXICO

ATLANTIC OCEAN

Boston's Samuel Adams, painted above by John Singleton Copley in 1772, is shown pointing at the charter of the Massachusetts Bay Colony. By the time he was forty, Adams had parlayed a Harvard education, a tidy inheritance, and a decent malt business into complete ruin. But he also discovered a sixth sense for public opinion, and by organizing the Sons of Liberty in 1765 Adams made himself one of the foremost early leaders of the fight for American independence. Revenue stamps, such as those below, had to be purchased with almost any printed matter, whether a deck of cards or a college diploma.

from the Ottawa Indians under the bold leadership of Chief Pontiac, whom the settlers accused of trying to drive them back east of the Appalachian Mountains. In an effort to placate the Indians and punish the colonists at the same time, the British Board of Trade proposed and the Proclamation of 1763 decreed that the Indians be allowed to keep the Appalachian region beyond a line on the mountains' crest that white settlers would not be allowed to cross until further notice. Not even the British paid much attention to the line.

The American colonists chose to ignore the order from faraway London and began migrating into the Ohio Valley. Angered by this latest defiance, the following year Grenville ordered British vessels into American waters to search for smugglers and punish them through admiralty courts set up in America with the authority to enforce the Navigation Acts, verdicts being rendered by royally appointed magistrates rather than by colonial juries who might be more sympathetic to their fellow Americans. Parliament imposed additional constraints on the colonies in rapid succession in the form of the Currency Act, which forbade colonists from issuing money, and the Sugar Act, which reduced tariffs on some trade but instituted new duties on a wide range of products as well as stringent collection procedures and severe fines for violations.

That did it for the colonists. Although most obeyed the acts, a significant and articulate minority protested loudly, including some individuals who would make names for themselves later, such as Boston's Samuel Adams, who warned that his region would not tolerate such treatment from the mother country. Even more noteworthy than the fine rhetoric was the Massachusetts decision to stop importing certain items from England, with the other colonies soon following suit. By the end of 1764, these rumblings began to have consequences in England, where Parliamentary support for the colonists was growing as British merchants with American trade interests protested that the legislative measures were hurting their businesses.

Nevertheless, the next year Grenville won passage of the Stamp Act, which levied a tax on Americans in the form of stamps that had to be purchased and affixed to newspapers, legal documents, marriage certificates, diplomas, almanacs, and—in an early attempt to profit from vice—on playing cards and dice. Because a similar tax imposed in Britain obviated any claims of colonial persecution, Grenville argued that the Stamp Act would be easy to enforce in America. Although most found it onerous, quite a few settlers had no objections to the legislation, and several of note appeared to embrace it; Virginia's Richard Henry Lee, who went on to become a leader of the revolution, tried to obtain a job as a stamp distributor, while Benjamin Franklin suggested various friends for similar posts. Neither foresaw the coming storm of protest, even though five years earlier Franklin had written, "They that can give up essential liberty to obtain a little temporary safety deserve neither liberty nor safety."

Patrick Henry, a young lawyer who had made himself spokesman for his colony's farmers, took the lead against the Stamp Act, proclaiming before Virginia's lower House of Burgesses that it violated the colonists' rights as Englishmen and should be rejected:

"Caesar had his Brutus; Charles I his Cromwell, and George III may profit by their example." When British loyalists shouted that this was treason, Henry replied, "If this be treason, make the most of it." News of his exhortations reached New England, where newspapers carried Henry's speech without mentioning that the Virginia House had only adopted four of Henry's proposals. Thus the press made one of the first in a long string of major impacts on American history. Fired by Henry's eloquent words, representatives from nine colonies convened the Stamp Act Congress, which met in New York to consider ways to fight the legislation. As the first session commenced, talk of revolution arose. Some colonies reached new agreements not to import various British goods, while vigilante groups calling themselves the Sons of Liberty formed in several communities to harass and occasionally assault anyone who sold or used the British stamps.

The tone of the congress was more moderate. The delegates opposed both the Stamp Act and the Sugar Act, but hesitatingly; they were, after all, Englishmen, citizens of the freest and most powerful nation in the world. Pennsylvania representative John Dickinson summed up the prevailing mood when he presented a series of declarations denying the British Parliament the right to impose taxes on the American colonies. Dickinson also affirmed the colonists' right of petition and their allegiance to King George III. A few delegates to the Stamp Act Congress were not so cautious: James Otis of Massachusetts decried "Parliament's injustices," insisting that "No parts of His Majesty's dominions can be taxed without their consent" and calling for a more radical document, while South Carolina's Thomas Lynch made a point of praising Patrick Henry. When the vote was taken, however, Dickinson's resolutions won by a wide margin.

The Relationship Collapses

While the Stamp Act Congress met in America, a Parliamentary crisis was brewing in London. The king and the prime minister had a falling-out over royal expenditures, leading to Grenville's dismissal in favor of his colleague, Charles Watson-Wentworth, the Marquess of Rockingham. Viewed from America, this change in government appeared to have been prompted by the sober proceedings of the Stamp Act Congress combined with the guerrilla activities of the Sons of Liberty.

Support for the colonists had indeed grown in Parliament but for other, more mercenary reasons. In the wake of the colonial trade legislation, the value of England's exports to America had fallen from £2.2 million in 1764 to less than £2 million in 1765, prompting members of Parliament from thirty British constituencies to call for repeal of the Stamp Act. George III was willing to acquiesce but did not want the colonists to perceive the repeal as a bow to their strength, so he accompanied it with a Declaratory Act asserting Parliament's right to levy taxes just like those in the soon-to-be-repealed Stamp Act. The British legislature went on to repeal sections of the Sugar Act as well before Rockingham was replaced by one of Britain's most open-minded prime ministers, who not by coincidence happened to be a strong

Many colonists protested the Stamp Act in raucous parades like the one in New York City depicted in the drawing above. Such demonstrations often degenerated into mobs running stamp agents out of town or even destroying their homes.

supporter of the colonists: William Pitt, who was made First Earl of Chatham one month later. In a speech to the House of Commons on January 14, 1766, he summarized his position on the colonies thus: "I rejoice that America has resisted. Three millions of people, so dead to all the feelings of liberty, as voluntarily to submit to be slaves, would have been fit instruments to make slaves of the rest." Four years later, Pitt would add to the House of Lords that, "I love the Americans because they love liberty, and I love them for the noble efforts they made in the last war."

Despite, or because of, England's cautious choice for prime minister, the change of government was perceived in America as yet another sign of weakness rather than of conciliation on the part of the mother country. By late 1766 it appeared to the colonists that London had bowed to Boston and Charleston; few had noticed, however, that Charles Townshend had been named chancellor of the exchequer, a position second only to prime minister—and that with Pitt not only ill but relegated as an earl to the House of Lords, Townshend was becoming the most powerful figure in England.

He did not stay out of the colonial spotlight for long. Like Grenville, Townshend insisted that the colonists pay what he determined was their fair share of the costs of empire, but unlike his diplomatically cautious predecessor, the ledger-minded chancellor boldly set forth a legislative program to take full advantage—and control—of the American economy. Under his plan, new taxes were to be levied on colonial imports of tea, paper, paint, and glass, with the monies collected going to the salaries of British civil servants stationed in America. Despite considerable opposition in Parliament, Townshend's program became law in November 1767. Shortly thereafter the government set up a Board of Commissioners of the Customs charged with directing collections and empowered to try cases without benefit of juries.

England's actions reignited the flames of rebellion. The same John Dickinson who had argued for restraint during the Stamp Act crisis now wrote "Letters From a Farmer in Pennsylvania to the Inhabitants of the British Colonies" in which he declared that Parliament was trying to strangle America's economy with arbitrary and unfair laws. While conceding as he had earlier that the British government had the right to pass such legislation, Dickinson also indicated that unless the laws were amended he would condone open opposition to them, including violence in the last resort. In 1768 he even went so far as to write "The Liberty Song," which included the lines, "Then join hand in hand, brave Americans all! By uniting we stand, by dividing we fall." At about the same time Boston's Samuel Adams, second cousin to future president John Adams, circulated a letter to other colonial revolutionaries similarly denouncing the Townshend program and suggesting that outright revolt might prove necessary if the British government did not change its position.

Angered by reports of such intransigence, England's newly installed secretary of state for the colonies, Lord Hillsborough, denounced the Americans as treasonous conspirators and dispatched troops to the revolutionary hotbed of Boston. It was an act Benjamin Franklin, then living in London as colonial representative, called "perverse and senseless"—not to mention counterproductive. London's toughening of its stance goaded Boston to do the same by reviving and expanding restrictions on British imports. It began to look as though both cities were edging toward a season of unrest.

Townshend died two months after his program was passed, leaving the exchequer to Lord North, an old and close friend of the king, who wanted to take a gentler approach to the colonists but was obliged to uphold his predecessor's policies. The next year Pitt resigned in ill health and was succeeded as prime minister by the Duke of Grafton, a young playboy, who knew so little about colonial affairs that he allowed the hair-trigger Hillsborough to take a lead role in his new cabinet. At this time of crisis, therefore, Britain was in the hands of leaders who were inexperienced, uninformed, and clumsy.

For the first time the colonists seemed to be gaining the upper hand. Their boycott of British imports was proving quite effective, even if it did cause domestic conflict between supporters and opponents along with the intended hardships on London and the northern Britain towns engaged in colonial trade. Britain's frustration spilled over in June 1768, when the HMS *Romney* attempted to seize the *Liberty*, an American ship used by Boston merchant John Hancock in his smuggling operations in the West Indies, in the Boston port. Residents of the port city responded by rioting and beating up customs officials, leading Lord Hillsborough to send two regiments of British troops to Boston from Canada to keep the peace. The heaviest blow to Britain, however, came in the spring of 1769, when an accounting revealed that the Townshend tariffs had returned £3,500 to Britain while losing some £7.3 million as a result of the ensuing trade boycott.

Fearful of what might happen next, Grafton suggested repealing the Townshend program and passing another Declaratory Act affirming England's right to enact such programs. The chancellor of the exchequer disagreed, arguing that to do so would betray England's weakness to the colonists. North's position prevailed and pushed him to the head of the government, officially when he became prime minister in 1770.

By then, however, North had begun having second thoughts, and on March 5 he announced that his government would not impose new taxes on the colonies. At the same time he allowed the lapse of the Quartering Act, under which British soldiers had been given the right to quarters in private households in America. This softness did not go unnoticed in the colonies. Everybody from Boston artisans to Piedmont farmers noticed that North's government seemed to be drifting in whatever direction the colonial winds blew.

The March to Revolution

The same day North tried to placate the colonists with a pledge of no new taxes from London, a mob of radical Americans unaware of the announcement

Even contemporaries found it hard to explain the sudden rise to prominence of British politician Charles Townshend, shown above in a portrait by an unknown artist. Edmund Burke called him the "lord of the ascendent," though his title was actually chancellor of the exchequer from 1766 until his death the following year. Townshend was the least experienced member of a caretaker government, yet he acted rashly to impose an array of import duties on the American colonies. The Townshend Acts were doomed to disaster, although Townshend would not live to realize it: he died of typhus two months after the acts were passed.

John Adams, in an undated portrait by Joseph Badger, right, became the colonies' strongest advocate for independence after an evening of treasonous conversation with his cousin, Samuel, on New Year's Eve, 1772. Prone to self-pity and often resentful of his colleagues, the Massachusetts lawyer continually recorded his turbulent feelings in diaries and letters. While most of Philadelphia was out celebrating General Washington's departure for Boston in June of 1775, Adams was telling his diary, "Such is the pomp and pride of the war. I, poor creature, worn out with scribbling for my bread and liberty, low in spirits and weak in health, must leave to others to wear the laurels which I have sown." However ungenerous Adams may have been to his fellowman, he proved himself more than loyal to the idea of American independence.

British troops disembark from a ship at the end of Long Wharf in Boston in a 1768 engraving made by Paul Revere, opposite top. The soldiers were charged with protecting customs officials harassed to the point that they couldn't collect the duties specified in the Townshend Acts. Royal Navy ships encircle the harbor in the picture, which offers a clear overview of the colonies' most prosperous port city. The Long Wharf, along which the redcoats can be seen marching, was the longest dock in the world when it was finished in 1710. Colonists circulated flyers such as the one shown opposite bottom, to blacklist merchants compliant with or even sympathetic to British rule.

attacked the customhouse in Boston, prompting a confrontation with British redcoats. The crowd began throwing hand-packed snowballs at the British sentries guarding the customhouse. The soldiers, goaded beyond endurance, began to fire, killing five people and wounding several others in what came to be known as the Boston Massacre. It was the first blood shed of the American Revolution.

But the rebellious attitude that had been spreading through the colonies was dampened by the news of North's concessions, causing a backlash among moderates who warned that the Sons of Liberty, an intercolonial association bent on resisting British law, presented a greater danger to America than did British taxes and troops. In October 1770, Boston's merchants announced that

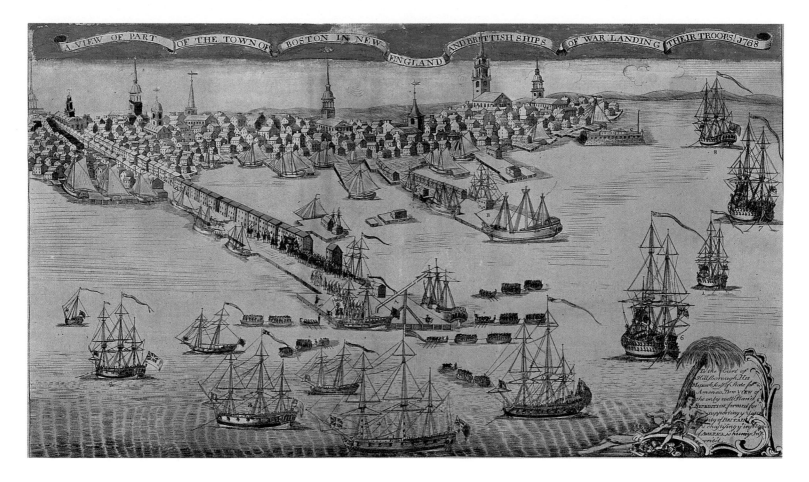

they would no longer abide by the boycott on British imports, and it looked as though the flames of rebellion had been snuffed out. Although some of the more ardent revolutionaries kept in contact through Committees of Correspondence that issued statements of colonial rights and grievances—Sam Adams pledging that "Where there is a Spark of patriotick fire, we will enkindle it"—no more significant incidents of violence would occur until late 1773.

During this reprieve North became more concerned with Britain's economic politics than with colonial discontent. The behemoth of British trade, the East India Company, was on the verge of insolvency. Because many leading British politicians were shareholders, saving it was of particular concern to Parliament. One potential solution seemed at hand: The company's London warehouse held more than 17 million pounds of tea, and if these stores could be sold, the East India Company might survive. North concocted an ingenious plan to make the most of the rescue attempt. The company would sell the tea in America at much lower prices than those offered by smugglers like Hancock who brought goods in from Dutch possessions in the West Indies. Even with the British tax, the company's tea would still be cheaper than any imported from the Dutch colonies. If everything went according to plan, the Americans would concede England's right to tax them in order to get the inexpensive tea, and the East India Company would be saved in the bargain.

But things did not go according to North's plan. The Sons of Liberty were convinced that North's plan was subterfuge to make the colonists continue to pay taxes; they were prepared to take direct action. Hancock, who hated

WILLIAM JACKSON,

an *IMPORTER*; at the

BRAZEN HEAD,

North Side of the TOWN-HOUSE,

and *Opposite the Town-Pump,* in

Corn-hill, BOSTON.

It is desired that the Sons and Daughters of *LIBERTY,* would not buy any one thing of him, for in so doing they will bring Disgrace upon *themselves,* and their *Posterity,* for *ever* and *ever,* AMEN.

Engrav'd Printed & Sold by PAUL REVERE BOSTON

| HAPPY BOSTON! see thy Sons deplore,
Thy hallow'd Walks besmear'd with guiltless Gore:
While faithless P——n and his savage Bands,
With murd'rous Rancour stretch their bloody Hands;
Like fierce Barbarians grinning o'er their Prey,
Approve the Carnage and enjoy the Day. | If scalding drops from Rage from Anguish Wrung,
If speechless Sorrows lab'ring for a Tongue,
Or if a weeping World can ought appease
The plaintive Ghosts of Victims such as these:
The Patriot's copious Tears for each are shed,
A glorious Tribute which embalms the Dead | But know FATE summons to that awful Goal,
Where JUSTICE strips the Murd'rer of his Soul
Should venal C——ts the scandal of the Land,
Snatch the relentless Villain from her Hand,
Keen Execrations on this Plate inscrib'd,
Shall reach a JUDGE who never can be brib'd. |

The unhappy Sufferers were Messʳˢ SAMˡ GRAY SAMˡ MAVERICK, JAMˢ CALDWELL, CRISPUS ATTUCKS & PATᵏ CARR

Killed. Six wounded; two of them (CHRISTʳ MONK. & JOHN CLARK) Mortally.

the British as much as he loved his profits, finally saw a chance to strike at the former while preserving the latter. On December 16, 1773, he and Sam Adams directed a group, most of whom were members of the Sons of Liberty, poorly disguised as Indians to board the British tea ships in Boston Harbor and to dump their cargo overboard. News of the "Boston Tea Party" spread quickly throughout the colonies, causing tea ships bound for Philadelphia and New York to turn back to Britain.

London was shocked and angered, even those members of Parliament who had so far been sympathetic to the colonists. King George III proclaimed, "We must master them or totally leave them to themselves and treat them as aliens," leaving no doubt as to which he preferred. Parliament bristled with loose, vengeful talk of sending a large expeditionary force to America to hang the rebels, level the settlements, and erect a blockade in the Atlantic to starve the ungrateful colonists. A few voices of reason also made themselves heard. Charles James Fox and Edmund Burke rose in the House of Commons to endorse punishing those directly involved in the tea parties, but warned against making a blanket indictment of all Americans. William Dowdeswell went so far as to predict war if severe punishment were inflicted across the colonies, and while North himself seethed at the "haughty American Republicans," he certainly didn't want to go to war with them.

Still, the prime minister had to do something, so in March 1774 Parliament passed the Boston Port Act, mandating that the city's harbor be closed until the colony paid Britain £9,570—about a quarter million pounds in today's money—for the lost tea. (The bill was not paid.) The next month North introduced the Massachusetts Government Act to suspend the colony's legislature, which became law in May. After that came a new Quartering Act as well as the Administration of Justice Act, which provided for trials in Britain of any colonial officials accused of capital crimes in the aid of the British government. At about the same time, Parliament passed a series of measures favorable to Canada, including the extension of its boundaries into the Ohio River Valley.

A firestorm of protest exploded in the colonies, where radical leaders sneered at the new laws as "the Intolerable Acts" or "the Coercive Acts." Sympathetic demonstrations took place in Philadelphia, New York, Charleston, and Newport, Rhode Island, while in Boston, Sam Adams demanded action from the Committees of Correspondence in the form of a complete embargo on British goods. In Virginia, an intelligent young plantation owner named Thomas Jefferson burst upon the revolutionary scene when he published his *Summary View of the Rights of British America,* which took issue with Parliament's right to legislate colonial matters on the grounds that "The God who gave us life, gave us liberty at the same time." Benjamin Franklin, on the other hand, warned of England's military might and urged caution, while John Dickinson similarly suggested that additional violence would only create more problems.

On September 5, representatives from every American colony except Georgia met in Philadelphia at what came to be known as the first Continental Congress. Radicals called for Sam Adams's trade embargo while moderates led by John Jay of New York and Joseph Galloway of Pennsylvania supported a strongly worded protest, but all agreed that some form of action

OPPOSITE PAGE: Paul Revere made this engraving of the Boston Massacre as a memorial to the five victims of the shooting on March 5, 1770. Even before the tragedy, most Bostonians resented the presence of armed soldiers in their city. The soldiers, for their part, were annoyed and intimidated by the sharp-tongued residents. Neither side, however, realized how strong the mutual antagonism had become until the wintry day in March when some five dozen colonists gathered before the customhouse, headquarters of the British Army. An eyewitness described what followed: ". . . a number of persons, to the amount of thirty or forty, mostly boys and youngsters, who assembled . . . near the sentry at the Custom-house door, damned him, and bid him fire and be damned; and some snow balls were throwed . . . I saw a party of soldiers come from the main guard, and draw themselves up . . . the people still continued in the street, crying, 'Fire, fire, and be damned,' and hove some more snow balls, whereupon I heard a musket go off, and in the space of two or three seconds, I heard the word 'fire' given . . . and instantly the soldiers fired one after another."

During the Boston Tea Party, patriots disguised as Mohawk Indians heaved 342 chests of tea overboard from three British ships newly arrived at the wharf, as depicted above in the 1846 color lithograph by Nathaniel Currier. Although the picture shows the operation taking place in the daytime, it actually occurred at night. In addition, the tide was out and the water so shallow that tea piled up in mounds higher than the boat decks. The large crowd that gathered to watch remained perfectly silent throughout.

had to be taken. On behalf of the radicals, Joseph Warren of Massachusetts introduced the Suffolk Resolves, declaring the Intolerable Acts to be in violation of the colonists' rights as Englishmen and urging the creation of a revolutionary colonial government. Much to his surprise, the resolves passed, if just barely. Galloway then put forth his Plan of a Proposed Union Between Great Britain and the Colonies, under which each American colony would control its internal affairs but would accept England's rule in all other matters. Just a few years earlier such a proposal would have been considered extreme, but in 1774 it seemed so moderate that the increasingly radical congress defeated it, although by only one vote. In its place the delegates accepted the Declaration of Rights and Resolves that conceded British rule but asserted American rights including Locke's "life, liberty, and property" as well as the right to self-government on internal policies and taxation. The declaration accepted royal veto power, but not Parliament's right to make legislation for the colonies. It was significant that the delegates were separating the king from his government; they would remain loyal to their monarch as true Englishmen, but they would not accept Parliamentary control, which was also their right as Englishmen. After all, opposing the king would amount to revolution, but opposing Parliament constituted a reform movement.

George III was infuriated at the whole business. To him, the very calling of the Continental Congress was proof of perfidy. "The New England governments are in a state of rebellion," he told North. "Blows must decide whether they are subject to this country or independent." The prime minister, however, was more disposed to peace than most of his countrymen and did not want to deliver the Americans an ultimatum. Joining with his secretary of state for the colonies, the Earl of Dartmouth, a known procolonialist, North approached Franklin in London to initiate talks aimed at easing tensions, while in Parliament, Burke, Chatham, and others worked for repeal of the Intolerable Acts. Burke repeated the gist of his first speech on conciliation with America on April 19, 1774:

> Reflect how you are to govern a people who think they ought to be free, and think they are not. Your scheme yields no revenue; it yields nothing but discontent, disorder, disobedience; and such is the state of America, that after wading up to your eyes in blood, you could only end just where you begun; that is, to tax where no revenue is to be found.

Burke and his fellow conciliators convinced Parliament to forbear laying any but external taxes, and only on those Americans whose own assemblies had already imposed internal taxation, but at the same time the body passed a resolution barring New England fishing boats from the North Atlantic after

The cartoon at left appeared in a London magazine in March 1775 under the heading "A Society of Patriotic Ladies at Edenton in North Carolina." It mocked the movement afoot in the colonies to boycott English products. The proclamation the women are signing, at center, reads, "We, the Ladies of Edenton do hereby Solemnly Engage not to Conform to that Pernicious Custom of Drinking Tea, or that we the aforesaid Ladies will not promote the Wear of any Manufacture from England until such time that all Acts which tend to Enslave this our Native Country shall be repealed."

This 1774 cartoon called "A Political Lesson" dramatizes the rough treatment Thomas Gage received from the colonies. The longtime commander of Britain's military forces in America, General Gage was married to an American and was presumed by those in London to understand both the terrain and the mentality of the thirteen colonies. Gage returned to London in June 1773. "He says they will be lyons whilst we are lambs, but if we take the resolute part, they will be very meek," the king wrote. In 1774, Gage was appointed governor of Massachusetts, with orders to shut down both trade and self-government in Boston until the colonists repaid the damage caused by the Tea Party. Jobs and food became scarce and most residents had no choice but to leave. Although the city's population dropped from 16,000 to 5,000 in just a few months, those Bostonians who remained were no more docile than the fiery steed in the picture.

July 20. Taken together, these moves sent the Americans very mixed signals.

When news of the former measure, known as the North Conciliatory Resolution, reached the British commander (now Massachusetts governor) in Boston, General Thomas Gage, he also received orders to strike a blow at the rebels. Gage learned of their whereabouts and sent troops to seize them and then destroy the supply facility at Concord. But that night Boston silversmith Paul Revere rode the twenty miles to Lexington to warn the radical leaders and everyone else along the way that the British were coming. As poet Henry Wadsworth Longfellow would later write in his homage to Paul Revere, "The fate of a nation was riding that night." When the British troops reached the town on April 19, 1775, they encountered an armed force of seventy, some of them "Minutemen," a local militia formed by an act of the provincial congress the previous year to be ready to fight on a minute's notice. Tensions were high and tempers short on both sides, but as the Lexington militia's leader, Captain John Parker, would state after the battle, he had not intended to "make or meddle" with the British troops. In fact, it was the British troops who were advancing to form a battle line when a shot rang out—whether it was from a British or colonial musket no one knows to this day. At the time neither side realized it was the first fired in the American Revolution. The lone shot was followed by volleys of bullets that killed eight and wounded ten Minutemen before the British troops marched on to Concord and burned the few supplies the Americans had left there. But on their march back to Boston the British faced the ire of local farmers organized into a well-trained embryo army, which outnumbered the British five to one, and shot at them from every house, barn, and tree. By nightfall total casualties numbered 93 colonists and 273 British soldiers, putting a grim twist on Sam Adams's earlier exclamation to John Hancock, "What a glorious morning for America." As one British officer reported back to London of the untrained American rebels, "Whoever looks upon them as an irregular mob will find himself much mistaken." Years later, Ralph Waldo Emerson wrote "Concord Hymn" to honor the Minutemen who had stood up against the 800 British troops:

The painting below, *First News of the Battle of Lexington,* 1847, by William Tylee Ranney shows horsemen riding through the Massachusetts countryside to rouse the Minutemen who would confront the British in Lexington on April 19, 1775. Watching a Minuteman go by his window in Concord, one Tory remarked, "There goes a man who will fight you in blood up to his knees."

George Washington at the Battle of Princeton by Charles Willson Peale, opposite, was completed in 1872. Washington himself designed the uniform, which, except for the sash and epaulets, was the same as the one he had worn in his Virginia Militia regiment before the war. A member of the Virginia delegation to the Continental Congress in 1775, Washington decided to appear in his uniform at the Philadelphia meeting as a show of patriotism and strength. Even so, he did not believe the conflicts at Lexington and Concord would necessarily escalate into full-scale war, and planned to return home after the congress. When the delegates decided that the regiments facing the British needed a commander, however, Washington was the obvious choice. Two of the most difficult personalities of the American Revolution, Ethan Allen and Benedict Arnold (pictured below), were both so eager for the honor of being the first man to enter the undefended Fort Ticonderoga that they finally had to agree to synchronize their steps and walk in side by side.

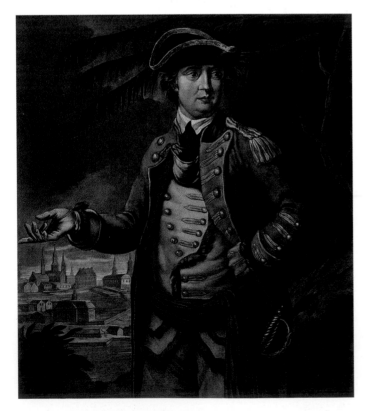

By the rude bridge that arched the flood,
Their flag to April's breeze unfurled,
Here once the embattled farmers stood,
And fired the shot heard around the world.

While Gage tried to regroup his forces, the rebel leaders came out of hiding to organize the American resistance. Confusion reigned for the next few weeks. After all, it looked to many colonists elsewhere as though a band of radicals had taken control of the Massachusetts government and entered on their own into a war with Britain. That was largely true, but it was a principled, well-organized, and rapidly growing band that already comprised 10,000 troops. Massachusetts next sent brave young Connecticut officer Benedict Arnold to attack and capture Fort Ticonderoga on New York's Lake Champlain, while Connecticut leaders convinced Vermont farmer Ethan Allen to commit his militia of "Green Mountain Boys" to the same purpose, and sent pleas for aid to the other colonies. Connecticut, New Hampshire, and Rhode Island responded by sending troops. Then Massachusetts dispatched its delegates to the second Continental Congress, hoping to find enough common ground with its fellow colonies to convince them to join the rebellion.

Independence

The second Continental Congress met in Philadelphia on May 10, 1775, the same day Arnold and Allen captured Fort Ticonderoga. In both places it was clear that the radicals were in command. At the congress, Dickinson urged moderation, but went unheeded as John Adams of Massachusetts called for a declaration of independence. On Lake Champlain squabbles broke out over who now owned Fort Ticonderoga. Was it Massachusetts or the united colonies? No one could say for certain because no one was in charge.

Recognizing the need for cohesion, John Adams set out to look for someone who could symbolize American unity, and found him in George Washington, whose service in the Seven Years' War had made him one of the most experienced military officers in the colonies and whose tenure in Virginia's House of Burgesses had established him as an implacable foe of British rule. Hoping that Washington would not only provide able military leadership but also unite every colony from Massachusetts to Virginia and every colonist from the most radical Son of Liberty to the most apolitical farmer, Adams proposed naming the gentleman who had represented Virginia at the first Continental Congress as general and commander in chief of the colonial army. He also figured that as a southerner Washington could bring his region into what so far had been mostly New England's fight. The well-heeled Washington accepted and set off immediately to join the continental forces in Boston.

The same day Washington received his commission, June 17,

The Battle of Bunker Hill, depicted at its very outset by Winthrop Chandler, began with a British assault on a collection of unproven continental regiments, June 17, 1775. About 2,500 British troops crossed the Charles River by ferry to march on the hills of Charlestown, where resistance was to have been weakened by gunfire from the navy ships at the mouth of the river. The battle plan seemed sound, but it resulted in disaster for the British side. The redcoats did ultimately take the hill, but not without a staggering loss of life.

1775, marked the first major engagement between colonial and British forces in Massachusetts. Known as the Battle of Bunker Hill, most of the fighting was actually on neighboring Breed's Hill, just outside Boston, fortified the day before by the Americans. It was a typical confrontation for the time: Britain's General Gage sent 2,500 red-coated troops up the hill, and the American flank commander ordered his men not to fire on them until they could "see the whites of their eyes." They didn't, and at first the British soldiers dropped in droves, but within half an hour the survivors had regrouped and mounted a second attack, then retreated again and mounted a third. By that point the rebels were low on gunpowder and had nothing to match the British bayonets. Although the British forces took the hill, in doing so they lost more than 1,000 men, while the colonies suffered only some 400 casualties. It was an imbalance that would make British generals more cautious in later engagements.

Back in Philadelphia, most of the delegates to the second Continental Congress still considered themselves loyal to the crown, if not to Parliament. On July 4, exactly a year before American independence, Dickinson put forth his "Olive Branch Petition," expressing hope that the colonies could end their differences with the mother country. On July 6, the congress adopted Dickenson's Declaration of the Causes and Necessities of Taking Up Arms, which denied that colonial independence was the goal of the congress while allowing that Americans might have to fight to secure their true rights as Englishmen. As late as January 1776, Washington himself was vowing to punish those in Parliament who had tried to curtail Americans' rights as subjects of the crown.

From the beginning, some rebels had insisted that American independence should be the goal of the conflict with England, but they were a small minority. That began to change in early 1776, when many colonists who accepted the idea of the war needed a concrete reason to fight—a prospective outcome that offered some foreseeable benefit. Such a goal was outlined in a forty-seven-page pamphlet that appeared on January 10, 1776. *Common Sense,* the work of a thirty-nine-year-old former British corsetmaker named Thomas Paine, postulated that the colonies were fighting for America, but beyond that "They scarcely know for what, and which, if it could have been obtained, would have done her no good." He went on to argue that Americans should not be dying over details such as "no taxation without representation" or to gain power within the British Empire, but rather to break free from Britain in order to create another civilization in the New World. Europe was corrupt and tainted by its past, Paine wrote, whereas America was fresh and pure; colonists who sought reconciliation with the mother country were therefore not only timid but foolish, an example of "perfect independence contending for dependence." The young pamphleteer minced no words in avowing that "Everything that is right or reasonable pleads for separation. The blood of the slain, the weeping voice of nature cries, IT IS TIME TO PART."

Until this point, appeals on all sides of the colonial issue, from Dickinson's calls for reconciliation to John Adams's arguments for independence, had been expressed in fairly calm and rational terms. Paine's pamphlet was by contrast highly emotional—and effective—in telling the colonists what they already knew but had not yet admitted: that they were no longer Europeans, and that the American Revolution had begun when they first left the old country for the new one across the Atlantic. Paine understood that true revolutions grow from the unfettered human spirit—and that logic and rationality are better suited to legislatures than to the barricades that must be manned to bring such governing bodies into existence. Passion sells better than dull reason, of course, and in the three months after it was first published some 120,000 copies of *Common Sense* were printed and distributed, a figure that reached half a million by the end of the revolution, or at least one copy for every family in America. "The period of debate is closed," Paine fatalistically announced. "Arms, as the last resource, must decide the contest."

A few months before Paine's pamphlet, Americans were learning that the British had been defeated at Charlestown, Massachusetts, and that General Howe had retreated from Boston. For the most part, the colonists were pleasantly surprised at their untrained, ragtag militia's successes against the much larger and more vaunted redcoat forces, a surprise that inspired growing confidence in America's potential as an independent nation. As John Adams put it ever so gently in a letter to his wife, Abigail, on May 17, "There is something very unnatural and odious in a government a thousand leagues off. A whole government of our own choice, managed by persons whom we love, revere, and can confide in, has charms in it for which men will fight."

On June 7, Virginia delegate Richard Henry Lee proposed a resolution "that

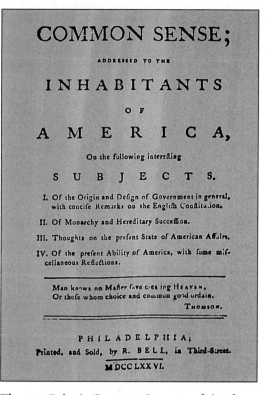

Thomas Paine's *Common Sense* explained America to Americans, pointing out the country's vast potential if only it were released from British control. The man who understood the colonies so deeply had been in America only a year when he wrote the piece. Issued in January 1776, Paine's words inflamed American opinion against Britain and won many over to the idea of independence.

Benjamin Franklin, painted by C. H. Peale in 1785, right, and Thomas Jefferson, in an 1898 Howard Pyle painting, below, were leaders not only of the American cause but of eighteenth-century thought as well. A generation older than most of the founding fathers, Franklin was liberal and tolerant, artfully diplomatic, and as witty as he cared to be in practically any situation. Thomas Jefferson had risen to prominence quickly after the publication of his pamphlet called *A Summary View of the Rights of British America* in 1774. Elected to the Virginia delegation of the second Continental Congress, he was noticeably quiet during the debates, but otherwise mingled amiably with the others. Over the winter, Jefferson worked steadily in his library at Monticello. When he returned to Philadelphia for the 1776 session, he was primed and ready to write the Declaration of Independence.

these United Colonies are, and of right ought to be, free and independent states." After four days of sometimes heated discussion a vote on Lee's proposal was postponed to allow time to line up support. Meanwhile, the confident radicals of the Continental Congress named a committee to draft it into a formal resolution: John Adams, Benjamin Franklin, Thomas Jefferson, Robert Livingston, and Roger Sherman. At the same time the congress agreed to act as the united colonies' temporary government until a more formal one could be established.

As the Continental Congress worked out the details of the latter agreement, the Committee of Five set to writing drafts of the independence resolution. Adams seemed the ideal author but demurred and let the task fall to Jefferson, explaining that "I am obnoxious, suspected, and unpopular. You are much the otherwise." And with good reason, as it turned out. The thirty-three-year-old Jefferson withdrew to his rooms in Philadelphia with a lap desk and re-emerged with an eloquent tract that would become the Declaration of Independence, with substantial editorial help from the rest of the committee.

As presented to the Continental Congress, the draft declaration consisted of two main sections after a preamble asserting that the Americans were indeed revolting in actions, not just rebelling with words. The first section outlined Jefferson's argument in philosophical terms that reflected the thinking not just of John Locke but also of the Enlightenment itself over the last century in England: that some truths are self-evident, and among them are "life, liberty, and the pursuit of happiness." The first part continued to the effect that governments are established to protect these rights, and that when they fail to do so they deserve to be overthrown—as was the case in 1776.

The second section of the draft was devoted to an unprecedented indictment of King George III, making it clear that the colonists no longer considered themselves Englishmen opposing Parliament but Americans opposing foreign rule of any kind. As Jefferson wrote, the king had overstepped his power and broken the bonds between colonies and crown, ruler and ruled, when he violated the colonists' rights as Englishmen, such as their right to take issue with Parliamentary acts.

The Declaration of Independence was written in a moment of urgency in 1776, but it has held its own ever since as the foremost statement of American ideals. It begins with these words: "When in the Course of human events, it becomes necessary for one people to dissolve the political bands which have connected them with another, and to assume among the Powers of the earth, the separate and equal station to which the Laws of Nature and of Nature's God entitle them, a decent respect to the opinions of mankind requires that they should declare the causes which impel them to the separation.

"We hold these truths to be self-evident, that all men are created equal, that they are endowed by their Creator with certain unalienable Rights, that among these are Life, Liberty and the pursuit of Happiness."

FOLLOWING SPREAD: In the 1875 colored engraving, members of the Sons of Liberty celebrate their new status as American citizens in 1776 by raising a Liberty Pole. Liberty Poles and Liberty Trees were erected as rallying points for patriotic speeches or for soldiers marching away to war.

John Trumbull, the artist who painted *Declaration of Independence in Congress at the Independence Hall, Philadelphia, July 4th, 1776,* below, finished the work in 1819 after more than thirty years of effort. The assembly depicted is the second Continental Congress, but the five men at the center command the moment as the committee responsible for drafting the Declaration: (from left to right) Ben Franklin, Robert Livingston, Roger Sherman, Thomas Jefferson, and John Adams. Jefferson is formally presenting the Declaration to John Hancock, who is seated.

Jefferson structured his draft this way deliberately. In the first part he appealed to the radicals who would accept nothing less than independence no matter what happened in London, while in the second part he tried to win over the moderates who viewed the conflict as a struggle over rights that had been seized by a particularly tyrannical king and who saw no reason to attack the monarchy as an institution. On the whole, as Jefferson later wrote, the object of the declaration was "not to find out new principles, or new arguments, never before thought of, not merely to say things that had never been said before; but to place before mankind the common sense of the subject, in terms so plain and firm as to command their assent, and to justify ourselves in the independent stand we are compelled to take."

That said, in truth Jefferson was also trying to appeal to another con-

stituency: foreign countries, especially France, which he and others hoped might come to America's aid if convinced that the colonists truly meant to separate from England, the longstanding enemy the French so despised.

On June 28, Jefferson's draft was presented to the Continental Congress, which debated and then edited it. The most important revision excised Jefferson's pointed attack on the slave trade, in which the Virginia slaveholder had charged the king with having "waged cruel war against human nature itself, violating its most sacred rights of life and liberty in the persons of a distant people who never offended him, captivating and carrying them into slavery in another hemisphere, or to incur miserable death in their transportation thither. This piratical warfare, the opprobrium of infidel powers, is the warfare of the Christian King of Great Britain."

But the southern delegates objected to this attack on a system they had found so profitable, and were joined in demanding its removal by a number of northerners who had also benefited from the slave trade. On July 2 the revised declaration was accepted for consideration by the congress by a vote of twelve to none, with New York abstaining (they approved five days later). The next day John Adams gushed in a letter to his wife, Abigail, that:

> The second day of July, 1776, will be the most memorable epoch in the history of America. I am apt to believe that it will be celebrated by succeeding generations as the great anniversary festival. It ought to be commemorated as the day of deliverance, by solemn acts of devotion to God Almighty. It ought to be solemnized with pomp and parade, with shows, games, sports, guns, bells, bonfires, and illuminations, from one end of this continent to the other, from this time forward forevermore.

His prediction was only two days off. On July 4 the Declaration of Independence was formally approved by the same twelve-to-zero vote. Exactly one year earlier, some of those who signed the new declaration had supported the Olive Branch Petition, but that seemed long ago. In the summer of 1776 every delegate to the Continental Congress represented a colony willing to sever ties with England. Copies of the declaration were sent across America, and on July 9 one reached New York City, where George Washington was preparing for a British attack.

CHAPTER 4

A New Nation

History all too often is written backward, starting with a momentous event and then tracing the steps that led to it. This certainly has been the case with the American Revolution, which has come to be regarded as the foregone conclusion of British rule. The facts indicate otherwise.

For several months after the Declaration of Independence in 1776, things looked grim for the Americans and rosy for a British victory. Britain seemed to have most of the advantages: better trained and more experienced troops, a larger and stronger economy, and the capital needed to mount and sustain a serious military effort. Apart from the advantage of fighting on its home turf, America's only significant asset—as would be proven again and again—was the simple fact that it lay some 3,000 miles from Europe across a tumultuous ocean that naturally restricted the size and supplies of any invading force.

In the late eighteenth century, however, Britain had the world's greatest navy, while America had only a handful of ships to engage the British on the open seas. Perhaps more important, the Americans were far from unified; after the War of Independence, John Adams estimated that a third of the population had favored revolution, another third had remained pro-British, and the rest were neutral. All three groups were motivated as much by economics as by politics. Those advocating revolution opposed British taxation on and appropriation

George Washington presided over the Constitutional Convention of 1787, as shown in this 1856 painting, *Washington Addressing the Constitutional Convention* by Junius Brutus Stearns. Washington had little to do with the actual drafting of the Constitution but everything to do with its unanimous acceptance, putting all his influence toward that end.

of the new continent's commerce and resources; those in favor of continuing British rule feared the loss of the mother country's financial and military safety nets, while those opting for neutrality just wanted to be left alone to conduct their own business, especially considering the odds. Every conflict has its share of fence-straddlers; it was the pro-British "loyalists," or Tories, whose opposition to the rebels almost turned the American Revolution into a civil war as well.

Some colonists maintained allegiance to the king out of gratitude, including local bureaucrats who owed their jobs to the British Empire, merchants who lived off British trade, and the most recent emigrants from the British Isles. Most, however, did so simply because they still considered themselves Englishmen and thus bound to be loyal subjects. Most Tories sympathized early on with the resistance and its procedural approach to justified opposition, such as through the stately Stamp Act Congress of 1765. When the colonial situation began turning ugly around 1774, however, many more Americans renewed their allegiance to the king. British taxation may have been obnoxious, they reasoned, but the rebels' increasing radicalism and resorts to violence were downright dangerous. Throwing tea into Boston harbor and skirmishing with British troops was not only ruffian behavior but also lawlessness that presaged a larger instability that could burst into civil war. It is not surprising that loyalist sentiment was concentrated in those colonies that had already suffered through bloody internal disputes such as the land riots in New York, New Jersey, Pennsylvania, and North and South Carolina earlier in the eighteenth century. In many areas old enmities drove colonists to take one or the other side just out of spite.

Class distinctions also played a part, particularly in the Carolinas, where wealthy plantation owners made up a large portion of the rebel ranks. Loyalists in western regions won support for the king from many common settlers who resented the effete easterners. This tactic spread, helped along by the Declaration of Independence itself. While economics may have started the revolution and fueled the internal discord that accompanied it, political philosophy came to the fore with the Declaration, its passionate excoriation of tyranny and privilege, and its lofty Enlightenment ideals. This very intellectualism, however, opened the way for loyalist leaders throughout the colonies to convince less educated farmers and tradesmen that the elitist rebels had little interest in the concerns of working men and women—unlike the king, apparently.

Among those who understood the Declaration's true potential to benefit all Americans was the forty-four-year-old George Washington, who also recognized how unlikely it was that the rebels could triumph over the British forces. In the summer of 1776, however, fretting about geopolitics was not Washington's job; commanding the Continental Army was. Of course, the way he commanded it was geopolitically brilliant: Washington's greatest achievement in the Revolution was to change the basic strategy in the fall of 1776 to "protract the war" rather than risk everything in one battle as Congress wanted. And he certainly knew how to rouse the troops; addressing his men six weeks before the battle of Long Island on August 27, the general said, "The fate of unborn millions will now depend, under God, on the courage and conduct of this army. Our cruel and unrelenting enemy leaves

us only the choice of brave resistance or the most abject submission. We have, therefore, to resolve to conquer or die." Still, Washington's initial efforts were hardly auspicious. In late August his troops lost several engagements with the redcoats in New York and on Long Island. In fact, the Americans barely escaped. They retreated to the north, crossed the Hudson River, and traveled through Pennsylvania.

Optimism was important for Washington, for after the Battle of Long Island morale was at a low ebb. But a young captain soon changed all that with a boost of rhetorical adrenaline. Twenty-one-year-old Captain Nathan Hale had been arrested by the British authorities for spying. The fearless Hale was marched to the gallows on September 22 in the British artillery park in New York City, and before his fate of death by hanging, Hale, adapting a line from Joseph Addison's *Cato,* boldly pronounced, "I only regret that I have but one life to lose for my country." The American Revolution thus had its first undaunted martyr, and over the ensuing years, troops would use this phrase as a rallying cry to ward off defeatism and dispair.

After another string of small defeats, Washington crossed the Delaware River on Christmas night and the next morning turned the tables by taking the British garrison at Trenton and the thousand-odd Hessian mercenaries who manned it. The Americans were desperate for a victory and they got one by sur-

British forces had complete control of New Jersey by the end of 1776 and ransacked homes at will, as depicted above in *Advance of the Enemy* by Alfred W. Thompson in 1885. Among the many houses not only looted but burned was Morven, the Princeton estate of Richard Stockton, a signer of the Declaration of Independence who was hounded into the countryside, captured, and persecuted. Stockton's inhumane treatment at the hands of the British became an international issue. In some cases such outrages turned Tories against George III, but across New Jersey, residents gave in to what seemed inevitable and swore public oaths of allegiance to the king in exchange for royal pardons.

The portrait of John Burgoyne, above, was painted by Sir Joshua Reynolds in 1766. In early 1777, Burgoyne responded to an invitation from the king to test the strategy he'd advocated "For Conducting the War From the Side of Canada." General Burgoyne did indeed march south from Canada, only to meet Horatio Gates and a much larger force on a field near Saratoga. Emanuel Leutze's *Washington Crossing the Delaware* (1851), left, has become a metaphor for the Revolutionary War, showing the general and his men setting out across the dark, chilly waters on Christmas night, 1776. The choice of Christmas as the date of attack was hardly sentimental: many of Washington's regular army soldiers were entitled to go home on January 1. In addition, he needed to make a strike before the river froze over completely and left Pennsylvania wide open to British invasion.

George Washington reviews the troops at Valley Forge in an 1883 painting by William B. T. Trego. The Continental army formed an island of want in the midst of plenty in the winter of 1777–78, forced to shadow the British occupation of Philadelphia fifteen miles to the east. General Howe's greatest worry in that city was maintaining discipline with so much luxurious living to distract the men. Meanwhile, General Washington drilled his starving troops, admonished them not to plunder food from nearby farms, and implored congress to send aid. All that arrived in Valley Forge with any regularity, however, was snow.

prising the Hessians. The German mercenaries did not think that the Continental army would attack in freezing winter weather, and they were under the weather themselves having celebrated Christmas with too much cheer. Washington, taking advantage of the circumstances, had his men wage a sneak attack. A week later Washington scored a smaller victory at Princeton.

Nevertheless, by the spring of 1777, Britain's military superiority had begun to look overwhelming. In February, British General John Burgoyne—a sometime playwright whose first comedy had been a hit in London two years earlier—got the go-ahead for his plan to bisect the colonies and isolate New England via a campaign in New York. He was to lead one army that would push south from Canada down Lake Champlain and the upper Hudson Valley (perhaps apocryphally with the general's mistress, thirty carts of baggage, and a supply of the general's private champagne in tow). A second army, under Lieutenant Colonel Barry St. Leger, would traverse the Mohawk Valley, while a third commanded by General William Howe would move up the Hudson River. Howe's prong of the attack never materialized. In July, instead of going up the Hudson, he opted to attack Philadelphia, leading 15,000 British troops by sea from New York, defeating Washington's forces at Brandywine Creek in Pennsylvania on September 11, and then forcing Congress to flee the then capital city. This was a signal victory, but it left Burgoyne to fight the northern army unaided, and by October he had to surrender. That winter marked the low point of the American effort. Washington led his troops outside the city into ill-supplied winter quarters at Valley Forge, Pennsylvania, where many died in lice-infested log shacks from starvation and the bitter cold.

Things went rather better for the Americans in New York and it proved a good thing for Burgoyne that he had a second career. On September 19, his 7,000 troops fought an American army led by Horatio Gates, with the aid of Benedict Arnold. The Americans soundly defeated the British at the Battle of Saratoga, which proved to be the war's key engagement not so much for its impact on America as for the impression it made in Europe. The Battle of Saratoga attracted what the rebels needed most: allies, whose entry into the conflict made an American victory begin to look less farfetched.

The French, still smarting from their defeat in the Seven Years' War, had been paying close attention to the colonial conflict. They had every intention of entering into another war with England, but this time the French wanted to be prepared, and had thus built up their navy and arranged for their heir apparent to marry Marie Antoinette of Austria in 1770 in order to cement the two countries. Fear of British domination of Europe brought Russia, Sweden, and the Netherlands into line, followed by several German states worried that King George III might have designs on central Europe. And now America seemed to be shaping up as a potential ally among England's own colonies.

France's foreign minister, Charles Gravier, the Count de Vergennes, had approached Spain in 1775 about cooperating in a plan to assist the American rebels, receiving interest from Madrid. The Spanish agreed with the French to furnish the Americans with secret subsidies. Vergennes organized a trading company to funnel such supplies to the Americans, and by the spring of 1776, France was routinely furnishing the colonists with guns and ammunition. The next year, colonial ambassador Benjamin Franklin arrived in Paris to win French support for the Revolution.

Franklin was one of America's great geniuses, like his colleague Thomas Jefferson a true Renaissance man of the Enlightenment. Born in 1706 in Boston, by the age of twenty-three Franklin, already a successful printer, bought a shoddy tabloid and turned it into a lively journal. Three years later he published the first edition of *Poor Richard's Almanack,* which would be the colonies' best-read annual publication for the next twenty-five years. A devoted husband and father of three who had a reputation for smoothness with the ladies, by the time Franklin contributed to the Declaration of Independence he had devised a profitable American postal system, founded the University of Pennsylvania, measured the Gulf Stream, discovered electrical polarity in a famously dangerous experiment involving lightning hitting a key tied to a kite string, and invented bifocal lenses, the lightning rod, and the potbellied Franklin stove still in use in rural New England houses.

For a while Vergennes held back, despite the formidable ambassador and his potent argument that the Declaration of Independence proved that Americans truly desired freedom from England, not merely economic and political accommodations from the mother country. Moreover, the intransigence of the British convinced Vergennes that London would not bow to talk of conciliation. The question remained whether the rebels could actually win a war against Britain, until Gates's victory over Burgoyne at Saratoga proved to France that

The Count de Vergennes, portrayed in this nineteenth-century steel engraving, was appointed foreign minister of France in 1774, at the beginning of the reign of King Louis XVI. Early in the Revolutionary War, Vergennes advised his young king to make secret loans to encourage the Americans' fight against Britain so that France could see how it would develop. Vergennes refrained from committing full support to the Americans until 1778, after they had proven themselves capable of winning the war. Making it clear that he favored the American Revolution only insofar as it could help the French crown, Vergennes wasted no sentiment on the republican cause. A decade later that cause would take hold in France as well, sparking the French Revolution and the violent overthrow of the king.

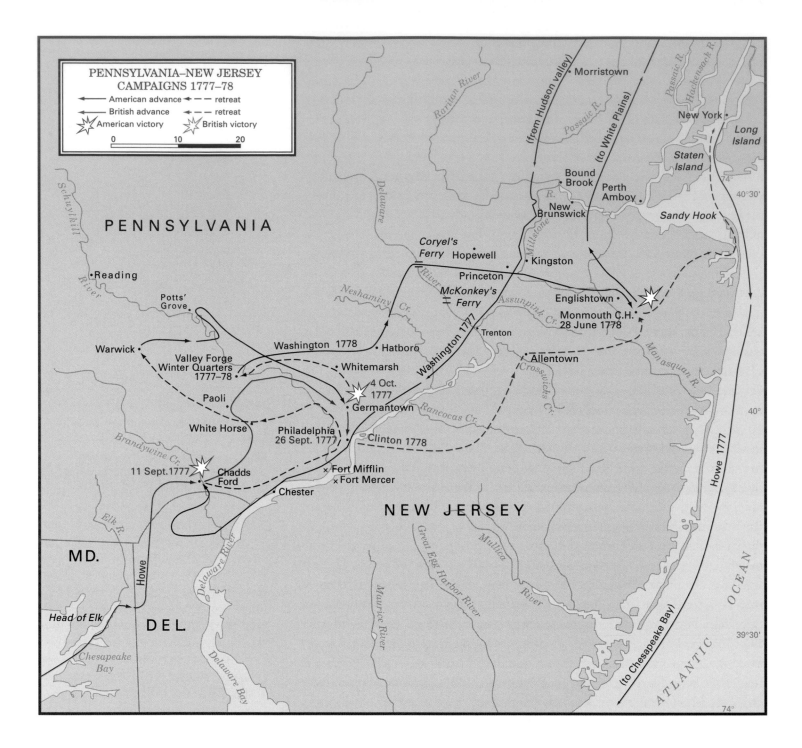

PENNSYLVANIA–NEW JERSEY CAMPAIGNS 1777–78

→ American advance ⇠ retreat
→ British advance ⇠ retreat
✦ American victory ✧ British victory

0   10   20

PENNSYLVANIA

Reading

Potts' Grove

Warwick

Valley Forge Winter Quarters 1777–78

Paoli

White Horse

Washington 1778

Hatboro

Whitemarsh

4 Oct. 1777

Germantown

Philadelphia 26 Sept. 1777

Clinton 1778

11 Sept.1777

Chadds Ford

x Fort Mifflin
x Fort Mercer

Chester

Brandywine Cr.

MD.

Howe

DEL.

Head of Elk

Chesapeake Bay

Delaware Bay

Schuylkill River

Delaware River

Elk R.

Neshaminy Cr.

Coryel's Ferry

Hopewell

McKonkey's Ferry

Princeton

Kingston

Englishtown

Monmouth C.H. 28 June 1778

Trenton

Washington 1777

Allentown

Crosswicks Cr.

Assunpink Cr.

Rancocas Cr.

NEW JERSEY

Great Egg Harbor River

Mullica River

Maurice River

Delaware River

Raritan River

Passaic R.

(from Hudson valley)

(to White Plains)

Morristown

New York

Bound Brook

New Brunswick

Perth Amboy

Staten Island

Long Island

Sandy Hook

Passaic R.

Hackensack R.

Millstone R.

40°30'

74°

40°

Manasquan R.

Howe 1777

39°30'

(to Chesapeake Bay)

ATLANTIC OCEAN

74°

The action around New York and Philadelphia in 1777–78 was precipitated by General Howe's rash decision to abandon the strategy of marching north to meet Burgoyne along the Hudson. Instead, Howe marched south to Philadelphia, where Washington's ragged forces could not defend the colonial capital. The victory proved to be meaningless, however; the new government simply moved to York, Pennsylvania.

they could. As Vergennes told King Louis XVI, "England is an enemy, at once grasping, ambitious, unjust, and perfidious. The invariable and most cherished purpose in her policies has been, if not the destruction of France, at least her overthrow, her humiliation, and her ruin." It was hardly surprising that before long Vergennes was telling his fellow nobles, "We must aid the Americans." After all, he had reason to hope that an American victory would mean French reoccupation of Canada and, with Spain, the Ohio and Mississippi valleys as well.

On December 17, 1777, Vergennes offered Franklin formal recognition and an alliance—just the steps needed to start the next round of Anglo-French hostilities—in return for America's pledge neither to seek nor to accept a separate peace with England. Franklin agreed, and by the second anniversary of the signing of the Declaration of Independence, Franco-American relations were as firm as either side could have hoped. Four days later a French fleet arrived in American waters to harass the British up and down the northern coast of the New World. The assistance proved a colossal disappointment when the French admiral refused to attack New York. Late in July and into August a joint Franco-American assault on Newport, Rhode Island, proved a downright fiasco: when the French put into Boston for supplies, a riot broke out in which one Frenchman was killed. The alliance tottered, but the French fleet left for repairs in the West Indies, promising to return the following spring.

The Americans and British battled to stalemate through much of 1778 to the east, but farther west the colonists did rather better. The British at Fort Niagara on Lake Ontario and Detroit on Lake Erie had enticed both Indians and colonial royalists to raid western settlements, prompting George Rogers Clark and 175 frontiersmen to spend the winter marching across icy wilderness flooded neck-deep to capture several British garrisons. The next summer Washington sent 4,000 troops against Tories and Iroquois Indians who were terrorizing frontier settlements in western New York, instructing that the Iroquois be not "merely overrun but destroyed." Meanwhile in the Kentucky territory, Daniel Boone and 30 other men aided by their wives and children held off more than 400 Shawnee Indians and their British and Tory allies. The effect of these encounters was to weaken the Indian tribes along the frontier and clear the way for further western settlements.

After the Battle of Saratoga, however, most of the fighting in America remained inconclusive until British General Henry Clinton mounted his southern campaign, beginning with the capture of Savannah, Georgia, on December 19, 1778. Throughout the next few months the British continued to advance through Georgia and into Virginia. Despite some harassment by American irregulars, Clinton captured Charleston on May 12, 1780, and shortly thereafter put all of South Carolina back into British hands. Flush with the success of his southern strategy, Clinton moved on to New York, leaving his best subordinate, General Charles Cornwallis, in charge of the southern campaign. It would not prove a smart move.

Cornwallis gave free rein to two overzealous cavalry officers who took to threatening to march over the Blue Ridge Mountains to North Carolina to hang revolutionary leaders. Upon hearing this, backcountry Americans attacked the British first, devastating loyalist forces at Kings Mountain on the border between the Carolinas and committing horrors of their own upon Tories who tried to surrender. This particularly fierce battle marked one of the turning points of the war in the South, because once the British proved vulnerable small farmers were emboldened to take up the cause via local guerrilla groups, which aided the American army in drawing Cornwallis and his troops across

Nathanael Greene, in a portrait by Charles Willson Peale, was perhaps Washington's most capable American-born officer. The sickly son of a colonial industrialist, he never received formal army training. Nonetheless, Greene was a military prodigy: when officials in his home state of Rhode Island recognized how naturally he took command of situations, he was promoted from the rank of private all the way to a command in the state's militia. Greene fought well at Brandywine and Monmouth, but he made his name by accomplishing something many thought impossible: he brought organization to the Continental army's quartermaster corps. But, as money ran out and frustration mounted in 1780, Greene came under personal attack in the Congress. About to lose a capable man in the squabbling, Washington promptly reassigned him to an even more challenging position—commander of the flagging Carolina campaign.

the Carolinas, expending British supplies and energy all the way. America's new commander in the south, General Nathanael Greene, conducted and won a brilliant war of attrition despite losing most of the individual battles.

Meanwhile in the north, George Washington was plagued by desertions. In Morristown, New Jersey, in May 1780 a mutiny born of sparse rations and serious arrears in pay came within a hair of destroying the American army and with it Washington's reputation. Money was one of the motives again in September, when Benedict Arnold, stewing over an official reprimand for his abuse of authority, made his name a synonym for "traitor" by attempting to sell out the West Point garrison he commanded and then joining the British Army. Such disloyalty was not confined to individuals. In January 1781, nearly 2,500 Pennsylvania veterans who had not been paid for years revolted after learning that new recruits were receiving bonuses; New Jersey's soldiers threw down their arms as well. It looked as though Washington would have to devote more time to fighting his own troops than to fighting the English.

Yet the Revolution went on as northern deserters were continually replaced elsewhere, such as by the Carolinas' backcountry irregulars—and the overall effect sapped British morale all the way to the top. Clinton and Cornwallis had a falling-out; the former thought the latter was conspiring to take

The British presented a strong threat in the Deep South, where they operated out of occupied territory in Georgia and South Carolina. But as the map below shows, the Americans rebounded in 1780–81, and the war that had started in the North finally ended in the South, at Yorktown, Virginia. For the Americans, the low point of the Carolina campaign came at Camden, South Carolina, where Cornwallis soundly beat Horatio Gates, the hero of Saratoga. Gates's replacement, General Nathanael Greene, arrived in December of 1780 and proved to be much wilier than Gates, using the terrain to his advantage to outmarch, if not outmatch, the British. Exasperated, Cornwallis and his forces moved up to Yorktown and paused in a defensive stance.

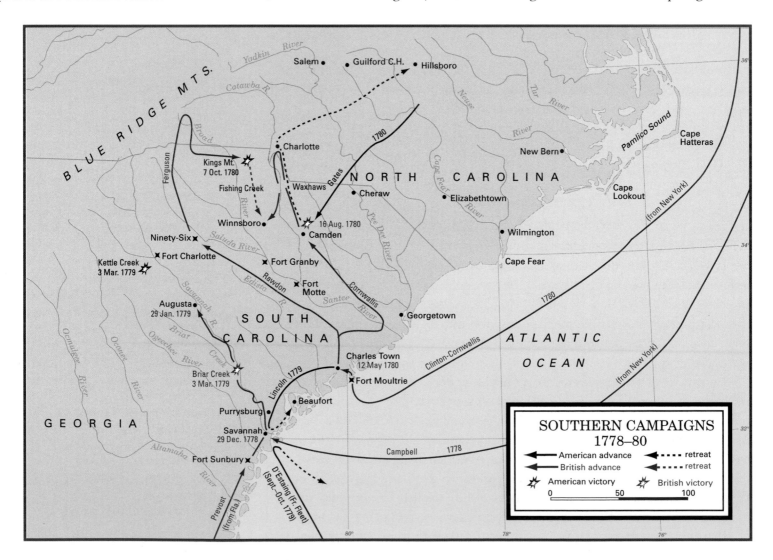

his place, while Cornwallis resented the lack of support he was getting from Clinton. In London, sick and tired in every sense, Prime Minister North yearned to be relieved of his duties; things were being bungled in America, and while King George III remained determined to continue the war, even he was beginning to see just how difficult victory would be. In other words, a ragtag American army fraught with deserters and itself on the verge of collapse was thwarting the superior forces of the world's greatest power, and it was causing dissension and division in the mother country.

By early May 1781 the last of the mutineers in the American army had been punished, the French were in place, and Washington was planning to move on the British. A year earlier a force of 5,000 French troops commanded by General Jean-Baptiste Comte de Rochambeau had landed at Newport, followed that next summer by a French fleet under Admiral François Joseph Paul de Grasse, fresh from successes against the British in the Caribbean. Thus bolstered by America's allies, Washington prepared to move south and meet Cornwallis before the British general could mount an autumn offensive.

Washington conferred with Rochambeau in late May and learned that a

This French engraving of the siege of Yorktown shows the French fleet under Admiral François de Grasse blocking the water route to the British position at Yorktown. Checked by American and French troops against escape by land, Cornwallis had done little through the summer of 1781 except dig in and await reinforcements by sea. It was General Rochambeau who recognized the opportunity to trap the British force by summoning de Grasse from the Caribbean. De Grasse defeated a British relief fleet making its way to Yorktown, then took over its position on the Chesapeake Bay. Washington and Rochambeau arrived soon enough to encircle Yorktown by land, after which Cornwallis retreated.

In John Trumbull's 1820 painting entitled *Surrender of Cornwallis at Yorktown,* General Charles O'Hara rides past two lines of American and French officers to formally surrender the British force at Yorktown, ending the siege and in effect the war. Stopping to face General Washington, O'Hara flashed a smile and explained that his superior officer, General Cornwallis, was indisposed. In reality, Cornwallis was too ashamed to go through with the surrender.

French fleet would sail to the Caribbean for military and trade reasons and then come north. Washington suggesed a Franco-American land attack on New York; Rochambeau argued for going after the garrison Cornwallis had established at Yorktown, Virginia. On July 10 the French and American armies met far up the coast at White Plains, and conducted combined operations around New York for a month. Then on August 14, word arrived that Admiral de Grasse was headed for Chesapeake Bay but would only remain there until October 15. Washington immediately agreed to Rochambeau's plan to attack Yorktown while the French fleet kept the British navy from reaching it. He headed south— leaving enough troops behind to make Clinton think an attack was planned on New York. The ruse went so smoothly that Clinton did not realize what had happened until Washington was past Philadelphia. (In mid-September, while Washington was in Virginia, he learned that on September 5 de Grasse had out-maneuvered the British fleet and sent them back to New York for repairs.)

The Franco-American army took its positions at Yorktown and began a siege on the morning of September 28; within two days the British were forced to retreat to an inner line of defenses. Washington's aide, Colonel Alexander Hamilton, led a fierce charge on the British left flank on October 14, and three days later Cornwallis was forced to admit his position was hopeless and that he was ready to negotiate.

On October 9—just as the regrouped British navy finally set sail from New York—Cornwallis surrendered. According to folklore, the British army band played a song called "The World Turned Upside Down" on the apocryphal Yorktown common green. Whether that was true or not, Cornwallis would later write, "All depended on the fleet. . . . Clinton promised one. Washington had one." Of course, Washington's fleet was largely French; America's small navy was capable only of making itself an occasional nuisance, such as through the heroics of Captain John Paul Jones, who in 1778 had sailed to the British coast and the next year captured and boarded a British frigate that had just crippled his own ship, prompting Jones's famous response to the call for his surrender, "I have not yet begun to fight." Then, an overall American triumph had seemed impossible so long as Britain ruled the waves, but things had changed by the autumn of 1781: thanks to the

Benjamin Franklin served as America's representative in Paris for almost two years before he was invited to call upon France's Queen Marie Antoinette (seated on sofa), an occasion depicted below. Arthur Lee, one of the other Americans present, was not impressed by the French court; of the moment captured below he wrote in his diary, "The commissioners went again to Versailles, to be presented to the queen. It was with great difficulty they could pass through an unordered crowd, all pressing to get into the room where the queen was, it being levee day. When they got in, they stood a moment in view of the queen, then crowded out again. They were neither presented nor spoken to, and everything seemed in confusion."

John Jay, in an 1805 painting by John Trumbull, was a lawyer and diplomat from New York who became a leading voice during America's transition from a colonial possession to an independent republic. From 1782 to 1784 Jay worked with Benjamin Franklin and John Adams in Paris to negotiate the end of the Revolutionary War and, even more important, the recognition of the United States as a sovereign nation. No three men could have had more disparate temperaments, but together they forayed into the treacherous world of European diplomacy and emerged with a treaty that acknowledged American independence.

French, the oft-defeated Washington had won the most important American victory since Saratoga.

When Lord North heard what had happened at Yorktown he moaned, "Oh, God, it's all over." It needn't have been. Britain still had powerful forces and many sympathizers in America and could have continued the war for many years—but not without funds, which Parliament refused to appropriate. The national debt had doubled since 1775, meaning new taxes would be needed to continue the war, and representatives to the House of Commons knew their constituents would have none of that. Those members who had opposed the war all along became more vocal about it, and others joined their ranks. Before long, both Clinton and Cornwallis were ordered back to Britain in an admission of military as well as financial weakness.

As early as 1779 the American Revolution had become a full-blown world war for the British. Britain and France had been going at each other around the globe, struggling for world domination from the Caribbean islands to India and West Africa. Spain had entered the war in June 1779, allying with France but not with the Americans after a series of British attacks on Spanish ships and colonies. The next year Britain declared war on the Dutch, who had been taking advantage of the conflict to renew their profitable trade in the West Indies, and in April 1782 the Dutch recognized the United States. Expensive confrontations with the Dutch and Spanish had continued around the globe and resulted in major successes in both India and the West Indies, but in February 1782 France captured St. Christopher just a week after Spain had taken Minorca and before news of either British defeat could reach Parliament, where a motion renouncing the American war failed by a single vote. King George tried desperately to rally his forces, but the defeats in the two islands drained supporters from his coalition. One of the staunchest, Lord Sandwich, left the government proclaiming that further fighting in America would be useless. When the cabinet minister for colonial affairs, Lord George Germain, resigned and renamed himself Viscount in recognition of his service, peace party leader Edmund Burke quipped that the war had produced nothing but calamities and peerages.

The rising tide of protest in Parliament could not be ignored, and on March 15, North lost a vote of confidence by nine votes. He resigned and was succeeded as prime minister by Lord Rockingham, an opponent of the war. Two members of the peace party, Charles James Fox and William Fitzmaurice, Lord Shelburne, joined the new government, as did several former supporters of the American conflict who believed the king had erred not so much in provoking the war as in losing it.

Peace talks were set to take place in Paris, where John Jay, the first member of the American negotiating team joined Benjamin Franklin in the summer of 1782. Despite the new nation's alliance with France, delegation head Benjamin Franklin had every intention of playing the French and British off one another. In September, for example, he proposed to the British negotiator Richard

Oswald that Britain recognize American independence, accept its boundary claims against Canada, and grant it fishing rights off Newfoundland and would be even better to admit responsibility for the war, cede Canada to the United States, and pay indemnities to Americans who had lost property in the conflict. If all this were done, the wily Franklin told Oswald, the United States would be left strong enough to act independently and thus not as, say, a French satellite.

Lord Shelburne, the new colonial minister, was not swayed by Franklin's supposed logic. He acknowledged that his country was down but refused to let it be counted out in the wake of England's recent victories in India as well as the opening created by the arrival of John Jay in Paris. Shelburne knew that Jay's family had fled France due to religious persecution, and that the American statesman had been suspicious of the French alliance from the beginning. What's more, Franklin had become aware of double-dealing on the part of France, which was not only holding secret talks with Spain over the fate of the Mississippi Valley but had also sent a secret delegation to London to discuss peace terms that would be unacceptable to the Americans.

Not to be outmaneuvered, in early September Franklin told Oswald that while negotiations could resume without American independence as a precondition, the talks would continue only if London acknowledged him as a representative of the United States rather than of a band of rebellious colonists. What Franklin was suggesting was that the new nation be allowed to conduct its own peace negotiations — at which any and all pertinent issues could be raised—without the French; after all, the Americans were not seeking independence from Britain in order to forge dependence on France. The British team accepted, and from then on Franklin was treated as a representative of the "Thirteen United States."

Perhaps the most important ingredient in the negotiations was the tacit recognition on both sides that despite the antagonisms of the past decade and beyond, America still had more in common with Britain than with any other country in terms of culture, religion, politics, and, of course, economics. Preliminary terms of the Treaty of Paris were agreed upon by the two countries on November 5: the Americans would forget about the rest of Canada, but would control the northwest territories and half of Lake Ontario as well as the fishing rights in each, while Britain would have access to the Mississippi River and citizens of both Britain and America would have equal commercial rights in the others' nation. Economic as well as political considerations lay behind each of these provisions: the British navy's presence on the Mississippi would deter French and Spanish ambitions in the area, while vigorous free trade between Britain and the United States would bind the mother country and its former colonies together in ways politics could not put asunder.

Not all the points made it into the final treaty: Ontario would remain part of Canada and the Royal Navy would not be granted license to sail up and down the Mississippi at will, but the rest of the terms were accepted in London and Philadelphia on November 30, 1782. French Foreign Minister Vergennes immediately pronounced the accord a violation of the Franco-American treaties of 1778. But Franklin was in the catbird seat and warned the French that pressing their points might anger the Americans into forming an alliance with Britain—

The ratified version of the Treaty of Paris, above, was signed on September 3, 1783. It included agreements to end a host of disputes among Europe's leading nations, including Spain, France, and the Netherlands, and guaranteed official recognition of the United States of America by each of those powers and, most notably, by Great Britain. The negotiations were exacting, but crucial: the Treaty of Paris took two years to complete and another thirty to test. Below, a medal struck in 1783 commemorated the Treaty of Paris and the return of peace to America.

and that it might thus behoove France to prove its friendship to the new nation, such as through a loan. Vergennes secured six million livres for the United States.

The American Congress ratified the Treaty of Paris on April 15, 1783, and the last British soldiers left New York on December 4. That same day, George Washington bade his officers farewell and returned to his plantation home in Mount Vernon, Virginia, rejecting talk of being named "King of the United States," a notion that had arisen among many who still could not imagine a nation where sovereignty would rest in the common people. The ensuing debate over what sort of government would best serve an independent republic based on freedom fired the construction of a constitution without precedent in world history.

The New Nation

At first, the United States operated under the Articles of Confederation formulated in the summer of 1776 not out of political philosophy but for expediency in time of war. When Richard Henry Lee had proposed independence in June 1776, he had also suggested writing a "plan of confederation" to be submitted to the colonies. Even before Jefferson had completed the Declaration of Independence, a committee of thirteen led by John Dickinson set to work on the plan, which was submitted to the Continental Congress on July 12 as the Articles of Confederation and Perpetual Union.

The Articles of Confederation actually provided more of a political and diplomatic alliance among the colonies than a constitution for a unified nation; in fact, it resembled today's charter of the United Nations more than the U.S. Constitution as we know it. Occasional meetings of diplomats from the various colonies could easily have accomplished what the first U.S. government did. Indeed, federal powers under the Articles were so limited that most Americans' lives would not have been much different had there been no central government at all. What the Articles did provide the new nation was a badly needed symbol of unity as well as a forum for representatives from each colony to meet regularly to discuss common problems. In fact, the document described the freest government the United States would ever know, perhaps one that better embodied the ideals of the American Revolution than the one created by the subsequent Constitution. Like the Declaration of Independence, the Articles reflected the distrust of powerful institutions of a more passionate time.

Dickinson's original draft of the Articles of Confederation provided for the new states to retain police powers, as well as the most important attribute of any government: the ability to exercise power over individuals. The states would be federated under a central government—actually little more than "a firm league of friendship"—that would function through a congress of representatives from the various regions of each former colony and whose decisions would be carried out by an executive council of state. The phrase "sovereignty, freedom, and independence" was added in April 1777.

Debate on the Articles continued through most of 1777. In the end, the amended document provided for even fewer powers than Dickinson had envisaged, indicating a clear victory for those who disdained too much authority. To insure that the central government would lack the power of coercion, the Continental Congress did away with Dickinson's proposed executive council of state—the new Confederation would have no executive branch. Each of the thirteen states would have one vote in the new U.S. Congress, and the assent of nine would be required to implement important decisions; amendments to the Articles could be made only by the unanimous approval of all state legislatures. The right to issue currency would be shared by the central government and the individual states. The Congress would not have the power to raise armies, or regulate commerce, although it would control the foreign relations of the United States, including the "right and power of determining on peace and war," of "sending and receiving ambassadors," and of "entering into treaties and alliances." The terms regarding foreign affairs were written to cover the conduct of the Revolution, however, and would be difficult to enforce in time of peace. By the same token, it would be virtually impossible to enforce the Articles' prohibition on any state raising an army or navy without the permission of Congress. The states would be able to make Congress keep its promise not to deprive any state of its western territories.

The amended Articles were sent to the states for ratification, but Maryland rejected the draft because of the clause on western lands. Thus the document was amended again to allow for the creation of new states out of frontier territories. Maryland accepted the revised Articles, and the government thus created began operating on March 1, 1781, as the Revolution was winding down.

It would be unfair to blame the weakness of the Confederation for all of America's immediate postrevolutionary problems, most of which would have cropped up under any new government. No constitution, for example, could have stopped the sharp economic depression that followed the Revolution and its profound impact on commerce; besides, far worse downturns would hamper the economy early in the nineteenth century, when the nation had a much stronger government. By the same token, the disdain many foreigners felt for the new nation grew more from the perceived weakness of its economy than from that of its government, a perception that would continue under the Constitution, which was designed to forge a stronger central government than that defined by the Articles of Confederation.

A more meaningful assessment of the Confederation can be gleaned from an examination of how the central government handled the powers it actually had, the most important of which was the disposition of America's western territories—a pressing issue considering the new nation's rapid expansion. Policies clearly were needed. Before long, American pioneers would cross into trans-Appalachia, so some means of governing them would have to be established. Because the states had granted the western territories to the Confederation, a system also had to be devised to handle private claims on the lands in question. It was the sort of disposition that, properly conducted, would provide the central government with much-needed capital.

Charged with formulating policies regarding the western lands, Thomas Jefferson wrote or inspired most of the legislation pertaining to the region. Thus he not only set the pattern for American expansion over the next century and a half, but he also became the most important figure of the Confederation era

In 1981, the bicentennial of the Articles of Confederation was commemorated on a U.S. stamp. The Articles were drafted largely by John Dickinson and amounted to little more than a friendship pact among the new states. According to Robert Morris, the documents gave Congress the "privilege of asking everything" and the states "the prerogative of granting nothing."

through accomplishments that rank with his service during the Revolution, and may perhaps be his greatest contribution to the new nation.

Not that it's easy to judge: Jefferson's remarkable achievements were hardly confined to politics and governance, to which he contributed such items of genius as the Declaration of Independence with its stirring prose and high ideals unequaled before or since on either count. As spectacular an intellect as Benjamin Franklin had, Thomas Jefferson's shone even brighter; this son of a wealthy Virginia plantation owner studied so many sciences, arts, and humanities that he might have been taken for a dilettante had his knowledge of each discipline not been so deep. In addition to his mastery of the biological sciences, engineering, agriculture, and archeology, among other matters, Jefferson spoke seven languages and was a brilliant architect, as can be seen in the Virginia capitol, on the campus of the University of Virginia he founded, and in Charlottesville at his fabled home, Monticello.

He did not cut much of a figure, despite a height of six feet three inches topped by red hair. The trappings of polite society held little appeal for Thomas Jefferson, as evidenced by his informality and tendency to receive visitors in a tattered robe and slippers down at the heel—a habit he continued as president, even when meeting with beribboned (and appalled) foreign dignitaries. Despite his genteel background, Jefferson devoted his talents to opposing the legacies of the British aristocracy and of Europe's established churches, leading him to write to a friend on January 16, 1787, "Experience declares that man is the only animal which devours his own kind; for I can apply no milder term to the governments of Europe, and to the general prey of the rich on the poor." Jefferson put his beliefs into practice by devising a more humane criminal code, creating a complex system of public schools, and at one point trying to put the brakes on slavery, even while continuing to keep slaves of his own, ostensibly in fear that American agriculture depended on slave labor but in fact because he was broke and his creditors would not let him sell or free them. Jefferson was above all an agrarian who feared that too much growth in cities would divide the new nation between powerful merchants and poor laborers whose reliance on others for their living would lay them bare to economic exploitation and political manipulation. Taken together, his instincts were decidedly libertarian; as he once said, "I am not a friend to a very energetic government."

This was obvious when Jefferson tackled the question of America's western lands. His first suggestions, which appeared in the Land Ordinance of 1784, specified a three-stage process for admitting new territories into the Confederation and eventually leading them to full statehood. It was a revolutionary notion because under the European model, such as the British practiced in Canada, the lands would have become colonies of the thirteen United States and their populations treated as subjects unentitled to the rights of Americans. Jefferson's plan was designed to help the United States avoid such a mistake.

And that wasn't the only innovation. Jefferson's original concept in the Land Ordinance of 1784 also included the abolition of slavery in new territories after 1800, reflecting growing sentiment against the horrific practice. Unfortunately, Jefferson's antislavery provision was defeated by a single vote in Congress, and the Land Ordinance of 1784 never went into effect; a simi-

OPPOSITE PAGE: **Thomas Jefferson was painted in 1801 by Caleb Boyle standing before the Natural Bridge, near Lexington, Virginia, a phenomenon that fascinated him all his life. "I sometimes think of building a little hermitage at the Natural Bridge (for it is my property)," he wrote to a friend from Paris in 1786, "and of passing there a [part] of the year at least." Engineered not by man but by the waters of Cedar Creek 215 feet below, the bridge was one of the natural sights that Jefferson recommended Europeans take in when they visited America.**

lar law regarding disposition of the western lands without mentioning slavery was adopted instead. This plan, the Land Ordinance of 1785, devised by a committee at the same time Jefferson was crafting his ordinance, provided for the lands in question to be marked into townships six miles square and divided into thirty-six sections of 640 acres apiece. One section would be reserved for educational facilities, while the rest would be auctioned off to the highest bidders at a minimum price of a dollar per acre. Jefferson had hoped the West would be settled by small farmers, but the new plan clearly favored land speculators, whose wealth helped them find friends in Congress. When Jefferson left America to become minister to France in 1785, the real estate–minded gained power, and as a result their plan passed as the Northwest Ordinance of 1787 over some objections but with little difficulty.

As could be expected, speculators purchased enormous tracts of land to resell to individual settlers. Among the largest such firms was the Ohio Company of Associates organized by Manasseh Cutler, a future member of Congress from Connecticut backed by colleagues from other states as well as European banks. Thanks to lobbying, political manipulation, and the know-how to take advantage of currency fluctuations, Cutler's group managed to obtain land at an average price of about eight cents an acre. In time, the Ohio Company would control more than 1.5 million acres of the American Midwest. Another million acres went to a group headed by New Jersey Congressman John Symmes, while five hundred thousand acres was sold to the Scioto Company formed by New York and New England speculators and congressmen backed by Dutch and French bankers.

Although they had purchased the land cheap, these groups and other investors put enough money into the West to be concerned whether an orderly enough government could be established to make settlements not only possible but profitable. Thus the speculators supported Cutler's modified 1785 version of Jefferson's original ordinance, which also provided for territories to become equal states in three stages. At the time, however, the land companies had no interest in the unexplored southwest, so in order not to complicate matters the new document applied only to the northwestern territories and, of course, without Jefferson's antislavery proposals. This Northwest Ordinance of 1787 passed with the support of the speculators and a few disappointed Jeffersonians, and became the model for America's expansion across the continent. The legislation enabled the then-"northwest" territories of Illinois, Indiana, Michigan, Ohio, and Wisconsin to enter the nation as states in the next generation.

Angry farmers in western Massachusetts follow Daniel Shays in an insurrection in 1786–87, below. The drawing shows a small force of troops repelling Shays' attempt to capture an arsenal, although most of the fighting took place between the rebels and state troops. Governor James Bowdoin published his intention to prevent and suppress all such riotous proceedings in the proclamation shown opposite page. Shays' Rebellion convinced Americans throughout the states that their new country was vulnerable to further outbreaks under the weak Articles of Confederation, opposite page. "Influence is not government," George Washington wrote to a friend. "Let us have a government by which our lives, liberties and properties will be secured, or let us know the worst at once."

Even with sales of these western lands the new nation experienced financial difficulties throughout the late eighteenth century. Repeated currency devaluations and the collapse of the continental dollar led many to distrust paper money in favor of gold and silver, which Americans either hoarded or deposited in banks overseas. Several states found it impossible to collect taxes to pay for ongoing expenses; before long debtors demanded currency inflation and insisted that creditors accept the depreciated paper money as full payment of debts. When banks and local governments in some communities attempted foreclosures on homes and businesses, debtors began resorting to violence against the authorities, raising fears that a new revolution might erupt over economic matters.

In a last-ditch effort to forestall further violence, several states issued more paper money as legal tender. This resulted in a rash of lawsuits by creditors; the most significant took place in Rhode Island in 1786, when a court decided in favor of a plaintiff who refused to accept paper currency. This precedent emboldened creditors in other states to demand an end to currency inflation, leading debtors to fight back again. By the summer of 1786 the threat of violence loomed large across the United States.

Matters were worse in some places than others, of course, and among the worst was Massachusetts, the very cradle of violent American radicalism. Its farmers had suffered more than those in other states from the loss of trade with Europe, and foreclosures mounted. Poor farmers burdened with debt appealed for help to the state legislature, which turned a deaf ear. When the legislature adjourned in July 1786 without having taken any action on their behalf, debtors organized protest rallies in several of the hardest hit communities. By September the protesters had united under the leadership of Captain Daniel Shays, a veteran of the Revolution who would command the slapdash rebels in several engagements with the state militia. Massachusetts Governor James Bowdoin was so alarmed that he denounced the debtor farmers as criminals and sent reinforcements under General Benjamin Lincoln to quell Shays' small force. The captain and his followers firmly believed they were fighting for the principles of the Declaration of Independence. Bowdoin maintained that if Shays was not put down anarchy would ensue and destroy the state and eventually the nation as well. After little more than one volley, Lincoln crushed Shays' Rebellion, forcing its leaders to flee and its troops to disband. The very existence of the uprising, however, made political and business leaders in every state wonder whether governments that permitted such events should be strengthened or replaced.

Toward a Constitution

The economic depression that followed the Revolution in America reached its nadir in the summer of 1786. After that, the domestic economy and the new nation's foreign trade began a slow, sporadic climb. This commercial upturn was due not to the actions of Congress, which met irregularly and often failed to achieve a quorum for weeks at a time; neither did it arise from executive or legislative actions by the states. Rather, the depression ended when Europe began to demand more American trade and as the supplying

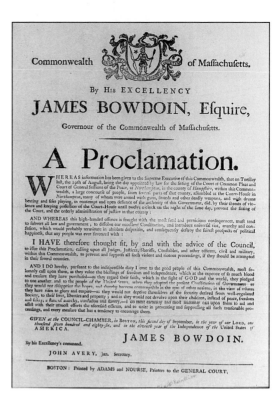

farmers and merchants learned to live with both peace and independence.

The most significant adjustment was the establishment of friendly relations among the various states. This form of national unity grew, as so many of America's defining characteristics would, from commercial concerns. Under the Confederation each individual state retained control over its own commerce, which made coordinated trade unwieldy to organize. Although there were few instances of states trying to erect tariffs or other barriers to trade, commercial clashes did take place between New York and its New England neighbors as well as among the mid-Atlantic states. Before long, however, most states acknowledged the need for firmer commercial guidelines, which prompted representatives from Virginia and Maryland to meet in March 1785 to work out an agreement governing trade on the Potomac River. The conference was such a success that the Maryland delegation suggested the resulting accord be expanded at a regional conference including Delaware and Pennsylvania. Virginia's representatives, driven by one James Madison, countered by suggesting the invitation be extended to all the states, to which the Marylanders agreed. The national conference on commerce was scheduled for September 1786 in Annapolis, Maryland, and Madison and others set to sending out invitations.

At the same time, Congress was discussing how to

Frail in appearance, James Madison compensated for his small stature with a bouncy walk meant to make him seem larger and more robust. A student of politics and history, Madison first worked with Thomas Jefferson on the Constitution for their home state in 1776, and remained associated politically with his fellow Virginian. At the Constitutional Convention of 1787, James Madison drafted most of the U.S. Constitution, crafting its language as precisely as possible. After the convention, he teamed up with John Jay and Alexander Hamilton to write *The Federalist Papers,* a series of essays that helped convince the states to ratify the Constitution. Madison and Hamilton went on to become bitter opponents, Hamilton leading the Federalist party that favored strong national government, while Madison remained with Thomas Jefferson in forming the more populist Anti-Federalist party.

amend the Articles of Confederation to make the central government work better. Some representatives were acting on the need to end friction among the states in order to present a common front to foreign countries; others were more interested in establishing efficient, binding means of controlling commerce and obtaining revenues from it. The dispute came to a head when New York blocked a movement to amend the Articles to allow for tariffs and New Jersey refused an amendment to insure the states made their payments to the national treasury. On the eve of the Annapolis Convention scheduled to begin September 11, 1786, the prospects for interstate cooperation looked slim.

Despite their differing opinions on trade policy, both New York and New Jersey had representatives at the Annapolis meetings, as did Delaware, Pennsylvania, and Virginia. Massachusetts, New Hampshire, North Carolina, and Rhode Island also sent delegates, but they did not arrive in time for the four-day conference. The brevity of the sessions was hardly due to animosities. On the contrary, from the very beginning the opinion was unanimous that the Confederation government had to be strengthened. New York delegate Alexander Hamilton suggested that a general convention be held in Philadelphia the following year "to devise such further provisions as shall appear to them necessary to render the constitution of the Federal Government adequate to the exigencies of the union" as well as to discuss the commercial problems that had led to the present meetings. Hamilton's recommendation was accepted by the delegates in Annapolis and sent to the Congress and the various states.

For the next five months political leaders in each state and the Confederation government discussed Hamilton's proposal as Shays' Rebellion and similar uprisings sparked fear of social upheaval. Thus encouraged to establish a government strong enough to put down insurrections as well as to make the Confederation's commercial clauses more workable, eleven of the states eventually agreed to attend the Philadelphia convention; only New Hampshire and Rhode Island failed to send delegates, but they fell in line soon after. In addition to the states, Congress agreed to a convention "for the sole and express purpose of revising the Articles of Confederation."

On May 25, 1787, enough state representatives had arrived in Philadelphia to call the convention to order. As some delegates left for the summer, others came to take their places; all in all, those who participated represented an accurate cross-section of each state's commercial, agricultural, and, of course, political leadership. Forty-three of the fifty-five attendees were or had been members of Congress, eight had signed the Declaration of Independence, and seven were or had been governor of their state. Although the Constitutional Convention defined the United States of America, some of the most important figures of the Revolution were not in attendance: Thomas Jefferson was serving as minister to France and John Adams as minister to Great Britain. Many radical revolutionaries were absent as well: Thomas Paine was on his way to Europe, where he would become a member of the French revolutionary government; Samuel Adams remained embroiled in the tempestuous teapot of Massachusetts politics, and Patrick Henry had refused when named to the convention.

Looking back over two centuries of perspective, it is clear that the impetus for the Constitutional Convention came from successful farmers and merchants who recognized that business would improve under a government that could issue a strong currency and establish a larger trading area. To achieve these ideal commercial conditions the delegates planned what amounted to a bloodless coup, for some their second in a dozen years. The first had sought independence from Britain and freedom from governmental controls, and had succeeded—all too well in the minds of some of those in Philadelphia. The second coup was thus aimed at throttling back the first to forge an even stronger central government.

Born in the West Indies, Alexander Hamilton had immigrated to America when he was twenty-two years old. As an artillery captain serving with the Continental army in 1776, he so impressed George Washington that he was invited to join the general's staff. Brilliant and conscientious, he remained at the center of national events for the rest of his life.

TRENTON 1789.
J. CALIFANO.
DESIGNED BY

CHAPTER 5

A MORE PERFECT UNION

It is understandable why many Americans looking back from the end of the twentieth century to the beginning of their nation consider the Constitutional Convention a gathering of political sages the likes of which has never been seen before or since. After all, this is how the story is usually told on TV and in the movies. What's more, the delegates actually did produce the most admired, imitated, and longest enduring constitution in human history, which was understood even at the time; not long after the meetings in Philadelphia no less an observer than Thomas Jefferson called the participants "an assembly of demigods."

But were these "founding fathers" really such extraordinary individuals, or does their greatness owe more to the demands of the times? Historians have been puzzling over this question for more than two centuries, trying to fathom the motives and actions of the storied early Americans who created the Constitution. The prevailing interpretation shifts with each generation of scholars, running a gamut of trends from the view of the founding fathers as

George Washington was hailed with affection on his ride through Trenton, New Jersey, in 1789, a scene captured in the folk painting at left by a local artist, J. Califano. En route to his inauguration in New York, Washington was preceded by young girls singing songs and spreading flowers in his path. A hankerchief, above, honors the first president.

just that in the best sense—selfless, high-minded idealists concerned only with the well-being of their offspring—to the opinion that they were a bunch of grasping would-be robber barons out only to line their own pockets. The truth, of course, lies somewhere in between, but one fact is inescapable: the delegates did not convene to engage in lofty debates over how to design a perfect new system of governance. Rather, they met to cobble together a charter that would be acceptable to all parties and would create a workable enough government to satisfy the needs of the time; they deliberately left it to future generations to modify the draft into something more elaborate. The goal was to devise a framework for resolving problems rather than for creating a utopia.

No system of government can be established without unity of principle as well as purpose, and the men who met in Philadelphia in 1787 did hold certain basic political truths to be self-evident. Paramount among these was the concept of limited government, particularly regarding economic matters. Next was majority rule, but only with the proviso that minority rights also must be preserved; after all, most of the founding fathers hailed from a minority themselves, even if their caste was the American version of aristocracy. Finally, the participants in the Constitutional Convention with few exceptions agreed that what were then the fundamentals of American society should be preserved. As opposed to their counterparts of 1776, these men were not revolutionaries but codifiers.

Unlike the soaring Declaration of Independence, the Constitution of the United States promulgates neither a strict theory of governance nor a doctrine on the relationship between citizen and state, nor does it contain a ringing proclamation of national purpose. It's much simpler than that: the Constitution is a set of rules with laws to back them up. After the majestic beginning of its preamble, little poetry graces the charter; its appeal comes more from ideas than emotions. Whereas scholars admire the soul-stirring eloquence of Jefferson's Declaration, they treasure the rational workability of the Constitution, through which men of different backgrounds but similar political principles devised the rules and built an arena for open debate over national issues. Thus the convention not only established a government but virtually insured that each generation would hold open debates aimed at adopting various new constitutional provisions.

It is interesting that during the proceedings not one of the delegates mentioned the absence of discussion about the primary issue for which the convention had been called: amending the Articles of Confederation, and this even though some of those present had been members of the Confederation Congress. Rather, early on, a vote was taken affirming the intent to adopt the Virginia Plan as a working model, in effect dumping the Articles. By June of 1787 it had become clear that the Confederation government was dying with no need for a final blow; its acceptance of the Northwest Ordinance within the month would prove to be the Confederation's greatest accomplishment as well as its last of any importance.

The Constitution would leave rather a greater legacy than even the participants in Philadelphia realized. Their first official act was to select the redoubtable George Washington as president of the convention—the only

American who commanded enough public respect to give the meetings sufficient authority and legitimacy. Although every schoolchild has been told that the "father of our country" was so great he fessed up to chopping down a cherry tree with his little hachet, it is curious that two centuries later Washington's personality is less fixed in Americans' minds than are those of Jefferson and Franklin; then again, the general lacked his more intellectual colleagues' talents for crafting brilliant prose through which to explain themselves and their ideas. His character instead must be drawn from eyewitness testimony and anecdotes. One of the more telling occurred during the fiercest fighting at Yorktown, when Washington had come under direct fire and a panicky colonel suggested the general "step back a little." The commander glared at his aide and replied, "If you are afraid, you have the liberty to step back." Many were the times Washington would thus demonstrate the leadership by example that made him such a perfect choice as the first U.S. president.

Born in Virginia in 1732, Washington grew up on a farm, studied mathematics, surveyed the primeval woods of the Shenandoah Valley as a teenager, and inherited substantial tracts of land when his brother died from tuberculosis in 1752. With no formal education Washington learned about the world from the merchants on transatlantic vessels which piloted up the Rappahannock River; he *never* set foot on European soil. Real estate would remain a prime interest: at the time of his own death, Washington would own 110,000 acres across Virginia, West Virginia, and Ohio. Physically imposing but with refined plantation manners, he pursued a military career from the French and Indian Wars through the Revolution and beyond that was nothing short of spectacular, as much for the resiliency he showed in defeat as for the brilliance of his victories. Resourceful, dependable, and stern but fair, he truly was a leader of men, perhaps because he was such a clear-headed pragmatist. By the mid-1780s, Shays' Rebellion and its fellows had brought many around to Washington's somewhat jaded view that "the few . . . who act upon Principles of disinterestedness are, comparatively speaking, no more than a drop in the Ocean." He added in 1786 that "We have, probably, had too good an opinion of human nature in forming our confederation."

The Constitutional Convention would benefit from its president's understanding that self-interest, particularly of the financial variety, made a far more potent motive for the public than ideology—and that clashes would thus continue among groups with divergent economic interests. Unfortunately, the president was prevented from making counterproposals. When one participant suggested that the American army be restricted to 5,000 troops at any given time, Washington could only whisper to a nearby delegate that an amendment would then be needed specifying that "no foreign army should invade the United States at any time with more than 3,000 troops."

Washington and his fellow Virginians, including James Madison and Edmund Randolph, comprised the delegation best prepared and most eager to dispense with the Articles and the Confederation government they described. On May 29, 1787, Randolph introduced a possible replacement dubbed the Virginia Plan, under which the states would be downgraded to a more subordinate role and a new national government created with a bicameral leg-

As governor of Virginia from 1786 to 1788, Edmund Randolph, above, counted Washington, Jefferson, and Henry among his constituents. Wealthy and well-born, Randolph was also an adept statesman. He asserted his leadership early at the Constitutional Convention, presenting the controversial idea that congressional representation should be based on population. Randolph's opponent on the issue was New Jersey's William Paterson, seen below in a late eighteenth-century engraving. Paterson was born in Ireland but grew up in Princeton, New Jersey, where his family operated a store. Serious and hardworking, Paterson studied at Princeton University and became a lawyer in 1769. His "New Jersey Plan" caused a protracted argument that resulted in the final makeup of the Senate.

Samuel Jennings portrayed Liberty as an educated woman in this allegorical painting entitled *Liberty Displaying the Arts and Sciences* in 1792. He anticipated that with independence an accomplished fact, Liberty in America would next have to turn her attention to the rights of enslaved African-Americans. Women, too, were ignored in the debate over rights and representation at the Constitutional Convention. Patriots such as Mercy Otis Warren and Abigail Adams expressed their ideas freely in letters to Thomas Jefferson, John Adams, and other influential men, but were denied an official voice in the national debate and a vote in the new not-quite-democracy.

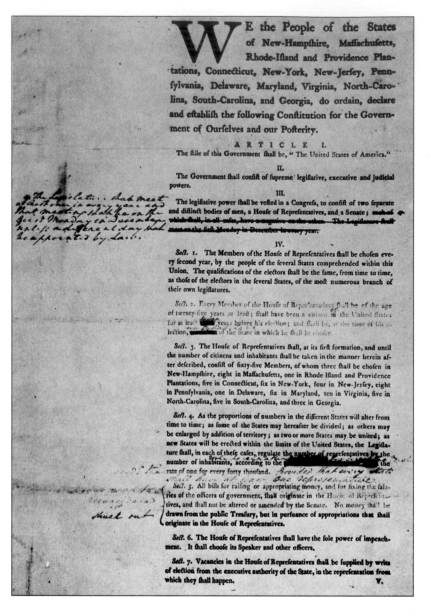

The first page of one of Washington's draft copies of the Constitution includes notes on proposed changes. Toward the end of the convention, the delegates realized that the Preamble should not include a list of the states present, since no one could be sure in advance that all the states would ratify the document.

islature elected by the states according to their respective populations, meaning the larger states would dominate. This legislature would select an executive—the American version of a European monarch—as well as the judges in a new federal court system. Understandably, the smaller states opposed the Virginia Plan and instead supported William Paterson's New Jersey Plan, which was more in line with the convention's stated purpose of amending the Articles of Confederation rather than replacing them outright. Under Paterson's scheme, each state would have equal representation in a Congress with broader powers to impose taxes, regulate foreign and domestic commerce, and pass national laws superseding those of the states as well as to select the members of the executive and judiciary branches—but all on behalf of the states. Neither plan was acceptable to all parties, as both Randolph and Patterson were well aware when they presented their drafts, which were designed merely as springboards for debate.

It would be the thirty-six-year-old James Madison, possibly the brightest in the firmament of political philosophers at the convention, who would take the lead role in drafting the Constitution that was eventually adopted. Frail and just topping five feet six inches, the studious scion of a wealthy, slave-owning Virginia plantation family had such a high tenor he shied from speaking in public—until the convention inspired him to risk embarrassment in the name of principle. The Princeton University graduate quickly became the force driving the proceedings, using his considerable eloquence to sway others to his arguments. Afraid he might look too passionate, Madison asked a friend to tweak his coattails if he seemed to get too carried away while speaking. After one especially impassioned peroration he fell to his chair in exhaustion, then chided his friend for having failed to pull at his coat. The friend replied, "I would as soon have laid a finger on the lightning." One delegate even wrote of Madison that "Every person seems to acknowledge his greatness," small stature, squeaky voice, and all.

After four sweaty months of six-hour debates six days a week, the various delegations did what they had intended all along and fashioned a compromise agreeable to all. An upper house known as the Senate would represent the states with two members from each, while a lower House of Representatives would represent the people by districts determined by population. A less Solomonic accord was forged over the question of slave representation, regarding which the slave states argued that their human property should be counted in local populations but not for purposes of taxation, while the free states maintained the converse. In the end, the two sides reached the ridiculous but efficient agreement that each slave would be counted as three-fifths of a person for the purposes of both taxation and representation. It was a ludicrous bit of political legerdemain conjured up to maintain the peace and insure the prosperity of the new nation through a pragmatism that would characterize the United States throughout its history.

The Constitution devised at the 1787 convention, in retrospect, is nothing if not pragmatic, even conservative, in defining a government slow to incorporate change. In part this reflected the conventioneers' distrust of the sort of direct democracy in which an emotionally aroused populace could be swayed to follow leaders like the violent Daniel Shays. Instead, America's executive—the president of the United States—would be selected for a four-year term by an electoral college, the members of which the founding fathers intended would be independent of the citizenry. These same founding fathers could not, of course, foresee the emergence of political parties and all the tendrils they would grow into that citizenry. Their goal, in essence, was to create a government that was one part monarchy, one part oligarchy, and one part democracy.

Senators would be selected by each state's legislators for six-year terms, allowing them to act as a brake upon the lower House of Representatives, whose members would be elected by the public every two years according to voting franchises and procedures determined by each state. The House was designed to be close to the people for the same reason as Britain's House of Commons. Because the lower body would be responsible for taxes and other economic legislation, its decisions would be accepted more readily if its members were directly elected by the general public who paid the bills. Under the U.S. Constitution, however, to pass a bill into law both houses of Congress would have to approve it, whereupon it would be sent to the president, who also could either approve or veto it. The president would also nominate judges to the nation's highest tribunal; the Senate would vote to approve them for life terms, making the Supreme Court the ultimate recourse for both the public and the other branches of the government. (In time the Supreme Court would assume the power to declare laws null and void as unconstitutional, a right the Constitution itself did not accord.)

In fact, the document is vague on a number of important details in addition to the exact powers of the executive and judiciary as well as the hierarchy among all three branches. The relationship between the federal government and those of the states also was not spelled out, nor was that between the federal government and the American people. These matters were left to be worked out later. What the Constitutional Convention did establish was a fail-safe system of checks and balances to prevent abuses and concentrations of power wherever they might occur. If, for example, the public were to become unduly aroused over an issue and let it influence them in the biennial elections to the House and a third of the Senate, the holdover senators would be there to quell any overenthusiastic proposals; the electoral college would do the same for the presidency. Even if an upstart element held on long enough to gain control of both houses of Congress and then the executive branch, the Supreme Court's lifers would be in place and ready

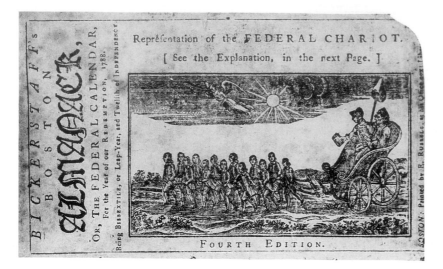

The 1788 cover of *Bickerstaff's Boston Almanack,* above, placed George Washington and Benjamin Franklin in heroic terms, being pulled in the "Federal chariot" by thirteen men. John Hancock, below, in a 1765 John Singleton Copley portrait, was an aristocrat who spent his early years in very humble circumstances. At the age of seven he was adopted by his wealthy aunt and uncle, and at twenty-seven he inherited Boston's House of Hancock, a thriving company in shipping, trade, and whaling. After some business setbacks, Hancock entered the revolutionary movement on the side of independence.

to hark back to precedents through their several generations to block any matter from getting out of hand. The bottom line, however, was simple: the Constitution was *the* supreme law of the land.

Above all, the members of the Philadelphia convention wanted to rectify the failings of the Confederation government, like its failure to guarantee the protection of property. Thus it is hardly surprising that the heart of the Constitution—Article I, Section 8, enumerating the powers of Congress—deals with economic concerns first, beginning, "The Congress shall have Power To lay and collect Taxes, Duties, Imposts and Excises, to pay the Debts and provide for the common Defence and general Welfare of the United States; but all Duties, Imposts and Excises shall be uniform throughout the United States." The next five paragraphs also deal with economic matters, giving Congress the rights to regulate commerce, coin and borrow money, set the standards for weights and measures, and establish bankruptcy laws; the four after that are only somewhat less directly geared toward commercial interests, according Congress the authority to establish post offices and routes, and "promote the Progress of Science and useful Arts, by securing for limited Times to Authors and Inventors the exclusive Right to their respective Writings and Discoveries," a capitalistic clause if ever there was one.

Because the convention delegates fully expected the legislature to dominate the executive and judicial branches, they put the most debate and greatest care into this section aimed at correcting the perceived failures of the Articles of Confederation. The founding fathers clearly intended to create a strong government for handling foreign as well as domestic matters, one that could "suppress Insurrections and repel Invasions." To that end, seven of the section's eighteen paragraphs, each of which states a power or powers of Congress, deal with the legislature's military rights and obligations. The final paragraph of Article I, Section 8, has been dubbed the "elastic clause" because it leaves so much room for maneuver, specifying only that Congress would have the authority "to make all Laws which shall be necessary and proper for carrying into Execution the foregoing Powers, and all other Powers vested by this Constitution in the Government of the United States, or in any Department or Officer thereof."

The seemingly sweeping rights accorded Congress in this section led some at the convention to fear that the new government would be strong enough to usurp power and turn to tyranny. These cautious delegates refused to accept the document without guarantees that Congress would be kept in check, such as through amendments spelling out the rights of citizens. When such assurances were not forthcoming, several delegates left without signing, promising to fight for the inclusion of such rights once the Constitution was submitted to the states for ratification.

Several would do just that successfully two years later, but on September 17, 1787, thirty-nine of the forty-two delegates remaining in Philadelphia

signed the charter for a completely new American government to begin operating as soon as the people—not the legislatures—of nine of the states approved it at special ratifying conventions called for the purpose. To indicate that the new federal government would be a republic of Americans rather than just another confederation of states, Pennsylvania delegate Gouverneur Morris rewrote the Preamble with jaw dropping resolve: "We the People of the United States, in order to form a more perfect Union, establish Justice, insure domestic Tranquility, provide for the common defence, promote the general Welfare, and secure the Blessings of Liberty to ourselves and our Posterity, do ordain and establish this Constitution for the United States of America."

None of the states could turn such a proposition down, and four days shy of a year later the Confederation Congress passed a resolution calling for the new government to take power, the first of several preparations for its own demise. Over the next few months the confederation government would also organize the first national elections under the new Constitution, further abetting its own gentle overthrow, which included nearly two months during which the new Congress waited for a quorum while America did without a central government.

Shaping the New Republic

To no one's surprise, in April 1789 the first electoral college unanimously voted George Washington as president—an honor that so far has not been repeated—and second-place finisher John Adams as vice president. His stellar career had turned Washington into a statue of himself: inchoate, reticent, forthright, and brimming with integrity. "The character and services of this gentleman are sufficient to put all those men called kings to shame," Thomas

L. M. Cooke's 1901 painting, *Salute to General Washington in New York Harbor*, illustrates the inauguration on April 30, 1789. Delegations of congressmen met the president-elect in Elizabethtown Point, New Jersey, and escorted him onto a barge rowed by thirteen oarsmen decked out in white. Gaily decorated boats and ships filled the harbor, a spectacle Washington appreciated, but found daunting. He described the scene in his diary: "The display of boats . . . some with vocal and some with instrumental music on board . . . the decorations of the ships, the roar of cannon and the loud acclamations of the people, which rent the skies as I passed along the wharves, filled my mind with sensations as painful . . . as they were pleasing." Declining to ride in a carriage, Washington walked through city streets lined with people, who fell silent and bowed in tribute as he passed.

Paine wrote in *The Rights of Man*. "He accepted no pay as Commander in Chief; he accepts none as President of the United States." By this time one of the richest men in America, Washington accepted the office reluctantly, but once having done so gilded it with aristocratic trappings including emblazoned coats of arms, elaborate formal receptions, and scads of attendants. But he can hardly be blamed for aping royal behavior to some extent; there was no other model. "I walk on untrodden ground," as he put it. "There is scarcely any part of my conduct which may not hereafter be drawn into precedent." The first chief executive of the United States decided to concentrate on three major areas: installing the new government and setting its precedents; formulating economic policies and programs designed to establish America's credit, and initiating diplomatic relations with the nations of Europe.

Among Washington's first acts was to create a cabinet of advisers along the British model. Washington chose Thomas Jefferson as Secretary of State, Alexander Hamilton as Secretary of the Treasury, Edmund Randolph as Attorney General, and Henry Knox as Secretary of War. "My movement to the chair of government," Washington wrote Knox, his former commander of artillary during the Revolution, that April, "will be accompanied by feelings not unlike those of a culprit who is going to his place of execution." At first

The core of the first presidential administration consisted of (from left to right) Secretary of War Henry Knox, Secretary of State Thomas Jefferson, Secretary of the Treasury Alexander Hamilton, and President George Washington. Knox, a Boston bookseller, caught Washington's eye during the early years of the war when he displayed a characteristic devotion to duty, using his spare time to study artillery books. Washington soon appointed him chief artillery officer and depended on him continually thereafter. Thomas Jefferson first met Washington in 1769 and knew him for thirty years. "He has often declared to me," Jefferson wrote of Washington, "that he considered our new constitution as an experiment on the practicability of republican government and with what dose of liberty man could be trusted for his own good; that he was determined the experiment should have a fair trial." The brilliant and mercurial Alexander Hamilton fed the president ideas on a range of subjects throughout his administration. Some people compared their rapport to that of a father and son. After Washington's retirement in 1797 and his death in 1799, Hamilton missed his mentor's steadying hand, becoming ever more tangled in political intrigue.

it wasn't clear whether the cabinet would be responsible to the president or to Congress, but Madison's advocacy of the former made it so. Nevertheless, for the next few years Washington stayed above the fray and in many ways acted the part of republican monarch while the savvy Alexander Hamilton took the prime minister's role and worked the political ends. This arrangement would cease when Washington left the presidency to more partisan successors.

In some respects the legislature was more prepared than the executive for the tasks ahead. Of the thirty-nine signers of the Constitution, fifteen served in the first Congress it established and thus had a good idea what was expected of them. Fortunately, the leading expert on the Constitution, James Madison, had been elected to the House of Representatives from Virginia and eagerly set to organizing the body in accordance. Unfortunately, he had no counterpart in the Senate.

The first Congress's most important act was passing the ten amendments called the Bill of Rights, the absence of which had nearly scotched ratification

The Constitution delineated the powers and the form of the nation's government, but the ten amendments known as the Bill of Rights, celebrated in the poster above (which commemorates its 150th birthday) and the contemporary pitcher below, pertained directly to its citizens. Submitted by James Madison to the very first Congress in 1789 and ratified in 1791, the Bill of Rights was of more interest to voters at the time than was the Constitution. Alexander Hamilton, seen on the opposite page in a portrait by John Trumbull, was against using the Constitution to describe individual rights, but by 1789 he was extremely busy with other matters, devoting himself to organizing America's financial structure.

of the Constitution. The version Madison introduced in June 1789 was accepted and ratified by the states by December 1791. This Bill of Rights—which borrowed from Britain's 1215 Magna Carta—guaranteed Americans' basic freedoms, including the rights to petition the government, to speak and publish opinions without fear of government reprisal, to worship freely, and to bear arms. The amendments were written as curbs on federal power, specifically delineating where the central government was not permitted to intrude. As the Tenth Amendment summed it up, "The powers not delegated to the United States by the Constitution, nor prohibited by it to the States, are reserved to the States respectively, or to the people."

The first Congress also passed the Judiciary Act of 1789, which established a federal court structure that has changed little to this day. The act provided for cases involving United States laws or treaties to be heard in thirteen district courts and appealed to three circuit courts, then finally to a six-member Supreme Court that would have the last word. More important, these federal courts were empowered to review the decisions of state courts and nullify any found to violate the Constitution. President Washington appointed the distinguished statesman John Jay as first chief justice of the United States Supreme Court, but during the next decade only four constitutional cases came up, and none created much stir.

In truth, and as ever in American history, highfalutin cogitation over matters of law and principle took a back seat to economic concerns. Happily, the young republic had the hard-nosed thirty-two-year-old Alexander Hamilton to make some deals and establish the nation's credit. At the time America was foundering financially under a $40 million debt inherited from the Confederation government, bonds from which had lost most of their value and left Americans distrusting their own currency. This hardly impressed the world's financial markets, which expressed a lack of confidence in the U.S. economy that made further borrowing out of the question. It would take Hamilton two years to turn the situation around and build a solid financial infrastructure for the new nation.

The thirty-two-year-old Hamilton, Washington's protégé since proving himself well before Yorktown, had worked his way into the vortex of the American aristocracy. Born out of wedlock in the Caribbean, deserted by his Scottish father, Hamilton eventually made his way to King's College (today's Columbia University) in New York and was noticed as a revolutionary pamphleteer before he joined the Continental army as General Washington's aide-de-camp. In 1780, he married the daughter of a patriot, General Philip Schuyler. After the war, he studied law, began a prosperous legal practice in New York, became a revenue collector, and a member of the Confederation Congress. His *Federalist* essays, published in New York newspapers, would play an important role in defending and promoting the work of the Constitutional Convention. Not that Hamilton's appeals were to humanity's better instincts; he once wrote and sincerely believed that "Men will naturally go to those who pay them best."

Despite the depth of America's debt, Hamilton dismissed suggestions that the nation default or declare bankruptcy, insisting that it could never recover

This British cartoon portrays ministers of the king's government about to kill the goose that lays the golden eggs, or trade with the young United States. England dominated postwar commerce with America, enforcing trade rules punishing to the U.S. economy. With American merchants and traders deep in debt to English commercial houses, some Americans favored war with England and renunciation of all debts. Calling that "fraud," Alexander Hamilton preferred to copy England, rather than war with it. He suggested that the country needed a national bank in order to succeed against Britain.

from either. Instead he proposed a multifaceted program to get more credit, beginning with the readily acceptable notion of repaying the nation's $11.7-million foreign debt through a new bond issue to replace the depreciated old ones. The Treasury Secretary's plan to pay off the domestic debt the same way was more controversial, as much of it was owed to Revolutionary soldiers, matériel suppliers, and patriotic individual bondholders—or to the speculators to whom these government IOUs had been sold. Hamilton saw no reason to shrink from rewarding those who had shown confidence in the new government by purchasing depreciated bonds in hope of someday redeeming them at face value.

Next Hamilton recommended that the federal government assume the states' debts in order to bind them together with the most compelling ties: purse strings. The suggestion outraged those states that held little or no debt, delighted the rest, and set Hamilton's many opponents to organizing against his plan, which also recommended creating a Bank of the United States, four-fifths of the stock in which would be sold to private investors in order to further cement the moneyed classes to the new government. Finally, the secretary proposed the Mint Act, passed the next year, which established a gold and silver standard that required the federal government to pay its debts in precious metals rather than dubious paper currency. In many ways the secretary's plan echoed that of the Confederation's superintendent of finance, Robert Morris, who in 1781 had obtained the charter for a Bank of North America to hold government deposits and make federal loans. Hamilton had supported Morris's design, and at the time wrote him that "a national debt, if it is not excessive, will be to us a national blessing."

Were Hamilton's plan implemented, the new government's total indebtedness would have amounted to some $75 million, at the time a seemingly staggering figure—even though it worked out to about $20 per American, or about one-sixth the arrears of Britain. Foreshadowing the way future politicians would brush off federal deficits tens of thousands times larger, Hamilton argued that the 1789 debt was not all that onerous considering America's commercial assets, revenues, and prospects; he added that the debt could be serviced through new tariffs, excise taxes, public land sales, and dividends from the proposed federal bank.

Such a mercenary—if smart and workable—scheme was bound to raise some hackles among those high-minded founding fathers who prided themselves on maintaining Enlightenment ideals. Madison and Jefferson led the opposition, pointing out that Hamilton's plan would in fact reward greedy speculators who had taken advantage of desperate investors by purchasing

their old bonds at a fraction of their original cost. In fact, upon Jefferson's return from France in 1789 and the assumption of his duties as Secretary of State the following year, he would spend his first year in office battling Hamilton's program and its supporters, dubbed "Federalists," by organizing the minority in Congress who disagreed with them. The task was made easier by the substantial number of representatives who considered the prickly Hamilton a personal enemy, politics aside.

But the debate transcended personalities. Broader objections were raised to the idea of the federal government assuming state debts as a scheme that would afford extremely uneven benefits. Led by Virginia, many of the Southern states had already paid off their obligations, unlike their Northern neighbors, or at least claimed to in fear that federal assumption of the debts would make the government too powerful. Yet, under Hamilton's plan, the Northerners would be forgiven their profligacy while the South would be saddled with a portion of the new national debt. Thus did partisanship, which had taken root in America even before the Revolution, begin to sprout, over

In 1791, the Bank of the United States opened for business in Philadephia. The establishment of the bank as a part of the government was one of the most bitter issues of America's first decade. Those who were against it said a central bank would align the government with the richest, most powerful segment of society. Thomas Jefferson, for one, argued that there was no provision in the Constitution for a federal bank. Alexander Hamilton's reply helped to carry the issue. It also opened the Constitution to broad interpretation by maintaining that the document conveyed "implied powers" as well as explicit ones. The Bank of the United States continued to be controversial throughout the early decades of the nineteenth century.

Frederick Kemmelmeyer's painting (opposite page, top) shows George Washington reviewing the army at Fort Cumberland before leading troops to quell the unrest during the Whiskey Rebellion in Pennsylvania. It was the only time in U.S. history that a president has led soldiers into action. In dire need of revenues, the federal government had placed a tax on whiskey, even homemade moonshine. The cartoon (opposite page, bottom) shows a tax collector who has taken a couple of casks of whiskey in lieu of money. As resistance to the tax grew, insurrections spread. Washington carefully abided by the Constitution in calling out a militia, derided as the "Watermelon Army" by the rebels. Two civilians were killed in incidents before things settled down.

money, of course. The Northern states, creditors, and foreign businessmen favored Hamilton's plan, while the South, debtors, and states' rights advocates generally opposed it. These factions were united philosophically as well as financially, with most who had favored the Constitution taking Hamilton's side and those who had fought for the Bill of Rights allying with Jefferson and Madison. Washington backed Hamilton's plan and made it his own, but he and others who preferred the ether above the fray hoped in vain that the divisions would not congeal into permanently contentious political parties.

A compromise was reached in which Hamilton agreed to limit the amount of debt the federal government would assume from any state and to pledge his supporters' agreement to establish the nation's permanent capital somewhere along the Potomac River in the mid-Atlantic region between the North and the South. In return, Jefferson and Madison would urge their followers to accept Hamilton's plan, which Congress passed soon thereafter. The Jeffersonians thus won the form of a symbolic victory, but Hamilton came away with the substance—especially considering that his "concession" on the capital site would help build Southern support for the United States as a new nation.

By this point Jefferson, who disdained the British, had become more than a little perturbed by Hamilton's Anglophile influence on the government. It was small wonder that the two came into conflict, as they harbored diametrically opposite hopes for the future of the United States. Jefferson's views were manifest in the Northwest Ordinance he had crafted, providing farmland to any American who wanted it; he had little use for cities and considered merchants and manufacturers mere facilitators for the farmers who produced a nation's true wealth. Hamilton, by contrast, outlined his vision in his economic program, which sought to erect a framework for a largely urban America devoted to commerce and industry. "Hamilton greatly admired the British," historian James Thomas Flexner wrote in *Washington: The Indispensable Man*.

Both George Clinton (left) and Aaron Burr (right) were entrenched in New York State politics at the end of the eighteenth century. Despite rising as high as vice president, they are remembered today not as leaders but as cunning politicians whose jockeying for power helped to carve out America's political parties. Born into a rich family, Clinton was elected governor seven times; Burr, an orphan, served in one of Clinton's administrations. Rivals, they both clashed with Alexander Hamilton, Clinton over issues such as states' rights, Burr for more personal reasons. Hamilton's denigration of Burr was relentless, and in 1804 Burr finally demanded satisfaction in a duel in which he mortally wounded Hamilton.

"He believed that upsetting the existing pattern of commerce—the lion's share was with Britain—would damage American prosperity, and also bankrupt the federal government, whose customs revenues depended on a flourishing trade."

Jefferson recognized that he would need powerful allies to suppress Hamilton, and in the summer of 1791 he and Madison toured New York and the New England states in search of recruits to their cause. In New York they met with anti-Hamiltonians such as George and DeWitt Clinton, who had built a political machine across the Hudson and Mohawk River valleys to oppose the one Hamilton and John Jay led in New York City. Aaron Burr, a brilliant lawyer devoted to the pursuit of money and power who was associated with the anti-Federalist Tammany Society in New York, eagerly joined forces with Jefferson and Madison, as did Pennsylvania Governor Thomas Mifflin, who also objected to the expansion of federal power Hamilton proposed. The Jeffersonian coalition also attracted a number of backcountry elements from across New England. By the end of the year these disparate "anti-Federalists" would evolve into the "Republicans," an embryonic but distinct political party (not to be confused with today's party of the same name, formed in Ripon, Wisconsin, in 1854).

Despite their substantial differences over ideology, policies, and the very direction the United States should take, both the Federalists and the Republicans supported Washington's re-election, giving him a second term as pres-

This undated portrait of William Pitt was painted by Gainsborough Dupont. The son of one of Britain's most prominent statesmen, "Pitt the Younger" was only twenty-four when he was asked to create a government and become prime minister in 1783. His administration was expected to last only three weeks, but he presided for over seventeen years—"A Kingdom trusted to a schoolboy's care," in the words of the day. With prudent fiscal policies and notably liberal social ones, he engendered the devotion of his nation. Yet, as all of Europe faced the specter of revolution in the 1790s, Pitt turned to dictatorial measures to stave off even the hint of unrest in England. He also pursued a belligerent foreign policy, leading his country through an almost continual state of war with the new French Republic after 1793.

ident by another unanimous vote in the electoral college. The surface harmony did not, however, last for long. In 1794 the division came to a head in the "Whiskey Rebellion," which broke out in western Pennsylvania when backcountry farmers angry over a new excise tax on distilled liquor refused to pay any federal taxes. Washington himself led a large army of 13,000 to crush the rebellion, but was embarrassed to meet no organized resistance. Still, the very existence of a tax revolt added a concrete aspect to the philosophical and political battle between Jefferson and Hamilton over the very foundations of the U.S. economy. But the trumpets never sounded. Instead, the two men would blare their differences on the international stage, as once again events in Europe spawned troubles in America—this time with a strong ideological cast that had been absent from the Anglo-French wars of the colonial era.

The New Nation and the World

In 1789, as the American Congress was debating the Bill of Rights, a bloody revolution erupted in France and toppled its aristocracy. By Washington's second inauguration in March 1793, King Louis XVI had lost his head to the French revolutionaries, who soon installed a vicious and disorganized government of ruffians who set about guillotining virtually all of France's nobles. William Pitt, England's young new prime minister, had disapproved of the French Revolution from its inception, but until the French monarch's execution he had been content to monitor the situation and enjoy the spectacle of a civil war within Britain's longstanding adversary. As the king's trial proceeded toward its preordained verdict, however, Pitt set to preparing for the inevitable: cutting off grain exports to France and asking Parliament for an increase in naval appropriations. Pitt's prediction proved right on February 1, 1793, when revolutionary France declared war on England, the Netherlands, and in March, on Spain. He then summoned a parade of diplomats and fashioned alliances with Austria, Prussia, Spain, Russia, and a smattering of lesser states.

Back in America, the only thing that had changed in the animosity between Thomas Jefferson and Alexander Hamilton was the primary bone of contention and the orientation of the adversaries. This time the offending pro-

gram was Jefferson's, with Hamilton serving as counterbalance: whereas the latter advocated institutionalizing America's new government and shoring up its progress, Jefferson was more interested in keeping America from backsliding into monarchism or anything like it. Although Jefferson had more sympathy for the French revolutionaries, he had no more desire than Hamilton that America be dragged into European squabbles. But while the two also agreed that the British should vacate the American Northwest, Hamilton was less insistent on the point than Jefferson, due to the former's belief that Britain was not only the bastion of constitutional governance in Europe but also America's most natural friend and ally should the need for one arise. What's more, the profit-minded Treasury Secretary was eager to develop American trade, which called for partners across the Atlantic. In contrast, and despite some lofty rhetoric regarding the ascendancy of France's downtrodden, Jefferson's primary economic interest was in the American West and its enormous spans of arable land.

The former king of France, Louis XVI, met his death at the guillotine on January 21, 1793, a scene shown in the contemporary engraving below. France's revolution and the renewal of its war with Britain pushed America to rethink its foreign policies. For George Washington, the French Revolution was of personal concern because his friend Lafayette was a leading participant. At first a hero in the new French Republic, Lafayette was eventually labeled an enemy, and deserted to the Austrians.

Edmond Genet, seen above in a portrait by Ezra Ames circa 1809, was the official envoy from France's new republican government to the United States. Charming and gregarious, Genet had been loyal to King Louis XVI, but he survived the French Revolution by proving himself to be just as loyal to the Republic. His mission in America was to obtain military support for the new government. At first Genet found Jefferson sympathetic, Hamilton antagonistic, and the populace wildly enthusiastic about him and his cause. George Washington, however, remained neutral. In frustration, Genet made the mistake of opposing the president's position, stirring up trouble, and making enemies out of the people who had once cheered him. Eventually, he lost even Jefferson's support.

As they had during the Confederation, the British continued to discriminate against American trade in the early years of the Constitution. Jefferson proposed retaliating in kind: if Britain limited American exports through quotas and tariffs, America should impose the same restrictions on goods imported from Britain. Although the United States needed British products more than the other way around, Jefferson knew he could count on those London merchants involved in the American trade to agitate for change. Hamilton was opposed to the entire approach in fear that it might jeopardize his economic program, which depended on revenues from tariffs and duties. The Treasury Secretary won the first round: when Madison introduced Jefferson's plan in the House, the Hamiltonians defeated it easily.

Hamilton himself used any and every means to thwart Jefferson's negotiations with the British. When the Secretary of State demanded Britain's withdrawal from the Northwest territories a few months later, he was told by minister to the United States George Hammond that would not happen until the U.S. government allowed British tradesmen to collect debts owed to them by Americans; Jefferson denied any impediments to such collections existed, bringing the talks to an impasse. Behind Jefferson's back, Hamilton wrote Hammond to assure him that Washington would not press the matter of Britain's withdrawal from the Northwest—a backdoor gambit that was ill-considered at best and treasonous at worst, especially as it contributed nothing to Jefferson's efforts to get the British out of the territories and to establish a more egalitarian relationship with London.

A month after Washington's second inauguration, Americans heard their first news from Europe after months of severe winter storms that had kept packet ships from crossing the Atlantic. It was not until early April 1793 that word finally arrived of King Louis XVI's execution, the rise of the radical Jacobins, and the threat to life and liberty presented by their reign of terror. The Hamiltonians immediately denounced the French Revolution, while the Jeffersonian Republicans either assumed the dire news was exaggerated or applauded the collapse of a monarchy. In fact, a few Jacobin societies sprang up in the United States, some members even affecting the courtesy title "citizen." For the most part, however, even most Republicans lacked enthusiasm for the brutal Jacobins.

The French miscalculated the American attitude and assumed a people who had just overthrown a king's rule would sympathize with their populist cause. Hard upon the arrival of the news from Europe, a new French minister to the United States landed in Charleston: Edmond Genet, who traveled extensively, recruiting soldiers and trying to gin up interest in an American attack on Spanish Florida and Louisiana. Angered by such French presumption as well as concerned about preserving America's neutrality in the European conflict, on April 22, Washington issued a neutrality proclamation to the effect that the United States would remain "friendly and impartial toward the belligerent powers." Genet continued his provocations nevertheless—until the Jacobins took a turn further left and declared him an enemy of the new French Republic, upon which he asked for and received asylum in America; before long he married a daughter of the governor of New York.

But the damage had been done. Genet's provocations ended by dividing the American public between pro-British and pro-French camps. Although it looked as though Anglo-American relations might improve after Jefferson left the cabinet late in 1793, this did not prove the case: clashes continued in the Northwest, and the Royal Navy took to seizing American ships bound for French ports. By the spring of 1794 some Americans began advocating a new alliance with the French. This was not in ideological sympathy with their revolution but rather for the same reason France had come to America's aid in 1776: so each could use the other for leverage against the British.

John Jay, whose hatred of the French made him perhaps the most pro-British official in America, was sent to Britain to negotiate a treaty in which Jay gave away a lot while gaining little for the United States. The British agreed to vacate the Northwest territories—something they had already pledged to do—but only if the Americans promised not to interfere with the region's fur trade. In addition, Americans would be compensated for any losses incurred when British ships stopped their vessels in the Caribbean, but the U.S. government had to assume all of the pre-revolutionary individual debts to British nationals. Furthermore, the United States had to agree to restrict its trade with France. As for the British, they were not made to compensate Americans whose slaves they had liberated during the Revolution, nor would the Royal Navy be required to end its practice of stopping American ships and impressing their seamen into service by claiming they were British subjects. In one of the treaty's few equal provisions, citizens of both nations would have the right to navigate the Mississippi River, an important point because Spain had begun to cause trouble at the mouth of the river in their port of New Orleans.

What came to be called Jay's Treaty—not as a compliment—reached Philadelphia, still the U.S. capital, in March 1795 and was ratified by the Senate in close to its original form. The Jeffersonians protested and branded Jay a traitor; even George Washington suffered bitter partisan attacks for the first time since he had taken office. In fact, as he neared the end of his second term he realized that his hopes of preventing political factionalism were doomed. However, Jay's Treaty did more good than harm: it averted what would have been a disasterous war with Britain; it got the British out of the Northwest, and settled both private and public debts on terms favorable to the Americans.

Jay's Treaty also produced an unexpected dividend. Fearing an Anglo-American alliance, the once-arrogant Spaniards suddenly showed interest in negotiating a treaty covering commerce on the Mississippi River, which sent U.S. minister to Britain Thomas Pinckney to Madrid in 1794 to start negotiations that ended in an agreement the next year. Under the terms of Pinckney's treaty both nations recognized the thirty-first parallel as the southern boundary of the United States, accepted the other's free navigation of the Mississippi, and agreed that for the next three years Americans would be able to use the port of New Orleans. This new treaty not only salved some of the burn from Jay's but also helped quench several secession movements that had fired up in the West. At the same time, it allowed Washington to leave office on a triumphant note.

Party politics grew progressively treacherous in the wake of the Washington presidency. The drawing at right shows two representatives, Matthew Lyon (a Republican) and Roger Griswold (a Federalist), assaulting each other in Congress in 1798. Its caption reads: "He in a trice, struck Lyon thrice/Upon his head, enrag'd Sir/Who seiz'd the tongs to ease his wrongs/And Griswold thus engag'd Sir."

South Carolina's Thomas Pinckney, below, served Washington as an officer during the war and as a diplomat in peacetime. While away on a mission to Spain, he was touted by Hamilton as a vice presidential candidate in the 1796 national elections.

The Rise of the Party System

Washington's decision to retire after his second term ended in 1796 brought the question of succession to the fore. He favored Vice President John Adams to take over, but Hamilton, the acknowledged Federalist leader, disagreed: Adams was neither wholly committed to the Treasury Secretary's financial program nor anti-French enough for his taste. What's more, Adams was friendly with Jefferson but thought his ideas on economics naive and his notion of agrarian democracy a pipe dream. But Hamilton was not prepared to challenge the will of George Washington, so he reluctantly supported Adams and put forth his own man, Pinckney, for the vice presidency. The Republican coalition of Virginians and Northerners bore its first fruits as a political party by selecting Jefferson as its presidential candidate and Aaron Burr for vice president.

Although the 1796 campaign was minuscule by today's media standards, the two sides attacked one another through newspapers with a bitterness bordering on libel that makes modern political mudslinging look like Socratic debate. Jefferson was called a "murderer under whom rape and pillage will be openly taught and practiced" as well as a dangerous revolutionary who would align America with France, while Adams was accused of harboring monarchical tendencies and a lust for power that would destroy the republic were he elected. The candidates themselves stayed aloof from the battle, eschewing speechifying in favor of working behind the scenes in an attempt to look detached and—well—presidential in the magisterial George Washington sense.

This allegory, painted on glass by an unknown Chinese artist, circa 1802, depicts George Washington as an angel ascending to heaven after his death in 1799.

CHAPTER 6

GROWING PAINS

John Adams would write of George Washington in 1811 that "If he were not the greatest President, he was the best actor of the presidency that we have ever had." Washington was followed in office, however, by a succession of men who did a great deal more than act the part. In fact, after he went home to Mount Vernon a quarter century ensued in which America was led by well-educated, democratic-minded, Revolution-tempered aristocrats who would prove the most brilliant generation of chief executives in American history: John Adams, Thomas Jefferson, James Madison, James Monroe, and John Quincy Adams. And the times called for no less. No matter the scale, it is one thing to launch an enterprise but quite another to keep it going, and what made the first generation of American presidents great was their remarkable ability to adapt revolutionary passions into workable policies.

On September 17, 1796, George Washington set forth his recommendations for America's future in a thoughtful and direct farewell address with ominous undertones, summarizing the state of the union bluntly. "The basis of our political system is the right of the people to make and to alter their constitutions of government," the outgoing president averred, adding, "Let me now . . . warn you in the most solemn manner against the baneful effects of the spirit of party. . . ." After excoriating political factionalism he then spelled out his (and Hamilton's) pragmatic if somewhat callous views on international relations:

New Orleans was a vibrant port city in 1803, as shown in this painting detail by Boqueto de Woieseri. The banner reads: UNDER MY WINGS EVERY THING PROSPERS. With the Louisiana Purchase, America gained its most diverse and multicultural city and a vast, uncharted territory. "You, the Americans, did brilliant things in your war with England," Napoleon said during the negotiations for the Louisiana Purchase. "You will do the same again."

The cartoon at right, reflecting the anti-French sentiment in the wake of the XYZ Affair, shows a profligate French agent approaching three honest American envoys in 1797. During the previous year French boats had seized more than 300 American merchant ships. The American envoys, Elbridge Gerry, Charles Pinckney, and John Marshall, traveled to Paris to discuss a diplomatic solution to the hostility, but three French agents, referred to later as *X, Y,* and *Z,* demanded a bribe of $250,000 to open negotiations. At the time, bribery was hardly new as diplomatic expedient. However, the affair marked a new low point in the deteriorating relations between the two fledging republics, France and the United States. Word of the French insult made many Americans demand war, and Pinckney's reply, "Not a sixpence, Sir!" has been a rallying cry for American military strength ever since: "Millions for defense, but not one cent for tribute!"

Observe good faith and justice toward all nations. Cultivate peace and harmony with all. . . . The nation which indulges toward another an habitual hatred or an habitual fondness is in some degree a slave. It is a slave to its animosity or to its affection, either of which is sufficient to lead it astray from its duty and its interest. . . . It is our true policy to steer clear of permanent alliances. . . . There can be no greater error than to expect or calculate upon real favors from nation to nation.

Coming whence it did, the prescription was not taken lightly, and Washington's successor devoted most of his single term to foreign policy matters, the very first of which ended in a rather messy final severing of America's long alliance. In December 1796, three months before John Adams was inaugurated as the second United States president, the French displayed their anger at the Jay Treaty's acceptance of British seizures of goods heading to enemy ports as contraband by treating American cargoes bound for Britain the same way. By March the French had plundered 300 American ships and, needless to say, ended their diplomatic relations with the United States.

The new president, hoping to smooth things over with the country that had made victory possible in the American Revolution, dispatched three envoys to Paris to work matters out with France's foreign minister, the grandiose political maestro Charles Maurice de Talleyrand, who once sneered after a visit to the United States, which he described as a country "with thirty-two religions and only one dish." But what a spicy "dish" it proved. Talleyrand waved the Americans off to deal with three representatives of his own—dubbed *X, Y,* and *Z,* in U.S. dispatches—who demanded a princely bribe of $250,000 before they would even start negotiating. The outraged U.S. delegation refused and broke off the talks. When Adams revealed the sordid details of France's behavior in the "XYZ Affair" in April 1798, Republicans as well as Federalists rose up to denounce the erstwhile American ally. Many cried for war, and Congress went along as far as recalling George

Washington to head the armed forces (with Hamilton as his second in command), which were enlarged for an unofficial two-year quasi war in which American and French ships went at each other's fleets across the Caribbean until Talleyrand cried uncle in 1800.

Once Adams had proved that despite its youth the United States was nobody's fool—and was building the muscle to ward off further foreign teasing—he turned to the domestic issues the French situation had set churning. Unfortunately, Adams reacted to the pro-French agitators with a bludgeon in the form of the Alien and Sedition Acts, which aimed, respectively, at ending foreign (i.e., resident "alien") dissent and at squelching domestic radicals who "write, print, utter, or publish . . . false, scandalous, and malicious . . . writings against the government of the United States." Thomas Jefferson rightly denounced the Sedition Act as a "gag law," and with Madison's help took to penning resolutions severely limiting federal power. Should the government exceed its authority as defined by the Constitution, Madison averred, the states would be duty bound to act against "the usurpations of Congress." Although only the legislatures of Kentucky and, of course, Virginia passed the resolutions, the measures did serve to rally the Republicans, who elected Jefferson as the third U.S. president in 1801, marking the first time in history that power had been passed democratically from one party in control to another.

Setting a pattern followed by virtually every chief executive after him, Jefferson moved toward the center of political opinion as soon as he took office. In his first inaugural address on March 4, 1801, in the new capital of Washington, D.C., he pledged "a wise and frugal government, which shall restrain men from injuring one another, shall leave them otherwise free to regulate their own pursuits of industry and improvement, and shall not take from the mouth of labor the bread it has earned."

In accordance with his belief that "what is practicable must often control what is pure theory," Jefferson tempered his usually inflammatory rhetoric with appeals for reconciliation, left Adams's Federalist administration pretty much as he had found it, and declared, "We have a perfect horror at everything like connecting ourselves with the politics of Europe." This made a great deal of practical sense at the turn of the century, when the upstart Corsican general Napoleon Bonaparte had taken command of France and begun eyeing the rest of the Continent and beyond. Americans' concerns deepened in 1801 when it was learned that Spain had ceded its Louisiana Territory, including the strategic port of New Orleans, to France, potentially enabling Napoleon to control commerce on the Mississippi as

Thomas Jefferson was sixty-two years old when Rembrandt Peale painted his portrait in 1805. Toward the end of his life, Jefferson chose three accomplishments for his epitaph that interestingly did not include the presidency or any other aspect of the "hated profession," as he once called politics. Instead, Jefferson's tomb lists his authorship of both the Declaration of Independence and the Virginia statute for religious freedom and his founding of the University of Virginia. Thomas Jefferson died in 1826, stoically persevering until the afternoon of July 4 so that he could have one more Fourth of July. His friend and sometime rival John Adams died the same day.

BRITISH POS[SESSIONS]

OREGON

Cape Disappointment x
Fort Clatsop
Clark's Point of View x
Cascades
The Dalles
Mt. Hood
Celilo Falls
Canoe Camp
Long Camp
Lolo Trail
Lewis and Clark Pass
Travellers' Rest
Three Forks
[Lemhi Pass]
[Bozeman Pass]

COUNTRY

Great Falls
White Bear Camp
Lewis 1806
Clark 1806
+ Pompey's Pillar
Mandan villages
Fort Mandan
(to St. Louis)
Arikara villages
Pike's Block House
North West House
North West House

LOUISIANA

Continental Divide
Lewis and Clark 1804
x Floyd's Bluff
x Council Bluff

SPANISH

Natural Boundary

PURCHASE

1803

Pawnee villages
Osage villages

Santa Clara de Asis
San Francisco de Asis
San José Guadalupe
Santa Cruz
San Juan Bautista
San Carlos Borroméo de Carmelo
Nuestra Señora de la Soledad
San Antonio de Padua
San Miguel Arcangel
San Luis Obispo de Tolosa
La Purisima Concepción
Santa Inés
Santa Barbara
San Buenaventura
San Fernando Rey de España
San Gabriel Arcángel
Cajon Pass
San Juan Capistrano
San Luis Rey de Francia
San Diego de Alcalá

Old Spanish Trail
Crossing of the Fathers
Third Stockade
+ Pike's Peak
Second Stockade
First Stockade
+ Spanish Peaks
Taos
Santa Fe
Albuquerque
Pike 1806
Wilkinson Party 1806

POSSESSIONS

PACIFIC OCEAN

San Xavier del Bac
El Camino Real
Gila River
Nogales
Santa Cruz
Arizpe
Ysleta
El Paso del Norte
Socorro
El Camino Real
Natural Boundary of Louisiana

(to Mexico City)

Presidio del Norte

Chihuahua

Sinaloa

Nacogdoch[es]
El Camino Real
San Antonio de Béxer
Presidio de Rio Grande
Laredo
Monclova
Pike 1807
(to Mexico City)
Saltillo

LOUISIANA PURCHASE
and EXPLORATION 1803–7

- • settlement   ⌑ military post
- ▲ Indian village   ■ U.S. trading post
- ∧ camp site   □ British trading post
- ⚘ mission   ⋯⋯ trail or road

EXPLORATION:
- •—•— W. Dunbar and G. Hunter 1804
- ←— M. Lewis and W. Clark 1804–1806
-      (←— return routes)
- —•— Thomas Freeman 1806
- – – Zebulon Pike 1805–6
- —— Zebulon Pike 1806–7
-      (←- - - return of Wilkinson party)

AARON BURR CONSPIRACY:
- ←— Burr route and capture 1806–7

0   100   200   300

Fort William
Lake Fort
● Grand Portage
Superior
rth West House
● Fond du Lac[Duluth]
rth West House
Sault Ste. Marie ●

Falls of St. Anthony
Fort Michilimackinac

INDIANA ●
Green Bay

MICH.
TERR.
1805-16

● Prairie du Chien
Detroit ●

Dubuque's
Lead Mines
Fort Dearborn
(Chicago)

Fort Wayne

TERRITORY
1805-9

OHIO

Cincinnati

St. Charles ● Wood River Camp
Fort Belle Fountaine ● Cabokia ● Vincennes
St. Louis ●
Ste. Genevieve ● Kaskaskia

KENTUCKY

Cape Girardeau ● Fort Massac

Nashville

TENNESSEE

Fort Pickering
(Memphis)

Arkansas
Post

MISSISSIPPI

TERRITORY

GA.

Quachita
Walnut Hills [Vicksburg]
1804-12

atchitoches ● Washington
● Natchez ● Fort Stoddert
Fort Adams Wakefield
Mobile FLA.
Opelousas ● SPANISH (to San Agustin)
Baton Rouge Pensacola
Attakapas ● New Orleans

GULF OF MEXICO

---

well as to push into the American West. When Napoleon decided instead that France's U.S. holdings would make too easy pickings for the British in the event of another European war, the French ruler offered not only New Orleans but the entire Louisiana Territory for $15 million; Jefferson abandoned his earlier constructionist arguments and jumped at the bargain. The Louisiana Purchase nearly doubled the size of the United States, and in time added substantial evidence to the argument that the nation is wise that values economic gain above military advantage. The Senate approved the purchase on October 20, 1803, and American expansion westward, the opening up of the new frontier, commenced at once.

President Jefferson proved clumsier at domestic politics. Between his election and his inauguration, the outgoing President John Adams had made a scad of "midnight appointments" to newly created judicial offices in an attempt to install Federalists where they could not be removed, but the new president was wise to the scheme and refused to deliver the commissions. Four of the denied appointees, including one William Marbury, sued the government in federal court, leading to the landmark 1803 decision in *Marbury v. Madison* that established perhaps the most important tenet of U.S. constitutional law: the Supreme Court has the right of "judicial review," or the final authority in deciding the constitutionality of laws passed by the U.S. Congress. It was a Federalist position vehemently opposed by Jefferson and his party. Thus the Republicans lost on the judiciary, but decimated the rest of Hamilton's framework by repealing the Alien and Sedition Acts, selling off government holdings in the Bank of the United States, and slashing the federal budget to bring down the national debt.

Europe, however, refused to let Jefferson concentrate on domestic matters. America remained officially neutral when tensions first began to heat up between Britain and France, but the booming U.S. traffic in military supplies to the French drew not only England's ire but its policy of seizing American ships headed for France. This led the U.S. Congress to retaliate by prohibiting the import of numerous British goods and in 1807 to the Embargo Act ending all U.S. trade with foreign nations. Vigorous protests from U.S. merchants forced Jefferson to repeal the act before leaving office—except regarding trade with Britain and France.

Fellow Virginian James Madison succeeded Jefferson in 1809, but not auspiciously. Whatever genius it had taken to write the Constitution proved ineffective when it came to running the country thus created. In 1810 the

In April 1803, the United States doubled in size through the acquisition of 827,000 square miles in the Louisiana Purchase, shown in the map at left. President Jefferson had confidence that the new lands would be productive, but he couldn't know for certain because no one had yet explored the area. In 1806, former Vice President Aaron Burr organized a network of conspirators and then sought British or Spanish support to take possession of the new territory; he was arrested along with a ragtag army on his approach to New Orleans in 1807. Burr's trial for treason, which riveted the nation, ended in acquittal.

The 1805 cartoon at right illustrates the effect of the war between Britain and France on American trade. Britain's George III, at left, and France's Napoleon Bonaparte, at right, brandish weapons meant for each other while they empty the pockets of U.S. President Thomas Jefferson, center. As a neutral nation supplying the combatants, America had initially prospered, but both France and Britain soon grew to resent the country's divided loyalties.

The lyrics of "The Star-Spangled Banner," below, were copied from a poem scrawled by Francis Scott Key as he watched the British attempt under Admiral Alexander Cochrane to level Maryland's Fort McHenry, September 13, 1814. Admiral George Cockburn, complying vigorously with orders to bring "hard war" to American soil, had destroyed the capital city of Washington the previous month. When Cochrane trained his guns on Fort McHenry and blasted away all night, whatever hope was left in the city of Baltimore was symbolized by the American flag waving over the fort. By morning, as Key wrote, "the flag was still there," and it was Cochrane who lost heart and left.

cagey Napoleon maneuvered Madison into pushing Congress to pass a bill removing the embargo on France but maintaining it against Britain, which led to high-seas skirmishes between U.S. ships and the Royal Navy. At the same time, land grabs by settlers in the Northwest territories had sparked ominous Indian uprisings—for which the settlers chose to blame the British. They pressed their point by sending hawks to Congress to demand increased military forces in preparation for a new war. Madison was forced to give in, and on June 1, 1812, he asked Congress—despite vociferous opposition from the Federalists primarily based in New England—to declare war on Britain over its trade violations and instigation of the Indians.

Although the motives behind it may have been specious and the immediate gains to be won unclear, the War of 1812 turned out well for the United States in the long run. Once again an ill-trained, poorly organized, ragtag gaggle of Americans hung on long enough to triumph over a superior but overextended British force despite serious early setbacks on land and sea. Although U.S. troops had secured the Northwest territories by 1813, in August 1814 a force of 4,000 British veterans landed in Maryland and marched on Washington, D.C., burning down the Capitol, the White House, and other government buildings before proceeding north to Baltimore. Their failure to take that city and its Fort McHenry inspired Washington lawyer Francis Scott Key, who watched the battle from a vessel in Baltimore harbor, to write "The Star-Spangled Banner," which would become the undeniably martial national anthem.

Meanwhile, on September 11, 1814, Thomas Macdonough's U.S. fleet won a decisive victory at the Battle of Plattsburgh Bay on Lake Champlain. This naval upset forced a shell-shocked British army to retreat into Canada. Late in 1814 American and British diplomats met in Belgium to end the war.

After months of negotiation, they signed the Treaty of Ghent on December 24—unaware that a decisive battle was about to begin in New Orleans. The British fleet from Jamaica was stopped in its tracks at the port city by General Andrew Jackson and his assemblage of Tennessee and Kentucky riflemen, free blacks, and various other irregulars. Ensconced behind cotton bales piled high, the Americans just kept firing on the advancing British troops, inflicting 2,037 casualties while losing only twenty-one of their own men. "This was a stupendous victory," the Andrew Jackson biographer Robert V. Remini wrote. "It was the greatest feat of American arms up to that time." The Battle of New Orleans not only ended the War of 1812 and made Jackson a national hero, it also sent American nationalism soaring by proving that the former colonial uprisings had been no fluke: once again they had managed to beat Europe's best, even if the ensuing peace treaty resolved none of the issues at hand. The Battle of New Orleans demonstrated that the United States had both tenacity and strength to defend its right to nationhood.

After the U.S. victory at New Orleans, the Federalists' antiwar, anti-government harangues began to look near treasonous, and support for the party dwindled. Hamilton's basic ideas fared better: President Madison and the Republican Congress quietly adopted the notion of a strong central government with the authority to regulate everything from defense to infrastructure. Another like-minded Virginian, James Monroe, succeeded Madison in 1817 and espoused centrist positions so widely acceptable that he was re-elected without opposition. The "Era of Good Feelings" that began under Monroe and continued under his handpicked successor, John Adams's son John Quincy Adams, grew from the Republican lock on American politics as the sole party remaining after the Federalists' demise.

The absence of domestic discord allowed President Monroe, a former Secretary of State, to focus on international questions such as who owned the eastern part of Florida, the rest of which had been annexed from Spain in 1810. In 1818, Andrew Jackson and his troops crossed into Spanish-controlled Florida as if they owned it. The next year the United States in fact did, courtesy of a treaty under which Spain ceded its American territories in exchange for the U.S. government's assumption of $5 million in Spanish debts to U.S. citizens.

The problem now was how to keep Europeans out of the Americas. The president drew a line in the Atlantic in December 1823, when he pronounced what would be called the Monroe Doctrine. In this doctrine the United States promised to fight those European nations that attempted "to extend their system to any portion of this hemisphere." Europe's leaders may have scoffed at such presumption from the not-quite New World, but Monroe's proclamation established a precedent that would bedevil international affairs for generations: the United States pledged to guarantee freedom throughout the Americas whether it was wanted or not, thus gaining an excuse to intervene at will in the internal affairs of its southern neighbors.

The portrait of James Monroe, above, was painted by Gilbert Stuart in 1817. Monroe, a Virginian, had served under George Washington in the Revolutionary War. As president from 1817 to 1825, he tried to follow the example set by Washington, keeping himself above the rough and tumble of partisan politics. By the end of his term in office, however, Monroe worried that he had done little to be remembered in history. The ideas that later became known as the Monroe Doctrine were among his initiatives in his tenure to make a difference: the doctrine permanently connected Monroe's name with American expansionism.

In October 1823 President James Monroe wrote this letter to Thomas Jefferson requesting an appraisal of the policy later known as the Monroe Doctrine. Jefferson gave his blessing, telling Monroe that the proposal "involves consequences so lasting and effects so decisive of our future destinies" as to rekindle his interest in political subjects. Just as Jefferson predicted, the Monroe Doctrine, strong words from a young country, did have profound consequences later in the century.

Sectional Crosscurrents

At the time, however, the Monroe Doctrine had little immediate effect beyond focusing America's attention inward—and thus westward. When John Quincy Adams took office on March 4, 1825, it was alongside a nineteenth Congress that evinced little interest in foreign affairs and a great deal in the frontier territories. The currents in thinking at the time were encapsulated by three figures whose grand oratory and commanding leadership allowed them to tower over their generation: Henry Clay and Daniel Webster of the House of Representatives and Vice President John C. Calhoun.

At forty-eight, Kentucky's whip-smart Henry Clay had already made a substantial mark on American politics, having been elected Speaker of the House at age thirty-four on his first day in Congress in 1811. In 1820 he had championed the Missouri Compromise, a Band-Aid on the slavery issue that had heated up a year earlier when the territories of Maine and Missouri applied for statehood, the latter as a slave-owning state. A furor erupted when a New York congressman tried to amend Missouri's petition so as to ban further introduction of human property in the new state and to gradually emancipate the slaves already there; if the statehood bill passed with the amendment, the South's slave states would lose their numerical parity with the free states and become a minority in the Senate, as they already were in the House due to the North's larger population. The Southern states maintained that Congress had no right to make abjuring slavery a prerequisite for joining the Union. Northerners countered that it was the legislature's moral duty to ban slavery from any new state. The Missouri Compromise sought to appease both sides by admitting Maine as a free state and Missouri as a slave state, thus maintaining the balance; the rest of the lands acquired in the Louisiana Purchase would be divided at the latitude of 36 degrees, 30 minutes, with slavery banned above it and allowed below it. Peace was struck for the moment, but the dichotomy was cast. As the seventy-seven-year-old Thomas Jefferson wrote of the Missouri Compromise to a friend on April 22: "But this momentous question, like a firebell in the night, awakened and filled me with terror. I considered it the knell of the Union." It did wonders, however, for Clay's career, painting him as "the Great Compromiser" who could be called upon to forge any accord needed among the various sections of the United States.

Representative Daniel Webster of Massachusetts, a barrel-chested giant with the voice of a lion and a mane and manner to match, had been elected to the legislature in 1812 as a Federalist, and at first had supported sectional laws in the belief that the South would prove powerful enough to dominate the federal government and impose its policies on other regions. As Northern industry had continued to grow bigger and stronger, however, Webster changed his mind, and by 1825 he had become a nationalist like Clay.

Webster had his match in John C. Calhoun of South Carolina, whose spectacular intellect and complete lack of humor were driven by an overweening passion to do what he saw as his duty to his beloved South. As Clay described him, Calhoun was "tall, careworn, with furrowed brow, haggard

and intensely gazing, looking as if he were dissecting the last abstraction which sprung from a metaphysician's brain." The intense zealot, who as vice president also presided over the Senate, had voiced nationalist sentiments earlier in his political career when he still harbored hopes that the South could capitalize on its cotton fields and develop a large-scale textile industry. When this failed to materialize and the North instead took the lead in business and manufacturing—as well as an interest in the West—Calhoun sprang to the defense of his region, opposing efforts to tie the states closer together and the high tariffs that would be needed to finance any such attempts.

In December 1821, Calhoun, then Secretary of War, had thrown his hat into the presidential ring to succeed Monroe alongside several fellow claimants who had regional backing of their own: Secretary of State John

Daniel Webster, left, grew up in New Hampshire but spent most of his political career representing Massachusetts. Nominally a Whig and geographically a New Englander, he was never firmly tied to any single political philosophy—a fact that led some people to suspect the depth of his convictions. No one doubted his intellect, though. An immensely popular orator and an icon of the nation, he—to his disappointment—never became its president.

South Carolina's John C. Calhoun, above, was handsome, with a noble brow, firm jaw, and eyes that "burned like stars from a deep cave." Raised on a cotton plantation in South Carolina but educated at Yale, Calhoun rose quickly to national prominence. However, after being frustrated in two runs at the presidency in 1824 and 1828, he devoted the rest of his life to a pro-South agenda that started with states' rights and ended with an outright approbation of slavery.

The undated portrait of Andrew Jackson, below, is attributed to Ralph Earl. Jackson grew up on a farm in South Carolina, the youngest of three brothers. His father died before he was born, and his mother managed the farm until the outbreak of the Revolutionary War, when one by one the boys left to fight. Andrew was fourteen when he joined the army in 1781. By the time he returned home, his mother and brothers were all dead. At twenty, Jackson inherited a large sum of money from a relative in Ireland, and he spent at least part of it studying law. After his triumph at the Battle of New Orleans in 1815, he was an object of fascination wherever he went; today we would say Jackson had star quality.

Henry Clay, right, depicted in a portrait after a painting by Samuel S. Osgood, had only three years of formal schooling as a boy in Virginia, but he read so much on his own that he was a respected lawyer by the time he moved to Lexington, Kentucky, where he also became a professor. Representing a border state, Clay was known as "the Great Compromiser" because he so often reconciled the North and South during his many years in Washington. With his affable personality and strong gift for oration, he became a glamorous figure in his day.

Quincy Adams, a New Englander; Henry Clay; and Clay's rival for the West's support, Andrew Jackson of Tennessee. Jackson was and remains the hardest to peg; those who backed him seemed to see whatever they wanted to in the hero of the War of 1812. His military triumphs, of course, appealed to all Americans; hailing from Tennessee, he had the support of the trans-Appalachian region; because he opposed Clay's economic program, he attracted Calhoun's anti-nationalists; a few remarks made some see him as a champion of the small businessman being squeezed by large northeastern conglomerates, while others considered him an agrarian opposed to industrial society. The one common thread running through all these perceptions was the image of Jackson as an establishment outsider: born into poverty and orphaned at fourteen, he had the rough-hewn manners of the common man who had to work for a living, unlike the string of well-educated gentlemen squires who had held the presidency since its inception.

In fact, Jackson did believe that the government had been used as a tool by the upper economic classes to the detriment of the country as a whole, and detested this Hamiltonian approach as much as he opposed Jeffersonian intellectual elitism. A tall, proud, short-tempered man tough and leathery in both appearance and manner, "Old Hickory" bore scars from British bullets and a chip on his shoulder that only looked as big as his head: Jackson, who had clawed his way through law school, was in fact shrewd and smart as well as a "most roaring, rollicking, game-cocking, horse-racing, card-playing, mischievous fellow," as one of his former classmates had described him. In other words, he was the perfect exponent of America's rugged new Western temperament.

In the presidential election of 1824 (the first under the "second party system" created when Clay and Adams assembled what would come to be called the Whig Party) no candidate captured a majority of the popular vote; Jackson, the only candidate with support from all but one region (New England), won a plurality. Adams came in second in the electoral count, but once he received the backing of fourth-place finisher Clay he claimed the election. When Adams then named Clay Secretary of State, however, the smell of a "corrupt bargain" arose and fouled the air of the entire Adams administration. Calhoun, who had dropped out of the race early, was elected vice president; Calhoun's understanding that he could keep the job in a subsequent Jackson administration made it clear that the Tennessean intended to have friends in high places when he challenged Adams in 1828. And Jackson went out of his way to make friends in every place. Martin Van Buren, a scion of upstate New York's "Albany Regency" of polititians, brought his substantial following among the working classes; Monroe's retired Treasury secretary, the ailing but popular William Crawford, roused himself to support Jackson and to encourage other Jeffersonians to do the same.

This cartoon from the *U.S. Weekly Telegram* portrays two American stereotypes created by the "Tariff of Abominations." The emaciated man on the left is a Southerner; his ship is docked and his warehouse empty because the tariff has dried up the foreign markets for his goods. The man on the right is a Northerner, fat and happy, standing beside his busy factory. In fact, the tariff was as unprofitable for many New England shippers as for the Southern planters, but it was the latter who started rumbling for secession in 1828.

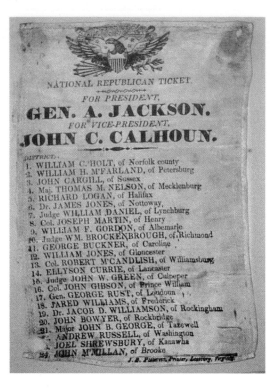

The 1828 ticket of Jackson and Calhoun, endorsed by a long list of dignitaries on the poster above, won a bitter fight against the incumbent president, John Quincy Adams. Calhoun had been Adams's vice president, but worked openly against him during their term of office. The photograph of Thomas Hart Benton, below, was taken in the late 1840s, near the end of his tenure as senator from Missouri. Benton's life and career closely followed Andrew Jackson's. Friends at first, they ended up dueling in 1813, leaving Jackson wounded. They eventually mended the relationship and Benton became Jackson's staunchest ally.

All the while, Jackson managed to steer clear of most of the issues, but he couldn't sidestep the question of tariffs. So he gave his backing to a clever, if clumsy, political ploy. In the spring of 1828, Jacksonians in Congress introduced a bill imposing extremely high tariffs on raw materials, a move designed to please the middle states while drawing opposition from Southern farmers as well as Eastern industrialists. If the measure passed, Jackson could claim credit for it among its supporters; if it failed he could complain that his plan had been stymied by selfish regional interests. Either way, he would win converts in the middle states while Calhoun held his Southern coalition together. As Representative John Randolph of Virginia remarked, the bill "referred to manufactures of no sort of kind, but the manufacture of the President of the United States."

To the surprise of many and the chagrin of Calhoun, the measure passed. As expected, the tariffs were far too high for the South to swallow, leaving Calhoun adrift without a paddle. Feeling betrayed, he penned—anonymously until three years later—the *South Carolina Exposition and Protest,* in which he argued that the tariffs were unconstitutional and that their imposition could well inspire the state to secede from the Union. Calhoun opined that every state had the right to declare acts of the federal government null and void within its boundaries in order to protect its citizens' rights. This doctrine, dubbed "nullification," had scant effect in 1828, but it would provide intellectual ammunition to sectionalists for a generation.

For all of today's complaints about negative campaigning, the election of 1828 was probably the nastiest in U.S. history. The Adams camp alleged that Jackson's wife had never divorced her first husband; Jackson's supporters responded with the charge that as an ambassador Adams had bought women for the Russian czar. Once the mud had settled, Jackson won handily, taking 178 electoral votes from New York, Pennsylvania, and the South and middle states while Adams garnered only 83 from New England. Although the president-elect was by this point a wealthy plantation owner who kept many slaves, the self-made Old Hickory managed to pass himself off as a man of the people. It was the right posture for the time: the electorate had grown substantially as suffrage had been broadened, giving all white males the right to vote as well as to hold public office. At the same time, state constitutions had been moving the nation closer to truly representative government by letting the voters rather than the legislatures choose their delegates to the electoral college. Those elitists who argued that these newly enfranchised, mostly poor voters—not to mention Jackson and his followers—were crude vulgarians unfit to govern seemed to have a point on Inauguration Day, March 4, 1829, when the new president invited the masses who had turned out to see him into the White House, which they promptly trashed, frat-party style.

Even some of Jackson's friends were soon put off, including holdover Vice President John Calhoun. Their first clash came over Missouri Senator Thomas Hart Benton's proposal to lower land prices in the West, a move opposed by Easterners fearful of a labor drain into the frontier territories. Senator Samuel Foot of Connecticut quickly countered with a resolution to limit sales of Western land. In the ensuing debate Senator Robert Hayne of South

Carolina, speaking for Calhoun, threw his support to Benton, charging that the North was trying to rob the West of its land just as it had tried to rob the South through the tariff bill of 1828. An alliance of the South and West against the Northeast was brewing, but Daniel Webster, now a senator himself, skillfully headed it off, diverting the discussion from economics to philosophy by attacking Hayne's advocacy of states' rights. As a result, the ensuing Webster-Hayne Debate of 1830 had less to do with land sales than with the very nature of the Union, a change in focus that earned Webster the president's gratitude, if briefly.

Political intrigues suffused the Jackson administration from every direction. By the spring of 1830 the administration had split into Jackson and Calhoun camps, much to the amusement of Clay, Adams, and other rivals of both. Martin Van Buren, Jackson's Secretary of State, saw his opening to seal the favor he had been currying with the president, and suggested that he and another friendly cabinet member resign to give Jackson an excuse to dismiss the entire lot. The plan was implemented and the cabinet rid of all Calhoun's supporters by the time both sides had begun to prepare for the momentous election of 1832, the main issue in which would be the very foundations of the U.S. economy.

This painting by G. P. A. Healy shows Senator Daniel Webster making the greatest speech of his career in response to Senator Robert Hayne of South Carolina. Hayne contended that each state was a sovereignty unto itself and enjoyed the right of nullification, or the rejection of federal laws it opposed. Webster's reply was an eloquent, sometimes sarcastic, indictment of nullification. The much anticipated speech was four hours long; parts of it were memorized by students in the North for generations, including the line "Liberty and Union, now and forever, one and inseparable."

When the first generation of Americans to be raised under the Bill of Rights reached adulthood in the early 1800s, the ideal of religious freedom came into full flower. In a country busily expanding in nearly every way, the result was an open frontier of religious thought and invention. While the vast majority of citizens described themselves generally as Protestants, from 1820 to 1850 they scrambled into an array of new sects that were distinctly of and by the American people.

Even the established denominations began to transform themselves with innovations that were peculiarly American. The firebrand style of evangelism, copied from a series of forceful sermons delivered at Yale in 1802, brought a new type of personalized religious experience to the farthest edges of civilization. The most popular would pit two separate denominations in huge preaching contests—an astounding 25,000 people attended one such contest in Logan County, Kentucky, in about 1823. The people expected the show of their lives and they got it, as the Methodists set up one camp and the Presbyterians another, each then setting their star preachers to work. Over the course of three days, converts fell about, rolling, crying, and praying in the ecstasy stirred up by the fury of the sermons. (For the record, the Presbyterians "won" that revival, toting up the greater number of conversions.)

Evangelists re-invigorated their staid sects, but other Americans invented entirely new beliefs within the Christian fold. More accurately, for true believers, they did not invent anything but conveyed messages directly from heaven. At a time when religion provided glamour in everyday life, hundreds of new religious sects gelled in the early nineteenth century; several have lasted to the present day. The fact that a high proportion of the new leaders were women indicates that religion was not yet among the country's established, unyielding institutions, such as, for example, academia, medicine, or the law.

The Shakers, founded in the 1740s in England and brought to America by an English immigrant named "Mother" Ann Lee, reached their peak from 1830 to 1850, with nineteen communities from Maine to Florida. Lee, who died in 1784, was considered the female embodiment of Christ: a perfect balance of the genders. Admired for the pure quality of their spirituality, the Shakers were best known for espousing celibacy, a policy that contributed to the decline of the sect.

Joseph Smith founded the Church of Jesus Christ of Latter-Day Saints after a series of visions starting in 1820 gave him possession of a set of biblical plates made of gold. Smith translated the plates into *The Book of Mormon* in 1829. The Mormons were notably controversial, even at a time of hot-blooded religious quarreling. After Joseph Smith was killed by a mob in Illinois in 1844, most of his followers made their way to a new home in Utah.

The early 1800s spawned new sects that predicted exact dates for the Second Coming of Christ. One of the most widely accepted was March 21, 1843. When it passed without event, a believer named Ellen Harmon had a new vision, and her fervent belief in an eventual Second Coming led to the formation of the Seventh Day Adventists. Another of the lasting American denominations was the Christian Science Church, founded in the 1870s by Mary Baker Eddy.

At the same time that thousands of people were exploring the new, open spaces of American religion, a small group of writers near Boston was leading the way into another awakening, one that was simultaneously spiritual, intellectual, and literary. Commonly called the Transcendentalists, they sought to transcend the boundaries between self and universe, between human being and nature. For Ralph Waldo Emerson, the dean of the group, qualities such as self-reliance, nonconformity, and imagination made any person equal to his or her universe. Shirking many of the narrow definitions of science—and logic, which he abhorred—Emerson's was a humanistic response to the world. His wholesome, optimistic view was delivered through important writings, but also through lecture tours that made the handsome New Englander an idol in his day.

One of Emerson's protégés in 1845 was Henry David Thoreau, a well-read but unemployed young Harvard graduate. Thoreau had an unusual love of nature: he was not a scientist intent upon classifying nature, but a man who gloried in its unexplained surprises. Having a cabin on Walden Pond, not far from Concord, Thoreau lived there for just over two years in the company of himself and the natural universe around him. He was not a recluse, but sallied into Concord nearly every day, and received visitors as well. Thoreau wrote an account of his happy sojourn, *Walden,* that not only served as an extension of Emerson's views, but also as a continuing reminder of the fullness of a life touched constantly by nature.

As a literary movement, based as much on clear, relaxed writing as on viewpoint, Transcendentalism embraced the novelists Nathaniel Hawthorne and Herman Melville, as well as the poet Walt Whitman. Yet the excitement of ideas grew just as much out of debate as isolation and the Transcendental Club met regularly for wide-ranging, unpredictable discussions. "It was like going to heaven on a swing," said one participant. In addition to the five writers already mentioned, Bronson Alcott (Louisa May's father) and Margaret Fuller were considered core members.

Fuller, a well-educated woman, was so certain of herself that she frequently asserted, "I now know all the people worth knowing in America and I find no intellect comparable to my own." Most people, male or female, concurred with that assessment, yet for a long time, Fuller could not find a suitable position. Eventually, she made a steady living by holding "conversations" (or discussions) for Bostoners interested in history, literature, and philosophy. She also initiated the Transcendentalist magazine, *The Dial*, which was published from 1840 to 1844.

The Transcendentalists have always retained the worldwide respect they first earned in the 1830s and 1840s. The fresh voice they gave to American letters, along with the breathless beliefs of the new messiahs and even the sweaty shoutings of the first evangelists, all proved early on that America was going to be a country with ideas of its own.

The artist Tom Lovell set his painting of Henry David Thoreau in a glade of trees near Walden Pond in Massachusetts. Thoreau lived in a cabin on the pond for about two years—an escape from the profanities of modern life that he later wrote about in Walden. *No recluse, Thoreau both visited friends in nearby Concord and received callers at the cabin. He was especially popular with children, including young Louisa May Alcott and her sisters, who frequently walked out to see him at Walden Pond.*

A Whig cartoonist drew Andrew Jackson as "King Andrew the First," above, making a play on one of the powerful president's more derisive nicknames. Jackson's own party saw him as a hero in the cartoon at right entitled "General Jackson Slaying the Many Headed Monster"; Jackson had once called the bank "the hydra of corruption." His chief nemesis was the bank's president, a Philadelphia aristocrat named Nicholas Biddle, who is shown wearing a top hat. Jackson's confidant, Martin Van Buren, is standing in the middle of the picture, helping to wrestle the serpent. In 1832, Jackson had told Van Buren that "The bank is trying to kill me, but I will kill it." Eventually he succeeded.

Taking It to the Bank

The 1832 election was among the most contentious and important in U.S. history, not least for firming up the nation's political labels. As early as 1828 Henry Clay's supporters had begun calling themselves National Republicans while the Jacksonians stuck with Democratic Republicans, soon to be shortened to Democrats. Calhoun's followers either fell in with Clay or went looking for a third option after their man resigned the vice presidency to accept the Senate seat to which South Carolina had elected him. At national conventions, held for the first time by both major parties, the Democrats nominated Jackson and Van Buren and the National Republicans Clay and John Sergeant. Jackson won in a landslide, 219 electoral votes to 49 for Clay.

No sooner were the results known than Calhoun's South Carolina issued its Ordinance of Nullification declaring the tariffs of 1828 and 1832 null and void within its boundaries. If necessary, the state announced, it would secede from the Union rather than pay the tariffs. Jackson responded by sending reinforcements to two federal forts on Charleston harbor, and a bloody confrontation looked imminent. While Calhoun and Webster attacked the problem through sonorous debate in the Senate, Clay took to his desk and fashioned a compromise in which South Carolina would accept the tariffs with the understanding that their rates would be lowered over the next ten years. Clay's arrangement was accepted as an interim solution, but the issues of nullification and states' rights to leave the Union remained unresolved—and ominous.

The president, however, was more interested in a political crusade inspired by personal experience. In 1804 his land speculations in Tennessee had left him on the verge of bankruptcy, and it had taken years of painful

sacrifice to extricate himself from near financial ruin. Jackson, as a result, trusted neither banks nor the paper money they printed. Thus to Andrew Jackson the Second Bank of the United States represented nothing less than an unholy union between excessive government and overprivileged aristocracy—a view the public shared, as the president's easy re-election had proved. His struggle against the bank formed the central focus of the 1832 campaign and was in fact the most important aspect of Jackson's administration, not to mention the most characteristic, at least in his eyes: a grand-scale battle waged by the common man against business interests powerful enough to control the economy and thereby the nation. The outcome, unfortunately, was characteristic of all political undertakings fueled by obsession: long-term failure and a situation worse than the one it replaced.

In its thirty-six years of operation, the Bank of the United States had grown into the nation's largest and most conservative financial institution, issuing most U.S. currency and backing it with gold, making loans, conducting foreign exchange, and tightening the money supply when necessary to squelch inflation and speculation. The bank's sound money policies had given the United States a stable currency and created confidence in government securities overseas, but its caution had also sparked complaints that the bank was holding the economy back. The bank applied for a new charter in 1831 to replace the one scheduled to expire in 1836. When the bill for recharter was passed by Congress in 1832, President Jackson blasted it with a veto followed by an all-out assault. In 1833 he ordered all federal funds to be withdrawn from the Bank of the United States and deposited in selected state banks. Although the central bank did not disappear, it shrank radically and was incorporated as a state bank in Philadelphia. The attainment of Jackson's primary goal proved disastrous: as soon as the federal funds were out of the bank, unemployment and interest rates soared in the absence of government regulation. Although the federal deposits into various state banks created economic booms in some areas, particularly in the West, the expansion came mostly from land speculation and the indiscriminate issuance of paper money by state and local banks.

Jackson was troubled by this sudden flow of currency, which prompted him in the summer of 1836 to put out the Specie Circular announcing that henceforth the government would accept only gold and silver in payment for federal lands. In addition, the surplus funds resulting from the 1832 tariff were distributed among the states beginning the next year. The combination of the Specie Circular's announcement, the nation's unfavorable trade balance, and the fact that bank withdrawals would be needed to pay for the distribution of the surplus led to a rapid contraction of currency and in its wake a financial panic that guaranteed hard times ahead. In fact, the depression that began in 1837 lasted into the early 1840s and would prove the most severe economic downturn in U.S. history to that point.

Jackson, nearing seventy and keen to return to his Nashville plantation, the Hermitage, opted to get out while the getting was good, leaving his hand-picked successor to take the heat. In 1836 the Democrats duly nominated Martin Van Buren for the presidency. The Whigs—formerly the National Re-

Martin Van Buren, in a painting by Jeremiah Nims, was born in upstate New York, the son of a poor farmer. He attached himself early in his career to Jackson: both were self-made men who rose to prominence in the nation's political arena in the 1820s. Together, they founded the Democratic Party: the charismatic Jackson, dead set in his beliefs, and the wily Van Buren, whose apparent "non-committalism" gave rise to national joking. Determined to pin Van Buren down to an opinion, any opinion, an acquaintance once said to him, "Nice day, isn't it?" The "Red Fox" replied, "Well, it might be; and it might not be, I once saw a day like this that. . . ."

publicans and still in favor of a strong federal government focused on economic growth—named several candidates in the hope that each would win his region's electoral votes, which could then be aggregated behind a single candidate in the electoral college contest. It didn't work: Van Buren won, although he may well have wished he hadn't.

Problems and Possibilities Beyond the Borders

Although matters of finance and infrastructure remained important issues, during the next generation westward expansion and the future of slavery took their place at the forefront of political discourse. The former's inexorable progress could not be ignored; the latter couldn't either, thanks to the clashes between the cotton culture of the South and the growing industrial base of the North. Both subjects raised the cardinal issue left unsettled after the Jackson era: the very nature of the Union.

In one of his last acts as president, on March 3, 1837, Jackson extended diplomatic recognition to the Republic of Texas. Within six months the newly created nation asked to be annexed by the United States, but its petition was denied by Northerners fearful of adding another cotton and slave state, with its likely votes against high tariffs, infrastructure improvements, and a strong central bank.

Texas had actually come into existence as an independent entity eighteen years earlier, when under the terms of the Adams-Onís Treaty the United States had abandoned its claims to the territory in return for Spanish concessions in Florida. Two years later the Spanish governor of the region granted an American, Moses Austin, the right to settle 200 families in Texas. More Americans soon arrived, leading to clashes with settlers from what would become the Mexican Empire in 1822. Bloody armed struggles broke out between the two groups in the early 1830s, but by 1835 the American population in Texas had swelled to 35,000—ten times the number of Mexicans in the territory. The Americans began agitating for representation in the Mexican government, but instead its president, General Santa Anna, dissolved his own national legislature, declared himself dictator, and headed north with an army 6,000 strong. At San Antonio he ran into fewer than 200 American and Texan irregulars, including Davy Crockett, entrenched inside the Alamo, an abandoned Franciscan mission. The following thirteen-day siege was so bloody that at one point the American commander traced a line in the dirt with his sword and said to his men, "Those prepared to give their lives in freedom's cause, come over to me." Every last one did, including the pneumonia-stricken Indian fighter Colonel James Bowie, who asked that his sickbed be carried over the line.

In the end Bowie, Crockett, and all but five others were killed when the Mexican troops overran the fort, but "Remember the Alamo" would become a rallying cry for Texas patriots. (Over the ensuing years, the Alamo would grow into an American myth of valor and courage, inspiring a cottage industry of racoon-skinned caps, hokum, jingoistic paeans, and B-grade Hollywood films.) Thus inspired, they made Andrew Jackson's tough military protégé Sam Houston, former governor of Tennessee, commander in chief of a new Texas army, which needed only fifteen minutes on April 21, 1836, to overwhelm Mexican forces at San Jacinto and capture Santa Anna. The Mexican dictator bought his release by signing a treaty recognizing the independent Republic of Texas, which immediately elected Houston president and then asked the United States for annexation. Most Americans were thrilled by Texas's successful struggle for independence, viewing it as the triumph of white Protestanism over Catholic Mexicans.

At around the same time farther north, the Canadians were also expanding west, leading to talk of an eventual union between at least parts of that country and the United States. Van Buren managed to avoid the international wrangling on both borders, but his administration never recovered from the disastrous economic situation it had inherited and he lost the 1840 presidential election to Whig William Henry Harrison, who also never had to deal with foreign or any other problems: he contracted pneumonia from standing outside in a cold rain at his own inauguration and died a month later. Harrison was succeeded by his vice president, John Tyler, who created fissures in the Whig Party by turning out not to be the Clay puppet everyone thought he was. Thus it was with scant political support that Tyler had to face America's deteriorating relations with Britain over western Canada and with Mexico over Texas. For the first time in a generation, in 1844 foreign policy questions—this time regarding America's potential expansion—became pressing issues in the national election.

The Democrats split their support between Van Buren, who opposed annexing Texas, and John C. Calhoun, who supported it; the party wound up compromising on James K. Polk of Tennessee, a Jackson protégé who supported the "reoccupation of Oregon" and the "reannexation of Texas" but who was not a Calhoun man. The Whigs went with Henry Clay, while the upstart Liberty Party, which opposed annexation but was more interested in the issue of slavery, selected James Birney as their candidate. Polk won by a slim popular vote margin, but the real surprise was the showing of the abolitionist third party. Birney received few votes overall, but nearly half were in the key states of New York and Massachusetts; had his supporters voted for Clay, who held a similar position on Texas, the

Even as a Mexican state from 1821 to 1836, Texas recruited American settlers with posters such as the one below. The settlers' refusal to abide by Mexico's 1830 ban on slavery was one of the reasons that Texas seceded from the country in 1836.

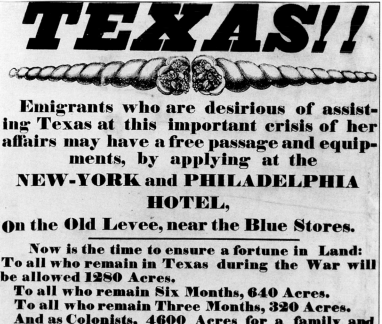

TEXAS!!

Emigrants who are desirious of assisting Texas at this important crisis of her affairs may have a free passage and equipments, by applying at the NEW-YORK and PHILADELPHIA HOTEL,

On the Old Levee, near the Blue Stores.

Now is the time to ensure a fortune in Land: To all who remain in Texas during the War will be allowed 1280 Acres. To all who remain Six Months, 640 Acres. To all who remain Three Months, 320 Acres. And as Colonists, 4600 Acres for a family and 1470 Acres for a Single Man.

New Orleans, April 23d, 1836.

The image of President John Tyler, left, was painted by G. P. A. Healy. After Harrison died in 1841 the Whigs were surprised to discover that they neither controlled nor much liked his successor, John Tyler. A graceful, well-born Virginian, Tyler considered himself above convention, whether social or political. His primary goal, a bill enforcing the annexation of Texas, was pushed through Congress by his successor, James Polk, whose portrait, right, was painted by Max Westfield. Taking office at the age of forty-nine in 1845, Polk was the youngest president up to that time. He was a Tennessean, so much cast in Andrew Jackson's mold that he was known as "Young Hickory." Polk worked twelve-hour days and took only one vacation during his presidency; deeply fatigued, he stuck to a campaign promise to serve only one term, and died only three months after leaving office.

Whigs would have captured New York and the election. The real significance of the 1844 election, then, lay in the revelation that combining Clay's federal-centered economic program of protective tariffs, a national bank, and government-supported infrastructure improvements with the anti-slavery platform of the Liberty Party could make for an effective coalition against the Democrats—and would sixteen years later.

The annexation of Texas by the United States was approved and scheduled for the last days of the Tyler administration, but the matter turned out not to be quite resolved. Mexico wanted the border at the Nueces River, while the United States thought it should bisect the Rio Grande 150 miles farther south. Mexico protested and broke off relations with the United States, and in May 1845 General Zachary Taylor was dispatched to southern Texas at the head of an "army of observation." When Mexico rejected a fairly generous U.S. offer to negotiate the dispute, Polk ordered Taylor to advance into the disputed territory in January 1846. Mexico protested and relations grew even more strained.

The president, however, wanted to tackle a similar controversy in the North first, this one with Britain over the question of Oregon's border with Canada. Just as the Northern states refused to fight for Texas because it had both cotton and slavery, the South wanted nothing to do with Oregon because it had neither. It appeared that unless Polk was prepared to make some compromises he might wind up with wars on both borders at the same time.

The British, however, had no interest in going to war over an untamed and mostly uninhabited area, and Polk accepted a compromise that set Oregon's boundary at the forty-ninth parallel. The settlement drew criticism from the North and West, but it left the president free to concentrate on the more important problems brewing in Texas.

The Mexican War

Polk decided to declare war on Mexico in May 1846. It was a move that might have been harder to justify had U.S. and Mexican troops not already clashed in the disputed territory, each side blaming the other for starting the bloodshed. The war officially began on May 13 and would last nearly two years. "It is for the interest of mankind that its [the United States'] power and territory should be extended—the farther the better," poet Walt Whitman wrote in a *Brooklyn Eagle* editorial expressing the gung-ho Manifest Destiny view of Mr. Polk's war. But many intellectuals—most famously the abolitionist Henry David Thoreau—saw the war as an illegitimate design to extend slavery. In 1846, his war dissent well known, Thoreau was arrested for refusing to pay a Massachusetts poll tax on moral grounds. His one night in prison motivated him to write his most famous essay, *Civil Disobedience* (1849), which became a key text for future nonviolent movements, including Mahatma Gandhi's in India and Martin Luther King Jr.'s in the United States: "How does it become a man to behave toward this American government today?" Thoreau asked. "I answer that he cannot without disgrace be associated with it."

The battles went well for the U.S. troops from the start, even though they faced a force four times larger fighting on its own terrain. In the summer of 1846 Colonel Stephen Kearny took the New Mexico capital of Santa Fe, then pushed west to join Commodore Robert Stockton and Captain John C. Frémont, who gained control of a good deal of California. Within a few months U.S. forces had seized much of the disputed territory north of the eventual border between Mexico and the United States. In fact, the conflict might have ended earlier had Taylor not been more interested in winning the 1848 Whig presidential nomination than the Mexican War. When Taylor's line in the north bogged down, Polk sent General Winfield Scott to the south at the head of a second army, which landed at Vera Cruz in March 1847 to conduct the first U.S. amphibious military operation. It was a smashing success: the Mexican commander surrendered within the month, and Scott and his 10,000 troops set out for Mexico City which he entered in September. Along the way they were ambushed by Santa Anna at the mountain pass of Cerro Gordo, but U.S. troops turned the tables and captured 3,000 Mexican prisoners, their matériel and provisions, and, just for effect, the Mexican president's clothing as well. Scott continued on while Taylor concluded the campaign in the north in February, 1847 with his victory at Buena Vista.

By January 1848, Mexico was eager for peace, and the Treaty of Guadalupe Hidalgo was signed the next month. Under its terms Mexico agreed to recognize the Rio Grande as its border with Texas and to cede Arizona, New Mexico, and upper California to the United States in return for $15 million and the assumption of debts owed by Mexicans to Americans, which amounted to another $3.25 million. Over 1.2 million square miles were added to the Union. The United States had won land, although the victory would create problems through the next decade and beyond.

With the Treaty of Guadalupe Hidalgo—ratified by a 38 to 14 Senate vote—the United States all but spanned the continent south of Canada, and

Richard Caton Woodville painted *War News From Mexico* in 1848, the year the Treaty of Guadalupe Hidalgo ended the Mexican War. The circumstances surrounding the treaty were almost comic, because war news took so long to arrive in Washington. President Polk, a Democrat, had been suspicious from the start that his Whig generals, Taylor and Scott, were each executing the war in anticipation of a presidential run. Polk was right, but long lags in receiving war news only exacerbated his paranoia. In February 1848, the non-diplomat, Nicholas P. Trist, signed a very real treaty in the town of Guadalupe Hidalgo. Even though the Mexican War was also called Mr. Polk's War, the president found out about it at the same time as the man holding the paper.

at scant cost to boot. Fewer than 1,800 U.S. soldiers had been lost in battle during the Mexican War, and military expenditures came to less than $98 million. It seemed a small price to pay for the glory of fulfilling the dream of Manifest Destiny to extend to the Pacific Ocean—or, as journalist John Louis O'Sullivan had defined the idea in 1845, "Our manifest destiny is to overspread the continent allotted by Providence for the free development of our yearly multiplying millions." The war gave definition to the American republic. "Who can calculate the value of our glorious Union?" Polk proudly asked. "It is a model and example of free government to all the world, and is the star of hope and haven to the oppressed of every clime." And in the bargain the United States had trained an army of efficient soldiers, many of whom would make use of their military talents in the Civil War.

The Schism Over Slavery

Underlying both border disputes, of course, was the matter of slavery and the growing calls for an end to the vile practice. A few Americans had advocated abolitionism since the first twenty Africans had been dragged in shackles off a Dutch ship to Jamestown, but it was not until the 1830s that the moral argument started to spread. It had taken new root in 1822 when Denmark Vesey, a free black man, nearly succeeded in organizing a mass slave revolt in Charleston. Soon thereafter abolitionist agitation increased in the North, sparked largely by Boston intellectuals devoted to social reform. In 1828 William Lloyd Garrison, editor of a newspaper that preached temperance, joined the anti-slavery ranks and three years later launched *The Liberator,* which would become an influential abolitionist journal. Although few read it at first, the South considered the newspaper so incendiary that the state of Georgia offered $5,000 for Garrison's capture. "On this subject, I do not wish to think, or speak, or write with moderation. . . ." Garrison, who had already been jailed in Baltimore for his ardent abolitionism, wrote from Boston on January 1, 1831. "I am in earnest—I will not equivocate—I will not excuse—I will not retreat a single inch—AND I WILL BE HEARD."

Also in 1831, Nat Turner, a Virginia slave, led an insurrection that failed to free those involved but succeeded in precipitating a debate in the state legislature over the future of slavery, during which some spoke openly in favor of abolition. Turner—who, with his followers, killed fifty-seven white men, women, and children—evaded capture for six weeks, but was eventually caught, tried, and executed as were seventeen other slaves involved in the insurrection. Unfortunately, abolitionist voices were drowned out by those preaching fear of violent black rebellions, and the anti-slavery movement dwindled throughout the South. In the rest of the country, however, abolitionists and defenders of slavery grew ever more polarized, with the conflict coming to a head in the dialogue over the future of the new far West.

The subject of slavery was officially broached in 1846 when Polk asked Congress to appropriate $2 million to help buy land acquired from Mexico. David Wilmot, the Democratic congressman from Pennsylvania, introduced an amendment to the bill to prevent the formation of slave states in any part of the

The Liberator, above, was the first publication to demand freedom for slaves, or "American citizens who are now groaning in servile chains in the boasted land of Liberty," in the words of William Lloyd Garrison, *The Liberator*'s vociferous publisher. Garrison used any tactic he could to promote abolition, including trying to scare Southerners with the nightmare possibility of a slave revolt. In August 1831 a slave named Nat Turner did rebel, leading a band of five dozen followers on a rampage through Virginia. Fifty-seven whites were killed before Turner was finally captured, a scene depicted in the undated woodcut at right. Turner was hanged, but the specter of his deeds terrified the South for generations.

Panning for gold, a forty-niner peers into the silt of California's American River in the photograph by L. C. McClure, opposite, taken in 1850. Within the span of just over one week—January 24 to February 2, 1848—two major events occurred: the United States acquired California in the settlement of the Mexican War, and gold was discovered at John Sutter's mill in the northern part of the territory. If the Louisiana Purchase had seemed a bargain, California was a boon, part of a whole package of territories costing just $15 million: by 1853, California had yielded $500 million in gold. The Gold Rush gave a new start to thousands of arrivals each month and accelerated settlement of the West when California became a state in 1850.

new territory. Although this Wilmot Proviso was defeated, it would reappear in various forms throughout the coming years. At the time, however, Calhoun responded by reprising his nullification argument of 1828 and proposing a series of resolutions proclaiming Congress had no right to legislate on the slavery issue—amid hints of secession if his resolutions were not accepted. With this, the Democrats split asunder over the question of slavery in the territories.

But Americans have a genius for political haggling, and a few of that ever-useful breed of lawmaker—the moderate activist—set to looking for middle ground. Stephen A. Douglas, a silver-tongued Democrat from Illinois who had been elected to the House of Representatives in 1842, for example, called for "squatter sovereignty," also known as "popular sovereignty," under which a territory's inhabitants would have the right to decide for themselves whether or not to permit slavery. Douglas saw the traffic in humanity as a political issue, while both the abolitionists and slavery's Southern defenders considered it a moral one as well. Therein lay the problem, although it was not recognized at the time. By the 1850s, tempers ran not only high but also deep, creating an atmosphere far different from the relative calm of 1820 when Clay had steered the Missouri Compromise through Congress.

Other complications also seeped into the stew. In July 1847, just before Scott entered Mexico City, Brigham Young and some 150 Mormon followers had arrived at the Great Salt Lake in what is now Utah. Forced from their homes by religious intolerance in the East and Midwest, the Mormons had crossed half the continent in search of the right place to practice their beliefs,

and in the Salt Lake area they found their promised land. It was certainly promising from an economic standpoint: astride one of the few existing routes to California, northern Utah was an ideal location for selling provisions to travelers heading farther west.

Another economic factor entered the picture in January 1848, when gold was discovered on John Sutter's property on the American River in the foothills of northern California's Sierra Nevada Mountains. The precious earth didn't stay secret for long, and by the late summer thousands of Easterners had set out for the gold streams. By then it had become clear that California, which more than 100,000 people immigrated in 1849 alone, would soon ask for admission to the Union as a free state, with the anti-slavery Mormons' new settlement, dubbed Deseret, close behind. Thus, while only a few months earlier it had looked as though the Mexican treaty would mostly benefit the South, in late 1848 it appeared that the North had actually gained the most from it. By the end of the year, Minnesota and Oregon as well as California and Deseret seemed likely to ask for admission as free states, and the South grew alarmed.

The burgeoning sectional antagonism all but wiped out the nationalistic sentiment the Mexican War had engendered and threatened to bring down what many in the North considered the utterly successful Polk administration. In addition to having led the nation to victory in an inexpensive and in the end profitable war, the workaholic president also had racked up an impressive record of legislative accomplishments. The Independent Treasury Act, for example, had set up a replacement for the Bank of the United States that worked nearly as well and that would serve the nation with only slight modifications until 1913. What's more, as he had promised in his 1844 campaign, Polk had also pushed through the Walker Tariff to lower the rates of its despised predecessor.

Richard Caton Woodville's 1849 painting, *Old '76 and Young '48*, shows a spent veteran of the American Revolution listening to a soldier of the Mexican War as the rest of the family looks on. From the grand wave of his hand, the soldier is probably speaking about expansion, the fighting cause of his generation.

Yet despite his considerable achievements, many were unhappy with Polk. Northern Democrats regarded him as pro-South, while Southerners were beginning to realize that the Mexican War had really served to benefit the North. When he was first elected, Polk had said he wanted to serve only one term and would not accept renomination. In 1848 he got his wish.

The United States was certainly not alone in its internal dissension. A new revolutionary spirit was roiling the entire Western world in 1848, once again creating a zeitgeist determined by economics, in this case the collapse of international credit. The same year Karl Marx and Friedrich Engels wrote their *Communist Manifesto*, populist revolts stoked by high unemployment, poor harvests, and rampant cholera broke out across Europe and ended in calls for German unification, the first fracture lines in the Hapsburg Empire, and the formation of new republics in France, Rome, and Venice. Although the old order—the pope, the Hapsburgs, and the Russian czar—managed to put most of the uprisings down within a year, the damage had been done; the bourgeoisie, or merchant class, had begun to make its political presence felt.

Just as the Europeans were rising up against their monarchies and aristocracies as much for interfering with commerce as for the related ethical issue of denying the people political rights, Americans went into their 1848 elections sharply divided over both the economic and the moral ramifications of slavery. The schism extended into the parties as well, particularly among the Democrats, where radicals of both Northern and Southern persuasion began to gain adherents.

Seeking the middle ground, the party nominated Senator Lewis Cass of Michigan, one of the early proponents of squatter sovereignty, with General William O. Butler of Kentucky for vice president. The Whigs, who had won their only national victory to date with war hero William Henry Harrison, tried the same ploy with Mexican War general Zachary Taylor. Taylor was supported at the bottom of the ticket by Millard Fillmore, an unremarkable former congressman who had lost New York's gubernatorial race in 1844 and was serving as the state's comptroller. The 1848 Whig platform was more a paean to Taylor than a statement on the issues, which was only fitting seeing that the general refused to say what his positions on the issues were. It would not be the last time the tactic worked.

Many voters were unhappy with both of the major party candidates. Northerners who favored abolition or at least the Wilmot Proviso joined the Liberty Party; a new "Liberty League" put forth Gerrit Smith until these and other like-minded groups united into the Free Soil Party behind former president Martin Van Buren. The Free Soil ticket drew enough votes away from Cass to give Taylor the election, once again raising tempting possibilities for new political coalitions.

Taylor surprised many by delivering a long inaugural address in which he hinted that some of the lands gained in the Mexican War might emerge as sister republics to the United States. Widespread opposition made him drop the idea quickly and instead assume leadership of the popular-sovereignty supporters whose candidate he had just defeated in the election. His shift in focus was short-lived: Taylor died after only sixteen months in office. Millard Fillmore, the new president, immediately allied himself with Daniel Webster and Henry Clay in pursuit of a compromise to save the Union.

In 1850 Clay devised another of the trade-offs on which he had built his reputation, a proposal to admit California as a free state in which both sides would make some gains and take some losses: Texas would relinquish its claims on parts of New Mexico (a border dispute left over from the Alamo days), but the federal government would compensate the state by assuming all public debt incurred there prior to annexation; the District of Columbia's

Zachary Taylor, above in a photograph circa 1850, was a hero of the Mexican War. He was a slaveholder, but a notably kind one, and with nothing against abolitionists: an ideal candidate to sit on the fence of the slavery issue. In the 1848 presidential race Taylor's running mate was Millard Fillmore, seen below in a photograph by Mathew Brady. Fillmore was a self-educated and self-made New York lawyer known for his impeccable manners and appearance. The team was elected, but Taylor died during his second year in office, leaving Fillmore at the helm of a nation already drifting toward civil war.

In 1805 a Shawnee shaman named Prophet, who had failed to cure his people of the new diseases introduced by Europeans, traversed the Ohio Valley to warn his fellow Indians of the need to embrace their traditional culture and avoid the white man's perils. Prophet's message fell on eager ears, reassuring tribe members who felt intimidated by white culture and drawing converts to his opposition toward the federal government's policies. Along with his older brother, the magnetic and physically imposing warrior Tecumseh, whose name meant "Cougar Crouching for His Prey," Prophet swayed his followers to refuse to leave lands claimed by the U.S. government and by 1808 had abandoned his message of spiritual renewal in favor of active resistance against whites. Two years later Tecumseh would take over as Shawnee leader on the more compelling platform of unifying the various tribes on the grounds that only an Indian federation could forestall the encroaching white settlers. "Brothers—we are friends; we must assist each other to bear our burdens," Tecumseh exhorted as he traveled from the Great Lakes to the Gulf of Mexico in search of support for his cause. "The blood of many of our fathers and brothers has run like water on the ground, to satisfy the avarice of the white men. We, ourselves, are threatened with a great evil; nothing will pacify them but the destruction of all the red men."

But as historian Peter Nabokov wrote in *Native American Testimony*, Tecumseh's "gathering storm never broke." Instead, he was killed on October 5, 1813 in Canada as he fought alongside the British against his longtime enemy General William Henry Harrison in the Battle of the Thames.

With Tecumseh died the organized Indian resistance. By 1820 tribes across the United States had been forced to give up their lands—nearly 200 million acres for pennies apiece. Yet the white settlers wanted more for even less as commercial farming blossomed in the Midwest and the South's booming cotton plantations called for ever more land. Efforts to co-opt the Native Americans by educating them in the ways of the white man largely failed as the Indians found the efforts useless and insulting.

In 1824 President James Monroe wrote Congress concerning the notion that all Indians should be "removed" to areas west of the Mississippi River. Monroe agreed with this proposal to protect Native Americans from invasion while allowing them the independence to carry out their own "improvement in civilization," provided that the Indians were settled peacefully and with their consent. The southern tribes would have none of it; they wanted to stay on their remaining ancestral lands. The dispute had arisen in Georgia, which in the 1820s charged the federal government with failing to fulfill its 1802 promise to remove the local Indian populations after the state renounced its claims to the west. When the Georgia state legislature ordered the seizure of tribal lands in 1828, a year later the Cherokee tribe launched an original suit in the Supreme Court to prevent the state from taking their lands. In 1831, in *Cherokee Nation v. Georgia*, Chief Justice John Marshall ruled that under the Constitution Indian tribes had no standing to initiate an original suit in the Court, but by the same token they had a right to their lands. President Andrew Jackson disagreed and continued trying to purge

the Cherokee. Through the Removal Act of 1830 Congress gave him the means to do so by resettling resisting tribes west of the Mississippi. Some Indians complied; but when the evacuation order came in 1838 most refused to move, upon which President Martin Van Buren ordered federal troops to round them up. Some 20,000 Cherokee were removed and put in detention camps or brought to Oklahoma under military escort along the notorious Trail of Tears, where almost one-fourth of them died from disease and exhaustion. In the end, the Indians gave up some 100 million acres of territory east of the Mississippi for $68 million and about thirty-two million acres west of the river.

Despite the finer ideals that supposedly defined the United States, there was little change throughout the nineteenth century in the white man's belief that Indians were inferior people destined either to "rise above" their culture into white society or to disappear. Andrew Jackson likened Indians to wolves, and General Philip Sheridan is reputed to have said, "the only good Indians I ever saw were dead. " Unfortunately, most non-Native Americans agreed with both views. Whites sought to remove Indians for a variety of reasons, although most were interested solely in the tribes' lands and were essentially oblivious to concerns about the rights or culture of the people they were displacing. After all, Manifest Destiny justified shoving any obstacle aside. Although various well-meaning missionaries worked to assimilate Native Americans into white American society, these attempts failed as well, and, in fact, only contributed to the destruction of the Indian tribes and their culture.

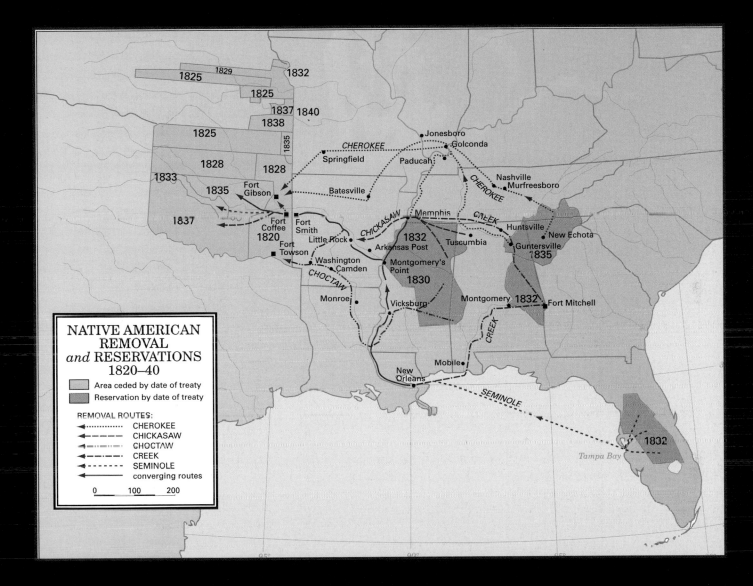

NATIVE AMERICAN
REMOVAL
and RESERVATIONS
1820–40

Area ceded by date of treaty
Reservation by date of treaty

REMOVAL ROUTES:
CHEROKEE
CHICKASAW
CHOCTAW
CREEK
SEMINOLE
converging routes

0   100   200

The map above illustrates the displacement of five major tribes in the South starting in 1820. The time period was one generation after the invention of the cotton gin in the 1790s. Ignorant farming techniques depleted the soil on cotton plantations along the coast, and planters felt they had no choice but to reach west toward new lands. President Andrew Jackson reacted by signing the 1830 Removal Act, allowing the government to force Indians to surrender their legally held lands in exchange for new reservations west of the Mississippi River. The Choctaws, Creeks, and Chicksaws went first: many of them in chains. The Cherokee, however, placed their faith in the judicial system. Priding themselves on a tradition of education and respect for the law of the United States, the Cherokee pleaded their case before the Supreme Court. They were victorious. Chief Justice John Marshall wrote the opinion upholding their right to the land. President Jackson and his successor, Martin Van Buren, ignored the court ruling. Under armed guard, the Cherokee were removed west. After fighting a second war with the United States in the 1830s, the Seminoles—who thrived in the swampland of Florida—were also placed in Oklahoma.

The cartoon above shows former president Martin Van Buren trying and failing to straddle the two predominant political parties of 1848. Neither fought hard for abolition and so a group of New Englanders prevailed upon Van Buren to accept the nomination of a new party, the Free Soilers: "Free soil, free speech, free labor, and free men!" They believed that all new states should be free of slavery; so did Van Buren, but his resolve on the issue was never adamant enough for fervent abolitionists.

In the drawing by R. W. Whitechurch after the painting by P. F. Rothermel, opposite, Henry Clay rises in the Senate chamber to deliver a series of resolutions later called the Compromise of 1850, which staved off disunion and fostered a spirit of reconciliation throughout the country. The debate over the compromise witnessed the last great moments of three aging warhorses of American politics: Clay, John C. Calhoun, and Daniel Webster. Calhoun died before the resolutions were passed. Clay and Webster retired soon thereafter, each wracked with illness.

slave trade would be ended but its practice of slavery guaranteed, while Congress would enact a strict fugitive slave law and assert that it had no right to interfere with slave trade between the states. Turning to the Northern Whigs, Clay pointed out, "You have nature on your side," meaning that New Mexico's climate insured the state-to-be's exclusion from the cotton culture.

Clay's Compromise of 1850 set off one of the grandest dramas in U.S. political history. A few weeks before he died, Calhoun rose from his deathbed, emaciated and wrapped in blankets, and had his speech read by fellow senator James Mason to answer for his region, rejecting the compromise and instead suggesting a constitutional amendment assuring that the South would never be crushed by the nation's other sections.

The shrunken but still leonine Daniel Webster also added his faltering voice to the calls for compromise, intoning, "I wish to speak today, not as a Massachusetts man, nor as a Northern man, but as an American. . . . I speak today for the preservation of the Union." The sixty-eight-year-old Webster continued, "Never did there devolve on any generation of men higher trusts than now devolve upon us for the preservation of this constitution, and the harmony and peace of all who are destined to live under it." Although some attacked the senator from Massachusetts for supposedly betraying Northern interests, Webster's ringing address may well have swung some waverers to support Clay's compromise.

All had not yet been heard from in the great debate. Mississippi's forty-one-year-old Senator Jefferson Davis spoke against the compromise, proposing instead that the line defined by the Missouri Compromise be extended to the Pacific with the understanding that slavery would be permitted everywhere south of it—a move that would have negated California's request to be admitted to the Union as a free state. Representative R. Barnwell Rhett of South Carolina went further and called for secession rather than compromise of any sort. Senator William Seward of New York, meanwhile, refused to consider the new fugitive slave law, in which he was joined by the even more virulently anti-slavery Senator Salmon Chase of Ohio. "All legislative compromises [are] radically wrong and essentially vicious," Seward said, asserting the existence of a "higher law" than even the Constitution provided.

In the end, after the initial defeat of Clay's Omnibus Bill in July, it was a second effort on the part of the younger generation led by Stephen Douglas that pushed the Compromise of 1850 through Congress in September using the brilliant political maneuver of splitting it into five separate bills and finding the votes to pass each on its own merits. Still, the compromise marked the last hurrah of the Jacksonian generation, the likes of which would never be seen again.

Among the last of his era and a politician to the very end, Henry Clay quit the Congress in 1852 but died a few months before his resignation went into effect. John Crittenden, who had taken over Clay's seat the last time he had left it, in 1842, replaced him again in 1855. Over the next five years the new senator, age sixty-eight, would put forth a series of compromises in the Clay tradition, but like his old friend he was always ready to settle for half a loaf, and the times were no longer ripe for trade-offs or for politicians disposed to make them. Younger, more ideologically obdurate men had taken charge of the nation's destiny.

CHAPTER 7

COTTON VERSUS CLOTH

P olitical currents alone do not determine the progress of a nation. In
fact, the bulk of the evidence suggests that economic forces have always
had a far deeper influence on the course
of history, simply because business is the
prime motivator of politics. As the French
social analyst Alexis de Tocqueville wrote
in 1840 in part two of his often-quoted study *Democracy in America,* "The love
of wealth is therefore to be traced, as either a principal or [an] accessory motive, at the bottom of all that the Americans do; this gives to all their passions a
sort of family likeness."

Throughout the history of the world as well as of the United States this financial incentive has led to a great deal of good, but it also has stirred up a
great deal of trouble. In the late eighteenth century, for example, a commonality of economic interests had brought the various states together, but a half century later it was a divergence of commercial concerns that began tearing the
young nation apart.

By the 1850s the cultures of the North and the South had become increasingly distinct for myriad reasons, from the varying national, religious, and political backgrounds of their populations to the differences between their climates,

**Life on a Southern plantation is idealized in the watercolor *The Plantation,* at
left, painted by an unknown artist around 1825. Invented in 1793, the cotton
gin, above, increased tenfold the efficiency of the crop's processing. As soon as
word of its invention leaked out, neighboring planters in Georgia broke into Eli
Whitney's shop to steal his patent models.**

HAULING THE WHOLE WEEK'S PICKING

William Henry Brown's *Hauling the Whole Week's Picking* depicts African-Americans bringing cotton back from the fields. In Mississippi a field slave picked an average of 130 to 150 pounds of raw cotton per day, six days a week, in a harvest lasting from August to January. Some planters tried to increase productivity by staging races and offering prizes, which could double or even triple the amounts picked.

topographies, and resources—and therefore to the incongruous businesses and industries the two sections developed in adapting to these divergent local conditions. Just how the North and the South evolved into entities disparate enough to go to war can be traced through the economic factors that made antagonism inevitable. Between the Revolution and the Civil War, centrifugal and centripetal forces swirled the United States into a maelstrom; sectional differences kept becoming sharper while advances in industry, transportation, and communications continued to connect the various regions into an ever more national economy, and the nation continued to grow: the five million Europeans who immigrated to America between 1820 and 1860 were more than the entire U.S. population at the time of the first census in 1790. These developments had at least as much to do as politics with determining whether the states actually were united and had a future as one nation. "There is plenty of room, yet," immigrant John Down who moved to New York from England wrote to his wife in August 1830, "and will be for a thousand years to come."

The Old South

Only at first glance is it surprising that throughout the Revolution and Confederation periods, and even well into the early national era, abolitionism was more prevalent in the South than in the North. The reason was simple: slave owners couldn't help but realize that keeping human chattel was far less economical than hiring white labor. If a slave fell ill or grew too old to work, more often than not his master would care for him out of the same sense of appreciation that filled plantation pastures with retired plow horses. Hired laborers, on the other hand, could be downsized without guilt when they were no longer needed. What's more, whenever a slave died, his owner's substantial investment in him was lost. As early as 1790 this cold economic reality had led many Southerners to believe that slavery would, and should, disappear before long. Of course, virtually no one in the South advocated letting any eventually

freed blacks stay in the country to which they had been abducted; instead it was assumed they would somehow be returned to Africa or the West Indies.

This pragmatic view gave way to an even colder and more calculating attitude within a generation. Not only would the South change its mind and stake its very soul to retain slavery, it would pledge to do everything possible to weld its system onto the nation by finding a way around the moral mandate against the slave trade. The reason for the South's abrupt reversal on and sudden ardor toward slavery was a spindly plant bearing seed pods full of fluffy white fibers that could be made into many useful things.

Cotton had been a relatively minor crop in colonial America. Although its potential as the woof of a strong, versatile fabric was well established, the fluffy stuff was just too hard to weave into cloth compared with the stiffer natural fibers used to make linen and wool fabrics. By the late eighteenth century, however, England's Industrial Revolution had begun to change that with the invention of new steam- and water-powered looms for the mass manufacture of textiles—the most popular of which proved to be cotton fabrics, which created a demand for the raw crop.

Although weaving cotton cloth was no longer an obstacle, the problems of gathering and processing the cotton bolls remained. Slaves provided a ready solution to the former, but they could never prove cost-effective at the latter: only "short staple" cotton grew naturally in mainland America, and it required far more labor to remove its seeds than the seeds of the Bahamas' longer fibered "sea island" variety. Southern planters in search of a cash crop to replace tobacco, which had exhausted the soil along the East Coast, tried to cultivate sea island cotton, but the climate wasn't right to grow it in the quantities needed to meet demand. The only answer was to find a way to extricate seeds out of short staple cotton more efficiently and thus more economically.

That became possible somewhat by chance in 1793, when Eli Whitney, a large, hawk-nosed, recent Yale graduate, accepted a job tutoring the children of a Georgia plantation owner. In between his teaching duties, he took the time to observe and learn about cotton cultivation, and within ten days came up with a simple machine—little more than a roller with wire teeth—that could separate the seeds from short staple cotton quickly and thoroughly. Whitney's design was the prototype "cotton engine," which would become better known by its abbreviation, the "cotton gin." The device's impact was enormous. Whereas a well-trained slave could tear the seeds from one pound of cotton a day, just about anybody could operate a cotton gin and yield fifty pounds of product in the same amount of time. Whitney turned down an offer of a "hundred guineas" for the gin and instead devoted his energies to acquiring a patent and "perfecting the machine."

In very short order cotton gins cropped up everywhere throughout the Southern seaboard states, spreading rapidly westward. Aspiring cotton growers surged across the Appalachians into the West, brutally forcing Native Americans off their land. The cotton boom was in full force by 1830, with plantations springing up in the fertile fields of Alabama and the rich silt of Mississippi. Whitney's design thus enlarged Southern society and became the most conspicuous invention in U.S. history to that point. The cotton gin made processing the much-in-demand crop for sale to textile manufacturers profitable enough to far offset the high costs of keeping slaves to pick the bolls; Whitney's invention therefore guaranteed the continuation of Southern slavery as well as the spread of its cotton culture west into those regions temperate enough to grow the suddenly golden crop. By 1821 cotton had overtaken tobacco as America's largest and most profitable trade commodity, ringing up $20 million in sales compared with $5 million for that year's tobacco exports. In 1860 annual cotton exports were valued at $192 million, while those of tobacco weighed in at only $16 million; in fact, by that year cotton brought more foreign money into the United States than all other exports combined. The Southern ports through which the crop made its way to Europe, such as New Orleans and Mobile, Alabama, began to grow faster than the nation's busiest shipping center, New York City.

But this new prosperity was built on the toil of slaves, who were forced to bend their backs and blister their hands picking the fluff from the bolls for Whitney's gin to process. The increased demand for the fruits of their labor naturally drove up the price of slaves: field hands who went for $300 in 1790 commanded upward of $2,000 in the 1850s. Even though only one in four Southern households owned or rented human beings, between 1790 and 1850 the number of slaves in the United States rose from 700,000 to nearly 4 million, most of whom were bought to work on the largest cotton plantations; among an overall Southern population of about 8 million, fewer than 1,000 families owned more than 50 slaves.

From a distance, throughout the first half of the nineteenth century the plantation South looked quite prosperous—not far from the genteel image of "Tara," later popularized by Margaret Mitchell's best-selling novel *Gone With the Wind*. But however lovely, this "moonlight-and-magnolias" image was built on less than solid foundations. In reality, social divisions ran deeper in the cotton-fueled South than anywhere else in the nation. In fact, the gulf between the plantation aristocrats and the region's poor white farmers was as wide as that between no-

Thomas S. Noble's 1860 painting, *Last Sale of Slaves on the Court House Steps*, opposite, shows a woman and her baby being sold at an auction in Missouri. Most of the slaves in Missouri worked on plantations growing cotton, hemp, or tobacco, but some worked in mines or were even leased for factory work. As cotton production expanded west into Louisiana and especially Texas, traders swept through Missouri looking to buy slaves by the thousands. Such wholesale trade was despised by some slaveholders, but it continued nonetheless, and in St. Louis, auctions were held at the county courthouse. According to a contemporary account of trading there, the auctioneer might introduce the bidding on a woman such as the one in the picture by saying, "How much is offered for this woman? She is a good cook, good washer, and a good, obedient servant. She has got religion."

bles and serfs in Europe's Middle Ages, and about as likely ever to be bridged. Had it not been for the fear of slave uprisings among whites of all strata, class war might well have erupted in the early nineteenth-century South.

Even the region's most ardent partisans recognized the need to do something about its growing social problems. South Carolina's great statesman John C. Calhoun himself—the section's most forceful proponent and defender of slavery—openly criticized some of the leanings of his beloved home region. Throughout his prominent career as a congressman, senator, cabinet member, and vice president, Calhoun had maintained that the South's concentration on cotton, which required only planters and slaves, was squeezing out poor whites who had no role in producing the precious fiber. Calhoun therefore called upon the South's powerful cotton growers to stop exporting their crop to the North and Europe and to build manufacturing industries that would keep everyone employed instead. His arguments went unheeded, even when he anticipated Marx and Engels by forecasting a nation-rending conflict in which Northern in-

A small farm, neat as a pin, is the subject of the woodcut at right, which was originally printed in a book called *A New Guide to the English Tongue*. (Note the man sitting on the cloud, demonstrating the workings of lightning.) The scene shows rural American life at its most ideal. A common perception was that Northern farmers worked their own land, while Southerners dallied and let the slaves do the work. In reality, the majority of Southern farmers worked a small field by themselves, or toiled side by side with one or two slaves. A more significant difference between the farmers in each region was that Northerners rotated crops, while Southerners planted the same one, usually cotton, every season, leaving the soil depleted after about a generation.

dustrialists and Southern planters would have to work together against their respective wage-earning "white slaves" and owned black slaves united against the ruling classes of both sections. Calhoun's nationalism only changed when he saw some of its deleterious effects on the South; once it had become clear that the North was progressing faster, he reverted to a sectional partisanship that in the hands of his successors would lead to civil war. The last words the dying Calhoun uttered on March 31, 1850, were, "The South! The poor South! God knows what will become of her!"

The Industrial North

Until the middle of the nineteenth century, most people in the northern and middle states were devoted to agriculture, with only a small percentage employed in manufacturing and other businesses. In fact, before the Civil War, New York and Pennsylvania comprised the nation's breadbasket, providing the bulk of the nation's foodstuffs. That began to change in the 1840s and 1850s when soil exhaustion, social pressures, and the lust for cheap land drove Northeastern farmers into the Midwest, which also attracted foreign immigrants eager to till their own plots in freedom.

The Industrial Revolution derailed this bucolic dream, making as great an impact on Northern agriculture as the cotton gin had on the South. Before the 1830s, Northern crops were planted and harvested by human hand and animal labor aided by only a few simple tools. As the decade commenced, an estimated 70 percent of America's workforce, including nearly 1.5 million slaves, were plowing soil. The inefficiency of the process kept most farms quite small, usually as family operations that required—and could afford—hired help only for brief stints at planting and harvesting time. There had to be a better way, and before long a few ingenious farmers invented the tools to enable one.

In 1831, Virginia farmer Cyrus McCormick produced the first working model of a reaper, a wheat-harvesting machine so fast and efficient it increased productivity more than a dozenfold overnight: whereas a farmer using a hand sickle could harvest half an acre of wheat per day, two people working a McCormick reaper could cover twelve acres a day. By the time he patented his invention in 1834, McCormick faced competitors, but the demand for reapers was so great that there was plenty of business for everyone, especially the flexible: when more and more wheat farmers moved to the Midwest, McCormick followed, closing his rural Virginia operation and setting up shop in Chicago in 1848, where he built a factory that eventually grew into the company International Harvester. Using interchangeable parts, McCormick was soon producing 5,000 reapers a year, with demand far outstripping supply. Before long John Deere, who invented the steel plow, entered the field manufacturing 13,500 machines in 1856. McCormick and Deere had transformed a region that had been wilderness into a Garden of Eden, a global breadbasket which became the envy of Europe.

By the 1860s the invention and manufacture of new farm implements had made U.S. agriculture the most mechanically advanced in the world. The impact resonated even deeper. Indeed, to some extent the Civil War was started by the cotton gin—which changed Southern agriculture to encourage the continuation of slavery—but won by the reaper, which enabled the North to outproduce the South and afforded many farmers the free time to fight in the Union Army. Ironically, the cotton gin was invented by a Northerner and the reaper by a farmer from the South. The reaper was not solely responsible for the industrialization of agriculture, but without McCormick's invention, harvesting would have remained primitive for decades to come. Still, it was not until the 1950s that the number of tractors superceded the number of horses working America's farms.

Even before McCormick invented his machine, the North had begun to industrialize, particularly in New England and mostly in the form of textile factories. As important as domestic agricultural innovations had been, Northern commerce was brought even further along by ideas that had sprung from England's Industrial Revolution. Several English textile entrepreneurs had come to the United States at the turn of the nineteenth century in hopes of profiting from the former colonies' proficiency at picking and ginning cotton; several succeeded despite situating in the North, and benefited all of America by establishing prosperous yarn- and wool-manufacturing industries in New York and Rhode Island. By the time the United States and England had returned to war in 1812, U.S. yarn factories employed thousands of workers and operated on $40 million in investments, although such manufacturing concerns still represented only a drop in the economic bucket. According to the 1810 census, in a labor force of 2.3 million, nearly 2 million people worked in agriculture and only 10,000 in the textile industry.

The War of 1812 helped to shift that imbalance. The Northern textile factories were forced into overdrive to provide yarn and cloth to Americans ac-

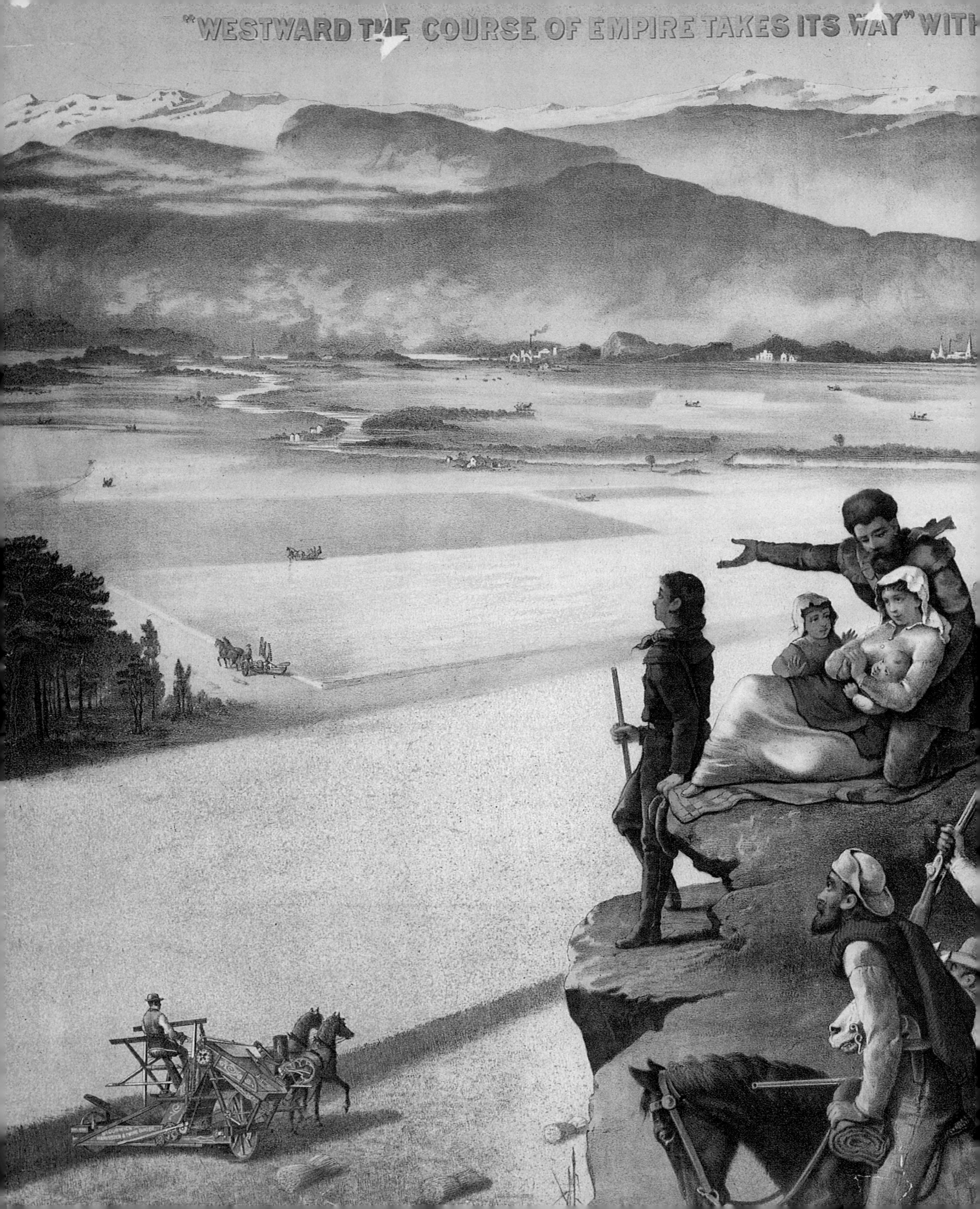
"WESTWARD THE COURSE OF EMPIRE TAKES ITS WAY" WITH

CORMICK REAPERS IN THE VAN.

The panorama at left was printed by the McCormick Reaper Company of Chicago. Having invented the reaper in 1831, Cyrus McCormick seemed content to build machines for the local market in Virginia until an archrival named Obed Hussey began to dominate the new industry nationally. In the early 1840s McCormick finally awoke to the reaper's potential and became one of America's most aggressive businessmen. One of his hallmarks was a huge advertising budget, with a breadth never before seen. McCormick ads were shrewd propaganda pieces celebrating the American ideal, such as the near replica of Emanuel Leutze's famous painting, *Westward the Course of Empires Takes Its Way*. The ad is just like its model except in one instance: the lush valley is already planted, and is being harvested by McCormick reapers.

customed to buying those products from England as well as to supply fabrics to the military for making uniforms. After the war ended, the English tried to regain their markets by dumping cheap textiles in the United States, causing many domestic factories to fail, but most were reorganized and resumed doing business stronger than ever.

Other commercial concerns flourished as well. Oliver Evans, a brilliant American inventor who in 1785 had designed a flour mill that required only two men to do everything from load the grain to package the processed flour, went on to establish the U.S. iron industry. Although European imports would remain necessary through the Civil War, by 1860 the United States was producing more iron than France and the Germanies combined. Between 1820 and 1840 alone the number of Americans working in manufacturing industries doubled, while the number of urban dwellers more than doubled as well. The machine-tool industry, in particular, caused an explosion in consumer goods as Waltham watches, Yale clocks, and Singer sewing machines became commonplace household items. The industrial revolution was being felt even in rural Indiana hamlets and backwood Kentucky towns. Much was gained, but something was lost as well; as New York writer Washington Irving had sighed as early as 1832, the "march of mechanical invention is driving everything poetical before it." Irving's sentiment was echoed profoundly in 1854 when naturalist Henry David Thoreau published *Walden* rallying against what he perceived as the dehumanizing quality of industrialization: "Men think that it is essential that the *Nation* have commerce, export ice, talk through a telegraph, and ride thirty miles an hour," Thoreau complained, ". . . but whether we should live like baboons or like men is a little uncertain."

The New West

Neither the cotton culture of the South nor the young industries of the North could have prospered as they did without demand for their products from the growing West, however defined. Throughout the nineteenth century continuing expansion kept pushing Americans farther and farther toward the Pacific Ocean, resituating the Western frontier every step of the way; whereas in 1690 backcountry Virginia and northern New York had been considered "the West," by the end of the nineteenth century that designation belonged to the trans-Rocky Mountain area. The frontier itself was defined by the U.S. Census Bureau as the farthest western area inhabited by two to six people per square mile and would continue to shift until 1890, when it officially disappeared with a census count showing a thicker population than that all the way to the Pacific.

The westward migration had been made possible by the exploits of Captain Meriwether Lewis and Lieutenant William Clark, whom Thomas Jefferson had dispatched to see what lay beyond the Mississippi. Their twenty-seven-man "Corps of Discovery" had left St. Louis to head up the Missouri River in 1804. Their guide for most of the trip was Sacajawea, a Shoshone woman who also proved to be a valuable translator. Along the way, they met Indians who shared local hunting and skinning techniques, and just six months after setting out, the party sent a barge back East bearing such novelties as the magpie and the prairie dog. After crossing the Continental Divide and surviving hardships from grizzly bear attacks to a paucity of provisions, Lewis and Clark sailed down the Snake and Columbia rivers to the Pacific Ocean and then headed home, checking out the gorgeous Yellowstone area on the way back. The most important accomplishment of their two-and-a-half-year journey was the defanging of America's far West: the explorers' descriptions of friendly Indians and abundant fur-trading opportunities erased fears and boosted interest in the previously uncharted territories.

That interest took off in the wake of an 1820 land law that not only brought down the price of Western land but halved the minimum parcel size to 80 acres, which meant that a family seeking to settle could buy a plot for as little as $100. More laws reduced the prices even further, eventually to just over twelve cents an acre. The results were predictable: 68,000 acres of public land had been sold in 1800, but fifteen years later the figure had climbed to 1.3 million acres, and in 1818 land sales reached a zenith of 3.5 million acres, about the total area of Connecticut. By 1860 more than half of the nation's growing population lived in trans-Appalachia, with ever more people spreading even farther west, beyond the Mississippi and all the way to the Pacific Coast. It was an inevitable development considering the numbers, which had been doubling every twenty-two years or so: from 4 million in 1790, America's population had swelled to more than 23 million by 1850.

Of course, neither the "frontier" nor the overall West had ever been unoccupied, as Native American societies had been established throughout the region for generations. In some ways, the frontier could be defined as wherever the earliest pioneers encountered Native Americans and their separate, non-European cultures—not that many frontiersmen had much use for the European-inspired Eastern establishment. However romanticized in Western novels and John Wayne movies, more often than not the frontiersmen were antisocial misanthropes who wanted nothing but to be left alone by civilization and all its trappings, from farms and businesses to neighbors and family ties. "Solitaires, sociopaths, compulsive travelers, boys who failed to grow up, found their way inevitably west, where they could pass for normal citizens," English writer Jonathan Raban observed in *Bad Land* (1996). "Fear of long-term attachment, to anything or anybody, was not a disability out here, where the peculiar economy of the region depended on a labor force of willing rolling stones."

These loners were forced farther west by the early pioneer families who followed in their wake, usually poor but at least second-generation Americans who had been struggling in the country's midsection and were desperate for free or at least cheap but arable land to settle on. Very few immigrants headed for the frontier immediately upon arriving in America, as few could afford the costly journey. As a result, most of Ohio's settlers came from western New York and Pennsylvania, while those who continued on to Illinois came largely from Ohio and the neighboring states that had themselves lately been considered "the West." Whatever their origins, the nomadic early pioneers generally carved their farms from wilderness they tamed and planted over several years, rarely bothering about titles to the land. If the lawful owners appeared, the squatters would just move farther west and start over again.

The *Lowell Offering,* above, was a literary magazine produced by the female workers at mills in Lowell, Massachusetts. Established in the 1820s, the Lowell mills were designed as much to cultivate young ladies as to produce fabric. The workers, predominantly girls in their teens, lived in strictly maintained boarding houses, took classes in academic subjects, and earned a fair income. Lowell was unique, however. Few textile factories that followed in the nineteenth century offered anything except work and wages.

Below, Lewis and Clark brought peace medals on their 1804 expedition, to be used as gifts for Indian chiefs. One side the coin had an image of President Thomas Jefferson, while the other depicted a handshake. Largely scientific in purpose, the Lewis and Clark expedition emphasized discovery, rather than conquest. A dutiful journal keeper, Lewis brought back volumes filled with descriptive passages. For example, an April 25, 1805 entry, would inspire future generations to move West: "[T]he whole face of the country was covered with herds of Buffaloe, Elk, & Antelopes; deer are also abundant but keep themselves concealed in the Woodland. the buffaloe, Elk, and Antelope are so gentle that we pass near them while feeding, without appearing to excite any alarm among them, and when we attract their attention they frequently approach us more nearly to discover what we are, and in some instances pursue us a considerable distance, apparenly [sic] with that view."

These brave souls—fired by the new American dream of an unspoiled place to call home—favored log cabins because they were easy to build and because they required very few nails, which were so expensive on a squatter's budget that, if forced to move on, families would burn down their cabins to recover the nails from the ashes. After these hardscrabble squatters came more prosperous and permanent settlers who bought the titles to their land and established communities, industries, schools, and churches—after which the areas so civilized came to be considered part of the East or Midwest rather than the western frontier. Some families did caravan westward for religious reasons: Christian settlers crossed the windswept Great Plains and treacherous Rocky Mountains by Conestoga wagon to bring the word of Jesus Christ to the wilderness. Mormons lead by Bringham Young escaped religious persecution in Ohio, Missouri, and Illinois because of the assertion of divine sanction and their embrace of polygamy. When Young first saw the Great Salt Lake Valley on July 24, 1847, he immediately recognized it as the new Zion he had seen in a vision. "This is the place!" Young exclaimed. There, in modern day Utah, Young, head of the Quorum of the Twelve Apostles, the Mormon governing body, established a prosperous agricultural settlement as well as a religious colony.

Pioneer spirit was endemic by 1841 when John Bidwell shepherded the first wagon train along the Oregon Trail from Independence, Missouri, to California, the so-called land of perennial spring and boundless fertility. Bidwell had organized an expedition for 500 anxious emigrants, but as departure day neared, all of them canceled out. Undaunted by this setback, Bidwell eventually signed up three adventurers and rounded up sixty-three more along the way. "Our ignorance of the route was complete," Bidwell later admitted. "We knew that California lay west, that was the extent of our knowledge." Although the arduous twenty-four-week journey almost cost Bidwell his life—forced to eat mules to survive—California turned out to be the Promised Land of his dreams: he eventually found gold in the Feather River near Sacramento, owned the largest ranch in the territory, and after California became a state in 1850, he became a U.S. congressman.

Fortune did not shine so brightly on the Donner party, a group of about ninety emigrants who left Springfield, Illinois, in the summer of 1846 for California. All went fairly well until the expedition's leader made the fatal blunder of attempting to cross the Sierra Nevada in late October. Heavy snowfall forced the Donner party to burrow down at Truckee Lake for the winter. Left with no provisions some of the emigrants resorted to cannibalism to stay alive. "The flesh of starved human beings contains little nutriment," Lewis Keseberg, a survivor, later explained of his horrible ordeal. "It is like feeding straw to horses. I can not describe the unutterable repugnance with which I tasted the first mouthful of flesh. There is an instinct in our nature that revolts at the thought of touching, much less eating, a corpse."

It wasn't long before the contagious pioneer spirit industrialized the Midwest. Just as the South's cotton-friendly climate and the North's abundance of swift streams and coal deposits for powering factories determined what businesses would thrive in each, the Midwest's vast grass plains made it a natural for the cattle industry. By the 1830s meatpacking centers had grown up in

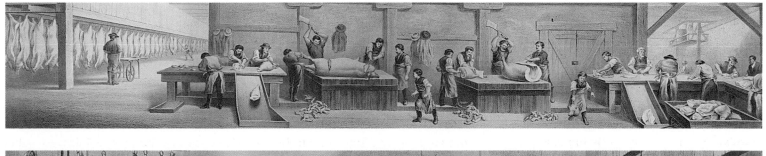

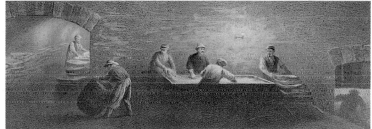

Chicago, Louisville, and St. Louis as well as in Cincinnati, which became the first U.S. industrial complex when its local meatpacking industry spun off businesses based on cattle by-products such as sausage-casing plants and glue, candle, and soap factories. One of America's most successful companies to this day, for example, took root in Cincinnati when candlemaker William Procter and soap manufacturer James Gamble came together in 1837 to form Procter and Gamble, now a thoroughly diversified international conglomerate but back then just a particularly forward-thinking local purveyor of household necessities.

At about the same time, Cincinnati also took the lead in the ever successful distillery business, using locally grown grains to make alcoholic beverages. When a large number of German immigrants settled in the Midwest in the 1840s and 1850s they expanded the industry with their fatherland's knack for brewing beer, a specialty that spread throughout the region wherever Germans put down roots. The breweries and distilleries they founded sold their refuse to local farmers for pig feed, just one example of how cooperation among Cincinnati's wide-ranging business concerns enabled each to thrive.

The success of early Midwestern industry owed as much to technological innovations as to shrewd commercial amity. The meatpacking business, for example, could not have prospered as it did without the development of means to pack and preserve its products. This was a more important consideration in America than in Europe due to the far greater distances goods had to travel from manufacturer to consumer. Advances in the preservation of perishable foodstuffs enabled distributors to expand into ever larger mar-

The scenes above show various stages of production in a meatpacking plant in Cincinnati. Abattoirs pioneered the division of labor in manufacturing, which later led to assembly line techniques. "When I started in the packing business, it was all straight sailing," wrote a Chicago merchant in the 1890s. "But when we get through with a hog nowadays, he's scattered through a hundred different cans and packages, and he's all accounted for. It takes doctors, lawyers, engineers, poets, and I don't know what to run the business."

kets, further adding to the incentive behind innovations that would push America far ahead of Europe in the food-processing business. Experiments with tin cans, for example, had begun as early as 1815, and by 1860 they were widely used across America. In 1853 New Yorker Gail Borden, who two years earlier had invented the dehydrated meat biscuit, developed a way to condense milk so that it could be canned, stored, and transported over long distances without spoiling.

Turnpikes, Canals, and Steamboats

Americans' push to the western edge of the U.S. continent and the economic boom that resulted depended upon the development of reliable, fast, and cheap transportation. No section of the country—the North with its industries, the Northwest with its commercial agriculture, or the South with its cotton and tobacco—could have flourished as all three did had it not been for new and inexpensive ways for each to get goods to market as well as to bring in needed but non-indigenous resources and products. In fact, it was the period's remarkable advances in transportation that drove nineteenth-century U.S. economic development, forming the bases for a number of major industries and spawning myriad others through spectacular gains in efficiency. In the single generation between 1825 and 1855, for example, the speed of land transport quintupled while its costs fell 95 percent.

The development of the transportation system in the United States was owed in large part to the can-do spirit that Alexis de Tocqueville had described in 1835 when he wrote that "America is a land of wonders, in which

The engraving below shows a section of the turnpike that ran between Baltimore, Maryland, and Yorktown, Virginia. Private companies led the way in building paved or planked turnpike roads from 1792 to 1860. Though the routes cost up to $10,000 per mile to build, they often brought returns of 10 or even 15 percent per year to investors. Despite the toll of about a dime every six miles, turnpikes were considered a necessary luxury for stagecoaches, teamsters, and even drovers with herds of cattle. John Quincy Adams noted that before the Boston–New York Turnpike was built, the trip took seven days if one traveled from early morning until 10 P.M. each day. The turnpike cut that time in half.

everything is in constant motion and every change seems an improvement. The idea of novelty is there indissolubly connected with the idea of amelioration. No natural boundary seems to be set to the efforts of man; and in his eyes what is not yet done is only what he has not yet attempted to do." That certainly proved the case with the nation's roads and waterways before the mid-nineteenth century. Echoing the problem fifteenth-century Europe had faced when its dilapidated, ancient Roman roads proved insufficient to accommodate a growing population moving ever farther inland, the expanding United States needed better thoroughfares than the sorry and incomplete paths that had been constructed during the colonial era. Routes were so poor the founding fathers had built a four-month cushion between the presidential election and inauguration to ensure that new chief executives would be able to take the oath of office on time. Roads such as those George Washington had traversed from Mount Vernon to New York in 1789 were actually no more than foot trails widened by pack animals and usable only a few months out of the year, as rain or snow turned them into impassable rivers of mud. These horrendous roadways made sea traffic, although often farther, both faster and cheaper than the overland option. For example, early in the national era it cost seventy-five cents a barrel to ship flour from New York to

Robert Fulton's first workable steamboat, the *Clermont,* was the subject of the painting, above, by Pavel Petrovich Svinin. Fulton, a former art student, launched his first steamboat on the Seine in Paris, but the engine fell through the hull into the river. Returning home to America, Fulton enlisted a wealthy partner, Robert Livingston, and launched the *Clermont* on the Hudson in 1807. Propelled by a 28-horsepower engine, the *Clermont* made the journey upriver from New York City to Albany in a record thirty-two hours. "The devil is on his way up-river with a sawmill on a boat!" shouted a Dutchman from the shore.

George Caleb Bingham painted *Boatmen on the Missouri*, opposite, in 1846 to show the rafters who supplied great steamboats with wood for fuel. The wide, inviting Missouri River was heavy with steamboat traffic in the nineteenth century, though it could be even more capricious than the Mississippi, changing course on a whim. On one famous occasion, a steamboat chugged downstream past the same town twice, without ever going in the opposite direction. Having just waved it good-bye, the townspeople were shocked to see it again, coming around the same bend as before. Out of sight downriver, the boat had been caught in a backflow, as the Missouri suddenly cut a new channel for itself through the surrounding cornfields.

Boston, while transport over a land route half as long cost five dollars a barrel.

Well before the advent of the South's cotton culture and the North's manufacturing industries, the new nation's leaders had recognized the need for better, cheaper, and faster ways to transport both goods and people. President Washington himself had presided over the groundbreaking for a turnpike (so called after the rotating pikes that permitted vehicles through after the toll was paid) in Pennsylvania that would be paid for by user tolls, and in 1806, during Thomas Jefferson's administration, Congress had approved the construction of a National Turnpike to link Ohio to the East, or at least to Maryland and Virginia. That year federal aid to transportation projects amounted to a mere $2,000, but the next year it had risen to $56,000—still not a staggering figure, but enough of an increase to show how much the government's interest in a national infrastructure had grown.

In truth, by the beginning of the nineteenth century, concern over transportation had grown to the point that Secretary of the Treasury Albert Gallatin asked Congress for substantial appropriations to construct roads and canals as well as to improve facilities on rivers and in harbors. The War of 1812 scotched Gallatin's ambitious plan, but its spirit lived on: in 1817 federal expenditures for transportation had mounted to $361,000, and ever since then the central government has played a major role in improving the nation's infrastructure. States and localities, however, did even more in the early nineteenth century. New York constructed some 3,000 miles of toll roads, with other states not far behind, while several private turnpikes were built with funding from philanthropists who just may have had some commercial interest in the ventures. In any case, by 1820 most of the Northeast's major cities were connected by some 4,000 miles of reasonably good toll roads.

That said, the turnpikes still couldn't handle heavy loads or be used year-round, which were the main reasons Gallatin had also asked Congress to appropriate funds for building canals. These disbursements were not approved, but that did not deter the State of New York, where there had been talk of a canal uniting the upper Hudson River with Lake Erie since the Constitutional Convention—and where several companies had been formed just to undertake such a project. Once federal funding proved unforthcoming in 1817, the New York legislature voted to create the waterway as a joint venture between state and private interests; the necessary investments would come from foreigners intrigued by the idea, farmers who would benefit from a canal to take their goods to market, and speculators who owned land in the affected areas. Among these sources enough money was raised to begin construction on a 363-mile-long waterway, which was completed in 1825.

The resulting Erie Canal was a smashing success in every way, including some that had not been foreseen. In 1818, it had cost $100 to transport a ton of freight from Buffalo to New York City; once the canal was in operation the price fell to $15. The faster means of transport drove the prices of New York farm goods down, while its lower cost enabled the state's total trade volume to double between 1818 and 1827. Villages sprang up all along the new route, and small towns burst into cities; land values rose, of course, and speculators enjoyed ample returns—as did investors. The Erie Canal showed

a profit from the very start, which is hardly surprising considering that before the canal began operating, Midwestern shippers had to send their exports through Montréal, which was closed to water traffic by ice four months out of every year. The Erie Canal not only opened New York directly to the Midwest, making the port city the most prosperous and commercially significant in the nation, but it also sparked a boom in canal construction fueled by $100 million in capital investments by 1840. Before long, canal mileage in the United States had reached 3,300—an increase of 2,000 miles in ten years. Unfortunately, as so often has been the case in the wake of staggeringly successful capitalist endeavors, canal overbuilding caused many such ventures to fail both commercially and as investments.

Unlike canals, which required constructing, America's major rivers were there for the navigating. The invention of the steamboat allowed shippers to take advantage of this natural resource, and the vessels began to fill the waterways shortly after inventor Robert Fulton, borrowing ideas from others, piloted the *Clermont*—his prototype—up the Hudson River on August 9, 1807. Within a few years of this epical voyage, steamboats plied the Great Lakes as well as larger rivers such as the Missouri and Mississippi, on which they first appeared in 1811 to make the trip downstream from Pittsburgh, Pennsylvania, to New Orleans. Until the 1850s steamboats carried more freight than railroads. The extra costs of steamboats made them uneconomical for transporting cargo as opposed to passengers, however; still their numbers multiplied rapidly. In 1815, only seven western river steamboats were in operation, but by 1850 there were 638 and New Orleans had become the nation's leading port for exports. The burgeoning river traffic made it look as though the West might shortly be bound economically to the South.

Railroads and the Telegraph

The sway of the steamboat was forestalled, however, by an even greater innovation: the railroad. But unlike the reaper and the cotton gin, the railroad did not enjoy overnight success. Early versions of the concept involved horse- or mule-drawn carts pulled along iron strips fastened to wooden rails, while other experiments tried wind-driven sails to push the carts forward.

The first locomotives imported from England proved worthless, but by 1830 several American-built engines worked well enough to reveal the full potential of railroads on the Baltimore & Ohio line, a thirteen-mile track built by Baltimore businessmen fearful that the Chesapeake & Ohio canal then being extended would divert inland trade from Maryland to Virginia. By the time the B&O railroad had been completed in 1830, the developers of the C&O canal had admitted defeat and abandoned their construction plans.

By 1840, dozens of railroad companies had been chartered and begun operating. Although the United States boasted just under 3,000 miles of tracks, in many places their mere existence led to the abandonment of turnpikes and canals, which railroads superseded by dint of speed. As early as 1832 steam-powered freight railroads could move at six miles an hour compared with canal boats' even more leisurely pace, which topped out at four miles per hour; ten years later railroads offered transport at fifteen miles per hour compared with steamships' best pace of ten miles an hour. The North had begun to shrink, thanks to the speed of rail transport; whereas it had taken a sloop thirty-six hours to sail from New York to Albany in 1817, in 1841 a train could cover the same distance in just ten hours. By the beginning of the Civil War era, railroads would become the nation's biggest business, with $1.25 billion invested in the various lines that were broadening commercial markets with an efficiency turnpikes, canals, and steamboats could not even approach.

In 1850, the United States had 9,000 miles of railroad tracks, which a decade later would grow to 30,000, mostly in the North and Midwest, which

A famous race was staged on August 28, 1830, between a horse-drawn car and a locomotive, as celebrated in the print below. The course was one of the longest rail lines in the country at the time, the Baltimore & Ohio, boasting thirteen miles of track in eastern Maryland. The locomotive—nicknamed the Tom Thumb, because it was smaller than imported British steam engines—passed the horse at a clip. It broke down before the finish, though, and the horse won. Nonetheless, the race made converts of many Americans, who would embrace railroad transportation with fervor in the middle of the nineteenth century.

The 300 Americans who flocked to Seneca Falls, New York, on July 19–20, 1848 launched the organized women's rights movement in the United States. In their six-volume 1881 *History of Woman Suffrage,* editors Elizabeth Cady Stanton, Susan B. Anthony, and Matilda J. Gage called the Seneca Falls Convention the "inauguration of a rebellion such as the world had never before seen." What distinguished the gathering and the suffrage campaign that grew out of it from prior women's rights efforts was the public organization and execution. Earlier American feminist intellectuals such as Fanny Wright and Margaret Fuller had written and spoken on the subject but had not worked to turn their protest into a wider crusade. The planners of the convention, inspired by the rallies, lectures, and legislative hearings of the abolitionist and temperance movements, were no longer content just to write their views; they wanted action, and they wanted it now.

The movement's beginnings were deceptively modest: five middle-class married women sat around Jane Hunt's tea table at her home in Waterloo, New York, in July 1848, lamenting the social inferiority of women and tossing about the possibility of a convention to "discuss the[ir] social, civil, and religious conditions and rights." Two of the guests, intellectual firebrand Elizabeth Cady Stanton and Quaker activist Lucretia Mott, had already found common cause while attending the World Anti-Slavery Convention in London eight years earlier, at which they had protested women's exclusion from active participation in the proceedings and resolved to hold a women's rights conference when they got home.

That, however, would have to wait while the just-married Stanton threw herself into homemaking and childrearing while Mott continued to electrify audiences on the anti-slavery lecture circuit. A second meeting in 1848 though brought immediate results. The five women sent a notice to a local newspaper announcing a women's rights convention to be held in just six days in nearby Seneca Falls. It was a measure of the reformist zeal of the times as well as of the activist spirit of the hosting western New York State community that despite the short notice some 260 women and 40 men attended, including noted abolitionist Frederick Douglass.

The organizers were prepared. In an attempt to frame some fitting resolution for the occasion they seized upon the Declaration of Independence, paraphrasing its introduction to include women as well as men in its claim of universal and inalienable human rights—substituting "mankind" for "King of Great Britain" in the litany of wrongs to be addressed. As the document proclaimed, "The history of mankind is a history of repeated injuries and usurpations on the part of man toward woman, having in direct object the establishment of an absolute tyranny over her." The litany of grievances in what its authors called the Declaration of Sentiments was long and bitter. The list of reformist resolutions was equally sweeping, demanding that women gain the right to own property; to make contracts; to testify in courts of law; to exercise free speech; to obtain educations; to get divorces; to gain child custody; to secure equal participation in trade, the professions, commerce, and religion; and, of course, to vote.

The participants convened in the Wesleyan Chapel in Seneca Falls to give and hear speeches, including Elizabeth Cady Stanton's reading of the Declaration. Ironically, considering the leading role suffrage would play in the women's rights movement for the rest of the century, all the resolutions passed unanimously except the one demanding the vote, which many feared was so outrageous it would make the conference a laughingstock. The resolution finally squeaked by only after persistent lobbying by Stanton and Douglass, who wisely pointed out that other rights could be realized only if women had the power to elect lawmakers themselves.

The Declaration of Sentiments was signed by a hundred brave souls and "extensively published, unsparingly ridiculed by the press, and denounced by the pulpit," as noted in the *History of Woman Suffrage,* while its signatories were mocked as Amazons and barren old maids (even though Stanton eventually had seven children and Mott five). Some of the petitioners withdrew their names but others went on to help spearhead a grassroots movement that only grew as the controversy spread. Women across the country began holding local meetings, airing grievances never before discussed, and organizing petition drives to persuade legislatures to pass laws favorable to women. In feminism's antebellum heyday, a National Women's Rights Convention was held every year but one between 1850 and 1860.

After the Civil War, when feminists optimistically expected to be given the vote at the same time as the freed slaves, they were dismayed to learn that according to Congress it was the "Negro's hour" and so women would have to wait their turn indefinitely. Worse, the Fourteenth and Fifteenth Amendments, ratified in 1868 and 1870, gave the vote to all "male citizens," black and white—for the first time explicitly denying women the rights of citizenship in the Constitution. "If that word 'male' be inserted now," Stanton wrote despairingly, "it will take us a century at least to get it out." In the end it took not a century but fifty years and the passage of another constitutional amendment.

Elizabeth Cady Stanton addressed the first Woman's Rights Convention on July 19, 1848, in Seneca Falls, New York. Mrs. Stanton had received the finest education available to females in the early 1800s, graduating from Emma Willard's Seminary in upstate New York in 1832. However, she resented the fact that she couldn't go on to college and ably debated that fact with the young lawyers who worked with her father, who was a judge. While on her honeymoon in London in 1840, Mrs. Stanton found herself barred from attending an antislavery meeting, solely because of her gender. Another American, Lucretia Mott, was also shut out of the meeting; the two immediately began an eight-year effort to organize the Seneca Falls Convention, a landmark event in the history of human rights. At Mrs. Stanton's insistence, it included the first formal call for female suffrage. Mrs. Stanton continued to work toward equal rights for women until her death in 1902. Eighteen years later, women received the right to vote in America's national elections.

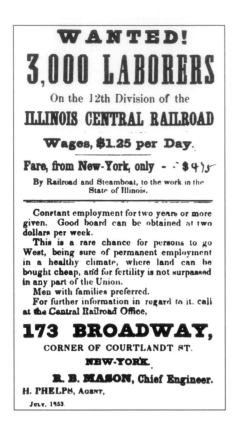

WANTED!
3,000 LABORERS
On the 12th Division of the
ILLINOIS CENTRAL RAILROAD
Wages, $1.25 per Day.

Fare, from New-York, only - - $4)5

By Railroad and Steamboat, to the work in the State of Illinois.

Constant employment for two years or more given. Good board can be obtained at two dollars per week.
This is a rare chance for persons to go West, being sure of permanent employment in a healthy climate, where land can be bought cheap, and for fertility is not surpassed in any part of the Union.
Men with families preferred.
For further information in regard to it. call at the Central Railroad Office,

173 BROADWAY,
CORNER OF COURTLANDT ST.
NEW-YORK

R. B. MASON, Chief Engineer.
H. PHELPS, Agent,
July, 1853.

The Illinois Central Railroad used the poster above in 1853 to recruit thousands of men to help lay new lines in the Midwest. The rail companies required laborers to build the railroads, as well as settlers to purchase excess acreage. By recruiting men with families, they filled both needs. Many of the workers, especially in the 1850s, were recently landed immigrants from Ireland.

held a strong advantage over the South in other forms of transportation as well. Some historians have opined that it was the disparity in railroad distribution—more than any other single factor—that determined the outcome of the Civil War, and they have a point: throughout the 1840s and 1850s more Midwestern goods reached markets down the Mississippi River route to New Orleans than were transported through the Great Lakes and Erie Canal to New York, but by 1860 the rail links between the American heartland and New York, Philadelphia, and Boston had shifted the balance of Midwestern trade from the South to the Northeast. Thus it was Chicago, connected to New York by railroads, and not St. Louis, a great Mississippi River port tied to New Orleans, that became the largest and most powerful city in the Midwest. But the railroads also had another effect on the North: they made life faster and louder. As New England writer Nathaniel Hawthorne lamented, the locomotive "comes down upon you like fate, swift and inevitable," bringing "the noisy world into the midst of our slumbrous peace."

Railroads quickened the pace of American life not only by forging physical connections between cities but also by inspiring the creation of a fast, long-distance communications system that strung the first wires of the ever evolving information age. As has been true of so many of the world's greatest technological innovations, high-speed indirect communication was invented because business concerns demanded it: running an efficient railroad required far more coordination than managing a canal, including the ability to set and maintain schedules and to report conditions and problems between various points on rail lines. Thus was the telegraph devised to meet the railroads' needs.

In 1832, while heading home from a trip to Europe, artist Samuel F. B. Morse happened to fall into conversation with a fellow traveler who had a great interest in electricity. Their talk inspired Morse to conduct some electrical experiments of his own, and in 1838 he perfected his resulting creation, the telegraph, organized a corporation to promote it, and attempted to obtain government support to put it into operation. He was granted enough federal funds to run a wire between Baltimore and Washington, D.C., over which Morse sent the first public telegram in May 1844. It read, "WHAT HATH GOD WROUGHT," a question the information age has been begging ever since. Despite the experiment's success, the federal government declined to appropriate any more money for it. Morse didn't despair but took the capitalist route and licensed his invention to businessmen who recognized its potential. The telegraph system thus created had limited value early on, as other versions were invented that were incompatible with any of their fellows, much like today's high-speed computer modems. Nevertheless, by 1853 more than 23,000 miles of telegraph wire were up and running, and so were a handful of powerful regional communications companies, some of which united to form Western Union in 1856. Five years later telegraph poles would extend all the way to the West Coast, making national telecommunications a reality that not only ensured smooth operation of the railroads but also enabled near immediate communication among businesspeople in most major cities.

When the history of U.S. transportation is compared with that of slavery, one fact leaps out: commerce was connecting the United States while sectional politics divided the nation. After all, the bonds of business afforded gains for everyone. The United States had enjoyed strong economic growth throughout the first half of the nineteenth century with only minor downturns during the Napoleonic Wars, the War of 1812, and in the wake of President Jackson's ill-considered assault on the central banking system. Overall, before the Civil War every section of the country was growing economically despite the political tensions among them that would threaten to sever the bonds forged at the Constitutional Convention. But as of 1860 some 84 percent of the South's labor force still worked in agriculture, compared with 40 percent in the North—while the South produced only 9 percent of the country's manufactured goods. Reduced to its simplest terms, the problem was that the Southern economy had become dependent on cotton and thus on slave labor, and was being outpaced by a dynamic industrial North growing ever more convinced that slavery was not only morally abhorrent but so cost-inefficient that it was holding back the economic progress of the entire nation.

In the lithograph below, a train brings materials to a shoe factory circa 1870. In the middle of the century, manufacturers complained that they couldn't find ready capital because so much money was devoted to building railroads. Industrial capacity shot up later in the century, though, in part because the extensive rail system made moving a carload of almost anything between regions or even between factories as easy as mailing a letter.

CHAPTER 8

THE SPLIT OF
THE UNION

In many ways the Civil War was an inevitable step in the country's quest for economic as well as spiritual unity. Most Americans today think of the war between the states as an ideological battle over the morality of slavery—and to an extent it was. The clamor of the Industrial Revolution rendered antique the appalling practice of owning human beings as chattel, even though doing so remained a wildly profitable proposition for some Southern platation owners. The Industrial Revolution made it clear that two very antithetic societies had flourished in the United States—one above the Mason-Dixon line and the other below—which would conform to the new age of specialization and urbanization in polar ways. Between 1837 and 1858, the antislavery territories of Michigan, Iowa, Wisconsin, and Minnesota achieved statehood. Combined with Ohio, Indiana, and Illinois they collectively formed the third major section of the United States, for by 1860 the population of this "middle border" region exceeded eight million—nearly matching those of the traditional Northeast and the antebellum South. Senator Stephen A. Douglas of Illinois called this robust new region a "swelling power that will be able to speak the new law of this nation." Without slavery, the dark clouds rising between the sections might well have been negotiated away through the ordinary compromises of politics. With slavery, they were insoluble.

The march toward disunion had begun to come to a head with the Compromise of 1850, among the provisions of which was the harsh new Fugitive Slave Law promised by Henry Clay. Under the terms of the law, suspected runaway slaves would be denied trials by jury and their status determined by federal commissioners. A presumed fugitive would not be permitted to testify on his own behalf and could be turned over to his self-proclaimed owner on no more evidence than the so-called master's affidavit. In some cases, what this meant was that men long free could be sent back into slavery. This was not a

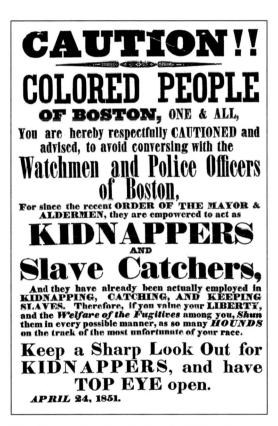

The County Election, left, painted by George Caleb Bingham in 1851–52, depicts the increasing tension surrounding the slavery issue in the mid-nineteenth century. The violent emotions surrounding the landmark vote that determined the fate of slavery in Kansas and Nebraska reverberated throughout America. Starting in 1851, the tough new Fugitive Slave Law had made life more precarious for African-Americans even in free states. The poster above warned "the colored people of Boston, one and all," of the risk of kidnapping.

Percentage of slaves in total population (by county) 1860:

50% or over

10-50%

under 10%

no slaves or unsettled

As the map shows, the routes of the Underground Railroad were a loosely knit network of about 3,000 Northerners willing to give temporary refuge to runaways. The railroad was a humanitarian response, but it did little to relieve the overall problem; in a slave population of more than 4 million, fewer than a thousand escaped each year.

rare occurrence, seeing that the law was written to insure commissioners received larger fees when they found for masters than when they freed alleged runaway slaves.

The Fugitive Slave Law had two noticeable effects on the North. First, the anti-slavery states did not shrink from making their distaste known and passed measures to nullify the law within their boundaries, thus widening the sectional gap. Second, the even less complacent abolitionists tightened the organization and sped up the pace of their "Underground Railroad" through which escaped slaves were helped flee to freedom via a series of safe houses reaching from the South to Canada, whence fugitives would not be extra-

dited back to the United States. Elijah Anderson, the black "general superintendent" of Underground Railroad operations in northern Ohio, for example, supposedly managed to guide more than a thousand slaves to freedom between 1850 and 1855; similarly, John Mason, himself an escaped slave who had been recaptured only to run north once more, helped some 1,300 other slaves find freedom. The most famous of the railroad's "conductors," Harriet Tubman, who was born a slave in Dorchester County, Maryland, circa 1820, made nineteen dangerous trips into the South to assemble groups of slaves and bring them to the North and to Canada. Of course, the presence of so many former slaves among the movement's organizers served only to raise hackles higher in the white South.

The potential success of the Compromise of 1850 was further hampered by the serialization of Harriet Beecher Stowe's dramatic novel *Uncle Tom's Cabin* in an anti-slavery newspaper in 1851 and again by its publication as a hardcover national best-seller a year later. In the abolition classic, she warned that the "great and unredressed injustice" of slavery had rendered America ripe for civil war. Stowe, daughter of a respected New England family that had produced numerous prominent ministers, gave a florid account of plantation life that conveyed strong abolitionist sentiments. To many readers the book's protagonist, Uncle Tom—a good and loyal servant who eventually is clubbed to death—represented the typical black slave, while the villain, heartless and greedy overseer Simon Legree, seemed to stand for nearly all white Southerners. That Stowe had made Legree a Yankee who worked in the South was largely overlooked by the novel's admiring public, who preferred to see it as an anti-Dixie treatise. By mid-1853 more than 300,000 copies of *Uncle Tom's Cabin* had been sold, a figure that even today would be impressive—and that at the time made Stowe's moralistic melodrama the most influential American literary work since Tom Paine's pamphlet *Common Sense,* and seemingly no less of a call to direct action.

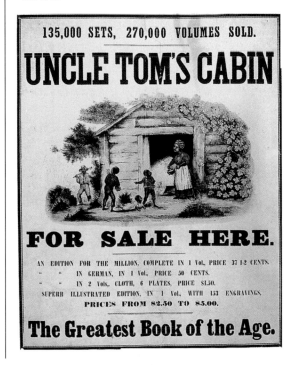

On the forty-ninth ballot, the 1852 Democratic Convention suddenly turned to a dark horse candidate, Franklin Pierce, touted on the campaign banner at right. In 1842, Pierce had resigned from the U.S. Senate for personal reasons. Unexpectedly called back to Washington, this time as president, he was still fighting an array of personal problems including occasional bouts with alcohol, the death of his only child, and the subsequent depression suffered by his wife. Pierce was a disappointing president, and his administration palpably strengthened Southern resolve on the issue of slavery. One of his opponents in the presidential election of 1852 was Winfield Scott, in an undated engraving below. A lifelong soldier, Scott's military career spanned more than fifty years. Born before the Constitution was written, he was a hero of the War of 1812, a veteran of the gruesome Black Hawk War in the 1830s, a commanding general in the Mexican War, and an able general in chief of the Union Army at the outset of the Civil War.

It was in this heated climate that the U.S. political parties met in 1852 to select their candidates for the presidency. The Democrats once more sought a compromise choice even though any agreement on slavery was looking ever less likely. In the end, the party turned to a "dark horse," a term coined by Britain's future Prime Minister Benjamin Disraeli in an 1831 novel describing the finish of an actual race wherein "A dark horse which had never been thought of, and which the careless . . . had never even observed in the list, rushed past the grandstand in sweeping triumph." The Democrats' 1852 long shot was Franklin Pierce of New Hampshire, a former congressman who supported the overall compromise, including the Fugitive Slave Law. In a further attempt to curry Southern favor the convention adopted a pro-expansion platform based on Manifest Destiny and selected William King of Alabama as Pierce's running mate.

The Whig Party also had supporters in both sections of the country, but its overall Northern tilt and the Democrats' nomination of a New Englander to top their ticket led a few Southerners to defect to the Free Soil Party and its candidate, John Hale of New Hampshire. Clearly sectional discord was severing the Whigs into Southern and Northern wings, which began refusing to cooperate with each other. Worse yet, the deaths of President Zachary Taylor (1850), Daniel Webster (1852), and Henry Clay (1852) had stripped the party of a towering national leader. The Whig platform, little more than a warmed-over rewrite of the party's issue-free 1848 version, was more a tribute to the candidate than a statement on the issues. Again seeking unity via a certified war hero, the Whigs nominated Pierce's former commanding officer, the vaguely anti-slavery General Winfield Scott of Virginia, whose positions were nearly as inchoate as Zachary Taylor's four years before except for his view of the Southern states as "our wayward sisters." The distinguished military records of both candidates hardly put a damper on negative campaigning. At one point, for example, one of Pierce's campaigners was inspired to call Scott "a carbuncle-faced old drunkard."

Faced with a choice between Pierce plus the Compromise and Scott with who knew what, the nation opted for the former. This time, however, even if all of Free Soiler Hale's votes had gone to the Whigs, Scott still would have lost to Pierce, although in a much closer contest. As it was, Pierce came into office with a substantial mandate, and as expected his administration was dominated by Southern Democrats led by Jefferson Davis of Mississippi, who became Secretary of War and, more importantly, the new president's chief adviser.

Although few Americans today have much sense of the presidency of Franklin Pierce, a number of important issues in addition to slavery and the future of the Union cropped up during his administration, including the crucial economic ones of building a railroad to the Pacific Ocean and trade opportunities far beyond that. When he took office in 1853 Pierce was only forty-eight, the youngest president to that point as well as a supporter of the Democrats' "Young America" movement, which went Manifest Destiny one better and eagerly advocated the global spread of U.S. democracy, beginning with the annexation of new territories. Pierce was thus in both the mood and the position to reap the fruits of his predecessor's approval of Commodore Matthew Perry's expedition to Japan, which arrived in Tokyo in 1853. For two centuries, Japan had been closed to U.S. trade, but that changed quickly after Perry's dazzling display of American weaponry and know-how, from demonstrations of the cannons on his ships to official U.S. gifts of firearms, telegraphs, and even a model train. All the Japanese

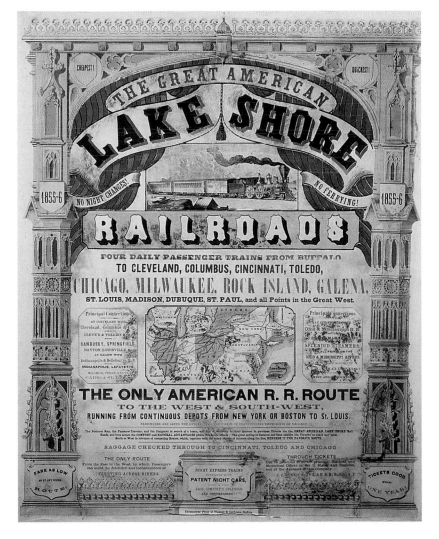

Under the Compromise of 1850, the nation reached a kind of status quo in which the South might retain slavery, while most new territories developed without it, as indicated on the map. In the mid-1850s, however, the compromise broke down. To survive the ensuing political struggle, proslavery forces felt compelled to control the majority of new states. Economically, however, slavery didn't make sense in the grain-growing areas of the northern plains, nor in the ranch lands of the Far West. It did thrive on its own in eastern Texas and in developing areas of Louisiana and Arkansas. In order to fill needs there—and to take up the surplus in agriculturally exhausted regions back East—the domestic slave trade began to flow west, as the map shows. Some groups of slaves were transported by boat, but most walked. Often numbering in the hundreds or even thousands, they marched in chains under the stern authority of slave drivers.

WASHINGTON

OREGON
(1859)
free by Oregon Act 1848

free by
Oregon Act
1848

International boundary (Adams-Onis Treaty) 1819–45 (Texas annexation)
Mexican cession (Treaty of Guadalupe Hidalgo) 1848

TERRITORY

NEBRA

TERRIT

free by Missouri
open to slavery by
Act

1845

CALIFORNIA
(1850)

UTAH TERRITORY
open to slavery by Compromise of 1850

1845

1820

NEW MEXICO TERRITORY
open to slavery by Compromise of 1850
[free 1850]

open to slavery by Act of
Annexation to New
Mexico Territory
1853

MEXICO

PROGRESS *of* ABOLITION *and the* SLAVE TRADE
1820–60

Free State by admission to Union   Slave State by admission to Union

Free State by gradual abolition   Territory open to slavery by
                                       Act of Congress
Free Territory by Act of Congress

() date of abolition by State Constitution

[] date of abolition by Territorial Constituion

• major port or center of slave trade   —— overland route of slave traffic

◦ District of Columbia (slave trade   – – sea route of slave traffic
abolished by Compromise of 1850)

0   200   400

45°
30°
15°
105°

ADA

UNORGANIZED
free by Missouri
Compromise 1820

MINNESOTA
(1858)

MAINE
(1780)

820
aska

WISCONSIN
(1848)

MICHIGAN
(1837)

VT.
(1777)

N.H.
(1783)

NEW YORK
(1799–1827)

MASS.
(1700)

CONN.
(1784–1848)

Boston

free by Missouri
Compromise 1820

IOWA
(1846)
free by Missouri
Compromise 1820

R.I.
(1784–1842)

Newport

SAS TERRITORY
Missouri Compromise 1820
by Kansas Nebraska Act 1854
[free 1859]

1820
1837   slave by Platte
Purchase in
violation
of Missouri
Compromise

ILLINOIS
(1818)

INDIANA
(1816)

OHIO
(1803)

New York

Long I.

PENNSYLVANIA
(1780–1850)

NEW
JERSEY
(1804–46)

Wheeling

MD.
Baltimore

DEL.
Annapolis
Washington, D.C.

exas 1845

LAND

St. Louis

Louisville

Frankfort

Alexandria

VIRGINIA
Richmond

Jefferson
City
MISSOURI

KENTUCKY

Petersburg
Norfolk

INDIAN TERRITORY
(UNORGANIZED)

ARKANSAS

Nashville

Knoxville

NORTH   CAROLINA

Salisbury

TENNESEE

SOUTH
CAROLINA

Wilmington

MISS.

Tuscaloosa

GEORGIA

Charleston

Tuskegee
Montgomery

Savannah

TEXAS

Vicksburg

Jackson

ALABAMA

Madisonville

Vidalia Natchez

Mobile

Pensacola

Tallahassee

Jekyll I.

Amelia I.

Baton Rouge

New Orleans

LOUISIANA

St. Augustine

Galveston
Matagorda
Port Lavaca

Grand
Island

FLORIDA

Nassau

BAHAMA
ISLANDS

Florida Keys

Havana

CUBA

The placard above trumpeted a convention for "free state voters" to assemble in hasty opposition to the proslavery minority that had taken control of Kansas in 1855. Although Kansas counted fewer than 300 slaves in its population, the battle over legalization of slavery there ignited violence in the territory and riled abolitionists in the East. "It rekindled the zeal, stimulated the activity, and strengthened the faith of our old anti-slavery forces," observed Frederick Douglass from New York State. Another act of violence that galvanized Northern feelings was the beating of Senator Charles Sumner, shown in the lithograph above right. Sumner, a leading Republican senator, had made a speech critical of Senator Andrew Butler of South Carolina. In retaliation, Butler's nephew stalked into the Senate on May 22, 1856, and beat Sumner senseless. Over the course of his three-year recuperation, many pointed to Sumner's empty Senate seat as a symbol of out-of-control Southern zeal.

had to offer in return was silk and sumo wrestling, and before long Tokyo agreed to a U.S. consulate as well as to wide-ranging commercial relations.

Along similarly expansionist lines, in 1854 Pierce would resuscitate former President Polk's plan to acquire Cuba, the alluring sugar island ninety miles from the Florida coast that would continue to bedevil the United States and particularly another young president, John F. Kennedy, a century later. Pierce offered Spain $130 million for Cuba with the vague threat that the island would be taken if not sold. But a presidential envoy's presumptuous missive to that effect—declaring that if Spain "actuated by stubborn pride and a false sense of honor refused to sell," the United States would be "justified in wresting" Cuba away—was leaked to the press and set Northerners sputtering over what they perceived as slave-crazed Southern imperialism, which laid the notion to rest until another day.

Thwarted in his attempts beyond the U.S. borders, Pierce became more interested in making use of the West's vast natural resources than he and his fellow Young Americans had ever been in slavery, although it was the lust for expansion that brought the matter fully to the fore: if the United States were to grow along the tracks of new railroads, some decision would have to be made about slavery in the areas those tracks would cross. In accordance with his capitalistic Young American views, in 1853 Pierce concluded the $10-million Gadsden Purchase of 45,000 square miles of Mexican desert along the U.S. border in present day Arizona and New Mexico—the most logical route for a transcontinental railroad to traverse the South. Stephen Douglas, an architect and manager of the Compromise of 1850, suggested overcoming the confounding political obstacles by allowing the settlers of the territories to be traversed—Kansas and Nebraska—to decide whether they would be slave-owning or free under the concept of "popular sovereignty." Relentless Southern pressure forced Douglas to keep capitulating until his bill came right out and overturned the Missouri Compromise prohibiting slavery north of 36°30' latitude, upon which it won the support of both Southerners in Congress and the Pierce administration and was passed in May 1854 as the Kansas-Nebraska Act. The Douglas-sponsored bill clearly left "all questions pertaining to slavery in the Territories . . . to the people residing therein."

Nebraska presented no problems, but Kansas turned into an ideological battleground between the sections. By 1855, clashes had erupted between Northern and Southern factions in the U.S. heartland that escalated into a full-blown guerrilla war early the next year. In the mid-1850s actual violence routinely broke out not only among neighboring farmers and merchants but also inside the halls of Congress, where America's elected representatives took to carrying pistols as a matter of course. One House member from South Carolina, Preston Brooks, actually beat a fiery antislavery Massachusetts senator, Charles Sumner, with his gutta-percha cane on the floor of the United States Senate in May 1856. But even the caning spectacle in Washington dimmed next to what was going on in the Kansas territory the same month, where radical abolitionist John Brown was leading raids on pro-slavery settlements sparked when 700 pro-slavery ruffians attacked the Free Soil town of Lawrence. Outraged, Brown—an Ohio sheep farmer and Calvinist drifter of stern Old Testament visage and manner who had settled in Kansas to join his sons and pursue business opportunites as a surveyor—assembled a half-dozen followers, including four of his boys to plot retaliation. Three days after the Lawrence raid, Brown and company, using surplus artillery swords brought from Ohio, hacked to death five supposedly pro-slavery settlers along Pottawatomie Creek even though not one of those murdered owned a slave or had anything to do with the attack. Despite his portrayal by poet Stephen Vincent Benét, whose celebrated 1928 verse *John Brown's Body* would address his noble intent, Brown had a lust for vengeance and a taste for vigilante actions that precipitated further bloodshed. The Pottawatomie murders set off a firestorm of violence in the Kansas territory, with small guerrilla bands clashing at Black Jack, Franklin, Fort Saunders, and other towns. The evasive abolitionist, considered a "maniacal villian" in the South, eventually escaped to Canada and started planning a slave insurrection back in Dixie. Kansas, meanwhile, continued to be a battleground: by year's end 200 people were dead and $2 million in property damage had been done, causing the territory to be dubbed "Bleeding Kansas." Territorial Governor John W. Geary managed to contain the wholesale violence by calling in thousands of federal troops, and by 1858 Kansas rejected the pro-slavery LeCompton Constitution. Still, the bleeding continued until the outbreak of the Civil War.

With such a background to the election of 1856 it's small wonder that the parties were more polarized than ever, the litmus test being the Kansas-Nebraska Act and whether it should be overturned. The situation was further fragmented by the emergence of a new "third" party born of bigotry fostered by the large influx of immigrants at the time. The xenophobic faction was officially called the American Party but better known as the "Know-Nothings" for their secret password, "I don't know." As the *Cleveland Plain Dealer* explained in 1854, "When one Know-Nothing wishes to recognize another, he closes one eye, makes an O with his thumb and forefinger and places

James Buchanan, above, was the Democratic candidate for president in 1856. A Pennsylvania lawyer with Southern sympathies, he was a mild, malleable man. His opponent was adventurer John C. Frémont, below, the standard-bearer for the new Republican Party. Former Senator Thomas Hart Benton was John Frémont's father-in-law but campaigned heartily for eventual winner, Buchanan, whose appeal he described succinctly: "Never a leading man in any high sense, but eminently a man of peace."

his nose through it, which, interpreted, reads eye-nose-O—I know nothing." Apparently so, for the Know-Nothings nominated Millard Fillmore, the unpopular former president, on a downright offensive anti-Catholic platform that promised harsh restrictions on immigration, particularly of Irish Catholics.

But fringe giddiness was only part of the peculiar electoral equation of 1856. The Whig Party headed for doom when its seams began to split as Southern members endorsed Fillmore. The Democrats took the wiser route of ignoring both slavery and Kansas and forgoing their best and brightest but most contentious choice, Stephen Douglas, in favor of James Buchanan, a foppish lightweight whose recent absence from the country (as minister to Great Britain) just happened to cloud most of his stands on the issues. The Democratic platform did, however, dub Douglas's Kansas-Nebraska Act "the only sound and safe solution of the slavery question" and promoted the expansionist policies favored by the Southern states. With this the Democrats became in part a Southern party, sending its Northern wing migrating to yet another new coalition blended of Free Soilers and Northern Whigs who called themselves Republicans. This new party denounced the Kansas-Nebraska Act and selected dashing Georgia-born Mexican War hero John C. Frémont—a western explorer who had helped free California to join the United States while looking good the whole while—as its presidential candidate despite, or perhaps because of, his relative lack of political experience.

This time the presidential choice was clear-cut: a Frémont victory would bring Kansas into the Union as a free state, while Buchanan would usher it in as a slave state. But slavery as a moral question still was not a central national issue except to a few radical Northern abolitionists and their fire-breathing Southern opponents; in 1856 the more important matter was the related question of the extension of slavery into the territories. Thoughtful Southerners understood that their very way of life depended on the perpetuation of slavery, and that unless the practice were permitted to spread, new states would vote with the North on economic and other federal issues and in time might even try to end slavery wherever it persisted. What's more, many of these modern sons of the old South also believed that because the question of secession had never been resolved, leaving the Union remained a state's right under the U.S. Constitution.

The most moderate candidate, Buchanan, won courtesy of a solidly Democratic South that had the numbers over the North's new Republican Party, some support for which had been leached by Fillmore, who garnered eight electoral votes from a substantial popular tally. In the end Buchanan received only 45.3 percent of the popular vote, the lowest victory margin since 1824. Yet it remained to him, the last U.S. president to have been born in the eighteenth century, to try to forge a compromise acceptable to all sections to avoid what appeared nearly inevitable in 1856: civil war.

The Widening Breach

Andrew Jackson must have spun in his eleven-year-old grave. He had never liked the man who would become America's only bachelor chief executive to

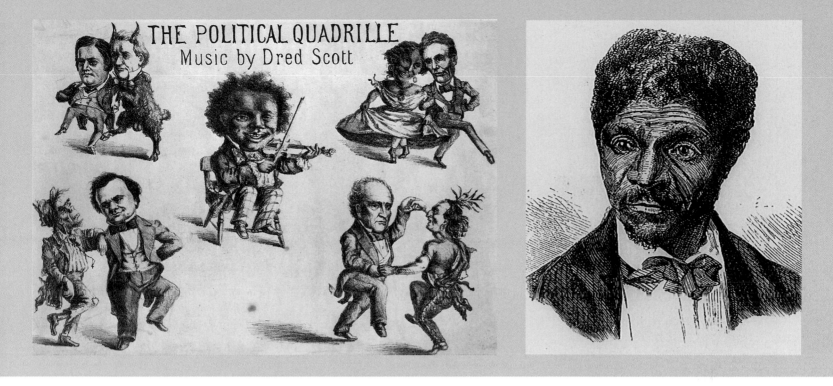

THE POLITICAL QUADRILLE
Music by Dred Scott

date: when President Polk had named Buchanan as Secretary of State in 1845, Jackson had denounced the choice. "But you yourself appointed him minister to Russia in your first term," Polk pointed out. "Yes, I did," Jackson rejoined; "it was as far as I could send him out of my sight, and where he could do the least harm. I would have sent him to the North Pole if we had kept a minister there."

The sixty-five-year-old commander in chief-elect inspired confidence in few and shortly showed why. Amid a swirling turmoil the likes of which the United States had never seen before and fortunately has not since, on March 4, 1857, President James Buchanan delivered an inaugural address stressing America's wealth and power and advocating the promotion of both via rapid repayment of the national debt. He also spoke of the needs to beef up the armed forces and to build a transcontinental railroad; then he endorsed popular sovereignty and condemned abolitionist agitation, obliviously calling slavery "happily a matter of but little practical importance."

Two days later U.S. Chief Justice Roger Brooke Taney indicated otherwise when he handed down the verdict in the case of *Dred Scott v. Sandford*. Scott, a slave, had been transported from Missouri to Illinois and then to the Wisconsin Territory (later Minnesota) before being returned to St. Louis, where in 1846 he had sued for his liberty on the grounds that his prior residence in non-slave states had made him free. A Missouri jury found in his favor, but the state supreme court overturned the verdict, which eventually reached the U.S. Supreme Court. Abolitionists across the nation took up his cause, but speaking for the majority Taney claimed that because Scott was a slave and therefore not a citizen of the United States, he was not entitled to bring suit in a federal court. The most chilling aspect of Taney's opinion was its finding that "The right of property in a slave is distinctly and expressly affirmed in the Constitution. . . . No word can be found in the Constitution which gives Congress a greater power over slave property or which entitles

Dred Scott, above, sued for his freedom in Missouri after his owner died. He lost his case when the Supreme Court ruled that he had no right to sue because a slave or a descendant of a slave was considered property and therefore could not be a U.S. citizen; moreover, the federal government had no power to exclude slavery in the territories. After the Court's decision, Scott was sold to a sympathizer who promptly gave him his freedom. But the 1857 case unleashed a storm of protest throughout the North and further polarized the issues in the 1860 election. The cartoon above left shows each candidate dancing with a political partner to the music of the Dred Scott decision: (clockwise from bottom left) Stephen Douglas with an Irish immigrant; John Breckinridge with outgoing president James Buchanan; Abraham Lincoln with a black woman; and John Bell with an Indian.

property of that kind to less protection than property of any other description."

The South had won a major victory there alone, but things got even better. Taney also argued that even had Scott had the standing to bring his case he would have lost on the grounds that the Missouri Compromise was unconstitutional. "Congress could not exclude slavery," Taney wrote, since to do so would violate the due process of law guaranteed by the Fifth Amendment; thus Congress could have "only the power coupled with the duty of . . . protecting the owner in his rights." For the first time since *Marbury v. Madison* in 1803, the Court had declared an act of Congress unconstitutional. Even though Congress had repealed the Missouri Compromise via the Kansas-Nebraska Act three years earlier, now the Court had challenged the very concept of popular sovereignty; if slavery could not be legislated out of a territory by Congress, then it certainly could not be abolished by a territorial government established by that Congress.

In other words, through the *Dred Scott* case the Supreme Court declared that no region had the right to legislate slavery out of its jurisdiction. What this meant was that all territorial restrictions on the abhorrent practice were invalid, as was popular sovereignty. The South's radicals had won the national debate, leaving their Northern opponents incensed and dealing a blow to the great silent majority of moderates throughout the United States, who wanted only a stable environment in which to go about their business. The *Dred Scott* decision alarmed most Northerners and the fear of "slave power" spread like wildfire. "There is such a thing as the slave power," warned the *Cincinnati Daily Commercial*. "It has marched over and annihilated the boundaries of the states." Abraham Lincoln, in fact, first gained national prominence by his eloquent attacks on "slave power."

By this point Southern partisans had begun to take the idea of secession seriously. This, of course, raised the question whether the region could prevail in the war that might be ignited by its departure from the Union. After all, no one could deny that the South had a smaller population than the North, fewer factories for producing the tools of war, and a far inferior internal transportation system. By the same token, the South's ruling aristocrats could harbor legitimate hopes of support from their like-minded cousins at the helms of several European nations, who had been given cause to fear the United States as a substantial power in the wake of the Mexican War. Logic dictated that if the South seceded successfully, other regions might follow—and half a dozen or more North American countries would pose far less of a threat to the European powers than one large, united nation.

In fact, Europe had been given reason to fear the United States beginning in 1854, when the young nation had started to enjoy an economic boom. The combination of the discovery of a seemingly endless fount of gold in California and the outbreak of the economy-threatening Crimean War in Europe that year brought foreign gold pouring into America for safekeeping, nearly doubling the U.S. money supply from what it had been a decade earlier.

By the summer of 1857, however, the U.S. economy had begun to slow down to the point of a depression that would last through most of the next year. When the expensive three-year Crimean War between Russia and Britain,

France, and the Ottoman Empire ended in 1856, demand for American grains plummeted and with it the trade goods' prices, much to the detriment of Northern and Midwestern farmers who had been expecting inflation instead. At the same time, speculation in cotton futures caused that commodity's price to rise, brightening the South's economic prospects. Northern textile manufacturers faced the dilemma of whether to pass on raw materials at the new, higher prices in the midst of a market so weak that many mills had to lay off part of their workforces. The confusion led to bank runs and a panic on Wall Street that caused a depression particularly bruising to the North, which the South took as a sign of the rival region's overall weakness. Because cotton planters conducted the bulk of their financial business with European banks, the domestic depression had scant effect on the South; in fact, cotton prices kept climbing thanks to increased European demand in the wake of the Crimean War.

Southerners jubilantly jeered the seemingly prostrate North. "The wealth of the South is permanent and real, that of the North fugitive and fictitious," crowed Governor Herschel Johnson of Georgia. Going the next step, on October 14, 1857, the Charleston, South Carolina, *Mercury* inquired, "Why does the South allow itself to be tattered and torn by the dissensions and death struggles of New York's money changers?" Although the depression had brought down a few Southern banks as well, no panic had ensued and recovery had come quickly. Even Senator James Henry Hammond of South Carolina, who a year earlier had cautioned against a sectional war he thought the South could not win, trumpeted the region's new doctrine, proclaiming to Seward in the Senate in March 1858: "No, you dare not make war on cotton. No power on earth dares make war on it. Cotton is king!"

Southern newspapers also chimed into the cry, asserting that a sectional war would lay the North to waste financially: laid-off workers would revolt and side with the South, while opposition to them among Republicans and Know-Nothings would lead to class warfare. According to this scenario Northern banks and railroads would fail while the South could withhold its cotton from the market, causing economic distress in Europe and obliging governments there—already hoping for the dissolution of the United States— not only to recognize the new Southern government but to come to its aid. So ran the fantasies of those considering secession in 1858.

But 1859 saw an event that would escalate the sectional animosities past the point of no return. On October 16, John Brown led a small band to raid the arsenal at Harpers Ferry, Virginia (now West Virginia). Unopposed they seized control of two bridges in the quiet town, the federal armory and arsenal, and a rifle shop nearby, then waited sanguinely for a slave uprising to rip through the South. The day after the raid, Colonel Robert E. Lee ordered Lieutenant J. E. B. Stuart and a company of Marines to overrun the building where Brown was holding a number of hostages. A week later, the captured Brown assumed the role of martyr and refused to plead insanity. On October 31, a jury found Brown guilty of criminal conspiracy, murder, and treason. The abolitionist replied three days later, "I believe that to have interfered as I have done . . . is no wrong . . . but right. . . ." On December 2, John Brown walked to the gallows as Southerners cheered and Northerners mourned the impending

Abraham Lincoln and Stephen Douglas are shown debating in Charleston, Illinois, on September 18, 1858, in Robert Marshall Root's *The Lincoln-Douglas Debate*. Before an audience of 1,500, Lincoln denied that he "had ever been in favor of making voters of the negroes, or jurors, or qualifying them to hold office, or having them marry with white people." It is generally agreed that Lincoln meant these remarks to placate voters in the southern part of the state, but they came to haunt his reputation as the Great Emancipator after the Civil War.

death of a saint. "This will be a great day in our history, a date of the new revolution—quite as needed as the old one," Yankee poet Henry Wadsworth Longfellow predicted in his diary. "As I write, they are leading old John Brown to execution. . . . This is sowing the wind to reap the whirlwind, which will come soon."

The national outlook after Harpers Ferry seemed ominous, but nothing has characterized U.S. history so much as the phenomenon of statesmen rising to meet the occasion. At no point has this been more evident than in the election of 1860, when the soul and indeed the very existence of the United States was at stake; as Thomas Jefferson had foreseen in a 1787 letter he wrote regarding slavery, "This abomination must have an end, and there is a superior bench reserved in Heaven for those who hasten it."

More than forty different editions of the Lincoln-Douglas debates have been published since the two Senate candidates first argued the future of slavery in 1858. Transcripts, which include descriptions of laughter, heckling, and cheers from the crowd, were made by reporters representing both pro-Lincoln Republican newspapers and pro-Douglas Democratic ones. Historians have studied the differing texts ever since, trying to assess just exactly what each man said. An 1860 book (the title page is shown below) boasts that it was "carefully prepared by reporters of each party." Whether read about in newspapers or books or heard in person, the Illinois debates propelled Lincoln to the forefront of the national debate on slavery.

POLITICAL DEBATES

BETWEEN

HON. ABRAHAM LINCOLN

AND

HON. STEPHEN A. DOUGLAS,

In the Celebrated Campaign of 1858, in Illinois;

INCLUDING THE PRECEDING SPEECHES OF EACH, AT CHICAGO, SPRINGFIELD, ETC.; ALSO, THE TWO GREAT SPEECHES OF MR. LINCOLN IN OHIO, IN 1859,

AS

CAREFULLY PREPARED BY THE REPORTERS OF EACH PARTY, AND PUBLISHED AT THE TIMES OF THEIR DELIVERY.

COLUMBUS:
FOLLETT, FOSTER AND COMPANY.
1860.

Happily, there was also a desk in the White House for him. The presidential contest of 1860 would indeed prove momentous, and so would the congressional races that set it up—particularly one 1858 state election that brought to the forefront of America's greatest debate the individual who would save the Union: Republican Abraham Lincoln, who became a national figure only after he lost a senatorial election in Illinois. His opponent was the incumbent Senator Stephen Douglas, who at the time was regarded as the Democrats' likeliest next presidential candidate, largely because four years after introducing the Kansas-Nebraska Act he had somehow regained the goodwill of moderates in both the North and the South. Illinois Republicans could not have known the full import of the decision that lay before them in 1858 when they faced a choice of Senate candidates between John Wentworth, who as Chicago's new mayor was the first Republican to lead any large city, and Abraham Lincoln, who had retired to his private law practice after one term in the House of Representatives. But Lincoln's political positions were clear. He had criticized the *Dred Scott* decision and was opposed to the extension of slavery into the territories, yet was no friend of the abolitionists; rather, he was perceived as a moderate believer in free soil and an opponent of popular sovereignty, and in the end he won the nomination.

Lincoln's story ranks among the clearest examples of just how possible it was in America to rise to the top on the strength of an idea and having the courage to stick to it. Born in a log cabin in Kentucky in 1809 and raised on hardscrabble farms in Indiana and Illinois, Lincoln had enjoyed less than twelve months of formal schooling spread over several years. He had taught himself not only to read but to study the right texts to develop a tight, kinetic prose style that would make his speeches perhaps the finest in the history of the presidency. He learned the political arts on his own time; the tall, skinny, and prodigiously unattractive Lincoln had worked on farms, ferries, and flatboats before he was elected to the Illinois legislature at the age of twenty-five. After that he studied law, was admitted to the state bar two years later, and stayed in the legislature until 1842; he was elected to the U.S. Congress in 1846. Six years after his voluntary retirement from the House of Representatives, Lincoln returned to politics only because the Kansas-Nebraska Act dug at the very principles at the bottom of his soul.

In a letter to a friend dated October 3, 1845, Lincoln had written, "I hold it to be a paramount duty of us in the free states, due to the Union of the States, and perhaps to liberty itself (paradox though it may seem), to let the slavery of the other states alone; while, on the other hand, I hold it to be equally clear that we should never knowingly lend ourselves, directly or indirectly, to prevent that slavery from dying a natural death." Yet on July 1, 1854, he had expressed a world-wearier wit on the subject that led him to write, "Although volume upon volume is written to prove slavery a very good thing, we never hear of the man who wishes to take the good of it, by being a slave himself."

In the best American tradition of political upstarts with something to say, Lincoln challenged Douglas to a series of debates for the Senate seat from Illinois. The ensuing Lincoln-Douglas debates did far more than inform the 1858 Illinois senatorial contest; they laid out the fundamental views of the man who eventually would hold the Union together for all the right reasons. Four years earlier, on October 16, 1854, Lincoln spoke in Peoria, Illinois, in response to Senator Douglas's defense of the Kansas-Nebraska Act:

> This declared indifference, but, as I must think, covert real zeal, for the spread of slavery, I cannot but hate. I hate it because of the monstrous injustice of slavery itself. I hate it because it deprives our republican example of its just influence in the world; enables the enemies of free institutions with plausibility to taunt us as hypocrites; causes the real friends of freedom to doubt our sincerity; and especially because it forces so many good men among ourselves into an open war with the very fundamental principles of civil liberty.

Although Lincoln shifted his position somewhat according to his audience, sounding decidedly antislavery in northern Illinois and more muted on the subject in the southern part of the state, wherever he went he succeeded in tarring Douglas, who had been married to a slave-owning heiress, as a captive of Southern interests. Of course, for all his erudition Douglas made Lincoln's arguments easier by trying to support the *Dred Scott* decision and popular sovereignty at the same time, a clear contradiction. Realizing he had to take a firmer stand Douglas, in what came to be known as the "Freeport Doctrine," more or less came out against *Dred Scott,* averring that the people of a state could pass laws against slavery if they so desired. Although this enabled him to win the Illinois Senate seat, it also assured Douglas of Southern opposition to his getting the Democratic presidential nomination two years later. Lincoln may have lost the senatorial race, but in doing so his arguments forged a new national coalition.

Long riven by slavery, the nation's political structure finally splintered in 1860. The Democratic Party split into Northern and Southern factions after failure to agree on a candidate forced it to adjourn its convention from Charleston to Baltimore. The Republicans did better at hanging together, but only as quite a different party from that of four years earlier. The Republican ranks swelled with Northern Whigs, Midwestern German immigrants who viewed abolitionism as an extension of their fight for freedom in Europe, and Eastern businessmen eager for the economic opportunities denied them by the Southern-dominated Congress. Other Republicans joined the Constitutional Union Party. Where the Republicans of 1856 had been concerned primarily with slavery and land policies, in 1860 the party's interests, in addition to slavery, included issues on internal improvements, tariffs, fiscal and monetary matters, immigration, and a spectrum of other issues more familiar to Henry Clay's Whigs than to the Free Soilers of the early 1850s.

A host of Republican candidates united to take on front-runner William Seward, who had accumulated many enemies during his long political career as governor of and senator from New York. Seward in fact had a great many good ideas and would go on to prove himself in Lincoln's Cabinet. In a speech during the Republican primary campaign, for example, he demanded of those who would coddle the South: "Did any propertied class ever reform itself? Did the patricians in old Rome, the noblesse or clergy in France? The landholders in Ireland? The landed aristocracy in England? Does the slaveholding class even seek to beguile you with such a hope? Has it not become rapacious, arrogant, defiant?" But no amount of ability and passion could make up for Seward's lack of support within his own party, and Lincoln managed to make enough deals to win the nomination on the third ballot. The convention then selected Hannibal Hamlin of Maine as its vice presidential candidate.

The cartoon at left shows Abraham Lincoln using his long legs to dart ahead of his three opponents in the 1860 "political race" for the presidency. Right behind him is Stephen Douglas, "the Little Giant," who had beaten Lincoln in the Illinois Senate race two years before. A Democrat, Douglas ran for president on a moderate platform and lost Southerners radically committed to slavery. They backed John Breckinridge, shown running behind Douglas. The fourth candidate, John Bell, ran for the new Constitutional Union Party, which was against secession no matter the outcome of the slavery issue. As the only candidate adamantly against the extension of slavery, Abraham Lincoln sprinted to victory, drawing 59 percent of the votes in the electoral college.

Sheet music, below, rushed to press in 1860, encouraged dancers in the South to do "The Secession Quick Step." The nation was on alert from December 20, 1860, when South Carolina became the first of seven Southern states to declare itself seceded from the United States, until April 12, 1861, when shots were fired on the U.S. Army at Fort Sumter. Individuals and special conventions attempted to negotiate a solution, even as both sides considered the possibility of war. "The man does not live who is more devoted to peace than I am," Abraham Lincoln told a New Jersey audience in February 1861. "None . . . would do more to preserve it. But it may be necessary to put the foot down firmly."

Respectfully dedicated to the MINUTE MEN of GEORGIA

Secession Quick Step

The SOUTH, The WHOLE South, and NOTHING but the SOUTH.

NOLI ME TANGERE!!

by Herman L. Schreiner of MACON, Georgia,

also by the same Author:

"Cotton Planters CONVENTION Schottish." &c. ~ "JULIA Schottish." &c.

MACON, GA.
Published by John C. Schreiner & Sons.

But the Republicans couldn't just walk into the White House. Even as the Republicans were nominating Lincoln in Chicago, a small group of old Whigs and Know-Nothings met in Baltimore, named themselves the Constitutional Unionists, and nominated Senator John Bell of Tennessee for the presidency—all the while calling for unity, oddly enough, but without presenting any specific ideas as to how to bring it about. Elsewhere in Baltimore a dispirited group of Northern Democrats convened and selected Stephen Douglas as their candidate. Five days later, the party's Southern wing had nominated James Buchanan's vice president, John Breckinridge, for the top job under the Democratic banner.

The campaign was long and vigorous, but by the early autumn of 1860 it looked as though no candidate could hope for a majority of the electoral votes and that the contest would be decided in the House of Representatives. The Southerners swung into action to create a new coalition. Jefferson Davis, for example, believed that if no candidate won outright, the supporters of Bell, Breckinridge, and Douglas might be able to unite behind a relatively unknown compromise choice such as Horatio Seymour of New York or Alexander Stephens of Georgia, either of whom could use his anonymity to ignore the sectional pressures and devote his administration to healing the wounds threatening to bring down the Union. As the election approached, some of these compromise interests did come together when a Lincoln victory looked ever more likely, but Douglas would have none of it. Although he had always opposed what he considered Lincoln's abolitionist radicalism and still adhered to the idea of popular sovereignty, Douglas rejected the very notion of trying to take the presidential election away from the public to let the Congress sway it one way or the other on the crucial issue of slavery. "By God, sir," he exclaimed to Representative Edward McPherson of Pennsylvania, "the election shall never go into the House; before it shall go into the House, I will throw it to Lincoln." He never had the chance, as Seward had predicted earlier when Douglas was still hoping to secure the Democratic nomination: walking home together from the Capitol one evening after Douglas had delivered a fiery diatribe against "nigger-worshipers," Seward had presciently and properly pointed out, "Douglas, no man will ever be President of the United States who spells 'Negro' with two g's."

Lincoln received a plurality of the popular vote as well as a majority of the electoral vote, all of his tallies coming from the Northern and border states. In fact, he wasn't even on the ballot in ten of the Southern states. Lincoln won the nation's highest office with less than 40 percent of the popular vote, the smallest mandate since John Quincy Adams had become president with only 30.5 percent. But sometimes politicians do know best: even had all his opponents united behind one candidate, Lincoln still would have come out on top in the electoral college.

Jefferson Davis, left, was elected president of the Confederate States of America on February 9, 1861. "England will recognize us," he promised an audience on the eve of his inauguration, "and a glorious future is before us. The grass will grow in Northern cities, where the pavements have been worn off by the tread of commerce." Davis was an experienced statesman, having served as Secretary of War in the Pierce administration, but he believed so fervently in the rightness of Southern secession that he underestimated the odds against its success. Kentucky's Senator John Crittenden, at right in a painting by G. P. A. Healy, took a far dimmer view of the South's chances and offered one of the many last-minute compromises heard during the winter of 1860–1. It was rejected, of course.

Secession

Unlike Andrew Jackson, who under similar if not quite as serious circumstances had threatened to invade the South, President Buchanan proved unable or unwilling to lead his rejected administration and divided party. In his annual message to Congress on December 3, Buchanan had more or less sighed that although he did not believe in the right of secession, he knew that the coercion of states was illegal and would thus do nothing to block any Southern attempts to leave the Union. Instead, he blamed militant Northerners for instigating the controversy and called for a constitutional amendment to guarantee slavery not only where it already existed but in the territories as well. This set the Republicans to jeering and prompted Secretary of State-designate Seward to parody the lame-duck Buchanan to the effect that, "It is the duty of the President to execute the laws—unless somebody opposes him; and . . . no State has the right to go out of the Union—unless it wants to."

On December 20, 1860, in response to the election of a president "whose opinions and purposes are hostile to slavery," South Carolinian delegates, meeting in Columbia, voted to secede from the Union, which was soon followed by Mississippi, Florida, Alabama, Georgia, Louisiana, and Texas. The outgoing president finally roused himself to take a stand; when South Carolina authorities demanded the withdrawal of the federal forces that had moved into Fort Sumter for security reasons on December 26, Buchanan proclaimed, "This I cannot do; this I will not do." He even dispatched a steamship with supplies and reinforcements to Fort Sumter, but it was driven away on January 9, 1861, when South Carolina forces in Charleston Harbor opened fire. It was an undeniable act of rebellion the weary president chose to ignore in favor of finishing his term quietly.

Abraham Lincoln sits for Mathew Brady, opposite, later in his administration. His first inaugural address, delivered to a nation already divided, was a pathetically humble plea for time. "No administration," he assured his constituents, "by any extreme of wickedness or folly, can very seriously injure the government in the short space of four years." In private, however, Lincoln admitted that time was up: "The tug has to come," he wrote in letters to friends, "and better now than any time hereafter."

On February 4, 1861, the secessionist states opened a convention in Montgomery, Alabama, that was attended by moderates as well as radicals. Just as those of the latter stripe had initiated the American Revolution and those of the former had carried it through, so now the Southern revolution turned away from its fire-breathers toward individuals who might appeal to a broader cross-section of public opinion. Thus Jefferson Davis was selected as president of the new Confederate States of America with Alexander H. Stephens of Georgia as vice president. Although he was fairly moderate, it is doubtful that Davis could ever have won a popular election. A well-born Mississippian who had graduated from West Point and served as Franklin Pierce's Secretary of War, Davis was prickly and dismissive of anyone who didn't bow and scrape for his favor. On February 8, the secessionist convention ratified a constitution based on that of the United States but stressing the powers of the individual states and guaranteeing the rights of slaveholders.

In the spirit of his predecessor, the Great Compromiser Henry Clay, Senator John Crittenden of Kentucky kept hoping for reconciliation. On December 18, he had proposed an omnibus measure not unlike the Compromise of 1850 that would reestablish the Missouri Compromise line of 36°60', strengthen the Fugitive Slave Law, and enact a new constitutional amendment stating that Congress had no power to legislate on the matter of slavery where it already existed nor to abolish it from any state. Crittenden's proposal was supported by Douglas and other moderates but opposed by Seward on the one side and Davis on the other, as Mississippi had not yet seceded. For a brief moment, Crittenden's compromise offered hope of saving the Union. But then President-elect Lincoln decided that while he would accept most of the provisions, he remained adamant against any extension of slavery into the territories.

Meanwhile in the House, both Republican and Democratic members put forth compromise measures, all of which echoed the Crittenden plan as far as strengthening the Fugitive Slave Law. A constitutional amendment safeguarding slavery where it existed was proposed and passed in committee, while a bill was passed admitting New Mexico into the Union as a slave state. The House compromisers even submitted a Thirteenth Amendment containing the slavery guarantees, but Republican opposition came together to kill the measure.

As Lincoln's inauguration approached, the moderates in Congress tried another path to reconciliation when Virginia and other Southern border states organized a "peace convention" to put the Union back together. Twenty-one states sent delegates to the conference, which opened in Washington, D.C., on February 4 and was presided over by John Tyler, the former president. In line with Crittenden's proposal, the convention recommended the extension of the Missouri Compromise to the Pacific and the admission of new states from the territories without the approval of concurrent majorities from the slave and free states. But when brought to Congress this plan was defeated in the Senate and never reached the House.

On February 28, a few days before Lincoln's inauguration, the House accepted an amendment guaranteeing slavery in the states where it existed; the Senate passed it the morning of March 4. That two-thirds of the nation's legislators voted for the amendment showed just how broad a spectrum opposed

The 1864 Mathew Brady photograph opposite shows a Virginia arsenal lined with cannon in the background and ammunition in the foreground, one of many installations seized by the South during the winter of 1860–61. Stockpiling such matériel all winter, the South prepared for war in earnest. Confederates even managed to requisition supplies from sympathetic officials in the lame-duck Buchanan administration—and what they couldn't obtain for free, they purchased from naive or greedy merchants in the North. Though slower than the South to organize, the North possessed far greater capacity in war industries.

the idea of a war to abolish slavery; in fact, by the end of the congressional session Colorado, Nevada, and Dakota would be made into territories without so much as a mention of slavery—measures supported even by Republicans.

For the first time in America's young history, the artists of compromise who had always characterized its politics—so essential in a nation of so many divergent interests and populations—seemed to have lost their touch. Congress had failed. But then along came Lincoln, apparently not a moment too soon even for the man he replaced. As Buchanan, the departing president, told his successor that March 4: "If you are as happy, my dear sir, on entering this house as I am in leaving it and returning home, you are the happiest man in this country."

Abraham Lincoln has been called many things, but "happy" has never been among them. Immediately upon taking office the brilliant but angst-ridden new president set out to appear conciliatory yet firm. He would not seek to abolish slavery where it already existed and was even willing to guarantee its continuance through a constitutional amendment, but he would not permit it to spread into the territories and denied outright any constitutional right of secession. "There needs to be no bloodshed or violence," Lincoln proclaimed, "and there shall be none, unless it be forced upon the national authority." In other words, the president denied that any secession had taken place, thereby indicating that if war were to come the Confederacy would have to shoot first.

Lincoln spent the next month organizing his government and expanding upon his ideas. He was determined not to widen the gulf between the sections any more than was absolutely necessary; he understood that any action against the secessionists would only strengthen their hands in their own states, where a sizable portion of the public still favored the Union. More important, Lincoln wanted to avoid antagonizing the border slave states that had not seceded. Other crucial considerations arose as well, chief among them that the North had no sense of unity; despite the Republicans' sweep of the section, most Northerners were hardly eager or even willing to go to war just to keep the territories free of slavery. Finally, Lincoln had to deal with the political and constitutional questions of secession. If there were a war, there would have to be a peace, and how might such an accord be formulated—and between whom? Would the Confederacy be treated as a foreign country, and would the South be considered a conquered land when the inevitable occurred? Would it have to be occupied by U.S. armies, as would be the case after, say, a conflict with Canada or Mexico? Lincoln couldn't help but agonize over the likelihood that even though the remaining United States might win a war against the Confederacy, neither side could win a peace that would reunite the people of the two sections.

For this reason Lincoln promulgated his view that the Deep South was still part of the nation. The president was willing to accede to the explanation that because revolutionaries had seized control of Southern state governments by illegal means, everything they had done was the work of traitors rather than of legitimate political leaders; once matters were resolved, because the Confederate states had never really left the Union, there would be no need to re-admit them. Lincoln would not ask Congress to declare a war as provided in the Constitution, and although the legislature was entrusted

with the power of the purse, the president would spend money as needed and ask for the appropriations later. In fact, he would do whatever it took to preserve the Union, even if that included silencing enemies, exiling dissidents, and suspending constitutional guarantees. As Lincoln would write to journalist Horace Greeley in August 1862: "My paramount object in this struggle is to save the Union, and is not either to save or to destroy slavery. If I could save the Union without freeing any slave, I would do it; and if I could

Highly Important News from Washington.

Offensive War Measures of the Administration.

The President's Exposition of His Policy Towards the Confederate States.

A WAR PROCLAMATION.

Seventy-five Thousand Men Ordered Out.

Thirteen Thousand Required from New York.

Call for an Extra Session of Congress.

Preparations for the Defence of the National Capital.

The Great Free States Arming for the Conflict.

Thirty Thousand Troops to be Tendered from New York.

Strong Union Demonstrations in Baltimore.

THE BATTLE AT CHARLESTON.

EVACUATION OF FORT SUMTER.

The New York Herald printed the somber headlines, above, on April 16, 1861. When the news of the attack on Fort Sumter first reached the Senate, "there was a solemn and painful hush," according to Jacob Fox, who was there, "but it was broken in a moment by a woman's shrill voice from the spectators' seats, crying 'Glory be to God!' . . . the fierce cry of joy that the question [of slavery] had been submitted to the decision of the sword."

save it by freeing all the slaves, I would do it; and if I could do it by freeing some and leaving others alone, I would also do that."

Never in the history of the nation had a president behaved so high-handedly and taken so many actions of dubious legality; in fact, Lincoln's interpretation of "executive privilege" far exceeded any of the secret power-grabbing Richard Nixon would try to get away with more than a century later and that would lead to his resignation. But President Lincoln felt in his heart any means were justified that ended in preserving the Union, even if that meant overlooking a few legalities. For example, if the Southern states were indeed still in the Union they had the right to be represented in Congress and their citizens had the right to vote in elections. But of course the states that had seceded no longer sent representatives to the national legislature. This meant that Lincoln's Congresses always lacked quorums and thus every measure they passed and the president signed was illegal by his own definition, and so were the presidential and congressional elections in which the Confederate states did not participate.

Still other considerations added to the reasons for Lincoln's admittedly unconstitutional actions. For example, his principled but subtle and broad mind grasped that a declaration of war on the South would have been tantamount to recognizing the Confederacy, opening the door for other countries to do the same—and perhaps to ally with the Southern nation as the section's leaders hoped and encouraged by withholding shipments of cotton to England and France, creating shortages that would be sure to get the Confederacy's power noticed in Europe. The plan backfired: Europe had plenty of cotton in storage as well as a bumper crop coming in from Egypt. Had that not been the case the South might have succeeded in driving cotton prices high enough to finance the purchase of overwhelming supplies of war matériel. As it turned out, by the time the Confederacy had raised the money to make such purchases, a Northern blockade was in place that kept most ships from getting through.

But the South's dreams of victory rested largely on other factors. For starters, the Confederacy would be fighting on the strategic defense, a far easier sort of war to conduct than one of conquest, and had what were believed to be superior military forces. Many U.S. career officers who were Southerners would resign their commissions to command Confederate troops. Moreover, whereas the North was divided over the central issue of slavery, the South was far more united in favor of the institution, affording hope that the border slave states would join in the secession along with sympathetic portions of the West. For his part, Lincoln knew to the contrary that not only was the Northern population greater but its economy was more self-sustaining and stronger in industrial production, meaning its armies would be larger, stronger, and better supplied to boot. There were a few other points the Confederates had not considered. For example, while it was true that Europe needed Southern cotton, depending on harvests around the world it might need Northern wheat even more. In addition, many Europeans could not stomach the idea of slavery, opening the way for Lincoln to draw popular backing for the Union and its ideals.

In hindsight it would appear to many that the Confederacy never had a prayer of winning a war against the North, but it did not seem that way at the time. Indeed, had just one or two things gone differently in three or four battles the North might have been obliged to sue for peace, in which case Lincoln today would be regarded as a bungling usurper rather than as one of the greatest figures in history. But he seemed destined to fill the bill a prescient John Quincy Adams had outlined in his diary entry for February 24, 1820: "Slavery is the great and foul stain upon the North American Union, and it is a contemplation worthy of the most exalted soul whether its total abolition is or is not practicable."

Not that even the most exalted soul imaginable would have an easy time of it. President Lincoln's vacillations on the subject early in his term encouraged his opponents, some of whom were members of his own cabinet and whose insubordination would plague the rest of his administration. Secretary of State William Seward, Secretary of the Treasury Salmon Chase, and Secretary of War Simon Cameron, for example, had all vied for the Republican nomination and each still thought himself better suited to the presidency than Lincoln. Their arguments seem laughable now, but only in retrospect is Lincoln's genius fully apparent. Lincoln created a cabinet according to individual merits and talent, even its members were rivals. His reasoning was that it is better to have one's critics and rivals inside your house where you can watch them rather than having them outside throwing stones.

The moment of truth came soon enough. Early in Lincoln's administration the federal garrison at Fort Sumter was running so short of supplies it demanded either restocking or abandonment. Commanding General Winfield Scott favored withdrawal, and Lincoln considered such a move acceptable if it would encourage the loyalty of the border states. But anti-Confederate sentiment was growing in the North, where withdrawal might be taken as a sign of weakness, so Lincoln decided to relieve and reinforce Fort Sumter. The Confederate authorities in Charleston regarded this as an act of war and fired on the fort on April 12, 1861. The next day the Union garrison lowered its flag and surrendered; the implacable war between the states had begun, and the Union could claim that the South had struck the first blow. The Confederates allowed the soldiers to leave the port on unarmed ships while the citizens of Charleston celebrated wildly in the streets.

President Lincoln proclaimed that "combinations too powerful to be suppressed by the ordinary course of judicial proceedings" had violated the laws of the United States. He therefore called upon the states to put forth a militia of 75,000 men for three months' service—a modest request that betrayed the Union's hopes for a short war—and asked for a special session of Congress to meet on the symbolic date of July 4. Despite the diligence of able politicians in the 1840s and 1850s to avert a split of the Union, slavery proved to be an issue that could not be compromised.

Shortly thereafter the border states found themselves obliged to choose sides. Virginia, Arkansas, North Carolina, and Tennessee joined the Confederacy when Lincoln's call for troops signaled an impending invasion. The Confederate capital was moved from Montgomery to Richmond, and several noted Virginia generals including Robert E. Lee, Thomas J. Jackson, and Joseph E. Johnston joined the South's cause. But the farmers and mountaineers in the

The power of an emotional moment still stirs in Thomas Nast's painting, *Departure of the Seventh Regiment for the War, April 19, 1861*. This scene is in New York City, but the same excitement surrounded departures throughout the North and South, as America prepared go to battle in the Civil War. Many of the men in Nast's painting were killed in the Confederate victory at Bull Run.

western part of the state, where slavery was little practiced, opposed secession from the Union and were eventually organized into West Virginia as a federal war measure. Although neighboring Kentucky was by contrast largely pro-South, Lincoln kept it loyal to the Union by stating that the war was not being fought to free slaves and by promising not to invade—unlike the small force of Confederate troops whose minor incursion into the area had rattled its population. A few months later, however, a large portion of the Kentucky militia joined the Confederate forces, a split that was echoed in Missouri, which for the next four years was wracked by its own internal civil war. Among the border states only Delaware allied firmly with the Union. (Maryland, another

slave-holding border state, did not secede because Lincoln sent in troops in order to protect Washington, D.C.) For the most part there was no clear line demarcating loyalties in the American Civil War but rather a jagged division ripping through states, through counties, and even through families.

The Civil War Begins

On April 17, Confederate President Davis authorized privateers to seize Union ships. Two days later U.S. President Lincoln ordered a blockade of Southern ports from the Carolinas to Texas, thus recognizing the existence of the Confederacy and the state of belligerence with it in fact, if not in theory. On May 13 Britain proclaimed its neutrality in the American conflict but recognized the Confederate States of America as a separate belligerent power; Lincoln interpreted this as a hostile act, even though in essence he agreed with the rationale of the English. It would not be long before Lincoln's hopes for a short war and easy reconciliation were dashed. In July, General Irvin McDowell marched toward Richmond at the head of a hastily trained force of 30,000 Union soldiers hoping to attack and defeat a numerically inferior Confederate force commanded by the dashing General Pierre G. T. Beauregard, but a second Southern army led by General Joseph Johnston outmaneuvered McDowell and on July 21 made a stand at Bull Run a few miles from Manassas Junction. Washington politicians and officials turned out in holiday spirit to watch the battle, which ended quickly in a rout of the North. Although the Confederate commanders had made one or two tactical blunders, they had also demonstrated skill and ingenuity, particularly General Thomas J. "Stonewall" Jackson. The South rejoiced when the ragged Union forces limped home in shock at their first major disaster on the battlefield. While the North worried that Washington D.C. might soon be taken by Stonewall Jackson, some jubilant Confederates knew victory at Bull Run would be short-lived. "The vast preparation of the enemy," wrote one Confederate soldier, had created a feeling of pragmatic "despondency" among Southerners. Both sides regrouped after Bull Run and prepared for a long and truculent conflict.

General Pierre G. T. Beauregard, above, was the South's first military hero, commanding the opening shots fired on Fort Sumter and capturing the victory with gentlemanly dispatch. A Louisianan of Creole background, he had trained at West Point and remained a student of military engineering. After leaving Fort Sumter in Confederate hands, he reported north to direct defenses in Manassas, Virginia, where Confederate forces were collected. At first they were positioned on a plateau overlooking the town and its rail yards. Upon arriving, Beauregard ordered them moved. He had correctly recognized the natural strength of a high ground along a creek called Bull Run, which would be the site of the first major battle of the war.

CHAPTER 9

THE CIVIL WAR

Virtually no one on either side foresaw just how long the American Civil War would go on and just how horrendous it would be. Not that the realization would likely have changed any thing; the defeat at Bull Run may have dispirited the Union and dashed its hopes for a quick victory, but rather than making Lincoln reconsider, the fiasco only hardened his resolve. The president demoted Irvin McDowell and named thirty-four-year-old George B. McClellan, a West Point graduate who had been working as a railroad executive before the war, to replace the retiring Winfield Scott, as general in chief of the Union armies in November 1861. Enthusiastic, ambitious, and smart enough to recognize that his hastily assembled forces were ill prepared for combat, McClellan immediately withdrew from any imminent attack and concentrated on training his troops. Congress authorized the military to swell to 500,000 men, some 100,000 of whom joined McClellan's new Army of the Potomac.

Lincoln trusted his meticulous and methodical new commander and at first accepted his arguments for a pause in the fighting. But in time the diminutive young general would take on Napoleonic airs, convinced that he was destined to be the future leader of the Union. McClellan continued to win

W. W. Chaloner's *Cavalry Charge at Yellow Tavern, May 11, 1864*, left, captures the bravery of horse soldiers in the Civil War. This battle turned into a desperate shoving match as J. E. B. Stuart's Confederate corps blocked the route to Richmond against Union troops under General Philip Sheridan. When Stuart was mortally wounded, the South lost one of its foremost military leaders. Shown above is ammunition as the soldiers received it.

The cartoon, below left, depicts General George B. McClellan as "the youthful Napoleon." Named general in chief in 1861 when he just thirty-four, McClellan made a good initial impression by whipping a disorganized Union army into superb fighting shape. Yet McClellan was a disappointment, letting his great army stagnate over long periods of time. Other commanders proved to be even worse until Lincoln finally discovered Ulysses S. Grant, shown in an undated photograph by Mathew Brady, below right. Tough and realistic, Grant had few illusions about war; he just wanted to win. Named general in chief in March of 1864, Grant led a cadre of other aggressive, no-nonsense officers such as William T. Sherman, Philip Sheridan, and George Thomas. *Farragut's Fleet Passing Through the Forts Below New Orleans,* opposite top, was painted by Mauritz F. H. Dehaas in 1867. It shows the most decisive naval operation of the war: the April 1862 capture of the South's leading port. Even as Admiral David Farragut's Union ships anchored outside the city, the mayor of New Orleans was trying to quell panic by means of the handbill, opposite bottom.

widespread praise even when he proved no Napoleon; what no one recognized at the time was that he was much too cautious and loath to attack unless pressed into it. Lincoln's general in chief in fact became known for sending the president the same report nearly every week: "All quiet along the Potomac."

Such was not the case with many of the Union generals. A hard-drinking, cigar-chewing, brigadier general—thirty-nine-year-old West Point graduate Ulysses S. Grant, who had been working as a shop clerk in Galena, Illinois, when the war broke out—was put in command of a large base in Cairo, Illinois, whence he was ordered to mount an attack on the South. Early in 1862 Grant moved south with Flag Officer Andrew Foote's gunboat flotilla, their object being to divide the Confederacy in two and conquer it from there. From the very beginning the fighting went well for the Northern troops, who captured both Fort Henry and Fort Donelson on the Tennessee and Cumberland Rivers respectively. After three days of bombardment on Donelson, Grant demonstrated what would become his legendary mettle when he received a message from the fort's Confederate commander asking for an armistice. Grant replied, "No terms except an unconditional and immediate surrender can be accepted. I propose to move immediately upon your works." Thus the Union general acquired the nickname "Unconditional Surrender Grant," and quickly proved it apt. After taking the forts he pursued the withdrawing Confederate forces, and in April encountered and devastated them in a bloody battle near a meetinghouse called Shiloh Church in Pittsburg Landing, Tennessee, that finally repulsed the Southerners.

The battle claimed 25,000 dead or wounded between both sides—more casualties than had resulted from the Revolution, the War of 1812, and the

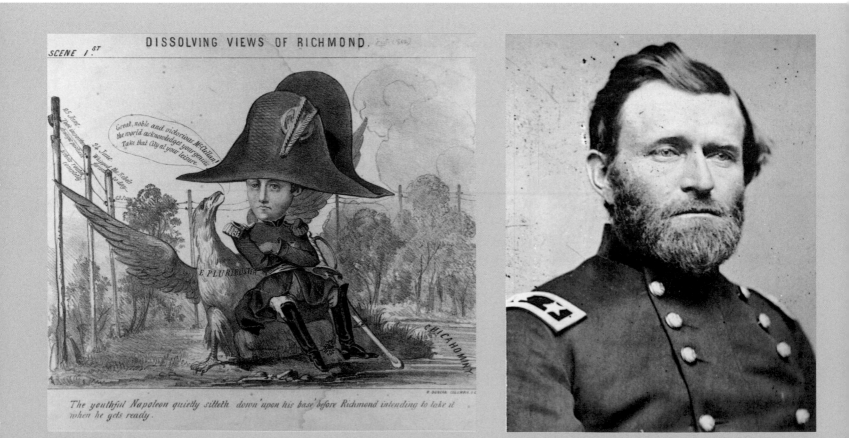

DISSOLVING VIEWS OF RICHMOND.

SCENE 1ST

Great, noble and victorious McClellan! the world acknowledges your genius. Take that City at your leisure.

E PLURIBUSTER

CHICAHOMINY

The youthful Napoleon quietly sitteth down upon his base before Richmond intending to take it when he gets ready.

Mexican War combined. The improved accuracy of modern rifles, along with the rudimentary medical knowledge of the time made the Civil War the most destructive in world history up to that time. Union soldier Oliver Wendell Holmes (later Supreme Court Justice) spoke for many when he wondered whether the "butcher's bill" was worth it. Despite the Union's victory, some charged that the North's losses would have been far smaller had the general not committed a series of slipups that critics ascribed to his drinking. When told of this, Lincoln said simply, "I can't spare this man; he fights." By the late spring the Union victories in the West under Grant's command nearly compensated for the lack of action in the East. As one perhaps apocryphal anecdote has it, Lincoln exclaimed, "If I knew what brand of whiskey he drinks, I would send a barrel or so to my other generals."

There was no need of such liquid inspiration in the Union's naval forces, which had been charged with cutting the Confederacy's overseas supply lines. By the spring of 1862 the U.S. Navy had established several strategically positioned bases in the South despite starting with only forty-two ships to blockade more than 3,500 miles of coastline. At the same time, the navy began running powerful new river gunboats, also with the goal of disrupting the enemy's commerce. The most important Union naval victory took place in April, when Flag Officer David G. Farragut—in the same spirit that two years later would have him command his crew to "Damn the torpedoes; full speed ahead!"—threaded his flotilla through shore-based Confederate cannon fire

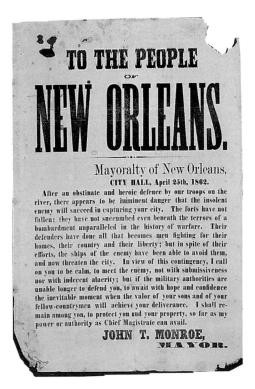

TO THE PEOPLE OF NEW ORLEANS.

Mayoralty of New Orleans,
CITY HALL, April 25th, 1862.

After an obstinate and heroic defence by our troops on the river, there appears to be imminent danger that the insolent enemy will succeed in capturing your city. The forts have not fallen; they have not succumbed even beneath the terrors of a bombardment unparalleled in the history of warfare. Their defenders have done all that becomes men fighting for their homes, their country and their liberty; but in spite of their efforts, the ships of the enemy have been able to avoid them, and now threaten the city. In view of this contingency, I call on you to be calm, to meet the enemy, not with submissiveness nor with indecent alacrity; but if the military authorities are unable longer to defend you, to await with hope and confidence the inevitable moment when the valor of your sons and of your fellow-countrymen will achieve your deliverance. I shall remain among you, to protect you and your property, so far as my power or authority as Chief Magistrate can avail.

JOHN T. MONROE,
MAYOR.

and took New Orleans, the South's largest city and busiest port. In June, Union forces would claim Memphis, another major trade center on the Mississippi. The ensuing transatlantic and river blockades crippled Southern trade and with it the section's overall economy, which was exactly what the Union intended.

Given the contrast with the dynamic successes of Farragut and Grant, before long Lincoln grew frustrated with McClellan's dilatory approach—at one point remarking, "If McClellan is not using the army I should like to borrow it"—and ordered him to mount an attack at once. The general got the message and moved south with 130,000 troops on what came to be called the Peninsular Campaign, which got within five miles of Richmond, Virginia, before the advance was halted by a brilliant attack under a new Southern army commander, Robert E. Lee, that forced McClellan into a hasty retreat.

By this point Lincoln had had enough and replaced his ineffectual general in chief with Henry Halleck, who combined three small Union forces and put them under the command of another pompous and baffled general, John Pope. This new Northern army clashed with the Confederate forces of Thomas J. "Stonewall" Jackson and Lee in late August at the Second Battle of Bull Run—and was soundly defeated by them. The daring, romantic Confederate cavalry leader J. E. B. Stuart particularly distinguished himself in the engagement by raiding Pope's headquarters and absconding with his fancy dress uniform. Even without such cheekiness the Jackson-Lee combination would have been formidable; the former was almost pathologically dedicated, and the latter a strategic genius. As one of his colleagues remarked of the well-born Virginian who would bedevil the Union despite the shortcomings of his own armies, Robert E. Lee would "take more chances, and take them quicker than any other general in this country." Lincoln responded to the challenge Lee posed by recalling McClellan to command the Army of the Potomac to defend the U.S. capital of Washington, D.C., just a hundred miles from the Confederate capital at Richmond.

On September 17, 1862, however, the Union enjoyed a triumph over Lee in the Battle of Antietam on the most gruesome day of the entire war; the day-long clash near Sharpsburg, Maryland, ended with more than 12,000 Federal and 11,000 Confederate casualties in the cornfields, the woodlots, and the dirt road known as "bloody lane." As one Union soldier said: "No tongue can tell, no mind conceive, no pen portray the horrible sights I witnessed this morning." Lee, however, escaped across the Potomac and, true to form, McClellan refused to pursue him promptly, whereupon Lincoln replaced him yet again, this time with General Ambrose E. Burnside, a handsome but incompetent officer best remembered for his bushy side whiskers, which forever after would be known as "sideburns." Burnside marched south at the head of a massive force to meet Lee and his Army of Northern Virginia at Fredericksburg on December 13. Despite its overwhelming superiority in numbers, Burnside's army was decimated—just as the Union's situation was deteriorating in the West, where the Confederates outmaneuvered and outfought the Army of the Cumberland at the Battle of Murfreesboro in central Tennessee. As the formidable Lee watched the Union assault of Fredericksburg fail from his position, he commented to General James Longstreet: "It is well that war is so terrible, or

we should grow too fond of it." Confederate General Jeb Stuart echoed this sentiment as he surveyed the carnage at Fredericksburg as the entire town smoldered in a cold white fog. It was, he said, "the saddest sight I ever saw."

The Moral War

By the end of 1862 the war had taken on a moral dimension missing at its start. Like virtually every military conflict in all of world history, the American Civil War had economic issues at its heart, but since those issues were inextricably bound with the institution of human bondage in one half of the country, the conflict had to become deeply ideological. As the poet and philosopher Ralph Waldo Emerson had warned in an 1841 essay: "If you put a chain around the neck of a slave, the other end fastens around your own." How true that would prove for the South, as would Emerson's musing in a speech five years later that "I think we must get rid of slavery or we must get rid of freedom."

Of course, Emerson was a man notoriously ahead of his time, and it took a while for most Americans to come around to his way of thinking. In fact, as late as 1860 few Northerners advocated the actual abolition of slavery, including Abraham Lincoln. As black leader Frederick Douglass—who would later appropriate Emerson's line about slavery's reciprocal chains—observed at the time: "Mr. Lincoln proposes no measure which can bring him into antagonistic collision with the traffickers in human flesh."

The truth was that in the beginning Lincoln thought very much as a man of his time. Soon after he called for volunteers in the spring of 1861, for example, the hundreds of free blacks who tried to enlist in the Union armies

Fallen Confederate soldiers lie along the Hagerstown Pike in the photograph above, taken after the Battle of Antietam, September 17, 1862. It was the most vicious single day of fighting in the war: two determined armies colliding on a relatively small patch of farmland in the hills of western Maryland. The Union Army, still holding the advantage at the end of the day, was sorely criticized for failing to press forward. However, the stubborn fighting of soldiers like those above had exhausted the aggression of both sides.

From his first speech in 1841 until his death in 1895, Frederick Douglass, above, lent an eloquent voice to the debate over African-American rights. During the Civil War he was adamant that blacks should serve in the armed forces, both for their own sake and for the sake of a Northern victory. General Benjamin Butler, below, a former state legislator from Massachusetts, extended the protection of the Northern army to Southern blacks by calling them "contraband of war." Although this policy succeeded because it treated people as "property," it released many slaves from bondage and gave them the freedom to fight or work.

were turned away as a matter of policy. The policy did not hold for all branches of the military out of cold necessity; a shortage of sailors forced the Navy Department to enlist blacks, and not just a few: by the end of the war in 1865, one of every four Union sailors was black. But the army was a different matter. The forward-thinking Frémont tried to liberate slaves so they could become soldiers in the district under his command, but his attempt was rebuffed by the administration. General William Tecumseh Sherman, however, was authorized to "employ fugitive slaves in such services as they may be fitted for." Sherman took advantage of the offer, using the men as laborers. General David Hunter used escaped slaves as soldiers, forming the all-black 1st South Carolina Volunteer Regiment in the late spring of 1862 and declaring free all slaves in Florida, Georgia, and South Carolina. Lincoln quickly overruled Hunter and his black regiment was disbanded. Out of Hunter's effort, however, grew the first black regiment officially allowed into the U.S. Army. It was commanded by the unflappable Thomas Wentworth Higginson: Unitarian ministry abolitionist, promoter of John Brown, and close friend of Emily Dickinson.

It would take a general who was far better at politics than military matters—Benjamin Butler of Massachusetts—to come up with a solution to the problem of freeing slaves to fight. Because slaves were considered "property," Butler ingeniously reasoned, they could be confiscated from conquered territories as "contraband of war." Thus as the Union's military governor in New Orleans, Butler hired some captured slaves as teamsters and organized others into three battalions of Louisiana Guards, which so scandalized Southerners that some took their protest all the way to President Lincoln himself.

By then, however, Lincoln had become disinclined to keep excluding blacks from the Union armies for two purely pragmatic reasons: the shortage of troops and the burgeoning support for emancipating the slaves. And Lincoln was nothing if not practical, as he had indicated in his summer 1862 letter to Horace Greeley, pledging either to free the slaves or guarantee their continued captivity, whichever would be likeliest to save the Union. "I shall do less whenever I shall believe what I am doing hurts the cause," Lincoln had written, "and I shall do more whenever I shall believe doing more will help the cause. I shall adopt new views as fast as they shall appear to be true views." As it turned out, this attitude made Lincoln exactly the right man at the right time to lead the United States; as he had once admitted, his positions were determined by events, and events were moving in the direction of emancipation.

And quickly, too. On April 16, 1862, Congress had passed a bill ending slavery in the District of Columbia. Lincoln approved the measure and went even further by abolishing slavery in the territories on June 19 and a month later declaring that all slaves who had fled Confederate masters into Union-held territory were officially free. The reasoning behind his actions was completely in character, more shrewd than high-minded: Lincoln was directing the Union so as to win favor in Europe, which he considered more important than sowing fear of slave rebellions in the South, and of far greater significance than the moral questions about slavery. The president clearly had not reached the Emerson level of enlightenment; upon liberating the slaves Lincoln thought it might be best to relocate them, perhaps to the Caribbean.

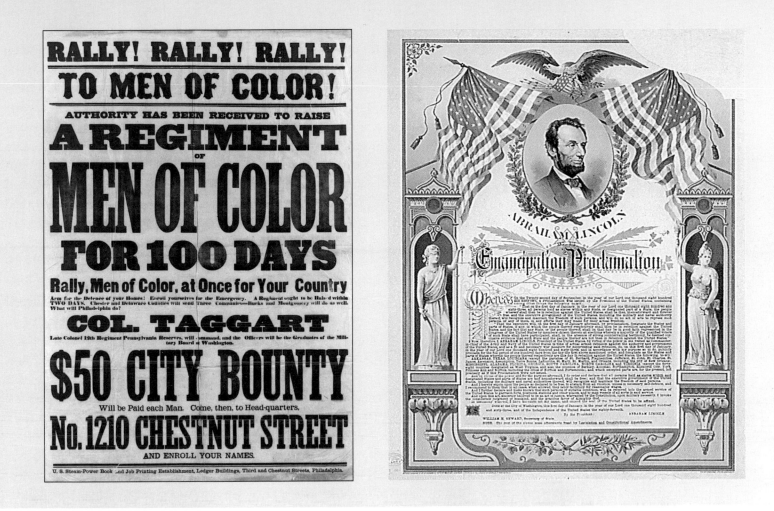

On July 17, Congress authorized the acceptance of blacks into the Union Army as well as the Navy and soon after passed a measure freeing all slaves in those areas of the South invaded by Northern armies owned by "rebels," as supporters of the Confederacy had come to be called in the North. Before the end of the year several black army regiments were organized and acquitted themselves well in battle; by the end of the war nearly 180,000 troops would serve in the Union's 166 all-black infantry units, many of them slaves who had escaped to the North in order to join up. African-American soldiers performed superbly in such Civil War battles as Overton Hill and Chafin's Farm in Virginia; Honey Hill, South Carolina; Nashville, Tennessee; and the brave but bloody debacle at the Crater near Petersburg, Virginia.

Politics and public opinion demanded that, to keep it from looking like an act of desperation, the next step toward abolition be held back until another major Union success. That victory came in mid-September at western Maryland's Antietam Creek, a triumph Lincoln capped five days later with the Emancipation Proclamation—in truth a rather cautious document that freed slaves only in areas in rebellion against the federal government. The Proclamation was delivered shortly after Antietam largely as a morale booster: a little over a year after the First Bull Run, many were questioning the rationale for war. By turning the war into a moral crusade—ending slavery—Lincoln was providing his Union soldiers with a compelling reason to fight. The Emancipation Proclamation was really a hollow document. The decree did not take

The call to arms issued in Philadelphia, above left, appealed to "men of color" to fight in the Union Army. After the Emancipation Proclamation took effect in 1863, Lincoln consented to the raising of Negro regiments and by the end of the war the Northern forces had been augmented by nearly 180,000 black soldiers. The elaborate copy of the Emancipation Proclamation, above right, was printed as a poster for the wall of a home or school. Announced in September 1862 but not effective until January 1, 1863, the Proclamation was carefully constructed to entice Confederate states to return to the Union, yet not to antagonize border states. The document did not free all slaves, just those in states still in rebellion. It did not induce any Confederate states to change their allegiance, but by the end of the war Lincoln's words applied to a region and spoke at long last for the whole nation: "all persons held as slaves . . . henceforward shall be free."

A Union volunteer posed for the photograph above decked out in his uniform. Inexperienced soldiers on both sides of the conflict rapidly lost their idealism on the battlefield. Edmund Patterson of the Ninth Alabama Infantry had been a book salesman in May 1861; in July he was in uniform on the banks of Bull Run in Virginia. "It looks as if someone is to be hurt, by their issuing ammunition to the men," he wrote a few days before the battle. "These are the first 'Cartridges' that I have ever seen, and is it possible that we actually [are] to kill men? Human beings? That these cartridges were made purposely for one poor mortal to shoot at another?"

effect until January 1, 1863, so it would be null and void in the event the war had ended by then. Still worse, despite its exalted reputation in history, in practical terms Lincoln's proclamation in and of itself didn't free a single slave. Not only was it of dubious legality as a war measure, but the proclamation did not cover slaves in the Union, the border states, or those parts of the Confederacy under Union control—only those in the South, which no longer recognized U.S. laws. In fact, after issuing it the president continued to offer slaveholders compensation for their chattel and to reiterate his support for the notion that freed blacks would best be resettled outside the United States. Still, despite its flaws, abolitionist William Lloyd Garrison, who once compared Lincoln to a "wet rag," lauded the Proclamation as an "act of immense historical consequence."

Not all Northerners were as progressive as Garrison when it came to emancipation. As guarded in tone and limited in scope as it was, the Emancipation Proclamation sent a wave of fear rippling through the North. Like some similarly hypocritical civil rights "supporters" a century later, even those who advocated the abolition of slavery certainly didn't want any hordes of newly freed blacks parading into their neighborhoods and settling there. Lincoln himself repeated yet again his grotesque notion of sending the freedmen to colonies in the islands and even suggested that the Northern states could enact legislation to prevent blacks from moving in; as he put it, "Cannot the North decide for itself whether to receive them?"

The president's own home state could, apparently. Illinois passed a law to exclude black settlers and debated a measure to enforce it by way of thirty-nine lashes on the back of any who crossed the state line. The political wrangling inspired anti-black violence to erupt in Chicago and spread to Peoria and beyond to Toledo, Cincinnati, Philadelphia, New York, Boston, and nearly every other large city in the North and Midwest. The situation deteriorated to the point that Indiana and Ohio stationed guards at their borders to keep blacks out.

The war on the ground continued to go badly for the North; the Union armies had proven unable to so much as contain the Confederate forces, much less defeat them. All these stewing troubles boiled over in December 1862, when Lincoln had difficulty putting down a revolt by Republican Senators over members of his own cabinet. Enlistments in the military had fallen off to the point that the government had to resort to a draft. (The Confederacy had been obliged to resort to the draft even earlier than the North.) Of course, some civilians were apparently more equal than others: in 1863, all men between the ages of twenty and forty-five were subject to be summoned to service, but would-be draftees with the means could get out of it by hiring a substitute or simply paying the government $300. Among the 776,000 men called up by the Union draft, 314,000 received exemptions for physical disabilities; 74,000 paid mercenaries to take their places; 87,000 coughed up the $300 commutation fee; and 161,000 simply refused to show up. Only 46,000 men actually reported to serve their country.

The draft faced strong opposition throughout the North in part because it allowed the rich to stay safe at home while the poor had to go off and fight for a cause that happened to include the middle and upper classes' economic interests. More important, those who were conscripted generally were not too keen on risking their lives to emancipate a bunch of slaves—not that many of the Union volunteers were either. Opposition to the combination of the draft laws and the Emancipation Proclamation built up and spilled over into both violence and pacifism throughout the North.

Those who opposed the war or supported the South, called "copperheads"—poisonous snakes eager to strike at the Union—came together and grew strong under the nominal leadership of Clement L. Vallandigham, a former Ohio congressman who upon losing his seat in 1862 had joined the "Order of American Knights"—the sort of group that had been prohibited by the 1798 Sedition Act—whose members opposed the Civil War and sought peace with the Confederacy. Vallandigham was arrested for treason and opposing the Union war effort on May 5, 1863, which fired a storm of protest from antiwar Democrats that raged even fiercer when he was tried in a court-martial rather than a civil proceeding. Many shouted that Lincoln had assumed dictatorial powers even before this outrage—and it was true that the president had subjected others to equally arbitrary arrests, suspended habeas corpus (the law safeguarding individuals from illegal detention), and harassed and even closed down newspapers that criticized his administration. A growing number of Northern Democrats and others who opposed the Emancipation Proclamation and the draft charged that Lincoln was not sav-

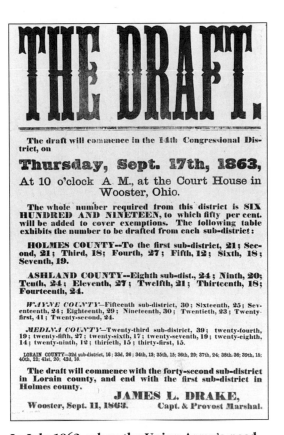

In July 1862, when the Union Army's need for soldiers outpaced the number of incoming volunteers, Congress passed the Militia Act requiring the states to provide militia for federal service. The following year, the federal government still found itself in need of soldiers, so Congress instituted the draft (as evident on the poster above). In the meantime, however, the draft remained an issue and almost incited a second civil war among Northerners. Pacifists, anti-Lincoln activists, certain industrialists, and many others opposed to the war rallied together against the Union effort. In politics, the antiwar sentiment turned openly seditious. The 1863 cartoon at left depicts leading "peace Democrats" of the North as copperheads (a variety of snake indigenous to the South) set to strike the Union. In many towns across the North organized militias even ambushed Union soldiers on leave.

Police fire on a mob protesting the draft in New York City in the undated woodcut above. The controversial draft, initiated in 1863, drew protests in many cities across the North, but in New York the tension exploded in draft riots that started on July 13 and lasted for three more days. Agitated by misguided politicians, low-wage workers burned buildings and looted stores as large parts of the city fell completely out of control. The riots took a far more disturbing turn, however, when dozens of uniformed soldiers and African-American civilians were beaten in the streets. In several cases, innocent blacks were killed by the mobs. To quell the rioting, army troops soon arrived from Gettysburg, where they'd been in a far larger battle only twelve days before.

ing the Union but destroying the freedoms Americans had been promised in the Bill of Rights—and they had a point.

These controversies drew to a head in New York, the center of Democratic opposition to the war. That spring a large contingent of the port city's longshoremen had gone on strike and been replaced by newly freed blacks; early in July many of the consequently unemployed white men were drafted into the Union armies. In their view the president was asking them to risk life and limb for the very men who had taken their jobs, a perception that sparked already existing racial prejudices to break out into four days of violent anti-draft riots that left 119 dead, most of whom were white. At this point it looked not only as if the North's hoped-for slave revolts would fail to materialize but that the South's dreams of Northern class warfare would.

The War Drags On

For all his failings and excesses—and both were considerable—Lincoln proved up to the task he had set for himself. Six months earlier, in January 1863, he had replaced the disappointing Burnside with General "Fighting Joe" Hooker.

A serious military man, at one point Hooker had opined that the nation needed a dictator, and it was in a letter to him that Lincoln made his view known: "Only those generals who gain successes can set up dictators. What I now ask of you is military success, and I will risk the dictatorship."

Hooker responded as Lincoln intended and marched south at the head of a Union army some 130,000 strong, only to be outwitted by Robert E. Lee's tactics on May 1–5 at Chancellorsville, Virginia. In a battle during which Stonewall Jackson was accidentally mortally wounded by his own soldiers from a North Carolina regiment, Lee mauled Hooker. A grievous Lee, devastated that he lost his best general, headed north to Pennsylvania, while Hooker, who had actually comported himself rather well, fell to quarreling with General in Chief Henry Halleck and was soon replaced by George G. Meade. On July 1, Meade and Lee went at it on the fields of Gettysburg, Pennsylvania, for three days that ended in a Union victory on the fortuitous

The Battle of Gettysburg was portrayed by Paul Philippoteaux in a cyclorama, or circular painting, one detail of which is shown below. General Robert E. Lee's Confederate army was deep in Union territory on the first day of July 1863, when it met the Union Army under George Meade for three days of ferocious fighting. The South largely dominated the first two days of the battle, but failed in its attempts to secure a victory on the third day. Lee retreated with his army to Virginia. Many people have wondered if the presence of Stonewall Jackson, so often successful against Union forces, might have led to a different result for Lee at Gettysburg.

Four score and seven years ago our fathers brought forth, upon this continent, a new nation, conceived in Liberty, and dedicated to the proposition that all men are created equal.

Now we are engaged in a great civil war, testing whether that nation, or any nation, so conceived, and so dedicated, can long endure. We are met here on a great battlefield of that war. We have come to dedicate a portion of it as the final resting place of those who here gave their lives that that nation might live. It is altogether fitting and proper that we should do this.

But in a larger sense we can not dedicate—we can not consecrate—we can not hallow this ground. The brave men, living and dead, who struggled here, have consecrated it far above our poor power to add or detract. The world will little note, nor long remember, what we say here, but can never forget what they did here. It is for us, the living, rather to be dedicated here to the unfinished work which they have, thus far, so nobly carried on. It is rather

for us to be here dedicated to the great task remaining before us—that from these honored dead we take increased devotion to that cause for which they here gave the last full measure of devotion—that we here highly resolve that these dead shall not have died in vain; that this nation shall have a new birth of freedom, and that this government of the people, by the people, for the people, shall not perish from the earth.

President Lincoln's final version of the Gettysburg Address, left, was written in his own hand. Lincoln began the speech with the now famous line: "Four score and seven years ago our fathers brought forth, on this continent, a new nation, conceived in liberty and dedicated to the proposition that all men are created equal." Presented at the scene of a battle more horrific than others only in its sheer scope, the message from Lincoln hoped to raise the struggle to a cause worthy of such carnage: democracy. He reiterated the Constitution in a way that made it as much a nineteenth-century document as an eighteenth-century one. In doing so, he gave Americans a loyalty to something even more important than their country itself, and that was to its form of "government of the people, by the people, for the people."

date of July 4. Lee was forced to withdraw, having suffered almost 4,000 killed and approximately 24,000 missing and wounded. Federal losses were just as daunting. Reporting to Jefferson Davis on Gettysburg, Lee offered his resignation; Davis refused. But Meade did not pursue Lee, which set Lincoln to looking for yet another new commander for the Army of the Potomac. Lincoln wanted a general capable of delivering a death blow.

Lincoln would find his man in the unlikely form of the rough-edged Ulysses S. Grant, who had been claiming victory after victory in the West. "Vicksburg is the key," Lincoln had instructed Admiral David Porter regarding the Mississippi port city that commanded the great river from its majestic bluffs. "Let us get Vicksburg, and all that country is ours. The war can never be brought to a close until that key is in our pocket." The indomitable Grant went after the strategic prize with a series of operations that had begun in December 1862. After several attempts to capture the city from the river and another by cutting a channel to allow gunboats to traverse the river beyond the range of Confederate artillery, Vicksburg remained impregnable. Determined to capture the Confederate stronghold, Grant decided the only way to take the city was by siege, which the general and his troops did. The tenacious citizens of Vicksburg took refuge in caves dug into the hillsides, where they suffered from the sweltering heat, inadequate provisions, and constant bombardment. Finally, on July 4, 1863—the same day that marked Meade's victory at Gettysburg—the six-week siege ended. Grant had succeeded in severing Texas, Arkansas, and Louisiana from the Confederacy, putting the vital Mississippi River transportation corridor in Northern hands. "The Confederacy, after Gettysburg and Vicksburg, never regained the military initiative," historian Stephen E. Ambrose would write in *Americans at War* (1997). "From hindsight, perhaps, the final outcome . . . was now inevitable." The capture of Vicksburg was a classic strategy that made Robert E. Lee nervous. Grant's next objective was no less than the destruction of the Confederacy's east-west transportation and communications systems, a goal he planned to achieve by taking the railhead

OPPOSITE PAGE: Stonewall Jackson is shown with General Lee in *The Last Meeting of Lee and Jackson* by Everett B. D. Julio, finished after Jackson had died of wounds received at Chancellorsville in May 1863. "Could I have directed events," General Lee had written to Jackson a few days before his friend's death, "I should have chosen, for the good of the country, to have been disabled in your stead." After Gettysburg, General Lee would extend the war through brilliant maneuvers, but they were nearly always defensive in nature.

at Chattanooga, Tennessee, a major distribution point for the South's war matériel and other supplies. Union General William Rosecrans had already captured the city, but when he moved south to a creek in Georgia called Chickamauga, he was outsmarted and his forces outfought by those of the Confederate commander Braxton Bragg. But when Grant arrived in October it was with additional troops and command of all the western armies.

By the time Grant launched his attack it was supported by something else as well: dwindling public antiwar sentiment and growing patriotism inspired by Lincoln's majestic Gettysburg Address of November 19—a mere 270 breathtakingly poetic words dedicating the Pennsylvania battlefield to those who had fought and died on it that still ring with a brighter clarity than can be found in any other expression of America's purpose since the Declaration of Independence. Lincoln's point, often repeated but never quite so well, was to convince the public that the Union was fighting for the very principles upon which America had been founded. Southerners, of course, believed that self-determination included the right to choose their own government.

While the president tended to public opinion and national purpose, Grant in Chattanooga summoned Hooker and William Tecumseh Sherman and their armies, and on November 25 they drove off the Confederate forces. The same general who had spent his summer cleaving the Confederacy from north to south had now done the same from east to west, thus proving himself the military leader Lincoln had been seeking since he took office. Although it would become clear that Grant was matched by Lee in terms of audacity and sheer brilliance, he enjoyed the considerable advantage of understanding that with the overwhelming forces at his command neither was needed, a point his predecessors had failed to grasp and that had led to their downfalls. Unlike them, Grant kept his strategy simple, something now possible due to waning Confederate resources.

In March 1864 Lincoln summoned Grant to Washington to take command of all the Union armies. Halleck was demoted to serve in a central staff role, while Sherman was promoted into Grant's old position at the head of the western forces and Meade was kept on as a nominal commander of the Army of the Potomac. The shuffling of personnel ushered the war into a new and more costly phase.

On May 4, Grant crossed Virginia's Rapidan River to meet Lee's 60,000 veterans with a Union army of more than 120,000 well-trained and fully equipped troops. Meade's Army of the Potomac headed into an area known as the Wilderness; there Lee attacked, and for two days the opposing armies slugged it out, both suffering heavy casualties. Grant then pressed ten miles southeast to another bloody battle near Spotsylvania. The Northern forces continued advancing south until they were just ten miles outside Richmond at Cold Harbor, where Grant sent waves of troops against the Confederates but they were slaughtered by Lee's army. The Southern commander appeared to have outmaneuvered his Northern counterpart, who had lost 60,000 troops in just one month—but who had the manpower to keep pushing ahead and in the process laid waste to most of the Army of Northern Virginia.

In the West, meanwhile, William Tecumseh Sherman—his middle name a tribute to the turn-of-the-century Shawnee Indian chief who had tried to unite the West's native tribes—and his 100,000-strong Armies of Ohio, Cumberland, and Tennessee marched from Chattanooga to Atlanta to take on the 60,000 men commanded by Confederate General Joseph Johnston, whose résumé included the victory in the first Battle of Bull Run as well as the defeat at Vicksburg. Johnston's troops proved no match for the Union's far larger forces, which captured Atlanta on September 2, 1864, and burned it nearly to the ground. Ten days later Sherman would explain his incendiary tactics in a letter to the mayor of Atlanta, writing that, "You cannot qualify war in harsher terms than I will. War is cruelty, and you cannot refine it." In a commencement address given fifteen years later Sherman would add that "War is hell," and he certainly made it so for the citizens of the South. While Grant continued wearing down his foe in the East, Sherman's scorched-earth approach turned him into the Union's new military hero and gave Lincoln the victory he needed to bolster his chances for re-election.

The photograph above shows the Atlanta railroad depot after it was obliterated by Union troops under the command of General William T. Sherman. After taking Atlanta in September 1864, Sherman used the city's excellent rail connections to relocate part of his army and to send wounded soldiers home. As the last authorized train rolled out, Sherman's men started dismantling the depot, blowing up its store of ammunition, destroying its machine shops, and pulling up the rails. As the Union troops moved east on their "March to the Sea," they left a city that would be of no further use in the war.

Lincoln's Second Administration

Today it may seem that only the most obtuse Civil War–era American could have failed to recognize Lincoln's greatness and to wholeheartedly support him, but that was certainly not the case in 1864. In fact, his own party's division over Lincoln's military strategy had fractured the Republicans and given the Democrats an opening to pick up seats in the 1862 congressional elections. Although most Republicans favored such successful administration initiatives as the transcontinental railroad, high import tariffs, liberal western land policies, and a new central banking system, many disagreed over the nature of any peace that might be made with the Confederate rebels.

Lincoln proposed a plan to allow each secessionist state to form a new government that could assume power once 10 percent of its white citizens who had voted in 1860 had taken an oath of allegiance to the United States. "Radical Republicans" in Congress—who were particularly radical in their enthusiasm to expand capitalism and abolish slavery—opposed the idea; they had not sacrificed their sons and brothers in a bloody war to hand power back to the same interests that had controlled the South prior to 1861. In fact, these Radicals wanted vengeance. What's more, they feared that the return of the Confederate states to Congress would result in enough votes to block the progressive economic programs favored by the Republicans' largely cap-

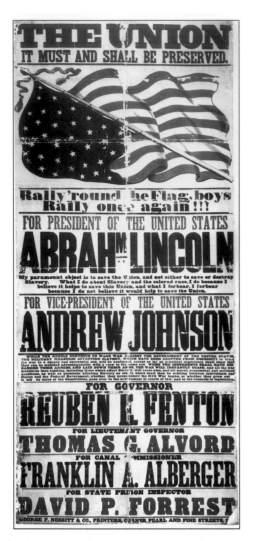

Abraham Lincoln chose Andrew Johnson to be his running mate in 1864, as broadcast on the election poster above. Johnson, a Tennessean, was the only senator from the South to remain in his seat throughout the Civil War.

italist constituencies. Most in the party did agree on one thing, if not for the same reasons: suffrage for freed blacks. Some Republicans sincerely believed it was morally imperative to free the slaves and extend to them all the rights of U.S. citizenship, including the vote; others supported the idea on the grounds that freedmen would show their gratitude to the party of their emancipators by voting Republican no matter what, insuring a long stretch of minority status for the Democrats.

In July 1864, the Radicals in Congress pushed through the Wade-Davis Bill, providing for secessionist states' re-admission to the Union only after they had accepted emancipation of the slaves and a full majority of their voters had sworn allegiance to the United States. In addition, the bill barred all former Confederate officials from voting. Lincoln responded to the Wade-Davis measure with a pocket veto, and his party's internal struggles went on.

There was no shortage of Radical Republicans eager to oppose Lincoln for the party's 1864 presidential nomination. Horace Greeley, the same editor to whom Lincoln had so eloquently expressed his passion to preserve the Union, started a movement behind Treasury Secretary Salmon Chase, who did not seem loath to run. Benjamin Butler, now in command of an army and buoyed by his longstanding advocacy of abolitionism, also had supporters for a presidential bid, as did John C. Frémont and any number of less stellar political and military figures.

But Lincoln still enjoyed enough popularity among the rank and file to win out over the Radicals, who withdrew from the party and named Frémont their candidate when the Republican National Committee gave its backing to the incumbent president. Shortly thereafter the ever pragmatic Lincoln assembled a coalition of both Republicans and Democrats into the Union Party, which gave him its nomination with Democrat Andrew Johnson of Tennessee on the bottom of the ticket. The remaining Democrats crafted an antiwar platform and selected George McClellan and Representative George Pendleton of Ohio to run on it.

At first it appeared that McClellan had a shot at winning even after Frémont dropped out of the race; the nation was weary of war and almost desperate for a leader who could put an end to it. Lincoln recognized this yearning to the point that he prepared to leave office. In a sealed memorandum opened after the election, the president wrote that he would cooperate with a McClellan administration and would ask his cabinet to do the same. Then came the news of Sherman's brutal triumph in Atlanta, the greatest in a string of Union victories that by election day had brought the North new hope that the war had entered its last phase and would soon be won.

A fresh wave of enthusiasm for the president enabled Lincoln to win re-election with 2.2 million popular votes to McClellan's 1.8 million and by 212 electoral votes to 21 for the Democrat, who managed to capture only Delaware, Kentucky, and New Jersey. Lincoln won the rest of the North and swept the Midwest and border states, although McClellan made impressive showings in Illinois, Indiana, New York, Ohio, and Pennsylvania. It was not lost on Republican politicians that a swing of only 50,000 votes, combined with the united support of a reconstructed South, would have put a Democrat in the White House in 1864. The party therefore pressed for a Reconstruction pro-

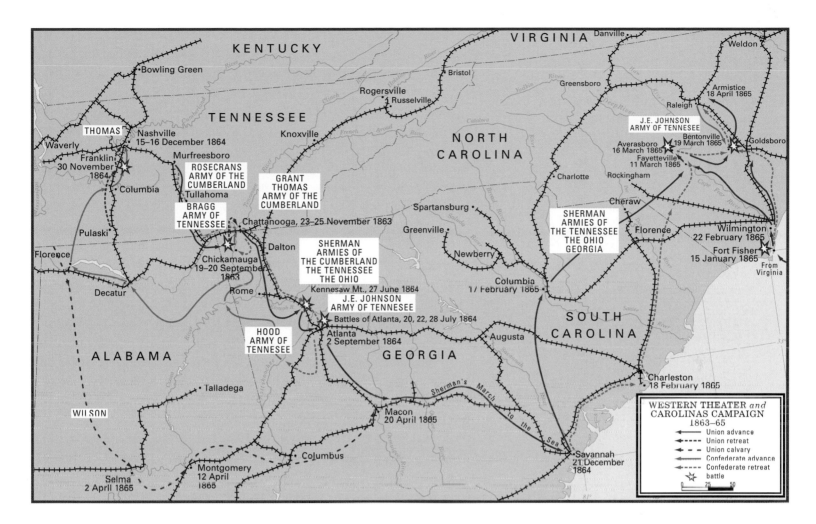

The map above shows how Union successes in the West allowed General William T. Sherman's armies to divide the Confederacy in two during 1864 by marching from Chattanooga to Savannah. Despite constant skirmishes with Confederate troops, Sherman's forces moved east with unstoppable momentum. An aggressive commander, Sherman was meticulous about maintaining strong supply lines even while reducing extraneous baggage. On the final, unopposed leg from Atlanta to Savannah, Sherman's orders stipulated that "the Army will forage liberally on the country." It did so, voraciously, and Southerners never forgave Sherman for the way his men stripped northwest Georgia bare.

gram that would create either a Republican South in the United States or none at all; the Democrats came to back Lincoln's more moderate plan, which they believed would insure them of at least some political power after the war.

The End of the War Between the States

The Confederacy finally began to crumble between the 1864 election and Lincoln's second inauguration on March 4, 1865. Sherman left Atlanta in November 1864 and conducted his renowned March to the Sea through Georgia and into the Carolinas, ordering his troops to "forage liberally on the country" for supplies and anything else they fancied, which inspired the looting and burning of virtually every private house the Unionists passed along the way. Shortly after Sherman's army arrived in Columbia, the South Carolina capital went up in flames that most Southerners believed had been set deliberately—and unnecessarily for any military purpose other than turning the area into a useless wasteland to show the rebels just how badly they were losing.

Sherman's rampage flattened the lower South and finally tore some holes in its spirit. Deserters fled the Confederate armies in droves, leading the Confederacy to go so far as to approve the enlistment of slaves into its armed forces, thereby removing one of the South's primary motives for rebelling in the first place. A few Dixie politicians attempted to negotiate a peace that would lead to Confederate independence, but Lincoln naturally rejected their offers out of hand.

The president had never glossed over his ardor for the United States to remain united, and in his second inaugural address he again attempted to salve the nation with an eloquent summation of his philosophy and plans for putting it into practice: "With malice toward none, with charity for all, with firmness in the right as God gives us to see the right," he exhorted, "let us strive on to finish the work we are in, to bind up the nation's wounds, to care for him who shall have borne the battle and for his widow and his orphan, to do all which may achieve and cherish a just and lasting peace among ourselves and with all nations."

Apparently oblivious to the compassionate approach of his commander in chief, by the end of March 1865 Sherman was in North Carolina and took up the pursuit of Johnston's dispirited forces. Within days Robert E. Lee gave up his evasive maneuvers and on April 9 capitulated to Ulysses S. Grant at Virginia's Appomattox Court House, where Lee surrendered the remaining 27,800 troops of the Confederate Army of Northern Virginia. Seventeen days later General Johnston gave up his 39,000 soldiers to Sherman in North Carolina; the very last rebel troops turned themselves over to the Union on May 26, and the Civil War was over.

After being present at Lee's dramatic surrender at Appomattox Courthouse on that fateful day in 1865, an exhausted Littleberry Walker laid down his rifle and journeyed back to Sumter County, Georgia, traveling mainly on foot, passing ragged clusters of Rebel amputees hobbling on bayonet crutches, others with arms or heads swathed in bandages, all heading in the same direction: home. Upon arriving in Atlanta, a stunned Walker found a city smoldered in ruin, the handiwork of Sherman's "scorched earth policy." (One hundred and twenty years later, Walker's great-grandson, thirty-ninth president Jimmy Carter, would construct his Carter Center, a humanitarian organization dedicated to diplomatically resolving global conflicts, on the very hilltop overlooking Atlanta on which General Sherman once stood.) Upon leaving Atlanta, Walker continued south, anxious for the cool comforts of his Dixie home. Unfortunately he returned to Sumter County only to learn that his father had died and that the family farm was teetering on the brink of bankruptcy. One suspects Inman, the main character of novelist Charles Frazier's *Cold Mountain* (1997), spoke for the battle-hardened Civil War veterans like Walker, when he lamented that "What you have lost will not be returned to you. It will always be lost. You're left with only your scars to mark the void. All you can do is go on or not. But if you go on, it's knowing you carry your scars with you."

But one essential question remained unanswered: the fate of African-Americans. Nearly 180,000 black soldiers had joined the Union cause, infusing it with new vigor. The answer should have been apparent to anybody who witnessed the site of the U.S. Colored Troops marching into Richmond, the Confederate capital, singing "John Brown's Body." These troops stopped at the city's slave pens where they were joined by hundreds of liberated men, women, and children. Togther they broke into song, an old spiritual, "Slav-

As the Civil War wound down, dreadful tales of horror and deprivation perpetrated by Confederates in charge of Union prisoners shocked the nation. The worst facility was a twenty-six-acre prison compound located ten miles northeast of Americus, Georgia, at the insignificant Southwestern railroad stop town of Andersonville. The site of Andersonville was chosen late in the war, in November 1863, because of its remoteness from the battlefront, its mild climate, and the ready availability of food and water. The stockade within Anderson Prison, as the compound was called, was named Camp Sumter. The parallelogram-shaped prison facility, a huge corral constructed in an oak and pine forest through which a creek ran, was overcrowded and mismanaged from the start, eventually housing 35,000 in an area planned for 10,000. Many of the Yankee prisoners perished after only a few days in the camp from rancid pork, polluted water, virulent diseases, chronic scurvy, diarrhea, and dysentery, which all turned healthy young Union men into skeletons. Medical supplies could not be found, hardtack rations were stolen by the Confederate guards, vegetables were almost nonexistent, and lice-ridden prisoners were ill clothed and blanketless.

Because of starvation, unsanitary conditions, and rampant disease men died so fast that often their limp, bony bodies lay in muddy stockade streets for hours, flies covering their festering, gangrenous sores, before work crews could bury them, sometimes as many as twenty to a grave. Those unconscionable prisoner-of-war abuses were the fault of the Confederate soldiers, who sold or kept for themselves the scarce food and supplies delegated for the Yankees. The Confederate soldier considered to be the most reprehensible and responsible for the deplorable cruelties at the prison was the brutish Swiss-born Captain Henry Wirz, the commander of Camp Sumter, whom MacKinlay Kantor portrayed in his 1955 Pulitzer Prize-winning novel *Andersonville* as a human demon. Recent revisionist scholarship exonerates Captain Wirz from such charges as deliberately exterminating prisoners, but his name will forever be associated with ruthlessness and grisly dereliction of duty.

After standing trial for war crimes, with hundreds of Union survivors of Andersonville telling their anguished stories of what it was like to be one of Wirz's living dead, the camp commandant was found guilty in 1865. With great fanfare General Lew Wallace, head of the military commission and future author of *Ben-Hur*, ordered Wirz hanged—the only Confederate sentenced to death—in the courtyard of the Old Capitol Prison in Washington, D.C. "With that pronouncement one frail Swiss immigrant went to the gallows and Andersonville came to signify all that was evil in the hated Confederacy," historian William Marvel noted. The acrimonious war crimes trial that ensued after the conflict further inflamed Northern fury and aroused knee-jerk defensiveness in the South to the point that the mere mention of Andersonville triggered barroom brawls. Today, visitors can walk peacefully among the 12,912 Union dead buried at Wirz's Andersonville prison site, which is maintained today as a stark monumental memorial now for all POWs everywhere.

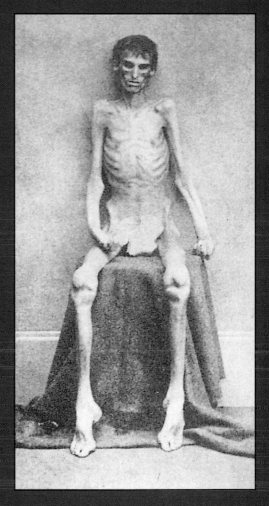

A Northern prisoner-of-war was photographed in 1865 at the Andersonville prison camp in southwest Georgia. Such pictures were used to support charges against the camp's commandant, Henry Wirz, the only Confederate officer executed after the war.

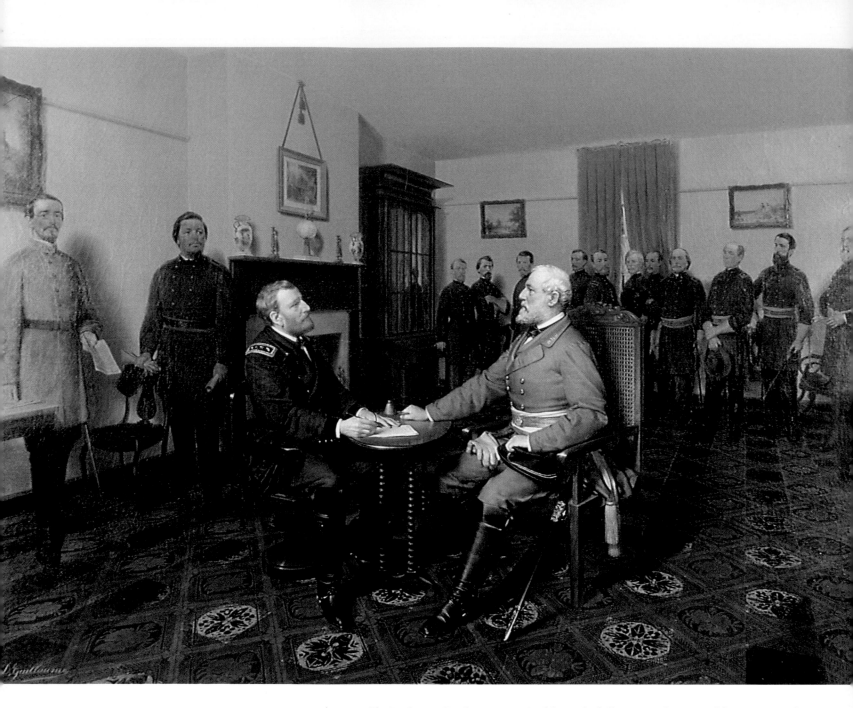

ery Chain Done Broke at Last." Although full citizenship would not come for another one hundred years, it was clear that day in Richmond that the Freedom Train had left the station and the struggle for racial equality had begun.

Reconstruction

In strictly monetary terms the war devastated both sections of the United States, which saw its national debt balloon from $90.6 million in 1861 to $2.84 billion four years later. The direct costs of the war to the Union amounted to more than $3.2 billion, while the Confederacy owed upwards of $2 billion. But it is impossible to calculate the total cost of the Civil War, as no formula can figure the worth of a life, and the human losses were staggering. The war claimed the lives of 370,000 Union soldiers and 260,000 Confederate rebels; another 275,000 of the former and 100,000 of the latter went home maimed or otherwise injured. The blood shed on both sides would stain American politics for the next three generations.

Every life wasted in the conflict marked a loss to the nation, but one reached the strict definition of tragedy: the death by assassination of President Abraham Lincoln, after which the nation ached all the more for the sheer ludicrousness of the killer's motives and execution. On April 14, 1865, in the middle of a comic play Lincoln and his wife had taken a break to attend at Ford's Theater in Washington, D.C., noted young actor John Wilkes Booth crept into the presidential box and shot the man who had held the United States together through its most trying time. Lincoln died the next morning, the victim of a Confederate sympathizer with a known violent streak, that hardly leached the agony from Booth's vile act, which among other sins crushed the last slim chance for any foreseeable reconciliation between the sections of the nation.

At the time of the president's death new governments had been established in the secessionist states of Arkansas, Louisiana, and Tennessee, while Virginia was in the process of reconstructing its state administration according to the terms of Lincoln's 10 percent plan. Congress had recessed, but not before indicating that it was prepared to take Lincoln on in the next session—a task that suddenly looked much easier after the politically skillful and now revered president had been dispatched by an assassin and replaced by Vice President Andrew Johnson.

The new president, a remarkable man in his own way, soon found himself in serious trouble. Born into poverty and apprenticed to a tailor early in his teens, Johnson could not read or write until after he married and his wife took the time to teach him. Illiteracy obviously did not hinder the political career of the Union-supporting Jackson Democrat, who had been serving as war governor of Tennessee when the Union Party tapped him to be Lincoln's running mate in 1864. Johnson had formulated his career upon chastising the wealthy planters and championing the South's small farmers. Lincoln's assassination sent fear through the Southern aristocracy, who were former slave owners and thus saw Johnson as worse than a Yankee.

Although one major gain for America occurred under the Johnson administration—Secretary of State William Seward's 1867 "folly" of arranging to purchase Alaska from the Russians for $7.2 million, or two cents an acre for a resource-rich area twice as big as Texas—his presidency was a fiasco overall. Johnson harbored an abiding hatred for the Southern plantation class as well as an appalling bigotry toward blacks. Although he had no quarrel with the practice of slavery in the South, Johnson opposed its extension into the territories for the same unworthy reason he had offered during the war when he said, "Damn the Negroes; I am fighting these traitorous aristocrats, their masters." As a result, once he took office Johnson quickly clashed with the Radical Republicans over the extent of the president's control over the South.

Johnson took a stand by offering amnesty to all but a few Confederate leaders, provided their states abolished slavery. Those states, however, tacked

Louis Guillaume's painting, opposite page, commemorated the very moment that the Army of Northern Virginia ceased to exist as General Robert E. Lee, at right in the painting, formally surrendered to General Ulysses S. Grant on April 9, 1865. The remainder of the Confederate armies continued fighting for a few more weeks, but the meeting between Lee and Grant signaled the inevitable end of the war. In the North, the celebration of the surrender started on April 10, as proclaimed in Detroit on this poster below.

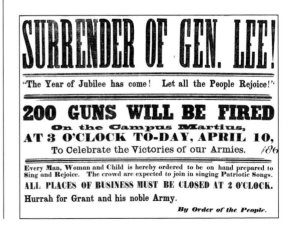

Lincoln Borne By Loving Hands on the Fatal Night of April 14, 1865 was painted by Carl Bersch. Bersch was on his balcony preparing to sketch the ongoing celebration in Washington at the end of the Civil War when the revelry suddenly stopped, and the cry arose that the president had been shot. Bersch watched as Lincoln was carried away from Ford's Theater by five or six men. "I recognized the lengthy form of the president by the flickering light of the torches, and one large gas lamppost on the sidewalk," Bersch wrote. "The tarrying on the curb and the slow, careful manner in which he was carried across the street gave me ample time to make an accurate sketch." Lincoln was taken to a private home, where he died the following morning.

on anti-black provisions that enraged Congress, which took to passing new legislation over Johnson's veto. Looking for any pretext to get rid of the troublesome new president, when Johnson fired Secretary of War Edwin M. Stanton in February 1868 without Senate approval, the House of Representatives voted to impeach him. The Senate then put the president on trial for having violated the Tenure of Office Act, but failed to convict him by a single vote on each of two counts. Johnson lost his bid for renomination nevertheless, and once he had been successfully removed from office the congressional Radicals took full control of the national debate.

The previous year, Congress had revived the Radical Republican agenda by passing the Reconstruction Acts, which divided the South into military districts and permitted readmission to the Union only after embracing emancipation and seeing to it that a majority of their voting citizens swore allegiance to the United States. In effect, what this did was redefine the Confederate states as "conquered provinces" subject to the will of Congress, which soon made sure the South was reoccupied by Union troops authorized to enforce military rule. Even more humiliating to the once proud masters of vast plantations, in order to apply for readmission to the Union the former rebel states had to assent to what they considered the odious Fourteenth Amendment, which defined the qualifications for U.S. citizenship and prohibited states from passing any legislation that would deprive "any person of life, liberty, or property without due process of law" or of the "equal protection of the laws."

Most of the South swallowed its pride and cried uncle. By the early summer of 1868 all but three of the former Confederate states had been readmitted to the Union and the Thirteenth and Fourteenth Amendments officially added to the Constitution. Less than a year later, as though to make sure everyone had gotten the point of the last one, Congress passed and the next year the states ratified the Fifteenth Amendment, guaranteeing the vote to all adult male citizens, white and black.

The Radical Republicans also dominated their party's 1868 presidential convention, where they condemned the disgraced Johnson and defended their own Reconstruction program. Although the nation was at peace and its prospects for prosperity bright, the Republicans blanched at what the election might bring. They knew they could count on the South now that blacks would be voting there, but feared that even their solid support might not prove enough to carry many states. In the North, meanwhile, the Democrats had by no means been inactive, and the possibility existed that pro-Johnson Republicans might join with them to defeat any Radical candidate. After all, the Republicans had never been the majority party before the war, and Lincoln had won in 1864 largely by catching the wind from Grant's military triumphs.

Thus it was that the Radicals rejected their own and turned to Ulysses S. Grant, the Civil War's most visible hero and as such the most popular figure throughout the North and Midwest. As insurance the Republicans nominated Schuyler Colfax, the Radical Speaker of the House, for vice president—not a small consideration seeing that Grant had absolutely no political experience and that on the few occasions when he had voted before the war he had

Andrew Johnson, in an undated photograph below, was born in poverty, trained to be a tailor, and once courted a girl by sewing a quilt with her. At eighteen he moved to Tennessee, where he married Eliza McCardle, a sixteen-year-old who had been schooled at a private academy; she taught her new husband to write and add. Antagonistic toward the aristocracy, he was unable to cooperate with any one group in Washington and ultimately failed as president.

done so as a Democrat. At this point, Grant, content to savor a ride on his own coattails, proclaimed, "Let us have peace," and campaigned as a representative of both America's military prowess and its magnanimity in victory. He could afford to take the high road; with troops still keeping military control over the South and its blacks preparing to vote, Grant had no reason to doubt that he would win the election.

The Democrats, of course, were entitled to no such confidence. With little else to run on, the delegates to the party's convention prattled about a "new departure" and nominated pallid ex-Governor Horatio Seymour of New York for the presidency even though in his speech to the delegates he had announced that "I must not be nominated by this convention as I could not accept the nomination if tendered, which I do not expect." But accept it he did—and then proved himself an even less known quantity than the Democrats had bargained for.

Turning to politics' old standby, the Democrats tried to emphasize economic issues such as the money supply and the tariff on imports, throwing their full support to "greenbacks"—paper dollars without the backing of gold or silver that the Treasury had issued during the war in the amount of some $450 million. Like the institution of an income tax and the sale of government bonds, greenbacks had been printed as a means of financing the North's war effort. Part of these issues had been redeemed, but more than $356 million remained in circulation, used mostly by farmers and other debtors as a cheap means of paying off mortgages and other obligations. Hoping to win the support of these farmers and other financially strapped Americans, the Democrats got behind Representative George H. Pendleton's "Ohio Idea," under which the federal government would support the inflated currency, including the paying off of its bonds in greenbacks. This plan held great appeal for debtors in the West as well as for the poor in the East, and the Democrats thought that if their votes could be added to those of whites in the South they might have a shot at winning the White House. There was only one problem: their candidate turned out to be a "hard-money" man who openly denounced greenbacks, which threw the Republican Party into utter disarray.

In the end, Grant's cockiness almost proved unjustified. Although he won with 214 electoral votes to Seymour's 80, he beat the Democrat in the popular tally by only 3 million to 2.7 million votes—a narrow margin of 53 percent. Despite the best efforts of the military Reconstruction effort, Seymour took both Georgia and Louisiana, but thanks to the presence of Union troops in the South to enforce black suffrage Grant captured all the other former Confederate states that participated in the election, without which he would have lost the election. The close outcome of the contest forced the Republicans to acknowledge that without soldiers in place to keep the region honest the Confederacy's old regime might well rise back into power and negate some of the gains the

The cartoon above portrays President Andrew Johnson being crushed by "Volume 14" of the U.S. Constitution. Johnson's disagreement with Congress over the Fourteenth Amendment—guaranteeing civil rights for all—and its use in controlling Southern states was a divisive issue in the 1866 congressional elections. After months of heavy campaigning, the results dealt a decided blow to Johnson. The Radical Republicans who ruled Congress during his administration ruined Reconstruction, and then very nearly ruined Johnson in the impeachment proceedings of 1868.

The U.S. Mint issued its first paper bills, such as the dollar above, in August of 1862. In financing the Civil War the country learned to use and trust greenbacks, a new type of currency that would accelerate the economy after the war.

The cartoon above depicts President Ulysses S. Grant as a wealthy conqueror being carried in a giant carpetbag on the breaking back of the "Solid South." Elected with strong support from African-American voters in the South, Grant perpetuated Reconstruction policies not because he believed in them but because he put his trust in politicians who benefited by them.

Union had fought so hard to win—and many Northerners feared that any return of white Democratic control in the South would mean radically different economic programs coming out of Washington, and not ones to their liking.

The Pain of Healing

Unfortunately for their party, the Republicans found no champion in the president they had just elected, who entered the office in 1869 on a wave of public goodwill the likes of which had not been seen since the days of George Washington and never would be again. But as formidable a military commander as former General Grant may have been, he proved an utter disaster as the chief executive of the United States. In fairness, his considerable failures were exactly those one might expect from a wily army man who had no experience on the far more shadowy political battlefield. Grant blithely went on misjudging men and their motives and avoided dealing with his confusion over the complexities of political issues by escaping to the racetrack, drinking heavily, or both. Perhaps Grant's *New York Tribune* obituary (July 24, 1885) summed up his White House tenure best: "The greatest mistake of his life was the acceptance of the presidency."

Grant's insufficiency for the office seems especially unfortunate when one looks back at all the opportunities he missed. To effect Reconstruction the postwar president could have sought accommodation with the South's white population, as no one would ever have dreamed of calling him anti-Union. By the same token, Grant's popularity in the North would have made it hard for anyone there to protest had he tried to create a new society with room for freed blacks as well as for scalawags (the South's derisive term for fellow whites who cooperated with Reconstruction governments) and carpetbaggers (another pejorative term, denoting Yankees who for their own profit headed south to "help" with Reconstruction).

By Grant's inauguration in March 1869 the U.S. economy and the business and commercial concerns driving it were growing at a remarkable pace, branching along the ever expanding railroads into a financial system of unprecedented intricacy and technological sophistication. This booming new economy threatened more traditional commercial pursuits such as agriculture and small industry and therefore quickly began to have an impact on U.S. politics. Grant's inability to deal with these massive evolutionary changes may have been his greatest failure as president. Instead of seizing the moment and building popular support for regulating these wild new forces and mustering the legislative backing to create federal safeguards against the trend toward commercial wrongdoing, Grant opted against even trying to sort the problems out and by his inaction created several new ones.

Southerners naturally regarded the scalawags and carpetbaggers with resentment bordering on loathing. Not only had the Yankees razed their plantations, but they also had destroyed Dixie's way of life by making America's first effort to resolve its oldest and most insidious problem of race relations. Although he was an unsuccessful president, Grant did better with Reconstruction than he did with economic issues, especially considering that by the time he took office the racial lines had hardened across the occupied South into animosities that made real peace between whites and blacks pretty much unattainable.

The South's blacks, most of them former slaves, were poorly organized, untrained in the day-to-day game of politics, and in most areas unequipped to demand their new rights without military and political aid from the North. Nevertheless, blacks and their allies would trade victories with the recalcitrant whites in the South during the Grant years. In 1870, for example, a South Carolina governor who favored blacks' political involvement was impeached, convicted, and replaced by a new state executive who immediately reversed his predecessor's policies. But that same year the same state sent J. H. Raincy to Washington as the first black member of the House of Representatives. Another African-American, Hiram Revels of Mississippi, entered the Senate, and over the next six years every former Confederate state except Arkansas, Tennessee, and Texas would include blacks in their congressional delegations, while not one Northern state elected a single black man to the national legislature. Before the end of Reconstruction twenty-two blacks would serve in the U.S. Congress, although none rose to prominence in Washington.

The situation was quite a bit better below the national level. Blacks were elected to the legislatures of every one of the Confederate states and came to dominate only that of South Carolina. In not one, however, did blacks gain the representation called for by their actual numbers. This disparity arose for two reasons: white racist organizations and what came to be slurred as "Uncle Tomism." As for the first, many Southern blacks were intimidated from voting by hate groups such as the Ku Klux Klan that prevented blacks from achieving equality by terrorizing them before elections and in some areas by controlling the polls and counting ballots. The second reason is in some ways even more disturbing. Some black leaders eager for reconciliation with their white neighbors entered into misbegotten alliances with seemingly friendly white politicians, which usually ended in broken promises from the whites that led to freedmen's subjection to still more new "black codes" aimed at keeping them from enjoying their full rights as citizens. Due to "black codes" former slaves were forced to carry passes, observe curfews, live in housing provided by landowners and forgo seeking meaningful employment.

Some of the states did quite well under black ma-

The lithograph below, *From the Plantation to the Senate,* celebrates African Americans who excelled professionally, including some who were elected to Congress after the Civil War. They are, starting from the left: Senator Hiram R. Revels (Mississippi); Representative Benjamin S. Turner (Alabama), the Reverend Richard Allen (an early abolitionist), Frederick Douglass (a publisher and statesman), Representative Josiah T. Wells (Florida), Representative Joseph H. Rainey (South Carolina), and William Wells Brown (a novelist). In all, twenty blacks were elected to the House of Representatives and two to the U.S. Senate during Reconstruction.

jority rule, framing constitutions that remained in force long after Reconstruction ended. Public school systems were established and legal machinery put in place across the South that were noted even at the time for their progressiveness and sophistication. A few black-dominated legislatures, however, grew as venal and corrupt as any white political cabal, which to the willfully obtuse indicated that blacks were unprepared for citizenship, much less political power. South Carolina in particular spawned a cesspool of a state government under black control—although it really didn't look so bad in an era when "Boss" William Tweed of New York presided over a political machine that regarded criminal activity as part of its daily routine. This was also a time in which individual members of President Grant's administration helped themselves to the public till in amounts that eclipsed the theft of all the dishonest freedmen combined. Instead of denouncing corruption, Grant defended his cronies as essentially honest: an attitude which diminished his popularity.

By 1876, as the Grant administration was nearing its welcome end, the war-weary North began to indicate that it no longer favored military control of the South. In 1876 the U.S. Supreme Court had declared in *U.S. v. Cruikshank* that although the Fifteenth Amendment guaranteed every male citizen the right to vote regardless of race, color, or previous servitude, Congress could not constitutionally prevent Southern states from denying blacks the vote through literacy and property-ownership requirements. Congress did pass a well-intentioned Civil Rights Act in 1875 forbidding discrimination by race in public facilities, but even its supporters knew the act was unenforceable—and they would be proved right when it took Congress another eighty-two years to pass further civil rights legislation. And Grant did have some success: taxes were cut by $300 million, the national debt reduced by $435 million, and many "pork barrel" congressional appropriations were cut.

In 1876 the Republicans' post-Grant military fatigue led the party to nominate Governor Rutherford B. Hayes of Ohio, a moderate on Reconstruction best known for sponsoring civil service reforms. The Democrats selected a similarly unspectacular presidential candidate on their second ballot: New York Governor Samuel Tilden, who also was considered a reformer despite his powerful business connections.

Vapid candidates notwithstanding, the election of 1876 turned into one of the filthiest and most peculiar in U.S. history. Tilden received 260,000 more votes than Hayes, but "irregularities"—fraud, violence, and intimidation that kept some quarter million likely votes from being cast—committed by Republicans in the South and Oregon effectively stole the election from the Democrats. A commission was named to investigate the alleged wrongdoing, but it was followed only by more chicanery and a Democratic filibuster in the Senate.

Two "ghouls," as the Ku Klux Klan called themselves, posed for the photograph above in 1868. Formed in 1866, the Klan was obsessed with intricate rituals that gave disenfranchised Southerners a sense of power and purpose. It soon grew into a lawless "invisible empire," using violence to intimidate African-American voters as well as carpetbaggers and scalawags.

In the end, Republican leaders and Southern Democrats came together in the fine American tradition of compromising in the interests of commerce. The Republicans agreed to end Reconstruction and award several lucrative railroad construction contracts to Southern firms, in return for which the Democrats agreed to end their filibuster and let Hayes become president—a deal struck only a week before his inauguration. The swirling political cesspool that followed the Civil War muddied the fact that in the year that marked the centennial of the Declaration of Independence, Southern blacks were abandoned by the same Republican Party that had done so much to free them from slavery. It would be the last time the Grand Old Party was perceived as holding any appeal for many African-Americans. Thus the nation ended over fifteen years of a destructive civil war and difficult reconstruction without establishing full freedom for African-Americans. "Although the freed man is no longer considered the property of the individual master," the political pundit Carl Schurtz lamented, "he *is* considered the slave of society."

A family of workers bring in the crop somewhere near Savannah in the photograph below. Labor was in short supply after the war and recovery was slow. Cash-poor white families on most plantations couldn't afford to pay outsiders and had to do their own picking. Even when they were offered money, many former slaves declined fieldwork; the old system had just been too harsh.

CHAPTER 10

POSTBELLUM AMERICA

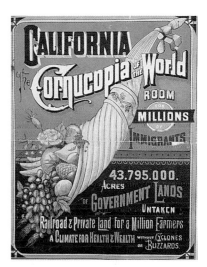

For all the massive changes the Civil War sent coursing through America, perhaps the most powerful was the lasting hold of its memory. Not until the early twentieth century would a generation come to political maturity with no recollection of the war, and even then it was never far from the focus of the nation's political thinking—not as long as the Republicans kept "waving the bloody shirt" every four years and the Southern Democrats grew misty-eyed whenever they heard a dirgelike version of "Dixie." As late as 1920, some 244,000 Civil War veterans were still living, several of whom were in Congress, while Union hero Oliver Wendell Holmes sat on the U.S. Supreme Court. As D. W. Brogan, an astute observer of national trends, would write: "The impact of the Civil War on American life and American memory can hardly be exaggerated. It is still 'the war.'" Brogan expressed this opinion in 1944—during World War II. Not until the last Union and Confederate veterans died out in the 1940s would the national memory be truly rid of the Civil War.

But some of the upheaval the war had wrought proved decidedly for the nation's good. The poet and historian Carl Sandburg noted that before the Civil War official documents had read, "The United States are . . ."; after the war they proclaimed, "The United States is. . . ." People no longer referred to themselves as "Georgians" or "New Yorkers" but as Americans. Although

John Gast's 1872 painting *The Spirit of the Frontier* shows Liberty accompanying the pioneers heading into the frontier, on foot, on horseback, and in trains, stagecoaches, and wagons. The advertisement above was published by a railroad in the 1880s to entice immigrants to southern California, where 43 million acres awaited them.

the pace of recovery was glacial, once the passions of the Civil War did begin to simmer down, America turned its full attention back to its usual business, which was, of course, business.

The war was not the only source of social upheaval in the second half of the nineteenth century. In fact, the period between the assassination of Abraham Lincoln in 1865 and the inauguration of Woodrow Wilson in 1912 witnessed the complete transformation of American life. The Indians were subdued, making the always romantic West seem even more appealing to settlers than it had before. Getting there became easier, too, thanks to the railroads, which sent their tracks shooting like vines across the United States. The railroads became the symbol of a vibrant U.S. economy, uniting the nation physically, broadening its commercial markets, and prompting the growth of big business. In the years between Lincoln's assassination and Wilson's inauguration, the amount of capital invested in manufacturing multiplied by a factor of twenty-two, while the number of industrial workers surged from fewer than 2 million to 6.6 million. This sudden growth sparked the labor movement and led to discontent on America's farms, where resentment grew at the government's perceived slights of agriculture in favor of manufacturing interests.

Cities were rapidly becoming the centers of U.S. life and underwent radical transformations in the wake of a new wave of immigration. Further changes resulted from a rash of inventions that spawned new industries, many of them the outgrowth of the greatest wonder of the age: electricity. An overall picture of the new society that was developing emerged in the 1890 census, which showed that for the first time in the nation's history the value of manufactured goods exceeded that of farm products.

Taking inflation into account, the gross national product (GNP) more than quadrupled between 1869 and 1914, while per capita income rose by approximately 250 percent. These figures cannot, of course, be considered precise, since between 1869 and 1878 the vast majority of Americans still lived on farms, and the statistics do not take into account the foodstuffs they consumed or the products they used for clothing and shelter. Once a large portion of the farming population became wage earners instead, their productivity was more easily quantified and their contributions to the GNP thus soared; similarly, whenever a rural area turned urban its per capita income figures shot up as well, a pattern that dominated the U.S. economy from the end of the Civil War to the eve of World War I. It was during this period that the United States turned from being a largely rural nation of farmers into a burgeoning industrial and economic monolith that would go on to become one of the world's great superpowers—and in time the only one.

Presidential elections immediately after the Civil War reflected new domestic economic concerns in several ways, the first and most obvious manifesting itself in 1876 when several farm groups organized the Greenback Party, which put up candidates for the next three elections, none of whom won a single electoral vote. That may have owed to the party's platform, which was strongly in favor of reissuing greenback currency and remonetizing silver. But the Greenback Party's mere existence proved that monetary matters had become a major consequence to the voting populace.

Postbellum America was a different world from the one that would take its place fifty years later. It was a world without electric lights, telephones, moving assembly lines, or cameras, not to mention automobiles or elevated urban train lines. The elevator had been invented by E. G. Otis just before the Civil War, but hardly any were in operation, in part because few buildings were tall enough to need one. Neither business nor residential districts boasted concrete sidewalks, and few houses had indoor plumbing. Most consumer goods were produced and purchased locally.

All this would change, and the prime agent behind the change was already the nation's largest and most lucrative industry: railroads. The romance of a lonesome train whistle calling across a black night in the heartland remains with us to this day, thanks to country songs and hobo stories, but to the generation that saw its birth the railroad was as glamorous and magical as the airplane would be in the early twentieth century and as the space shuttle is today. Of course, the real significance of the advent of rail transportation is not that it became fast, cheap, and easy for people to travel from farm to city—few chose to make the return trip—but that it provided local businessmen throughout the country the opportunity to move products cheaply and thus to sell their goods in many more markets, which spurred the growth of large commercial conglomerates.

Although most farmers didn't have the means to go into cities to shop, before long the rail distribution system brought the cities to them via the Sears, Roebuck and Montgomery Ward mail-order catalogs and through traveling salesmen from the John Deere, McCormick, and Case companies eager to sell farm equipment. The same railroads that carried grain to market from rural areas also brought meat from the Midwest to the East, along with every other product from machine tools to shoes to beer. The nation's spreading railroad network combined with parallel developments in communications technology—the telegraph and eventually the telephone—to stimulate many businesses to look beyond local customers to regional and even national markets; as the costs of transportation and communication plummeted, customer bases broadened.

The very nature of the transformation affected by the new U.S. industrial order, however, ensured that the urban, industrial North and the substantially rural, agricultural South would remain politically polarized. In the former, social and political debate centered on labor issues, immigration, and the problems of overcrowded cities; in the latter, the greatest worries remained racial divisions and an agrarian economy dependent upon the vagaries of markets as determined by the financial centers in large Northern cities.

Naturally, many Southerners began to bristle at the erstwhile enemy's

The arrival of the Sears, Roebuck and Company catalog, such as the 1897 edition above, was a noteworthy event in many rural American homes. The "wish book," as it was known, was not only a merchandising tool, it was a form of national communication regarding both new styles and inventions. Richard Sears, the former watch salesman who started Sears, Roebuck, tried to cater to any and all customers, offering items ranging in price from two cents to thousands of dollars. In addition, the company encouraged sales to immigrants by accepting orders written in any language.

Edgar Degas painted *Bureau de Coton à la Nouvelle-Orléans* ("Cotton Brokerage in New Orleans"), right, during a visit to America in 1873. A native Parisian, Degas had roots in New Orleans: his mother came from a prominent family there and his brother, René, settled in the city in 1865. Many of the artist's relatives traded cotton for a living, and he included some of them in the painting. The cotton trade was slow to return in the South, partly because it was the only crop known to most regions and the land was eventually exhausted. In the circa 1900 photograph below, George Washington Carver (right) did more than anyone else to resuscitate Southern agriculture. A longtime professor at the Tuskegee Institute, he vastly enlarged markets for such alternative crops as peanuts, soybeans, and sweet potatoes by deriving new products from them. His most famous, of course, is peanut butter.

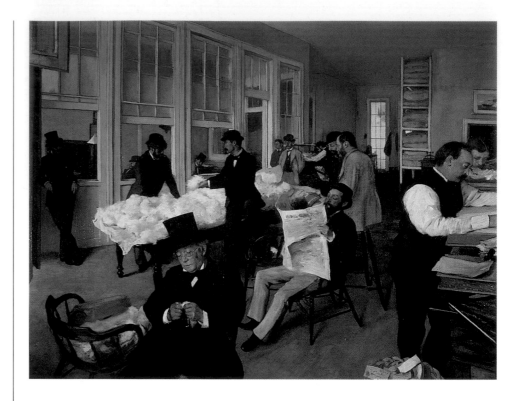

control over business and commerce. As Mark Twain accurately noted in *Life on the Mississippi* (1883): "In the South the war is what A.D. is elsewhere; they date from it." Yet a new generation of Southern entrepreneurs was anxious to put its Confederate past to rest. In the 1880s the editor of the *Atlanta Constitution,* Henry Grady, began arguing for the development of a "New South" based on the Northern industrial model, but at first the old South mentality proved highly resistant to any such notion. Agriculture remained the economic focus, with cotton still at its center, although scientist George Washington Carver did manage to convince many black farmers to diversify with peanut crops when the demand for cotton began to fall off and the South's plantations started to shrink. Before long the old Southern aristocracy's devotion to doing things as their fathers had done began to lose its appeal, while the ideas of Grady and his fellow "redeemers" looked better and better.

Consequently, "New South" cities like Birmingham, Richmond, and Atlanta became vital centers of industry in the late nineteenth century, rivaling many of the more important Northern industrial towns in manufacturing productivity. In fact, between 1869 and 1909 the South's rates of industrial output and worker productivity rose faster than those in the North, as the tobacco, timber, and cotton textile industries boomed, spurred after 1879 by the explosive growth of railroads that finally connected the region with reliable transportation. As many black farmers and laborers migrated West to escape the racial animosities still so prevalent in the South, white laborers moved from the plantations to the textile factories and slowly began to adjust to the industrial, urban way of life already so common among their neighbors to the north. Naturally, as the two regions drew closer economically and thus socially, their politics began to merge as well. "National unity" became the rally cry of the era, as demonstrated at the 1876 centennial celebration where Confederate and Union soldiers exchanged captured flags. Newspapers revived the notion of American exceptionalism and Manifest Destiny to bolster patriotic fervor. America basked in a frenzy of self-adulation which was seen as a gallant moment of national apotheosis. This contrived explosion of nationalism was probably best captured in the Reverend Josiah Strong's *Our Country* (1885) where he insisted that God favored the Anglo-Saxon race, and the United States was his holy kingdom. "As America goes," Strong claimed, "so goes the world."

The Invisible Government

To most Americans in the second half of the nineteenth century, the importance of politics was in direct proportion to its proximity: local government had the most impact, then state, and finally the distant federal authority. Mayors and after them state governors were not only better known but enjoyed more power and prestige among their constituents than did the congressmen and senators who represented their interests before the national government. Understanding their audiences, newspapers across the United States sent more reporters to city hall than to Washington; the capital was still a small, muddy, provincial city where little of noticeable importance was seen to go on.

The federal government was, after all, of quite modest scope. In 1871 it employed 51,000 civilians—only 6,000 of them stationed in Washington—with 42,000 men in the armed forces. By 1914 the federal workforce would swell to 401,000 civilians and 166,000 servicemen, but still only 40,000 of the former worked in the capital, the rest being distributed around the nation in the postal, customs, and other localized services. What's more, until the invention of air-conditioning in 1911, the federal government worked more or less part-time, with employees of all branches taking summers off to escape the heat, humidity, and occasional malaria scares of the swamp along the Potomac River upon which the nation's capital had been built. Of course, this unbearable sultriness could not have lasted as long as the vacation the Fifty-third Congress took in 1869, when it adjourned on April 10 and didn't return until December 6—eight months during which not a single piece of national legislation was passed. Over the years the sessions would be lengthened, but only gradually.

Throughout the postbellum period, the federal budget was impossibly small by today's standards. In 1865, the last year of the Civil War, government revenues totaled $333 million and expenditures $1.3 billion, some $1.1 billion of which went to the armed forces. By 1886 federal spending would bottom out at $242 million. In 1914, revenues amounted to $725 million, nearly half of which came from taxes on alcohol and tobacco; expenditures came to the same figure, almost half of which went to the military.

In the late nineteenth century presidents hardly occupied the center of political life as they do today. Congressional leaders actually exercised more power, although it was also true that the nation's debate on political issues crystallized every four years during the presidential campaigns, some of which generated considerable heat, if little light. No chief executive between Lincoln and Theodore Roosevelt particularly distinguished himself, in part because of the domination of Congress. While the Republicans for the most part held the White House and the Senate, Americans showed their basic lack of partisanship by giving the Democrats pretty much equal standing in the House of Representatives and by denying any presidential candidate a landslide election.

The political stakes have seldom been lower; in fact, American life would not have been appreciably different if Democrat Samuel Tilden had won the 1876 presidential election instead of Republican Rutherford B. Hayes, as their beliefs and policies were more or less the same. Hayes trumpeted this bipartisan ideal at his presidential inauguration on March 5, 1877: "He serves his party best who serves his country best." All of the elections of the late nineteenth century were remarkably close, in part because of the candidates' similarity and in part because political affiliations often remained carved in stone and passed from father to son. Until the turn of the century, political loyalties were based largely on wartime allegiances and the economic issues that had defined them: the South was solidly Democratic and the North and Midwest Republican. Religion played a role as well, as most big-city Catholics adhered to the Democratic Party while old-line Protestants voted Republican. The small swing vote thus became quite important, and each party went out of its way to woo the few independents, spending ever more money on presidential campaigns.

It wasn't necessarily well spent, as the presidents of the period had little to do—they were chief executives in the strictest sense. Republican James A. Garfield, elected in 1880, didn't have a choice, as he died ten weeks after being shot by a deranged officer five months after taking office. Garfield had been murdered by a man who failed to get a patronage job in the federal government from the newly elected president. The words Garfield had uttered in 1865 to calm a crowd in New York that had just learned of Abraham Lincoln's assassination rang just as true, if not as momentously: "Fellow citizens! God reigns, and the Government at Washington still lives." And so it did in 1881: Vice President Chester A. Arthur succeeded Garfield and proved that it really is possible to grow into the office by abandoning his former cronies in New York's corrupt political machine and signing civil service reform legislation aimed at putting an end to the spoils system. Apart from that, however, President Arthur hardly seemed busy enough to justify spending so little time on politicking that he did not win his party's nomination in 1884.

In 1884 it was probably only marginally better that Democratic candidate Grover Cleveland won the election: he was honest and able, while his Republican opponent, James G. Blaine, was dishonest and able. Although Cleveland again won a plurality of the popular vote in 1888, he lost to Republican Benjamin Harrison in the electoral college—but Cleveland returned to unseat Harrison in 1892, becoming the only president to serve nonconsecutive terms. Cleveland also had the distinction of being the only Democrat to become president between James Buchanan in 1857 and Woodrow Wilson in 1913.

Rutherford B. Hayes, below, served as America's nineteenth president from 1877 to 1881. Combining a valiant Civil War record with his position as one of Ohio's richest men, he entered politics and earned a reputation for honesty. When Hayes was nominated for president in 1876, outgoing president Ulysses Grant described him as "a flat-footed Republican who never apologizes for his party." Running against Samuel Tilden, an aristocratic New Yorker, Hayes actually received fewer popular votes. The count in the electoral college also seemed to tilt toward the Democrat, but Hayes's backers engineered a victory out of the disputed validity of the returns in four states. Even before the inauguration, the Hayes administration was stained with scandal.

The presidential election of 1884 raised issues that remain the stuff of punditry today. In the absence of any other pressing matters, the contest came down to the question of the candidates' character or lack thereof. Bachelor Democrat Cleveland was alleged to have seduced a widow, fathered her child, refused to marry her, and paid her off, leading to the popular taunt, "Ma! Ma! Where's my pa? Gone to the White House. Ha, ha, ha." At the same time Republican Blaine was said to have had his hand in the public till all the time he was in Congress, twisting laws to his advantage when he served as Speaker of the House, and worse, such as selling railroad bonds on commission while crafting related legislation. But like so many prominent men of America's so-called Gilded Age, Blaine regarded politics as a branch of business, although even one particularly unsavory political boss quipped that he wouldn't campaign for Blaine because "I do not engage in criminal practice."

Cleveland, a minister's son, believed that government *should* and *could* be honest. Whatever his personal failings, Cleveland was best known for a determination to stamp out corruption that made him many powerful enemies, some in his own party. As governor of New York, he took on the notoriously corrupt Tammany Hall machine and won the presidential nod at the 1884 Democratic convention because, as the delegate who nominated him said, "We love him most for the enemies he has made." As one Chicago columnist explained the public attitude that still characterizes U.S. politics: "We are told that Mr. Blaine has been delinquent in office but blameless in private life, while Mr. Cleveland has been a model of official integrity, but culpable in his personal relations. We should therefore elect Mr. Cleveland to the public office which he is so well qualified to fill and remand Mr. Blaine to the private station which he is admirably fitted to adorn."

Once in office Cleveland repeatedly clashed with the Senate and only

The drawing above at left shows President James Garfield at 9:30 A.M. on July 2, 1881, just as he was shot and mortally wounded by a disgruntled office seeker named Charles Guiteau. In office for five months when he was shot, Garfield died in September 1881. His successor was Chester Arthur, shown above right in a portrait by Daniel Huntington. Arthur, a popular lawyer from New York City who never held elected office except as Garfield's vice president, oversaw an untroubled and quiet administration.

managed to get anything done by getting on somewhat better with the House of Representatives. A story of the time relates that one night Cleveland—the only president to be married during his term in the White House—was awakened by his wife's cry, "Wake up! I think there are burglars in the house." The president is said to have replied sleepily, "No, no, my dear. In the Senate maybe, but not in the House."

Cleveland would not face any major problems until his second administration began in 1893. In the interim, the United States was looked after by Republican Benjamin Harrison, who was so underwhelmed by his own election in 1888 that he went to bed before the results were announced. When asked why, the president-elect replied, "I knew that my staying up would not alter the result if I were defeated, while if I was elected I had a hard day in front of me. So a night's rest seemed the best in either event." Once inaugurated, Harrison worked in his office only from 9 A.M. to 1 P.M. Monday through Friday; after lunch and on weekends he went for strolls, played billiards, or whatever else he felt like, including occasionally greeting sightseers taking the White House tour. Never again would an American president enjoy as much leisure as the nation's focus on business allowed in the late

1880s. The tenor of the era was best encapsulated by an old Benjamin Franklin aphorism: "No nation was ever ruined by trade."

The Transcontinental Railroads

It wasn't just peace that gave presidents so little to do; prosperity dimmed the immediacy of politics as well, and good times had come to America courtesy of the railroads that opened the West and created national markets by transporting raw materials to factories and their products to consumers. Simultaneously, of course, the rail companies themselves comprised a powerfully expanded market for iron, steel, and lumber.

Railroad mileage had increased every year of the antebellum era, and by the end of the war more than 35,000 miles of track were in place, much of it financed by foreign capital, particularly from Britain. The federal government had helped build the transcontinental railroads, construction of which began during the Civil War, with massive contributions of federal funds and land since 1862. In 1869 the Central Pacific was joined to the Union Pacific at Promontory Point, Utah, and the bridge to the Far West was complete. This rail link between the two coasts spurred construction of more transcontinentals, while in the East and South railroads snaked into virtually every town. In 1869 the net capital worth of stock in railroads was $1.7 billion (adjusted for inflation into 1909 dollars); in 1909 that figure had grown to $10.5 billion.

America's railroad titans—Charles Crocker, Jay Gould, Grenville Dodge, E. H. Harriman, Mark Hopkins, Leland Stanford, Cornelius Vanderbilt, Henry Villard, and others—presided over enormous business empires and harbored the national and even global ambitions that such success so often inspires. They accumulated vast wealth and held on to it through tactics that were nothing if not direct. Cornelius Vanderbilt, for example, upon discovering that two associates had abused the power of attorney he had given them to the substantial detriment of his interests, dictated the following letter to them: "Gentlemen: You have undertaken to cheat me. I won't sue you, for the law is too slow. I'll ruin you." In short order Vanderbilt had indeed thwarted and embarrassed these erstwhile associates and recaptured control of his company. But the pure capitalist rapacity of the industrial giants of the nineteenth century can best be summed up in Jay Gould's response to an impending labor strike in his southwestern railroad empire: "I can hire one half of the working class to kill the other half."

While not the greediest, perhaps the most talented of America's railroad barons was James Hill, creator of the Great Northern Railroad, the only transcontinental constructed without government funding and the only one never to fall into bankruptcy. His financial acumen made Hill more than a railroad tycoon; he soon became a powerful regional developer, and in the process of conducting his business opened the Northwest to numerous settlers and commercial enterprises.

Toward the end of the Civil War, Hill, a Canadian entrepreneur who had gone to St. Paul, Minnesota, entered into the Mississippi and Red River trade and by natural progression into midwestern railroads to bring goods to his

Grover Cleveland had taken responsibility for fathering a son out of wedlock in 1874, a scandal that burst into the 1884 presidential campaign, as shown in the cartoon, opposite top. Cleveland immediately implied that as a bachelor at the time, he had only assumed the responsibility in the place of a married friend—the mother had indeed named the baby for Oscar Folsom, one of Cleveland's closest friends. The old disgrace failed to level Cleveland's reputation and he was victorious at the polls. However, in making a bid for reelection in 1888, Cleveland was surprised by Benjamin Harrison, the winner in a close contest. *The Lost Bet,* opposite bottom, was painted in 1893 and illustrates how a crowd on one New York street received the news of Benjamin Harrison's victory. Harrison did not receive as many votes as his opponent, Grover Cleveland but managed to take the election anyway, based on the tally in the electoral college.

When the lines of the Central Pacific (left) and the Union Pacific (right) finally reached each other at Promontory Point, Utah, on May 10, 1869, as shown in the photograph above, a momentous accomplishment was marked: railroads snaked all the way across America. "The Chinese laid the rails from the west end and the Irish laborers laid them from the east end, until they met and joined," wrote former Union Major General Grenville Dodge, chief engineer of the Union Pacific. The "golden spike" that finished the job was connected to telegraph wires so that each strike of the hammer would register the news to both coasts. Unfortunately, the company officials given the honor of driving the last spike kept missing it, and the chief engineers had to take over. "Then it was declared that the connection was made and the Atlantic and Pacific were joined together never to be parted," reported Dodge.

steamships. The depression that had begun in 1873 was ending in 1879, when midwestern grain production reached record highs; it was the right time for a man with ambitions regarding the West's open opportunities to push his dreams across the nation. The Northwest in particular attracted Hill: Rich in natural resources, densely forested, and sparsely populated, the vast territory between Minnesota and Oregon represented a challenge for developers on a scale that only the Moon and Mars offer today. In 1889, Hill recapitalized his regional railroad, renamed it the Great Northern Railway Company, and drove it to the West Coast, reaching Seattle in 1893.

Hill's unflagging success and ballooning fortune inspired him to even more grandiose visions than just establishing a transcontinental railroad: now he wanted to make it pay off. Thus the hard-driving capitalist sent agents to Europe to distribute leaflets calling for "Everybody: Farmer, Stock raiser, Dairyman, Fruit-grower, Lumberman, Mechanic, Merchant, Professional Man" to come to "A Home in the Land of Opportunity" across the ocean. Hill's company offered promising farm families and individual laborers reduced fares to America and on to the Northwest, help in finding land and settling it, and agreements to transport their produce to markets in the East. At the same time, Hill went into partnership with lumber tycoon Frederick Weyerhaeuser to develop the northwestern timber industry, which by 1914 would turn out 20 percent of the nation's wood products.

Like many of his fellow industrial titans, Hill was not content with domestic operations; like the first Europeans who had discovered America and its enormous economic potential, he looked for further gold in trade routes to the Orient and its 500 million potential consumers. He therefore extended

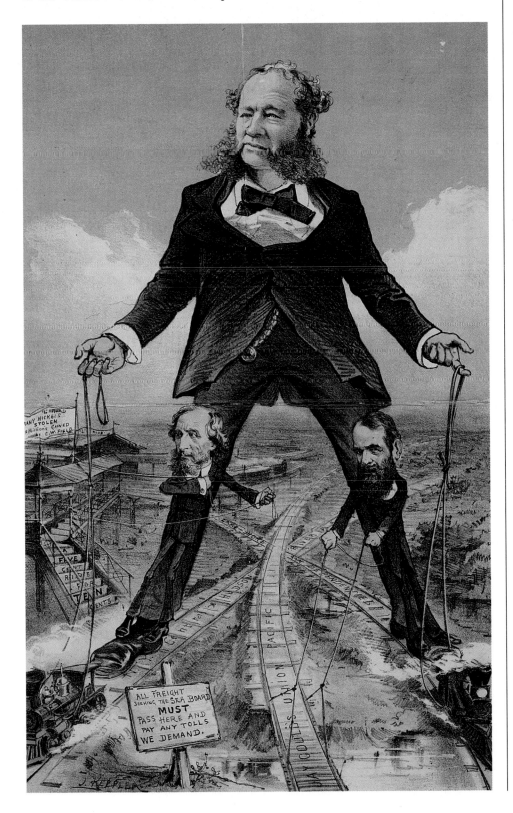

James Hill, photographed circa 1910 in the Rocky Mountains, above, and William H. Vanderbilt (Cornelius's son), caricatured at left, were two of the "robber barons" who presided over the expansion of American business after the Civil War. Hill was in the freight transportation business in St. Paul in the 1870s when he entered the railroad business, eventually building one of the most respected lines in the nation: the Great Northern, running from St. Paul to the Pacific. Leonine in appearance and manner, Hill brought farsighted practices to the railroad field at a time when it was riddled by speculation. Vanderbilt, the son of New York's richest man, toiled as a farmer until he was middle-aged. After entering the railroad business under his father's aegis, he built up the New York Central, a vital link in the nation's rail system. Asked about his decision to discontinue a mail train upon which the public depended, Vanderbilt retorted, "The public be damned!" It was a comment by which Vanderbilt, and his era, would be remembered.

The map at right illustrates the growth of American rail lines in the last half of the nineteenth century through a system of public subsidies based on land grants. Railroad builders received huge tracts in return for completing their lines, as indicated. Note, however, that the companies received only every other square mile within the bands shown on the map; the rest remained in the public domain. Because settlers preceded the railroads to some tracts in the "primary" land granted by the government, indemnity zones were set aside to guarantee that the companies could receive the full acreage to which they were entitled. Some companies chose to keep their primary lands for speculative reasons, but most expended great effort to sell it, placing advertisements as far away as Europe. The notion of making land grants to private companies was controversial, especially in view of the fact that a line as ambitious as the Great Northern Railway, running westward from St. Paul, had been constructed without any public funding whatsoever. Whatever the means, however, the nation acquired a full transportation system—with more than 250,000 miles of new track—in the short span of a half century.

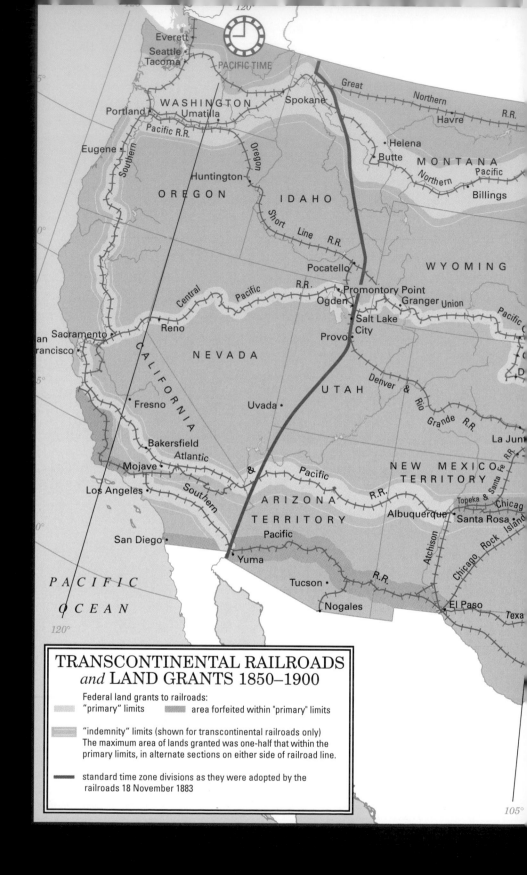

TRANSCONTINENTAL RAILROADS *and* LAND GRANTS 1850–1900

Federal land grants to railroads:
"primary" limits   area forfeited within "primary" limits

"indemnity" limits (shown for transcontinental railroads only)
The maximum area of lands granted was one-half that within the primary limits, in alternate sections on either side of railroad line.

standard time zone divisions as they were adopted by the railroads 18 November 1883

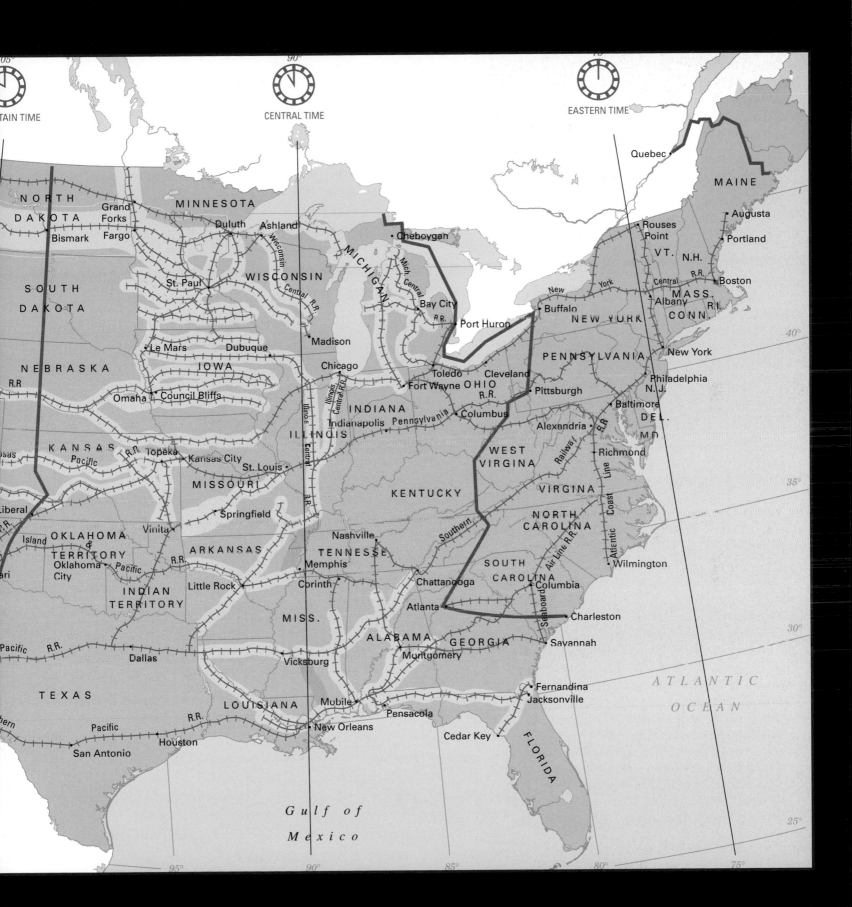

MOUNTAIN TIME

CENTRAL TIME

EASTERN TIME

Quebec

MAINE

NORTH DAKOTA
Grand Forks
Duluth
Ashland
Cheboygan
Rouses Point
Augusta

Bismark
Fargo
MINNESOTA
WISCONSIN
Wisconsin Central R.R.
MICHIGAN
Mich Central
Bay City
VT.
N.H.
Portland

SOUTH DAKOTA
St. Paul
Madison
Port Huron
R.R.
Buffalo
New
York
Central
R.R.
Albany
MASS.
Boston
R.I.
CONN.

NEBRASKA
Le Mars
Dubuque
IOWA
Chicago
NEW YORK

R.R
Omaha
Council Bliffs
Indianapolis
Pennsylvania
Toledo
Fort Wayne
Cleveland
OHIO
R.R.
Pittsburgh
PENNSYLVANIA
New York
Philadelphia
N.J.

KANSAS
Pacific
Topeka
Kansas City
St. Louis
INDIANA
Columbus
Alexandria
Railway
R.R
Baltimore
DEL.
MD.

Island
MISSOURI
ILLINOIS
Illinois Central R.R
KENTUCKY
WEST VIRGINIA
Richmond
VIRGINIA
Coast
Line
35°

Liberal
R.R
Springfield
Nashville
NORTH CAROLINA
Atlantic

OKLAHOMA & TERRITORY
Oklahoma City
Vinita
Pacific
ARKANSAS
TENNESSE
Southern
Chattanooga
SOUTH CAROLINA
Columbia
Air Line R.R.
Wilmington

ari
INDIAN TERRITORY
R.R.
Little Rock
Memphis
Corinth
Atlanta
Seaboard
Charleston

Pacific
R.R.
MISS.
ALABAMA
GEORGIA
Savannah

TEXAS
Dallas
Vicksburg
Montgomery
Fernandina
Jacksonville
ATLANTIC OCEAN

Pacific
R.R.
LOUISIANA
Mobile
Pensacola
Cedar Key
FLORIDA

hern
San Antonio
Houston
New Orleans

Gulf of Mexico

25°

Buffalo once numbered in the tens of millions on the prairie lands of the West, but as shown in N. H. Trotter's painting *Held Up by Buffalo* (circa 1880), they were pushed out with the coming of the railroads. Slaughtered for sport and as a policy to deny Plains Indians their primary food source, and then exterminated to make room for pioneers, buffalo numbered only 549 in 1889. Many buffalo were shot only for the tongue, others for hides; most carcasses, however, were left to decay in the sun or freeze in the cold.

his distribution network overseas to Yokohama and Hong Kong, sending steamships full of lumber and goods collected from other manufacturers eager to tap a new market: cotton, grain, iron ore, and coal, all of which the United States could sell cheaper than anyone else thanks to the natural abundance of each. James Hill made a fortune as well as his greatest contribution to the nation by opening U.S. trade with the Orient; whereas the United States sent total exports of $26 million to Asia in 1896, just nine years later the figure rose to $135 million, while imports climbed from $95 million to $175 million. The financial daring and capitalistic visions of men such as Hill had at least as much to do as strictly political developments with how America progressed. If a poll had been taken in 1890 to rate the "greatest builder," the ever-popular Hill would have beaten the other railroad financiers by a wide margin.

The Cattle Frontier and Indian Wars

The same entrepreneurial daring the railroad titans demonstrated existed in various nonindustrial concerns as well. For example, in 1860 the United

States was comprised of 31.5 million people and 17 million cattle. The cow population of Texas tilted the balance more than any other state, with 2.9 million head of cattle for 604,000 people. Although most of the fresh meat consumed in America was still raised locally, the ranchers of east Texas began sending beef across the country; cowboys gathered the free-roaming cattle, drove them in herds to Galveston, and sold them for the then-princely sum of six dollars a head to traders who then transported the cattle across the Gulf of Mexico to New Orleans. Profits could be so high that a few enterprising ranchers risked cattle drives all the way from Texas to Chicago and then shipped them by boxcar on to California. The exploits of these bold-spirited cowboys inspired a cultural genre that remains the stuff of movies and fiction today: the Western, with its sepia images of bravery and loneliness and that quintessentially American variety of wanderlust that never ends but just fades into the sunset. "We have no class structure, we don't even sense it, we don't even know what it means," historian Frank Tannenbaum noted. "The national hero is not a prince, not a king, not a rich man—but a cowboy."

The cattle business had taken a downturn during the Civil War when many cowboys joined the military and left the cattle to roam the plains unmolested. Thus when the cowpunchers returned to Texas in 1866 they found their ranges fat with mature, overfed bovines ripe for the roundup. The oversupply of cattle drove down prices in Texas but not up North, where prosperity and a greater demand for beef raised prices close to ten times those in Galveston. Fortunes were there for the taking by anyone who could find an economical way to transport cattle from Texas to the East, past Indians, buffalo, disease, and farmers who did not like herds of cattle thundering across their cropland. Much of the trouble and expense of moving cattle was eliminated in the late 1870s, when refinements to the refrigerated railroad car allowed beef to be sent East as steaks and hindquarters, which saved space as well as a great deal of bother and, of course, money. During the next few years, as U.S. cattle ranges spread north and west from Texas into Colorado, the Dakotas, Montana, and Wyoming and the number of head sent East quadrupled, the industrial and agricultural regions of the country became more tightly bound economically. Unfortunately, the era of the true cattle kingdom—large ranches, owned by single families with thousands of cattle

Guide maps such as the one below helped cowboys move large herds across the West. At first cattle drives headed from Texas all the way to eastern Kansas but by the mid-1860s they were effectively blocked by farmers trying to grow crops in the area. In 1867 a cattle broker named Joseph McCoy realized that cowboys could avoid farm country altogether by making better use of the railroads. He picked out a whistle-stop town called Abilene in central Kansas and invited ranchers to bring their herds there for transport straight through to Chicago. Copying the success of Abilene, other depots became cow towns, and railroad companies published guidebooks in order to attract business.

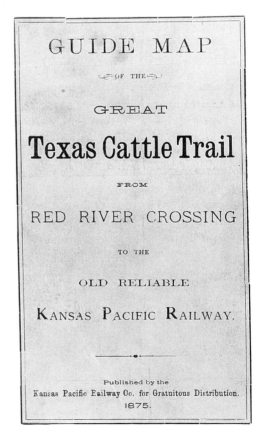

GUIDE MAP

OF THE

GREAT

Texas Cattle Trail

FROM

RED RIVER CROSSING

TO THE

OLD RELIABLE

KANSAS PACIFIC RAILWAY.

Published by the
Kansas Pacific Railway Co. for Gratuitous Distribution.
1875.

and spring roundups for branding—ended with the Great Blizzard of 1888. The "open range" concept no longer made sense. Beef cattle were raised on much smaller, barbed wire stockyards—and with it went the glamour of the mythological West. Cattle had become big business with new slaughterhouses in the rail towns of Omaha and Chicago—not Texas and Montana.

By 1890 the census would show that the American frontier—and open range—had disappeared into the Pacific, thanks largely to the transcontinental railroad that now connected California to New York. But the massive undertaking that would turn the country into an economically united nation had a brutal consequence: during construction of the railroad the Native Americans along the way were rounded up and relocated to reservations in the Great Plains.

Beginning in the 1860s, the federal government had slowly abandoned its previous policy of treating much of the West as a vast Indian reserve, introducing a system of smaller, separate tribal reservations where Native Americans would be forced to concentrate—meaning they would also be forced to exchange their nomadic ways for a settled, agricultural life. Some Native Americans, such as the Crow of Montana and the Pueblo of the Southwest, calmly accepted this grim fate. Others, including the Dakota Sioux and the Navajo of Arizona and New Mexico, initially opposed the new policy, but to no avail.

The remaining tribes, however, with a combined population of nearly 200,000 in the Northern Plains, made clear most Native Americans' determination to resist such brutal and inhumane treatment. From the 1860s through the 1880s these tribes—the western Sioux, Cheyenne, Arapaho, Kiowa, and Comanche on the Great Plains, the Nez Percé and Bannock in the northern Rockies, and the Apache throughout the Southwest—squared off with the U.S. Army in a final battle for the West.

The most notorious and bloodiest outbreaks of Indian resistance against the new policy took place between the western Sioux tribes and the U.S. Army in the Dakotas, Montana, and Wyoming. The trouble started when U.S. Indian agents proved incapable of keeping the Sioux on the reservation, which fueled increasing pressure from would-be settlers and developers for the army to take action. Thus in 1874 General William Tecumseh Sherman sent a force under Colonel George Armstrong Custer into the Black Hills of the Dakota Territory (now South Dakota) on the edge of the Great Sioux Reservation. Muscular and mustachioed with shoulder-length chestnut curls, the thirty-four-year-old Custer had been a celebrity since his days as an impetuous Civil War officer; now he had traded in the gold braid of the Union for a fringed buckskin uniform set off by a crimson scarf. Flamboyant and vainglorious, he had just published an autobiography titled *My Life on the Plains* (1874), casting himself in the mythic tall-tale tradition of Daniel Boone and Jim Bridger.

Custer's ostensible mission in South Dakota—whose so-called "badlands" had been described as "a part of hell with the fires burnt out"—was to find a suitable location for a new fort and to keep a watchful eye on renegade Indians. In fact, however, his cavalry regiment's primary objective was to

Kicking Bear, a Native American who fought at Little Bighorn in 1876, painted the aftermath of the battle at left. In late June, Colonel George Custer, at the head of the Seventh Cavalry, was moving aggressively through the Black Hills of what is now South Dakota. Having opened the Black Hills as gold territory two years before, Custer was aware of the pressure from private interests to move the remaining Indians out of the hills to free the area for mines and railroads. Custer pressed forward against the Sioux on June 25, 1876, over the ridges overlooking the Little Bighorn River. Around noon, a large force led by Crazy Horse overwhelmed Custer's ill-situated battalion, killing all 263 men. The watercolor below shows Custer at center, dressed in buckskin, with his hat beside him. The four victors standing over him are Sitting Bull, Rain-in-the-Face, Crazy Horse, and Kicking Bear.

confirm rumors that there was gold in the Black Hills, where the army had a deliberate plan to force land concessions from the Sioux. In November 1875, when government negotiations to buy the Black Hills broke down because the Sioux refused to sell, President Ulysses S. Grant and his generals decided to just clear entry to the gold mines. The administration announced that by January 31, 1876, any renegade Indians who were not on a designated reservation would be hunted down by the army and taken to one by force.

Certain Native American tribes refused to return to the reservations, and Custer, under the command of General Alfred Terry, ordered his troops to mobilize for an assault. In June 1876 he led one group of the 600 soldiers of the Seventh Cavalry to the Little Bighorn River area of Montana, a stronghold of Indian resistance. On June 22, seriously underestimating the Sioux enemy led by the legendary Chiefs Crazy Horse and Sitting Bull, Terry unwisely divided his forces, and Custer and his 263 men advanced recklessly against a company of Indians encamped along the Little Bighorn—a company later estimated at 2,000 warriors. In short order the heavily outnumbered U.S. troops found themselves surrounded and under heavy fire; in the slaughter that ensued, Custer and his entire army were annihilated. Two days later another cavalry company came upon the carnage and buried the dead soldiers where they had fallen. Only a single life was saved: a horse that had belonged to one of Custer's captains.

But the Sioux triumph would be short-lived. Crazy Horse's surprising victory at Little Bighorn served only to stoke the U.S. Army's fire to round up the Indians. After taking over the tribe's reservations the U.S. Army sent further expeditions to hunt down renegades in Montana, where troops harassed various Sioux bands for more than five years. Troops attacked Native American camps in the dead of winter and destroyed all their supply lines in an unrelenting effort to drive the Indians onto reservations. When that wasn't enough, the troops took to slaughtering the vast herds of buffalo that once roamed the plains, thereby wiping out the Indians' primary food source and spelling the end of their nomadic freedom. In time even the famed Sitting Bull, a leader at Little Bighorn who had led his tribe to Canada to escape the U.S. Army, was forced to surrender in 1881 for lack of provisions. Still worse, for a time after his surrender, Sitting Bull was made to suffer the humiliation of appearing as a freak attraction in entertainer Buffalo Bill's traveling Wild West Show. As historian Page Smith later noted: "Viewed in the light of the widespread public reaction of horror and anger, Little Bighorn may have been the costliest victory ever suffered by a people fighting for survival against enormous odds. The voices of that not inconsiderable company that espoused the cause of the Indians were drowned out by those who pressed for a 'final solution' to the Indian problem."

The bloody massacres that characterized so many of the reservation roundups greatly reduced the Native American populations, allowing the non-Indian westward expansion to continue with one less obstacle. As the nineteenth century drew to a close, any fear of a Native American menace in the West had become a memory. And the notion of the U.S. government's helping to "civilize" native peoples was viewed by honest journalists as a complete, holocaustic farce. As E. L. Godkin noted in *The Nation*: "Our philanthropy and our hostility tend to about the same end, and this is the destruction of the Indian race . . . the missionary expedient may be said to have failed."

The Western Farmers

Ultimately, farmers would settle and carve up much of the West while civilizing its manners, but for a while the mining industry made it the Wild West, spawned by the sudden influx of prospectors followed by those who preferred to dig gold from the miners' pockets: barkeepers, prostitutes, con artists, hustlers, and thieves. After the frenzy of the 1849 California gold rush had died down, bigger lodes of gold and silver were discovered in Colorado and Nevada, but they were so deep that miners had to cooperate to get at them. Mining companies therefore sprang up in both states to dig shafts hundreds of feet into mountainsides; within twenty years one Nevada lode alone yielded more than $300 million in gold and silver.

Most miners continued to move on to stake new claims, unlike the farmers of the nineteenth-century American West who owned the titles to their land through the Homestead Act of 1862, which insured that their rights would be upheld by federal marshals in the event a dispute arose. Plus, the farmers had an even stronger ally: the railroads, which had an interest in their success at providing crops to take to market and in their need for supplies and the occasional luxury item. But the partnership between farmers and the

railroads would collapse before long and set the stage for political battles in the 1890s.

The widespread manufacture and distribution of newly invented farm implements changed American agriculture after the Civil War, making it more profitable and strengthening farmers who could afford the new technology while pushing out those who could not. Cheap barbed wire introduced in 1874 slashed the price of fencing, which previously had often cost more than the land it marked off; redesigned windmills powered pumps to dredge precious water from beneath the surface of the windswept Great Plains, and improvements in plows, thresher machines, and combines reduced labor needs by half for harvesting corn, to a tenth for oats, and to a twentieth for harvesting wheat. As a consequence, labor costs fell by 70 percent and more.

The new farm machinery was, however, so expensive that it was economical only on holdings at least twice the size of the 160 acres settlers could

The Sylvester Rawding family posed on their homestead in Nebraska in the 1886 photograph above. Because lumber was expensive on the prairie, most pioneers built homes of sod. It was "Nebraska marble" to the pioneers, who could slice it quite easily into bricks for the walls of a house. Constructing a roof was a challenge, though, so most sod houses were dug into the side of a hill, as was the Rawding's. Families stayed in sod houses for a dozen years or more while tending to other priorities in establishing a farm. Farmers would use lumber to build corrals for stock long before they would indulge in the luxury of a frame house.

Deadwood, South Dakota, is shown above in 1876, the year it was founded. The new town was in a canyon in the Black Hills, an area considered sacred by the Sioux. Colonel George Custer opened up the lands in 1874, stirring up hostilities that would later haunt him, but that soon led to the discovery of gold. One of the thousands of adventurers drawn to the lawless town of Deadwood during its first year was "Wild Bill" Hickok, a celebrated marksman. A few months later, the local *Black Hills Pioneer* printed a laconic report: "Died, in Deadwood, Black Hills, August 2, 1876, from the effect of a pistol shot, J. B. (Wild Bill) Hickok, formerly of Cheyenne, Wyoming." Shot in the back of the head while playing cards, Hickok's death endures as one of Deadwood's legends.

obtain under the Homestead Act. What's more, farms of every size faced the same problems that plagued the West's cattle ranchers: weather, foreign competition, transportation costs, and overproduction. The last proved the most insidious when produce prices fell, prompting debt-ridden farmers to plant even more to compensate, which drove prices even farther down. Between increased domestic production and growing foreign competition, the prices of agricultural products began to plummet in 1867, falling to half and below by 1896. The prices of farm machinery also dropped, as did the interest rates on most farmers' debts—but that hardly kept farmers from bristling at the fees railroads charged to transport their crops, which sometimes exceeded the market value of the produce itself. As one regional farm newspaper decried: "There are three great crops raised in Nebraska. One is a crop of corn, one is a crop of freight rates, and one is a crop of interest. One is produced by farmers who by sweat and toil farm the land. The other two are produced by men who sit in their offices and behind their bank counters and farm the farmers."

Despite the poignant image of the struggling individual farmer mortgaging body and soul to keep his family going, banks generally would not even consider making loans to such marginal concerns. Instead, most borrowers were those prosperous enough to repay their loans; most of the debt taken on was not for sustenance but for expansion, be it in land, livestock, or machinery.

It is little wonder, then, that the farmers of the American West, like some of the eastern laborers whose goals for prosperity they shared, organized into a political force. Like the laborers, many farmers tended to ascribe their troubles to urban America, particularly its banks; several organizations stooped so low as to turn xenophobic, blaming the foreigners they said were allied with Wall Street. The increasingly militant farm groups called for restrictions on immigration and for the nationalization of banks and railroads as well as for lower tariffs that would enable foreign competition to lower prices on domestic manufactured goods. Along with the labor organizations, farmers aimed to curb the power of businessmen.

The End of the Frontier

Among the less noticed momentous events of 1893 was a quiet meeting of the American Historical Society in Chicago, where thirty-two-year-old University of Wisconsin scholar Frederick Jackson Turner proclaimed the end of the western frontier and the need for a new American mission now that the continent had been conquered. Contradicting those who held to the "germ theory" that America had been born in Europe and merely raised in the New World, Turner postulated that the United States had forged a unique spirit from its push against every frontier—a spirit that would die without further barriers to cross, especially as the end of the frontier meant more trouble for farmers in the form of higher prices for ever less available land. Many interpreted Turner's seminal article, "The Significance of the Frontier in American History," to recommend that a "new frontier" had to be found overseas. Doubting that the "expansive character" of the United States had ceased, Turner wrote that "the American energy will continually demand a wider field for its exercise."

Thus the question presented itself: what to conquer next? Did the United States need to continue its pattern of growth and expand overseas, extending statehood and guarantees of equality for all to territories there? Or was there an alternative with the new frontiers being created in urban New York, Boston, Philadelphia, and every other port city, where foreigners were alighting from steerage in droves to make new lives for themselves? There was, indeed, another option. The challenge of the future would be America's expansion into new technologies and business structures, which would in time make the nation stronger and more prosperous than any forays into empire ever could have. A "deluge of wonders" was changing America, and it was not cowboys and politicians that would propel the nation into the next century, but barnyard tinkerers, trained engineers, college professors, and wild-eyed tycoons.

Below, barbed wire was advertised as "the greatest invention of the age," and for farmers on the open range it may have been. J. F. Glidden, himself a farmer, invented the first widely used type in 1874 after seeing an exhibit on wire fencing at a county fair in Illinois. Replacing lumber, especially in areas where forests were scarce, barbed wire allowed farmers to keep livestock for themselves or, just as important, to keep cowboys and cattle drives from trampling their fields. Although cowboys had a habit of clipping through it, barbed wire soon enclosed the open spaces of the West.

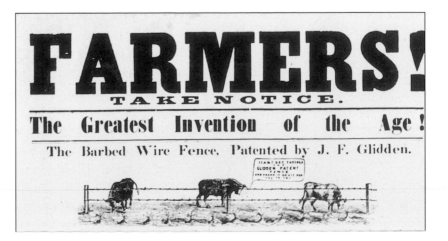

CHAPTER 11

THE RISE OF AMERICAN INDUSTRY

I n 1889, the United States was still too much of a work in progress to be harboring imperial ambitions. Besides, there was an enormous amount of profit to be made by concentrating on business at home. Just how young the nation was in the centennial year of George Washington's first inauguration can be traced through the history of the powerful Adams family of Massachusetts. It had taken only four generations to get from founding father John Adams, the second president of the United States, through *his* son John Quincy Adams, the sixth president, and through his son Charles Francis Adams, the U.S. ambassador who kept Britain neutral in the Civil War, to *his* son Henry Adams, the scholar who in 1889 authored the multivolume *History of the United States of America.* If it is true that "all experience is an arch to build upon," as written in *The Education of Henry Adams* (1907), then the Adams family was America's dynastic scorekeeper.

Henry Adams was very much aware of how vastly the nation had changed since his great-grandfather's day. When he wrote his history of Jefferson, the United States had become a major industrial power virtually unrecognizable as the crude, untamed land of a hundred years before, when

Thomas Anshutz painted steelworkers spilling out of a large mill in *The Ironworkers' Noontime,* left, in 1880. During the late nineteenth century, the insistent growth of corporations combined with the demands of competition to force intolerable burdens on workers in many industries. Unions arose in response, pitting themselves against the titans of business, even before the government did. One of the strongest labor unions was the United Mine Workers, whose emblem is shown in a colored lithograph, above.

more than two-thirds of the American population had lived within fifty miles of the Atlantic Ocean yet in surprising isolation from one another. As Adams wrote of the young republic: "Bringing New England nearer to Virginia and Georgia had not advanced even with the aid of a direct ocean highway. In becoming politically independent of England, the old thirteen provinces developed little more commercial intercourse with each other in proportion to their wealth and population than they had maintained in colonial days. The material ties that united them grew in strength no more rapidly than the ties which bound them to Europe. Each group of states lived a life apart."

How things had changed in a century. It may have taken a civil war to bring the states together by testing how far they could be pulled apart, but it was commerce and industry that would weld the nation's bonds permanently. National politics before the turn of the twentieth century were largely determined by a blossoming industrial economy, and can best be understood by first examining the massive changes it brought to American society. The United States was evolving, both internally and in its external perception by the rest of the world; England's ragtag New World colonies of yore had in a mere century united into one of the planet's most industrially advanced nations, and as such was well on its way to becoming a major global power.

In retrospect that development seems inevitable, perhaps even the logical extension of Manifest Destiny: Once the United States spanned the continent, it only made sense that the nation would start taking advantage of the vast natural resources it had uncovered along the way. After all, America's lands offered an embarrassment of riches: millions of acres of timber forests, mines brimming with gold, silver, and copper, and huge deposits of iron ore ready for the smelting. More important, America's greatest natural resource— its people—proved more than up to the task of making use of and therefore profiting from the land's bounty. In addition, the rise of science, particularly Darwinism, fostered an attitude of competitive individualism that helped catapult America headstrong into the twentieth century.

In the four decades following the Civil War, the United States demonstrated a genius for invention that made England's Industrial Revolution look quaint. Between 1860 and the turn of the century the U.S. Patent Office registered half a million new inventions, including significant discoveries at the rate of about one every five months from Thomas Alva Edison alone. In the best American entrepreneurial tradition, Edison had turned innovation into a systematic process at his "invention factory," founded in Menlo Park, New Jersey,

Thomas Edison had not slept for five days when he was photographed in 1877, below. Edison was so undisciplined as an Ohio youth that he could neither stay in school nor hold a job. Yet after he enjoyed his first success as an inventor in 1869, with a vote recording machine, he applied himself ferociously to work, resting only about four hours in a typical day. Edison would eventually obtain more than 1,000 patents, including those covering the incandescent light and the motion picture. In 1876, Edison even pioneered the research laboratory, as it is known today, coordinating a large team of specialists to solve problems in applied science. One of the first results was the phonograph.

in 1876 and staffed by the best and brightest engineers he could find. The brightest of them all, of course, was Edison himself, who followed up his design for the first electric light-bulb by forming the Edison General Electric Light Company (which eventually became General Electric) to power those bulbs in every home and business across the nation. With funding from several large banks he succeeded in doing just that. By 1898 nearly 3,000 power stations across the country generated electric current that consumers could tap into to turn night into day and that businesses could use to drive trolley cars, subways, and industrial machines. "I don't care so much for a fortune," Edison once told a reporter, "as I do for getting ahead of the other fellow." By insisting that persistence could overcome almost any obstacle, Edison, the indefatigable inventor-tinkerer, became the archetypal hero of the new age.

Alexander Graham Bell, above, arrived in Boston from Scotland in 1871. The son of a famous linguist, Bell taught elocution to the deaf. However, he had been inventing useful items since the age of eleven and was soon at work on several communications devices, in partnership with a patent attorney. By 1876, Bell had a working telephone and the beginnings of a tightly controlled business empire. He also continued his work in the education of the deaf, and was two-year-old Helen Keller's first teacher. He earned her enduring love by finding a way to reach her; he later recommended young Annie Sullivan as her resident teacher.

A decade earlier George Eastman had begun marketing his cheap and easy Kodak cameras to a public still giddy over the most valuable patent ever granted in the United States. Scottish immigrant Alexander Graham Bell's telephone, which was operable in 1876 and by the turn of the century had launched the American Telephone and Telegraph Company (AT&T), spread instantaneous communication to every region of the country. These advances in technology combined with innovations in workplace productivity to produce a boom in industrial efficiency. By the early 1900s, for example, Frederick W. Taylor's time-and-motion studies of steelworkers had grown into the broader commercial philosophy of "Taylorism," which sent productivity soaring by analyzing tasks back to their fundamentals.

For all the latest inventions, however, the U.S. economy continued to revolve around the railroads, especially since the advent of the refrigerated rail car that had so broadened markets for agricultural products. The ongoing demand for new railroad tracks spawned an entire new industry: steel, thanks largely to Scottish immigrant and U.S. railroad executive Andrew Carnegie, who showed that it was possible to rise from impoverished beginnings in Allegheny, Pennsylvania, to become the richest man in the world by taking advantage of opportunities.

As a teenage telegraph messenger, Carnegie had made his abilities known to every prominent businessman to whom he delivered a message. At the age of twenty-four, he was named superintendent of the Pennsylvania Railroad's western operations. He parlayed this expertise into making a name for himself during the Civil War, developing the Union's military telegraph system, and, after the war, he turned his attention to investing. With a small but impressive fortune and a pledge to let "nothing . . . interfere for a moment with my business career," he delved into the local iron business in Pitts-

Andrew Carnegie, left, and John D. Rockefeller, right, were among the richest men in America at the turn of the century, and perhaps the most despised as well. Each quit active participation in business while still in his fifties to attack a problem just as challenging as making a huge fortune: giving it away so that every dollar would do the most good. The Carnegie Trust and the Rockefeller Foundation became lasting models for philanthropy not only in spirit but in structure. However, the rare generosity exhibited by Carnegie and Rockefeller in their later lives belies the ruthlessness of their earlier business careers. As Harry Truman, who was raised in the era the two magnates dominated, would assert in a bitter speech before the Senate in 1937, "No one ever considered Carnegie libraries steeped in the blood of the Homestead steelworkers, but they are. We do not remember that the Rockefeller Foundation is founded on the dead miners of the Colorado Fuel and Iron Company and a dozen other performances."

burgh, which he greatly expanded. Then, in 1872, he met Sir Henry Bessemer, who had invented a cheap and easy new way of removing impurities in iron to make steel, a far lighter, stronger, and more durable metal than iron alone.

Armed with his own ironworks and the Bessemer process, Carnegie set out to produce steel faster and cheaper than ever. Never one to pass up an opening, he took advantage of the great Chicago fire of 1871 by turning the rebuilding of the city into a laboratory and showcase for his new product, erecting steel skyscrapers and other edifices the likes of which the world had never seen, proclaiming, "The day of iron is past; steel is king!"

Andrew Carnegie bought the best talent and built the most advanced steel mills, which quickly took over the industry and made him incredibly wealthy. At the time there were scores of steel plants in the United States, but America's first million-dollar company, Carnegie's steel mill in Homestead, Pennsylvania, doubled the output of its nearest competitor by combining the Bessemer process with ruthless cost-cutting and efficiency measures that pushed earnings to $2 million a year. Carnegie's employees averaged eighty-four hours of brutal toil at less than $10 a week, making railroad tracks as well as beams and girders for Chicago's skyscrapers and New York's Brooklyn Bridge. By 1890 their efforts boosted Carnegie's personal fortune to more than $100 million (well over $1 billion in today's dollars), which made him the richest American of his time as well as the natural spokesman of the industrial aristocracy of the Gilded Age. Within a few years Carnegie's mills would produce more steel than all of Great Britain and allowed him to further revolutionize the industry by slashing prices and branching into specialty products such as steel wire and fencing.

Carnegie was nothing if not single-minded. When a visiting socialist carried on to him about the evils of capitalism and the desirability of a fair distribution of wealth, Carnegie asked his secretary for two figures: the total value of his assets and the latest estimate of the world's population. After some arithmetic he told the secretary, "Give this gentleman sixteen cents. That's his share of my wealth." By the same token, however, Carnegie's motto was "The man who dies rich dies disgraced," and he did spread his wealth through enormous bequests to good causes, giving scientist Marie Curie $50,000 for her research on radium and far more to the research-oriented Carnegie Institute of Technology that would become Carnegie-Mellon University. Late in life, Carnegie was determined to give away as much money as possible, setting up hundreds of Carnegie Free Public Libraries across the United States, desperate to shed his image as a leading "robber baron" of the age.

Steel, however, was hardly the only source of America's growing industrial might: There was oil as well, and another titan to marshal its power in John D. Rockefeller. The founding father of one of the country's great commercial dynasties started his empire by merging with or buying out other oil refineries while diversifying into pipelines, barrels, and storage facilities. Rockefeller and five partners had formed the Standard Oil Company of Ohio in 1870 and let nothing thwart its eventual domination of the industry, even if that meant slashing prices, bribing or spying on competitors, and crafting sweet deals with the railroads not only to discount costs but to actually pay to ship Standard's products. Like Carnegie, Rockefeller was interested in only one thing. As he told his family when he found out they planned to surprise him on his birthday with an electric car for tooling about his vast estate: "If it's all the same to you, I'd rather have the money."

The cartoon below entitled "Next," published in *Puck* in 1904, portrays the Standard Oil Company as a mean-tempered octopus strangling the government and anything else within its long reach. By 1880 "the Standard" controlled 90 percent of the oil-refining capacity in the United States, a fact for which the president, John D. Rockefeller, felt no need to apologize. He usually said very little in public, preferring to let his actions speak for him, but in 1907 he wrote, "We did not ruthlessly go after the trade of our competitors and attempt to ruin it by cutting prices or instituting a spy system. We had set ourselves the task of building up as rapidly and as broadly as possible the volume of consumption." Whether by diligence or guile, the Standard eventually grew too large, however, and the Supreme Court broke it up into smaller companies in 1911.

The cartoon at right entitled "The Bosses of the Senate" by Joseph Keppler was published in 1889, showing business monopolies, or "trusts," had become so bloated that they dwarfed even the U.S. Congress. The power of the monopolies stirred the anger of reformers such as Kansan Mary Lease, who proclaimed in an 1890 speech that, "It is no longer a government of the people, by the people, and for the people, but a government of Wall Street, by Wall Street, and for Wall Street. The great common people of this country are slaves and monopoly is the master."

And have it he did. With Standard Oil's expansion beyond Ohio stymied by state laws, Rockefeller needed a means of entering new markets, and found it in 1881 when his company's chief counsel concocted the "trust," under which a corporation's stockholders would entrust their shares to the control of a central board of trustees. In exchange, the stockholders would get certificates of interest in the trust in the corporation that offered sizable dividends while violating none of the state laws against one company owning another in the same business. The Standard Oil Company of Ohio formed America's first major trust in 1882, handing Rockefeller centralized control of the oil industry and creating an entity that would play a role in U.S. finance and politics for generations to come.

At first only a handful of trusts operated on a national scale, but that would change in 1888 when New Jersey passed a Holding Company Act and removed most of the barriers to corporate organization. The rest of those barriers would tumble in 1890 with passage of the Sherman Antitrust Act, which proscribed cartels and thus encouraged companies to merge formally into corporations. A boon to big business came in 1895 when the U.S. Supreme Court ruled in the case of *United States v. E. C. Knight*, in which the government sought the dissolution of the American Sugar Refining Company on the grounds that it was a conspiracy devoted to the restraint of trade. The Court, however, found that although the company controlled 90 percent of all U.S. sugar refining it was engaged in manufacturing rather than in commerce, and thus was not subject to antitrust law. The ruling seemed to suggest that most industrial corporations need not fear prosecution under the Sherman Act.

Incorporations boomed in both number and size. Across the nation the trend toward expansion was most obvious in the very names companies gave themselves. Whereas in the past most commercial concerns had been named for their founders or locations, the new flood of corporations tended to include the designations American, National, General, and even International. Industry swelled with monikers such as American Tin Plate, American

Car & Foundry, American Woolen, American Steel Foundries, Distilling Company of America, National Biscuit, National Steel, National Sugar Refining, International Silver, and International Harvester. These were not merely semantic changes: among other developments, the creation of large corporations spawned new business structures such as "middle management," a layer of bureaucracy designed to serve as liaison between workers and company owners.

The financial structure of these industrial corporations differed substantially from that of the trusts, as the former were defined by selling securities to the public to raise capital. By contrast, the earlier trusts had issued no public shares; only when trust members wanted to liquidate their positions did they sell their certificates on the open market. The new industrial corporations encouraged familiarity with their operations and "went public" just as they do today, through underwritings and initial public offerings of stock to anyone who had the means to invest.

This new way of doing things provided business—and power—to Wall Street, as the nation's financial center in New York had come to be known. Influential investment bankers, such as John Pierpont ("J. P.") Morgan, could raise millions of dollars for the companies in their "constellations" while denying funds to those they considered poor risks. Without them the creation of large enterprises would have been difficult if not impossible, as the enormous sums corporations required could be obtained only in New York, London, and the world's few other major financial markets. It is little wonder that opponents of the new system considered the "money trust" the most powerful and insidious of all.

Many felt the same way about J. P. Morgan and his fellow financial wizards, especially when they proved even mightier than the leading industrialists. For example, when Andrew Carnegie's tactics finally began to seem too ruthless, his competitors appealed to Morgan as the only man who could stop the steel tycoon. And so he did. A genius at mergers and acquisitions, the Merlin-like Morgan succeeded in buying Carnegie out for an initial bid of $492 million, which made the latter one of the richest men on earth and created the world's first billion-dollar holding company, United States Steel. When Carnegie lamented that he should have held out for another $100 million, Morgan averred, "Andy, I would have paid it."

Such gamesmanship between powerful individuals was hardly uncommon and had a disturbingly deep impact on the nation's economy and on the lives of its people. At a time when the United States imposed no income tax and there was little government regulation of business, companies merged into corporations and made entire industries into monopolies, increasingly concentrating wealth and power in the hands of just a few men and thus widening the gap between the scant "haves" and the many "have-nots." Although this aggressively pure form of capitalism undoubtedly helped America develop into an industrial monolith, it sprang from a dubious interpretation of Charles Darwin's theory that the evolution of species was determined by the "survival of the fittest." English philosopher Herbert Spencer led the charge that poverty was the result of laziness or some other defi-

J. P. Morgan, above, circa 1890s, was the most powerful banker of his time. Born in Connecticut in 1837, he absorbed the art of international finance from his father, Junius Morgan, a banker with ties to London. John Pierpont Morgan then established his own reputation as a deal maker during the consolidation of industries such as steel and railroads. After inheriting full control of the House of Morgan in 1890, he was in a position to increase its business dramatically, even as he assumed an unofficial role as America's supreme financial arbiter and authority. Twice, in 1893 and 1907, the federal government appealed to Morgan for leadership in times of financial crisis. Some of Morgan's influence emanated from his fortune, but most of it grew from the strength of his personality; a stern Yankee, he claimed that the only factor he considered in making a loan was the character of the borrower. Old-fashioned in many ways, he nonetheless managed to carry the U.S. banking system almost single-handedly well into the twentieth century.

The cartoon at right, "The Jaws of Monopoly Power," was printed circa 1890. Many Americans feared that monopolies would inevitably grow so large they would be uncontrollable. Until Theodore Roosevelt entered the White House in 1901, the issue did not receive any presidential attention, a situation that encouraged the conviction that the monopoly monster was bigger and stronger than Washington.

OPPOSITE PAGE: A family from Italy was photographed at Ellis Island (top); a health inspection card like the one pictured (bottom) was absolutely necessary for entry into America. An immigrant named Bianca De Carli, who arrived from Italy in 1913, later recalled her mental turmoil as her ship approached New York harbor: "We were impatient, but yet patient; we were nervous—how do you say, confused, *agitato*—because we were still not sure of passing through. A thousand times during the last day or two I put my hands on my passport and papers, which I kept wrapped in a handkerchief under the front of my dress. This was just to make sure they were still there."

ciency and success the result of natural selection among human beings, a belief known as Social Darwinism. Some corporate titans took this designation as one of the chosen few as a public trust. Carnegie, for example, began preaching a "gospel of wealth" urging the rich to work on behalf of the poor. But others used it to justify their distaste for the working classes and to claim that labor organizations were sacrilegious and had to be suppressed. Their position unfortunately held up against the best arguments of more egalitarian thinkers such as writers Henry George and Edward Bellamy, who decried corporate capitalism and called for the redistribution of wealth, the nationalization of railroad and utility companies, and civil service reform. Bellamy's utopian novel *Looking Backward,* in particular, championed a benign socialism as the next evolutionary step for providing citizens with services and material needs.

The New Immigration

The rise of corporations changed the nature and scope of the U.S. economy, but the late-nineteenth-century influx of immigrants revolutionized the nation itself. In 1880 there were 50.3 million Americans, of whom 6.7 million, or 13 percent, had been born elsewhere; that year 457,000 new immigrants arrived in the United States. The mark was broken the next year and again in 1882, when 789,000 landed in America. This "new immigration" would expand throughout the 1890s, boom late in the decade when prosperity returned after a brief depression, and result in a U.S. population of 92.4 million in 1910. Although the number of foreign-born residents had grown only to 13.5 million, or 15 percent, their impact was far greater than that of earlier influxes because most of the new immigrants settled in cities and concentrated in ethnic neighborhoods that transformed urban life. Two-thirds of the immigrants who arrived in the 1880s were from Germany, Great Britain, Ireland, and Scandinavia; by 1900, however, slightly over one-third would be from Russia, Italy, and Austria-Hungary.

More than a million immigrants came to the United States in 1910, more than 90 percent of them Europeans. Smaller numbers arrived from Canada, Mexico, the British West Indies, Turkey, and Japan; as might have been expected, non-whites faced far more prejudice. As President John Mitchell of the United Mine Workers wrote in 1909: "The demand for the exclusion of Asiatics . . . is based solely on the fact that as a race their standard of living is extremely low, and their assimilation by Americans impossible." Laborers and their unions generally opposed immigration on the grounds that newcomers willing to accept low pay would take jobs from native-born Americans, while manufacturers favored it for the same reason: immigrants were a cheap source of labor. This did not seem to bother most new arrivals at first. Even though immigrants made less money for the same work as native-born Americans, the wage scale was far higher than that in Europe and opportunities for education and advancement were much better. Moreover, those who arrived after 1898 found themselves in the first great U.S. economic boom, during which social and financial mobility made the American Dream attainable for the majority of immigrants from overseas as well as from America's own farms.

More immigrants were male; some came hoping to make enough money to send for their families, while others planned to make fortunes to take back home. Most arrived poor. Between 1899 and 1910, for example, the average amount of cash in a European immigrant's pocket was $21.57; only the English and French landed with an average of more than $50 apiece.

Millions of displaced persons immigrated to the United States, including more than a million persecuted Jews. Many others were not so much pushed out of Europe as they were pulled toward America by exaggerated tales of "streets paved with gold," plentiful good jobs, cheap land, and, best of all, freedom from government restrictions on enterprise, commerce, and every other kind of pursuit of happiness. The United States was seen as a prosperous land of occupational opportunity, endless possibility, and social mobility. Reports of the wonders of the New World were spread not just by family members who had already made the crossing but also by agents for U.S. businesses who traversed Europe offering credit to those willing and qualified to come to the states to work for their companies.

The map at right shows the density of foreign-born residents throughout the United States from 1900 to 1920. It also indicates dominant religions, by state. In the early twentieth century, when immigrants were more likely than ever before to come from southern and eastern Europe, many native-born Americans resisted what they perceived as the changing fabric of the population. The leading citizens of many major cities organized "protective organizations" to lobby against further immigration; the effort succeeded in imposing new curbs that were enacted into law in 1924. However, not all immigrants remained in America; hundreds of thousands returned to their native countries each year. With improvements in transportation it was possible to work seasonally in America or to stay just long enough to build a nest egg. Some of those returning were so proud of their stint in the United States that they "Americanized" their names: "Chicagovich," for example.

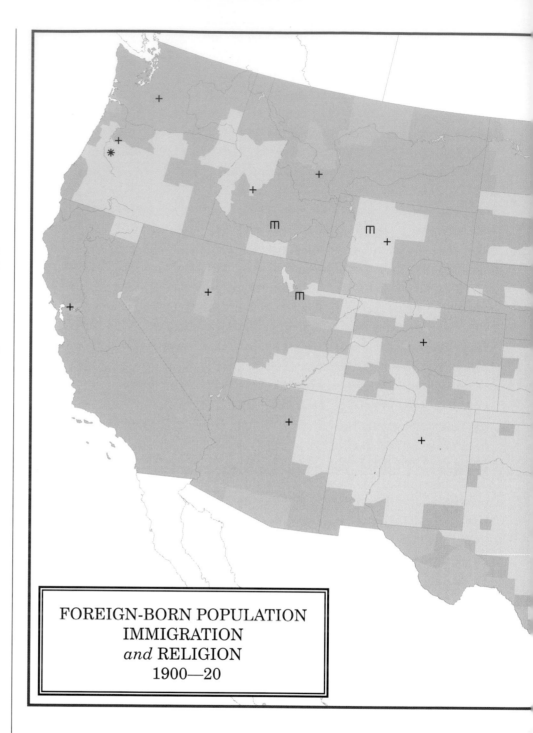

FOREIGN-BORN POPULATION IMMIGRATION *and* RELIGION 1900—20

This influx of immigrants between 1870 and 1920 had also transformed America from a basically Protestant nation into a society of Protestants, Catholics, and Jews. In fact, Catholics represented almost half the population of Buffalo, Cleveland, Chicago, and Milwaukee. Three-quarters of all immigrants over the age of fourteen could read and speak their native languages, but this aggregate average does not reveal the educational disparity among the various ethnic groups. While more than half the immigrant Turks, southern Italians, and Mexicans were illiterate, one-quarter of the Jews and Greeks and less than one percent of the English could not read or write. Labor and professional skills were similarly distributed, with only the English account-

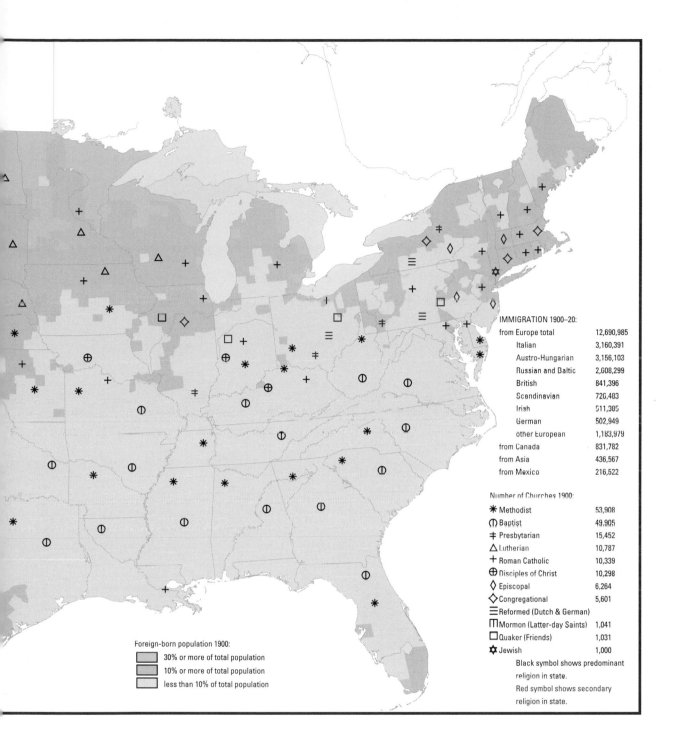

IMMIGRATION 1900–20:

from Europe total	12,690,985
Italian	3,160,391
Austro-Hungarian	3,156,103
Russian and Baltic	2,608,299
British	841,396
Scandinavian	726,483
Irish	511,385
German	502,949
other European	1,183,979
from Canada	831,782
from Asia	436,567
from Mexico	216,522

Number of Churches 1900:

✳	Methodist	53,908
⋔	Baptist	49,905
ǂ	Presbytarian	15,452
△	Lutherian	10,787
+	Roman Catholic	10,339
⊕	Disciples of Christ	10,298
◇	Episcopal	6,264
◇	Congregational	5,601
≡	Reformed (Dutch & German)	
�	Mormon (Latter-day Saints)	1,041
▢	Quaker (Friends)	1,031
✡	Jewish	1,000

Black symbol shows predominant religion in state.
Red symbol shows secondary religion in state.

Foreign-born population 1900:

- 30% or more of total population
- 10% or more of total population
- less than 10% of total population

ing for a sizable professional class of 10 percent of its quarter-million immigrants to America between 1899 and 1910, most of them seeking better wages and fewer class distinctions.

Opened in 1892, New Jersey's Ellis Island was the nation's busiest immigration station at the turn of the century, at its peak processing as many as 5,000 people a day. Because most of the newcomers were almost destitute, few could afford to settle very far from where they had disembarked. Thus nearly a third of all immigrants from 1899 to 1910 traveled across the river to New York, most of them in New York City, which quickly became the world's largest and most ethnically diverse metropolis. By 1910 almost half

H. G. Wells described the Grand Hall at Ellis Island, above, as "quietly immense." Ellis Island was by far the busiest port of entry. Inching through numerous checkpoints and inspection stations, immigrants made their way into the United States.

of the population of New York's borough of Manhattan was foreign-born, as were those of Boston, Buffalo, Chicago, Cleveland, Detroit, and San Francisco, while non-natives made up more than 60 percent of the populations of rapidly growing urban areas in Massachusetts, Minnesota, and New Jersey. If, as many writers of the time believed, the nation's future could be found in its cities, then it looked as though immigrants would control that destiny.

A Changing Nation

The changes wrought by new immigration of the late nineteenth century were not, however, confined to foreigners; the exploding U.S. economy prompted internal population shifts as well. Wanderlust has always been one of America's defining traits, and high mobility characterized natives at the turn of the twentieth century as much as it did the newcomers from other lands. But whereas a half-century earlier the vast majority of relocations had been from one rural area of the nation to another, in 1910 most of the moves were from farms to cities. Beleaguered Midwestern farmers made their way to Chicago and joined the swelling immigrant population that in time would see one out of four native-born Americans living in states other than their birthplaces. The full sweep of the migration can be drawn from the U.S. Census, which in 1880 showed 14.1 million Americans living in areas described as urban, with 6.2 million residing in cities with populations exceeding 100,000. By contrast, in 1910 there were 42 million urban dwellers, of whom 20.4 million lived in cities of more than 100,000 people.

The sheer size of the migration from both within and without made the integration of immigrants into America's emerging urban fabric one of the most pressing issues of the early twentieth century. And despite nervous anticipation of conflict, the assimilation of white foreigners and rural Americans was surprising for its ease as well as its speed.

The main reason for their quick absorption was the immigrants' embrace of their new country's language, customs, and values. Some of those who

Below, a monumental traffic jam halts all types of vehicles at an intersection in Chicago in 1905. The need to relieve urban congestion inspired huge investment, both public and private. In 1887 engineer Frank Sprague created an industry when he succeeded in replacing mule-drawn cars with electric trolleys. "Lincoln set the slaves free; Sprague set the mule free" was his motto. Only ten years later, electric trolley lines crisscrossed 20,000 miles in cities around the country. As shown in the photograph, however, an electric trolley did not go any faster than a horse-drawn one when it was stuck in traffic. To remedy that, New York and Chicago built elevated train lines, while Boston completed America's first subway in 1898.

made a point of adapting to American ways took pride in becoming "Yankees" and looked with contempt upon the "greenhorns" who had not yet learned to fit in. Those who were unwilling or unable to adjust to their adopted country's culture often opted for ethnic ghettos, which soon made many growing cities, and New York in particular, seem more like patchworks of nationalities than unified societies. In 1910, for example, it was possible to cross Manhattan from the East River to the Hudson or from the Battery north to Thirty-fourth Street without hearing a word of English.

To most new Americans, and especially to their children, success seemed attainable by learning the rules and obeying them. Young immigrants as well as the children of native-born farmers who had moved to the cities devoured Horatio Alger's stories of poor boys whose honesty and effort as well as sheer luck and pluck led them to wealth and respect by way of the good fortune that supposedly came to all who played by the rules. This was only the most glittering of the immigrants' traditional paths to the American Dream, and many made it come true by entering into professions and serving members of their own communities before making the leap into the larger society.

Another route to prosperity was employment through political agencies that offered good jobs in exchange for votes and funds and the services required to obtain both. Yet another option was admitted criminal activity, both within ethnic communities and outside them. Finally, there was the great equalizer that still lures the inner-city youth of today with the promise of riches and fame: sports, particularly the few athletic endeavors that somehow managed to escape racial prejudice, perhaps because certain ethnic minorities had proved so much better at them than anyone else. In boxing, for example, a stereotype had developed of the Irish as such fine fighters that immigrants from South America and Eastern Europe took to calling themselves "Battling Bob O'Doul" and "Terrible Tim O'Brien" and the like. Still, when a black man, Jack Johnson, became world heavyweight champion in 1908, it caused much distress among white fans. For some reason racism in sports did not extend to horse racing; several trainers and most of the best nineteenth-century jockeys were black, including those who rode eleven of the Kentucky Derby winners between 1875 and 1895. America had truly become multicultural: in New York, Pittsburgh, or Chicago one could dine on Italian or Mexican cuisine, listen to Irish folk music or African-American jazz, attend Yiddish theater or Austrian opera all in the same evening.

It was business, however, that played the greatest role in many immigrants' transition into American culture. At the turn of the century large-scale government intervention in the lives of individual citizens was still two generations off. Federal, state, and municipal assistance programs were unknown in 1910, when there was still no income tax and total federal expenditures amounted to less than $700 million. Some cities had charitable organizations devoted to helping the needy and speeding the poor into jobs and thus the economy, but these were private enterprises rather than government programs.

Although their entry seemed smooth, the huge influx of immigrants at the turn of the century raised issues that echo to this day. Before the new immigration, most newcomers to the United States had been Protestant; now the majority were Catholic, Jewish, or Eastern Orthodox. Some observers fretted that two Americas seemed to be taking shape, one a native-born, rural, Protestant, literate, and middle-class nation, the other composed of poor, foreign-born, illiterate, urban Catholics and Jews. As crime and gang violence intensified in most of the nation's cities, the vital question arose whether the process of Americanization could take hold before the two disparate nations came into conflict. As Republican Senator Albert Beveridge of Indiana warned: "If law and order are not maintained, then surely the nation will be doomed."

Opposition to Immigrants

Americans had been wrestling with immigration policy since the brief heyday of the Anti-Masonic Party in the early 1830s, but in 1911 the issue took on a new urgency. The U.S. Congress jumped into the debate by appointing a joint committee on immigration that presented a massive report, along with recommendations for improvements such as excluding certain classes of immigrants, establishing quotas for each port of entry, and instituting a literacy test for all newcomers.

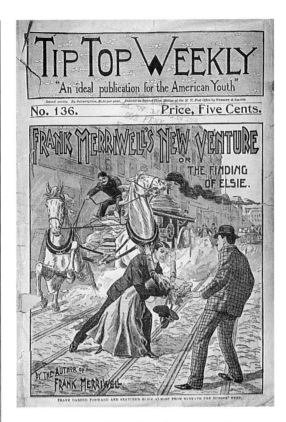

Inexpensive publications known as "penny dreadfuls" such as the one above often featured stories in which hard work, ingenuity, and honesty were richly rewarded. Many American children read them avidly; others, however, were too busy to read, working long hours at tedious jobs. In 1890, Jacob Riis photographed "Bohemian Cigarmakers at Work in Their Tenement," left.

Longtime labor leader Samuel Gompers is shown above in an undated photograph. Gompers started working in a cigar factory in 1863 at the age of thirteen and led his first strike there fourteen years later. A tough-speaking man, he rose to prominence by protecting skilled workers against both the greed of capitalists and the onslaught of unskilled labor. Though born in England himself, Gompers came out loudly against immigrants, especially those from Asia. He remained at the head of the American Federation of Labor almost continuously for 38 years, until his death in 1924.

This report was applauded and endorsed by a wide spectrum of political leaders, from conservative Republican Elihu Root to Socialist leader Eugene V. Debs and American Federation of Labor (AFL) leader Samuel Gompers (himself an English immigrant), who feared that immigrants' acceptance of low wages would harm American workers. Similarly, Senator Robert La Follette of Wisconsin, who would go on to lead the Progressive Party, blamed foreigners for what he perceived as an increase in immorality in the nation's cities, while novelist Jack London wrote slightingly of the "dark pigmented things, the half castes, the mongrel bloods, and the dregs of long conquered races." Even such a forward thinker as President Theodore Roosevelt was troubled about the potential dilution of his nation's Anglo-Saxon heritage. "There is no room in this country for hyphenated Americanism," Roosevelt told a group of New Yorkers in 1915, "The one absolutely certain way of bringing this nation to ruin, of preventing all possibility of it continuing to be a nation at all, would be to permit it to become a tangle of squabbling nationalities."

By the second decade of the twentieth century, restrictions on immigration had become part of the reformist creed, if not openly then couched in rhetoric and proposed legislation. Even those who eschewed racial arguments found other reasons to bar foreigners from America's shores. Prohibitionists claimed they were immoral drunkards, middle-class progressives denounced them as dangerous radicals, and churchmen whispered of white slave traffic and the harsh treatment some immigrants suffered under the still extant indentured servitude system, which inspired the rationale that it was more humane to keep some people out of the United States than it was to let them enter. Only big business, which craved cheap labor, argued for maintaining the tradition of open access to anyone who wanted to come to America—not that the tradition hadn't developed a few loopholes. Federal legislation restricting immigration was already on the books, prohibiting the entry of those deemed morally, mentally, or physically unfit, while labor unions had lobbied successfully for laws against importing foreign workers to perform contract labor.

In the years following the 1911 report of the congressional committee on immigration, so-called progressive reformers and their allies in the churches and labor unions fought hard for a bill excluding illiterate foreigners, which would have barred one in four applicants from entering the United States. A measure incorporating a literacy requirement would not be passed until 1917 over the veto of President Woodrow Wilson, however, by which time the flood of immigrants had dwindled to a steady stream. The last year to usher in more than a million immigrants would be 1914; two and three years later World War I would drive the number down to fewer than 300,000. In addition, in 1918 Congress would pass a law excluding anarchists and those advocating the overthrow of the government. In 1918, the first full year of the restrictions, only 110,000 foreigners would be admitted to the United States; three years later the first quota law was added, further limiting immigration to 3 percent for each nationality recognized in the 1910 census, with a cap of 357,000. The new immigration was over.

The Rise of Black America

Of course, none of these restrictions applied to black Americans, who faced cultural barriers of a more political nature as the United States continued on its march to economic dominance. Toward the end of the nineteenth century state legislatures passed segregationist "Jim Crow" laws (named for a popular character at minstrel shows), which separated the races and effectively denied blacks the vote not only throughout the South but in other parts of the country as well. The race question turned federal in 1896 when the U.S. Supreme Court used the case of *Plessy v. Ferguson* to declare segregation legal so long as facilities provided both races were "separate but equal" in quality.

In other words, by the turn of the century African-Americans had become second-class citizens in everything but name, as that was prohibited by the Fourteenth Amendment to the Constitution. But in fact blacks were barred from many desirable jobs, such as in textile mills, as well as from juries, which helps to explain why blacks received far harsher penalties for committing the same crimes as whites. Worse still, attempts by blacks to gain real equality were often overwhelmed by the Ku Klux Klan, whose brutal attacks ranged from tarring and feathering to lynchings, more than a hundred of which were reported in every year of the 1890s, mostly in the South. A mere generation after their emancipation, African-Americans were again being forced to fight for the civil rights they supposedly already had.

According to the 1910 census, some 10.2 million blacks lived in the United States, a figure that may be low due to incomplete reporting from black areas of the rural South at the time. No matter how significant their numbers, whatever steps black Americans took to change their financial status, values, way of life, and even appearance did not get them far on the path to socioeconomic advancement. Foreign immigrants had reason to hope they—or at least their children or grandchildren—could leave the ghettos and enter the American mainstream, but blacks were effectively excluded from the middle class. Not even the best efforts of organizations such as the now venerable Urban League, formed in 1910 to help Southern blacks adjust to city living in the North, could do much to clear the way toward equal, or any, opportunities for African-Americans.

Blacks were divided about how to resolve the dilemma of race in the United States. The largest group reacted to the widespread racism of the time by conceding the impossibility of integrating into the mainstream and working instead to build their own communities, versions of the American Dream that were usually defined as isolation from whites. Another segment of the black population pursued the sort of assimilation to which all immigrant groups seemed to aspire, while a small but vocal third segment despaired of ever fitting into American society and advocated blacks' return to Africa.

Fortunately, the most pragmatic approaches to the problem of racism found spokesmen of true greatness. In 1903, black intellectual leader W. E. B. Du Bois opined that, "Easily the most striking thing in the history of the American Negro since 1876 is the ascendancy of Mr. Booker T. Washington,"

The playbill above advertises a performance by the white actor Thomas D. Rice as "Jim Crow." Rice based his characterization on an elderly African-American street entertainer he had seen in Louisville, Kentucky, in 1828. With a dancing step and wide smile, Rice and his many imitators played "Jim Crow" in minstrel shows for almost a century. Entertaining and ingratiating, the character came to represent the only personality many whites would accept in a black man. In the late nineteenth century, the phrase "Jim Crow" took on a new meaning when it was used to describe a system of laws designed to keep African-Americans in Southern states as subservient as the character for which they were named.

Booker T. Washington is shown below delivering a speech at the opening of the Cotton States and International Exposition in Atlanta in 1895. Washington had been born a slave in Virginia in 1856 and was raised without formal schooling. Nonetheless, he craved knowledge and found ways to learn how to read, eventually working his way through college. In 1881, Washington founded the Tuskegee Institute in Alabama, where he strived to produce a middle class of black workers. He believed fervently in education for African-Americans, yet in his speech in Atlanta he reasoned that "agitation of questions of social equality is the extremist folly," since progress for African-Americans would come as the "result of severe and constant struggle" and not "artificial forcing." The applause from the audience, composed entirely of whites, lasted almost as long as the fifteen-minute speech.

and it was no exaggeration; Washington wielded more power and influence than any African-American between Frederick Douglass and Martin Luther King, Jr.

In the aftermath of the Civil War, former slave Washington attended the Hampton Institute, where he learned the value of a practical education aimed at providing students the wherewithal to make a living. The institute's founder, General Samuel Chapman Armstrong, stressed the importance of hard work, savings, home equity, and family, maintaining that while political and social equality for blacks was important, it was not as essential as uplifting their own communities, the top priority before going on to other goals.

Although Washington bristled at the way blacks were treated in America, he realized how impenetrable the problem was and took up Armstrong's cry. He found a platform for his views in 1881 when he founded the Tuskegee Institute, a business and agricultural school for blacks in Alabama, and then hit the road to make speeches assuring whites they had nothing to fear from a hard-working, industrious black population that had no interest in integrating itself into middle-class American society. "In all things that are purely social we can be as separate as the fingers, yet one as the hand in all things essential to mutual progress," Washington told a largely white and approving audience at the Atlanta Exposition in 1895. Addressing himself to his fellow blacks, he added, "To those of my race who depend on bettering their condition in a foreign land or who underestimate the importance of cultivating friendly relations with the Southern white man . . . I would say, 'Cast down your bucket where you are'—cast it down in making friends in every manly way of the people of all races by whom we are surrounded. Cast it down in agriculture, in mechanics, in commerce, in domestic service, and in the professions." It was, of course, the same appeal offered to foreign immigrants. What Washington meant was that anything could be attained by any American who applied himself—anything, that is, except the full political and civil rights guaranteed by the U.S. Constitution.

In 1900 Washington organized and became the first president of the National Negro Business League, which encouraged blacks to start businesses that would be patronized by other African-Americans. He outlined the ways and means of accomplishing this in his book *The Negro in Business,* and blacks soon started a large number of enterprises, from groceries to hotels to insurance companies to banks, virtually all of which served black communities exclusively. Although many whites nodded approvingly at Washington's apparent success in pursuing economic progress rather than civil rights, some blacks derided him as an "Uncle Tom" for backing off the cause of full equality. It is true that while Washington railed against bigotry and inequality in his correspondence, in public he was all reason and open to compromise.

To some extent the strategy worked. Washington urged the nation's political leaders to extend a hand to the black population, which given the fresh memory of the Civil War meant allying with the Republicans. And the party responded. President William McKinley, inaugurated in 1897, named more blacks to federal positions than ever before. McKinley's successor, fellow Republican Theodore Roosevelt, went even further out of his way to court blacks, inviting Washington to dine at the White House, to the shock and outrage of many whites. By then it was firmly established that blacks with political or business ambitions could best find help through the kind offices of Booker T. Washington.

But not all African-American leaders agreed with his conciliatory approach. W. E. B. Du Bois, for example, acknowledged Washington's influence but criticized his preaching "a gospel of work and money to such an extent as apparently almost completely to overshadow the higher aims of life." Educated at Tennessee's Fisk University, the University of Berlin, and Harvard, where he earned three degrees including his doctorate, Du Bois believed that African-Americans needed to focus on what he called the "talented tenth," the top percentile of achievers he hoped could gain enough education to become the new leaders of black America. Unlike Washington, Du Bois saw no reason to hold off on the struggle for full equality. "The problem of the twentieth century is the problem of the color line," Du Bois boldly declared in a speech at the first Pan-African Conference in London. Convening like-minded whites as well as blacks at Niagara Falls, Ontario, in June 1905, he drew up a manifesto for action; the "Niagara Movement" called for black suffrage, freedom of speech, and the abolition of all race-based discrimination.

Although the Niagara Movement enjoyed only limited success, it did bring the descendants of antebellum white abolitionists together with latter-day black intellectuals in a new activism. Such forward thinking whites as philosopher John Dewey, social reformer Jane Addams, and novelist William Dean Howells joined with Du Bois and other blacks in 1910 to organize the National Association for the Advancement of Colored People (NAACP), which included a legal committee that concentrated on challenging racial laws and in so doing won several significant triumphs. Nevertheless, it was Washington who extolled the mounting victories in the peaceable war for equality, while Du Bois kept talking about all the obstacles still to be surmounted. But the two great black leaders only appeared to be at odds; later it would become clear how much they agreed upon, although Washington's influence would remain such that he completely overshadowed Du Bois until his death in 1915. By that time there was virtually no mixing of the races in America's cities, particularly in the North. But there had sprung up numerous black communities that if not quite as wealthy as their white counterparts were mirror images of them, complete with professionals, entrepreneurs, skilled workers, and a large lower class of unskilled laborers. The message which the NAACP tried to convey to white America came from Booker T. Washington himself: "You can't hold a man down without staying down with him."

W. E. B. Du Bois, above, was a leading American intellectual of the twentieth century. In 1895, Du Bois became the first African-American to earn a doctorate from Harvard University. An elitist at a time when any show of pride was discouraged in a black man, Du Bois continually encouraged the top 10 percent of African-Americans, the "talented tenth," in his phrase, to take their place in the ranks of American intellectuals. After helping to found the NAACP, he edited its publication, *Crisis,* from 1910 to 1934 and became a nationally known author. In 1961, at the age of ninety-three, Du Bois concluded that relations between the races in America had barely improved at all during his long lifetime. He accepted a job in Ghana, Africa, and died there two years later.

Turn-of-the-century students attend a chemistry class in the photograph above, taken at the Tuskegee Normal and Industrial Institute in Alabama. Founded in 1881, Tuskegee was modeled after the Hampton Institute in Virginia, where the primary emphasis was on punctuality, grooming, and other forms of daily discipline. As the early graduates began to establish solid careers in teaching, agriculture, industrial engineering, and nursing, Tuskegee earned a national reputation for excellence. "It is at the bottom of life we must begin, not the top," was the pragmatic philosophy of Booker T. Washington, the president. "Nor should we permit our grievances to overshadow our opportunities."

The Organization of Labor

In time the working classes of both races produced a social and political movement that gave the lie to the notion that a few rich individuals determined the course of the nation's progress toward economic supremacy. In fact, considering the late nineteenth century's crowding of blacks, immigrants, and former farmers into America's cities, the rise of industrial corporations, and the ongoing evolution of the railroads, it is little wonder that unions began to organize to protect workers from the rapacity of unfettered capitalism. As Wendell Phillips noted in an 1871 address entitled "The Foundation of the Labor Movement," what the workingmen of America wanted was "short hours, better education, cooperation in the end and, in the meantime a political movement that will concentrate the thought of the country on this thing."

Not that labor organizations had much standing at the time. In fact, most Americans shied from the mere idea of unions, remembering the terrorist activities of the "Molly Maguires" of the 1870s, a group of disgruntled Pennsylvania coal-field workers who had taken their name from a violently anti-British Irish patriot and followed her example by crusading for the rights of workers through intimidation, assault, and murder. Ten of the Molly

Maguires were hanged in 1876. The next year witnessed the Great Railroad Strike, America's first major interstate worker revolt with violence erupting from Pennsylvania all the way to Chicago. Wage cuts had provoked railroad workers in Baltimore to walk off their jobs and onto the tracks, sparking a mob mentality that quickly spread from Baltimore to Martinsburg, West Virginia, and beyond, inspiring railroad employees along the way to destroy millions of dollars' worth of their employers' property, derailing trains and burning railyards. The strike touched hundreds of towns and cities, left more than 100 dead, and forced President Hayes to order in federal troops to quash the violence, which succeeded primarily in souring the public's view of labor. The worst violence occurred on July 21 in Pittsburgh where troops bayoneted and then fired on demonstrators, killing ten and wounding dozens of others. Nevertheless, as labor leader Samuel Gompers put it, "The railroad strike of 1877 was the tocsin that sounded a ringing message of hope for us all."

Twenty years later less obvious factors would contribute to the growing labor movement as well: the examples of unions abroad, the social awareness spawned by Marxism and other forms of socialism, and, perhaps most important, America's deflationary economy of the mid-1890s. With these motives behind them, the many strikes of the period resulted as much from management's attempts to slash wages as from labor's efforts to raise them—although another major impetus grew from the violent contrast between the harsh living conditions of most workers and the lavish circumstances enjoyed by those who owned the businesses for which the workers toiled.

The new immigration both helped and hindered the spread of unionization. Although some unions sprang up that were composed mostly of newcomers to the United States, one of the primary reasons behind most worker organizations was the desire of native-born laborers to restrict foreigners' entry into the American workforce. At the same time, however, many immigrants arrived with strong European concepts of labor solidarity and organization that contributed greatly to the early successes of unions in the economically booming United States. And the unions thrived with a simple two-pronged message: better conditions and higher wages for workers.

Contrary to popular perception, poor working conditions played only a minor role in the growth of labor unions. After all, the main reason foreigners had been drawn to America's cities was to enjoy the opportunities they offered, which also attracted native-born farmers who willingly exchanged the round-the-clock demands of the land and the precariousness of factors beyond their control—weather, interest rates, commodity prices, and the like—for the relative security of what seemed an almost leisurely seventy- or eighty-hour workweek.

By modern standards, however, the plight of turn-of-the-century industrial laborers was horrendous beyond belief. They toiled in environments choked with pollution on equipment that was downright dangerous. Industrial accidents were commonplace, and rare was the veteran railroad worker who still had a full complement of fingers. Worker compensation was unheard of, as were retirement plans and medical insurance, while chronic unemployment fueled the constant threat of replacement by cheaper labor. Most

The engraving opposite top shows a Chicago meat-packing plant in 1882. Meatpacking was a national enterprise, uniting the suppliers of the West with the markets of the East through the processing plants of Chicago. It inspired awe among other industrialists, who tried to copy its assembly-line techniques. However, the pressing drive to efficiency eventually led to the fall of the industry's reputation. In 1906, Upton Sinclair's book *The Jungle* shocked the country by describing the effects when productivity overwhelmed all other concerns, including quality and safety, at a Chicago meatpacking plant. The acceleration of the Industrial Age wore heaviest on children. The picture above shows children operating looms in a mill; opposite bottom, Lewis Hines photographed boys laboring in a glass factory. Jacob Riis took the photograph at right, and titled it "Two Ragamuffins Didn't Live Nowhere." It was included in his 1890 book *How the Other Half Lives.* A best-seller, the book forced readers to look at lives and faces, like those of the boys pictured, otherwise forgotten in the fast-moving Gilded Age.

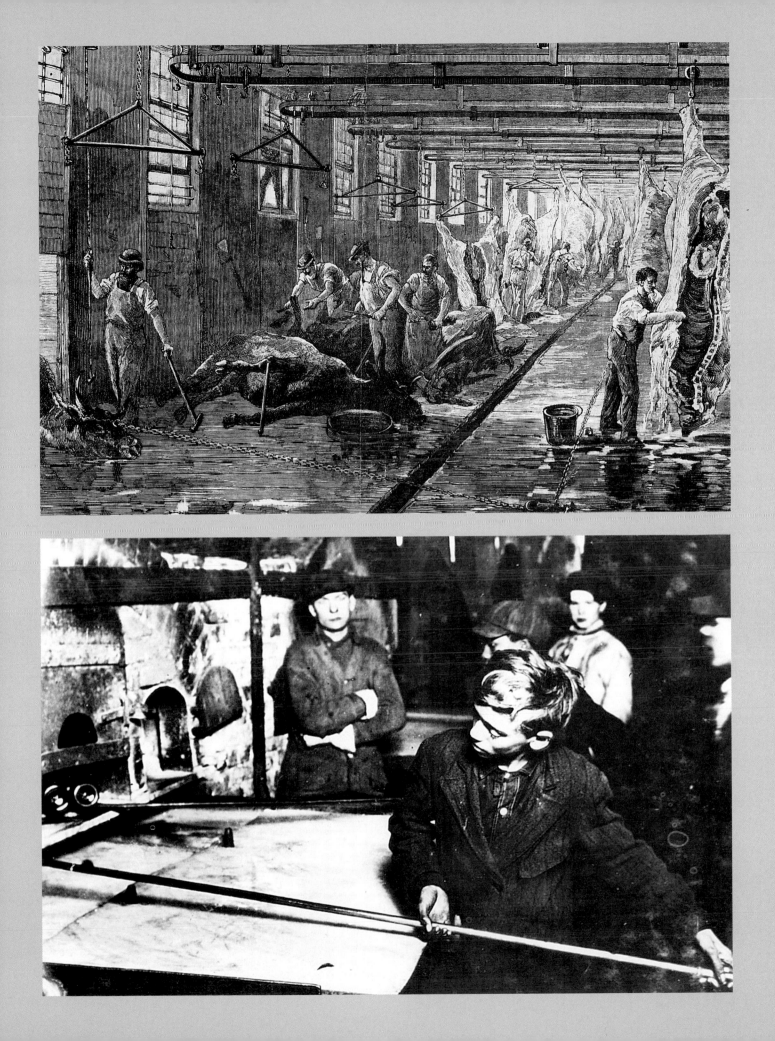

THE GOSPEL OF THE KNIGHTS OF LABOR.
" We work not selfishly for ourselves alone, but extend the hand of fellowship to all mankind."— *Mr. Powderly, at Richmond.*

Joseph Keppler drew the sardonic cartoon above in 1886, showing Terence Powderly, head of the Knights of Labor, fulfilling his promise to "extend the hand of fellowship to all mankind." A scab worker receives the back of his right hand, while an employer is shown the back of his left. The Knights of Labor was an industrial union, a type of organization that embraced a wide array of workers, as opposed to a trade union, which was defined by job description.

appalling of all was the routine hiring of child labor, which allowed preteen boys and girls to be dragged out of schools and into sweatshops and steel mills, a practice so heinous that the call for a constitutional amendment forbidding child labor became one of the most important causes of the late nineteenth century, although no legislation was passed concerning it until the early twentieth century.

Adults were hardly better off, as Upton Sinclair so hauntingly testified in his lurid 1906 novel *The Jungle*, a devastating exposé of Chicago meatpacking plants. "There would be meat stored in great piles in rooms; and the water from the leaky roofs would drip over it, and thousands of rats would race about on it," Sinclair wrote in his novel, causing President Theodore Roosevelt to order a sanitation investigation which led to passage of the Pure Food and Drug Act and the Meat Inspection Act. Urban overcrowding in the shadows of steel skyscrapers that blotted out the sun made coming home to their disease-riddled tenement houses just another long, grim test of endurance for the unskilled laborers who spent their days toiling over noisy machines in sweatshops seemingly designed to crush the human spirit.

These and other factors pushed the drive toward unionization, but none with as much force as the march of technological progress, which led to the replacement of common laborers by skilled operators of machine tools and construction equipment. Whereas the unskilled and largely uneducated workers had never had much bargaining power, the evolution of a more complex workplace that called for greater skill and training created a workforce that demanded and got more power in the marketplace.

At first, specialized local unions enjoyed more clout than the better-known national confederations of labor. The more pragmatic regional organizations, heirs to the craftsmen's guilds of Europe's Middle Ages, sought specific concessions such as higher wages and proved more successful in attaining their goals than did the more ideological groups with wider aspirations to alter America's social fabric. Still, the gains of the former gave hope to the latter.

The first national union in the United States had been formed in 1866 and was followed by several more successful ones, both open and supposedly secret—including the Knights of Labor. Formed in 1869, by 1886 the Philadelphia garment-cutters' guild had attracted some 700,000 members from America's adult population of 35 million with its calls for eight-hour days, a prohibition on child labor, graduated income and inheritance taxes, government ownership of railroads and banks, and restrictions on immigration. That year some 610,000 workers participated in various strikes that reached epidemic proportions due to wage reductions in the face of hard economic times. Severe strikes disrupted the coal fields of Ohio and Pennsylvania in 1884, prompting the formation of a national labor movement and contributing to the Democratic presidential nomination of Grover Cleveland. That same year, labor pressured the Democratic House of Representatives to pass a measure creating a Bureau of Labor within the Department of the Interior that for the same reason managed to squeak through the Republican-controlled Senate and be signed by Republican President Chester Arthur.

Despite the politicians' attempts to make peace, labor unrest continued to grow and break out into strikes more and more often. Public opinion waffled between sympathy for the downtrodden workers and fear that their disgruntlement would spill over into violence. In 1886 the Knights of Labor led the most important strike of that year against the Gould system of railroads in the Southwest. Although the action lasted two months and paralyzed any number of industries, it ended with few gains of consequence for the workers. Still, the Knights were undeterred and led a series of strikes against other employers, most significantly at the McCormick Harvester Company in Chicago after 1,400 workers were locked out by management when they demanded eight-hour days at a wage of $2 a day. Police who were called in killed several workers in the course of quelling the uprising, which led to another protest a few days later at which a bomb exploded, mortally wounding seven officers. The remaining police opened fire, resulting in eight killed and 100 wounded including a number of officers.

When McCormick's management tried to replace its employees with scabs, the workers attacked. The resulting riot ended in the indictment and conviction of several alleged anarchists, four of whom were hanged. In a similarly violent vein, in 1892 strikes broke out at both the Coeur d'Alene silver mines in Idaho and at Andrew Carnegie's Homestead Steelworks in Pennsylvania; federal troops were called out to quell the former, while at the latter an anarchist pumped two bullets into the general manager, Henry Clay Frick, in an unsuccessful attempt to assassinate the hatchet man Carnegie had allowed to turn Homestead into a camp of armed thugs hired to take on the unions. Nevertheless, public opinion turned against the strikers when the Pennsylvania state militia was called in to put an end to the unrest; the steel unions would stay suppressed for decades. Labor's gains would be diminished even further in 1894, when President Cleveland was called upon to send several thousand special deputies to Chicago to put down a strike against George Pullman's luxury railcar company, which had refused even to explain its recent layoffs and wage cuts to workers, who had responded by

Eugene Debs, shown in the cartoon below, led the American Railway Union in 1893 on a prolonged strike against the Pullman Palace Car Company in Chicago. The strike was also broken up by federal troops, and Debs was sentenced to a short jail term for disobeying a court-ordered injunction forbidding interference with the Pullman's converging of rails.

A family of Gypsies, above, remains cheerful despite meeting an unexpected delay at Ellis Island. With roots in ancient India, at least a half-million Gypsies emigrated from various nations in Europe, finding a permanent home in America. The family shown arrived from Serbia.

Since its very founding the United States has been haunted by two contradictory impulses: what historian Arthur M. Schlesinger, Jr., described as "the curse of racism" and the hopeful metaphor of "the melting pot." The latter term, interestingly enough, was taken from the title of a 1908 play by Israel Zangwill, an English author of Russian-Jewish origin. *The Melting Pot* tells the story of an idealistic young Russian-Jewish composer living in New York whose artistic ambition is to pen a memorable symphony about the harmonious interweaving of the races in America. His personal ambition, meanwhile, is to marry a Christian woman named Vera, because in America, religion was no deterrent to love. "America is God's crucible, the great Melting Pot where all the races of Europe are melting and reforming," Zangwill's Cervantes-echoing character David Quixano exclaims. "Here you stand. . . in your fifty blood hatreds. . . . A fig for your feuds and vendettas! Germans and Frenchmen, Irishmen and Englishmen, Jews and Russians—into the Crucible with you all! God is making the American."

President Theodore Roosevelt, who attended the Washington, D.C., premiere of *The Melting Pot*, was bully about the drama, the patriotic finale of which involved a single, guiding star twinkling above a replica of the Statue of Liberty's torch as a choir launched into a rousing rendition of "America."

Newspapers reported that when the chorus ended Roosevelt shouted from his box, "That's a great play, Mr. Zangwill; that's a great play." Weeks later Roosevelt's enthusiasm hadn't dwindled, and he told the author, "I'm not a Bernard Shaw man or Ibsen man, Mr. Zangwill. No, *this* is the stuff." Zangwill's play was received glowingly nationwide, packing crowds into theaters in every downtown for an evening of uplifting, patriotism. To many—such as social reformer Jane Addams of Chicago's Hull-House—*The Melting Pot* had rendered America "a great service" by reminding citizens of the "high hopes of the founders of the Republic."

Thirty-eight million people immigrated to America between 1820 and 1924—the year that entry was severely restricted by federal law. Over that span, the top five emigrant nations were Germany, Italy, the United Kingdom, Ireland, and Austria-Hungary. While there were certainly peak years for immigration, often owing to some natural or man-made disaster in Europe, the percentage of foreign born in the U.S. population remained at approximately 14 percent during the decades from 1860 to 1920. The melting pot seems to have struck on that proportion naturally, a figure that worked amid the realities of America's continuing growth and economic need.

Since the Theodore Roosevelt era,

"melting pot" has come to mean "the process by which immigrants become Americanized" as well as "a nation that assimilates all nationalities and cultures," according to *New York Times* language columnist William Safire. But as many social commentators have noted, the United States may fit the definition more in reputation than in fact. Most immigrants throughout American history have settled in cities, where work has always been easier to find, and have tended to cluster together in ethnic communities that follow the ways of their native villages and provinces. These self-created ethnic communities afford immigrants familiar-seeming havens from the rough and tumble of American urban life. Whereas newcomers felt hard pressed in the workplace to speak English and "act American," in their neighborhoods they could speak their native languages, eat their accustomed foods, and enjoy the music of their homelands. "If the 'melting pot' had completed its work," journalist Henry Fairlie wrote in 1947, "there would be no 'ethnics.'" As then-Governor Thomas E. Dewey told journalist John Gunther in 1947, "New York City is not a melting pot; it's a boiling pot." Daniel Patrick Moynihan and Nathan Glazer would make much the same point in *Beyond the Melting Pot,* their 1963 study of immigrant assimilation in New York: many of the city's various ethnic populations went out of their way to remain

separate from the wider American culture. The truth of this study is supported by the ethnic appeals and ticket-balancing efforts practiced by virtually every big-city politician.

In the 1960s the melting pot metaphor would be applied to African-Americans as well as to foreign immigrants. President John F. Kennedy, in a 1963 speech on civil rights, called Jim Crow laws that denied blacks equal access to public and private facilities "a daily insult which has no place in a country proud of its heritage—the heritage of the melting pot, of equal rights, of one nation and one people." Three decades later, however, the vogue of the melting pot would be replaced by acceptance of and in fact a preference for what would be called multiculturalism—in which American society was seen less as a homogeneous fondue and more as a salad of many individual ingredients tossed together but retaining their separate identities.

organizing a Pullman boycott in twenty-seven states. Unlike Pullman and his fellow tycoons, however, the workers did not enjoy such easy access to the president.

By this point the American business community was more than a little troubled by labor in general and in particular by the Industrial Workers of the World (IWW), a radical group whose members were called "wobblies" that cried for a workers' revolution. The IWW attracted up to a million supporters by World War I, and its virulent agenda presented middle-class America with a threat of revolution that seemed a real possibility. The preamble to the IWW constitution, ratified in Chicago in June 1905, minced no words: "The working class and the employing class have nothing in common. There can be no peace so long as hunger and want are found among millions of working people and the few who make up the employing class have all the good things of life." By contrast the American Federation of Labor (AFL), formed in 1886 by a group of craft guilds and headed by Samuel Gompers of the cigar-makers' union, seemed substantially less disturbing. The AFL focused on what Gompers considered labor's most immediate objectives: wages, factory conditions, and above all the institution of an eight-hour workday. Once a socialist, Gompers had come to believe that the best way to improve the lot of labor was via a loose organization of workers skilled in various crafts whose individual unions would devote themselves to obtaining "more" from the employers in each industry. "The labor of a human being is not a commodity or article or commerce," Gompers would say. "You can't weigh the soul of a man with a bar or pig iron." Gompers deliberately kept the AFL out of politics and took great pains to appear both reasonable and respectable. It worked. By 1917 the AFL comprised 3 million members and had become the most viable labor organization in the world—and what a very different world it was from the quaintly agrarian, isolated nation Abraham Lincoln had taken such pains to hold together just fifty years earlier.

The unprecedented reach of the railroads resulted in enterprises so large they demanded the creation of the corporate structure to manage them, which inspired admirers in other industries to follow suit. Unlike sole proprietorships and partnerships, these new business organizations followed not the whims of individual owners but the decisions of boards of directors elected by and answerable to shareholders. As a consequence, corporations boasted far greater stability—after all, they were designed to operate indefinitely despite changing casts of owners and managers. For all the gains this new business structure brought to the American economy, however, something was also lost in the rise of corporations, and that loss left a gap for the labor movement to fill. Workers were becoming ever more aware of their growing distance from management as impersonal corporate bureaucracies took the place of the almost filial relationships employees had enjoyed with the owners of small operations in the antebellum years, and they began to see themselves as powerless cogs in enormous industrial machines. It did not take long for laborers to realize that at least some power in the workplace could be reclaimed only if they joined together into a collective force united in its goals and sympathetic to all its members, particularly those worst off.

As labor leader Eugene V. Debs urged workers to proclaim along with him, "While there is a lower class, I am in it; while there is a criminal element, I am of it; while there is a soul in prison, I am not free."

Meanwhile, other changes large and small were brewing across the United States. In 1893, Charles and Frank Duryea of Springfield, Massachusetts, designed the first American gasoline-powered automobile; the unfortunately ahead-of-his-time William Morrison of Des Moines, Iowa, tested the first electric car, based on an alternating-current motor designed earlier in the year by Nikola Tesla, an immigrant from Croatia who was likely as great an inventor as Thomas Edison but who remains less well-known simply because he was a far worse businessman.

Further up the industrial line in 1892, large and violent labor strikes broke out at silver mines in Idaho and at Andrew Carnegie's Pennsylvania steelworks; meanwhile, the Ohio State Supreme Court ordered John D. Rockefeller's Standard Oil Company of Ohio to sever its connections with the Standard Oil Trust, spelling the beginning of the end for America's first great monopoly (In 1911, the United States Supreme Court ordered a much more extensive breakup of the Standard Oil Trust). But the Fifty-second Congress's accomplishments were not so laudatory: spurred by racial prejudice stewing in a public threatened by what one New York newspaper called "those disgusting habits of thrift, industry, and self-denial" among Chinese immigrants—habits evidenced most offensively by their willingness to accept low wages for hard work—both houses also passed, and President Benjamin Harrison signed, an extension of the Chinese Exclusion Act of 1882, which banned the entry of any additional Chinese laborers for the next ten years.

Yet patriotism was welding the nation together, and many immigrants were taking part in the red-white-and-blue jubilee. When John Philip Sousa, son of a Portuguese immigrant from Spain, composed "Stars and Stripes Forever" in 1897, three hundred thousand dollars worth of sheet music was quickly sold—including hundreds in a large San Francisco Chinatown emporium. All Americans, it seemed, shared one thing in common: adjusting to the new industrial, scientifically pragmatic order of things which was propelling Old Glory forward.

A WORD OF CAUTION TO OUR FRIENDS, THE CIGAR-MAKERS.

Through the smoke it is easy to see the approach of Chinese cheap labor.

The cartoon above warned cigar makers not to use Chinese labor in 1877. Trade unions, fearful of competing with cheap labor, supported restrictions against immigration in the 1870s and 1880s. In 1850, fewer than 1,000 people of Chinese descent were living in the United States; by 1870, the number had risen to more than 100,000, due mainly to the steady work building western railroads. The Chinese called America *Mei Kwok* ("the beautiful land"), but by the 1870s the beauty was marred by overt prejudice, especially in California. Tensions rose, and in 1882 President Chester Arthur capitulated to pressure by groups such as the Workingman's Party and signed the Chinese Exclusion Act that banned immigration from China and denied citizenship to those Chinese who were already residing in the United States.

HAVANA HARBOR

ADMIRAL SICARD

CAPTAIN SIG

CHAPTER 12

BEYOND MANIFEST DESTINY

RECOVERING THE DEA

The America that marched briskly toward the twentieth century was unrecognizable as the fledging agrarian republic of a hundred years earlier. The United States had become more sophisticated socially and technologically, far more powerful economically, and as a consequence more ambitious globally. In 1898, America would demonstrate a new rapaciousness fed by this sudden might, trumping up the dubious Spanish-American War that ended seventy-five years of peace with Europe and not incidentally turned the United States into an imperial power. As one astute observer would note, "A beaver has given birth to an eagle—and a damn hungry one."

It was, of course, the United States' sudden rise to economic preeminence that made the nation's confidence possible. The federal government floundered at first over how to rein in the excesses of booming corporations already rich enough to wield real clout, but before long political leaders would be elected who knew a good thing when they saw one and would forge mutually beneficial relationships with the industrial and financial titans who were making America so prosperous and powerful. Fortunately for society, the workers who made most of the contributions to that prosperity had

The lithograph at left, by an anonymous artist, shows the horror of flying bodies and exploding metal as the U.S.S. _Maine_ blew up in Havana harbor, February 15, 1898. The powerful battleship had been moored in the unfriendly waters to pressure Spain into improving conditions in Cuba. When the ship exploded, killing 260 men, America placed the blame on the Spanish and rushed into war.

The Carnegie Furnaces in Braddock, Pennsylvania, above, were enormous, yet they constituted only a small corner of Andrew Carnegie's empire. In the 1890s, when no more than $1,000 a year was considered an excellent middle-class salary, Carnegie's annual income was $7.5 million, putting him in a class almost by himself.

begun to realize they had the numbers as well as the burgeoning political know-how to make their interests known and to form movements and elect candidates who would take those interests into account and regulate big business.

Political Crosscurrents

Of course, it took a shaking-out period before America's political, business, and public interests settled into productive cooperation. After the Civil War, as immigration and industrialization transformed the United States into an ever less familiar society with ever less familiar problems, the government seemed ever less up to guiding the nation progressively or even effectively. In the two decades between Ulysses S. Grant and William McKinley, a mediocre run of U.S. presidents—Rutherford B. Hayes, James A. Garfield, Chester A. Arthur, Grover Cleveland, Benjamin Harrison, and Cleveland again—reacted to America's building social and economic upheaval with an almost curious passivity and a complete lack of foresight. By the last decade of the nineteenth century the public began to take notice.

Before long the public also began to take action, starting with the debt-ridden farmers eking out harsh lives from the Old South to the Midwest. The first politically influential farmers' organization had its beginnings in hayrides and hoedowns: the Grange, officially known as the "Patrons of Husbandry," which had been founded in December 1867 by Oliver Hudson Kelly and six others to help farm families brighten their drab existence with social activities such as dances, fairs, and lectures on farming techniques. By 1875 the Grange had some million members spread across 20,000 local chapters, most in the Midwest, South, and Southwest. Although at first apolitical, in time the Grangers' socializing evolved into economic and then political coordination. Having discovered that by organizing into cooperatives they could get volume discounts on supplies, storage facilities, and transportation to market for their crops, by the early 1870s the Grange was sending lobbyists to state legislatures to argue for "Granger laws" putting caps on equipment and storage prices. In 1887 the U.S. Congress took notice of the farmers' concerns and growing power to make them heard by creating the Interstate Commerce Commission to regulate commercial trade across states—a bow to the public's right to exert some control over the doings of private enterprises.

By that point a decade-long depression in prices for agricultural products had fertilized the growth of other cooperatively owned farmers' groups, which the press took to merging with the Grangers into "the Alliance Movement." Between 1886 and 1892 these new organizations— including the million-member Southern Alliance—multiplied and acquired strength through the booming number of voices questioning the traditional capitalist practices that kept farmers poor and made financiers rich. What would become the most powerful group, the National Farmers' Alliance that had sprouted in the Midwest and Great Plains in 1880, took its members' concerns beyond agricultural economics and into national politics a decade later. These agricultural activists blamed their economic woes on the plutocrats and their new industrial order, which stole from farmers—Thomas Jefferson's "chosen people of God"—the fruits of their backbreaking toil. Forming the People's Party, they took on the Democrats and Republicans who so far had been making the policies that determined the quality of farmers' lives. Perhaps most significant in the long run, the alliance brought new sounds into grassroots American politics—soprano and alto voices. As one observer wondered at the burgeoning organization, "Wimmin is everywhere."

On July 2, 1892, the new People's Party held its presidential nominating convention in Omaha, Nebraska. A collection of mostly Midwestern farm, labor, and reform organizations and local political groups, these "Populists" called for an already familiar litany of reforms including secret ballots, immigration restrictions, and the direct election of presidents and senators as well as the nationalization of banks, railroads, and telegraph lines. Their most important plank, however, advocated the free and unlimited coinage of silver at sixteen ounces for one ounce of gold. The Populists argued that adopting this silver standard would not only boost the nation's mining interests but inflate U.S. currency overall and thereby stimulate the economy. Opponents of the plan maintained that it would drive gold from circulation and that if the United States became the only major industrial economy using silver as a

Adlai Stevenson, above, was elected vice president when Grover Cleveland, opposite page, regained the presidency in 1892 after having served already from 1885 to 1889. Democrats were back in the White House, but under Cleveland's conservative, pro-business leadership it was hard to distinguish them from Republicans. The similarities in the party lines were lost on neither the rising Populist Party nor entrenched magnates such as Henry Frick, who wrote to Andrew Carnegie after the election, "I cannot see that our interests are going to be affected one way or the other by the change in administration." Cleveland's alignment with big business continued through his term and led to a split in the Democratic Party in the 1896 election.

medium of exchange, foreigners would refuse to trade with American companies, investors would flee, and ruin would quickly ensue. But the Populist platform amounted to more than just silver and a recital of reforms; in fact, it stopped just short of calling for an economic revolution for subtly paranoid reasons. As one section of the third party's rather overwrought convention platform read:

> We meet in the midst of a nation brought to the verge of moral, political, and material ruin. Corruption dominates the ballot-box, the Legislatures, the Congress, and touches even the ermine of the bench. The newspapers are largely subsidized or muzzled, public opinion silenced, business prostrated, homes covered with mortgages, labor impoverished, and the land concentrating in the hands of the capitalists . . . A vast conspiracy against mankind has been organized . . . If not met and overthrown at once it forebodes terrible social convulsions . . . or the establishment of an absolute despotism.

The People's Party nominated former Union General James B. Weaver of Iowa for the presidency and, for balance, former Confederate General James G. Field of Virginia for the vice presidency, and asserted its intention to displace either the Democrats or the Republicans as one of the nation's two dominant political organizations. But the Populists threatened not just America's leading parties but its very social order; in the South, black as well as white farmers united behind Weaver's candidacy, and blacks played a substantial role in the party's organization, to the distress of many outsiders. Thomas Nugent, the People's Party nominee for governor of Texas in 1892 and 1894, spoke for many angry farmers when he denounced "Wall Street" and "big bankers and moneylenders" as heinous villains bent on destroying the "common man." Critics wrote off such political figures as Weaver, Field and Nugent as rabble-rousers, "hayseed socialists" with a flare for demagoguery.

The Democrats, meanwhile, had already met in Chicago and nominated a ticket of Grover Cleveland and former Assistant Postmaster General Adlai E. Stevenson, while the Republicans had renominated Benjamin Harrison with aristocratic diplomat Whitelaw Reid for vice president. The Prohibition Party, which four years earlier had gathered a quarter million votes and since had grown faster than any other political organization in the country, nominated John Bidwell of California on a platform calling for the coinage of silver, the nationalization of railroad and telegraph companies, and draconian immigration restrictions as well as the prohibition of alcoholic beverages. All in all, the Prohibitionists were essentially Populists, but sober. In addition, for the first time the left-wing Socialist Labor Party, founded in 1877 with a base among urban immigrants, entered the presidential fray, nominating Simon Wing of Massachusetts.

In the end in 1892, Democrat Cleveland became the only U.S. president in history to win a nonconsecutive second term, by a popular vote of 5.6 million and an electoral count of 277 to Harrison's tallies of 5.2 million and 145 and Weaver's 1 million popular and 22 electoral votes. The Prohibitionists captured 271,058 popular votes that should fairly be added to the Populists' total; the leftists made a puny showing.

Cleveland's second administration went from an inauspicious start to a disastrous end. Just before he took office the Philadelphia and Reading Railroad failed, and three months after his inauguration the stock market plummeted and set off the panic of 1893, the worst depression the United States would suffer until the greatest one of the 1930s. In 1893 alone more than 600 banks failed and 74 railroads went into receivership, including such former successes as the Northern Pacific, the Union Pacific, the Erie, and the Atchison, Topeka and Santa Fe. Matters became even worse in 1894; gold drained from the U.S. Treasury to lending banks both domestic and foreign, and before long it looked as though the United States might not be able to meet its financial obligations. Meanwhile, unemployment had tripled from 1 million in the summer of 1893 to 3 million a year later. Homelessness was widespread during the Panic of 1893, and "tramping" the country begging and stealing food became an occupation for tens of thousands of hungry souls. President Cleveland nevertheless continued to expound the belief in "laissez-faire" government that he had explained at his second inauguration: "While the people should patriotically and cheerfully support their government, its functions do not include the support of the people." The states felt much the same way, and left it to individual communities' churches and charities to provide relief for the jobless, whose numbers gave the lie to the no longer convincing notion that poverty resulted from laziness and nothing else.

In March 1894, Jacob S. Coxey of Massillon, Ohio, a populist champion of unemployment relief, his wife, and his son (actually named Legal Tender Coxey) led 500 protesters to Washington, D.C., where they demanded that the government issue $50 million in paper money and take on a number of public works projects to help those who could not find jobs. Later in the year Congress responded by passing a bill providing for the coinage of silver, but couldn't muster enough votes to override Cleveland's veto. Although the economic situation improved somewhat in 1895—when J. P. Morgan stepped in by selling $65 million in U.S. bonds in Europe—the nation's fiscal jitters persisted.

The instability of the economy gave rise to one of the most dramatic and difficult debates in U.S. financial—and social—history: silver versus gold as the nation's monetary standard. The majority of Republicans favored keeping gold as the sole guarantee behind U.S. currency; not only was it the international standard, but it was a proven foundation of the "sound money" that led to prosperity and confidence in business. The "silverites," by contrast,

The 1894 cartoon above left shows Jacob Coxey leading his ragtag army against the Napoleonic forces of Washington politics. Coxey was a smalltown businessman from Ohio who accused the government of ignoring the concerns of the working class. His announcement early in 1894 that the next petition he sent to Washington "would be wearing boots" became a lightning rod for the frustration of many people, especially in the midst of a continuing depression. Coxey's army of several hundred walked to Washington, but found very little there except more frustration. Coxey was arrested for trespassing the very first day, when he mistakingly took a shortcut across the Capitol lawn. After three months, the only thing his followers managed to get out the government was train fare back to their hometowns. The cartoon above right, published in 1893, suggests that an American currency based on silver as well as gold would be as shaky as a bicyclist riding on mismatched wheels. While the debate over the currency standard was a serious issue in the mid-1890s, the cartoon also reflects the bicycle fad, which peaked during the last decade of the century.

argued for the U.S. Treasury to coin all the silver available to it regardless of foreign economic standards, on the theory that this would increase the nation's money supply, drive prices up, and boost the overall economy—or so the silverites hoped. But the real significance of the debate lay in its division along class as well as regional lines, pitting the debt-laden farmers of the South and West against the prosperous industrialists and financiers of the commercial Northeast.

Midway through 1895, the prosilver forces got together to plan their strategy. Some favored allying with the Republicans and others with the Democrats, but many thought independence made the most sense. In any case, given the economic turmoil a Populist victory looked plausible in 1896. The upstart party had attracted votes from all three constituencies—Republicans, Democrats, and Independents—in the 1894 congressional elections, and by so doing increased its support by some 40 percent. In fact, the new Fifty-third Congress had a silverite majority, but its members were well aware that any bill endorsing a two-metal monetary standard would be quashed by a presidential veto. The opposing forces therefore decided to wait and take on the monetary issue in the 1896 presidential election.

Although the silver question dominated the campaign, it was hardly the only significant issue in the last election before the turn of the century. America's economic evolution had been so swift that the nation's business concerns had already begun to press up against the borders dictated by Manifest Destiny. When Cuban opposition leader José Martí effectively began a colonial war against Spain on February 24, 1895, the U.S. Congress passed a resolution supporting the rebels and urging President Cleveland to offer his peacemaking services. Distressed at the widespread destruction of U.S.-owned property on the island, Cleveland instead adopted an essentially neutral policy, officially opposing the rebellion but pressing Spain to grant Cuba various freedoms leading to independence. (In fact, American sugar planters in

Cuba began secretly funding Martí hoping to force Spain to leave the island.) Although the imperial movement was nearly imperceptible at the time, the United States had begun to push toward new frontiers beyond the borders suggested by the world's two greatest oceans—and most of the pushing was by the strong arms of big business.

The Election of 1896

At about the same time that the United States began to seem too confining for some commercial interests and the politicians they supported, at a far humbler level American ingenuity was churning out advances that would prove their full significance only in the years to come. In 1896 inventor Samuel Langley at the Smithsonian Institution got a steam-powered, mechanically propelled, heavier-than-air model plane to fly 3,200 feet, a motion picture created by Thomas Edison was shown in New York, and a new gold rush ensued after the discovery of huge lodes of the metal in Alaska's Klondike region. Still, the nation's focus had not yet broadened to the larger scope of what America was becoming through its technological and economic breakthroughs, and remained fixed on the upcoming presidential elec-

Below, a photograph taken in 1896 shows lawyers marching in a New York parade favoring "sound money," or the gold standard. The bitter controversy of the 1896 election centered around the value attached to U.S. currency. "Free Silver" Democrats, mostly Westerners and Southerners, were in favor of issuing money backed by abundant silver, while "Gold Standard Republicans," centered in the North, wanted to control the currency more tightly by supporting it with the scarcer metal. Businessmen and manufacturers were jittery at the very thought of losing the gold standard.

Above, a youthful William Jennings Bryan was caricatured as a biblical prophet after his "Cross of Gold" speech ignited the Democratic convention of 1896. To many people, the God-fearing Bryan had gone too far, using Biblical symbols to project his wholly secular politics, and the cartoon shows him as a peddler hawking such wares. Nonetheless, as the pace of urbanization quickened across the nation, Bryan reached out to those left behind: farmers and small-business owners. "Burn down your cities," he told a rapt convention, "and leave our farms, and your cities will spring up again as if by magic; but destroy our farms and the grass will grow in the streets of every city in the country."

tion and the proposal for a two-metal monetary standard that defined it.

The U.S. political scene had not seen such disorganization since 1860, and talk of civil war arose again. This time, however, the dispute was not between Northern free states and the slaveholding South; in 1896 conflict was brewing between "the people" and "the plutocracy" in every region. With a virulence unprecedented even during the Revolutionary War, class warfare had come to the United States, leading Marxists and other socialist sympathizers to whisper of impending revolution. Boiled down to basics, rural Americans distrusted smooth-talking city folk, while urban dwellers characterized Jefferson's so-called honest "yeoman farmers" as backward rubes, dumb hayseeds, and country bumpkins.

The Republicans convened in St. Louis in mid-June only to see their leaders from silver-producing states, led by Senators Henry Teller of Colorado and Richard Pelligrew of South Dakota, threaten a walkout if the convention endorsed the gold standard. Despite the threat, Ohio party boss Mark Hanna rallied the conventioneers solidly behind gold, getting the Republican Party to proclaim it was "unreservedly for sound money" and would continue to be so until the unlikely event that an international agreement to coin silver was reached. In addition, the Republican platform called for a protective tariff on imports, the independence of Cuba, and the construction of a transisthmus canal through Central America. With this, Teller and his hundred-odd followers marched out, declaring they would choose and support a silverite candidate in the general election. The convention then nominated Governor William McKinley of Ohio for the presidency with New Jersey politician Garret A. Hobart at the bottom of the ticket.

The selection of the gold-minded McKinley put pressure on the Democrats, who met in Chicago on July 7. The greatest influence on the convention was exerted by Governor John Peter Altgeld of Illinois, who had clashed with Cleveland over the president's decision to put down the Pullman strike in 1894 and whose forces covertly rode the incumbent out of the Democratic Party by throwing their support to silverite former Congressman Richard Bland of Missouri. As expected, the convention lined up behind the silver standard, leading gold-backing Democrats to make noises about walking out and forming a separate party with their own candidate. In the end, Bland lost the nomination during the platform debate to the charismatic and evangelistic thirty-six-year-old William Jennings Bryan, a handsome, silver-throated and silver-minded Baptist former congressman from Nebraska who attended the convention on a press pass and electrified the gathering with what would become known as his "Cross of Gold" speech, in which he proclaimed that "You shall not press down upon the brow of labor this crown of thorns; you shall not crucify mankind upon a cross of gold." The delegates were swept away, nominated Bryan, and waved good-bye to the gold Democrats. "More than any one I have known," wrote the journalist Fredric Howe, "he represented the moralist in politics. He wanted to change men. He was a missionary; America was a missionary . . . He was the *vox ex cathedra* of the Western self-righteous missionary mind."

Less than two weeks later a rattled People's Party convened in St. Louis. The Populists had expected the two major parties to name gold candidates, leaving their silver supporters to join the upstart third party and bring it a major electoral victory. When this scenario failed to develop, talk arose of nominating labor leader Eugene V. Debs, but he rejected the idea. Finally, the Populist convention turned to the Democrats' own William Jennings Bryan, which sparked more than a little protest. After all, the Democratic candidate's platform mentioned nothing about nationalizing railroads and banks, included a vaguely antitrust plank, and but for its strong pledge on silver was more a rehash of old programs than a blueprint for the future. Nevertheless, the Populists also nominated Bryan, although to assert their distinction from the Democrats they chose one of their party's stalwarts, former Congressman Thomas E. Watson of Georgia rather than free-silver advocate Arthur Sewall of Maine for the vice presidency.

The presidential campaign of 1896 was among the most dramatic and colorful in U.S. history, a David-versus-Goliath contest that introduced the personality-oriented politics, which has since become the norm. The image-savvy "great commoner" Bryan staged the first "whistle-stop" campaign, traveling across the nation by train to address crowds from the platform. McKinley, by contrast, followed Hanna's direction and stayed home, occasionally delivering prepared texts to visiting delegations of supporters. Behind the scenes, however, Hanna also courted the not inconsequential black vote on behalf of the Republican Party, while gold-supporting employers of all political persuasions warned their workers that if Bryan was elected their factories would be closed the next day. Hanna even hired talented writers to bombard the nation with reams of books, pamphlets and position papers that painted Bryan as a dangerously messianic simpleton.

The scare tactics worked: McKinley won in a landslide of 7.1 million popular votes and 271 in the electoral college to Bryan's 6.5 million popular and 176 electoral votes. The outcome showed the extent to which the country was still rent asunder by region. Although Bryan captured the South and West, he lost every state north of the Mason-Dixon Line and east of the Mississippi. But the nation was divided in more ways than those left over from the Civil War. Urban workers, for example, saw little to be gained from inflation and gave the Republicans more of their votes than usual, as did Catholic and Jewish voters disturbed by the antiforeign element in Populism; blacks, moreover, proved more solidly Republican than ever. A full 79.3 percent of the electorate turned out to vote in 1896—a smaller portion than had elected Abraham Lincoln in 1860, but more than in any contest since and a full quarter more of the enfranchised than would go to the polls a century later.

President William McKinley, above in a 1900 photograph, had served under Rutherford B. Hayes during the Civil War and followed him into Ohio politics afterward, eventually winning the 1896 and 1900 presidential elections. A reserved, very private man, McKinley was held in affectionate regard even by his political enemies. One of the most negative remarks ever made about him came from his future vice president, Theodore Roosevelt, who remarked that "McKinley has all the backbone of a chocolate éclair." However, Elihu Root observed more cunningly that McKinley always got his own way, even if he had to let others take credit for ideas he had held all along.

Although it appeared to some observers in 1896 that the United States had decided on a Northern-style urban nation rather than a rural one of Southern flavor, memories of the Civil War in fact remained as important in the election as the debate over silver. But McKinley would be the last Civil War veteran to serve as president; what the Americans of 1896 could not foresee was that the harsh times of the past two decades were coming to an end, as was the country's isolationism. Those recent inventions that had seemed such curiosities—the automobile, the airplane, the motion picture—would soon alter the fabric of American life to a far greater extent than anything mentioned in the debates of the 1896 presidential campaign.

Prosperity

In addition to American ingenuity, plain old luck helped to turn things around and set the U.S. economy soaring. In 1896 it became clear that former Secretary of State William Seward's 1867 purchase of Alaska had been no folly: news of a gold strike in the Klondike region reached the continental United States in January 1897 and precipitated a deluge of miners into the area. Six months later a cargo ship would dock in San Francisco bearing $750,000 in Alaskan gold, followed three days later in Seattle by a ship carrying another $800,000 worth of the metal. As novelist Jack London wrote in *Call of the Wild*, men by the thousands were "rushing into the Northland" and "groping in the Artic darkness," frantic for "yellow metal." Alaska's output of gold would top $10 million in every one of the next eight years, after which the lodes were tapped out.

Equally good news for U.S. commerce had arrived in the summer of 1896 with reports of the failure of India's wheat crop, followed six months later by the even better news that Europe's harvests were the Continent's worst in a decade. As a result, between 1895 and 1904 the price of wheat doubled on the international market.

Naturally, the crop failures overseas boosted demand for American grain and produce, which led the country to a return to prosperity that coincided with McKinley's crushing victory. These events did not bode well for the People's Party. After all, the Populist movement had been born of low farm prices and had risen on farmers' belief in the panacea of currency expansion and the inflation that would result from the issuance of silver dollars. In 1896 the debate over the U.S. monetary standard had divided the nation into warring political camps, but by 1898 farm prices had climbed and were still rising, and the nation's currency was expanding through gold rather than silver—a development, appreciated by both farmers and businessmen, that spelled the end of the agrarian uprising that had been simmering since the depression of 1873. The Populists hung on a while longer but were essentially finished as a force in U.S. politics.

The promise of an imminent economic boom was only dimly perceived by the McKinley administration in its first months, so the new president set about doing whatever he could to fulfill his party's campaign promises by ending the supposedly ongoing recession. Immediately after taking office he called a special session of Congress to ask for that old standby for alleviating economic distress: a higher tariff on imports. By the time the new Dingley Tariff was passed in July the financial pall had already begun to lift, mostly for other reasons, but McKinley's successful efforts to push the tariff through won him not only respect among his fellow politicians but credit among the public as the wonder-worker who had revived the U.S. economy.

The Spanish-American War

The economic wonders—no matter their actual origins—slowly began to inspire a certain American arrogance toward the rest of the world that some would say has characterized the nation ever since. Where Manifest Destiny had earlier referred to America's preordination to spread across its continent from the Atlantic to the Pacific, by the end of the nineteenth century the idea had expanded to include more imperial ambitions and the foreign policies to execute them. The growing advantage in the U.S. balance of trade with other nations—combined with a stellar history of military success in the face of supposedly stronger foes and the continuing federal investment in military readiness—made historians and intellectuals swarm to the notion that the United States was destined for eventual global dominance. According to the Darwinian tenet of the "survival of the fittest," these thinkers maintained, a great future lay ahead for the nation that had evolved into the world's fittest

The cartoon below imagines a melee of land speculation after America's annexation of Hawaii in 1898. The potential for territorial expansion had been a sensitive issue in Washington ever since 1893, when American residents on the islands led a revolt that overthrew Queen Liliuokalani and the longstanding Hawaiian monarchy. The treachery involved in the revolt sickened Grover Cleveland, who refused to support annexation during his administration. President McKinley, however, thought that the United States needed Hawaii "just as much and a good deal more than we did California." His stewardship of the annexation treaty through Congress was one of the hallmarks of his administration.

economy in little more than a century of existence. And now that vigorous economy craved new markets to conquer and profit from.

In the quarter century following the Civil War the United States faced a number of problems from abroad, but none had amounted to more than a passing diversion from the more pressing tasks of industrializing and urbanizing the nation. After some bickering early in the antebellum period, claims were settled against Great Britain for damages wrought upon U.S. shipping by Confederate destroyers fitted in British ports; after similarly considerable controversy, disputes over the U.S.-Canadian border and fishing rights in Alaskan waters were settled; in 1889 Secretary of State James Blaine presided over the first session of the eighteen-member Pan-American Congress he had helped found, which proved ineffectual itself but served to lay a foundation for inter-American cooperation; when Germany provoked clashes over Samoa the same year, President Harrison refused to risk war, and in 1893 President Cleveland similarly ignored arguments to annex the Hawaiian Islands, although he did intervene to help end a boundary dispute between Great Britain and Venezuela in 1895. All the while the United States maintained steady pressure on Spain to do something about the smoldering independence movement in Cuba, which loomed as an ever larger problem as Eastern business interests began talking of the eventual U.S. acquisition of the Spanish island just seventy miles off the coast of Florida.

While there appeared to be a pattern in these international maneuvers, it was deceiving. Judging from the political debate, it looked as though the United States was most concerned with Latin America but had a growing interest in the Pacific, while there seemed to be little or no engagement by either the nation's government or its businesses with Europe, Asia, or Africa, which together contained most of the world's population. But the numbers indicate otherwise: since the Civil War, U.S. businesses invested $50 million in Cuba—$30 million of it in sugarcane plantations—while commercial investments in Europe amounted to $151 million and to $200 million in Mexico.

In 1895 Cuba's restlessness erupted into a full-blown revolution against Spanish rule that grew more violent over the next three years. By 1898 the situation had deteriorated to the point that for the first time American lives and property appeared to be in real danger. After all, the United States conducted more trade with Cuba than Spain did, which meant it had more compelling claims on the island. So at the beginning of the year President McKinley sent the battleship U.S.S. *Maine* to protect American interests

The cartoon below, which appeared in *Puck* magazine in 1898, depicts Uncle Sam standing hand in hand with Cuban Liberty, watching Spanish conquistadores depart on a galleon. Spain had claimed control over Cuba ever since Columbus's first visit in 1492, and had long used the island as the anchor of a lucrative empire. By 1898, however, Cuba was in the throes of annihilation, losing a quarter of its population in just three years as a result of famine and a brutal rebellion. Experts on the subject refrained from pinning all the blame on Spanish mismanagement, but Americans went to war doing just that, most acting out of sincere humanitarian concern. Some, though, merely liked the idea of pushing the Spanish out of the Western Hemisphere at long last.

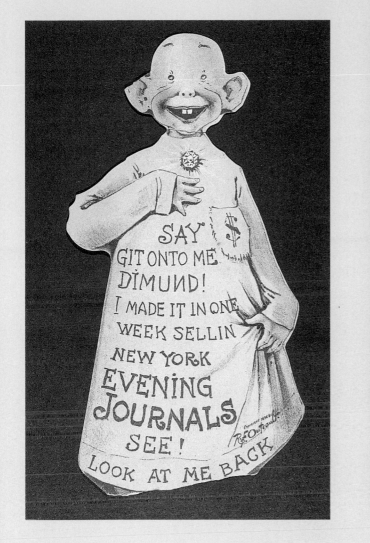

there. But on February 15 the ship was sunk in Havana's harbor after a mysterious explosion that left 260 dead. Although President McKinley wanted to avert war with Spain over Cuba, the rally cry "Remember the *Maine*!" caught on like wildfire as American citizens demanded revenge for the deaths. Historian Dexter Perkins would later note that "never was there a clearer case of war brought about by public opinion." The U.S. makeshift naval court that investigated the *Maine*'s explosion determined on March 28 that Spain was guilty of either criminal negligence for mining Havana harbor or malicious intent of destroying the *Maine* by torpedo. The noninterventionist McKinley's diplomatic options were greatly reduced by this devastating naval report, which in essence was interpreted as a declaration of arms. (In actuality, the Spanish had not mined or torpedoed the U.S.S. *Maine*. This verdict was handed down in 1976 when the Rickover Commission determined that the battleship was sunk by an internal accident—a boiler explosion.)

But in 1898 Americans were whipped into a war frenzy by the press, which at the time had descended to a sensationalistic approach so tawdry it was given a name, "yellow journalism," after the unprecedented colored ink Joseph Pulitzer's *New York World* splashed on its tabloid front page to highlight history's first comic strip, "The Yellow Kid." Pulitzer and a fellow news-

The original "Yellow Kid," above left, was a popular cartoon character of the 1890s. His hue inspired the phrase "Yellow Journalism," for any unrestrained effort to increase circulation, after the *New York Evening-Journal* rapaciously snatched the cartoon from a rival paper. The character's name soon attached as well to William Randolph Hearst, in a 1906 photograph above right, the owner of the *Journal.* "The Yellow Kid" of the newspaper wars, Hearst would do anything to sell his tabloid, from helping police solve gruesome murders to stirring the events that led to the Spanish-American War. James Ford, a *Journal* writer, said of the enigmatic Hearst, "When peace brooded over the city and nobody was being robbed or murdered, he would come down to the office with despondency written on his face . . . but the tidings of some new crime or disaster would rouse him to instant action."

paper tycoon William Randolph Hearst of the *New York Evening-Journal* happened to be embroiled in a vicious circulation battle at the time, and turned the sinking of the *Maine* into an excuse for demanding war in the interest of boosting their papers' readership. Both publishers contributed mightily to the wave of anti-Spanish sentiment that swept the nation, printing jingoistic articles and editorials embracing the threat of war under banner headlines like "Remember the *Maine*! To Hell with Spain!" Suddenly Cuban independence from Spanish rule became a national obsession. Ardent expansionists—evoking the Monroe Doctrine—relished booting Spain out of the Western Hemisphere.

Despite the growing public outcry stirred up by Pulitzer and Hearst, for two months President McKinley shied away from entering into hostilities, which won him the adulation of those who feared that a war with Spain over Cuba would mark the beginnings of American imperialism and the end of the nation's democratic vision. For its part, Spain had no desire to fight the United States, and made broad concessions including a unilateral cease-fire, giving the United States the right to decide the nature and length of the armistice, an autonomous government for Cuba, and international arbitration of the matter of the *Maine*. Nevertheless, egged on by the yellow press the cries for war mounted at home until McKinley—who, as one congressman quipped, "keeps his ear to the ground so close that he gets it full of grasshoppers much of the time"—felt sufficiently threatened by the public's ire and the divisions in his own party that he submitted a war message to Congress on April 11, 1898. Eight days later the House and Senate passed a joint resolution declaring Cuba free and demanding Spain's withdrawal from the island, yet also disclaiming any hegemonic ambitions on the part of the United States. But best intentions aside, the nation had embarked upon an imperialism that would alter America's very definition of itself and its reasons for existence—and that would in time make it the world's strongest and most imitated democracy, if not always the best liked. On April 24 Spain declared war on the United States; the following day Congress formally did the same against Madrid retroactive to April 21.

The Spanish-American War lasted six months and ended when U.S. troops moved beyond Cuba and into Puerto Rico, another Spanish-controlled island in the Caribbean. The fighting in Cuba likely would not have dragged on so long but for the incompetence of General William Shafter and a number of War Department procurement scandals. But the flamboyant and brazen Colonel Theodore Roosevelt and his "Rough Riders," who famously charged up and took San Juan Hill and Kettle Hill—on foot, because their horses hadn't made it over in time from Florida—brought the fight for Cuba to a glorious conclusion. Despite the general successes in the combat and the public's continuing enthusiasm for the newspapers' war, there was also substantial domestic opposition to the conflict sparked by suspicions that it had actually been concocted by and for U.S. commercial interests. Such famous and exalted icons as educator Charles Eliot, industrialist Andrew Carnegie, and philosopher William James protested what they considered an unnecessary, unjust, and just plain foolish war. Fighting Spain, author Sherwood Anderson observed, was "like robbing an old gypsy woman in a vacant lot at night after a fair." Nevertheless, despite protests, the fighting continued, with Puerto Rico falling to General Nelson Miles's U.S. forces in late July.

What John Hay, the future Secretary of State, would call the "splendid little war" had spread far beyond the Caribbean; in fact, its most significant engagement may have been the battle for the Philippines, which Spain had controlled since founding Manila in 1571. There, on May 1, 1898, Commodore George Dewey led U.S. forces in the Battle of Manila Bay—almost offhandedly telling the captain of his flagship, "You may fire when you are ready, Gridley"—and destroyed the entire Spanish flotilla without losing a

OPPOSITE PAGE: William Dinwiddie took the photograph titled "Col. Theodore Roosevelt and the 'Rough Riders' at the top of San Juan Hill after its capture, July, 1898." Roosevelt is at left of the flag. The Rough Riders, known officially as the First Volunteeer Cavalry, were the stuff of colorful legends even before they left for battle in Cuba. Millionaire sportsmen joined Ivy League athletes and Western cowboys in ranks that perfectly reflected the types of men Roosevelt knew best. The Rough Riders acquitted themselves well in Cuba, helping to turn American fortunes around near Santiago by valiantly attacking a larger force. First they charged up Kettle Hill—"the best moment of anybody's life," eyewitness Stephen Crane called it—and then up San Juan Hill, the most famous incident of the war.

Below, Theodore Roosevelt was painted in his soldier's garb by U.S. Army private Charles Johnson Post. Roosevelt was Assistant Secretary of the Navy when the Spanish-American War started; he resigned immediately in order to join the fight and proving a fearless officer. In November 1898, Roosevelt was elected governor of New York and he was on his way to the presidency.

Rufus Zogbaum's painting shows Commodore George Dewey on the bridge of the *Olympia*, flagship of the U.S. fleet in the Pacific. Even before war was declared in April 1898, Dewey was preparing his Asiatic Squadron for a possible attack on the Spanish fleet in the Philippines, a measure considered suicidal by most observers. However, in Manila Bay on the morning of May 1, the Americans destroyed ten Spanish ships without sustaining serious damage to a single U.S. ship. By noon, the Spanish were ready to surrender.

single U.S. ship and suffering only one casualty. The American forces then formed an alliance with Filipino guerrilla leader Emilio Aguinaldo, and soon controlled several key points across the islands. In early July at Santiago, Cuba, the U.S. achieved another lopsided victory over a Spanish fleet. The U.S. triumph was announced on July 4; three days later, while the nation was still celebrating, McKinley quietly annexed the Hawaiian Islands. Undermanned and ill-equipped Spain sued for peace. The combatants signed an armistice on August 12, thus ending a war that should be called the Spanish-American- Cuban-Filipino War.

Although the United States had gone to war to free Cuba, its troops had wound up in Puerto Rico, the Philippines, and several other Pacific islands as well. "If old Dewey had just sailed away when he smashed that Spanish fleet," McKinley complained to his friend Chicago newspaperman H. H. Kohlsaat, "what a lot of trouble he would have saved us." Faced with this unexpectedly wide-ranging victory, McKinley decided to make the most of the situation and annex everything but Cuba, which would become a virtual U.S. protectorate. Under the Treaty of Paris signed on December 10, 1898, the Philippines were ceded to the United States for $20 million, while the U.S. Army remained in Puerto Rico and the various Pacific islands. Secretary of State William R. Day, upon signing the Treaty of Paris, is purported to have twirled a large globe in his office and said, "Let's see what we get by this." What the United States *got* was an overseas empire.

The treaty's provisions kicked up America's first major foreign policy debate, over no less a question than whether the United States should expand beyond the natural borders of its continent. Before the Spanish-American War few had expressed designs on the Philippines or any other Spanish possessions, but Dewey's smashing victory had inspired U.S. businessmen to drool at the prospect of bases near vast new Asian markets for their products. As Republican Mark Hanna, a senator from Ohio, exclaimed: "If this be commercialism, for God's sake let us have commercialism!" Bolstering the capitalist argument was the even more specious claim by religious missionaries that it was America's duty to "civilize" and "save the souls" of its "little brown brothers" in less advanced circumstances. John Hay, meanwhile, could quite rightfully boast that the Spanish-American War had healed the wounds of the Civil War: victories in Manila Bay and Santiago Harbor had unified the nation like never before.

The rush toward imperialism sparked a countermovement that considered the acquisition of the Philippines a violation of America's most basic principles, such as the Monroe Doctrine's isolationism and the belief in self-government for all nations, and would afford the United States nothing but unforeseen problems in the bargain. In 1899 the various groups that had risen in protest against the Treaty of Paris united into the American Anti-Imperialist League, which attracted members as diverse as industrial titan Andrew Carnegie, labor activist Samuel Gompers, and mild-mannered philosopher William James, who was driven to sputter, "God damn the United States for its vile conduct in the Philippine Isles!" The conquest of people, these anti-imperialists argued, violated the sacred concept of self-determina-

tion as postulated in the Constitution and the Declaration of Independence. As James so indelicately noted, America was about to "puke up its heritage."

But the treaty was ratified nonetheless, and the United States suddenly found itself with an empire. Optimists—including many eager businessmen—looked forward to a Caribbean Sea transformed into a large American lake dotted with tourist resorts and bustling sugar factories, and even more

American soldiers march into Manila in August 1898, the last offensive action of the Spanish-American War. Even while fighting in the Caribbean to liberate Cuba, the United States was maneuvering in the Pacific to seize the Philippines as spoils of war. Dewey's naval victory in May had given America control of Manila Bay and one army base on land, but the capital city and the rest of the country had remained in Spanish hands. The invasion posed a delicate challenge, not so much because of the light resistance put up by the Spanish occupiers but because of the presence of a large, anxious army of Filipino rebels on the outskirts of the city. The U.S. Army may have marched freely into the surrendered city in mid-August 1898, as shown left, but it would then expend four years, $160 million, and 5,000 American lives in a vicious guerrilla war with the insurgents in the Philippines.

ardently to the potential construction of a transisthmus canal that would join the Atlantic to the Pacific and afford far quicker sea trade among the nations around both. Pessimists, on the other hand, looked with regret at the capitalist factory America was becoming and mourned the passing of what by 1899 already seemed a quaint age of agrarian innocence. Most politicians, naturally, sided with the former view: vigor had become the American way.

CHAPTER 13

IMPERIALISM AND REFORM

The nation entered the twentieth century with a bang—or, more precisely and even better, without one, for the United States was at peace after the successful Spanish-American War, and well on its way into an era of unprecedented prosperity. Americans were rapidly evolving from subsistence farming and railsplitting to manufacturing, commerce, and international trade. It was an age of dynamic, unfettered free enterprise, which brought forth transcontinental railroad empires, nationwide monopolies in steel, the birth of the automobile, and the consolidation of vast financial power on Wall Street. Yet amidst such sterling optimism lingered a deep concern that America's social fabric was unwinding, that not enough citizens were sharing in the good fortune. "Our production, our factory laws, our charities, our relations between capital and labor, our distribution—all wrong, out of gear," Thomas Edison wrote Henry Ford, "We've stumbled along for a while, trying to run a new civilization in old ways, but we've got to start to make this world over."

The makeover Edison wanted—known as Progressivism—emerged out of the new political realities that formed after the watershed election of 1896. As expected, the Republican Party renominated William McKinley for the presidency in 1900, justifiably claiming to have fulfilled its campaign pledges of four years earlier and promising voters a "full dinner pail" this time out. The incumbent boasted not only a credible national agenda but an abun-

Theodore Roosevelt, left, delivered a Fourth of July address at Grant's Tomb in New York in 1910. The former president was as magnetic as ever in his return as a political force that summer. "We grudge no man a fortune in civil life," he stated. "We should permit it to be gained only so long as the gaining represents benefits to the community." Roosevelt assumed for the government the moral right to judge business practices, and so ended the Gilded Age.

William Jennings Bryan is touted on the poster below as the Democratic nominee in the 1900 presidential election. Beaten by McKinley, Bryan would run again in 1908, his two campaigns straddling Theodore Roosevelt's presidency almost exactly. The two men, both in their forties, were alike in many ways: vigorous, moralistic, and popular. In politics, Roosevelt adopted so many of Bryan's issues over the course of his presidency that the suggestion of a great debate between the nation's leading Democrat and Republican actually brought laughter at a dinner they attended in 1905. "What's the use? They're both on the same side," jeered a voice from the crowd.

dance of personal charm; McKinley was a president who unabashedly walked the streets of the nation's capital, currying public favor with handshakes and tokens of flowers from his own lapel. Beneath his genial demeanor, however, in many ways McKinley departed from the model of his predecessors and operated less as an executive figurehead than as the leader of his party, making the crafty Gilded Age politician perhaps the first truly modern U.S. president.

Not that he would be remembered as such. McKinley's first vice president, Garret Hobart of New Jersey, had died in November 1899, and at the urging of New York Republican boss Thomas Platt, the president reluctantly accepted the idea of Theodore Roosevelt as his running mate in 1900. A hero of the recent war after having led a successful charge up Cuba's San Juan Hill, the colorful "Teddy" Roosevelt had been elected governor of New York in 1898. Once in office he immediately set about disturbing the status quo with his demands for political and bureaucratic reform, including the taxation of corporations and an end to the spoils system. Platt wanted him out of the state and therefore proposed him for the innocuous vice presidency, where he could do less harm to New York's Republican machine. What's more, the boisterous Roosevelt made a nice contrast with the rather subdued McKinley, who was so circumspect that upon a visit to Niagara Falls in 1901 he had taken great pains to walk less than halfway across the bridge between the United States and Canada to avoid becoming the first American president to leave the country during his term in office.

Unconcerned as ever with circumspection, the Democrats again selected William Jennings Bryan as their presidential candidate, further unsettling the Populists, who were already divided among three factions. One supported Bryan and lost its members to the Democratic Party, another remained independent and nominated Wharton Barker of Pennsylvania, while the third wing joined the new Socialist Party in nominating Eugene V. Debs.

The nation's overall peace and, more important, its prosperity produced the expected result: McKinley won with 7.2 million popular and 292 electoral votes to Bryan's totals of 6.4 million and 155. Despite their victory, the Republicans saw cause for concern; even running on a strong economy in the wake of a successful and popular war, McKinley had managed to attract only about 110,000 more votes than he had in 1896, some of which apparently came from Spanish-American War opponent Bryan. Socialist Debs, meanwhile, received 86,000 votes and Prohibitionist John Woolley a whopping 209,000, indicating the power of the movement that combined temperance with opposition to immigration. All in all, the various minor party candidates gleaned 395,000 votes, a significant enough 2.8 percent of the popular tally to suggest substantial public discontent with the country's two dominant political parties.

The colored engraving at left shows the close range at which President McKinley was shot, September 6, 1901, while greeting visitors at the Pan-American Exposition in Buffalo. The assassin, Leon Czolgosz, described himself as an anarchist, though his crime was assailed even by most anarchists, who considered McKinley a relatively harmless leader. The doctors marveled at the president's essentially kindly nature even in delirium and reported that he sang snatches from the hymn "Nearer My God to Thee" as he lay dying. Following his death, large crowds gathered all along the route taken by his funeral train, and many sang "Nearer My God to Thee" as the cars passed.

Early in his second term McKinley declared that under no circumstances would he run again, thereby making it clear that he intended to take a more politically independent stance—and proving his seriousness by coming out in favor of a series of reform programs. For starters, he made a number of speeches asserting that high tariffs were no longer defensible, proclaiming that "There is nothing in this world that brings people so close together as commerce." The president also alluded to the "trust problem" and suggested that businesses had a responsibility to the community at large and would have to start answering for any actions that indicated otherwise. Although he did not recommend any specific actions or legislation to curb the growth of corporations, McKinley hinted at enough concern to create a general sense that such restrictions were imminent. Addressing the Pan-American Exposition in Buffalo, New York, on September 5, 1901, McKinley said, "We must not repose in fancied security that we can forever sell everything and buy little or nothing. . . . Isolation is no longer possible or desirable. . . . God and man have linked the nations together. . . . The period of exclusiveness is over."

The next day President McKinley was shot in Buffalo by anarchist Leon Czolgosz. At first it seemed he would recover, but bungling on the part of his doctors led to McKinley's death eight days later, elevating Theodore Roosevelt to the presidency. There would be no McKinley reform crusade, nor his guidance over the legacy of the Spanish-American War. But that did not mean there wouldn't be reform or adequate leadership for dealing with the remains of the conflict that had thrust the United States upon the world stage.

The Problems of Empire

"Now look," sputtered McKinley's closest adviser and Svengali, Mark Hanna. "That damned cowboy is president of the United States!" Roosevelt could afford to ignore the Republican party boss and his brand of slick political packaging. He was and knew he was a genuine American prodigy of presidential caliber, and bully for him and the nation.

Indeed, for all his bluster Theodore Roosevelt deserves his place with Washington, Jefferson, and Lincoln in the giant national memorial at South Dakota's Mount Rushmore. In fact, the youngest U.S. president—Roosevelt was sworn in at age forty-two—put the infectious enthusiasm behind his seemingly perpetual toothy grin to good use for the nation, attracting Americans to his causes in much the same way as the second youngest chief executive, John F. Kennedy, would sixty years later.

The scion of an aristocratic New York family that spanned seven generations of America's history, Roosevelt, a frail and asthmatic child, devoted himself to building up his body as well as his mind to the point that few could keep up with him on either score. He had sojourned to the Great Plains in 1883 looking for storybook adventures—and he found them along the cottonwood banks of the Little Missouri River with randy scouts and weathered cowboys as his guides. Years later, in his autobiography, Roosevelt would describe the West he encountered in romantic prose: "It was a land of scattered ranches, of herds of longhorned cattle, and of reckless riders who unmoved looked into the eyes of life or death." Heroes came easily to Roosevelt and he took to these cowboys with an unprecedented zeal like a young boy living out a nickle novel fantasy. These rugged citizens of the Dakotas were imbued with the virtues Roosevelt ranked supreme: Emersonian self-reliance, Lincolnian honesty and Darwinian survivalist instincts. Before he assumed the presidency he had roped cattle in the Dakota Badlands, killed grizzly bears, mastered various martial arts, and prepared himself for an eventual retirement hunting big game in Africa and exploring the Amazon. As he told Chicago's Hamilton Club on April 10, 1899, "I wish to preach not the doctrine of ignoble ease, but the doctrine of the strenuous life. . . . Far better it is to dare mighty things, to win glorious triumphs, even though checkered by failure, than to take rank with those poor spirits who neither enjoy much nor suffer much, because they live in the gray twilight that knows not victory nor defeat." Given his vigorous proclivities, it is hardly surprising that unlike his predecessors Roosevelt regarded the U.S. Constitution not as putting limits on presidential power but as suggesting only what he could not do. It did not, for example, keep him from renaming the Executive Mansion "the White House."

Before he could get to the political, and in time the environmental, reform programs that actually interested him most, President Roosevelt had to face the question of what to do about the recent U.S. victory over Spain and the continuing tensions in the Philippines. The potential annexation of the territories accorded the United States under the Treaty of Paris posed dilemmas the imperial enthusiasts of 1898 had hardly anticipated. Were the inhabitants of these territories now Americans, or subjects of the United States? If they were Americans, it would only be logical to assume that one day they would become citizens of states of the Union. If they were not Americans on the grounds that the nation had no intention of admitting its new possessions as states, then was the United States no better than the European powers it had always attacked for subjugating native peoples?

The Treaty of Paris ending the Spanish-American War begged the question altogether, providing only that "the civil rights and political status of the native inhabitants hereby ceded to the United States shall be determined by Congress." The matter eventually fell to the Supreme Court, which interpreted the treaty's provisions inconsistently in a series of decisions that together decreed that the inhabitants of the new possessions had some, but not all, the rights of U.S. citizens. The divided Court distinguished between fundamental rights extended to all residents of the United States—those somewhat vague promises of life, liberty, and the pursuit of happiness, among others—and procedural rights, such as trial by jury, that are reserved for U.S. citizens. In addition, the Court decided that the new quasi-Americans clearly would not be entitled to the rights accorded inhabitants of states, such as the ballot.

The Supreme Court also drew distinctions between two kinds of United States–owned territories: incorporated and unincorporated. Those in the first category, such as Alaska and Hawaii, might one day be considered for statehood; those in the second, such as Puerto Rico and Guam, would not be so considered. The Philippines occupied a category of its own because it was to receive its independence at some future date. Naturally, economics had at least as much to do as politics and geostrategy with the disposition of the various U.S. territories. Alaska qualified for statehood not only for its longevity as a possession—Seward had completed its purchase in 1867—but for its abundance of oil, timber, minerals, and other useful natural resources. The Hawaiian Islands made the cut because of their location as a perfect way station for trans-Pacific trade. Puerto Rico, on the other hand, had been acquired largely with an eye toward its serving as a U.S. military outpost for guarding the Caribbean and any transisthmus canal that might be built, while Guam similarly had been acquired for its strategic defensive position between Hawaii and the Philippines and thence the rest of the Orient.

None of this sat well with either the Filipinos or the Puerto Ricans. In the Philippines, rebel leader Emilio Aguinaldo declared himself head of the nation and rallied his forces to continue fighting the Americans as they had the Spaniards, and by the time the insurrection ended more Americans had died in brutal combat with Aguinaldo's and other guerrillas than they had in the Spanish-American War itself. In 1902 the

Below, Filipino leader Emilio Aguinaldo boards a U.S. gunboat after he was captured in a daring raid by U.S. forces in March 1901. When the Americans first arrived in the Philippines to fight the Spanish in 1898, Aguinaldo assumed that they were there to help him fight for Filipino independence. Instead, the defeat of the Spanish led to a long period of guerrilla warfare between American soldiers and Aguinaldo's followers.

The color lithograph of John Hay, above, by Sir Leslie Ward, was published in England's *Spy* magazine in 1897. Hay's career in government started in Springfield, Illinois, in 1860, when President-elect Abraham Lincoln engaged him as a private secretary. He worked his way up as a diplomat in later Republican administrations and so impressed McKinley with his erudition and tact that the president named him Secretary of State in 1898. Hay was devastated by McKinley's assassination in 1901, especially as he had also been close to both Abraham Lincoln and James Garfield, two previously slain presidents. Roosevelt retained John Hay at the head of the State Department, even while handling many aspects of foreign affairs himself. As illustrated in the cartoon at right, Roosevelt considered himself "the World's Constable," policing rogue nations around the globe.

Philippine Islands were granted the right to form a legislature, and fourteen years later the Jones Act promised their independence in 1945. Puerto Rico got both more and less of a deal in 1902: while its goods were permitted into the United States duty-free, only after 1917 would its people be made U.S. citizens.

America's further forays into foreign affairs were not confined to imperialism; international trade remained if anything an even greater concern. As Britain, France, Germany, and Russia began to scramble to keep Japan's growing influence from spreading too far into China, in 1899 William McKinley's Secretary of State, John Hay, opted to go it alone toward China instead, implementing what came to be known as the Open Door policy. Like the Monroe Doctrine, Hay's policy pronounced America's intention not to meddle in the Orient and proposed instead that China be kept equally open to all nations. As Hay's circular letter of July 1900 stated, the U.S. wanted to "bring about . . . peace to China" and to "preserve Chinese territorial and administrative entity." The Open Door policy was born of U.S. eagerness to take advantage of China's vast markets, but its support for Chinese sovereignty also drew applause from American anti-imperialists.

Hay's successor under Theodore Roosevelt, Secretary of State Elihu Root, reinforced the Open Door policy in 1908 by coming out in favor of both "the independence and integrity of China" and "the principle of equal opportunity for commerce and industry in China" in an agreement reached with Japan, which had continued to grow in military and economic might. Root's concern for the sovereignty of foreign nations had been established some years earlier, when as Secretary of War he had helped President Roosevelt set up the modern U.S. military system, in which the nation pledged to "police the surrounding premises" of the Western Hemisphere. In one of its first such actions, before granting Cuban independence in 1902 the United States had reorganized the island nation's finances and added the Platt Amendment to the Cuban constitution, which gave America the authority to intervene in

Cuba's internal affairs in the event that either its independence or its order were threatened. Under the Platt Amendment, U.S. troops would occupy Cuba twice between 1906 and 1923.

For all the death, destruction, and international political reshuffling caused by the Spanish-American War, perhaps its most significant outcome was renewed U.S. interest in a transisthmus canal connecting the Atlantic to the Pacific by way of the Caribbean. The importance of such a waterway had become clear during the conflict with Spain, when the battleship U.S.S. *Oregon* had been forced to go from its base in San Francisco Bay south through the Pacific all the way to the nether tip of South America, through the Straits of Magellan, and back north to Cuba, a treacherous, storm-plagued, 13,000-mile journey that captured the public's attention through vivid newspaper reports. The evidence was clear that, although rapidly building one, the United States did not yet have enough of a navy to cover both its far-flung coasts at once, and the easiest and cheapest of the hard and costly solutions to the problem was to build a path between the oceans at the narrowest point dividing them: Central America. It was lost on no one that in aiding defense, a canal could also prove quite a boon to U.S. commerce.

In 1901 President Roosevelt entered into negotiations with Colombia for the rights to construct a canal across the Isthmus of Panama, which Bogotá then controlled. When the Colombian government rejected the U.S. proposal, Roosevelt denounced the "foolish and homicidal corruptionists at Bogotá" and threatened to get what he wanted by force. He got his chance a few months later when a revolution broke out in Panama, and U.S. forces aided the rebels by refusing to let Colombian troops into the areas they controlled. Within a few weeks, Panama was recognized as an independent nation and signed the Hay-Bunau-Varilla Treaty, granting the United States a zone in which to build a transisthmus canal. All this was Roosevelt's doing, as he was only too happy to boast, crowing, "I took the Canal Zone and let Congress debate." Roosevelt's boasting aside, the canal was built by huge steam shovels and the calloused hands of thousands of Caribbean laborers and American workers. Yellow fever claimed the lives of hundreds until Colonel William C. Gorgas wiped out the mosquito-breeding grounds at Colón and Panama City, virtually eliminating the disease from the isthmus. United States' engineers dug, dynamited, and clear-cut their way across the isthmus. The Panama Canal was formally opened to world traffic on August 15, 1914, and is considered an astonishing engineering feat.

As soon as the first negotiations with Colombia began, the United States found itself embroiled in Caribbean politics, and over the next generation U.S. Marines—and dollars—would become familiar visitors and often residents of the area. Usually it was with the best of intentions, such as the desire to spread democracy, end corruption, and improve the lives of the islands' people, but the U.S. incursions were always aimed at protecting commercial as well as strategic interests. For these reasons U.S. troops would occupy Cuba from 1898 to 1902, 1906 to 1909, in 1912, and again from 1917 to 1922; Haiti would become a U.S. protectorate in 1915 and U.S. forces would remain there until 1934; Santo Domingo (later the Dominican Republic)

Elihu Root, above, was a busy corporation lawyer in New York when William McKinley asked him to serve as Secretary of War in 1899. Even with no military or government experience, Root was able to reorganize the inefficent army. Serving as Theodore Roosevelt's Secretary of State from 1905 to 1909, he built on America's burgeoning military strength to expand its diplomatic influence, especially in Latin America and the Pacific. After Roosevelt met Germany's Kaiser Wilhelm in 1910, he told friends, "the Kaiser is an able man, a very able man . . . but not so able as Elihu Root!"

The *Oregon*, above, was commissioned in 1896, one of the first vessels in America's battleship fleet. An armored steel battleship such as the *Oregon* was the most advanced military weapon of the day—and remains quite contemporary in silhouette even more than a century later. By 1904 the United States had thirteen such battleships afloat and ten more under construction. As a result of its massive building program, America caught up to France, Russia, and Germany; among world navies, only Great Britain truly dominated, with its forty-four battleships. In total tonnage, the U.S. Navy had the third largest fleet afloat in 1904.

would become a U.S. protectorate from 1905 to 1924, and Nicaragua would stay under U.S. control from 1912 to 1925 and from 1926 to 1933. In each case, the interests of the United States had as much if not more to do with business than with empire. In 1912, for example, 2,000 U.S. Marines landed in Nicaragua to protect a government threatened by a revolution but, more important, to indicate the extent of U.S. financial interests in the area, which many businessmen were then eyeing as the ideal site for building operating bases near the Panama Canal.

The aggressive U.S. actions in Central America aroused many animosities and bred both fear and hatred of what was increasingly perceived as "the colossus of the North." Although the United States' motives were often altruistic as well as commercial, the nation's expanding military and economic prowess was driving it ever further into the affairs of other countries—whether those countries wanted that help or not. Decades before the United States would become mired in Vietnam, America had tasted the quicksand such outgoing foreign policy initiatives could lead to.

But Theodore Roosevelt was nothing if not outgoing. Despite his advice to "speak softly, but carry a big stick," in office Roosevelt spoke loudly and often from what he dubbed the "bully pulpit" of the presidency. In 1902, for example, when European nations tried by force to collect on debts from Venezuela, he waved the U.S. stick and warned them away. Two years later he enunciated the Roosevelt corollary to the Monroe Doctrine, which declared that the United States would intervene to protect Latin American nations from the kind of internal inefficiency and disorder that had led so many

The photograph above shows the Panama Canal under construction in December of 1904. The first effort to cut a canal through the Isthmus of Panama began in 1881, when a French company started work with the highest expectations, under the supervision of the same man responsible for the Suez Canal in Egypt. Panama's rugged terrain and jungle conditions proved far too much for the French, however, and the company collapsed. Theodore Roosevelt revived the project after he took office in 1901, but soon concluded that no private company in the world could overcome all of Panama's obstacles simultaneously: the deadly diseases and vermin, the rotting humidity, the steep landscape, and the heavy seasonal rains. Under such conditions, workmen on the canal viewed Panama as nothing less than the very specter of death, as illustrated in a 1904 Joseph Keppler cartoon at left. In 1907 President Roosevelt assigned the daunting project to the U.S. Army, which finally opened the Panama Canal in 1914. During the course of the work army doctors overcame two virulent diseases—yellow fever and malaria—an achievement with even more impact worldwide than the completion of the canal itself.

of them to default on payments of debt. By thus proclaiming that the United States would in effect act as guarantor of its southern neighbors' debts, Roosevelt thrust the nation far deeper into the affairs of Latin America.

The Progressive Movement

As vigorous an interest as he took in foreign policy, President Roosevelt was equally concerned with the country's domestic situation and still more with its future. He also had a public mandate to pursue initiatives regarding both; in fact, by 1901 he had achieved the status of a near idol at the head of his own cult of personality. After all, he had reinvigorated the U.S. presidency and changed the nation's role in global affairs—and besides, the youngest chief executive had a delightful grin and forthright manners hewn as much by his days wrangling cattle on the Dakota frontier as by those he had spent in the drawing rooms of New York society. The public was wowed, and pretty much went along with anything Roosevelt chose to do.

In his first message to Congress on December 3, 1901, the new president outlined his thinking on the important issues of the day. He called for action to deal with the "tremendous and highly complex industrial development" of the past century, including federal action if necessary. By the same token, however, he applauded America's corporate titans and supported their freedom from regulation, proclaiming that "The creation of these great corporate fortunes has not been due to the tariff nor to any other governmental action, but to natural causes in the business world, operating in other countries as they operate in our own." Thus in one speech Roosevelt effectively killed hopes for tariff reform and disappointed those who wanted to use it as a step toward government control of big business. In fact, he warned that "to strike with ignorant violence at the interests of one set of men almost inevitably endangers the interests of all."

And yet the aristocrat from Sagamore Hill in posh Oyster Bay, Long Island, added that "It is also true that there are real and grave evils, one of the chief being over-capitalization because of its many baleful consequences; and a resolute and practical effort must be made to correct these evils." In other words, President Roosevelt was calling for business reform and regulation while at the same time praising the very institutions that required them. To further assure the business community that he was not embarking on a crusade against them, the president consulted with conservative Republican patriarch Senator Nelson Aldrich of Rhode Island—known as Wall Street financier J. P. Morgan's "floor broker in the Senate"—prior to writing his first address to Congress, and made sure the press knew it. As a result and as intended, newspapers praised Roosevelt for being so "reasonable" and "judicious." Meanwhile, tycoons exhaled sighs of relief across the nation; compared to what McKinley had been suggesting, it looked as though Roosevelt might not be such an ardent reformer after all.

In fact, he was better—and exactly the right man for the times. Roosevelt served as president during a period of unprecedentedly rapid and unsettling change that had begun under McKinley. Unlike his predecessor, however,

Roosevelt appeared to see the forest as well as the trees more clearly than any of his contemporaries. The everyday lives of ordinary Americans were changing in major ways for any number of reasons: the new industrial order, the sudden interest in overseas expansion, the explosion of the cities, the troubles on the farms, the changing composition of the immigrant influx. Although apparent earlier, the magnitude and implications of these changes had eluded even the most astute observers of the time. The Populist movement may have been the most important attempt to restructure the United States in the late nineteenth century, but it had little to offer beyond palliatives derived from nostalgia for the simpler virtues of an agrarian society. Although workers' organizations such as the American Federation of Labor recognized the fact of a new industrial order, their programs for meeting it centered more on trying to create a "labor aristocracy" than on sweeping away the debris left by the old order and fashioning a new one designed to meet the needs of the emerging class of industrial workers.

International affairs were no less confused at the turn of the century. Up to the Spanish-American War, U.S. foreign policy had for the most part been formulated and carried out by political amateurs with little knowledge of international relations and less experience in actual power politics. In context, the main reason Theodore Roosevelt looms so large in U.S. history is that he was among the first individuals of any influence to understand and deal with the myriad new forces buffeting the United States.

By the end of his first term, Roosevelt would be dubbed a "Progressive" as the originator of what he called the "square deal." Like so many of the greatest political slogans, the terms had no precise definition. Those who declared themselves Progressives used the word to mean forward-looking, modern, and concerned with reform but neither radical nor violent and certainly averse to any undue alterations to the nation's basic institutions. To be Progressive also, however, meant to oppose big business to some degree; Progressives were those who acknowledged the increasing urbanization of the United States and wanted the government to take a more active role in dealing with the changes thus wrought both socially and economically. Adherents believed that government should be more responsible and responsive to the public than it had in the past, and should reflect the aspirations of the common man rather than the interests of business. Indeed, one of the most striking hallmarks of the movement was Progressives' belief that government had to play an ever larger role in the lives of Americans, which meant civil service could no longer be considered a mere pastime for the second sons and troublesome nephews who had lately been in charge of the nation's destiny. How these vast changes in the U.S. bureaucracy were to be accomplished, however, was the subject of considerable debate among the reformers.

Few Progressives evinced much concern for the plight of blacks or Native Americans, opting instead to flirt with high-minded socialism and vague schemes for utopia in their lifetimes. Unlike the Populists of a decade before, the Progressives did not make narrow appeals to one segment of the public against another; instead the movement tried to spread its banner wide

The photograph at right was taken on May 12, 1930, fifty years after Jane Addams founded the pioneering institution. Both Hull-House and Addams believed in attacking urban problems at their source—and in cities overcrowded with new arrivals, sheer ignorance was the source of much misery among the lowest classes.

enough for all, and in the process was forced to contradict itself. The greatest support for Progressivism came from the rising urban middle class that had the most to gain by adhering to the rules for climbing America's social and economic ladders. But it was also a movement of the "outsiders" against the "insiders," attracting the faded aristocrats who had seen their status sucked away by newly minted tycoons, the small businessmen threatened by what they deemed unfair competition from large corporations, and the working classes who felt themselves the victims of a conspiracy of greed conducted by "malefactors of great wealth," as Roosevelt would call them in

1907. In fact, the Progressives were not a new phenomenon, but the same people who had voted for both Democrat Grover Cleveland and Republican William McKinley.

As early as the mid-1880s the precursors of the Progressives had been preaching temperance and the "social gospel" that individual souls could be saved by improving the conditions of society that forced them to live immorally. The new discipline of social science offered the parallel argument that the country's problems could be alleviated by encouraging those better off to take a measure of responsibility for helping immigrants and the native poor. The secular approach proved even more effective with the establishment of "settlement houses," early community centers run by middle-class volunteers to aid the poor in the worst of America's slums. More than a hundred such houses would be established by the turn of the century, the best-known being social reformer Jane Addams's Hull-House in Chicago. "For action," Addams wrote in 1902, "is indeed the sole medium of expression for ethics." She would eventually be awarded a Nobel Peace Prize for her humanitarian efforts to help the downtrodden.

The Progressive reform movement gained in strength as America's urban blight became ever harder to ignore. New York's Tammany Hall political machine had gone on enriching its members via graft at the public expense, but the results of such corruption finally caught the nation's attention in 1911 when the Triangle Shirtwaist Company in Manhattan caught fire and its lack of safety provisions trapped hundreds of employees inside, mostly young women and children. Many of the workers—who toiled twelve hours a day for as little as $3 a week, less the cost of the needles, thread, and even electricity they used—jumped from the top stories; 146 people were killed, most of them young women. The public was outraged and began to agitate seriously for change, giving rise, among other things, to the Socialist Party and its leader, Eugene V. Debs.

Roosevelt's Reforms

As defined by historians, the Progressive era embraced three U.S. presidents: Theodore Roosevelt, William Howard Taft, and Woodrow Wilson, all of whom would oppose one another for the presidency in 1912 while Governor Robert La Follette of Wisconsin, who was if anything the most Progressive of all, would denounce the entire trio. In any case, the Progressive movement was bigger than any one leader, and there were reform movements in many states and cities led by men like Albert B. Cummins in Iowa, Hiram W. Johnson in California, Judge John Burke in North Dakota, James M. Cox in Ohio, and others.

The ideas of the Progressives were popularized by a subset of crusading journalists, including such noted scribes as Ida Tarbell, Lincoln Steffens, and Upton Sinclair, whose 1906 novel *The Jungle* had exposed many middle-class Americans to the horrors of the urban poor. Sinclair and his fellow reform-minded journalists quickly created a boom in the exposé industry, uncovering the rot under every rock in U.S. society from child labor to unsafe

On March 26, 1911, a fire broke out at the Triangle Shirtwaist factory in New York City; the photograph above shows the scene on the sidewalk outside in the midst of the tragedy. Of 850 employees, mostly foreign-born women, 146 died from the smoke and flames, from trampling at the few exits that were not locked or from leaping out the windows. While the catastrophe could have been averted had the managers followed existing regulations—such as keeping fire doors unlocked—the horror of the Triangle Shirtwaist fire led directly to stringent new laws regarding worker safety.

working conditions to unregulated food and drug products. Concerned that their efforts were going too far, President Roosevelt dubbed these crusading reporters "muckrakers," like those workers John Bunyan had described in his seventeenth-century opus *Pilgrim's Progress*. "The men with the muckrakers are often indispensible to the wellbeing of society," Roosevelt noted, "but only if they know when to stop raking the muck, and look upward to the celestial crown above them, to the crown of worthy endeavor." Many muck-rakers were in fact guilty of sensationalizing the news in order to aid their quest for social justice, but without them the public likely would not have become informed and incensed enough about the nation's social problems to demand broad reforms. Aiding the muckrakers was celebrated jurist Louis D. Brandeis, who had quit his corporate law practice and proclaimed him-self "the people's attorney" after the brutal response to the Homestead Steel-works strike of 1892. His devotion to "sociological jurisprudence," in which

Ida M. Tarbell, photographed in 1918, left, was a respected journalist. In 1901 she was asked to write about the Standard Oil Company for *McClure's Magazine* and it was expected that she would turn in a straightforward business story. But Tarbell had witnessed the company's marauding ways firsthand when she was growing up and her book, *History of the Standard Oil Company*, presented a disturbing view of big business, written from the perspective of those vanquished by it. Louis Brandeis, shown below in an Eben Comins painting, was a longtime Supreme Court justice. He began his career as a business attorney at the turn of the century but soon turned his understanding of law to social issues. As a former corporation lawyer he was particularly effective in attacking "the oligarchy" of investment banking dominated by J. P. Morgan.

PITTSBURG: A CITY ASHAMED

McCLURE'S MAGAZINE

MAY

LINCOLN STEFFENS'S exposure of another type of municipal grafting; how Pittsburg differs from St. Louis and Minneapolis.

THE END OF THE WORLD, by Professor Newcomb. A powerful story, yet a scientific prediction; pictures by the famous French artist, Henri Lanos.

IDA M. TARBELL on the Standard tactics which brought on the famous oil crisis of 1878.

SIX SHORT STORIES

PUBLISHED MONTHLY BY THE S.S. McCLURE CO., 141-155 E. 25th ST., NEW YORK CITY

McClure's Magazine in May 1903, left, was part of a revolution in journalism, packing three "muckraking" stories into the same issue. The January issue of *McClure's* had been the first to offer three such potent articles together. S. S. McClure, the editor, admitted the hard-hitting lineup had been a coincidence, but it was one that made readers stop and think. Explaining the magazine's impact, he wrote, "Capitalists, workingmen, politicians, citizens—all breaking the law or letting it be broken. Who is left to uphold it?" The answer, in *McClure's* and other magazines, was the crusading journalist.

THE SOCIALIST PARTY

SOCIALIST PARTY

1904

EUGENE V. DEBS   BEN HANFORD

FOR PRESIDENT   FOR VICE PRESIDENT

Above, a 1904 campaign banner for the Socialist Party featured Eugene V. Debs as the presidential candidate. Debs ran in every presidential election but one between 1900 and 1920. He was widely respected, perhaps because he was just as critical of most labor unions as he was of most businesses. Debs never came close to winning, but compiled a gratifying record by polling more and more votes with each successive election. Hanford, a longtime Debs loyalist, had created an apocryphal character named Jimmie Higgins in the course of many speeches and essays. Upton Sinclair later wrote a novel about Hanford's symbolic man, but it was Debs who cast him as the very heart of the Socialist Party: "Jimmie Higgins is the chap who is always on the job; who does all the needed work that no one else will do; who never grumbles, never finds fault and is never discouraged. . . . It takes the rarest of qualities to produce a Jimmie Higgins. These qualities are developed in the 'lower class' only. They are denied those who know not the trials and privations, the bitter struggle, the heartache and despair of the victims of man's inhumanity to his less fortunate fellow-man."

the law took into account the circumstances of the aggrieved, took Progressivism beyond the political arena and into the courts.

In truth, Progressivism needed a more broad-based advertisement than the human dynamo that was Theodore Roosevelt. His personality was so large that it overwhelmed the whole notion of Progressivism, to the point that some still think of it as whatever Roosevelt supported, which was hardly the case. In action, the president was usually prudent and slow to wield the big stick no matter how loudly he had spoken—and when he did it was more often with a smack on the wrist than a full body blow.

One example of the president's tendency to follow rough talk with gentle actions toward business occurred in 1902, when Roosevelt approved a case under the Sherman Antitrust Act against Northern Securities, a railroad holding company he saw the need to break up. Although that and subsequent moves would earn the president the badge of "trustbuster," in truth he was more than a little circumspect when it came to the prosecutions. Indeed, his successor William Howard Taft, who generally is regarded as friendlier to business than Roosevelt, instituted twice as many federal antitrust actions in his four years as president than Roosevelt did in close to eight. But Taft couldn't have launched any of the suits without Roosevelt's Northern Securities victory.

Also in 1902, Roosevelt intervened in a coal strike called by the United Mine Workers and appeared to favor the workers. The next year he created the cabinet-level Department of Commerce and Labor, which had the authority to investigate corporate practices and could even force companies to turn their records over to the government. Although conservatives in Congress paled at this prospect, Roosevelt alleged that Standard Oil's John D. Rockefeller was leading the opposition for nefarious purposes, which convinced Congress to enact the legislation.

By 1904 the country was prosperous and the popular president who seemed to know how to have it both ways won the Republican presidential nomination easily. The Democratic Party acknowledged that two-time loser William Jennings Bryan may not have been their wisest choice and turned to Alton B. Parker, a conservative New York judge best known for having supported Grover Cleveland. The Socialists nominated Eugene Debs again, and the Prohibitionists backed Silas Swallow.

Despite the nation's peace and prosperity, Roosevelt took his Democratic challenger seriously and went out of his way to obtain a mighty store of campaign funds by cultivating wealthy businessmen who proved more than happy to make hearty contributions: $250,000 from railroad giant E. H. Harriman, $150,000 from J. P. Morgan, and $100,000 from John D. Rockefeller's Standard Oil, among others. As far as big business was concerned,

Roosevelt—always careful to note the distinction between good and bad commercial monoliths—did not present too much of a threat compared with the alternatives. The corporate giants opened their wallets out of concern, but not about Parker; their real worry was Debs and the Socialist Party that called for nationalizing their companies.

They needn't have worried, but nonetheless continued to even after the 1904 election, which Roosevelt won by record tallies of 7.6 million popular votes and 336 in the electoral college to Parker's 5.1 million and 140 electoral votes (a popular falloff of 1.2 million from Bryan's total four years earlier). The biggest surprise, however, was Debs, who received no electoral votes but garnered 420,000 from the people, many from former Populists plus a significant number from both Democrats and Republicans who considered Progressivism too tame. The Prohibitionists did better than they had since 1888 with a tally of 258,000 popular votes, although their appeal clearly remained very limited. Such did not seem to be the case with the Socialists, who continued to discomfit American business by drawing more votes than ever before from an increasingly broader range of the electorate.

Roosevelt's second term was marked by a string of landmark reforms: the National Monuments Act, the Employers' Liability Act, and the conservation movement in general. Yet many critics charged that Roosevelt's reforms were mere window dressing. A typical example is the Hepburn Act of 1906, which expanded the powers of the Interstate Commerce Commission that regulated the railroads to give it authority over all kinds of communications as well. The legislation was opposed by conservative congressmen and hailed by Progressives. President Roosevelt played all the angles. He supported the measure but would not insist on an end to the questionable accounting methods the railroads were using to avoid prosecution under the act, nor would he speak out for tougher prosecution of wrongdoers. Through such clever tactics Roosevelt won the support of Progressive congressmen as well as those businessmen who favored greater regulation as a hedge against competition. In addition, he retained the confidence of the Hepburn Act's opponents, who were satisfied with the president's wink and nod that they could easily avoid the substance of the measure.

Newly elected Progressive Senator Robert La Follette, however, saw through Roosevelt's maneuvers and accused him of half-hearted reformism. Former Governor "Fighting Bob" La Follette actually knew what he was talking about: his "Wisconsin idea" of efficient and accountable government had been widely copied, and he was well known for his work toward reforms such as workers' compensation, beefed-up regulation of railroads, and environmental conservation. La Follette had the common man's faith in the judgment of the American people and the oratorical skills—and stamina—of an updated William Jennings Bryan. Most important, he had the courage of his convictions, and in voicing them both incurred the president's wrath and embarked on a campaign to take over the Progressive wing of the Republican Party. What the ideologically committed La Follette failed to grasp was what Teddy Roosevelt understood so well: America's burgeoning businesses had to be checked by government regulation, but their relative freedom to pur-

Theodore Roosevelt was arguably the most farsighted environmentalist ever to inhabit the White House. Contrary to some of his critics at the time, it was not to ensure himself of good big-game hunting that Roosevelt increased America's national forests by more than 450 percent, created five new national parks, established the first federal bird and game preserves, appointed conservationist zealot Gifford Pinchot as the first head of the new U.S. Forest Service, signed into law the Newlands Reclamation Act and National Monuments Act, assembled blue-ribbon commissions to study resource management, and claimed that "a grove of giant redwoods or sequoias should be kept just as we keep a great and beautiful cathedral." Naturalist John Muir may have been less accommodating toward development, Pinchot may have had a shrewder understanding of natural resource management, and Democratic Senator Francis Newlands of Nevada may have been more boisterous in promoting land reclamation, but only Theodore Roosevelt understood the big picture of how nature nourished the human psyche and how conservation meant protecting as well as managing the environment. To Roosevelt conservation was an empirical, scientific matter, with the nation's very survival at stake. "In utilizing and conserving the natural resources of the Nation, the one characteristic more essential than any other is foresight," the president noted in a 1907 speech in Jamestown, Virginia. "The conservation of our natural resources and their proper use constitute the fundamental problem which underlies almost every other problem of our national life." Roosevelt understood that trees were a

crop and fish a meal, and he believed that God had put natural resources on earth to be used, but he felt as ardently that these resources had to be managed properly in the *long-term* interests of the nation. Like John Muir and Henry David Thoreau, as a naturalist philosopher Theodore Roosevelt maintained that America's most pristine wilderness areas should be protected from man and his industries. Thus Roosevelt became America's innovator in conservation, as president instituting the first federal irrigation projects, wildlife refuges, national monuments, conservation commissions, and more. Above all Roosevelt was a preservationist determined to set aside land for the future—land for forest reserves, waterpower development, future parks and nature preserves—land equivalent in area to all the states from Maine to Virginia plus West Virginia. Looked at another way, the 150 national forests Roosevelt created between 1901 and 1909 amounted to more than 150 million acres, 100 times more land than the combined areas of France, Belgium, Luxembourg, and the Netherlands.

Roosevelt's can-do approach to conservation can also be seen in his creation of the first fifty-one federal bird sanctuaries. As governor of New York Roosevelt had insisted that the state ban apparel factories from using bird skins or feathers; birds in the trees and on the beaches were far more beautiful than on women's hats he proclaimed. Once he became president, of course, Roosevelt was in a position to do even more for the nation's birds. The first important step occurred in March 1903, after a group of ornithologists had come to lobby the president

at the White House. For some time these naturalists had been trying to protect the birds on Pelican Island off the coast of Florida, where plume hunters had been killing so many egrets and other birds that they were in danger of extermination. The ornithologists appealed directly to the president to save the birds. "Is there any law that will prevent me from declaring Pelican Island a federal bird reservation?" Roosevelt asked. The island was federal property, and he was told there was no law that would prevent the president from acting. "Very well," he said, "then I so declare it." Thus was established the first federal wildlife refuge.

Before long Roosevelt created fifty more bird sanctuaries scattered from the Gulf of Mexico to California and Maine and even in Alaska, Hawaii, and Puerto Rico. Without this presidential initiative, it is doubtful whether brown pelicans would still be in Louisiana, horned puffins along the Oregon coast, or that a hundred other species of birds would still be around. Roosevelt created the first four federal game preserves as well, including Oklahoma's Wichita Forest and the National Bison Range in Montana, both set up to save the bison from extinction. He also established five national parks, which protected Oregon's Crater Lake, the Indian cliff dwellings at Mesa Verde in Colorado, and other sites. Roosevelt fought unsuccessfully to make Arizona's Grand Canyon a national park, although he tried to declare it a national monument in 1908. In 1903 he had explained, "The Grand Canyon has a natural wonder which, so far as I know, is in kind absolutely unparalleled throughout the rest of the world. . . .

Keep this great wonder of nature as it is. . . . You can not improve it. The ages have been at work on it, and man can only mar it."

Roosevelt also signed the National Monuments Act on June 8, 1906. The law authorized the president, at his discretion, to "declare by public proclamation historic landmarks, historic and prehistoric structures, and other objects of historic and scientific interest that are situated upon lands owned or controlled by the Government of the United States to be National Monuments." Roosevelt established the first eighteen national monuments, beginning with Devils Tower, Wyoming.

Theodore Roosevelt worried that denizens of Manhattan, Philadelphia, and Boston could not understand the splendor of the American West and why it had to be saved. "To lose the chance to see frigate birds soaring in circles above the storm," Roosevelt wrote, "or a file of pelicans winging their way homeward across the crimson afterglow of the sunset, or a myriad of terns flashing in the bright light of midday as they hover in the shifting haze above the beach—why the loss is like the loss of a gallery of masterpieces of the artists of old time." Roosevelt understood that wilderness areas are America's national heirlooms. "Surely our people do not understand even yet the rich heritage that is theirs," he wrote in 1905. "There can be nothing in the world more beautiful than the Yosemite, the groves of giant sequoias and redwoods, the Canyon of the Colorado, the Canyon in the Yellowstone, the Three Tetons; and our people should see to it that they are preserved for their children and their children's children forever with their majestic beauty unmarred."

Theodore Roosevelt takes a ride through Yosemite National Park in California with John Muir, a naturalist who worked for the preservation of many American wilderness areas. Roosevelt was the first president to turn the environment into a national priority, telling Congress in 1907 that conservation constituted "the fundamental problem which underlies almost every other problem of national life." Some of those other problems also touched on matters close to Roosevelt's heart, including his fight to get rid of exploitative corporations and his equally vigorous campaign to preserve a sense of western frontier.

sue capitalism was and would continue to be an important element in the success of the new kind of nation the United States was evolving into.

Therefore a balance had to be struck, and Roosevelt did so artfully. He supported the Pure Food and Drug Act, prohibiting the sale or shipment of adulterated or fraudulently labeled foods and drugs, and the Meat Inspection Act, requiring federal inspections of all meatpacking houses engaged in interstate or foreign commerce. Again, what looked like a victory for Progressive reform was also a win for large corporations over their smaller competitors: for violators, the bill mandated severe penalties that could ruin and shut down a small company but amounted to little more than a nuisance for large ones. In consequence, the legislation put hundreds of small food and drug firms out of business, wiping out enough competition to give a significant boost to the sales of large manufacturers who managed to more or less toe the ethical line.

Similarly, Roosevelt's vaunted conservation measures enjoyed the support of both the environment-conscious Progressives and the biggest lumber concerns, which already had large reserves and regarded conservation initiatives as a boon in their struggles against timber-poor small operators. In short order the president, an ardent outdoorsman and naturalist, would lead the nation in conservation efforts by inspiring so much public concern over the abuse of natural resources that the nation's businesses had no choice but to go along. Even the president's attempts to strengthen the Sherman Antitrust Act, which among other things would have created a Bureau of Corporations with the power to investigate large companies for violations of the law, won the endorsement of J. P. Morgan and pretty much all the rest of Wall Street and big business, which hoped that being given a clean bill of corporate health would make them immune from future prosecution.

Then, in 1907, the nation underwent its worst financial panic since 1893, caused by the threat of wide-ranging bank failures in the wake of jitters in New York brought on by fluctuating demands on the nation's money supply. As he had fourteen years earlier, Morgan stepped into the breach and reorganized Wall Street's banks in an attempt to save the day. Frightened, Roosevelt had dispatched Treasury Secretary George B. Cortelyou to New York to work with Morgan, who for all intents and purposes ran the nation's finances throughout the emergency. The financier had his price: he wanted U.S. Steel, the giant corporation he had formed after buying out Andrew Carnegie in 1901, to be permitted to purchase the Tennessee Coal and Iron Company without fear of prosecution under federal antitrust laws. Roosevelt agreed to Morgan's fee, and the merger took place soon after. Again, Progressive critics charged that the president had sold out to Wall Street, and later a Senate

The commemorative tin plate above shows the winner of the 1908 election, William Howard Taft, also seen in the photograph on the opposite page. A native of Cincinnati with a background in law, Taft was one of Theodore Roosevelt's closest associates. He often said he wanted to be a Supreme Court justice, and his personality may well have been better suited to judicial reaction than to action in the executive office. However, the circumstances of 1908 made Taft turn down a seat on the bench in favor of the presidency. Voted out after one term, he eventually got his wish and was named Chief Justice of the U.S. Supreme Court in 1921, becoming one of the few former presidents to enter another branch of the federal government.

committee charged with investigating the matter implied in its concluding report that Roosevelt had indeed overstepped his authority. Whether he had or not, the economic panic was suppressed and a much-feared depression avoided. It was not the first and wouldn't be the last time pure capitalism pulled America's economy from the brink of ruin.

Pragmatically political as always, Roosevelt initiated no important new legal antitrust actions for the rest of his term, and in general limited his reform activities to rhetoric. As bully a pulpit as he found the presidency, Roosevelt knew better than to ride roughshod over the corporate interests that had long ago assumed the greatest influence on the nation. Instead, in his second term he used his executive powers—aggressively as always and in some areas almost radically, such as regarding conservation efforts—to make himself into a self-proclaimed mediator in those instances when the corporate world clashed with the public interest.

But true to his earlier word, Roosevelt did not seek re-election in 1908 and instead supported his Secretary of War, William Howard Taft, for the Republican nomination, against the wishes of the party's Progressive wing. "Get on the raft with Taft" became the GOP campaign mantra intended to convince citizens of their candidate's sober-minded virtues. The Democrats, still stinging from their defeat four years earlier, harked back to their liberal roots and put forth

Bryan for a third go, this time on a Progressive platform. In fact, the party adopted such a pro-labor stance that for the first time in its history the American Federation of Labor abandoned its nonpartisan policy and endorsed Bryan. The Socialists, of course, nominated Eugene V. Debs who insisted that workers were "the saviors of society" and "the redeemers of the race." Author Elizabeth Gurley Flynn later wrote that Debs was more "agitator" than a politician, a proletariat preacher who made sure that the "shame of servitude and the glory of struggle were emblazoned in the mind of every worker."

Taft won as easily as Roosevelt had in 1904, receiving 7.6 million popular and 321 electoral votes to Bryan's 6.4 million and 162, which bettered Parker's showing of four years earlier and more or less equaled the tallies Bryan had racked up in 1896 and 1900. To the consternation of conservatives and Progressives alike, Debs garnered 421,000 popular votes and Prohibitionist Eugene Chafin claimed 254,000.

In addition to his overriding ambition to one day become Chief Justice of the U.S. Supreme Court, William Howard Taft's most distinguishing characteristic was his obesity; Taft was so fat that on one occasion when he was bobbing on the waves off Massachusetts, a neighbor suggested to a friend that they should jump in as well. "Better wait," the friend replied. "The president is using the ocean." But the former Secretary of War and America's first governor-general of the Philippines was also a skilled administrator and a man of great personal charm—as well as one full of distaste for political machinations. Even his most ardent supporter, Theodore Roosevelt, had a few reservations, telling a reporter on Taft's inauguration day that "He's all right. But he's weak. They'll get around him. They'll lean against him."

Indeed, Taft ran into difficulties almost immediately upon taking office. The U.S. tariff on foreign imports had not been revised since 1897, when it had been increased sharply in an effort to boost the economy. Roosevelt had chosen to ignore the issue entirely as political dynamite. The Republican platform of 1908 had promised revisions to the tariff, which Taft and most other Americans assumed meant reductions; accordingly, the new president called a special session of Congress to deal with the matter. The Payne Bill, which lowered the tariff considerably, was quickly passed by the House and sent to the Senate, where conservatives turned it into a much higher tariff. La Follette and other Progressives fought this new Payne-Aldrich Tariff for three months while Taft watched from the sidelines. After the conservatives won out, the president conceded that the tariff ended up higher than he had hoped. In the end, his indecision on the matter won him the opposition of both Progressive and conservative Republicans.

This marked but one of several occasions upon which Taft managed to aggravate both wings of his own party. In 1909 the president and the Progressives finally broke over a dispute involving conservation, when Taft's Secretary of the Interior put a million acres of coal-rich public lands in Alaska up for sale, angering conservationists who alleged shady dealings designed to benefit J. P. Morgan's syndicate as well as conservatives who thought even more lands should have been taken out of the public domain. In addition, not only was Taft's antitrust program more vigorous than Roosevelt's had been, but he lacked his predecessor's political and public relations acumen for selling it. The president became increasingly unpopular, including with the predecessor who had handpicked him. In October 1911, Taft's Justice Department charged U.S. Steel with violating the Sherman Antitrust Act by acquiring the Tennessee Coal and Iron Company—an acquisition Roosevelt himself had agreed to. Angered by what he took as a personal slight, the former president sputtered that his successor "was playing small, mean, and foolish politics."

Taft also alienated more of the public than he won over with his pursuit of what came to be known as "dollar diplomacy," which comprised two basic policy thrusts: the encouragement of U.S. investment overseas and the protection of those investments by establishing what amounted to financial protectorates in nations noted for their financial inefficiency. In some cases this meant that Americans would take over the administration of customs services and local banks; in others it meant that U.S. troops would be deployed until Yankee-supervised elections put elements friendly to the United States in power. In some, such as Nicaragua, it meant both. As Taft's Secretary of State, Philander Knox, argued: "If the American dollar can aid suffering humanity and lift the burden of financial difficulty from states with which we live . . . all I can say is that it would be hard to find better employment."

To this most Latin Americans replied that such help usually meant near-complete foreign (in this case U.S.) control of their countries. At their best, the policies of both Taft and Roosevelt boosted the economic development of the nations the United States occupied: sanitary conditions were improved, roads built, banks set in order, and a general housecleaning carried out in the targeted countries' political and bureaucratic realms. At their worst, these American initiatives were barely disguised imperial interventions—perhaps a bit subtler and more generous than those of European nations, but imperialism all the same: an effort by the great white colossus of the north to "civilize" its supposedly inferior "little brown brothers" to the south.

Opposition to Taft's international and domestic policies continued to mount as his tenure drew to a close. In 1911, La Follette organized the National Progressive Republican League, a pretty clear indication that he planned to challenge Taft from within the party in 1912. Theodore Roosevelt also wanted the nomination; after all, it no longer violated his pledge not to seek reelection now that he had been out of office for a term. Heading into 1912, Roosevelt began talking about what in a 1910 speech he had called the "new nationalism," a model for an updated United States that acknowledged and accepted big business but that called upon a strengthened central government to act as counterbalance. This stance won Roosevelt the crucial support of business giants such as George W. Perkins, although most corporate titans went for Taft or Woodrow Wilson. La Follette made things easier by falling ill and opening the way for Roosevelt to seize command of the Republican's Progressive wing and battle his erstwhile friend Taft for the nomination directly. But the incumbent still had control over most of the party and won the Republican nomination in 1912—prompting Roosevelt to split off and organize the Progressive Party to run under, all but ensuring a victory for Democratic nominee Woodrow Wilson.

"Look up, not down—
Look out, not in—
Look forward, not backward—
And lend a hand."

Founders' Day
October 27, 1912

THE

Progressive Party

In 1912 Theodore Roosevelt loyalists followed the former president to the Progressive Party, wearing ribbons like the one above.

CHAPTER 14

THE GREAT WAR

During his 1912 campaign against incumbent Republican President William Howard Taft and Theodore Roosevelt, the former Republican president and current Progressive candidate, Democrat Woodrow Wilson made a point that resonated with the American people: "There is no indispensable man. The government will not collapse and go to pieces if any one of the gentlemen seeking to be entrusted with its guidance should be left at home." He was right, of course, and the very obviousness of his declaration offered the best evidence to that point that the United States had matured into a sovereign nation capable of enduring even the strongest shifting winds of political change. Yet history suggests that Wilson may have been as indispensable to his time as Abraham Lincoln had been to his a half-century earlier.

As expected after Roosevelt's third-party candidacy fragmented the Republicans, Wilson won the 1912 presidential election with a record 435 electoral votes, and the Democrats took control of both houses of Congress. Wilson received a majority of the popular tally in only fourteen states, however, and an overall total of only 6.3 million votes, fewer than William Jennings Bryan had garnered in any of his three campaigns. Playing spoiler,

George Luks' 1918 *Armistice Night* caught the unrestrained elation of Armistice night in 1918, left. Although reluctant to enter World War I, America had turned a cruel stalemate into an Allied victory by pouring 2 million soldiers into France. The most famous recruiting poster of all time, above, appeared in 1917. It was the work of James Montgomery Flagg, who used himself as the model for Uncle Sam.

The portrait of Woodrow Wilson above was painted by E. C. Tarbell. A first-term New Jersey governor, Wilson had no national political experience when he ran for president as a Democrat in 1912. Nonetheless, he managed to topple the two most prominent Republicans of the time: William Howard Taft, the incumbent, and Theodore Roosevelt, the former president who was leading a third party, the Progressives, also known as the Bull Moose Party.

Roosevelt took 4.1 million votes to Taft's 3.5 million, which together equaled the incumbent's tally in 1908. Perennial candidate Eugene V. Debs doubled his 1908 total to more than 900,000 popular votes, proving that socialism was indeed the fastest growing force in American politics. Heading in the opposite direction was the Prohibitionist Party, which again had nominated Eugene Chafin but this time received only 206,000 votes, a sharp drop-off from four years earlier that indicated the temperance movement was receding from its plateau. Despite the number of parties and the passions behind them, a clear indication of public discontent with the choices manifested itself in a voter turnout of 58.8 percent of those eligible—the smallest since 1836.

The new president was only the second Democrat to take up residence in the White House since the Civil War and the first to have been born in the South. A Virginia native raised in Georgia and South Carolina, Wilson had graduated from Princeton (then the College of New Jersey) and the University of Virginia Law School before earning a doctorate in government and history from Maryland's Johns Hopkins University in 1886. He entered upon an academic career that took him to the presidency of Princeton and on to the governorship of New Jersey, where he repudiated the conservative political machine that had put him in office to pursue a Progressive platform. Although Wilson was aloof and often sanctimonious, he was honest, imbued with a high-minded penchant for facts over platitudes. All the while his Presbyterian manners remained so mild that when asked by an aged aunt shortly after the 1912 election what he had been up to, the bespectacled Wilson shyly replied, "I've just been elected president." The aunt asked, "Oh, yes? President of what?" When Wilson answered, "Of the United States," his aunt snorted and said, "Don't be silly."

He wasn't: Woodrow Wilson had a carefully worked out agenda that he called the "New Freedom." Whereas Roosevelt had believed big government was needed to control big business, Wilson thought it made more sense if business had less power and thus generated less need for government. "The history of liberty is a history of limitations of governmental power, not the increase of it," he wrote. This does not mean that Wilson was a liberal. As historian Richard Hofstadter noted, Wilson was a conservative whose attitude toward labor was "generally hostile" and who believed Populists were cursed with "crude and ignorant minds."

The Wilsonian Vision

Rhetoric aside, Wilson would take advantage of his executive powers to a far greater extent than either Taft or Roosevelt, both of whom had been accused of overstepping their presidential bounds. The new chief executive explained his actions simply: "No one but the president seems to be expected . . . to look out for the general interests of the country." And Wilson's administration would prove that forceful executive leadership combined with control of Congress could prevent government gridlock: a flood of important legislation was passed in 1913 and 1914. For starters there was the Underwood-Simmons Tariff, which lowered rates on imports for the first time since the Civil War. Far more important than the tariff itself, however, was a single clause inserted at the insistence of Democratic Representative Cordell Hull of Tennessee; he and other Progressives believed that the Underwood-Simmons Tariff provided substantial enough cuts to usher sufficient competition into U.S. markets to break the power of the trusts—and that an income tax would thus be needed to offset the losses in tariff revenues. This marked the beginning of a fundamental change in the U.S. tax structure, from public lands, alcohol, and customs duties to levies on personal and corporate income.

Ever since 1895, when the Supreme Court had invalidated an income tax written into a tariff the previous year, reformers had worked for a constitutional amendment making one possible. Such an amendment had been passed by Congress in the first months of the Taft administration, sent to the states, and ratified in February 1913 as Taft was preparing to leave the White House. Under the new tax introduced in the Underwood Simmons Tariff, no one with an annual income below $5,000 (about $70,000 in 1998 dollars) had to pay taxes; in 1913, some 357,000 individuals filed returns that brought the government revenues of $28 million.

Another consequential measure passed during Wilson's administration was the act that established the Federal Reserve system, providing the country with a central bank that would have made Alexander Hamilton proud. With twelve district branches, the "Fed" seemed capable of breaking Wall Street's monopoly on American finance. Conservatives were content that they finally had their central bank, and Progressives pleased with its decentralized structure. The Federal Reserve Act of 1913 was just one of the reforms Wilson brought to the American banking system in his quest to stabilize the U.S. economy by putting the nation's money supply under federal control. "Wilson serenely ignored the torrent of abuse heaped on him by the big bankers," historian Samuel Eliot Morison would later observe, "and the Federal Reserve Act is clearly the crowning achievement of his domestic legislation."

After that, Congress passed the unprecedentedly detailed Clayton Antitrust Act as a club to use against unruly corporations, while exempting labor unions and farm cooperatives from its provisions. The Wilson-era Congress also established the Federal Trade Commission and gave it both information-gathering powers and the authority to issue cease-and-desist orders against those found in violation of federal trade laws. With an eye toward his re-election, early in 1916 Wilson picked up the pace of his government reforms of business and commerce. He extended federal intervention ever further into the workings of the U.S. economy, sponsoring laws to improve conditions for merchant seamen and railroad workers and to provide low-interest loans to farmers, and in 1916 he would push Congress to pass the Keating-Owen Act, the first federal law regulating the often unconscionable abuse of child labor. The reform measures President Wilson sponsored greatly expanded the federal government's role and gave it new tools for regulating the economy that would help reshape the very structure of American society.

Although Wilson was progressive in many ways, he was also a Democrat raised in the South, and was not completely able to transcend its racial bigotry. Blacks, who had received somewhat improved treatment under the

The cartoon, "He'll Make a Fine Picking," above, was drawn by N. R. Manz for the *Washington Herald* in 1913. It shows the attitude of President Wilson and Congress toward dominant business trusts. Wilson made a special appeal to Congress on January 20, 1914, maintaining that "business waits with acquiescence" for laws to fight the trusts, while freeing competition and access to capital. The partnership between the two branches was so effective that by autumn, Wilson was signing two landmark laws, the Federal Trade Commission Act and the Clayton Antitrust Act.

preceding Republican presidents, now lost a great deal of ground—to the point that Jim Crow laws were introduced into previously integrated Washington, D.C. Suddenly the federal government was segregated, with black and white workers assigned to separate offices, bathrooms, and drinking fountains. When black leaders protested these outrages, the president replied that the racial segregation was meant to prevent the possibility of "friction" in the federal workplace. He also refused to support a constitutional amendment regarding women's suffrage. For all his high-minded talk about bringing America's ideals of equality to every corner of the globe, Wilson somehow failed to realize that denying the full rights of U.S. citizens to women and blacks meant that his own nation was not safe for true democracy.

As his administration advanced, Wilson's own progressive pursuits were on the wane: he conducted fewer antitrust actions in 1914 than he had in 1913, and it appeared that his crusade against big business was slowing down. There were several reasons for this, beginning with the simple fact that the New Freedom approach had started to run out of ideas once Wilson more or less achieved the basic goals he had set out in his 1912 campaign. In addition, of course, there was the economy: the nation had experienced a recession in 1913, and Republicans had placed the blame on Wilson. Somewhat gun-shy as a result, the president feared damaging business confidence and eased up on reforms in both his statements and his programs. Happily, he had an excuse to turn his attention to other matters: troubles brewing in Mexico had called U.S. forces there, and a major war had erupted across Europe.

Moral Diplomacy

Wilson sincerely believed it was a national duty to provide the world with strong moral leadership on the grounds that America's principles were not those "of a province or of a single continent . . . [but] the principles of a liberated mankind." While earlier presidents had attempted to enlarge the scope of U.S. interests, none since the passing of the Revolutionary generation had done so in the name of spreading "the American way" to other nations. Presidents Polk, Grant, McKinley, and Roosevelt had pushed the U.S. agenda under cover of the Monroe Doctrine, Manifest Destiny, and what British poet Rudyard Kipling had dubbed the "white man's burden," but Woodrow Wilson harbored an almost messianic belief that the spread of democracy could save the world from humanity's worst instincts. He thus justified his administration's international interventions by asserting that his opponents were false leaders of people whose true voices, if heard, would agree with him instead; as he once swore in reference to the government of Mexico, he would "teach the South American republics to elect good men."

Others of such evangelical bent hastened to the cause. William Jennings Bryan—who had responded to J. P. Morgan's recent exclamation that "America is good enough for me!" by quipping, "Whenever he doesn't like it, he can give it back to us"—had thrown his support to Wilson at a critical moment during the 1912 Democratic convention and was rewarded with the post of Secretary of State. He and Wilson continued intervening in the Caribbean,

The 1913 *Punch* cartoon below chides President Wilson for his ineffectual stance against Mexico—Wilson responds to increasing Mexican unrest by merely wagging his finger, a policy he preferred to call "moral force." Wilson ultimately resorted to military force in Mexico with a 1914 operation in Vera Cruz, shown on the opposite page in a photograph of American troops raising the Stars and Stripes.

WOODROW ON TOAST

making Nicaragua a virtual protectorate and sending U.S. Marines to preserve the order and commercial opportunities in Haiti and Santo Domingo. Problems with other nations, however, proved less tractable: in 1913, over Wilson's objections, the California legislature passed anti-Japanese laws—including restrictions on land ownership by Japanese immigrants—that escalated tensions between the two countries to the point that Admiral Bradley Fiske warned that war with Japan was "not only possible, but even probable." The situation had certainly deteriorated since 1907, when President Theodore Roosevelt had sent a "great white fleet" of sixteen gleaming new battleships on a world tour that had stopped most conspicuously in Japan, where crowds had turned out to cheer and schoolchildren to sing "The Star-Spangled Banner" in carefully practiced English. Although the bully show of force had, as Roosevelt intended, announced a new era of U.S. naval might, it also had an unintended effect that would bedevil the United States for decades: the display sparked Japan to build up its own navy.

Another carryover from the preceding Republican administrations would present Wilson with the hardest international affairs test of his first year in office: unrest in Mexico, which could hardly be ignored in the wake of Roosevelt's and then Taft's vigorous meddling throughout Latin America. After thirty-four years under the dictatorial presidency of Porfirio Díaz, a liberal government forced his resignation in 1911. Two years later a group of generals led by Victoriano Huerta had seized power in Mexico. In the past the United States had recognized even such upstart governments, but Wilson was not about to go along with any illegal assumptions of national control, and less than a week after becoming president announced that the United States would not recognize Huerta's rule. In October 1913 he added, "We dare not turn from the principle that morality and not expediency is the thing that must guide us." Wilson therefore sent American agents to work with Venustiano Carranza, head of Mexico's constitutional movement, to help in overthrowing Huerta; in addition, the U.S. president imposed an embargo on munitions shipments to Mexico, recalled the U.S. ambassador, and proposed aiding "the submerged 85 percent of the people of that republic who are now struggling toward liberty."

Wilson didn't stop with threats. Upon learning that a German ship was

Wilson responded to outlaw Pancho Villa's actions by sending General John J. Pershing, above, to hunt him down; among the young officers in Pershing's expedition was George S. Patton. They never did catch Villa, who later retired from outlaw pursuits in exchange for a large pension from the Mexican Army.

about to dock at Vera Cruz to unload munitions, the president sent a force of U.S. Marines to occupy the Mexican port city on April 21, 1914. A brief skirmish ensued in which 126 Mexicans and 19 Americans were killed. The next day Huerta severed relations with the United States.

In August and without American assistance, Carranza's forces seized Mexico City, Huerta having fled the previous month. Rebel leaders Francisco "Pancho" Villa and Emiliano Zapata, a pair of shrewd peasant-born leaders, split with Carranza. Wilson did not take sides at first, but ultimately recognized the Carranza regime. The move proved a blunder: by year's end the so-called "bandit" Villa was conducting terrorist raids against both the Carranza government and American border towns. The outlaw Villa's revolutionary policies included land redistribution, opposition to the dominant Catholic Church, expropriation of foreign-owned property, and authorization for guerrilla raids across the U.S. border. Anxious to embarrass the U.S. "gringos" and angry at Wilson for supporting Carranza, in January 1916 Villa murdered 17 American mining engineers, then two months later raided Columbus, New Mexico, burned it to ashes, and murdered nearly 20 citizens. In March 1916, Wilson sent General John J. "Black Jack" Pershing to Mexico to capture Villa. Pershing and his 6,000 men would chase Villa without success until February 1917, when the president called them home in the face of even more demanding international problems.

American Neutrality

Although it seemed far away and even further afield from America's concerns, a crisis of what would turn out to be unprecedented proportions had been brewing in Europe since 1914—and the United States had become too rich and too powerful in international commerce to remain isolationist for long. The supposed "war to end wars" began on June 28, 1914, when Austrian Archduke Franz Ferdinand was assassinated by young Serbian nationalists, a misfortune that at the time hardly seemed a serious threat to European peace. But the winds of war often blow from unexpected quarters, and after a month of convoluted diplomatic maneuvering Austria-Hungary declared war on Serbia, and within a week every major European power was involved in the conflict except Italy, which joined the fray soon thereafter.

The main foes took sides as the Allies—France, Great Britain, Italy, and Russia—against the Central Powers of Austria-Hungary, Germany, and the Ottoman Empire—an alliance from which Itlay had defected after accepting a better deal from Britain via a secret treaty in 1915. Everyone assumed it would be a short war, and young men from all the involved nations scrambled to enlist in their respective armed services in hopes of snatching a share of glory before it was all over. They needn't have hurried: what would shortly be called "the Great War" turned into just that—the greatest conflict Europe had ever known in all its centuries of armed confrontation. By its end the Austro-Hungarian, German, Ottoman, and Russian empires would be no more, and nominal victors Britain and France would be greatly diminished in power, prestige, and wealth. More than 9 million soldiers and sailors would die; the Soviet

Union would appear, and the United States would become one of the world's leading powers. All in all, the Great War would mark the true beginning of the twentieth century, although few saw it as such in 1914. Among the rare prescient observers was Britain's Foreign Secretary, Viscount Grey of Fallodon, who on August 3 of that year stood at his office window in London watching the lamplighters do their job in St. James's Park and sighed, "The lamps are going out all over Europe; we shall not see them lit again in our lifetime."

Actually, he would see them relit in half a decade—before they would go out again six years after his death in 1933. Despite his pessimism Lord Grey sensed a depth of military resolve in the Central Powers that escaped most Europeans on the Allied side. Public passion actually ran higher in the United States, largely along ethnic lines: Irish-Americans were generally anti-British, while most in the East and South were pro-British; Jewish-Americans, noting that Zionism was strongest in Germany, were pro-German along with the French-, German-, and Russian-Americans. Wall Street and American business in general had close ties to London's financial markets and thus aligned with the Allies, especially as they seemed most likely to come out on top.

In a message to the Senate on August 19, 1914, however, President Wilson stated that "The United States must be neutral in fact as well as in name. . . . We must be impartial in thought as well as in action," as the European war was one "with which we have nothing to do, whose causes cannot touch us." Of course he knew such detachment was impossible, especially as he himself was pro-Allies and had told his secretary, "England is fighting our fight. . . . I will not take any action to embarrass England when she is fighting for her life and the life of the world." This attitude explains

Above, Archduke Franz Ferdinand, next in line to be emperor of Austria, was photographed with his wife on a tour of Bosnia about an hour before they were both assassinated on June 28, 1914. Austria, asserting that the assassins were Serbian, threatened war unless neighboring Serbia capitulated on a number of unrelated political issues. Germany backed up Austria, while Russia and France supported Serbia; Britain tried to remain neutral but eventually joined the others against Germany. No one was anxious to go to war, however—not even Austria. The attempts failed and the First World War began in early August.

the lukewarm U.S. response to the naval blockade Britain imposed upon German shipping in November 1914—and why in response to the State Department's tepid protest the British effectively sniffed that the Royal Navy was doing no more than the United States had in the 1860s to keep British goods from reaching the Confederacy.

Over the next two and a half years Wilson did what he could to assist the Allies while professing America's official neutrality in the growing conflict. Although the president maintained his insistence that all neutral parties had the right to trade with any nation, he lodged no protest against the British blockade in fear that taking issue with Britain's best weapon—its navy—might shift the balance of power to Germany. Thus by the end of 1915, U.S. neutrality was nothing more than a slogan: so much American matériel continued to pour into England that the United States in essence had become the Allies' quartermaster, to the substantial profit of American arms dealers—who but for the British blockade would readily have sold munitions to the Central Powers as well.

The official U.S. stance was not without consequences. Early in 1915, Germany developed a new way to even the score at sea: counterblockading Britain via some two dozen submarines (*unterseebooten*, or "U-boats"), which attacked without warning or mercy. President Wilson warned that he would hold Germany to "strict accountability" for any loss of American lives to U-boat attacks. Instead they did the next worst thing on May 7, 1915, sinking the British passenger liner *Lusitania* off the coast of Ireland on its way from New York to Southampton, killing 1,198 people—including 128 Americans. Wilson decried this "murder on the high seas" but held back from a military response, declaring, "There is such a thing as a man being too proud to fight. There is such a thing as a nation being so right it does not need to convince others by force that it is right."

Secretary of State William Jennings Bryan, who had argued for truly neutral U.S. protests against both the British blockade and the German U-boats, joined influential Senator Robert La Follette in pointing out that the Germans had sunk the *Lusitania* in a war zone and had also warned passengers of the threat beforehand. Furthermore, the much-disputed allegation that the *Lusitania* had been carrying munitions, making it a legitimate target, would later turn out to be true. When Wilson chose to ignore the evidence and sent a strongly worded note of protest to Berlin indicating his support for the proposal that U.S. banks float a $500-million war loan to Britain and France, Bryan resigned and was replaced by the openly pro-British Robert Lansing.

In 1916 the Democrats renominated Wilson on the slogan "he kept us out of war." Most American Progressives had quietly returned to the Republican Party, which gave its presidential nomination to former Governor Charles Evans Hughes of New York, a Progressive jurist who had made himself a national figure by exposing a raft of egregious insurance-fraud schemes in his home state. Hughes also promised neutrality, but the irrepressible Theodore Roosevelt discredited his fellow Republican by trekking around the country calling for a militant approach to the European situation. Wilson took a stance more in line with Roosevelt's belligerence than with the isolationist leanings of his fellow Demo-

The *New York Times* printed an extra edition to announce the news that the *Lusitania* had been attacked by a German submarine on May 7, 1915. The passenger liner had passed into blockaded waters fifteen miles off Ireland when a lone German U-boat fired a torpedo into its side. When the torpedo hit the *Lusitania,* "an unusually heavy detonation followed with a very strong explosive cloud," according to the ship's log. Fifteen minutes later, the 785-foot liner was completely underwater. Most of those onboard didn't have a chance: only 761 out of 1,959 survived. The news clipping superimposed on the front-page (lower right) warns ship passengers of the dangers of the seas.

crat Bryan. By the end of 1915 the president had been won over to the arguments of those who called for American "preparedness" for war and promised to build a "navy second to none" while urging Congress to double the army and beef up the National Guard in the event the United States was called upon to go to war to construct a democratic new world order.

Despite the advantages of an incumbent president, peace, prosperity, and a badly organized opposition, the Democrats nearly lost the election of 1916. Wilson garnered a popular vote of only 9.1 million to Hughes's 8.5 million and an electoral college margin of 277 to 254—the narrowest since 1876. Socialist candidate A. L. Benson, meanwhile, racked up more than half a million popular votes. Wilson thus received less than half the popular vote and, as he had in 1912, again lacked a clear mandate.

Nevertheless, he took a determined stance in an address to the Senate on January 22, 1917, in which he foreshadowed his intentions by proclaiming that "There must be not a balance of power but a community of power; not organized rivalries but an organized common peace." The president went on: "It must be a peace without victory. . . . Victory would mean peace forced upon the loser, a victor's terms imposed upon the vanquished. It would be accepted in humiliation, under duress, at an intolerable sacrifice, and would leave a sting, a resentment, a bitter memory upon which terms of peace would rest, not permanently but only as upon quicksand. Only a peace between equals can last." Wilson called instead for a cessation of hostilities followed by the establishment of "some definite concert of power which will make it virtually impossible that any such catastrophe should ever overwhelm us again."

On March 1 the State Department released a note the British had intercepted and turned over to the United States more than a month earlier. In it the German foreign minister to Mexico, Arthur Zimmerman, had proposed an alliance between Germany and Mexico with the object of restoring to the latter

Woodrow Wilson's 1916 presidential campaign took to the streets in his decorated van, right. In some ways reactionary and in some liberal, Wilson was hardly predictable. By 1916, when he was touted as the incumbent "who kept us out of war," the voters should have known that there was always more to Woodrow Wilson's thinking than he let on.

"the lost territory in New Mexico, Texas, and Arizona." The note also indicated that Germany had proposed a similarly beneficial alliance to Japan, and American hackles began to rise. Zimmerman's note to other German officials had recommended unleashing "new enemies on America's neck—enemies which give them plenty to take care of over there." Then, only a few weeks later, moderate Russian rebel leader Aleksandr Kerensky and his followers overthrew Czar Nicholas II and formed a provisional government that promised to continue fighting the aristocracy and to institute a Russian republic after the European conflict ended. Once Kerensky took power the Great War looked more than ever like a battle between Europe's democrats and its tyrants, which increased its appeal to Americans naturally sympathetic to the former.

On April 2, 1917, President Wilson addressed Congress to ask for a declaration of war, which the Senate passed on April 4 and the House two days later. "Armed neutrality is ineffectual enough at best," Wilson finally admitted. "The world must be made safe for democracy." He elaborated upon that often pilloried phrase by adding:

It is a fearful thing to lead this great peaceful people into war, into the most terrible and disastrous of all wars, civilization itself seeming to be in the balance. But the right is more precious than peace, and we shall fight for the things which we have always carried nearest our hearts—for democracy, for the right of those who submit to authority to have a voice in their own governments, for the rights and liberties of small nations, for a universal dominion of right by such a concert of free peoples as shall bring peace and safety to all nations and make the world itself at last free. To such a task we can dedicate our lives and our fortunes, everything that we are and everything that we have, with the pride of those who know that the day has come when America is privileged to spend her blood and her might for the

NOW, THEREFORE, I, Woodrow Wilson, President of the United States of America, do hereby proclaim to all whom it may concern that a state of war exists between the United States and the Imperial German Government; and I do specially direct all officers, civil or military, of the United States that they exercise vigilance and zeal in the discharge of the duties incident to such a state of war; and I do, moreover, earnestly appeal to all American citizens that they, in loyal devotion to their country, dedicated from its foundation to the principles of liberty and justice, uphold the laws of the land, and give undivided and willing support to those measures which may be adopted by the constitutional authorities in prosecuting the war to a successful issue and in obtaining a secure and just peace;

And, acting under and by virtue of the authority vested in me by the Constitution of the United States and the said sections of the Revised Statutes, I do hereby further proclaim and direct that the conduct [be to] observed on the part of the

Above, President Wilson addresses a joint session of Congress on April 2, 1917, to request a declaration of war. The resulting resolution (left) was passed in just four days. Wilson signed it and on April 6 the United States was at war with Germany. (The country didn't formally declare war on Austria-Hungary until the end of the year.) On the very eve of the declaration, President Wilson sadly predicted to a friend that upon entering the war the nation would lose its gift for tolerance: "The spirit of ruthless brutality will enter into the very fiber of our national life, infecting Congress, the courts, the policemen on the beat, the man in the street." In monetary terms, the country would spend $32.7 billion on its participation in World War I, more than the total the federal government had spent from 1791 to 1914.

principles that gave her birth and happiness and the peace which she has treasured. God helping her, she can do no other.

Whether she could or not, it is basically this determinist line of thinking to which one can trace, if indirectly, America's later involvements in Europe, Korea, Vietnam, Grenada, Nicaragua, Panama, and Iraq. "The world must be made safe for democracy," Wilson intoned and Congress quickly declared war against Germany by a margin of 373 to 50 in the House and 82 to 6 in the Senate.

World War I taught the United States how to conduct a multinational military engagement, and the United States taught the world how to win one: with better technology and overwhelming manpower. Germany's U-boat attacks on neutral as well as Allied ships in the Atlantic precipitated America's entry into the war and in consequence President Wilson's pledge to build a stronger navy. With democracy to be fought for and profit to be made, the U.S. shipbuilding industry did just that. But the United States put more than money into the European war: in May 1917 Congress passed the Selective Service Act to draft a million men to be trained into soldiers and sent to fight across the Atlantic. Some 24 million Americans registered for the draft, of whom over 2 million were called up and 2 million volunteered, 1.4 million of whom fought in France. The popular song "Johnny Get Your Gun" and an impressive array of government posters drew eager volunteers to the armed forces to, as one soldier put it, "see a little of the biggest scrap the world has ever known." The average soldier was white, single, about twenty-two years old, and was anxious to "kick the Kaiser" and come home a hero. Yet there were numerous exceptions: approximately 18 percent of U.S. soldiers were foreign born and 400,000 were African-American.

U.S. Army General John J. Pershing kept most of the fresh-faced "American doughboys" sent to France in extensive training until the spring of 1918, when the Germans began to push toward Paris. Then Pershing sent troops rushing to the front to block the German advances at several strategic points including the town of Amiens and the region east of the Marne River, where the Americans dealt the enemy one crushing blow after another. In mid-September a force of half a million U.S. soldiers and a handful of French troops had little trouble overrunning the Central Powers' stronghold at Saint-Mihiel. Two weeks later heavily armored U.S. divisions made the difference in the massive Meuse-Argonne Forest offensive, the Allied march to the railroad center that supplied the entire German front. The bloody battles raged until the first week of November, when the Americans made it to the center, cut the rail lines, and sealed the Allies' victory.

The trumph came at enormous cost: only the next World War would exact a higher toll than the one the United States had joined on April 6, 1917. America's participation in World War I would last nineteen months and send more than 2 million Americans overseas, 1.4 million of them to serve in France. More than 53,000 U.S. troops died in combat, while another 63,000 perished from disease and other causes. In comparison, 407,000 U.S. servicemen would die in World War II, 54,000 in the Korean War, and 58,000 in Vietnam (while more than half a million Americans gave their lives in the U.S.

These photographs show the unearthly battlefields created by World War I. Above, soldiers make their way across planking at Ypres in the Flanders region of Belgium in 1915; below, Scottish troops crawl through a trench. Horrific weaponry proliferated during the First World War: tanks, machine guns, flame throwers, armed airplanes, and long-range artillery such as the huge German cannon that could loft a shell seventy-five miles. To the soldiers the most appalling new weapon was poison gas, which maimed, blinded, and killed men in eerie silence; it was first used by the Germans on the Western front at Ypres in April 1915. In a letter found in the mud there, one soldier had written, "You do not know what Flanders means. Flanders means endless human endurance. Flanders means blood and scraps of human bodies. Flanders means heroic courage and faithfulness even unto death."

The map at left shows the progress of World War I during its first four full years of fighting, before America's entry. For close to three years Germany and its partners in the Central Powers fought World War I on four major fronts. On the Balkan front, where the war started in the summer of 1914, the opposing force was led by the Serbians. On the eastern front, the Germans faced Russian troops in battles centered in Poland. On the western front (where the Americans eventually were to meet the Germans), English and French troops in massive numbers held the Allied side of the battle line. The Austro-Italian Front was centered in the Tyrolean foothills. By the end of 1917, the Central Powers were poised to take control of all fronts, except perhaps the western one.

The western front stretched from the North Sea to the Swiss border, but most of the fighting took place in Belgium and northeastern France. British troops were stationed on the northern stretch of the line, defending the route to the English Channel. French troops were also present in the north, but were more concentrated on the southern section of the front: the route to Paris.

In the first months of the war, the Germans rushed to within eight miles of Paris before the Allies pressed them back. The front stalled along an arc that represented, not surprisingly, a midway line between the French capital and the German border. The western front did not shift significantly over the next three years, though it was contested on large and small scales; at the end of one of the fiercest engagements of the war, the Battle of the Somme, the line in that sector moved a mere eight miles.

Civil War). Joyce Kilmer perfectly summed up the unfathomable carnage in his 1918 war poem, "Rouge Bouquet": There lie many fighting men/Dead in their youthful prime/Never to laugh or love again/Nor taste the summer time. (He was killed in action in France on July 30, 1918.) In addition to the incalculable human losses, in today's dollars the financial cost of World War I to America amounted to some $32.7 billion, a quarter of which was financed by new taxes and the rest by a sharp increase in the national debt, which soared from $1.3 billion in 1917 to $26 billion in 1919. A fifth of that debt was held by individual Americans in the form of Liberty Bonds that were sold to the public to back a $3-billion war loan to the European Allies.

America at War

For all its horrors, World War I had at least one benefit for the United States: for the first time in its history, the nation had a chance to prove what it could do when its economy was opened full throttle. Not even during the Civil War had federal intervention in commerce been so vigorous or the government's relationships with business so close. Ironically, it was the Progressive movement's failure to rein in big business that allowed America's mighty industries to make the enormous contributions they did to the war effort—without which the nation would not have developed the overwhelming military prowess to put an end to the Great War in Europe.

The long-growing bond between America's public and private sectors was cemented by World War I. Just as Theodore Roosevelt had turned to J. P. Morgan when America had faced financial troubles eleven years earlier, in March 1918 Woodrow Wilson tapped Wall Street wizard Bernard Baruch to become chairman of the new War Industries Board, which supervised the production of necessary supplies and matériel and was thus the most important of all the government's mobilization operations. Like Morgan before him, Baruch was handed a virtual dictatorship over the U.S. economy; the board had the authority to requisition resources, command manufacturers, order new plant construction, and even fix prices with the president's approval. In very short order, factories that had been producing civilian goods began turning out munitions. Automobile plants, for example, converted to the manufacture of aircraft engines, while radiator factories switched to making long-range artillery.

Under Baruch's command thousands of businessmen went to work for the federal government, which forced politicians to take notice of their concerns—and their capabilities. Congressmen who had been staunchly antibusiness suddenly became circumspect in criticizing the corporations that were putting America at the top of the world order, and mergers that would have been rejected as attempts to create monopolies just a few years earlier were not only allowed but encouraged.

The national motives were undeniable, yet some irony remains in the fact that a president who had railed against big business ushered in a tacit cooperation between government and industry that would not be forgotten by the Wilsonians—including one Franklin Delano Roosevelt—who went to Washington to help with the war effort and who little more than a decade later would return with these experiences to formulate the New Deal. After the Great War, no presidential administration would be so foolhardy as to try to reverse the forward thrust of American business or to make a serious attempt to nationalize private industries; the great debate over the nation's economic forms and future, which had so occupied both the Populist and Progressive reformers of the prewar period, had been decided by the practical needs of a nation at war. The "military-industrial complex" that President Dwight D. Eisenhower would note with concern in his farewell address some four decades hence was actually born of World War I during the administration of a president who had come to office as a critic of big business.

Wilson thus remade the U.S. political landscape as well. When he became president his Democratic Party was known for its isolationism and the

The photograph below shows the Bethlehem (Pennsylvania) Steel Company's Projectile Shop No. 1, which produced three-inch artillery shells in 1918. Labor troubles plagued companies such as Bethlehem Steel, which was itself guilty of sidestepping the wartime regulation of an eight-hour day for workers. The maneuver sparked a strike that resulted in a three-month delay in deliveries of vital weaponry.

Female workers at the Midvale Steel and Ordnance Company in Pennsylvania are busy at work at right as photographed circa 1918. One million women entered the American workforce during World War I. Hopes ran high that they could make a significant contribution to the war effort while at the same time establishing themselves in high-paying jobs. "At last, after centuries of disabilities and discrimination," said a speaker at a 1917 meeting of the Women's Trade Union, "women are coming into the labor . . . on equal terms with men." But it was only temporary: the number of female workers was lower in 1920 than it had been in 1910.

Republicans for their protoimperialist internationalism. World War I turned the tables and made Democrat Wilson into the biggest booster of industrial America since Abraham Lincoln. As an academic Wilson had advocated the division of power, but the war forced him to realize that the president had to centralize power within his own grasp.

At right, Eugene V. Debs delivers a speech to the Ohio Socialist Party's 1918 convention in Canton. A former railroad worker from Indiana, Debs was an amiable man with an adamant opposition to big business. In Canton his message was to "resist militarism, wherever found," a phrase strong enough to result in his arrest under the Sedition Act for protesting U.S. involvement in World War I. A perennial presidential candidate, Debs pulled almost a million votes in the 1920 election even though he was in the midst of a twenty-month stint behind bars.

Wilson did just that with the help of Congress, which allowed the construction of a mammoth bureaucracy to conduct the U.S. war effort. In addition to Baruch's War Industries Board, the Food Administration was created to see to it that farmers produced more and civilians consumed less or grew their own crops in "victory gardens." Similarly, the Fuel Administration worked to fill the military's energy requirements by increasing production and cutting domestic consumption, while the U.S. Railroad Administration was more direct and just assumed control of the nation's railroads for the duration of the war. In that nineteen-month span, nearly 5,000 federal agencies were created to run the government and its new associations with business and labor, and the federal payroll doubled to more than 850,000 civil servants. Although much of this wartime machine was dismantled after the Armistice, a structure and the precedent remained for the federal bureaucracy to build itself back into a behemoth.

Not that the Great War was universally popular. Peace demonstrations broke out, particularly in German-, Irish-, and Scandinavian-American neighborhoods. Pacifist progressives Jane Addams and suffragist Carrie Chapman Catt founded the Woman's Peace Party. Jeannette Rankin of Montana, the first woman member of the U.S. House of Representatives, voted against American entry in World War I boldy stating, "I want to stand by my country, but I cannot vote for war. I vote No." Industrialist Andrew Carnegie, who in 1910 had created the Carnegie Endowment for International Peace with U.S. Steel bonds worth $10 million, bankrolled peace groups. The indominitable Henry Ford went so far as to send a "peace ship" to Europe in 1915 to lobby for a negotiated settlement. Robert La Follette opposed the conflict to no political detriment, but when Socialist Eugene V. Debs came out against it—his party vehemently opposed what it considered a capitalist war—he was jailed for violating the Sedition Act of 1918, which Congress had added to its legislation of patriotism via the Espionage Act a year before. Jingoism broke out everywhere. Motion picture houses showed the atrocities of "the Hun" to shocked citizens. Iowa's governor decreed it a crime to speak German in public, while across the country German and other immigrants were harassed, hamburger was redubbed "Salisbury steak," and some 1,500 Americans were arrested for breaches of national enthusiasm from complaining about wartime taxes to denouncing the draft. The government repression incited a considerable public backlash, including the foundation in 1920 of the American Civil Liberties Union, an organization devoted to protecting individuals' civil rights, even in wartime.

To combat the burgeoning antiwar sentiment the Wilson administration organized the Committee on Public Information chaired by Denver newspaperman George Creel, who had convinced the president that the best way to influence public opinion was through "expression, not repression," or pro-

Jeannette Rankin, above, was photographed on January 22, 1918, twelve days after the House of Representatives passed a resolution in favor of granting women the right to vote. The bill failed to get through the Senate that year, but eventually it worked its way through the constitutional process becoming the basis of the Nineteenth Amendment in 1920. Mrs. Rankin was noted for voting against American participation in both world wars. In fact, hers was the only vote against America's entry in World War II.

paganda rather than censorship. Creel and his committee launched a publicity campaign designed to feed war fever, enlisting more than 75,000 "four-minute men" to deliver brief but pointed patriotic speeches and a cadre of college professors to write tracts supporting America's position in the war. One such screed—Columbia University Professor Charles Hazen's "The Government of Germany"—attained a circulation of 1.8 million copies. After the war an undeterred Creel would boast, "Three thousand historians are at our call in the preparation of pamphlet material; virtually every writer of prominence is giving time to the work of the committee." Such coziness between government and academe would also draw a warning forty years later in President Eisenhower's farewell address.

Creel's most potent siren song celebrated the "Fourteen Points" Wilson presented in his State of the Union address to Congress on January 8, 1918, as an outline of America's aims in the war. Among other things, the president called for the removal of economic barriers between nations; "open covenants of peace, openly arrived at"; "absolute freedom of navigation upon the seas"; "a free, open-minded, and absolutely impartial adjustment of all colonial claims"; and the formation of a "a general association of nations . . . for the purpose of affording mutual guarantees of political independence and territorial integrity to great and small states alike." Although his Fourteen Points barely registered at the time with a public inclined to dismiss them as mere rhetoric, by issuing them Woodrow Wilson had in fact asked the United States to take on a global mission—one directly counter to the Bolshevik one already announced in Russia by V. I. Lenin. After the war American hatred for Kaiser Germany instantly switched to Communist Russia. Xenophobic Americans lashed out at individuals perceived as being "Red"—anarchists, wobblies, Socialists, pacifists, Communists, and reformers—creating a fanatical scare where citizens were forced to prove their patriotism.

In October 1918 Germany signaled to Wilson that it would accept the Fourteen Points as a framework for peace, and an armistice was arranged for November 11. A week later Wilson announced that he would attend the peace conference in person. As the president would explain in September 1919, "Sometimes people call me an idealist. Well, that is the way I know I am an American. America is the only idealistic nation in the world."

The End of the War To End Wars

President Wilson was hailed as a savior nearly everywhere he went in Europe on his way to the Paris Peace Conference. Once there, Wilson's hero status enabled him to win substantial concessions from the Allies, including self-determination for a dozen new countries from Austria to Yugoslavia and the formation of his beloved League of Nations, an international body the U.S. president had long dreamed of establishing as "definitely a guarantee of peace," as he described his vision to the delegates.

The Continent's Allied leaders, however, were less enthusiastic than their constituency about what some considered America's moral posturing; in any case, the winners were far more interested in punishing the losers by exacting onerous reparations than they were in forming some international body for preventing future conflicts. The conference included representatives from twenty-seven nations, but the "Big Four" participants were Wilson, British Prime Minister David Lloyd George, French Premier Georges Clemenceau, and Italian Premier Vittorio Orlando. Also in attendance was a young Vietnamese gentleman in a second-hand pinstriped suit who had come to Versailles to plead for the interests of his country. Shunned by the delegates, the young man—Ho Chi Minh—became a Communist who would model Vietnam's future on the recent Russian Revolution, to the long-term frustration first of France and then of the United States. The proceedings would turn up a few other harbingers of future conflict as well, most notably when it was revealed that the Allies had promised the same land in Palestine to both Zionists and Arabs. At the time, however, the interest of the participants and the public centered on the future of Europe, particularly of Germany; the rest of the world would have to wait—with one exception.

A year before the Paris Peace Conference began at the rococo palace of Versailles that King Louis XIV had built to his own glory, Vladimir Ilyich Lenin and his Bolsheviks had succeeded in overthrowing the Russian czar and establishing a socialist republic in November 1917. It was a momentous revolution that began with factory workers' strikes and ended by redefining the Western world until the close of the century. The vast Union of Soviet Socialist Republics that resulted would span twelve time zones and have as its goal a worldwide "workers' paradise" via communist revolution, the exact opposite of Wilson's idealistic vision of global democracy. Nevertheless, the still-forming U.S.S.R. would have to be taken into account in any treaty coming out of Paris to end World War I.

In the end Wilson got much of what he wanted in the Treaty of Versailles, although he did not manage to keep the Allies from imposing a harsh peace on Germany that permanently barred any rearmament and assessed reparations of $32 billion. A laconic Wilson, unsure if his leadership in Versailles had been successful, told his wife, "Well, it is finished and, as no one is satisfied, it makes me hope we have made a just peace; but it is all in the lap of the gods."

Unfortunately for Wilson the gods were not in his corner. The Senate refused to ratify the treaty. The upper house was divided into three camps: the Wilsonians; the "Reservationists," led by Republican Senator Henry Cabot Lodge of Massachusetts, chairman of the Senate Foreign Relations Committee, who wanted to alter parts of the treaty mostly for partisan purposes; and the Western and Midwestern "Irreconcilables," two Democrats and fourteen Republicans who refused to accept the Paris agreement on the Progressive principles of isolationism.

Below, the leaders of the "Big Four" victorious nations gathered at Versailles, France, in January 1919 to negotiate the terms that would formally end World War I. They were, from left to right, David Lloyd George, prime minister of Great Britain; Vittorio Orlando, premier of Italy; Georges Clemenceau, premier of France, and Woodrow Wilson, president of the United States. Wilson arrived in France with high hope that the conference would result in a new world attitude toward sovereignty and conciliation. By the time he left, however, he was exhausted by the prevailing atmosphere of petty deal making and stubborn revenge. Wilson's greatest triumph was that the resulting treaty created the framework for his League of Nations.

"This colored league of nations," Senator James A. Reed of Missouri complained in a fit of xenophobia, would include "black, brown, yellow and red faces, low in civilization and steeped in barbarism." The Senate voted on the treaty twice—with and without Lodge's "reservations" weakening the proposed League of Nations and America's participation in it—and both times the Wilsonians and the Irreconcilables joined to defeat it. Wilson refused to accept the changes, and in the end America did not become a member of the League of Nations its president had designed. On October 2, 1919, in the midst of his public campaign for the treaty, Wilson suffered a massive stroke that paralyzed him on one side and left him an invalid. For the next seven months his wife, the formidable Edith Bolling Galt Wilson, isolated her ailing husband and kept the public from learning that she was in effect carrying out the business of the presidency. When told by his physician that the Senate had voted the treaty down, Wilson replied, "Doctor, the devil is a busy man."

Even had he not fallen ill it is unlikely that President Wilson could have convinced the country to support the League of Nations. After all, Americans had reason to distrust foreign alliances after the Soviets released secret internal pacts showing the kind of wheeling and dealing that had taken place among the Allies in dividing the spoils of the Great War. Americans learned, for example, that most of the horror stories about German atrocities had been manufactured in London. An even greater disillusionment set in when the

In the 1920 cartoon at right, the Statue of Liberty points an accusing finger at the Senate for failing to ratify the Treaty of Versailles and for refusing to commit America to the League of Nations. Because of intense political wrangling and underlying isolationist sentiment, America backed away from the opportunity to take a full leadership position in world affairs after the First World War.

million-plus U.S. soldiers who had served in France returned home dejected by the experience and convinced that the French were no better than the Germans—among them one Captain Harry S Truman, who had spent close to a year in France. Most of these weary veterans agreed that entering the European war had been a mistake, and would never permit such a thing to happen again.

Isolationism

America's insular postwar mood was captured by popular *New York World* columnist Franklin P. Adams, who on August 1, 1924, wrote:

> Ten years ago this day the Great War did begin, and I mind how I was at Martha's Vineyard, and listened reverently to men I deemed wiser than I who said there could be no war at all, and if there were it would all be over in a month, and if it were not, Germany would

A ship brings thousands of African-American soldiers home from France in the 1919 photograph above. Black soldiers serving in segregated regiments brought courage to the western front. For example, Corporal Freddie Stowers of the 371st (Colored) Infantry Regiment was in the Champagne-Marne area of France on September 28, 1918, when he took the lead in advancing his squad toward a machine-gun nest. Moving through heavy machine-gun fire, Stowers finally managed to silence the gun nest. He was badly wounded, but led the squad past a second German trench line. Stowers died from his wounds, and his heroism was largely forgotten until 1991, when he was posthumously awarded the Medal of Honor.

be wiped off the face of the earth in two months. And they cited me figures to prove it, and I believed it all. And since then similar things have happened, and when men I deem wiser tell me things I believe them. But nowadays I find fewer and fewer men I deem wiser than I hold myself.

Both Woodrow Wilson and V. I. Lenin had died early that year, two men who had promised their peoples such bright futures in 1917 and had lived just long enough to see their visions thwarted: Lenin witnessed the instant evolution of his Soviet Union into a bureaucracy that hardly fulfilled the Marxist ideal, and Wilson saw his nation turn against his crusade for global democracy via sincere international cooperation. America was instead gripped by a red scare in 1919, perhaps best remembered by the xenophobic oratory of Attorney General A. Mitchell Palmer, who claimed that the "blaze of revolution" was "eating its way into the homes of the American workmen, its sharp tongues of revolutionary heat . . . licking the altars of the churches, leaping into the belfry of the school bell, crawling into the sacred corners of American homes, burning up the foundations of society." Palmer created the new Bureau of Investigation (renamed the Federal Bureau of Investigation in 1935) headed by the twenty-four-year-old J. Edgar Hoover to stamp out insipid radicalism. In 1919 Hoover's agency arrested hundreds of IWW workers and even deported "alien radicals" like feminist Emma Goldman. Due to such bullying during the 1920s the "left" was marginalized to the point of near extinction. "The war," historian Howard Zinn wrote in *A People's History of the United States,* "gave the government the opportunity to destroy the IWW."

By the autumn of 1924 the American public had turned firmly against the idea of both radicals at home and military entanglements abroad. As is so often the case, popular culture provided the best evidence of the nation's thinking through the hit Broadway play *What Price Glory?* by former war correspondent Maxwell Anderson and Marine Corps veteran Laurence Stallings, both in their thirties. Their critically acclaimed antiwar drama revolved around a company of U.S. Marines in France; its message came in a speech delivered by the character of a young lieutenant who returns from the blood-drenched front to company headquarters and screams at his commander,

And since six o'clock there's been a wounded sniper in the tree by that orchard angel, crying, "Kamerad! Kamerad!" Just like a big crippled whippoorwill. What price glory now? Why in God's name can't we go home? Who gives a damn for this lousy, stinking little town but the poor French bastards who live here? God damn it! You talk about courage, and all night long you hear a man who's bleeding to death on a tree calling you "Kamerad" and asking you to save him. God damn every son of a bitch in the world who isn't here. I won't stand for it! I won't have the platoon asking me every minute of the livelong night when they are going to be relieved. . . . I tell you, you

can shoot me, but I won't stand for it. . . . I'll take 'em out tonight
and kill you if you get in my way.

Then the lieutenant would break down, and on most nights, after a few
seconds of silence, the audience would rise to their feet, crying and clapping
and cheering. Five years after the armistice the nation was still sick of war.
What Price Glory? may have been a rhetorical question, but the play was a
loud reply to Wilson's 1917 call for a crusade to make the world safe for
democracy. The most memorable fiction in the immediate postwar period—
Ernest Hemingway's *A Farewell to Arms,* T. S. Eliot's *The Waste Land,* and
Ford Madox Ford's *No More Parades,* to name a few—all reflected a visceral
distrust for the mechanized barbarism which left Europe in ghastly ruins.
Idaho-born Ezra Pound spoke for a generation of disillusioned artists when he
lashed out at the "botched civilization of the post-war world." The public's embrace of these antiwar messages signaled the isolationism that would define
the nation's mood until 1941 as an antiwar sentiment that would go unmatched
until the Vietnam War half a century later.

The New Racism

More than 300,000 black Americans served in the U.S. armed forces during
World War I. Although their country had asked them to risk their lives for liberty and democracy, most returning black veterans did not personally experience either as civilians. Not that the situation had been much better in the
military: those blacks who had been deployed to France had found a more benign variety of racism there than they had been used to in America, but white
U.S. officers asked the French not to be too friendly with the black soldiers.

The unfairness of having been forced to bear an equal share of the nation's military burden and then coming home to segregation, discrimination,
and Jim Crow laws appalled many black veterans and led to racial tensions
that came to a head in 1919. The tinderbox of white fear was kindled by the
new and rapidly growing black populations in northern cities and the entry
of discharged black war veterans into the job pool. In the decade from 1910
to 1920, Detroit's African-American population grew by more than 600 percent, Cleveland's by over 300 percent, and Chicago's by 150 percent. This
mass migration from the Deep South—a land of lynching, low wages, share
cropping, and boll weevil–ravaged cotton crops—to the industrial north created a brush fire of racial violence across the country that summer; twenty-
five serious riots broke out, the most significant in Chicago, Illinois;
Knoxville, Tennessee; Longview, Texas; and Washington, D.C. The Chicago
uprising alone claimed the lives of 23 blacks and 15 whites and wounded
537 others. African-American poet Claude McKay of Harlem summed up black
rage in 1919, the year of the race riots:

If we must die—let it not be like hogs
Hunted and penned in an inglorious spot,

Above, an African-American victim of a Chicago race riot is carried into a police car, May 31, 1919. After the Russian Revolution racial tensions in America increased as any agitation in the black community was suspected of being fostered by Bolshevism. In Chicago that July the worst race rioting in America up to that time erupted when a black teenager was purposely drowned after drifting over to a "white" section of Lake Michigan.

While round us bark the mad and hungry gods,
Making their mock at our accused lot.

. . .

Like men we'll face the murderous, cowardly pack,
Pressed to the wall, dying but fighting back.

By the end of the long, hot summer of 1919 both races had come to recognize that the old solutions, whether the despicable Jim Crow laws or the moderately progressive programs of Booker T. Washington, who died in 1915, were no longer enough. To enraged blacks even the supposed militancy of the NAACP seemed too tame. Two groups with strikingly similar solutions to the racial tensions appeared on opposite sides of the spectrum. The less justifiable was the Ku Klux Klan, the racist hate group that had plagued Reconstruction and had been reorganized by William Simmons of Atlanta in 1915. The Klan offered a broad program aimed at "uniting native-born white

Christians for concerted action in the preservation of American institutions and the supremacy of the white race." But the Klan was not just antiblack; it opposed Catholics and Jews just as vehemently, and soon would conduct its most vicious crusade against foreign-born Americans. The new Klan spread beyond the South and in fact became strongest in the North and Midwest, with major centers of activity in Oregon and Long Island, New York; at its height in the early 1920s the movement boasted some 4 million members and was a potent force in national politics.

African-Americans remained the organization's particular target; as one Klan official stated, "We would not rob the colored population of their rights, but we demand that they respect the rights of the white race in whose country they are permitted to reside." The Klan's updated program, which was both clearly articulated and forcefully argued, demanded separation of the races in all respects, preferably enforced by a police state apparatus authorized to "keep the Negroes in their places."

On the other side of the racial debate, a "Back to Africa" movement had arisen in the nation's black communities. The notion had been mentioned since before the Civil War, most vocally by President Lincoln, but its earlier advocates had been more given to rage than programs, and none had attracted much of a following. This changed in 1914 when Marcus Garvey started the Universal Negro Improvement and Conservation Association in his native Jamaica. Two years later he brought his movement to the United States, where it quickly became popular among blacks looking for an alternative to the moderate approaches of Booker T. Washington and W. E. B. Du Bois.

Garvey believed that blacks had nothing in common with whites and argued that this should be a point of pride; instead of pursuing the immigrants' quest to join America's larger society, Garvey urged blacks to reject that white-dominated culture. He organized black-owned factories, small businesses, and even a steamship line that he hoped would soon be filled with blacks returning to Africa. Proclaiming that blacks had no future in America and could gain nothing from remaining in it, Garvey exhorted his followers to "Wake up, Ethiopia! Wake up, Africa! Let us work toward the one glorious end of a free, redeemed, and mighty nation. Let Africa be a bright star among the constellation of nations." By the eve of World War I his organization had branches throughout the United States, and by the early 1920s Garvey claimed more than 6 million followers who agreed that returning to Africa was a viable option for America's blacks. Although he may have been exaggerating the number, Garvey did command the largest black movement the nation had ever seen.

Marcus Garvey, shown below in New York City in 1922, was born in Jamaica, but was equally at home in the United States, Britain, or the Caribbean. As a reformer, Garvey offered a bold vision for African-Americans that he expressed in one of his poems, "The New Day": "The Negro slept a thousand years/While white men moved along." For a decade before 1925 Garvey moved African Americans along, encouraging them to think and act independently, especially in business ventures. However, his own tangled enterprises, built on capital invested by his many followers, turned out to be scams and he was convicted of mail fraud in 1925.

CHAPTER 15

THE JAZZ AGE

America has always had a penchant for labeling its decades, assigning them moods and values to celebrate the presumably different zeitgeists of each. Thus we recall the Depression of the 1930s, the War Years of the forties, the "Ozzie and Harriet" Generation of the fifties, the Protest Generation of the sixties, the Me Decade of the seventies, the Greed Decade of the eighties, and whatever slogan will be stuck on the end of the millennium. The 1920s, however, embraced a period so unique and colorful that it earned several monikers: Normalcy, the Roaring Twenties, the Unruly Decade, the Age of Flaming Youth, the Speakeasy Era, and the Jazz Age. Its young people were, as poet and expatriate Gertrude Stein told novelist Ernest Hemingway in Paris, "a Lost Generation of post-World War I modernists in search of humanistic values in a highly mechanized epoch." Whatever the era is called, for some it represented the last happy time in the nation's history, full of progress and suffused with a joyous innocence; for others, however, the 1920s marked an era of crime and disorder, lost opportunities, and a tendency toward excess that could lead only to disaster.

Ben Shahn painted nightlife in an urban speakeasy at left (detail). John Held, Jr.'s *McClure's* cover, above, depicts the uninihibited dancing and improvisational music for which the Jazz Age was named. Regarding life during Prohibition, a character in a 1925 book by Ring Lardner observed, "The night before it went into effect everybody had a big party on account of it being the last chance to get boiled. As these wds [sic] is written the party is just beginning to get good."

As John Dos Passos claimed in his novel *The Big Money,* the third volume of his trilogy *U.S.A.,* there were "two Americas": a repressive, "puritanical" nation hostile to anybody not imbued with rigid Protestant fundamentalism—such as Catholic immigrants, Jewish merchants, African-American sharecroppers, industrial workers, and sexually liberated women, and the other America of free-spirited liberals, female suffragists, wild-eyed anarchists, civil right activists, and soapbox socialists who helped spark a cultural and social renaissance. And Dos Passos was correct; the decade could rightly be characterized either way, depending on who and where one was in America. The 1920s played out far differently for a housewife in Peoria, a farmer in Ohio, a New York banker, a fisherman in San Francisco, a steelworker in Pittsburgh, and for each of the other 106 million individuals in the United States at the beginning of the decade, whose numbers would swell to 123 million by its end.

But stereotypes exist for the simple reason that generalities can be drawn about any segment of any society at any given time, while every era has widely shared characteristics by which it can be defined. In 1929, Robert and Helen Lynd pointed out those of America's 1920s in their book *Middletown: A Study in Contemporary American Culture,* which told the story of a typical small American city based on the authors' observations of Muncie, Indiana. Among the characters studied was a middle-aged mother of two teenage boys, the wife of a pipe fitter; her own mother had been a housewife, but this woman had to clean other people's houses six days a week to make ends meet in the style to which they wanted to be accustomed. As the Lynds described her, this Muncie housewife was as much as anyone the "typical American" of the 1920s. In her words:

I began to work during the war, when everyone else did; we had to meet payments on our house and everything else was getting so high. The mister objected at first, but now he don't mind. I'd rather keep on working so my boys can play football and basketball and have spending money their father can't give them. We've built our own home, a nice brown and white bungalow, by a building and loan like everyone else does. We have it almost paid off and it's worth about $6,000. No, I don't lose out with my neighbors because I work; some of them have jobs and those who don't envy us who do. I have felt better since I worked than ever before in my life. I get up at 5:30. My husband takes his dinner and the boys buy theirs uptown and I cook supper. We have an electric washing machine, electric iron, and vacuum sweeper. I don't even have to ask my husband

Above, in an undated photograph, a woman begins a load of laundry by filling a washtub with water, bucket by bucket. In most homes the water for such chores was cold and in many it had to be carried from an outdoor pump. The laundress or housewife would then lather each garment with a bar of soap, rub it against a metal washboard, turn it through a wringer to remove the excess water, and then hang it outside on a line to dry. She could take a break to do other housework while she waited to start the ironing. Before the advent of household appliances, laundering clothes for a family typically took a whole day.

any more because I buy these things with my own money. I bought an icebox last year—a big one that holds 125 pounds; most of the time I don't fill it, but we have our folks visit us from back East and then I do. We own a $1,200 Studebaker with a nice California top, semi-enclosed. Last summer we all spent our vacation going back to Pennsylvania—taking in Niagara Falls on the way. The two boys want to go to college, and I want them to. I graduated from high school myself, but feel if I can't give my boys a little more all my work will have been useless.

This nameless Midwestern woman would prove more perceptive regarding the changes taking place in post-World War I America than most of the celebrated social observers of the time. What she described was no less than the beginning of the true consumer society that has defined the United States ever since. The greatest upheavals of the decade were not those wrought by Prohibition, jazz, the Ku Klux Klan, or even politics; rather, the real leaps of the 1920s occurred in communications, transportation, labor-saving inventions, and the spread of consumer goods that were as "new and improved" as American life itself after the Great War.

The Twenties

The statistics tell the story. The U.S. gross national product, which stood at $74 billion in 1921, would rise to $104 billion in 1929; the nation's total wealth, estimated at $192 billion in 1914, soared to $367 billion in the last year of the decade. Whereas during the ten years before the war, American industries had spent an average of $6 billion annually on new plants and equipment, in every year from 1922 to 1929 that figure would exceed $11 billion. What this meant was more jobs, and not just for Muncie housewives who worked to buy the latest consumer goods and college educations for their children. Over the decade, workers overall would enjoy a nearly 26 percent increase in real earnings, the sharpest in U.S. history to that point.

As Americans' income rose, so did their consumption. In 1920 the nation used 57 billion kilowatt-hours of electricity; by 1929 the figure had more than doubled to 118 billion. The reason was the incredibly quick spread of electrification to homes: whereas in 1920 only 35 percent of U.S. households were wired, ten years later 68 percent were, driving residential demand for electricity over the decade from 3.2 billion to 9.8 billion kilowatt-hours per year. During the same period the number of homes boasting flush toilets rose from 20 to 51 percent, those with washing machines from 8 to 24 percent, and those with automobiles from just over 25 percent to 60 percent. These conveniences that improved the standard of living had far more than the booming stock market to do with Americans' optimistic view of both the present and the future in the years just after World War I.

For all the justified giddiness over its postwar prosperity, the United States of the 1920s faced the twin challenges of growing urbanism and a shrinking world. America had emerged from World War I powerful, secure,

Men and women work side by side in a large factory during the 1920s. As overall employment swelled, the postwar decade witnessed a growing phenomenon: women who went to work as a constructive way to use their extra time. With the advent of smaller family sizes and time-saving domestic appliances in the 1920s, a new type of applicant began to enter the workplace: the woman with excess time on her hands and an interest in working outside of the home.

confident, and far less agrarian than it had been. The 1920 census showed that for the first time more Americans lived in urban than in rural areas—and that the former were evolving far faster than the latter. Suburbs help to create "metropolitan areas" and older enclaves such as Cleveland's Shaker Heights, Detroit's Grosse Point, and Los Angeles's Beverly Hills grew tenfold, becoming centers of art and culture. The result was a major cultural clash barely evident at the time but that remains significant today.

The rapid transformation of America's urban areas was partly due to the speed of the technological and commercial advances the Great War had demanded. "There is no country in the world so efficiently governed as the American Telephone and Telegraph Company or the General Electric Company," New York advertising tycoon Ernest Elmo Calkins boasted. "Business has become the world's greatest benefactor." The economic boom naturally pushed U.S. business concerns to seek ever more and larger markets, and this meant looking overseas. Until World War I, the United States had rejoiced in its unique position as a resource-rich and self-sufficient nation protected from the rest of the world's problems by immense oceans on either side—which had always made it seem logical that America should pretty much ignore Europe and focus its foreign policies in the Caribbean. World War I changed all that, and after it U.S. isolationism would be no more than an outdated memory.

When the war ended in 1918 it appeared that France and Great Britain would dominate Europe and thus become the world's major powers. Into the early 1920s, London retained its status as the Western Hemisphere's greatest bastion of financial strength and international influence, but this was an illusion; by 1918 the United States had transformed from the world's largest debtor nation into its preeminent creditor, and New York had overtaken London as the globe's leading financial center. What's more, American firms had

The General Electric Company commissioned the noted artist Maxfield Parrish to create paintings for its promotional calendars, as in the example at left. Corporate advertising budgets increased dramatically during the 1920s, as did expenditures in a new line: public relations. The first full-time "PR" firm was founded by Edward Bernays in 1915 in the wake of the muckraking journalism that had compromised some of America's most powerful companies, including John D. Rockefeller's Standard Oil. Modern companies realized that they had to groom and promote their own best image on a continuing basis. Distributing beautiful calendars, free of charge, was one method among many.

seized control of formerly British-dominated markets throughout Asia and Latin America. Money, of course, meant international might, and although few recognized it at the time, America's newfound creditor status marked the beginning of the most prosperous period in the nation's history—and of its position as a global power.

Of course there were reactions against the changes transforming the nation, many from rural America toward a world that seemed to be leaving it behind. Farmers across the nation had suffered since the end of the war, when demand for agricultural products plummeted after the government no longer had to feed so many troops. During the 1920s American farmers' share of the national income shrank by nearly half as the federal government withdrew its wartime price supports for wheat and corn, and European farms resumed production. From the Great Plains to the Mississippi Valley, farmers were additionally burdened with decreasing yield per acre, overgrazing, flooding, deforestation, and drought. The desperate situation thus created led to calls for federal farm relief programs including such far-out proposals as the McNary-Haugen Bill, under which U.S. farm surpluses would be dumped on foreign markets to boost domestic commodity prices—which passed after three years of debate over President Coolidge's veto. At the same time, other industries in outlying areas also started to suffer: coal-mining operations faltered as natural gas and petroleum interests made inroads into the energy market, while textiles and many smaller rural business concerns fell into sharp decline. Fortuitous landowners who happened to strike oil in California, Texas, and Oklahoma became instant millionaires, the archetypal envy of the rural poor but characterized as crude buffoons in Edna Ferber's popular novel *Cimarron* (1929).

The backlash to these shifts took many grim forms across the American countryside, from the Ku Klux Klan to Prohibition to the 1925 Scopes "monkey trial," a legal circus that upheld a Tennessee law prohibiting the teaching of evolution in public schools. Yet to most thoughtful observers the real message of the Scopes case—celebrated in the acclaimed 1955 play *Inherit the Wind*—came from the losing side's arguments as declaimed by the rumpled but constitutionally compelling Clarence Darrow, who got his point across that the church had no business meddling in state-funded schools, to the considerable annoyance of opposing counsel William Jennings Bryan. In spite of the carnival atmosphere that grew up around the Scopes trial, the clash between Darwinism as articulated by Chicago agnostic Darrow and Creationism as argued by no less a heartland orator than Bryan cast a national spotlight on the larger phenomenon of religious "fundamentalism," illuminating its adherents' radical insistence that every word in the Bible was the literal truth and should be acted upon as such.

An equally intransigent philosophy oozed from Americans' worst instincts into "nativism," a widespread xenophobia that resulted in the strictest immigration laws in U.S. history. Fueled by white Protestants' mindless fears that because most recent immigrants were Catholics, Jews, or Mexicans, their assimilation would turn Americans into "a hybrid race of people as worthless and futile as the good-for-nothing mongrels of Central America and South-

eastern Europe," nativism grew to such hysteria that in 1927 Nicola Sacco and Bartolomeo Vanzetti were executed on dubious murder charges not so much because of their admitted anarchism as for their Italian heritage. (While their trial was a kangaroo court and there was a rush to judgment, it does appear today that both men were involved in the robbery and murders even if not the actual gunmen.) The rural United States in fact endured a rash of anti-black, anti-Semitic, and anti-Catholic incidents in the 1920s. Klan membership rose from 100,000 in 1920 to nearly 5 million "white male persons, native-born Gentile citizens of the United States" in 1924. Lynchings and beatings of African-Americans were so commonplace in the 1920s that Harlem intellectuals declared such states as Alabama and Mississippi "killing fields." As historian W. J. Cash noted of the Klan in the South, the rank and file "swarmed with little businessmen . . . the rural clergy belonged to it or had traffic with it almost *en masse*. . . . It was . . . at once anti-Negro, anti-alien, anti-red, anti-Catholic, anti-Jew, anti-Darwin, anti-Modern, anti-Liberal, Fundamentalist, vastly Moral, militantly Protestant."

Unfortunately, there was nothing new in this wave of paranoia; such ghastly bigotry had been an ugly stain on the nation's countryside throughout U.S. history. This time, however, as the situation worsened it also began to be corrected by the unstoppable spread of technology; the small-minded views of small-town America began to change when minds were opened by radio broadcasts from the larger world that rural electrification brought into every living room, by the relative affordability of automobiles that put that world within reach, and by the leisure time available thanks to the same modern conveniences that were making it possible for the housewife in Muncie to send her boys to college.

Above, the Ku Klux Klan marched boldly through the nation's capital in 1926. Fostering something it considered "Americanism," the Klan preached hatred against minority groups, strict personal morality, and prosecution of bootleggers. It dominated the politics of several states and was in complete control of Indiana by 1925. That year, however, the head of the regional KKK was convicted of second-degree murder in the rape and subsequent death of a twenty-one-year-old Sunday school teacher. The Ku Klux Klan lost its political power in the aftermath of the Indiana case and was unmasked as a highly corrupt, manipulative organization of bigots.

America's standard of living had begun its climb in the sprawling cities. Although World War I technically had brought an end to the Progressive Era, it did not halt the Progressive agenda or the wretched urban blight that had spawned it. In 1919 the same appalling conditions had sparked a wave of violent labor strikes around the nation that Congress ascribed to Bolshevik agitators spoiling for a workers' revolution, prompting a brief "red scare" that Communists were out to overthrow the U.S. government. As jurist and later Supreme Court Justice William O. Douglas wrote, "Ever since World War I our government has been increasingly lawless as it caters to popular fears, and indeed generates them by cries of 'subversion' and 'un-Americanism.'" The scare fortunately faded when the American public reacted more soberly to the shenanigans of a few anarchists than the government did.

American businesses for the most part took a less sanguine approach to the labor question, forcing their workers to disavow unions and refusing to deal with companies that used union labor. Many had the industrial muscle to get away with it, as a flurry of mergers in the 1920s put half of the nation's wealth under the control of some 200 corporations. But a number of these large enterprises tempered their demands on workers with "welfare capitalism," under which employees were given incentives such as opportunities to buy preferred stock and paternal care the likes of which had not been seen since before the Civil War—safety codes, spotless factories, good cafeterias, and collegial after-hours bonding activities such as choral groups and baseball teams. Most corporations went so far as to create a new bureaucratic layer of professional "middle managers" to facilitate a happy liaison between owners and workers—a business structure that even the most draconian downsizing efforts have since proven inadequate to dismantle.

The federal government, meanwhile, continued to some extent in the Progressive tradition. Between 1913 and 1920 the U.S. Senate passed and the states ratified three constitutional amendments that derived from nineteenth-century reform movements. The Sixteenth Amendment to the Constitution provided for an income tax, the revenues from which had helped to pay for the war and would soon finance a host of government programs. The Eighteenth Amendment, a short-lived product of rural temperance movements, gave America prohibition of alcoholic beverages, a failed attempt at legislating morality. The urban-born Nineteenth Amendment, by contrast, was purely laudable, long overdue, and the last, best gasp of Progressivism: it gave the vote to women, who by dint of superior longevity were, are, and always have been a majority of the population rather than a sector to be grouped with "other minorities."

The New Woman

The history of women's suffrage in America is long and convoluted, through no fault of the pioneers who worked so hard to attain it. In retrospect, as disturbing as it is that the United States didn't get around to abolishing slavery until the Thirteenth Amendment to the Constitution and then

Below, Elizabeth Cady Stanton and Susan B. Anthony sit for a photograph circa 1881. In the ferment of change after the Civil War the two had founded the National Woman Suffrage Association. Their dream was not achieved until after World War I, when women were granted voting rights in time for the 1920 election. Neither Mrs. Anthony nor Mrs. Stanton was alive to see the passage of the Nineteenth Amendment; they both died at the turn of the century.

took two more amendments to extend the franchise to African-American men, it is not that much less unsettling that the majority of the U.S. population was denied the vote until passage of the Nineteenth Amendment a full two decades into the twentieth century.

Some progress had been made earlier, but it was limited. After the Civil War, the Wyoming Territory adopted universal suffrage, women included; Kansas, however, considered amending its state constitution to enfranchise women, but the measure was soundly defeated. National feminist leaders such as Elizabeth Cady Stanton and Susan B. Anthony had campaigned for the inclusion of women's suffrage in the Fourteenth and then the Fifteenth Amendments, but had been denied both times. Undeterred, they had formed the National Woman Suffrage Association to continue the battle in 1869, and a year later they were joined by another group called the American Woman Suffrage Association, founded by Lucy Stone, that was dedicated to the quest for legislation permitting women to vote. The two groups united in 1890 into the National American Woman Suffrage Association and were soon joined by other women's rights organizations from around the nation; once brought together and coordinated, the suffrage movement began to make headway. In 1913 Quaker Alice Paul led a lobbying effort for a constitutional amendment giving women the vote, and six years later formed the National Women's Party.

For all the sincerity of these efforts, in the end it was America's entry into World War I and the prominent role women played in the war effort that made passage of the Nineteenth Amendment not only possible but certain. Once women had proven their capabilities by ably running the factories and

In the 1930s artist Ben Shahn looked back to the turn of the century for the painting above of Women's Christian Temperance Union (WCTU) marchers. The founder of the WCTU was Carrie Nation, a woman driven by a permanent rage against liquor in general and bars in particular. According to Nation: "It is very significant that the paintings of naked women are in saloons. Women are stripped of everything by them. Her husband is torn from her, she is robbed of her sons, her home, her food, and her virtue. And then they strip her clothes off and hang her bare in these dens of robbery and murder."

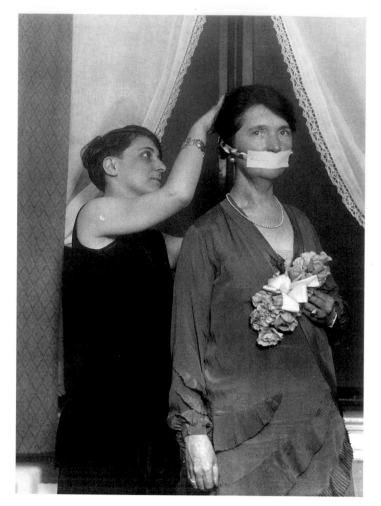

The photograph above shows the activist Margaret Sanger having her lips taped shut to prevent her from uttering so much as a word about birth control during a 1928 visit to Boston. Sanger, a social worker raised in Corning, New York, felt that high birthrates locked many families into a state of poverty. When she first began to promote family planning in about 1914, she was practically alone. Though constantly encroaching on wider moral issues, Sanger intended only to reduce unnecessary privation among the ignorant and poor. By the late 1920s, her message was widely accepted and her birth control clinics were allowed to remain open in poor neighborhoods of many large cities.

other workplaces vacated by men off fighting the war, America's daughters finally had not only the right to vote but also indisputable evidence of the absurdity of its ever having been denied them. One by one the states extended the franchise to women, and by 1918 a full fifteen had done so, some even having women serve in their legislatures—as did the U.S. House of Representatives, which its first female member had been elected, Republican Jeannette Rankin of Montana, in 1916.

Thus the only surprise was that it had taken so long when the U.S. Senate passed the Nineteenth Amendment giving women the vote by a margin of 56 to 25 on June 14, 1919. As the thirty-sixth state to ratify the amendment, Tennessee pushed women's suffrage through on August 18, 1920.

America's female population responded in a variety of ways, not the least significant being the emergence of the culturally and sexually liberated "flapper" who bobbed her hair, wore short skirts, smoked cigarettes in public, and drove a car she bought with her own wages. Women otherwise emboldened by the franchise dipped their toes into politics, lobbying Congress about traditional female concerns successfully enough to achieve passage of the nation's first federally funded health-care program, the 1921 Sheppard-Towner Maternity and Infancy Protection Act that established pre- and neonatal care centers to combat high infant mortality rates in rural areas. Similarly, activist and nurse Margaret Sanger of New York found many adherents as well as passionate, puritanical opposition to her American Birth Control League, which advocated contraception for any number of reasons, especially to help poor women avoid the burdens of unwanted pregnancy. As Sanger put it: "Women cannot be on equal footing with men until they have complete control over their reproductive functions."

Getting the vote and at least acknowledgment of the need for birth control did not, however, end the women's movement for full equality. Alice Paul now called for another constitutional amendment—which would arise again and spur the same national debate half a century later—providing that "equality of rights under the law shall not be denied or abridged by the United States or by a State on account of sex." As tame and self-evidently logical as such a proposal might seem, it splintered the women's rights movement in the early 1920s. Many supported Paul, but more believed that all the suggested amendment would accomplish was the elimination of the Progressive laws protecting women in the home as well as the workplace.

When the Supreme Court declared in the 1923 case of *Adkins v. Children's Hospital* that a minimum-wage law for women was unconstitutional as a trespass against the rights of management, the National Women's Party declared the decision a victory for equal rights, while other women's groups swore to fight it. But the era of such Progressive reforms had ended, and their likes would not resurface for another generation—and then they would be focused on a different agenda aimed at solving different problems.

A New World Order

As America continued on the path into prosperity cleared by its victory in World War I, politics seemed somehow diminished in importance, eclipsed by the mighty corporate engines that were driving the economy forward. Nevertheless, the presidential election of 1920 had its points of interest. President Woodrow Wilson, of course, had suffered a stroke on October 2, 1919, that left him able to do little in his last year in office. His Democratic Party was therefore confused as well as divided, but managed to nominate Governor James Cox of Ohio for the presidency and a well-bred young up-and-comer who had served as assistant secretary of the Navy during the war for the vice presidency: Franklin Delano Roosevelt of Hyde Park, New York.

The Democratic veep candidate's fifth cousin, former President Theodore Roosevelt, had been preparing to seek the Republican nomination and by 1918 had already organized a staff to raise funds and seek support for his campaign. Given the country's vigorous mood, the still bully sixty-year-old Roosevelt had a good chance to win both the nomination and the 1920 election. In fact, the history of the 1920s might have been far different had Teddy Roosevelt not died in 1919 and denied the nation a Rooseveltian revival—for the time being.

In his absence the Republicans turned to smooth, silver-haired Senator Warren G. Harding of Ohio and taciturn Governor Calvin Coolidge of Massachusetts. Although both major parties considered the League of Nations the most pressing issue of the day, candidate Harding chose to avoid it on the grounds that "America's present need is not heroics but healing; not nostrums but normalcy; not revolution but restoration . . . not surgery but serenity." In fact, the Republicans had chosen Harding in large part for just such vague moderation—as well as for his packaging potential on the cynical reasoning that he was handsome enough to win the hearts of the new women voters.

Because the Nineteenth Amendment had added 9.5 million women voters—nearly 40 percent of the total—to the electorate, it looked as though the 1920 contest might be decided by the allegedly gentler sex, who had long claimed they would inject a purifying element into the rough and tumble of U.S. politics. Such did not turn out to be the case in 1920. Although more than 28 million Americans voted compared with 18.4 million in 1916, a good part of the increase resulted from the return of war veterans to the polls and from the stir created by the League of Nations issue. Whereas in 1916 voter participation had been 61.6 percent of those eligible, in 1920 the turnout fell to 49.2 percent, the lowest since 1824. For all the work of the suffragettes to obtain the Nineteenth Amendment, not many women bothered to exercise their newly won right to vote the first time out.

Still, the better-looking man won in a landslide, 16.1 million popular votes to Cox's 9.1 million and 404 electoral votes to the Democrat's 127. Most surprising of all, Socialist Party candidate Eugene V. Debs who was in prison for sedition during the campaign, received nearly a million votes. In taking 60.8 percent of the popular tally, however, Harding became not only the first presidential candidate since 1908 to receive a majority but also set the record

The Republican candidate for president in 1920 was Warren G. Harding, top. A small-town newspaper publisher, Harding sought the party nomination on a shoestring budget but won it with canny advice from a lawyer named Harry Daugherty, who constantly positioned his man as a friendly alternative to the front-runners. Daugherty also made up slogans that suited the postwar yearning for stability, such as "Back to Normalcy" and the one on the campaign button above. After receiving the nomination Harding waged his entire campaign from the front porch of his house in Ohio. Exhausted by world affairs, America apparently liked the idea of having a small-town man in Washington, and Harding won the election easily.

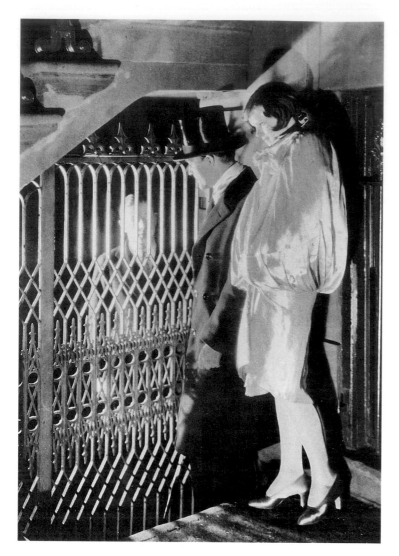

A couple dressed to the nines awaits entry to a speakeasy in the photograph above. Some speakeasies were swank nightclubs at which patrons were carefully screened. In working-class neighborhoods, by contrast, the speakeasy was typically located in one room of a private home and operated by a widow or divorcée and her children. "At first I just sold to the men who stayed here," explained a Vermont woman, referring to her boarders, "but naturally, more and more kept coming, you know how it is. Their friends brought other friends and I sold more drinks. Pretty quick, it got to be quite a business."

for the largest electoral victory in U.S. history to that point. Some interpreted the size of Harding's triumph as a repudiation of Wilson's global idealism, and in part they were right. More significant, however, was the extent to which the country remained Republican; Wilson's victories, after all, had owed more to the Progressives' fragmentation of the party than to any sudden shift away from traditional Republicanism. Nevertheless, Democrats and other critics warned that Harding would force a return to the days of William McKinley and the bucolic small-town America that seemed so far away from the bustling urban society that had sprung up in its place. What the critics ignored was that many of those who had voted for Harding agreed; after all, that was just what they wanted.

Prohibition Ends

What a seeming majority of Americans turned out not to want was Prohibition. In 1914 the temperance movement had succeeded to the point that five states had gone dry followed by four more the next year, which inspired the Prohibitionists to fight for the complete triumph they achieved in December 1917 with a constitutional amendment prohibiting the manufacture, sale, and transportation of alcoholic beverages, which sped through the House of Representatives by a vote of 282 to 128 and through the Senate 65 to 20. By the time the Eighteenth Amendment went to the states for ratification, twenty-seven of them had already enacted bans on alcohol. Mississippi was the first to ratify Prohibition, on January 8, 1918; on January 16 of the next year Nebraska became the thirty-sixth state to join in and made the Eighteenth Amendment part of the U.S. Constitution. Under it, as of January 16, 1920, "the manufacture, sale, or transportation of intoxicating liquors within, the importation thereof into, or the exportation thereof from the United States and all territory subject to the jurisdiction thereof for beverage purposes is hereby prohibited."

Congress then passed the Volstead Act, setting the parameters of what some would dub "the Noble Experiment" to legislate against intoxication. The act sparked considerable debate, its opponents arguing for the exclusion of beer and wine from the ban to make Americans more receptive to Prohibition, while its hard-line supporters saw victory within their grasp and refused to compromise. The latter won. There would be no more legal alcohol among the U.S. populace, a policy that oddly had been considered progressive in the nineteenth century. This was no longer the case once Prohibition actually took effect.

In 1920, shortly after the Volstead Act was passed, Congress appropriated $2 million to enforce the law; a year later rampant violations drove the budget to $6.35 million, which still proved insufficient to the task. By the end of

1922, "speakeasies," where alcohol was sold to trusted customers at outrageous prices, could be found in most neighborhoods in most American cities; bootlegging and associated corruption were on the rise, and Prohibition was not only an unpopular inconvenience but little more than a national joke. For starters, the Volstead Act was widely violated; for instance, the federal Prohibition Bureau estimated that some 22.6 million barrels of illicit beer alone had been produced and distributed in the United States in 1929, a full third as much brew as had flowed through the country legally in 1917. The American vocabulary was soon enriched with a host of memorable idioms of lawlessness and vice: clip joint, bathtub gin, white lightning, the real McCoy, to name just a few.

Although plenty of stills churned out moonshine in the backwoods of nearly every state during Prohibition, most of the large-scale bootlegging operations were run by organized crime syndicates that had grown up around gambling and prostitution and blossomed amid the lucrative new possibilities presented by Prohibition. More than a few of these ruthless outfits attained considerable power in such urban centers as Chicago, where gangsters such as the notorious Al Capone bribed their way out from under the authorities and amassed enormous fortunes from illegal activities. In 1927 alone Capone made some $60 million from his criminal pursuits; when convicted of tax evasion and sent to prison two years later, he complained that "I've given people light pleasures, and all I get is abuse."

Both large- and small-scale violations of Prohibition grew increasingly common as the 1920s wore on, continually adding evidence of the program's

Al Capone, shown at leisure at left, was raised in New York City, where he was linked to two murders before he reached the age of twenty. At twenty-one in 1920, he left for Chicago, where a particularly vicious gangster named John Torrio was already busy staking out territory in the wake of Prohibition. Together they gained most of the liquor business in the city, and controlled most other forms of corruption and crime as well. They also operated Chicago's leading speakeasies. Turf fights escalated, however, and finally became too frightening even for John Torrio—a situation Capone probably engineered. After Torrio went into hiding, Capone took over. "Scarface" Capone, a thug reviled even by other thugs, became symbolic of the criminal underworld that Prohibition helped engender in most American cities.

The battle to enforce Prohibition turned into a propaganda war in the 1920s. In the photograph above, federal agents in Philadelphia destroy caseloads of beer for the benefit of photographers, while the government continually issued posters such as the one shown below in its attempt to uphold the law. But liquor remained nearly as popular as ever and enforcement only clogged up court calendars, without discouraging violations.

failures. It was no secret that President Harding—who at one time opposed Prohibition but had come to support it for political reasons—was a drinker who never found much appeal in temperance, remarking "I am unable to see this as a great moral issue." Indeed, none of the presidents of the 1920s—Harding, Calvin Coolidge, or Herbert Hoover—considered the Prohibitionists anything but temperance fanatics who had to be humored in the name of politics. The ridiculousness of the nation's antialcohol policy became inescapable in the autumn of 1923 when the U.S. Justice Department complained that it had "been called upon to prosecute a member of the judiciary, prominent members of the American bar, high officials of federal and state governments. The sordid story of assassination, bribery, and corruption has been found in the very sanctums where the law was presumed to be sacred." Despite the mounting hypocrisy, Prohibition remained the law beyond the decade, although its end was foreseen in 1928 by Republican Congressman Fiorello La Guardia of New York, who made the pragmatic argument that if the Prohibitionists would not "stand up courageously and demand the hundreds of millions of dollars it will require to enforce Prohibition," then "it is our right to seek through proper, constitutional, and legislative channels a change in the law."

The Rise of Popular Culture

Prohibition's doom was foretold in America's postwar turn toward the Jazz Age sybaritism which novelist F. Scott Fitzgerald captured so poetically in his fiction and so tragically in his short life. It was a time when random hedonism flourished among those who could afford it, be it at lavish Long Island lawn parties as depicted in *The Great Gatsby* or in real life at ostentatious champagne bashes thrown by magazine magnate Condé Nast, a time soon jaded by nervous breakdowns and secret suicides symptomatic of the freewheeling age. In the spirit of the times the *Ladies Home Journal* admitted advertisements of lipstick while cigarette manufacturers dared to publish pictures of women smoking. "Today," social critic H. L. Mencken wrote, "the newsstands are piled high with magazines devoted frankly and exclusively to sex. Hundreds of writers make their livings producing this garbage; its merchandising has become one of the largest American industries." The loosening of morals reached revolutionary proportions in the art world: Sinclair Lewis's *Babbitt* (1922), for example, lampooned Christian hypocrisy while Sherwood Anderson's *Winesburg, Ohio* (1919) ripped off the veil of small-town America to expose widespread psychological dysfunctionalism. Artists everywhere were declaring the death of puritanical America and the rise of a new modernism that was highly sophisticated and sexually liberated. In 1924 Broadway burst into racy song with jazzy new musicals from such icons as Irving Berlin, Jerome Kern, Cole Porter, Richard Rodgers and Lorenz Hart, and George Gershwin, who topped off his three stage hits of that year with the premier of his remarkable *Rhapsody in Blue*. Meanwhile, Fletcher Henderson and Duke Ellington brought the Harlem Renaissance to uptown New York, while all-black Broadway shows like Eubie Blake and Noble Sissle's *Shuffle Along* (1921) ran for packed houses for most of the decade. Elsewhere on the nation's stages, vaudeville was declining from a prime that would disappear with the advent of a new form of popular entertainment.

When motion pictures first appeared, few took them seriously—including Thomas Alva Edison, who had invented the tools of the industry before the turn of the century but considered their products little more than idle diversions. The first Vitascope had been demonstrated in 1896 and the first real feature film, *The Great Train Robbery,* was produced in 1903, but it wasn't until the movies of director D. W. Griffith appeared that Americans began to regard the cinema as something more than a trifle. Griffith's *The Birth of a Nation*, released in 1915, had presented the Ku Klux Klan favorably and freed black slaves as near savages, creating a sensation and inspiring both black and white civil rights leaders to accuse the film of racism. Their charges had merit, but *The Birth of a Nation* also introduced such cinematic novelties as close-ups, action shots, panoramas, and montages, techniques that were immediately imitated and improved upon by others. Most significant, however, the very bigotry in Griffith's film proved the power of movies not only to attract the public but to excite its emotions.

By 1924, America boasted more than 20,000 movie theaters fed by Hollywood studios churning out some 700 features a year. The medium's popularity was staggering; the national population was 114 million, but weekly motion picture attendance was 126 million. Movie stars more recognizable than the president included "America's Sweetheart," Mary Pickford; swashbuckler Douglas Fairbanks, Sr.; "Little Tramp" Charlie Chaplin; and dreamboat Rudolph Valentino, whose *Four Horsemen of the Apocalypse* made the outrageous profit for the time of $4 million. Wild West romances, many based on the pulp fiction novels of Zane Grey, created a host of modern cowboys such as Tom Mix and Buck Jones, mavericks who always stood for justice, law, order, and the American way. Cartoons were popular courtesy of a Kansas animator named Walt Disney, whose mouse named Mickey tootled

George Gershwin, above, started out as a "song plugger," sitting in a little booth at a store and playing sheet music for prospective customers. He was later fired for playing his own songs on company time. Soon after, in 1917, he enjoyed his first big hit, "Swanee (How I Love You, How I Love You)," and after that no one would ever again be fired for playing George Gershwin's music. Gershwin remained at the forefront of musical composition for twenty years, blending styles and exploring different mediums in original and distinctly American ways. In addition to popular music, he wrote the score for the opera *Porgy and Bess* and orchestral works including *Rhapsody in Blue,* which debuted at New York's Aeolian Hall in 1924.

The Birth of a Nation, advertised in the poster at right, was an epic motion picture in an era of cheap one reelers. Released in 1915, it featured expert storytelling and cinematography on a Civil War theme. It also carried a racist message that helped further the cause of the Ku Klux Klan.

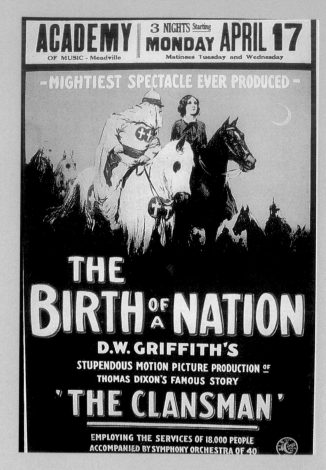

Charles Chaplin, below, and Mary Pickford, below right, were the most popular performers of the silent screen, winning unprecedented worldwide stardom. Chaplin, an unknown comic actor at the Mack Sennett Studios, was new to films in 1913, when he improvised the "Little Tramp" character shown here. "In all comedy business an attitude is most important," he wrote in his autobiography. "I was a tramp just wanting a little shelter." Mary Pickford also played the innocent in most of her movies, though neither she nor Chaplin was anything of the kind in real life. They drove hard business deals for themselves, founded United Artists (with Douglas Fairbanks, Sr., and D. W. Griffith), and did as much as anyone else to shape the movie business into a major industry.

his way into the American psyche in 1928's *Steamboat Willie*. Sound had come to the movies the previous year and as Al Jolson rightfully proclaimed in *The Jazz Singer*: "Wait a minute, you ain't heard nothing yet, folks."

The movies made the 1920s an era of hero worship that soon extended beyond the silver screen to embrace sports stars such as baseball's Babe Ruth, boxing's Jack Dempsey, and tennis champions Bill Tilden and Helen Wills. The greatest hero of all, however, was a man whose accomplishments transcended entertainment and made the world smaller and more commercially accessible than anyone had ever dreamed possible: aviator Charles Lindbergh, who in 1927 drove America wild by crossing the Atlantic nonstop and solo in his tiny monoplane *The Spirit of St. Louis*. Overnight twenty-five-year old "Lucky Lindy" had become a new kind of American royalty: the celebrity. Congress awarded "The Lone Eagle," a Medal of Honor, and flappers danced

George Bellows painted *Dempsey and Firpo* in 1924, above, to commemorate one of the most improbable moments in the history of boxing: when the underdog Luis Firpo knocked the great Jack Dempsey right out of the ring early in the second round of their fight on September 14, 1923. But Dempsey climbed right back into the ring to finish Firpo off. The popular champion had some help getting up, though, and it became a matter of controversy in the sports world. As reporter Bugs Baer put it in his column the next day: "If that had been Firpo in the aisles, they'd still be walking on him."

From 1897 to 1917, Storyville, a sixteen-block area of New Orleans that scoffed at Victorian mores, became the world's most famous red-light district. At the high point of its twenty-year existence Storyville hosted more than 2,000 prostitutes in a sort of theme park for vice created by Alderman Sidney Story, whose goal was not to promote licentious behavior but to corral it in one section of town. Managed by State Legislator Tom Anderson, Louisiana's foremost pimp, the bordellos and sex shows were closed down in 1917 at the insistence of the U.S. Navy Department, which feared venereal disease would spread among sailors leaving New Orleans for service in World War I. (Today, only five unmarked buildings remain of what was Storyville; the rest, even those with significant Edwardian and Victorian details, were razed in the 1930s and 1940s and replaced by a public housing project.) But the bordellos also had served as jazz music workshops for such legends as Ferdinand "Jelly Roll" Morton, Tony Jackson, Clarence Williams, and Joseph "King" Oliver. As historian James Lincoln Collier has noted, New Orleans was "drenched" in music during the Storyville years—including "ragtime," piano music that first appeared in the 1890s.

The king of ragtime was Scott Joplin, a native of Texarkana, Texas, whose "Maple Leaf Rag" sold more than a million copies in 1900. Joplin went on to compose dozens of sterling rags, including "The Entertainer," which would revive ragtime in 1973 via the Academy Award-winning movie The Sting), approaching his art as African-American classical music. Infuriated at what he considered cheap imitators such as Irving Berlin, who was claiming knockoff compositions like "Alexander's Ragtime Band," Joplin began printing instructions on his sheet music reading: "Do not play this piece fast." He died at age forty-nine in 1917, broke and in despair, but he left behind the ragtime syncopation that would help form the backbeat of jazz.

Jazz, born out of the postbellum Delta blues and other American roots music combining with other ingredients such as march music and ragtime, evolved into the artistic innovation of the century, thanks largely to pioneering genius Louis Armstrong—a master of improvisation on the trumpet and cornet. Armstrong, born on July 4, 1900, in a shack off Jane Alley in New Orleans, was weaned on the sounds of Storyville, whose brothels he would sit in front of as a boy to listen to the music. By 1922 Armstrong—nicknamed Satchmo (for "Satchelmouth")—had moved to Chicago with King Oliver's Creole Jazz Band and stunned audiences with the depth of emotion and natural inventiveness that emanated from his horn. "The guys never heard anything else like it," composer Duke Ellington recalled. Jazz became the music of the 1920s, reaching its zenith with such Armstrong tunes as "Dipper Mouth Blues," "Mabel's Dream," and "Heebie Jeebies." In jazz, African-Americans had created a modern art form that influenced not only American culture but also such European painters as Pablo Picasso and Henri Matisse. "Armstrong is the Prometheus of the blues idiom," trumpet great Wynton Marsalis would note toward the century's end, and it was through Satchmo that the United States made its impact on twentieth-century aesthetics.

Jazz had a profound influence, for example, on the so-called Harlem Renaissance, a period in the 1920s of extraordinary creativity among African-American writers and artists as well as musicians. "Our poets have now stopped speaking for the Negro—they speak now as Negroes," explained Alain Locke, the first African-American Rhodes scholar. "Where formerly they spoke to others and tried to interpret, they now speak to their own and try to express." The poet laureate of the Harlem Renaissance was Langston Hughes. Born in Joplin, Missouri, on February 1, 1902, Hughes, best known for his poem "The Negro Speaks of Rivers," celebrated the African descent of "my people" in his volumes of autobiography, plays, fiction, and short stories. "The night is beautiful," Hughes wrote in an appreciation of blackness. "So the faces of my people." He celebrated the African-American vernacular and insisted that the Delta blues were as powerful as Mozart, that jazz was a revolution in sound. According to Hughes, the "undertow of black music with its rhythms never betray you . . . strengths like the beat of a human heart."

One of the last members of the 1920 black writers' movement—Dorothy West, who died August 16, 1998, sixty years after she founded two respected literary journals—remembered, "We didn't know it was the Harlem Renaissance, because we were all young and all poor. We had no jobs to speak of, and we had rent parties to pay expenses." Although the Harlem Renaissance also produced other outstanding writers—particularly Richard Wright, Zora Neale Hurston, and Jean Toomer, whose 1923 novel Cane brilliantly explored African-American identity—Hughes was its shining star, the Walt Whitman of twentieth-century black America. And jazz, that hot improvisational stream of musical styles that produced such extraordinary musical talents as Miles Davis, Charlie Parker, Duke Ellington, Charles Mingus, John Coltrane, and Thelonious Monk, was the United States' gift to world culture—and remains an African-American art form as rich as the Mississippi River.

The Cotton Club was one of the premier nightclubs in New York City during the Harlem Renaissance of the 1920s. Featuring most of the nation's finest African-American performers, it drew well-heeled patrons of both races.

The Magnavox Reproducer and the Magnavox Power Amplifier

"These two devices have revolutionized Radio"

MAGNAVOX Radio equipment takes the feeble sound vibrations produced by your receiving set and builds them up into full, round tones in exact accordance with the original broadcasted speech or music.

The development of the Magnavox is one of Radio's spectacular achievements.

Magnavox R3 Reproducer and 2 stage Power Amplifier, as illustrated . . $90.00

R2 Magnavox Reproducer with 18-inch curvex horn: the utmost in amplifying power; requires only .6 of an ampere for field . $60.00

R3 Magnavox Reproducer with 14-inch curvex horn: ideal for homes, etc. $35.00

Model C Magnavox Power Amplifier insures getting the largest possible power input for your Magnavox Reproducer . . 2 stage $55.00 3 stage 75.00

Magnavox Products can be had from good dealers everywhere. Write for new booklet.

THE MAGNAVOX CO. Oakland, Cal. New York: 370 Seventh Ave.

MAGNAVOX Radio
The Reproducer Supreme

The advertisement above announced a radio revolution: the loudspeaker. Using previous "crystal sets," listeners had been forced to wear earphones. The first radio network, NBC, debuted on November 15, 1926, when listeners as far away as Kansas City stayed home and heard a whole evening of entertainment live from the Waldorf-Astoria Hotel in New York City.

a new step known as the Lindy Hop. In that celebrity-crazed age Lindbergh's views on everything from morality to medicine were taken seriously, as were boxer Gene Tunney's on Shakespeare and industrialist Henry Ford's on politics, all on the assumption that performance in one area had to carry over into others. The advent and rapid ascent of advertising stoked the trend, encouraging the public to emulate its heroes' and heroines' choices of dress, cigarettes, cars, and all the other items that defined what later generations would call "lifestyle." The Horatio Alger characters who had risen to the top through pluck and luck before the war had given way to the glamorously idle icons of the Age of Flaming Youth.

Even more significant were the national bonds forged by radio, which foreshadowed the cultural upheaval television would wreak thirty years later. Radio, which had been invented by Italian Guglielmo Marconi at the turn of the century and refined since by a number of Americans, was still in its infancy in the 1920s. The technology's chief proponent early in the decade was Secretary of Commerce Herbert Hoover, who believed it had the potential to develop into the world's most important communications medium. He waxed futuristic about how radio would tie the country together through national broadcasts of music, educational lectures, news reports, and discussions of serious issues, provided the medium did not fall into the hands of commercial interests. "I believe the quickest way to kill broadcasting would be to use it for direct advertising," Hoover averred in 1924. "The reader of a newspaper has an option whether he will read an ad or not, but if a speech by the president is to be used as the meat in a sandwich of two patent-medicine advertisements, there will be no radio left."

He proved wrong in a big way. Although radio was noncommercial at first—stations having been established by the Radio Corporation of America (RCA), Westinghouse, and other receiver manufacturers to give consumers a reason to buy their products—by the mid-1920s Alexander Graham Bell's already monolithic American Telephone and Telegraph Company (AT&T) had also built radio stations and, despite Hoover's admonitions, suggested "toll broadcasting," through which companies would pay for airtime on which to advertise their wares.

As of 1925 some 2.7 million American households owned at least one radio, a number that five years later climbed to 12 million. By that point a national radio network had been established by the Columbia Broadcasting System (CBS), founded in 1927, and two by the National Broadcasting Company (NBC), a subsidiary of RCA founded in 1926. In short order, radio broadcasts began to cut into moviegoing and the study habits of American teenagers as the medium began to fulfill RCA President David Sarnoff's prediction that the "radio music box" would become "a household utility."

The Merry Automobile

In 1916, 1.5 million automobiles were sold in the United States, a number that dipped during World War I but then rose to 1.9 million in 1920. By 1929 automobile sales reached 4.5 million and accounted for more than $3 billion

in sales at a time when the gross national product totaled $104.4 billion. In more concrete terms, in 1920 there were 9.2 million cars on the roads of America; by 1929 there were 23 million. In addition to its obvious effect on traffic, the automobile made the single most important impact on the U.S. economy; its manufacture employed 7.1 percent of the nation's industrial workforce and paid 8.7 percent of its wages. In addition, the production of automobiles boosted the aluminum, copper, chemical, glass, lead, leather, and petroleum industries as well as road construction and the rapid spread of service stations, outdoor advertising, and travel agencies. In retrospect, Detroit's boom seems mind-boggling. During the 1920s the nation spent approximately $1.5 billion on road construction alone, and in 1929 economist Wesley Clair Mitchell estimated that one in nine American workers was employed by the automobile industry or one directly connected to it.

Just as railroads had boosted the growth of cities in the nineteenth cen-

The automobile offered Americans freedom from train schedules and hotel costs as seen in the photograph above showing "auto-campers" in Boiling Spring camp grounds, Cleveland National Forest, California, circa 1920s. For many people, it was as if the American frontier had opened again. During the 1920s the national landscape itself began to change by catering to the new pioneers with "auto-camps," cabin colonies, drive-in restaurants, and gas stations. President Harding enjoyed automobile touring, while Henry Ford, Thomas Edison, and Harvey Firestone went on a series of well-publicized automobile tours together.

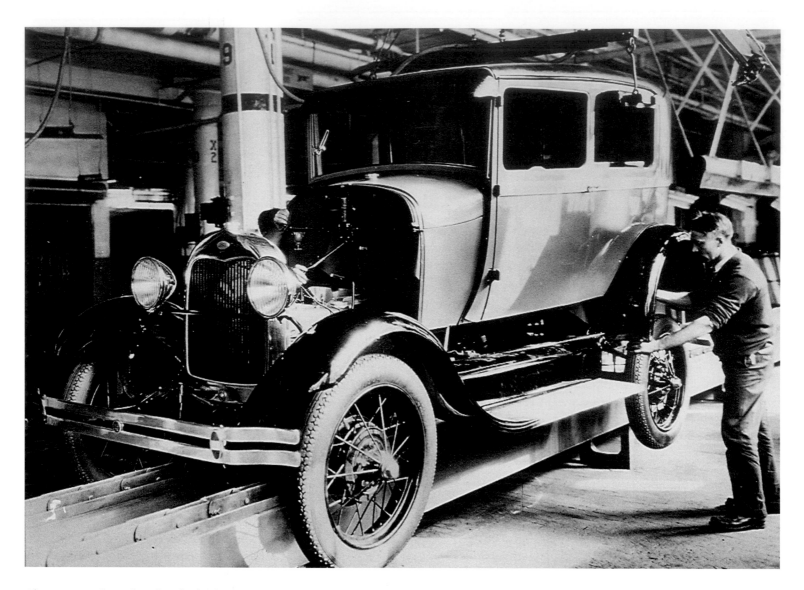

Above, a Ford worker fits the body on a Model T sedan circa 1926. The car shown is not black, as nearly all previous Model T's had been. In 1926 Henry Ford had finally allowed the use of other colors as part of a modernization scheme. To Ford, his Model T was "the perfect car," and he clung to the nineteenth-century ideal that it would therefore remain in production forever, like a pickax or some other unimprovable tool. Even as sales began a treacherous slide beginning in 1924, Ford stubbornly resisted the impetus for change. In 1927, though, he finally admitted that the Model T era was over and abruptly stopped making them.

tury by carrying raw materials into their factories and finished products out to market, in the 1920s the automobile encouraged movement away from city centers and into the new phenomenon of suburbia. Although America's great suburban exodus was still two generations off, as early as 1924 these family-friendly halfway points between city and country could be found in embryonic form around virtually every major metropolis in the United States. The advent of the automobile brought urban and rural America closer by encouraging traffic in other directions as well, giving farm folk easy access to nearby cities and everyone the means to venture far from wherever they had been born. Almost overnight everything from gasoline stations to billboards sprang up, transforming the American landscape forever. Detroit initiated the three-color traffic light in 1919 while state and federal highway departments began laying down asphalt roads at an astonishing rate. In 1926, a mild-mannered California innkeeper named Arthur Heineman opened the first motel, a term used only because he could not fit "Milestone Motor Hotel" on his welcome sign. By the decade's end the U.S. government was constructing 10,000 miles of paved highway yearly, a sign that the automobile was not a consumer product but a revolution.

The quick ubiquity of the automobile in America was owed largely to the foresight and pragmatic approach of one man: Henry Ford of Michigan, who dominated the U.S. auto industry throughout most of the 1920s. Although he unfortunately adhered to some of the nation's most vicious nativist causes, for the most part Ford was a product of Populism and a believer in the "common man" who saw the typical American as not unlike himself—a rugged individualist capable of improvising anything when the need arose and scornful of anyone who couldn't do the same.

Secure in his Midwestern understanding of the American public, Ford set out to give the public an uncomplicated and inexpensive car that would fulfill their spartan needs for transportation. The groundbreaking, mass-produced Model T that resulted had an elegant, simple, and extremely practical design: the motor was mounted for easy removal so farmers could put it to other uses, and its simple mechanisms allowed basic repairs to be performed by anyone who cared to master a few tools and principles. A relentless tinkerer with a musical ear for machines Ford began experimenting with the production methods of the Model T. His persistence paid off: in 1914 his new Detroit plant revolutionized U.S. industry by initiating the first assembly line. By 1926 Ford was making a Model T every 10 seconds. As if the moving assembly-line-manufactured Model T needed any more selling points, in 1915 Ford upped the daily minimum wage at his factory to $5 and cut the workweek from forty-eight to forty hours, which won his company a reputation as a friend of the working man while at the same time instituting measures that were good business. The high wage enabled Ford to hire the cream of the laboring class and to work them ever harder on the assembly lines that made the Model T so cheap. The Ford car that had sold for $845 when it appeared in 1908 had by 1925 changed through constant improvements on the basic design into a much better Model T that consumers could purchase—in black only—for $290, because, as Ford explained, "Every time I lower the price a dollar we gain a thousand new buyers." And so he did. More than 15 million "Tin Lizzies" were sold before the Model T was discontinued in 1927 after its popularity had plummeted with the appearance of snazzier and more technologically advanced offerings from various upstart automobile manufacturers. Detroit attracted all sorts of automakers including plumber David Buick, who began making cars, and the Dodge brothers, who specialized in parts.

The most successful of these was General Motors, whose president, Alfred Sloan, Jr., responded to the changing market with the Chevrolet, which combined updated automotive technology with more modern styling. Sloan boasted that the "Chevy" was well worth the $100 more it cost than Ford's Model T. In addition to an automatic ignition, a foot accelerator in place of Ford's hand-operated version, and a water-cooled engine that wouldn't boil over as the Tin Lizzie's radiator so often did, the Chevy came in a rainbow of colors. Henry Ford had designed the Model T for hardworking, no-nonsense Calvinists like himself, but Americans influenced by the glamorous images presented by movies and radio had grown more focused on fun and the fruits of their labor than on the labor itself. Compared with the new Chevy,

The cartoon, above, published in 1924, shows the Democratic Party trying to take advantage of the scandals of Harding's Republican presidency. The implication—that Republicans couldn't be trusted—failed to take root. The troubles in the Harding administration had never been partywide but limited to a very few scoundrels, including Attorney General Harry Daugherty, the lawyer instrumental in winning the White House for his pal Harding. Republicans rallied around Calvin Coolidge, who was nothing if not trustworthy, and retained the White House.

Two old adversaries were among those seeking the presidency in 1924: Robert M. La Follette of the Progressive Party, above, and Democrat William McAdoo, below. La Follette, a strong-minded liberal from Wisconsin, had nearly been expelled from the Senate for his opposition to Wilson's program of wartime finance. McAdoo, Wilson's Treasury Secretary, was the man directly responsible for that program. La Follette placed third in the election; McAdoo failed even to secure his party's nomination.

the Model T seemed drab and too much work to justify saving a hundred bucks, and the Ford Motor Company fell into decline as a result of its refusal to adjust to the changing desires of the American consumer.

The Republican Decade

Pretty much the same fate befell the Democratic Party midway through the 1920s. Although his administration would later be tainted by scandal, during his presidency Warren G. Harding was credited with several impressive accomplishments and overall was regarded positively. The Great War in Europe had been brought to a legal end through treaties, the anti-Communist hysteria of the immediate postwar period had faded, and Harding's new Bureau of the Budget had initiated a responsible fiscal program of tax and spending cuts and a balanced federal budget. Plus, reforms were not ignored. It was pressure from the White House, for example, that brought an end to the notorious twelve-hour workday in steel plants. Most important, the Harding administration fostered a sense of well-being across the country by emphasizing calm after two decades of social and international upheaval.

Unfortunately, Harding died from an attack of apoplexy in San Francisco on August 2, 1923, amid unfounded rumors of foul play on the part of Mrs. Harding to spare her husband the effects of expected revelations of corruption within his administration. Although there are indications that Harding had indeed uncovered some shenanigans that made him pledge to clean house just before he suddenly died, the rumors surrounding his demise remain unsubstantiated. In any case, Harding's death brought the almost comically quiet Calvin Coolidge to the White House. "Silent Cal" began his term by cooperating with Congress's investigation into the alleged Harding scandals and was relieved when the final report concluded that if there had been any corruption it was bipartisan, even if Harding's Interior Secretary, Albert Fall, did become the first cabinet member ever to be convicted of a felony, for taking bribes to extend certain private oil companies' secret leases on the government's petroleum reserves in Teapot Dome, Wyoming.

Seeing that the nation's mood was fairly content and the economy booming, it's hardly surprising that the laid-back Coolidge was content to let things go at that. This was, after all, the president upon word of whose demise a decade later poet and wit Dorothy Parker would inquire, "How can they tell?" But Coolidge was silent like a fox; as he had remarked shortly after Harding's death: "I think the American people want a solemn ass as a president. And I think I'll go along with them." For the most part he continued to pursue Harding's agenda, taking his only real interest in economy in government, which he made sure of. In 1924, the year after Coolidge entered office, annual federal expenditures amounted to $2.9 billion, and did again in 1928 when he stepped down. Similarly, where the national debt had risen above $22 billion when Coolidge took office, it had fallen below $17 billion by the time he left, and with the president's blessing Treasury Secretary Andrew Mellon pushed through tax cuts that encouraged further economic expansion. In an age of business, Coolidge ran the federal government like one, and it turned a profit every year of his presidency. It is ironic that it was the least voluble of presidents who best articulated the spirit of the nation when he told a conference of the American Society of Newspaper Editors in January 1925 that "the chief business of the American people is business."

As the 1924 campaign drew near, Coolidge remained personally popular, but his Republican Party was divided. The Senate leaders who had put Harding in the White House had been enraged by his successor's ignoring their calls for spending on pork-barrel projects. Erstwhile Progressives, meanwhile, considered Coolidge a profit-mad political troglodyte. Wisconsin Senator Robert La Follette, now sixty-nine, still headed the remains of the Progressives and served as the last symbol of Republican reformism, although he had little power within the party. As he had in 1912, La Follette challenged the sitting Republican president but was easily defeated at the convention, whereupon he formed a new Progressive Party and announced for the presidency on its platform of old-fashioned reform and isolationism, which still had considerable appeal for anti-Wilsonians and others with long memories. But the new Progressives were a movement of old people fronting an outdated candidate to lead a country that had abandoned his principles. The Socialist Party did endorse La Follette, but in 1924 its support counted for far less than it had before the war.

Although the Democrats were also divided, at least their problems were rooted in the present rather than in the past. The party was riven along the lines between the new urban America and the old rural one, a clash that manifested its depth in two major ways: Prohibition and the Ku Klux Klan.

Early in 1924 the leading candidate for the Democratic presidential nomination was William G. McAdoo, who had been Woodrow Wilson's Secretary of the Treasury as well as his son-in-law. McAdoo had some backing from labor and former Progressives but was considered friendly to business as well; he favored Prohibition, if not ardently, and as a Southerner by birth harbored despicable prejudices that earned him the support of the Ku Klux Klan as well as the unhelpful nickname "Ku Ku McAdoo." In any case his programs seemed well suited to the concerns of rural Americans, although he also had ties to urban voters. McAdoo's city connections could not compare, however, with those of reform-minded Governor Al Smith of New York, who remains best known for his quip in a campaign speech that, "No matter how thin you slice it, it's still baloney." At fifty-one, Smith was a pragmatic new breed of reformer who had no connection to either the prewar Progressives or the Wilsonian dreamers. Instead, his policies were founded in the realities of the new urban America; as governor of New York, for example, he had supported laws favoring labor unions, workers' compensation, and the extension of workplace rules to women. For all his innovations, however, Smith never had a chance to win the Democratic nomination; the sad bigotry that still plagued U.S. society prevented many voters from so much as considering casting their ballot for the first Catholic—vilified as a "rum-soaked Romanist"—ever to run for president of the United States.

Apart from Smith's attempt to break the glass ceiling of religion in U.S. politics, perhaps the most significant development to come out of the 1924

John Davis, above, was the Democratic standard-bearer in 1924, ultimately losing the election to Calvin Coolidge. Raised in West Virginia, Davis was a well-known corporation lawyer. He took an unbiased view regarding most issues, even those pertaining to his clients, and was one of the authors of the Clayton Antitrust Act of 1914. Returning to the bar after losing the election, Davis argued cases before the Supreme Court during the Truman administration.

In the 1925 photograph below, John Coolidge and his neighbors in Plymouth, Vermont, listen to his son Calvin's inaugural address on the radio. Twenty-six stations broadcast the speech, one of the first times radio was used to air a newsworthy event live. Two years earlier, Calvin had been visiting his father when they were awakened by aides who arrived in the middle of the night to inform the vice president that Warren Harding had died. The elder Coolidge, a justice of the peace, administered the oath of office and Calvin Coolidge became the thirtieth president of the United States, upon which he went back to bed.

Democratic National Convention in New York City was its national broadcast on radio, which for the first time made the entire country privy to political proceedings as they occurred. The Democrats did not disappoint their first nationwide audience: at the time would-be party nominees had to obtain two-thirds of the delegates' votes, and it soon became obvious that the convention was deadlocked. McAdoo and Smith held on through no less than 103 ballots, when the absurdity of the situation finally convinced both to agree to withdraw. The party then handed the nomination to John W. Davis, a former solicitor general and West Virginia congressman who had served as U.S. ambassador to Great Britain, with Governor Charles W. Bryan of Nebraska for vice president. Although Davis—known as the Wall Street "lawyer's lawyer," for better or worse—was capable, he clearly did not enjoy much support, and the Democrats fell into greater disarray than they had

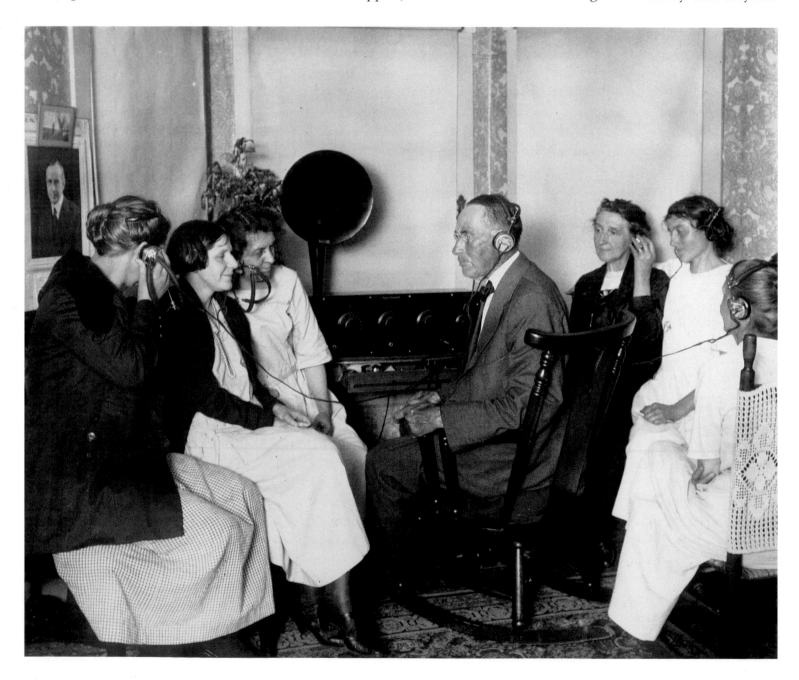

known since 1896, when their new vice presidential candidate's more talented brother William Jennings Bryan had topped the ticket. As popular comedian Will Rogers quipped, "I am a member of no organized political party: I am a Democrat."

Coolidge won easily, capturing 15.7 million popular and 382 electoral votes to Davis's 8.4 million and 136, none of the latter from any state north of Virginia or west of Texas. La Follette drew support from both major parties, racking up a popular tally of 4.8 million and the 13 electoral votes of his home state. Perhaps the most telling point of the 1924 presidential election is that a record low of only 52 percent of those eligible to vote bothered to do so, indicating an unprecedented degree of voter apathy that, sadly, has been routinely surpassed in recent elections. But there was a bright side: two women—Nellie Ross of Wyoming and Miriam Ferguson of Texas—were

Franklin Delano Roosevelt is shown with his sons, James and Elliott, set to launch a pair of model sailboats in 1920. After suffering partial paralysis from an attack of polio in August 1921, Roosevelt remained at home in Hyde Park, New York, for three years, surrounded by his family. By June of 1924, Roosevelt was ready to begin again. He made a stunning return to national politics at the Democratic convention in Baltimore, delivering a rousing speech in favor of Alfred Smith. Franklin Roosevelt showed himself and his party that he had emerged from a three-year convalescence a stronger candidate than he had been before.

At right is a mural painted in 1930–31 by Thomas Hart Benton as part of his *City Activities* series for the New School for Social Research in New York. The series represented Benton's first portrayals of modern scenes; he had long been known for his historical subjects. To Benton, the country was bursting with "energy and rush and confusion," qualities shown in the mural, with its well-muscled people and fast-moving inventions.

elected governors, a political reality undreamed of during World War I.

In 1924 politics in general was weakened by the lack of public interest, and even within the arena the Republicans were not as strong as Coolidge's victory might have indicated. This could be seen in the composition of the newly elected Sixty-ninth Congress: the Senate included 50 Republicans, 40 Democrats, and 6 La Follette Progressives, while the House of Representatives comprised 232 Republicans, 183 Democrats, and 20 Progressives. Although the Republicans remained in the majority, the legislature was no longer the party enclave it had been since the Civil War—nor was it any longer a rubber stamp for presidents of the "Grand Old Party," as Republicans had been calling themselves since the 1870s. In fact, in 1925 the Senate would twice reject Coolidge's ethically questionable choice for attorney general, and a year later would block the seating of two Republicans elected to the upper body through "campaign irregularities" in Illinois and Pennsylvania. Further evidence of Congress's independence from the White House mounted, but it didn't matter all that much seeing that the administration had no legislative agenda to push. In fact, Coolidge seemed disinclined to do much of anything but demand twelve hours of sleep a night in addition to his afternoon nap; as newspaper pundit H. L. Mencken noted: "[He] slept more than any other president, whether by day or by night. Nero fiddled, but Coolidge only snored."

Thus the next four years were quiet politically. Coolidge's younger son had died of blood poisoning during the Democratic convention, a loss the president had taken very hard. From that point on, the always retiring Coolidge was truly dispirited and indicated even less interest in governing, but he remained popular and likely could have won easy renomination and reelection in 1928 had he had any interest in a second full term.

The outcome of the 1924 presidential election suggested that what would be needed to wrest the White House from the Republicans four years later was a candidate who could unite the South and the Progressive forces. But as the nation basked in Republican-managed prosperity this hardly seemed possible, and the Democrats turned to lamenting their fate, some going so

far as to predict that their party would go the way of the antebellum Whigs and be replaced by some new political entity. Among the leading Democrats who despaired of his party's future was Franklin D. Roosevelt, who had returned to politics in 1924 after suffering a polio attack in the summer of 1921 that disabled him for life. Like many of his colleagues, Roosevelt believed the Democrats were doomed to indefinite minority status unless they could seize hold of a major crisis under a Republican administration, such as an unpopular overseas war or a major economic collapse, neither of which Roosevelt or anyone else deemed at all likely.

CHAPTER 16

THE GREAT DEPRESSION AND THE NEW DEAL

YEARS OF DUST

RESETTLEMENT ADMINISTRATION
Rescues Victims
Restores Land to Proper Use

The Great Depression of the 1930s struck America largely unaware. Hindsight, however, reveals a series of events and circumstances that make the collapse of the U.S. economy look utterly inevitable.

America's downward fiscal spiral was created by many factors, from social unrest to economic profligacy to political happenstance. The booming twenties were identified with the presidency of Calvin Coolidge, whose rejection of a second term with his surprisingly terse statement in 1927 that "I do not choose to run" seemed an omen that the halcyon era was ending. (In fact, President Coolidge's decision was determined largely by his anguish after the death of his fifteen-year-old son.) Years later Coolidge was embraced by fellow Republican Ronald Reagan as a great president for presaging the movement toward smaller government and reduced

O. Louis Guglielmi painted *Relief Blues,* left, in 1938. As an employee of the Works Project Administration, Guglielmi was familiar with government programs that tried to combat hopelessness during the 1930s. Few people remained unaffected by the Great Depression, however, and his painting shows the resignation and worry that hard times etched into the faces of one family. Ben Shahn's *Years of Dust,* above, depicted a destitute farmer on a 1936 poster for the New Deal agency that helped rural victims of disaster.

OUR NEXT PRESIDENT

HERBERT C. HOOVER

A Chicken *for* Every Pot

Wages, dividends, progress and prosperity say,

"Vote *for* Hoover"

taxes. Reagan went so far as to have Coolidge's portrait placed in the White House Cabinet Room next to Lincoln and Jefferson.

The Republicans had no trouble selecting a successor at their Kansas City convention: Herbert Hoover, the Secretary of Commerce under both Harding and Coolidge who had emerged from World War I as a hero because of his direction of humanitarian efforts to provide food and economic assistance to the war-ravaged countries of Europe, which gave him the ideal image of a fiscally conservative Republican with a compassionate concern for people. Hoover—who happened to be in England when the war broke out—spearheaded the effort to increase agricultural production and decrease the consumption of food in America so that armies and civilians overseas would not go hungry. Because of "Hooverizing," the United States was able to triple its exports of breadstuffs, meats, and sugar in 1918. When a critic had asked if he was helping Bolshevism by extending aid to famine-stricken Soviet Russia, Hoover had retorted, "Twenty million people are starving. Whatever their politics, they shall be fed!" Even Americans who had disagreed with the decision to enter the war could still applaud Hoover's work to alleviate some of the distress it had caused.

For his part, Hoover wanted to promote the American system of "rugged individualism"; after all, he was an example of it. The son of a blacksmith in Iowa, he was orphaned at nine but still managed to graduate from Stanford University as a mining engineer. By the age of forty Hoover had become the millionaire owner of one of the largest mining concerns in the world, but remained a devoted Quaker who believed in balancing his private gain with public service. The intelligent, efficient Hoover was perhaps the most admired American of his time, commonly referred to as the Great Engineer and the Great Humanitarian.

Beginning with his appointment to Harding's cabinet in 1921, Hoover had done much to turn the U.S. Department of Commerce into one of the most vigorous arms of the federal government. His goals, however, were almost anathema to true capitalism; Hoover considered competition wasteful and in many cases unnecessary, and urged businesses to cooperate with one another through industry trade associations and chambers of commerce. His idea was that cooperation would result in better products at lower prices as well as increased production that would lead to more and better jobs at higher wages. As Hoover saw it, everyone would gain from what he dubbed "the Associational Movement." As the GOP's presidential candidate in 1928, he promised a continuation of "Republican prosperity" that would lead to "a chicken for every pot and a car in every garage." "No one loved Hoover," Rexford Tugwell wrote, "but everyone—or nearly everyone—respected him. He was not a toady to business . . . he was more its best representative, its better embodiment."

The Democrats had nothing quite so appealing to offer. The party remained divided over Prohibition and the racist Ku Klux Klan. The convention chose Al Smith, the "wet" governor of New York and a Catholic from the streets of the city dominated by Tammany Hall—he was the only potential candidate with the name recognition to have even a chance of beating

Hoover. As Franklin Roosevelt, who had nominated his friend Smith, predicted to journalist Josephus Daniels before campaigning for his fellow New Yorker in the South: "I am doubtful whether any Democrat can win in 1928."

The issues seemed clear-cut. On the surface the 1928 presidential contest pitted a Protestant Republican friendly to big business against a Catholic Democrat keen on urban reform; the only commonality was that both Hoover and Smith were "new men" who eschewed the outdated ideologies of the past. Hoover's belief in active government cooperation with business seemed more appropriate to the realities of modern America than either Progressivism or Coolidge's laissez-faire approach; similarly, Smith's roots in aggressive urban reform were a far cry from Wilson's ideological Progressivism. In the end, however, the more business-oriented man won, 21.4 million popular and 444 electoral college votes to Smith's 15 million and 87. Most significant, the Republicans took five states below the Mason-Dixon Line to crack the "solid South" that had voted Democratic since Reconstruction. Apart from the Southern states that stayed in the Democratic column, Smith carried only Massachusetts and Rhode Island, losing even his home state of New York in the Republican landslide. "The plain truth is that Smith did practically nothing, except speak negatively on Prohibition, and in a somewhat amateurish way on farm relief," his erstwhile supporter Walter Lippmann complained. "His heart is all right, his character is all right, his head is all right, but his equipment is deplorable." In truth, with the average worker content and the average businessman thriving, most Americans were uninterested in change. As humorist Will Rogers quipped, "You can't lick this prosperity thing. Even the fellow who hasn't got any is all excited over the idea."

OPPOSITE PAGE: Herbert Hoover, pictured on a 1928 campaign poster, top, brought an impressive resume to his bid for the presidency. Raised in Iowa, he lived for a time in a sod house. In 1895, he graduated from Stanford University and then made his fortune as a mining engineer. At forty Hoover turned to public service, directing relief efforts in the aftermath of World War I. He was such an outstanding manager that people came to believe he could efficiently run and organize any enterprise. Succeeding through pragmatism (but ultimately limited by it), Herbert Hoover would never have made the promise on the Republican leaflet at bottom; "a chicken for every pot" just wasn't feasible. That slogan was coined by an advertising man in the Hoover camp.

The photograph at left, taken in 1924, shows three successive Democratic presidential nominees: John W. Davis (center) ran in 1924 and Alfred Smith (right) in 1928, both unsuccessfully, while Franklin D. Roosevelt (left) would run and win in 1932. In 1928 Roosevelt was still convalescing from the effects of polio when Smith asked him to run for governor of New York to bolster the national ticket there. At first Roosevelt protested that he was not well enough, yet he ultimately waged a victorious campaign that redefined him as a politician. "He listened," wrote Frances Perkins, who worked on the campaign, "and out of it learned what he later held with such conviction as a basis of action—that 'everybody wants to have the sense of belonging, of being on the inside,' that 'no one wants to be left out,' as he put it years later."

Hooverism

President Hoover was well aware of the nation's economic problems and quickly called a special session of Congress to deal with them. The first area tackled was agriculture, which had been ailing since the end of World War I. Among earlier efforts to do something about the farm situation was the McNary-Haugen Act, which Coolidge had vetoed after Congress passed it in both 1927 and 1928. The act would have established domestic prices for farm products at "parity" with the prices for all goods from 1910 to 1916, which had been bumper years for U.S. farmers; when prices fell below that level, the government would purchase the crops and sell them on the world market for whatever they would bring. But like his predecessor, Hoover opposed this approach as unwarranted government interference in the private sector. As he had said during the campaign: "My fundamental concept of agriculture is one controlled by its own members, organized to fight its own economic battles and to determine its own destinies." By this Hoover meant the creation of farmers' cooperatives and a federal farm credit system. He thus called for Congress to pass the Agricultural Marketing Act to establish a Federal Farm Board tasked with helping farmers market their products. The plan was for regional cooperatives organized among and controlled by farmers to purchase surplus crops from individuals and store them until prices rose, when they could be sold at a reasonable profit; the purchases would be financed by the Farm Board, which would control a revolving $500-million fund from which to make loans.

Agricultural price supports were only one of the contentious economic issues of the early Hoover administration. The tariff posed another problem: Democrats traditionally had favored low rates and Republicans higher ones. The GOP Congress had passed the Fordney-McCumber Tariff of 1922, which raised rates sharply. The higher tariff made it feasible for the United States to export more than it imported, and between 1922 and the end of the decade exports would rise by 26 percent while imports would increase by only 16 percent; in 1929 imports amounted to some $4.4 billion, while U.S. exports reached a record of $5.2 billion. The difference was made up in loans: foreign countries sold record amounts of bonds in New York, then used the revenues to finance their trade deficits with the United States.

Decline Sets In

The U.S. economy began to slow down late in 1928 and into 1929, most noticeably in the automobile and construction industries. Steel mills also reported lower orders, and many started cutting back on overtime while some were even obliged to lay off workers. Few panicked, however, thinking the downturn temporary, perhaps the result of seasonal trends or other transitory factors; a shutdown at the Ford Motor Company in Michigan, for example, was arguably due to the switch in production from the Model T to the Model A.

At the time, no one realized that America was heading into the worst eco-

nomic depression in its history, but today the gradual descent seems glaringly obvious. The great stock market crash of October 29, 1929—"black Tuesday"—was the worst sell-off of shares since 1907. It put an end to what had been a decade-long rise in stock values. But the market's downturn didn't last; after the first jitters, few investors took the crash as a sign that the good times were over, and stock prices recovered some ground throughout November and December. In fact, by Christmas the financial markets were no longer front-page news. Department store sales were good, and as analysts optimistically observed, unlike in previous panics not a single major bank had failed in October 1929. Americans' unawareness of what was about to befall them was clear on New Year's Day 1930, when the *New York Times* selected Admiral Richard Byrd's flight over the South Pole as the biggest news story of 1929, followed by the St. Valentine's Day massacre, in which Al Capone's alleged orders to execute six rival Chicago gangsters had been carried out, with the stock market crash coming in third. As historian Samuel

On October 29, 1929, America's financial markets plummeted. The photograph shows the scene on Wall Street that day as thousands of investors rushed to brokerages for news. Even though business leaders tried to prop up prices, the market sagged to yet a new low in November. Inevitably, the crash began to affect more Americans than the nation's two million stock investors. During the ten days leading up to Christmas 1929, one million Americans were told they had lost their jobs; by the second day of the New Year the figure had climbed to four million.

Eliot Morison later observed: "Economic analysis, a science then in its infancy, failed to discern the serious faults in American and European economics and their increasing vulnerability to shock."

The stock market crash of 1929 burst the bubble of uncontrolled speculation and business expansion. There were many causes for this economic precariousness, among them the loose regulation of the U.S. banking system. Another factor often cited is the dramatic upturn in consumer credit spending. Prior to World War I most goods had been purchased with cash; even homes were financed with modest mortgages. But beginning around 1923 the concept of "buy now, pay later" became popular as the advertising industry whetted appetites for products of every description. Easy credit convinced the middle class that there was no reason to defer the good life, or at least occasional instant gratification: by 1927 more than 85 percent of the furniture, 80 percent of the phonographs, 75 percent of the washing machines, 70 percent of the new and used cars, and more than half of the radios, pianos, sewing machines, vacuum cleaners, and refrigerators sold in America were purchased through payment plans.

Consumers made up for the difference between their wages and the costs of what they wanted to buy by borrowing against their future earnings. As long as prosperity continued, most of this installment debt could be met—but a wavering economy could bring it all crashing down. Yet times had been so good for so long that people had begun to get used to spending on credit; after all, from 1921 to 1928 the economy had enjoyed a generally upward spiral of increased production that created more jobs, which meant more wages that could be spent on more purchases, sending the spiral upward again. Once the direction reversed, factories' output would be reduced, meaning fewer jobs and thus fewer consumers able to make purchases,

The cartoon at right lampooned Herbert Hoover's attitude toward the farmers' losing battle against the Depression, showing the president relying on a scarecrow to spook the hard times away. When crop prices kept falling ever drastically, farm families by the thousands were ruined: it was a dire crisis when the price of a bushel of wheat fell to $1.01 in 1930, yet the same bushel was selling for only 33 cents two years later. In response, Hoover advised farmers to reduce their yields by about one quarter. When Kansas farmers tried to tell the chairman of Hoover's Farm Board that they couldn't do it without government help, he retorted, "I don't care what you do."

which would send the spiral spinning down to more cutbacks in production and employment. In addition, the prosperity of the 1920s had overlooked a large part of the country. More than half of all American families at the end of the decade were living on the edge of the subsistence level and could not afford the consumer goods factories were churning out. Their absence from the consumer credit revolution created a major imbalance between supply and demand that took another toll on the economy.

Financial troubles had begun to crop up overseas as well. After World War I Germany had been forced to pay large reparations to the Allies, some of which had been obtained from banks and other sources in the United States. The Germans paid the reparations out of these funds, which the Allies then used to repay loans made to them during the war. Once the economic situation in the United States forced Americans to stop lending to the Germans, the vanquished nation appealed for relief from its reparations payments—which if granted could have prevented the Allied debtors from servicing their own loans from U.S. sources.

At first both President Hoover and most of the country thought any major economic downturn would follow the pattern of those of the past, purging marginal businesses followed by reorganization and recovery. The president saw no need for government intervention in the economy, just as his predecessors had rejected it on similar occasions. He was pleased to follow Democrat Grover Cleveland's observation during the economic decline of 1893: "It is the business of the people to support the government, but it is not the business of the government to support the people." He listened to Secretary of the Treasury Andrew Mellon, who advocated a "do nothing" approach to economic lows.

Hoover did, however, recognize that some steps might be prudent, and called conferences of business and labor leaders at which he got both to pledge to maintain production and employment levels. In 1930 the president also signed the Smoot-Hawley Tariff, setting the highest rates on imports in U.S. history, in the belief the measure would insulate the country from foreign competition. Leading economists of the time warned that the action would instead invite retaliation from other governments. They were right. Within a year nearly all the countries with which the United States conducted important trade had raised their tariffs, dealing a blow to America's export industry that deepened the growing depression.

True to his classic Republican belief in nonintervention in the private sector, Hoover advocated nongovernmental relief efforts, but they proved inadequate. As more and more Americans were laid off from their jobs, the same man who had been credited with saving millions of lives through the relief programs he directed during and after World War I was now called heartless, seemingly unmoved by the sight of people starving in the streets. Hoover always asserted that he took his hands-off approach to protect American democracy, arguing that direct federal aid would have turned its citizens into government dependents who would take to electing whatever demagogue promised the best bread and circuses (as the Roman writer Juvenal had in his *Satires* in the first century). At one point Hoover complained to his pre-

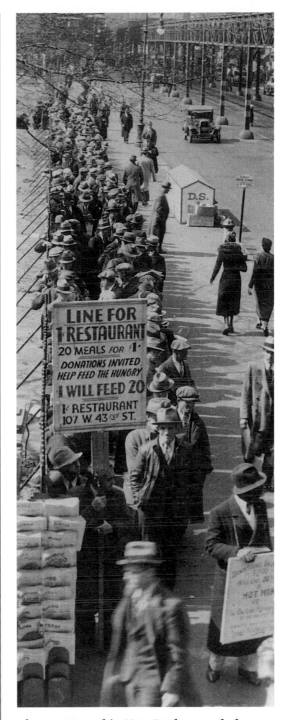

Above, a crowd in New York overwhelms a restaurateur's promise to feed twenty hungry people. During the Depression men of all professions joined the ranks of the homeless as they took to the road in search of work, usually after placing their families with relatives. In one case among many, a respected civil engineer was reduced to living in a vacant lot in Brooklyn, where the neighborhood children brought him table scraps. He was eventually arrested for vagrancy.

decessor that his work toward economic recovery seemed to be getting nowhere and that his critics were becoming increasingly vocal. "You can't expect to see calves running in the field the day after you put the bull to the cows," Coolidge reassured him. "No, but I would at least expect to see contented cows," Hoover sighed.

There were some signs of improvement in 1931, but hopes for a quick recovery were dashed in May when Austria's largest bank collapsed, sending ripples across the economies of Europe. A reflection of Europe's growing financial anxiety could be seen in the German election of September 1930: the Nazi Party received eight times the number of votes it had two years earlier. Most European nations were unable to meet the payments on their debts to the United States, whether for reparations or past-due war expenses. The defaults helped cause American banks to fail at a rate that went from 499 in 1928 to 659 in 1929 to 1,352 in 1930 and to 2,294 in 1931. The U.S. banking system was close to paralysis. The Federal Reserve System was little help; half of the United States' 25,000 banks did not even participate, and the Fed exerted only weak control even over its members.

The president now resorted to the claim that America had been just about to emerge from its depression when the troubles hit from abroad. It was the new international aspect of the financial crisis that called for new policies, Hoover argued, and on June 20 he recommended a moratorium on debt and reparations payments to help Austria and Germany avoid complete collapse. The move was instituted but failed; however, the president also had asked Congress for new means to combat the depression at home. With nearly two million men roaming the United States looking for jobs or handouts, *something* had to be done. In December Hoover initiated policies to help large banks organize the National Credit Corporation, designed to aid smaller financial institutions in danger of failure. When this proved inadequate, Hoover sent Congress a bill to create the Reconstruction Finance Corporation (RFC)—which was chartered in January 1932 with initial capitalization of $500 million and the authority to raise another $2 billion through bond sales—to lend money to railroads, banks, agricultural agencies, industry, and commerce. By the end of 1933 the RFC had aided more than 7,400 companies, mostly banks and railroads, with $1.8 billion in loans.

Although its advocates considered the RFC a creative attempt at cooperation between government and business, critics called it a "millionaires' dole" because it extended credit only to those financial institutions that could put up sufficient collateral. The agency's usefulness was further restricted in that it had no authority to purchase stock, which is what the truly troubled institutions needed most. All the RFC could do was hand out loans that only added to the debt crisis. No president to that point had gone further in using government to respond to an economic crisis, but in the end Hoover's efforts proved inadequate to the task. In a more or less laissez-faire capitalist economy, it would take more than mild government intervention to set things right.

And things had gone more than a little wrong. The happily consumer-oriented Middletowns, U.S.A., the Lynds had described just a few short years

ago had been transformed into dismal "Hoovervilles," as the grim shanty-towns that sprang up out of old crates and cartons came to be called somewhat less than good-humoredly. Hunger was rampant, and utter desperation permeated every aspect of American life. It is fitting that the Great Depression is still remembered through tattered, sepia-toned photographs of hollow-eyed boys in knickers and caps selling apples on street corners. Scapegoating was widepread as citizens wondered who was responsible for the greed and folly that caused the collapse of the stock market. It was a time of muted pleasures that led to depression in every sense; many formerly middle-class families from the cities to the countryside fell on hard times and everyone knew at least one friend or relative whose fortunes had fallen into hunger and homelessness. The black population was hit the hardest, as African-Americans who migrated from impoverished rural areas in the South

With no money for rent and nowhere to go for help, many unemployed people had to set up housing in the open, as in the New York City scene above. Because such camps bore testimony to the crisis long before the president would admit its existence, they were known bitterly as "Hoovervilles."

The so-called Bonus Expeditionary Force, made up of 15,000 World War I veterans left destitute by the Depression, camp out on lawn of the U.S. capitol on July 13, 1932. Gathering in Washington that summer, they set up temporary dwellings and begged their government for immediate payment of bonuses for service overseas. Hoover called out riot troops led by Chief of Staff Douglas MacArthur. Most Americans were sickened to see the army pitted so angrily against its own tattered veterans.

to cities in the North found no more opportunities there. "Everybody in America was looking for work," poet Langston Hughes recalled, "everybody moving from one place to another in search of a job." Not only did these migratory blacks for the most part fail to find jobs in the so-called Promised Land, they also faced virulent racism for even trying to "take" scarce employment away from whites. This new racial hatred spilled over in 1931 in the controversial Scottsboro case, in which nine black youths were convicted on questionable evidence of raping two white women on a freight train in Alabama. Four years later, the Supreme Court ruled that the exclusion of blacks from Alabama juries had denied the Scottsboro defendants due process of law, but at the time of the official trial, the case pointed up the viciousness of America's new racism. Blacks were not the only targets; Mexican and Native Americans also were persecuted for attempting to take scarce U.S. jobs; not surprisingly, women of all races saw their professional opportunities disappear as well.

The Great Depression's dramatic effects on American culture went far and deep. Nobel Prize–winning novelist William Faulkner published four of his best books in the 1930s, including *Light in August* (1932) and *Absalom, Absalom!* (1936), in the process creating a mythical Mississippi county, Yoknapatawpha, in which his main characters grapple with everything from race relations to economic disparity. It was all dust, no rain all across the Great Plains. A single dust storm on May 11, 1934 blew away 300 million tons of top soil, the equivalent of tossing 3,000 hundred-acre farms in the air. The Dust Bowl caused a mass migration of farm families to California's San Joaquin Valley, where 350,000 people searched for seasonal jobs at cattle ranches and citrus orchards. But perhaps these troubled times were best expressed in John Steinbeck's 1939 masterpiece *The Grapes of Wrath*, the grim yet oddly hopeful tale of the hardbitten Joad family's trek through the Dust Bowl from Oklahoma to California down Route 66—the famed "road of flight"—in search of jobs to feed themselves and their children. As Steinbeck realistically portrayed the Joad family's misfortunes, he also painted unforgettable portraits of American endurance. A devastating drought had ravaged the entire Midwest and South from Virginia to Oklahoma in the 1930s, ruining corn and hay crops and leaving no feed for cattle that died from eating dust-covered grass. It was the worst of times in the Shenandoah Valley, an old man told literary critic Malcolm Cowley, "since Sheridan laid waste" during the Civil War. Regardless of hard times, Ma Joad exhibited a bedrock true grit in the face of economic calamity: "We ain't gonna die out. People is goin' on—a changin' a little maybe, but goin' right on." As is so often the case with the hardest times in history, the period produced a wealth of great literature as well as the golden ages of both radio and the movies, which afforded suffering Americans a few escapist diversions they so desperately needed. Folk singer Woody Guthrie, in particular, wrote and performed hundreds of classic Dust Bowl ballads about impoverished Okies struggling with dispossession, underdogs who ended up building the Booneville Dam and laying out the Lincoln Highway. Guthrie—on whose guitar was painted the slogan "This Machine Kills Fascists"—like many others found a different sort of diversion in left-wing politics and the American Communist Party, the result of opposition to Hooverism or capitalism.

That opposition was growing. Demonstrating an inflexibility that was taken as an even greater dearth of compassion, the president opposed a plan to pay a cash bonus to World War I veterans that had first been passed by Congress in 1924—a move that in 1932 would have been smart not only politically but economically, introducing $2.4 billion into circulation that would have helped reverse the growing deflation. But Hoover continued to play the issue exactly wrong; when approximately 17,000 unemployed veterans organized a "Bonus Expeditionary Force" and marched on Washington in the summer of 1932, Hoover called out the army to scatter the peaceful marchers and the shantytown they had built in the shadow of the Capitol. The bonus marchers refused to move from their ragged camp along the Anacostia River, taunting the administration with chants like "Mellon pulled the whistle/Hoover rang the bell/Wall Street gave the signal/And the country went to hell." Soldiers commanded by General Douglas MacArthur and aided by officers Dwight D. Eisenhower and George S. Patton, Jr., descended upon the camp and burned it down, in the process killing an eleven-week-old baby with tear gas. Talk of revolution was in the air. MacArthur tried to excuse his actions by arguing that the bonus army was nothing but a bunch of Communists and criminals despite the evidence to the contrary. In any case the callousness of the government's action sounded the death knell for Hoover's already diminished political standing. As Franklin Roosevelt read about the bonus marcher beatings in the *New York Times* he realized that the "wonder" of Hoover was over, that the "engineer president" was now perceived as weak, inept, and doomed. Like his hero Thomas Jefferson, FDR was now ready to bring the country back in line with the principles of the average American.

A New Roosevelt

The 1932 presidential campaign took place in an atmosphere of national apprehension. Americans were looking for a bold leader to extract them from economic misery. There were those who warned it might be the last election held under the Constitution, that whoever became president in 1933 would have to lead or put down a revolution. That is exactly what happened, of course, but without the sinister cast the Cassandras had predicted.

The cartoon below shows the Republican Party as a large but tired man exhorting Herbert Hoover to "tear into" the 1932 campaign. If the party gave Hoover any push at all, though, it was in the wrong direction; even as America grew desperate in the face of the Depression, the Republican Convention concerned itself almost exclusively with a debate over Prohibition.

ROOSEVELT AND GARNER

The bumper plate above indicates the 1932 Democratic ticket's promise to repeal Prohibition. President Hoover, the Republican candidate, continued to support the ban on liquor despite his habit of stopping by the Belgian Embassy at cocktail time. (Embassies were officially considered foreign property, so alcohol was legal on their premises.) After the election and even before Franklin Roosevelt was inaugurated, Congress began the process of repeal, both houses casting votes in mid-February 1933. By December 5, the necessary number of states had ratified the Twenty-first Amendment canceling the Eighteenth Amendment; after that, Americans could have a drink even without access to foreign embassies.

The Republicans convened in Chicago to renominate Herbert Hoover despite his obviously slim chances of reelection. With no other ideas to turn to, the party's platform endorsed the Hoover record, claimed credit for solving the economic dislocation of 1929, and blamed current circumstances on troubles abroad. It was clear, however, that the American system was in desperate need of revamping and that Hoover was not up to the task. There was little enthusiasm even among Republicans for either the party's platform or its candidate.

The mood at the Democratic convention was strikingly different, and for good reason: party leaders knew that whomever they nominated would likely be elected, so there was no lack of candidates. Better still, the front-runner was Governor Franklin Delano Roosevelt of New York, who among other virtues boasted a magic name that evoked the memory of the revered Theodore Roosevelt, even if they did belong to different parties. Only the polio attack he had suffered in 1921 had kept the younger scion of the family from rising in politics faster; even so, the badly crippled Franklin Roosevelt had stayed out of public life only until 1924, when he delivered the speech nominating Al Smith—fruitlessly—at that year's Democratic convention. Four years later he won the governorship of New York by a narrow margin even as Smith was losing another attempt at the White House.

The patrician Franklin Delano Roosevelt was in some ways an odd choice for the man to solve the problems of poor Americans, as he had no knowledge of poverty himself. He came from a wealthy family and had the pedigree and jaunty habits of his blue-blooded class, including diplomas from Groton, Harvard, and Columbia Law School and membership in all the right establishment organizations. Yet with a ubiquitous cigarette holder thrust up from his grinning jaw, "FDR"—despite his physical handicap, which the press cooperated in keeping secret from the public—was as dynamic and vigorous as his adored cousin had been, which appealed to people of all socioeconomic classes. "If you've spent two years in bed trying to wiggle your big toe," FDR noted, "everything else seems easy." As he said in a campaign speech in Atlanta in May 1932, "These unhappy times call for the building of plans . . . that build from the bottom up and not from the top down, that put their faith once more in the forgotten man at the bottom of the economic pyramid."

Roosevelt won the Democratic presidential nomination easily after striking a deal with the forces of powerful Speaker of the House John Nance Garner of Texas, who was rewarded with the vice presidential nod. ("Cactus Jack" Garner later described the post as "not worth a bucket of warm spit.") Roosevelt broke tradition by flying to Chicago to accept the nomination in person, the first candidate of any party to do so. He electrified the convention with a speech asking America to show its compassion by providing a "more equitable opportunity to share in the distribution of national wealth." The Democrats, he exhorted, should make themselves into the "party of liberal thought, of planned action, of enlightened international outlook," and brought the delegates to their feet by concluding: "I pledge you—I pledge myself—to a New Deal for the American people." It sounded so good it didn't matter that it wasn't clear what Roosevelt meant. "Big business" interpreted the slogan as a direct attack on "capitalism," an ugly echo of William Jennings Bryan in 1896. A nervous Henry Ford went so far as to post notices all around his factories reading: "To prevent times from getting worse and to help them get better, President Hoover must be elected."

Some of the day's leading intellectuals were equally suspicious of FDR and migrated to Communist Party candidate William Z. Foster as the only true alternative to Hoover. One Communist petition proclaimed that Foster offered "a practical and realizable ideal, as is being practiced in the Soviet Union"; among those who signed it were such notable thinkers and writers as John Dos Passos, Theodore Dreiser, Sidney Hook, Lincoln Steffens, and Edmund Wilson. Slightly less radical intellectuals such as philosopher John Dewey, lawyer Morris Ernst, and theologian Reinhold Niebuhr supported Socialist candidate Norman Thomas in similar fear that Roosevelt would prove yet another tool of the capitalist "interests."

The intellectuals were ignored. The nation rejected the radical third parties and gave Roosevelt a smashing victory in which he captured all but six states to receive 472 electoral college votes to Hoover's 59. More significant, Roosevelt's 22.8 million popular votes beat Smith's 1928 tally by almost 8 million, while Hoover's total of 15.8 million popular votes represented a loss of 5.6 million from his count four years earlier. It was one of the most dramatic shifts in voting behavior in American history, although it had been foreshadowed by Smith's results the last time out. Although Socialist Thomas's 882,000 votes more than tripled his 1928 total, the tally was far below expectations given his vocal support and the economic crisis. Similarly, the Communists' Foster gained only 103,000 votes, proving that even at the depths of the worst depression in their nation's history Americans were not about to go in for drastic solutions. "America hasn't been as happy in three years as they are today," Will Rogers wrote in a column the day FDR took the oath of office. "The whole country is with him."

The Beginning of the New Deal

The U.S. banking system continued to crumble in the final days of the Hoover administration along with just about all the other indicators of the nation's economic strength. "We are at the end of our string," conceded the outgoing president as he prepared to leave the White House. He made a plea to Roosevelt before his successor's inauguration not to tinker with the currency, borrow heavily, or unbalance the budget.

But Franklin Delano Roosevelt had his own ideas. He stirred the rain-soaked audience at his first inaugural address on March 4, 1933 with a ringing declaration: "Let me assert my firm belief that the only thing we have to fear is fear itself—nameless, unreasoning, unjustified terror which paralyzes needed efforts to convert retreat into advance." He went on to declare that the old Republican regime was no more, that "the money-changers have fled

Peter Arno's cover for *The New Yorker* magazine, above, shows Franklin Roosevelt riding to his 1933 inauguration in the company of a dour Herbert Hoover. The polarity in the depiction was not exaggerated. To Hoover, Roosevelt was a "chameleon on plaid," trying to please everyone. To Roosevelt, President Hoover was a "solemn defeatist."

Above, Franklin Delano Roosevelt at his first inauguration, March 4, 1933. Roosevelt's speech was not a typical inaugural address, but a rallying cry in the midst of an economic emergency he compared in its urgency to an enemy invasion.

from their high seats in the temple of our civilization. We may now restore that temple to the ancient truths." Then the new president announced that he would call a special session of Congress to consider ways to end America's economic crisis. And should Congress fail to respond with the sort of legislation he had in mind, Roosevelt indicated with more prescience than he knew that a new approach might be in order: "I shall ask Congress for the one remaining instrument to meet the crisis—broad executive power to wage a war against the emergency as great as the power that would be given me if we were in fact invaded by a foreign foe."

FDR concluded his inaugural address with the reassurance that "We do not distrust the future of essential democracy. . . . The people of the United

States have not failed. In their need they have registered a mandate that they want direct, vigorous action." Franklin Delano Roosevelt offered just that. In his very first speech as president he gave substance to the New Deal, the collective term for the experiments his administration designed to prove that neither American democracy nor its brand of capitalism was obsolete. "We were all ideologists in those days," Malcolm Cowley wrote in his memoirs, "from Hoover on the right to the Trotskyites on the far left—all except Roosevelt, who was the only convinced and happy experimentalist." Modeling the semantics of his New Deal on Theodore Roosevelt's Square Deal and Woodrow Wilson's New Freedom, FDR proved a genius at bolstering the sagging confidence of the American people. He embraced the new science of public relations, holding an unprecedented number of press conferences, hiring the first presidential press secretary, and broadcasting his compassion for the country's suffering to every living room radio through his "fireside chats," which did much to ease the despair of the American people.

Overwhelmed by the force of presidential personality and popularity, the U.S. Congress passed Roosevelt's New Deal legislation, including measures designed to meet the immediate crisis, without much debate in the "first hundred days" of the new Democratic administration. On his first day as president, FDR ordered a national "bank holiday" and proposed the Emergency Banking Relief Act, which Congress passed overnight. The act did not nationalize the banks but rather gave them federal assistance to reopen if they proved strong enough after federal examination and certification and, if not, handed then over to federal "conservators" who would help them regain solvency. Roosevelt understood the importance of taking quick action to end the public panic. He also knew that his early moves were mere Band-Aids intended to stanch the economic bleeding until more comprehensive programs could be devised.

Roosevelt's New Deal programs were most remarkable for their number and their commitment to making the government an active instrument in ensuring social justice. The new president asked Congress to pass the Economy Act, which reduced federal salaries by as much as 15 percent and together with other cost-cutting measures carved some $243 million from the federal budget. Other proposals enacted programs that had been discussed a decade earlier. The Agricultural Adjustment Act of 1933, for example, was passed after a brief but bitter debate and established an Agricultural Adjustment Administration (AAA) to oversee a major farm-subsidy program under the parity principles of the 1927 McNary-Haugen bill. Under the AAA, farmers would be compensated for limiting their own production out of revenues from taxes on businesses that processed farm products for sale. But by the time the AAA began operating another bumper crop was sprouting, so the administration reluctantly ordered the destruction of some growing crops and the slaughter of some livestock to reduce surpluses. Given the number of Americans who were going hungry, this naturally sparked an angry response, some calling Agriculture Secretary Henry A. Wallace the "assassin of little pigs." Nevertheless, the AAA did succeed in boosting prices to the point that gross farm income increased by half in the first three years of the New Deal. Similarly, the

Pomo Chief Little John displayed his commitment to the NRA in the company of his great-great-grandson, Little Eagle Feather, in the photograph below left. After the NRA was declared unconstitutional in 1935, Roosevelt said privately, "We have got the best out of it anyhow. Industry got a shot in the arm. Everything has started up." Albert Bender created the poster below right, "CCC: A Young Man's Opportunity for Work, Play, Study, and Health," in 1935. The Civilian Conservation Corps (CCC), among the first of Roosevelt's New Deal programs, was enacted March 31, 1933, and lasted until World War II. Roosevelt established the CCC to give men aged eighteen to twenty-five a constructive form of work relief. The CCC became a symbol of a nation putting its resources to work again.

Farm Credit Administration succeeded in refinancing and thus keeping afloat about a fifth of all U.S. farm mortgages.

In addition Roosevelt pushed through legislation to create the Civilian Conservation Corps, designed to provide employment for young men in the national forests and on federal road construction and conservation projects. CCC Forestry Camps under the direction of the Departments of Agriculture and the Interior were established—1,300 by mid-June—to provide jobs, improve the nation's forests, and prevent soil erosion. The CCC camps were run by the U.S. Army, which imposed strict discipline on the recruits: men between the ages of eighteen and twenty-five who were single, unemployed, healthy, and without other resources. The CCC hired "local experienced men," many of whom were unemployed foresters and builders from the communities where the camps were located, to train and supervise the workers. "CCC boys," as they were called, received $30 per month plus room, board, and health care—leaving as much as $25 to be sent home to help support their impoverished families. Working with axes, two-man saws, shovels, pickaxes, and other hand tools, the CCC boys planted grass and trees, fought forest fires, cut hiking trails, dug canals, worked on projects to control erosion, and built structures from bridges to swimming pools. At its zenith in September 1935, the CCC had 502,000 men enrolled in 2,514 work camps. In the nine years of its existence, the CCC helped 2.9 million men learn about conservation firsthand.

Another innovation, the Federal Emergency Relief Administration (FERA), distributed $500 million to the states for relief efforts. Under the leadership of former social worker Harry Hopkins, the FERA encouraged states and localities to provide work to the unemployed. With similar goals the Home Owner Refinancing Act created the new Federal Housing Administration authorized to disburse $2.2 billion in capital to finance home mortgages and stave off foreclosures through the federal Home Owners' Loan Corporation. Also to help the small depositor, the Glass-Steagall Banking Act of 1933 separated commercial and investment banking from the personal variety and protected the latter by establishing the Federal Deposit Insurance Corporation, which guaranteed individuals' deposits under $5,000. Aimed further up the financial hierarchy was the Federal Securities Act requiring full disclosure from anyone who sold them; the following year the Securities Exchange Act created the Securities and Exchange Commission to monitor activities on Wall Street.

The most dramatic of the early New Deal programs, however, were the National Industrial Recovery Act and the Tennessee Valley Authority Act, which put the federal government directly into the workings of the U.S. economy to the point that in some areas it became the dominant factor. The National Recovery Administration (NRA) brought labor and management together to come up with regulatory codes that would obviate antitrust laws in the closest cooperative effort among government, labor, and management the nation had ever seen in peacetime. Eventually, some 2.3 million firms employing more than 22 million workers would operate under one or more of the 500-odd codes the NRA formulated. The agency also established the Public Works Administration, which provided employment on federally funded good works—but not enough to satisfy the president, who in time superseded it with the Civil Works Administration, which had only slightly more success. Overall, despite its sterling intentions the NRA had mixed results: its codes overlapped and were often confusing even if their formulation did convince the public that action was being taken. But the NRA's efforts grew into a bureaucratic nightmare, while the everyday annoyances of enforcing the codes angered business executives.

Other New Deal projects would prove more lasting, such as the Tennessee Valley Authority (TVA) established in May 1933. Designed as a model for regional development, the TVA program was intended to eradicate poverty from the Tennessee Valley through the development of cheap elec-

The cartoon above shows the resounding "OK" voters gave Franklin Roosevelt's New Deal programs in 1934. The *New York Times* called the midterm elections "the most overwhelming victory in the history of American politics." The newspaper summarized the mood of the nation in assessing one of the many anti-New Deal politicians defeated that year, a senator from Missouri: "It is pretty difficult to arouse much antagonism against an administration which has directly or indirectly assisted more than 500,000 persons in Missouri in the last eighteen months." The local politician swept into office to replace that senator was Harry Truman, who would be Roosevelt's vice president in 1945.

tricity. The effort was nothing if not grandiose, calling for the hiring of 40,000 workers to construct a series of dams to provide hydroelectric power to the region along with flood-control stations, fertilizer plants, and other projects geared to bringing prosperity to the area. Set up as a multipurpose public corporation, by 1936 the TVA had six dams either finished or under construction and plans for another nine on the Tennessee River to create the "Great Lakes of the South." The agency also spurred soil and forestry conservation efforts, developed new fertilizers, opened rivers to navigation, and attracted new industry, all the while sending cheap power coursing through the formerly rural valley.

Roosevelt's Second Hundred Days

In January 1935 the president informed Congress that all the initial New Deal relief programs would be ended on the grounds that "We must preserve not only the bodies of the unemployed from destitution but their self-respect, their self-reliance and courage and determination." Toward this end he recommended replacing the earlier programs with the Works Progress Administration (WPA), which would become perhaps the most enduring symbol of the New Deal.

Soon to take a place as one of FDR's most trusted advisers, Harry Hopkins was called over from the FERA to direct the vast program that in its first two years alone would oversee the construction of 36,000 miles of rural roads, 5,800 traveling libraries, 3,300 dams, 1,654 medical and dental clinics, 1,634 school buildings, and 105 airport landing fields—as well as 3,000 tennis courts and 103 golf courses that at the time did not seem so outlandish. Before long most of the nation's post offices would boast murals painted by WPA artists like Willem de Kooning, Jackson Pollack, and Thomas Hart Benton. The WPA also paid out-of-work writers including Saul Bellow, John Cheever, and Ralph Ellison to pen travel books covering each state and financed the Federal Theater Project, which put on some 1,500 productions with such talented actors as Burt Lancaster and Burgess Meredith in lead roles. The WPA was the broadest-ranging government works project in history, and critics were not far wrong when they argued that it was fraught with waste even if under it the relief rolls did decline such that by 1937 fewer than 4.5 million American families were receiving benefits under state and local programs.

To many political observers, Roosevelt's enthusiasm for programs such as the WPA indicated his adherence to the beliefs of English economist John Maynard Keynes, who had argued in 1930 that when the public stops making purchases for economic or psychological reasons the government must step in and spend money to "prime the pump." Although to Keynesians it appeared that this is what Roosevelt was doing through the WPA and similar agencies, such was not actually the case; in fact, FDR's economic ideas were rather conventional, and among the chief goals of his first term was ultimately to balance the federal budget. That his administration continued spending heavily on programs for a time indicated only that Roosevelt meant to use fiscal policy to alleviate suffering, not to end the Depression outright.

Deficit spending by the government to "prime the pump" of the economy was advocated by John Maynard Keynes, below, the most influential economic theorist of the post-World War I era. Formerly a proponent of laissez-faire economic policies, Keynes, an Englishman, gave top priority to full employment after 1929.

The WPA was followed by the National Labor Relations Act of 1935. At first FDR opposed the measure, claiming that its guarantees of union rights in collective bargaining would benefit one economic interest at the expense of another. In addition, the act would establish a National Labor Relations Board (NLRB) to supervise workers' dealings with management nationwide, which inspired fear even among some administration leaders that such a body would turn into an overseer for the entire U.S. economy. But the National Labor Relations Act proved popular among the labor rank and file, and soon after its introduction in Congress the president gave the bill his support.

The Revival of Organized Labor

The labor movement had for the most part been moribund throughout the 1920s due to indifferent leadership and the generally conservative tone of the nation. Although in 1929 the American Federation of Labor had more members—2.8 million—than before World War I, they represented a smaller percentage of the industrial labor force as AFL membership dropped throughout the Depression, bottoming out at 2.3 million in 1933 with another 650,000 workers in unaffiliated local unions. By the mid-1930s this would change radically, as unions began to grow ever more powerful—and militant.

As a result of pressure from a handful of reform-minded congressmen,

Above, artist Alfred Castagne sketches a construction site sponsored by the Works Progress Administration (WPA) in 1939. The WPA found useful employment for up to 3.3 million people a year, paying them the going rates for the work they were trained to do. Funding projects for everyone from professionals to unskilled laborers, the WPA maintained both the stability of the workforce and the dignity of the individual. Its primary purpose, however, was to dispense paychecks. When a politician tried to debate the long-term effects of government-sponsored employment schemes, WPA chief Harry Hopkins retorted, "People don't eat in the long run, Senator; they eat every day."

the legislation that established the NRA had stated that "employees shall have the right to organize and bargain collectively through representatives of their own choosing." This provision naturally stimulated unionization, but employers had wriggled around it by sponsoring their own company unions, a practice that seemed doomed with passage of the National Labor Relations Act and its establishment of the NLRB.

Debate over the act had helped widen a division within America's labor movement. Industrial unions had organized entire businesses and had grown much faster than craft guilds during the early years of the New Deal; for example, membership in the United Mine Workers union led by John L. Lewis had climbed from 50,000 to 500,000 in the space of two years, while the International Ladies' Garment Workers federation headed by David Dubinsky had only quadrupled in size. This trend couldn't help but trouble the leaders of the less militant craft unions, whose members feared that the scope of industrial unionization would revive the radicalism of the Knights of Labor of 1869. (The first unions in the nineteenth century represented skilled "craft" laborers whose abilities gave them leverage in dealing with their employers; less-skilled "industrial" workers hadn't begun to win widespread recognition until much more recently.)

At the 1934 AFL convention, over the protests of the pacifist craft unions, Lewis pushed through a resolution granting provisional charters to industrial unions. The following year he and other industrial union leaders formed the Committee for Industrial Organization, which the rest of the AFL refused to recognize. After the parrying that followed the dissident unions were expelled from the AFL in 1937, whereupon they formed the Congress of Industrial Organizations (CIO) and launched one of the most turbulent years in U.S. labor history. Among many other actions, in February of that year CIO-

Fletcher Martin painted *Mine Rescue,* below, in 1939. The work was part of a Treasury Department initiative to commission unemployed artists to decorate government buildings. Administered by a lawyer-painter named Edward Bruce, the program nurtured a generation of artists while placing remarkably few constraints on subject matter. The mural, though, was eventually removed from the Kellogg, Idaho, post office for which it was painted; local citizens felt it might upset those who had lost relatives in mine accidents.

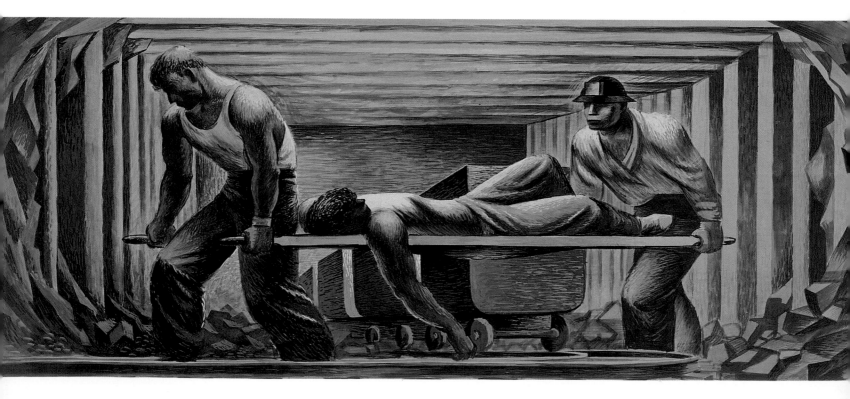

affiliated automobile workers tried a new tactic, the "sit-down strike," in which employees simply refused to leave their workplaces until they were granted collective bargaining rights. Many took this as an alarming spit in the eye of authority, but it did inspire General Motors to recognize the United Automobile Workers union as the negotiating agent for its employees.

Social Security

The most important legislation passed in 1935 was the ground-breaking Social Security Act, although it was hardly a new idea; Progressives had spoken of such a program as early as 1912, and many state pension and unemployment compensation programs were already in effect. Under terms of the new federal Social Security Act, however, nearly all employees and employers would be obliged to pay a payroll tax, the revenues from which would go into a reserve fund; workers who retired at age sixty-five would receive monthly disbursements from this fund of between $10 and $85, depending on their contributions, beginning in 1939. Employers would pay a new unemployment tax to provide benefits to those out of work through no fault of their own.

Social Security cards such as the blank one pictured above assured many Americans of an income in old age. The program also guaranteed assistance to fatherless children, the unemployed, and others in distress.

Social Security—which was passed by Congress on August 14, 1935—was neither structured nor sold to the American public as a welfare program; rather, it was a form of insurance plan that would pay benefits not according to need but based on the contributions workers had made to it. "You want to make it simple—very simple, so simple that everyone will understand it," FDR told Secretary of Labor Frances Perkins. "And what's more, there is no reason why everybody in the United States should not be covered. I see no reason why every child, from the day he is born, shouldn't be a member of the Social Security system. . . . This system ought to be operated through the post offices. Just simple and natural—nothing elaborate or alarming about it. . . . And there is no reason why just industrial workers should get the benefit of this. Everybody ought to be on it—the farmer and his wife and family. . . . I don't see why not. Cradle to the grave—from the cradle to the grave they ought to be in a Social Security system." Its comprehensive structure disarmed opponents who had at first asserted that Social Security was just another program to help the elderly poor on the middle class's nickel; in fact, it would prove the single most important piece of social-welfare legislation in U.S. history, what Roosevelt called the New Deal's "supreme achievement." And so it was, especially in its long-term effects as a retirement pension plan.

The Election of 1936

In 1933 and 1934 the U.S. Supreme Court had ruled favorably on the constitutionality of various minor New Deal measures. By 1935, however, the Court began hearing cases involving the more important laws and agencies instituted under the first Roosevelt administration, and a slim majority found that

In 1932 Louisiana's Huey Long, below, went on a speaking tour in support of Mrs. Hattie Caraway, a Senate candidate in Arkansas. Shepherding her to a surprise victory, Senator Long demonstrated his influence even outside his home state. As a politician Long employed the same techniques as Fascist leaders in Europe: he told people what their problems were, encouraged narrow self-interest, offered simplistic solutions, and delivered enough results in the short term to build momentum. Although Long had supported FDR at first, he soon became the president's most dangerous adversary and left little doubt that he was preparing to enter the 1936 presidential race, even titling his book, *My First Years in the White House.* In September 1935, however, Huey Long was assassinated by a relative of another Louisiana political figure.

some of them violated the United States Constitution. On May 27, in two landmark decisions, the Supreme Court declared certain parts of the New Deal unconstitutional: the president's authority to remove members of the Federal Trade Commission and the NRA itself, against which the Court voted unanimously. Eight months later the U.S. Supreme Court also invalidated the Agricultural Adjustment Administration, and shortly after that decided to negate a New York State law fixing minimum wages.

Roosevelt accepted these decisions with a mixture of anger and relief. The first arose naturally from his belief that his entire reform program was being challenged by what he would later call the Court's "nine old men" from the "horse-and-buggy" days. But the president would do little in response until after the 1936 election, in acknowledgment that the AAA and the larger NRA had not worked out very well, and that the Supreme Court had saved him the embarrassment of canceling the programs himself.

By then opposition to Roosevelt had also appeared from the political right. Backed by funds from such corporate behemoths as General Motors and the Du Pont chemical corporation, a group of anti-Roosevelt Democrats, Al Smith reformers, and conservative Republican businessmen calling themselves the American Liberty League charged the president with attempting to foist socialism upon the nation. The organization singled out the NRA, the TVA, and Roosevelt's other New Deal relief programs as being radical to the point of being un-American. It was to such criticism that Roosevelt's Second New Deal responded by attacking large corporate interests and wealthy individuals through tax reforms.

From other quarters, however, FDR faced criticism for failing to press reform faster and further. The most formidable challenge came from Senator Huey Long of Louisiana, a populist firebrand who had become the first white Southerner since Reconstruction to attract a national following. As governor from 1928 to 1931, as U.S. senator from 1932 to 1935, Long had ruled Louisiana with a meaty fist and taxed its large corporations heavily enough to pay for the construction of new roads, bridges, schools, hospitals, and other popular public works. Under the slogan "Every Man a King" and with a program promising to "Share the Wealth," the politician who liked to be called "Kingfish" offered every family a guaranteed income as well as a home—promises that could be funded only through the confiscation of large fortunes and sharp increases in taxes.

Nevertheless, Long appealed to unemployed, downtrodden, and rootless Americans across the nation. In fact, a secret Democratic poll indicated that if Long ran for president in 1936 he might be able to

siphon enough votes from Roosevelt to elect a Republican or at least to throw the contest into the House of Representatives—and if the economy took a significant dip before November he might even win the White House. But Long was assassinated on September 8, 1935, by the son-in-law of a Louisiana judge he had tried to remove, and with the Kingfish went any threat to FDR from the populist quarter. Still, the forces that had pushed Long to prominence remained and could not safely be ignored.

Not that there was any question Roosevelt would win a second term. The weakened Republican Party sent mixed messages by drawing up a conservative platform for 1936 and then nominating Governor Alfred Landon of Kansas, who had supported Theodore Roosevelt in 1912 and Robert La Follette in 1924 and had also accepted many of FDR's New Deal reforms. Long's diverse followers and other radical elements responded by organizing the Union party and nominating Congressman William Lemke of North Dakota as its presidential candidate alongside such other minor-party hopefuls as the Socialists' Norman Thomas and the Communists' Earl Browder.

For all the political wrangling, the Democrats emerged with an overwhelming victory, the magnitude of which surprised even Franklin Roosevelt. FDR won 27.7 million popular votes—60.6 percent of the total cast—as well as 523 electoral-college votes and every state except Maine and Vermont. The Republicans' Alf Landon scored a paltry 16.7 million popular votes and only 8 in the electoral college, while Lemke attracted fewer than 900,000 popular votes and the rest of the minor candidates even less significant numbers.

Although Roosevelt's popular tally of 1936 would not be surpassed until 1952 and his electoral-college total until 1984, and even though the Democrats that year gained control of the Senate 75 to 21 and of the House by 333 seats to 102, the Republican Party was hardly on its last legs. On the contrary, lost in FDR's tremendous second victory was the fact that Landon had garnered more popular votes than Hoover had in 1932.

Still, a handful of prescient observers noted that the nation's political balance had in fact shifted. Four years earlier it had remained a given that the United States was still mostly Republican, as had been the case since 1886, and that absent the Depression the party would once more have waltzed into the White House and most of the seats in Congress. In 1936, however, it looked as though the Republican alliance of Western and Midwestern farm-

Alfred Landon, shown above at a campaign rally in Des Moines, was the Republican presidential nominee in 1936. A likable man, Landon was a popular Kansas governor with a modestly progressive record. He was also the figurehead of a campaign propelled by an extreme wing of the party, the "American Liberty League," which unleashed vicious attacks on Roosevelt's New Deal. FDR regarded Landon's campaign as futile and desperate, yet during the last week of the campaign, the *Literary Digest* predicted Landon would be a big winner based on the results of a telephone poll. The magazine's miscalculation was emblematic of the state of the country during the campaign: it relied on a telephone poll even though a large number of voters couldn't afford telephones. On election day Landon won just two states, Maine and Vermont, and suffered the worst drubbing in electorial history to that time.

Above, Franklin and Eleanor Roosevelt ride to the inaugural ceremonies in 1937. When Franklin Roosevelt was first elected president in 1932, Eleanor prepared for a dull life in Washington presiding over state dinners and remaining hidden inside the White House. Within a month, however, she was deep in the Appalachian Mountain region, gathering information for her husband. Mrs. Roosevelt had a style all her own, arranging to visit people right in their homes or workplaces, putting them at their ease, and speaking with them like a neighbor. Throughout her husband's administrations, Eleanor Roosevelt cast her role as that of a domestic ambassador serving as a link between all types of Americans and their government.

ers, Northern conservatives, and large and small businessmen had been bested by a new Democratic coalition of Northern laborers and minorities, intellectuals, and, of course, the solid South. And so it was: the new Democratic alliance would hold throughout the thirty-six years between 1933 and 1969 with only one breach in the White House from 1953 to 1961, when Republican Dwight D. Eisenhower would be twice elected president not on account of his party but because he was among the U.S. generals who had made the most noticeable contributions to winning World War II. The U.S. Congress also remained in Democratic hands for most of this period.

The End of the New Deal

As it turned out, the presidential election of 1936 would mark the last hurrah of the New Deal. A little more than two weeks after his second inauguration, on February 5, 1937, Roosevelt proposed a reorganization of the judicial branch from the top down. Declaring the members of the Supreme Court too old to handle the flood of cases descending upon them, the president requested the authority to name replacements for every justice over the age of seventy, and after that for every judge of the same longevity on the nation's lower courts. Roosevelt's opponents—now joined by moderates and even New Dealers who had supported him in the recent election—immediately charged the president with a blatant attempt to "pack the Court" and disrupt the balance of power among the three branches of government. What's more, Chief Justice Charles Evans Hughes was able to demonstrate not only that the Supreme Court's calendar was not clogged but that under his leadership the Court had disposed of more cases than any other in the past century.

At the same time, however, Hughes was joined by Associate Justice Owen Roberts in his decision to "follow the election returns," a shift that allowed the more liberal members of the Court to hand down decisions favorable to the Roosevelt administration. Then conservative Justice Willis Van Devanter retired, permitting FDR to make his first appointment to the Supreme Court, which would shortly be followed by others. The president had notched a victory, but its price was the shattering of his New Deal coalition.

Not that the New Deal seemed necessary any longer: the economy appeared to be on the mend in 1936. The unemployment rate was down to 16.9 percent and would fall to 14.3 percent the next year, the lowest level since 1930; the GNP, meanwhile, was $82.5 billion and would rise to $90.4 billion in 1937, higher than it had been at any time since 1929. Fearing inflation, in fact, the Federal Reserve raised its standards for member banks and in other ways discouraged easy loan policies, while Roosevelt took similar steps to rein in the economy. After all, he had been elected with a mandate to bal-

The cartoon at left shows Franklin Roosevelt unveiling his 1937 plan to expand the Supreme Court. In the drawing, FDR is asking Harold Ickes, then head of the Public Works Administration but better known for his position as Secretary of the Interior (1933–35), for two new towers. In reality, it was not the building but the number of justices that the president tried to expand. "Unless the complexion of the Supreme Court can be changed, two or three elderly judges living in cloistered seclusion and thinking in terms of a bygone day can block nearly all the efforts of a popularly elected president," complained Harry Hopkins, a top administration aide. Nonetheless, Roosevelt's "court-packing scheme" was flatly rejected.

The photograph opposite is from the series *One Third of a Nation, New York City*, produced in 1938 by Arnold Eagle and David Robbins, under the auspices of the Federal Art Project. The Depression rebounded in the autumn of 1937 as Roosevelt cut government spending in an attempt to balance the budget. The Roosevelt administration had taken at least 5 million people out of the ranks of the unemployed, but more than 7 million remained, numbers that would not decrease until America entered World War II. The New Deal succeeded in easing America through the worst depression in its history, but it didn't alleviate the suffering of everyone.

ance the budget, and now set out to do just that, moving to cut expenditures while counting on larger revenues from the new tax law. In 1936 the government had spent $8.4 billion, the most since World War I, creating a budget deficit of $4.4 billion that was also the highest since the war. After Roosevelt's spending cuts, in 1937 federal government expenditures amounted to $7.7 billion, and a year later to $6.8 billion.

However fiscally prudent they may have been, these frugal policies resulted in the sharpest economic contraction in U.S. history, in which many of the gains achieved during Roosevelt's first term were lost. The president's critics jumped to charge that the New Deal had been a failure. FDR had no immediate answer and called another special session of Congress, which voted for new appropriations to take up the slack in employment and consumption. Roosevelt himself responded that the economic downturn of 1937 had been caused by intransigence on the part of business and launched the biggest attack on the corporate sector America had ever seen. He had slowly been souring on the nation's businesses, and had been influenced by labor and the left to consider whether perhaps it was the financial mavens who had caused most of the economic troubles. The president therefore nominated the zealous Thurman Arnold as assistant attorney general in charge of the Justice Department's Antitrust Division, and over the next five years Arnold instituted some 230 lawsuits against corporations charged with monopolistic practices. Roosevelt also asked Congress to establish the Temporary National Economic Commission to study the economy and recommend options for its reform and recovery. Proving its own honesty, the commission reported that U.S. business was more concentrated than ever, and that instead of promoting competition the New Deal had actually encouraged the growth of monopolies. Before the commission's recommendations could be implemented, however, both the president and Congress would have their hands full with World War II—which, ironically, is what in the end brought America out of the Great Depression.

The actual end of the New Deal came with the 1938 midterm elections, when Roosevelt's attempt to purge the Democratic Party of its conservatives backfired. Instead the Republicans bounced back from their disastrous showing two years earlier, retaking 7 Senate and 81 House seats along with the governorships of five states considered safely Democratic. As a result of this shift the Republicans could now join with anti-New Deal Democrats to block legislation emanating from the White House—and did just that, burying the New Deal under a series of legislative failures.

Nevertheless, Roosevelt still could claim to have salvaged American capitalism and reinvigorated the nation's faith in democracy. After all, he had led a massive reform effort that had realigned the relationship between the United States and its citizens by providing Americans with unprecedented economic and social guarantees courtesy of Washington. In the long run, Franklin Roosevelt's greatest contribution to his nation's evolution may have been drawing the public's focus to the executive branch, which Americans since that time have deemed responsible for every major national development, positive or negative. Whereas both Democrats and Republicans had

criticized Herbert Hoover as too activist in 1930, today he is pilloried for "failing to bring America out of the Depression," even though at the time no one had considered this the president's job—certainly not Grover Cleveland, Theodore Roosevelt, or Warren Harding, as evidenced by their responses to lesser economic crises. Today, recessions, riots, business triumphs and failures, and even foreign developments hardly within the control of the United States are all blamed on—or credited to—American presidents, who have the sea change wrought by Franklin Roosevelt and his New Deal to thank for the responsibility.

CHAPTER 17

WORLD WAR II

Not since the days that called for Abraham Lincoln had America found itself so in need of strong leadership as it did in the 1930s, when the nation found its guide in the irrepressible Franklin D. Roosevelt. Many eras have been defined by the outsized personae of certain leaders—Julius Caesar's Rome, Elizabeth I's England, Louis XIV's France, Bismarck's Germany—and such was the case with FDR in America's 1930s and early 1940s. The times required no less, as other strong rulers of varying character and motives had begun to make their moves on the chessboard of Europe.

Americans were not in any mood for international entanglements, as there were plenty of economic troubles at home to take care of. In the wake of World War I, the United States had grown more isolationist than ever, as shown by its high tariffs and strict immigration laws. Among the most clearly expressed, if least effective, indications of the nation's insular attitude was the signing of the Kellogg-Briand Pact of 1928, a pledge of permanent peace that French Foreign Minister Aristide Briand had proposed to Frank B. Kellogg, President Coolidge's eager secretary of state. Signed amid great ceremony with a foot-long golden pen, the agreement declared that its signatories "condemn recourse to war . . . and renounce it as an instrument of national policy." In time sixty-two nations would sign this Pact of Paris, although every one of them conveniently reserved the right to "self-defense."

The photograph at left shows soldiers from the 163rd Infantry Regiment of the U.S. Army racing across the beach at Wakde Island in Dutch New Guinea on May 18, 1944. The Pacific Theater constituted an immense naval battlefield, but military progress was realized one tiny island at a time. The poster above sells war bonds, much needed funds that were integral in winning the war.

At the end of the 1920s, President Roosevelt's thinking remained in line with that of the American public. A decade earlier he had agreed with and contributed to Woodrow Wilson's internationalist policies, including the decisions to aid the Allies and then to enter World War I. Similarly, as the Democratic vice presidential candidate in 1920, Roosevelt had supported America's joining the League of Nations. By 1933, however, the national and world situations had changed drastically, and pressing U.S. domestic needs demanded a less vigorous approach to international matters. The "squire of Hyde Park" did initiate some new foreign policies, but most of them had domestic ends as well. He devalued the dollar to make American goods more competitive abroad, for example, and despite fragile relations with Communist dictator Joseph Stalin, Roosevelt recognized the Soviet Union in the vain hope that it would become a new market for American products. At a 1933 international economic conference in London called by the League of Nations a year earlier, Roosevelt's sympathetic secretary of state, Cordell Hull, was instructed to oppose currency stabilization in order to further the American recovery. The U.S. position crushed the conference, which adjourned without doing anything about either issue.

At the same time, however, that the American government was happily proclaiming the nation's wish to be left alone, U.S. commercial interests had become increasingly enmeshed in foreign investments and markets, which inextricably linked the economy to events abroad such that they could not safely be ignored. In fact, the public's fierce isolationism resulted in part from the knowledge that the current U.S. depression owed in some measure to the financial miasma that had grown out of Europe's World War I debts and reparations and that was spawning some ugly political movements abroad. In hindsight, the worldwide economic downturn had a deleterious domino effect: depression and uncontrolled inflation in Germany inspired Hitler's National Socialism; depression in Japan helped give rise to imperialism, such as the conquest of Manchuria; and depression in Italy led to the seemingly efficient Fascism of *Il Duce*, Benito Mussolini.

It soon became obvious that the United States could not avoid the growing global tensions, especially as the evidence mounted that a dictator was on the loose in the middle of Europe. Shortly after he had taken power in Germany in 1933, the democratically elected Adolf Hitler had renounced the Versailles Treaty and begun to rearm. Fueled by vicious beliefs drawn in part from a skewed reading of Teutonic mythology, Hitler had instituted a policy of official anti-Semitism that led many German Jews to flee the country. But he also wrested Germany out of its long postwar depression, and by mid-decade was quite popular at home, as was his National Socialist Party—the Nazis. Hitler's success with his nation's economy drew admiration for some Nazi programs from around the world, as did the few effective propaganda Fascist policies of Italian dictator Benito Mussolini, who claimed to have made "the trains run on time." As the decade wore on and Hitler began his drive for conquest, of course, he found fewer and fewer defenders outside Germany.

The Roosevelt administration paid close attention to Hitler's activities for the next six years while pursuing overall foreign policies that looked more

isolationist than they actually were, such as the "good neighbor" policy of nonintervention the United States adopted in Latin American affairs. President Roosevelt continued the efforts of Hoover, who had worked to bring home the U.S. Marines his predecessors had stationed in Nicaragua and Haiti, by securing the withdrawal of those troops and in 1934 negotiating a treaty with Cuba to abrogate the 1901 Platt Amendment that had formalized a U.S. right to intervene in the island nation.

Roosevelt similarly refused to be embroiled in the Pacific. In 1934 he supported the Tydings-McDuffie Act, giving the Filipinos more control over their own affairs and declaring July 4, 1946, as the date for withdrawal of the last U.S. troops from the islands. Applauded for its statesmanship, the act also encouraged a burgeoning expansionist movement in Japan around the belief that any aggression on its part would not be blocked by the United States.

Roosevelt's early foreign policies matched the mood at home. In addition to growing more resentful toward the European nations that were defaulting on their U.S. debts, Americans blamed big business for the depression as well, many believing that the government had made international commitments in the First World War solely for the benefit of commerce. More important, a majority of Americans believed that businessmen—bankers and

Above, Adolf Hitler arrives to speak at a Nazi rally in Nuremberg in September 1934. After squandering a modest inheritance in his youth, Hitler lived as a hobo in Vienna before moving to Munich in 1913. He served as a messenger during World War I and decided to enter politics immediately afterward. Awkward and unappealing in social situations, Hitler discovered that when he made a speech, he came alive and so did his audiences. Despite mistakes that would have ruined any other politician, he propelled his career with orchestrated mass rallies as well as gangsterlike violence. Hitler was named chancellor of Germany in 1933. "That is the miracle of our age," he told one cheering audience, "that you have found me, that you have found me among so many millions! And that I have found you. That is Germany's good fortune!"

The Senate Munitions Investigating Committee, photographed above on September 7, 1934, analyzed the influence of industry on U.S. military policy; its members were, from left to right: James Pope, with glasses (Idaho); Chairman Gerald P. Nye (North Dakota); Walter George (Georgia); Bennett Champ Clark (Missouri), and Arthur Vandenberg (Michigan). The committee didn't draw any substantive conclusions, but it did establish Senator Nye as one of the country's leading isolationists. He habitually used Senate subcommittees as pulpits from which to charge that a British-Jewish conspiracy was maneuvering the United States into war. In 1941 yet another Nye subcommittee took aim at American movies. Noting that "it swarms with British actors," the senator accused Hollywood of fostering "a fear of Hitler." Nye was voted out of office in 1944.

munitions manufacturers in particular—had inspired the nation's entry into World War I and thus its international troubles. As a consequence, much of the public supported controls on business and limits on corporate influence in the interest of avoiding any new wars.

Isolationists began to get their way in April 1934 when Congress passed the Johnson Act prohibiting foreign governments that had defaulted on previous debts from borrowing any more money in the United States. At the same time isolationist members of the U.S. Senate engineered a special subcommittee to investigate the munitions industry; headed by Gerald Nye of North Dakota, it attempted to show that financial ties between New York and London had been the prime reasons behind America's entry into World War I. Although the Nye Committee failed to prove this allegation, it did produce evidence indicating that large U.S. corporations had indeed tried to influence the nation's military and naval procurement policies, and had continued to do so into the 1920s. Although nothing concrete was proven, the impression was left that the "merchants of death" and their political allies had conspired to make a war, foreshadowing the military-industrial complex President Dwight D. Eisenhower would warn of twenty years hence.

The resulting public disillusionment with military actions prompted passage of a series of acts designed to insure that the United States could never again be dragged into war. The first of these neutrality acts was passed in 1935 and stated that the president had the authority to assert that if war existed between two or more countries, as a neutral nation the United States could impose arms embargoes on all parties to the conflict. These policies had no effect on the Italo-Ethiopian War, which broke out earlier that year, as Ethiopia could not afford weapons and Italy didn't need them. Fortunately for America's oil companies, petroleum was not deemed war-related, so U.S. shipments of Italy's most important import continued unabated.

In 1936, Congress passed a second neutrality act extending the arms embargo and prohibiting loans or credits to belligerents. When the next foreign conflict—the Spanish Civil War—broke out later that year, however, the neutrality acts again proved useless, as they didn't apply to civil wars. But 1936 was an election year, and the United States actually avoided the Spanish imbroglio for isolationist reasons: Roosevelt's aides had advised him that assisting Spain's socialist government would anger Catholic voters. The war was considered a minirehearsal for World War II, particularly since Hitler's Luftwaffe bombed the Spanish town of Guernica—FDR wanted to avoid the conflict at all costs. Third and fourth neutrality acts were passed in 1937 forbidding Americans from traveling on ships registered to belligerent nations and prohibiting U.S.-registered ships from bearing arms. In 1939 a new, less restrictive neutrality act dictated that belligerents' ships could not depart U.S. waters unless their cargoes had been paid for in advance, a provision known as "cash and carry," which allowed friendly belligerents' ships to come to the United States and buy any supplies and matériel they wanted, provided they had the cash in hand.

During this time, and in fact since the Spanish-American War in 1898, few Americans gave much thought to Asia. They should have. By the mid-1930s, an increasingly militaristic Japan was on the march in China and Manchuria, but Roosevelt did not invoke the neutrality acts against it. Even when Japanese aircraft sank the U.S. gunboat *Panay* on China's Yangtze River in 1937 and then machine-gunned many of its survivors to death, the Japanese had to do no more than apologize and pay $2.5 million in reparations for the matter to be dropped. But considering America's isolationist mood, Roosevelt's hands were tied: with the nation mired in the Depression and his administration still brushing off the dust from the court-packing fight, FDR had reached the nadir of his presidency.

Situations evolve, however, and smart politicians evolve with them. Thus on October 5, 1937, Roosevelt signaled a change in his administration's attitude, observing in a speech in Chicago that "there is no escape through mere isolation or neutrality. . . . There is a solidarity and interdependence about the modern world, both technically and morally, which makes it impossible for any nation completely to isolate itself from political and economic upheavals in the rest of the world." Then the president turned to a particularly apt metaphor for isolating the enemy rather than oneself, explaining, "When an epidemic of physical disease starts to spread, the community approves and joins in a quarantine of the patients in order to protect the health of the community against the spread of the disease."

Not surprisingly, the quarantine speech got a chilly reception—only one in three people polled at the time agreed with the president. For one thing, Roosevelt had been rather vague as to which nation he had in mind, and for another he had failed to explain just how this quarantine was supposed to work. Although in January 1938 the House voted down a proposed amendment calling for a referendum before any U.S. declaration of war, it did so by a slim margin of 209 to 188 votes. A poll taken in April showed that 54

The 1939 cartoon below commented on the stubborn stance the United States adopted with its neutrality acts: not even the specter of democracy in need was supposed to affect America's avoidance of foreign wars.

The cartoon above shows U.S. foreign policy tangled up with Adolf Hitler despite the isolationism that was supposed to ensure the country's independence. "America First," the rallying cry of the isolationist movement, became the title of a song, as shown below. The America First Committee was organized in a wave of patriotism in 1940, but in actual operation, it seemed suspiciously pro-German. Its influence waned when Charles Lindbergh accused "the British, the Jewish, and the Roosevelt Administration" of pushing the U.S. toward intervention in World War II.

percent of those surveyed thought the United States should withdraw from Asia entirely, a majority that grew as the Sino-Japanese conflict that had begun early in the decade intensified. Undaunted, on May 17 President Roosevelt indicated his growing concern over the shakiness of world peace by signing a bill authorizing a two-ocean navy.

American isolationists now became more outspoken. Theodore Roosevelt, Jr., spoke for conservative Republicans by warning that "We must not permit ourselves to be stampeded in our foreign policy." Similarly, traditional New Dealer Raymond Moley, a professor who served as one of FDR's original "brain trusts," predicted that if the United States went to war, "free criticism will be restricted . . . industries will be nationalized . . . wages and hours will be fixed . . . profits will be conscripted." Ernest Hemingway spoke for many when he characterized World War I as "the most colossal, murderous, mismanaged butchery that has ever taken place on earth" and prayed there would not be a repeat performance. Yet more and more Americans began to believe that war in Europe could not be avoided, and that once it started the United States was bound to become involved. The situation was far different from that in 1914, when war seemingly had broken out absent-mindedly and almost accidentally; in 1938 the signs of conflict had been mounting for a decade.

The Road to War

As the 1930s progressed President Roosevelt could not help but be alarmed by what was happening in Europe and wonder whether isolationism in fact remained America's wisest foreign policy. After all, the evidence was mounting that Germany's self-proclaimed "Reichsführer," or emperor, harbored an excess of territorial ambition. In 1936, Hitler had reoccupied the Rhineland buffer zone across Germany's border with Belgium and France, which had been demilitarized after World War I. The same year he and Mussolini had intervened on the side of the Fascist insurgents in the Spanish Civil War. In 1938, Hitler again violated the Treaty of Versailles and annexed Austria, stating that all he was trying to do was bring all Germans under one flag. Then he took over Czechoslovakia's largely German-populated Sudetenland, a strategically important region that had been carved from the defunct Austro-Hungarian Empire, awarded to the Czechs under the Versailles Treaty, and taken away again with the consent of Britain and France at their Munich Conference with Hitler in 1938, where they appeased the German führer by abandoning the nation with the second strongest army in central Europe. Less than half a year later Hitler violated his promise that the Sudetenland would be his last territorial acquisition and ordered his troops to occupy the remainder of Czechoslovakia.

Thus there was good reason for President Roosevelt's heightening anti-isolationism, and he began to prepare the United States for war. In January

1939, FDR asked Congress to appropriate $535 million for the national defense. He got it, and that year federal spending rose to $4.8 billion. Military spending climbed from $1.2 to $1.4 billion—a figure that would rise to $1.8 billion in 1940.

Throughout the summer of 1939, the nation's leading magazines and newspapers split over whether the United States should risk war on behalf of Britain and France (no mainstream groups seriously considered any arrangement with Germany). Still, the debate over U.S. policies toward Europe did not really heat up until September 1, 1939, when Hitler invaded Poland. Realizing the extent to which they had been betrayed, the Allied powers of Britain and France declared war on Germany two days later, and World War II began.

Thus ended official American isolationism in everything but word. The United States could not ignore its "special relationship" with the British. The engineer who would keep that bond welded throughout the Second World War was the brilliant Winston Churchill, the British prime minister who was both the grandson of England's venerable Duke of Marlborough and the son of American beauty Jennie Jerome, the lively daughter of a prominent New York financier, who had become Lady Randolph Churchill. The prime minister put both his Yankee heritage and his substantial old-world charm to work on his equally aristocratic American counterpart, who would repeatedly find it as impossible to say no to Churchill as did the U.S. Congress—which the prime minister thoroughly disarmed in his first address to that body on December 26, 1941, when he quipped, "If my father had been American and my mother British, instead of the other way round, I might have got here on my own."

The first sign of what was to come from Roosevelt appeared on September 3, 1939, when he made a speech on radio promising that "This nation will remain a neutral nation," though unlike Woodrow Wilson, Roosevelt admitted that he could not ask every American "to remain neutral in thought as well. Even a neutral has a right to take account of facts. Even a neutral cannot be asked to close his mind or close his conscience." Yet Roosevelt concluded his speech by pledging that, "As long as it remains within my power to prevent, there will be no blackout of peace in the United States."

Indeed, America would stay neutral in the official sense for some twenty-seven months—throughout which Roosevelt took a consistently pro-Allied stance and did everything within his power short of actual aggression to aid in the fight against Hitler. In 1939 he called a special session of Congress to repeal the arms embargo provisions of the neutrality act to allow the Allies to purchase U.S. weapons on a cash-and-carry basis. In January 1940 Roosevelt asked for and got a defense appropriation of $1.8 billion. Two months later, Roosevelt maneuvered Congress into passing the nation's first peacetime draft law and concluded an arrangement with Churchill whereby fifty World War I–era U.S. destroyers were traded to Britain for naval bases in Newfoundland and the Caribbean. As Churchill slyly explained to his nation's House of Commons on August 20, 1940: "The British Empire and the United States will have to be somewhat mixed up together in some of their affairs for mutual

In the company of Adolf Hitler, Italy's Benito Mussolini, gives the Roman salute to a passing parade, above. At their first meeting in 1934, Hitler had been disdained by the more established Mussolini, a Fascist who had swept into power in 1922. Ostentatious and extroverted, Mussolini wanted to be known as *Il Duce* ("the leader"). The ties between the two dictators were reflected in the Rome-Berlin Axis, which began as an idea in 1936 and solidified into a military pact in 1939.

and general advantage. For my own part, looking out upon the future, I do not view the process with any misgivings."

Churchill was right to be optimistic for despite powerful isolationist feeling in America, there were significant countercurrents of domestic opinion. Active internationalists at the League of Nations Association, a citizen lobby group whose members tended the flickering flame of Wilsonian idealism, sought to adapt their convictions to new circumstances. Clark Eichelberger, the energetic national director, formed the Committee to Defend America by Aiding the Allies and persuaded William Allen White, a Pulitzer Prize–winning newspaper editor of the Emporia, Kansas *Gazette,* to serve as chairman. Their first aim was to repeal the neutrality acts. Likewise, playwright Robert Sherwood, a Roosevelt speechwriter, took up the interventionist case by taking out newspaper advertisements entitled "Stop Hitler Now."

Marching to War

In 1939, it looked as though the next year's presidential election would revolve around the success of the Democratic president's foreign policies. Republican Senator Robert Taft of Ohio represented those who opposed both the New Deal and a blank check for aid to the Allies, but he faced opposition from several intriguing dark horses, including Wendell Willkie, an Indiana farm boy of Will Rogers-like wit who had grown into a successful New York utilities executive and who until the previous year had been a Democrat. Willkie, sarcastically dubbed by FDR's Interior Secretary Harold Ickes as "the barefoot boy from Wall Street," had captured the interest and then the support of powerful Eastern internationalists, including influential *Time* magazine publisher Henry Luce, which certainly couldn't hurt in the first presidential campaign to be covered on the radio by the national broadcasting companies. What's more, Willkie knew a good thing when he saw it and was smart enough to latch on. In general he supported Roosevelt's foreign policies, and upon winning the Republican nomination came out in favor of most of the New Deal programs with the proviso that if elected he would administer them more efficiently.

The big question for the Democrats in 1939 was who would succeed FDR, as it was assumed he would adhere to precedent and decline to seek a third term. But by early 1940 it appeared that Roosevelt had other plans, which he made clear by dropping Vice President John Nance Garner from the ticket in favor of Agriculture Secretary Henry A. Wallace, whose Iowa-bred progressivism held more appeal for the party's left wing.

Despite the concern over a third term, Roosevelt won the election handily, with 27.3 million popular votes and 449 in the electoral college to Willkie's 22.3 million and 82. Although the Democrat's victory was clear-cut, Republicans could take some cheer from the fact that the president had received 500,000 fewer votes than in 1936 while their man Willkie had attracted upward of 5.6 million more than Alf Landon four years earlier. Of course, the opposition party also couldn't help but notice that its revival was most likely due to Willkie's embrace of some of FDR's policies.

Whatever the motives behind it, a spirit of sporadic bipartisanship was in the making. More important, it was becoming increasingly obvious that the American people were preparing for war, at least psychologically, as was shown less than a month after the 1940 election by a poll reporting that only 39 percent of those surveyed still thought America's entry into World War I had been a mistake, compared with 64 percent two years earlier.

On January 1, 1941, Roosevelt worked late in his small study on the second floor of the White House. Accompanied by his adviser Harry Hopkins, speechwriter and playwright Robert Sherwood, and his speechwriter, Samuel Rosenman, he was putting the final touches on his State of the Union message, which he would deliver before a joint session of the Congress on January 6. There remained only the question of how to close the speech. After a long silence, the president began dictating what became his famous declaration of hope for "a world founded upon four essential human freedoms"— freedom of speech and expression; freedom of religion; freedom from want; and freedom from fear. These were, he said, not a vision for "a distant millennium" but "a definite basis for a kind of world attainable in our own time and generation."

Such was the power of Franklin Roosevelt's personality that he managed to turn America from a nation of provincial isolationists into one of forward-thinking globalists. As William Allen White declared with remarkable foresight, the president had given the world "a new magna carta of democracy." The Four Freedoms, which became the moral cornerstone of the United Nations, marked, White wrote, "the opening of a new era for the world." The tables had been turned: isolationist voices like aviator Charles Lindbergh, Senator Burton Wheeler, and Chicago Tribune publisher Robert McCormick were becoming obsolete. Of course, Roosevelt had a great deal of help from the Axis powers of Europe, whose mounting outrages shocked the American people. In the spring of 1940, after capturing Denmark and Norway and the sea lanes through them, Hitler had sent tank divisions supported by airpower on a blitzkrieg, or "lightning war," to conquer Belgium and the Netherlands in just eighteen days. On June 22, France fell to Germany, and with only Great Britain remaining between Hitler and the United States, Americans began to seriously rethink their isolationism.

As the Axis nations' power grew, the United States increased aid to the Allies and accelerated its own preparations for war. When Britain could no longer afford to buy U.S. goods on a cash-and-carry basis, Roosevelt proposed and after a month-long debate Congress passed the Lend-Lease Act in March 1941, granting the chief executive the authority to lend, lease, exchange, sell, or in any other way transfer arms or other war matériel or supplies to "any country whose defense the president deems vital to the defense of the United States." Designed at the time as a way to shore up the Royal Navy, the Lend-Lease Act would in time provide for the transfer of more than $50 billion in goods from America to Allied nations, particularly Britain.

The world crisis was now crescendoing. As 1941 opened, the massive German air assault on England continued, and Hitler made unrelenting efforts to extend his grip on the Continent. In March, he forced Bulgaria and

At right, Wendell Willkie, the Republican presidential candidate in 1940, leads a parade through his hometown of Elwood, Indiana. Willkie campaigned against the prospect of an unprecedented third term for Franklin Roosevelt. Many Democrats sided with him on that issue, as expressed on the placard above. Even FDR's former mentor, Al Smith, declared himself a "Democrat for Willkie."

Yugoslavia to join the Axis, and when the compliant Belgrade government was promptly overthrown by a coup d'état, he declared war on Yugoslavia, using Italian and Hungarian troops alongside his German forces. The previous November, Italy invaded Greece, which conducted a tenacious defense with help of British troops until the introduction of larger German forces broke the organized resistance and led the British to withdraw.

In May 1941, Roosevelt proclaimed an "unlimited national emergency" in response to the sinking of U.S. ships by German submarines in the North Atlantic, even if in most cases the unfriendliness had started with the American captains pursuing German submarines in an "undeclared war." German forces in Africa were also advancing through Libya toward Egypt and the supreme prize of the Suez Canal. In June, Hitler and Mussolini responded by charging the United States with belligerent acts; shortly thereafter Roosevelt froze all German and Italian funds invested in the United States.

Germany added to the tension on June 22 by attacking the Soviet Union. That massive German onslaught made an already highly fragile situation across the globe much more volatile. Britain's ability to hold out against German bombers and submarines still hung in the balance. Now German troops were slicing deep into Russia, and Japan stood poised to attack in the Pacific. Without hesitation, FDR immediately pledged Lend-Lease aid to the Soviet regime. When the inevitable criticism for helping the Bolshevik dictatorship arose, Undersecretary of State Sumner Welles replied that "any defense against Hitlerism" was justified.

On July 7, U.S. troops occupied Iceland to prevent its use by Germany as a naval or air base. The next month Roosevelt held a series of secret meetings with Churchill on warships off the Newfoundland coast. The two leaders released the Atlantic Charter, which set forth a list of common war aims in broad terms, including "the final destruction of the Nazi tyranny" as well as Roosevelt's Four Freedoms. Probably the most compelling statement of the war, the charter enunciated "certain common principles" on which the Anglo-American democracies "base their hopes for a better future for the world." Perhaps more important, the two leaders established, as Robert Sherwood would later write, "an easy intimacy, a joking informality, and a moratorium on pomposity and cant and also a degree of frankness in intercourse which if not quite complete, was remarkably close to it." Despite its cozy relations with Churchill's Britain, the United States was still officially neutral.

It would not remain so for long. The Germans increased their military activities in the North Atlantic in September 1941, and the next month a U-boat sank the U.S. ship *Kearny,* killing eleven U.S. sailors. On October 27, Roosevelt declared to the nation that "The shooting has started," and announced that he had ordered the U.S. Navy to sink upon sight any German ship found in American waters. The president proved right three days later when the U.S. destroyer *Reuben James* was sunk, claiming the lives of more than one hundred American servicemen. A formal declaration of war seemed in-

In the photograph below, taken during the winter of 1940–41, women march in front of the White House against Roosevelt's proposed Lend-Lease program, through which America was to supply Great Britain (and eventually the Soviet Union) with war matériel. The bill, given the patriotic number "1776," was assailed by isolationists, who feared it would lead to the sacrifice of America's young men. Roosevelt's response, delivered in a fireside chat on December 29, 1940, was that "We cannot escape danger, or the fear of danger, by crawling into bed and pulling the covers over our heads. . . . A nation can have peace with the Nazis only at the price of total surrender." The same night, the Nazis unleashed a particularly heavy bombing raid on London in an effort to push Roosevelt's speech out of the next day's headlines.

Arctic Ocean

15°   0°   15°   30°   45°

Pechenga
(Petsamo)

• Murmansk

KOLA PENINSULA

White Sea

Lofoten Is. • Narvik

Allied Landings
April–May 1940

• Tornio

SWEDEN

• Oulu

• Nurmes   Lake
                Onega

Atlantic

60°

• Namsos

Trondheim •

**FINLAND
1941**

• Vassa

1940 USSR

Lake
Ladoga

• Vyborg
(Vijpuri)

Andalsnes •

Helsinki •

• Leningrad

Faeroe Is.
(Danish)
British occupied
1940

Ocean

**NORWAY
1940**

• Turku

• Tikhvin
• Novgorod

Shetland Island
(British)

• Bergen

Tallinn •

Lake
Peipus

Orkney Island

Scapa Flow

• Oslo

• Stavanger

• Stockholm

ESTONIA

Baltic

LATVIA

Reykjavik •

ICELAND
British occupied 1940

UNITED

KINGDOM

• Aberdeen

Glasgow • • Edinburgh

Riga •

Sea

LITHUANIA

• Aalborg

North

**DENMARK
1940**

• Minsk

N. IRELAND
• Belfast

IRELAND

Dublin •

GREAT

BRITAIN

• Manchester

Sea

• Copenhagen

• Kiel

MEMEL
TERR.
1939

**EAST
PRUSSIA**

Kaunas
•
Königsberg • Vilna •

• Gordno
Danzig •

• Bialystok

• Pinsk

Birmingham •

Bristol •   • Coventry

Plymouth •   London •
Southampton •

English Channel

Dunkirk •

Brest •

**FRANCE
1940**

• Le Havre

• Paris

Nantes •   *Loire*

Seine

NETHERLANDS
1940
• Amsterdam
British evacuation
May-June 1940   • Rotterdam

BELGIUM
Brussels
1940

• Hamburg
• Bremen

RHINELAND
occ. 1936

LUX.
1940

• Essen
Cologne •

RHINELAND 1938

• Frankfurt

• Stuttgart

Strasbourg •

• Stettin

• Lubeck

• Berlin

• Posen

• Warsaw

**POLAND
1939**

• Lublin

Lodz •

• Kassel   **GERMANY**

• Leipzig

• Dresden

• Breslau

• Krakow

• Lvov

• Brest Litovsk

• Tarnopol

SUDETENLAND 1938

• Prague

**CZECHOSLOVAKIA
1939**

Pilsen •

**HUNGARY
1940**

Budapest •

ROMANIA 1940

BESSA
1940 U.

• Munich

**AUSTRIA
1938**

Graz •

Szeged •

• Oradea

• Ploesti

45°

Bay

of

Biscay

Bordeaux •

• Vichy

**VICHY FRANCE
1940**
unoccupied

Lyons •

Toulouse •

Marseilles •

• Toulon

PORTUGAL

Corsica
(Fr)

• Lisbon

• Madrid

SPAIN

Balearic Island
(Sp.)

*Strait
of Gibraltar*   • Gibraltar (Br)
• Tangier

Rabat •

SP. MOROCCO

French Fleet sunk
3 July 1940

• Oran

**MOROCCO
1940**

• Algiers

**ALGERIA
1940**

• Bern

SWITZ.

• Innsbruck

• Milan

• Trieste

Venice •

Zagreb •

Belgrade •

Subotica •

Bucharest •

• Ruse

• Bern

Po

• Genoa

Zadar
(It.)

**YUGOSLAVIA
1941**

Sarajevo •

Nis •

Sofia •

**BULGARIA
1941**

• Plovdiv

• Split

Adriatic Sea

Danube

Skoplje •

• Kavalia

Durazzo • • Tirana

• Salonika

Aegean

ITALY

Rome •

• Florence

Naples •

• Foggia

Taranto •

British
air strike
11 Nov. 1941

**ALBANIA
1939**

Valona •

Ioanninia •

Missolonghi •

**GREECE
1941**

• Patras

Athens •

Sea

Dardanelles

Sardinia

*Tyrrhenian
Sea*

Palermo •

Sicily

• Messina

• Catania

Battle of Cape Matapan
27 March 1941

Cape Matapan

Crete
(Gr.)

• Bizerte
• Tunis

*Malta
(Br.)*

Mediterranean Sea

**TUNISIA
1940**

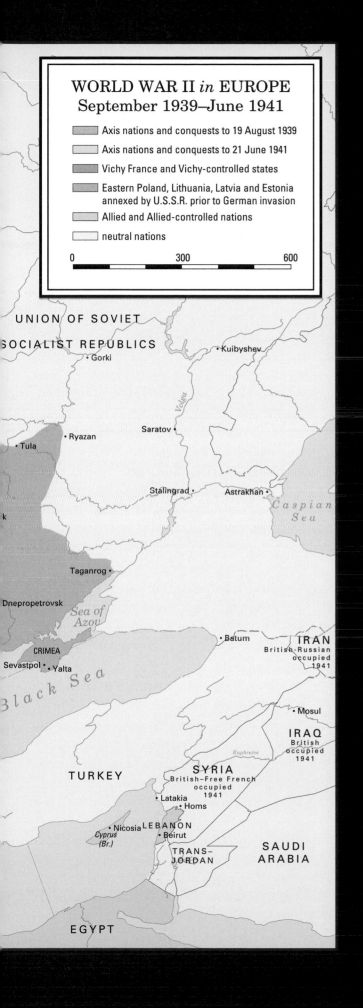

UNION OF SOVIET
SOCIALIST REPUBLICS
• Gorki   • Kuibyshev

Volga

Saratov •

• Ryazan
• Tula

Stalingrad •   Astrakhan •

Caspian Sea

k

Taganrog •

Dnepropetrovsk
Sea of Azov

CRIMEA
Sevastpol • • Yalta

Black Sea

• Batum   IRAN
British-Russian
occupied
1941

• Mosul

IRAQ
British
occupied
1941

Euphrates

TURKEY   SYRIA
British–Free French
occupied
• Latakia   1941
•• Homs

• Nicosia LEBANON
Cyprus   • Beirut
(Br.)
TRANS-   SAUDI
JORDAN   ARABIA

EGYPT

The map at left depicts the conquest of Europe by Germany and its Axis partner Italy during the first two years of World War II. In the mid-1930s, Hitler had tested the international reaction to German expansion by shouldering his way into such places as the Sudetenland (now the Czech Republic), the Rhineland, and Austria. Western countries grumbled, but none tried to stop him. Even as Hitler signed peace treaties with Britain, France, and the U.S.S.R, he was accelerating his military buildup into a national obsession. By September 1, 1939, his glistening new German Army had finished parading in peace pageants and national festivals. On that day, it stormed into Poland.

Two days later, the leaders of Britain and France declared war on Germany. London was blacked out the same night in anticipation of an air raid. "We shall win," commented a doctor surveying the eerie scene from the roof of a hospital, "We shall win because every man and woman in this hospital is at his or her post in the dark—quiet, determined, efficient, prepared for the worst, uncomplaining, certain that we shall win in the end." As it turned out, London was not bombed that night: after Germany took possession of most of Poland (the U.S.S.R. claimed an eastern section), it paused in its aggression. The winter of 1939–40 was known as the "phony war" because the Allies did not take very much direct action, either. They concentrated on construction of a defensive arc, the Maginot Line, along the Franco-German border.

Throughout the spring of 1940, Hitler resumed his conquests. Germany turned the blitzkrieg that had worked so well in Poland to the west, conquering Denmark and Norway and the next month the Netherlands and Belgium. The Maginot Line proved to be pathetically ineffective, and the Germans marched almost as easily into France, which surrendered in June. The British Army just barely escaped annihilation, rescued with the help of a civilian armada at Dunkirk.

On June 22, 1941, Germany attacked its supposed ally, the U.S.S.R., marching brilliantly through the initial Soviet resistance toward the important cities of Stalingrad and Leningrad. Before Hitler captured either one, the Soviets would prove themselves just as determined to win as the British. At the end of 1941, though, Hitler was so giddy over his conquests that he brashly declared war on the United States in the aftermath of the attack on Pearl Harbor. By doing so, he provoked a third enemy that would prove unwilling to lose.

evitable, and by November the public was prepared for a call to arms such as Woodrow Wilson had sent to Congress in 1917.

World War II finally engulfed America on December 7, 1941. The aggression came not from Germany, however, but from Japan, with which U.S. relations had deteriorated throughout the Hoover and Roosevelt administrations as a result of Japanese expansion in Manchuria and China and American opposition to it. By 1938, official U.S. protests against Japanese actions had become commonplace, and on July 1 of that year Secretary of State Cordell Hull had successfully appealed to America's munitions manufacturers to stop selling their wares to Japan in a sort of "moral embargo." This and other such actions played a large part in convincing Japan's leaders to join the Axis alliance, upon which President Roosevelt embargoed exports of scrap iron to Japan and boosted U.S. loans to China.

By early 1941, some members of the Democratic administration were convinced that a war with Japan was at least as likely as one with Germany; in fact, there was an indication of exactly how it would come about, as U.S. Ambassador to Japan Joseph Grew had reported to the State Department in January that according to a Japanese source "Japanese military forces planned . . . to attempt a surprise mass attack on Pearl Harbor using all of their military facilities." Nevertheless, at the time the European war and particularly the German threat so occupied Roosevelt's time and energies that little was done in the first half of 1941 to prepare for war in the Pacific.

By the summer, however, the threat from the East could no longer be ignored. Japan had taken control of much of Southeast Asia and was moving on Malaysia and the Dutch East Indies (today's Indonesia)—the loss of which would deprive Britain and the United States of the islands' vital exports of rubber and tin while providing the Axis powers with a desperately needed source of oil.

Following the unauthorized Japanese occupation of French Indochina (today's Vietnam) on July 24, Roosevelt froze all Japanese assets in the United States. It didn't work. From August to December the Japanese continued preparing to attack while at the same time pursuing negotiations with Washington. The balance shifted toward war in mid-October when Japan's relatively moderate premier was replaced by belligerent War Minister Hideki Tojo; although by the end of November both sides recognized the futility of further talks, the Japanese continued sending fresh emissaries with new proposals—and its fleet in the direction of Hawaii. On December 1, Tokyo's Privy Council voted for war against the United States, as decided and initiated four

Below, a seaman aboard the HMS *Sheffield*, en route to Murmansk in the Soviet Union, operates a signal lamp covered with ice in the frigid Arctic air. Facing the Nazis alone on the eastern front, the Soviet Union was in desperate need of U.S. weaponry, ammunition, and food, yet its only viable ports in the early years of the war were Murmansk and Archangel, on the northern coast. The risk of attack was high, especially in the early years of the war. German U-boats, along with airplanes based in Norway, sank twenty-two of the thirty-three ships in one convoy bound for Archangel in 1942.

I address myself to Your Majesty at this moment in the fervent hope that Your Majesty may, as I am doing, give thought in this definite emergency to ways of dispelling the dark clouds. I am confident that both of us, for the sake of the peoples not only of our own great countries but for the sake of humanity in neighboring territories, have a sacred duty to restore traditional amity and prevent further death and destruction in the world.

Franklin D. Roosevelt

****

months earlier, beginning with a surprise attack on the U.S. military installations at Pearl Harbor, which commenced on the morning of Sunday, December 7, 1941.

The U.S. garrison on the island of Oahu, ill-prepared and disorganized, was astonished by the wave of Japanese attack planes that sank or damaged nineteen U.S. ships and claimed some 2,400 American lives. Indeed, had the Japanese pressed on they probably could have captured the islands without much of a struggle. Surprised themselves at the extent of their success, the attackers instead withdrew. In fact, the assault on Pearl Harbor was a strategic blunder because none of the U.S. Pacific Fleet's three aircraft carriers was present at Pearl Harbor, and all the sneak attack accomplished was uniting the American people in a crusading zeal that sustained them throughout the war. Soon millions of Americans wore enameled lapel pins proclaiming they would "Remember Pearl Harbor."

Some Americans, however, immediately suspected Roosevelt of somehow having invited the attack in collusion with Churchill as an excuse to get the United States into the war on the Allied side. Following its historical pattern, the nation found it hard to believe that its forces could have been so roundly defeated without the help of some internal conspiracy, rumors of which persist to this day. Investigations of the U.S. response to the attack on Pearl Harbor both during and since the war have indeed revealed blunders, accidents, and breakdowns in communication, but no evidence of conspiracy or foreknowledge by FDR. In any event, Japan's attack on the Hawaiian bases accomplished in minutes what Woodrow Wilson had needed months to attain in 1917: a United States commitment to a foreign-born war.

After a stirring address by the ever-persuasive President Roosevelt, the Senate unanimously approved a war resolution against Japan, which only one member of the House—Republican Congresswoman Jeannette Rankin of

On Saturday, December 6, 1941, President Roosevelt sent a plea for peace, above left, to Japanese Emperor Hirohito. FDR devoted most of that afternoon to writing the lines in hope of avoiding war "for the sake of humanity." As it turned out, the message was delayed for ten hours in Tokyo. By the time the emperor received it, the assault on Pearl Harbor, directed by General Tojo, above right, was irreversible.

Without a moment's notice, Pearl Harbor turned from a quiet port into a war zone on the morning of Sunday, December 7, 1941, above. The enemy force of 31 ships and more than 350 planes approached Hawaii undetected and delivered what was later called on Tokyo radio "an annihilating blow" to Pearl Harbor and other bases in the islands. Six battleships were sunk or disabled, almost 200 airplanes were destroyed, and some 2,400 people killed. The Japanese simultaneously attacked the Philippines, a U.S. territory, as well as the British possessions of Hong Kong and Malaya. Winston Churchill telephoned Franklin Roosevelt immediately to confirm the report regarding Pearl Harbor. "It's quite true," FDR answered. "We are all in the same boat now."

President Roosevelt, left, signs a declaration of war against Japan on December 8, the day after the attack on Pearl Harbor. At 12:30 P.M. on that day, he addressed a joint session of Congress, requesting a war declaration along with the funding to back it. The speech was short—almost curt—in part because Roosevelt did not want to weaken morale by detailing the extent of the damage to the U.S. Pacific Fleet. Within minutes, both houses voted approval of the declaration, Roosevelt signed the document, and America was at war with Japan. "Remember December 7th" would remain a rallying cry throughout the war, as on the poster below.

Montana—voted against. On December 11, Germany and Italy also declared war on the United States, making things easier for Congress: that same day both houses voted unanimously to recognize a state of war with those Axis nations as well. The attack on Pearl Harbor had permanently shattered America's sense of security, and the United States entered World War II unified as never before. Whereas sizable minorities had opposed every previous U.S. war, after December 7, 1941—which Roosevelt called "a date which will live in infamy"—virtually every American agreed that it was time to go all out for victory. As George Orwell accurately noted on BBC radio upon hearing FDR's January 6, 1942, State of the Union Address, America had made a "complete and uncompromising break . . . with isolationism."

The Arsenal of Democracy

World War II would do for the United States what seven years of the New Deal had been unable to accomplish: extricate the nation from its Great De-

.. we here highly resolve that these dead shall not have died in vain . . .

REMEMBER DEC. 7th!

pression. The numbers tell the story. In 1940, the GNP was $99.7 billion, still some $4 billion less than in 1929, while the unemployment rate was 14.6 percent, more than quadruple what it had been then. But mobilizing the U.S. armed forces and providing aid to the Allies sent production soaring and unemployment plummeting, such that by 1942 the GNP had reached $159 billion and the jobless rate had fallen to 9.9 percent. In 1944, the last full year of World War II, America's GNP had shot up to $211.4 billion, unemployment had sunk to 1.2 percent, and the United States had become the world's arsenal of democracy.

Americans responded to their president's call with a vigorous enthusiasm that had the side benefit of righting the U.S. economy. Shortly after Pearl Harbor, Roosevelt had spoken hopefully of producing 50,000 airplanes a year; in 1943 the U.S. aviation industry delivered 84,400, and 95,200 the next year. Overall, U.S. manufacturing output increased by 128 percent from 1939 to 1944, a period during which U.S. factories churned out more than 300,000 aircraft, 77,000 ships, 86,000 tanks, and 2.7 million machine guns—the matériel that helped the

The photograph above shows construction of a Liberty ship, the SS *Joseph Teal,* at one of Henry Kaiser's shipyards. To meet a critical need for the standardized freighters known as Liberty ships, Kaiser revolutionized an age-old process, building ships largely on land and from prefabricated pieces. Soliciting time-saving ideas from everyone—ranging from professors at M.I.T. to the workers at his yards—he cut construction time for a complete ship to an astonishing eighty and one-half hours by 1944. Germans could not possibly sink them as fast as Henry Kaiser could build them.

Allies win the war. Of course, paying for the war effort drove the federal debt from 50 percent of the gross national product in 1940 to 122 percent of the much higher GNP in 1945. New factories mushroomed in wheat fields and swamplands. At Willow Run Creek near Detroit, Henry Ford build a seventy-acre aircraft plant called the "most enormous room in the history of man." Aviation hero Charles Lindbergh dubbed it the "Grand Canyon of a mechanized world."

A large portion of America's wartime industrial and economic success was attributed to the role played by women. As the boys and men marched off to war, 6 million women stepped forward to do their jobs. The U.S. government indicated the nation's desperation for laborers by urging women to "Do your part—free a man for service" on posters promoting the idea of "Rosie the Riveter," a gorgeous model bursting out of a grease-monkey uniform and brandishing a wrench. Norman Rockwell painted Rosie as a muscular Amazon for the cover of the *Saturday Evening Post*. The genuine article was the amazing Rosie Bonavita, who with minimal assistance pounded 3,345 rivets into the wing of a bomber plane in a record six hours. As eager to get out of the house as they were to aid the war effort, women responded to the call to service in overwhelming numbers, in one year increasing their presence in the workplace by half. By 1944 more than a third of all American women, including 24 percent of the married ones, had entered the workforce, many breaking into traditionally male jobs in construction, railroads, trucking, and every other sort of heavy industry. Happy to be liberated from the kitchen and making money on their own, many women would not want to give up their jobs when the men came back home.

Perhaps the low point of FDR's domestic wartime policy was his creation of "relocation camps" for the more than 100,000 people of Japanese ancestry living in the United States, of whom 80,000 were native-born Americans, or Nisei. In February 1942, the Roosevelt administration, under pressure from Western politicians who feared that some Nisei were engaged in espionage activities, rounded up these citizens, forced them to sell their property at low prices, and shipped them off to desert camps in a so-called "national security exercise" distinctly reminiscent of the U.S. Army's nineteenth-century Native-American removal policies. This evacuation policy—based on the racist premise that "a Jap is a Jap"—was ruled constitutional by the U.S. Supreme Court in 1944. Forty years later Congress deemed the Nisei relocation policy an ugly by-product of "war hysteria, racial prejudice and failure of political leadership." The internees were each compensated with a $20,000 apology check.

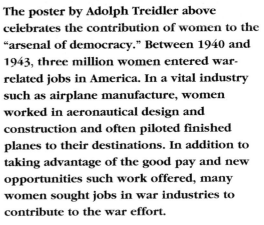

"THE GIRL HE LEFT BEHIND" IS STILL BEHIND HIM She's a WOW

The poster by Adolph Treidler above celebrates the contribution of women to the "arsenal of democracy." Between 1940 and 1943, three million women entered war-related jobs in America. In a vital industry such as airplane manufacture, women worked in aeronautical design and construction and often piloted finished planes to their destinations. In addition to taking advantage of the good pay and new opportunities such work offered, many women sought jobs in war industries to contribute to the war effort.

The Battles Begin

While the effort at home was an immediate and continuing success, World War II itself went badly for the Allies throughout most of 1942. The Germans continued advancing into the Soviet Union and across North Africa while the Japanese captured the Philippines and then swept down through the South Pacific islands to land in New Guinea and threaten Australia, and east toward Hawaii, and west to India. But in a series of key battles in far-flung corners of the globe, the Allies managed to stop the Axis advance in mid-1942 and into 1943. The first of these engagements took place in the Pacific theater in June 1942 at Midway Island just a thousand miles northwest of Hawaii, where a Japanese task force led by Admiral Isoroku Yamamoto was

America's race relations were a disgrace during World War II, and pleas for tolerance and unity generally went ignored. Prejudice against Jews did not so much decline as go underground as a natural consequence of the nation's war against the viciously anti-Semitic Adolf Hitler, but in its place antiblack bigotry flared up among white Americans. The reasons were obvious, if the converse of those had inspired similar race hatred after Reconstruction and World War I.

During the Great Depression, blacks had been the last hired and the first fired, and even into 1940 black unemployment had remained high as whites took the first jobs in the new war-related industries. By the end of the year, however, labor shortages in large Northern cities arose as an increasing number of men went into the armed services, which led many Northern employers to lure able-bodied black men from the South with the promise of good jobs at high wages. The top destinations included New York, Chicago, Pittsburgh, and Los Angeles, but it was Detroit—long the nation's "motor city" and now the hub of heavy ordnance and bomber production—that experienced the largest influx of new black workers.

The sudden proximity of different races kindled the bigotry already simmering in cities into violence. Several riots erupted in 1942, followed by more the next year in virtually every major urban area. In February 1943 a white mob attacked several black tenants at the Sojourner Truth housing project in Detroit, and that summer some 10,000 white rabble stormed the streets of Beaumont, Texas, beating blacks and burning their homes. In Los Angeles a group of black and Mexican "zoot-suiters" deemed undesirable for no more than sporting loud garb, long hair, and their own slang were brutalized by middle-class whites, including several dozen servicemen.

The tensions exploded into mass race riots in Detroit in late June, leaving twenty-five blacks and nine whites dead and thousands of both races injured. Entire city blocks were destroyed while Mayor Edward Jeffries, Jr., and Michigan Governor Harry Kelly were paralyzed by fear and indecision. Bands of vicious white youths roamed the streets, beating every black they could catch, and soon the blacks reciprocated. Factory production ground to a halt, but Kelly tried to stop federal troops from entering the city in hopes that his state forces could cool the situation. After a week of sporadic rioting, looting, and arson, however, the governor relented and allowed President Roosevelt to send two military police battalions into Detroit. There wasn't much left for them to do, as by then both races had tired of the violence and the uprising came to an end.

Still, the Detroit Times called the riots "the worst disaster which has befallen Detroit since Pearl Harbor," while the German and Japanese press reported that the violence signaled the beginning of a new American revolution that would force the United States to abandon the war overseas. "We'd better be frank about this," warned moderate black leader Louis Marin. "The race riot and all that has gone before have made my people more nationalistic and more chauvinistic and antiwhite than they ever were before. Even those of us who were half liberal and were willing to believe in the possibility of improving race relations have begun to doubt and, worse, they have given up hope." Adam Clayton Powell, New York's sole black city councilman, warned that what had happened in Detroit "easily could be duplicated here in New York."

Determined to keep that from occurring, Mayor Fiorello LaGuardia took to the airwaves to notify New Yorkers that anyone who fomented violence would be dealt with harshly. The situation stayed tense but quiet until August 1, when a black soldier was shot in a scuffle with white policemen in Harlem. A riot immediately erupted for the exact reasons violence would break out in Los Angeles almost fifty years later when a jury acquitted white policemen of beating black motorist Rodney King, showing how little America's racial attitudes have matured. In 1943, however, Mayor LaGuardia handled the tinderbox in Harlem better than L.A. officials would theirs in 1992, immediately isolating the area and preventing white mobs from entering. LaGuardia's police arrested looters and arsonists quickly and effectively, prompting even black leaders to praise the city's restraint. At the same time, however, those leaders warned that additional violent outbreaks were inevitable unless something was done about what they termed the racist nature of American society. The point could not be denied: so long as racial discrimination existed in civilian and military life, the nation could not truly claim to be a beacon of democracy in the fight against Hitler and Tojo—and until that changed, blacks would become increasingly militant in their battle for social justice at home.

The photograph above was taken in June 1943, when race riots broke out in Detroit. The African-American man in the center of the picture is under attack from the hoodlums surrounding him. Thirty-four people died in the Detroit riots.

Griffith Bailey Coale painted the scene from the Battle of Midway, above, which took place in the Pacific, June 3–6, 1942. Even before the war started, Admiral Isoroku Yamamoto had predicted that he could "wreak havoc for a year," with the hope that that would be enough to knock the United States out of the war. Throughout the first half of 1942, the Japanese Navy did enjoy a string of successes, and was planning to deal a final blow to the U.S. Pacific Fleet at Midway Island. Instead, it was the Japanese fleet that was devastated, a dramatic reversal in the momentum of the war in the Pacific.

outmaneuvered by a U.S. fleet commanded by Admiral Chester Nimitz. The Japanese lost four aircraft carriers. Had the Japanese won at Midway, they could have taken control of the entire central Pacific; as it was, they were forced to withdraw from the region. "At one stroke," Churchill would write after the war, "the dominant position of Japan in the Pacific was reversed," although this was clear only in hindsight. The Japanese would go on to victories in the south and west Pacific, but their defeat at Midway lifted the danger to Hawaii.

Back in the European theater, another key battle took place on the Volga River at what Russia had called Volgograd and the Soviet Union had renamed Stalingrad in honor of its current dictator. German troops led by General Friedrich von Paulus swept through southern Russia in the summer and early autumn of 1942, seemingly on their way to a breakthrough across the Volga River to the Caspian Sea. Had they made it, Hitler effectively would have torn the U.S.S.R. apart, gaining valuable oil reserves in the bargain.

But as the forces of Russia's Czar Alexander I had against Napoleon's equally ill-considered incursion late in 1812, the Soviets made a determined stand at Stalingrad in mid-September and maintained it for more than four bitter winter months, despite resources the Germans poured into the battle. The Red Army thus won its greatest victory: of the more than quarter-million German soldiers who had marched into Stalingrad, over 90,000 survived to be captured. The battle broke the back of the German invasion and was the turning point in the war on the eastern front. By the time it ended in February 1943, Stalin would have every right to exhort his fellow Allies to attack Germany immediately from the west to take some of the pressure off the Soviet front.

While the fighting was still intensifying on the outskirts of Stalingrad, the Germans also clashed with the British in North Africa. In late October 1942 the armies of Germany's sly "Desert Fox"—General Erwin Rommel—met

those of his British counterpart, General Bernard Montgomery, at the Egyptian town of El Alamein; after two weeks of fighting the Germans were forced to withdraw. Churchill may have deserved part of the credit. Before the battle he had summoned the rather high-handed Montgomery to suggest that the general study some logistics, only to hear him dismiss the notion that he should bother with such technical details. "After all, you know, they say that familiarity breeds contempt," Montgomery sniffed. "I would like to remind you," the prime minister replied, "that without a degree of familiarity we could not breed anything."

Although the British lost more men and matériel at El Alamein than did the Germans they defeated, they stopped the Axis advance on Alexandria just as the Allies launched an invasion of North Africa. Had Hitler broken through the Allies at both El Alamein and Stalingrad, the two pincers of Germany's eastward movement might have joined for a march on British-owned India—and the Axis powers might have won the war.

The Allied Victory

Encouraged by events on every front, in June 1942, Roosevelt and Churchill met in Washington to plan for sweeping the Axis forces from North Africa in preparation for a massive Allied assault on Europe later. To lead these unprecedented offensives the Allies selected U.S. Army General Dwight D. Eisenhower, who just a year earlier had been a lieutenant colonel conducting training maneuvers in Louisiana. But his plans and their execution had captured the notice of Chief of Staff General George C. Marshall, who kept a list of officers he intended to promote to top command posts if and when war came. As soon as it did, Marshall had tapped Eisenhower to work on strategy at the War Plans Division. By the spring of 1943, the military prodigy was a lieutenant general and in command of the Allied Forces in North Africa, which invaded the region in November 1942 and with the help of gung-ho generals Omar Bradley and George S. Patton ingeniously sent the Germans packing in May 1943. Seven months later Eisenhower was made Supreme Allied Commander in the European theater and sent to England to prepare for the invasion of France.

While Eisenhower was still fighting the battle of Tunisia, however, Roosevelt, Churchill, and the Allies' Combined Chiefs of Staff met at Casablanca, Morocco, to discuss the next phase of the war. Stalin was too busy on the eastern front to attend, but sent word reiterating how ardently he desired a second front to be opened in western Europe. Despite the Soviets' urging, at

Below, General Erwin Rommel was photographed in February of 1941 on his way into Libya in command of the German Afrika Korps. He proved effective during the 1940 German blitzkrieg in France, after which Hitler rewarded him with the chance to develop a tank corps patterned on Rommel's own ideas. In the desert, the Afrika Korps embarrassed the British Eighth Army, pushing it east almost to Cairo. A mystique soon developed around Rommel, and soldiers on both sides began to believe he was invincible. In 1942, however, General Bernard Montgomery revitalized the British force and led it to a crucial victory over Rommel's Afrika Korps at El Alamein. In 1944 Rommel was privy to an impending plot against Hitler's life, and perhaps was even behind it; in any case, he did nothing to stop the eventual assassination attempt, for which Hitler allowed him to swallow a lethal dose of poison rather than face trial.

General Dwight D. Eisenhower, below right, had recently been named Allied Commander of the North African campaign when this photograph was taken in March 1943. General George S. Patton, below left, was in charge of II Corps in the American army attached to the campaign. A strict disciplinarian, Patton used his men so effectively in North Africa that he was given an even wider command in the invasion of Italy later in 1943. His men, however, often felt that "Old Blood and Guts" Patton cared less about their survival than about his reputation. General Eisenhower never led men in the field during World War II, but proved himself a master at operational command.

Casablanca Churchill persuaded the Americans to postpone the eventual cross-Channel invasion until after an attack on the "soft underbelly of the Axis" in Italy and Sicily. Roosevelt and Churchill left Casablanca with the U.S. president's announcement that the war would end only upon the "unconditional surrender" of all the Axis powers—a reassurance to Stalin that Britain and the United States would not negotiate separately with the Nazis, who could not be defeated without Soviet cooperation.

Stalin did not, however, get his wish of a quick Allied incursion on the western front; in fact, the campaigns in Italy would delay the invasion of France by nearly a year. The Churchill-inspired assault began on July 10, 1943, when a 140,000 U.S. and British troops landed in Sicily under Eisenhower's command. General George S. Patton's Seventh Army and Bernard Montgomery's British Eighth Army stormed across the island, capturing it on August 17. The victory proved troublesome, however; on July 25, Italy's king had removed Mussolini as premier, and once Sicily was secured, set up a new regime that offered not only to surrender but to join the Allied side. The natural suspicions this created prolonged negotiations for more than a month—during which time Hitler inundated Italy's strategic areas with German reinforcements. In consequence, the Allied assault on the Italian mainland met considerable German resistance as well as mountains and winter weather that kept the Americans from taking Rome until June 5, 1944.

While the invasion of France continued to be postponed through the winter and spring of 1944, the U.S. and British air forces tried to further demoralize Germany with brutal bombing raids over industrial areas and urban centers such as Berlin and Leipzig. These aggressive maneuvers, combined with the fighting in Italy, were intended to divert Germany's attention from the covert Operation Overlord that Eisenhower was planning for what would be chosen as "D-Day"—the massive invasion of German-occupied France on the sixth of June 1944. The most ambitious military assault in human history seemed so uncertain of success that in the event of failure Eisenhower kept a statement for the press in his wallet reading, "My decision to attack at this time and place was based upon the best information available. If any blame or fault attaches to the attempt, it is mine alone."

The invasion's success, of course, attached to many, especially all those who had managed to keep it quiet enough to completely surprise the enemy. When the first brave soldiers of the U.S. Army's Second Ranger Battalion stormed the beaches of Normandy and scaled the sheer cliff of Pointe du Hoc, American paratroopers dropped the night before had already taken their places behind the Germans, who were utterly unprepared and in the end overrun. The situation elsewhere among the Allied invasion forces was more chaotic; in fact, the D-Day invasion nearly failed as cloud cover wreaked havoc with air and

At left, a letter from General Dwight D. Eisenhower, supreme commander of the D-Day operation, rallied the soldiers on the eve of the battle. Above, soldiers wade toward a Normandy beach from a landing craft on the morning of June 6, 1944. "We were all happy and smiling, telling jokes, and yelling," wrote one seaman who made the crossing, "But as soon as we dropped our ramp, an 88-mm came tearing in, killing almost half our men right there."

The overview above shows matériel being unloaded at Omaha Beach on France's northern coast, June 7, 1944. Only one day into the D-Day invasion, the beach had already become a huge artificial port. D-Day, also known as Operation Overlord, involved 3 million Allied soldiers in all of its phases. The exact details were somehow kept secret during planning, even though it was no secret at all that the Allies were expected to make an assault on Nazi-occupied France eventually. Fooled by a decoy operation farther east, the Germans were completely surprised by the location of the D-Day landings when they began on June 6. Nevertheless, Allied losses were heavy. The first soldiers to reach Omaha Beach were pinned at the water's edge for hours; finally, reinforcements helped the push forward, but nearly 5,000 men died in the effort. By the end of the day, almost 150,000 Allied troops had arrived on the Normandy beaches.

sea operations. In the end, however, the Germans could not withstand the overwhelming Allied forces, who in the space of one week took a beachhead sixty miles long by putting a million troops, a half-million tons of supplies, and over 170,000 vehicles on it. After another two months of bitter fighting, Allied forces liberated Paris on August 25, and despite a forceful German counterattack, by mid-September most of France and Belgium were free of enemy troops and it was clear that the European war was entering its last phase.

In the autumn, however, the fighting bogged down on the borders of Germany and stayed there all winter. The Nazis staged a last blitzkrieg on December 16, 1944, when they advanced through the frozen Ardennes Forest along a fifty-mile forward bulge in their line in Belgium and Luxembourg. "We are having one hell of a war," General Patton cabled home. The fierce, month-long Battle of the Bulge finally turned in the Allies' favor the day after Christmas when the weather cleared and the Allied planes could attack German tanks. In January 1945, Stalin launched a final offensive against Hitler from the east. As the British and Americans swept into western Germany and the Soviets swarmed in from the east, Churchill warned Eisenhower that if Stalin got to Berlin first the U.S.S.R. would gain dangerous leverage over the postwar division of Europe. The U.S. general said he was more interested in ending the ground war first, and Churchill's appeal to the ailing President Roosevelt was turned back to his supreme allied commander. Eisenhower considered General Omar Bradley's estimate that liberating Berlin before the Soviets did would cost 100,000 American lives, decided it would be a "pretty stiff price to pay for a prestige objective," and left the way open for the U.S.S.R. to do so instead. The Red Army had already occupied eastern Germany and Czechoslovakia.

In February 1945, the "Big Three"—Roosevelt, Churchill, and Stalin—met at Yalta, a seaside resort in the Crimea, to hold the next in a series of meetings to plan Allied strategy and sketch the world's future. Victory in Europe now appeared imminent, but the Alliance was divided by basically different approaches to treatment of the German enemy, Russian participation in the Pacific War, establishment of the United Nations organization, and control of Poland. When Roosevelt expressed the hope that the Yalta conference would last less than a week, Churchill replied, "I do not see any way of realizing our hopes about world organization in five or six days. Even the Almighty took seven." After all, the U.S.S.R. controlled much of eastern Europe, including all of Poland, which FDR and Churchill considered the key to the region. The Soviets joined the West in a Declaration on Liberated Europe that spelled out plans for free elections and democratic programs for the newly liberated territories—although in actuality the Soviet Union had already

In February 1945, the Allied leaders, photographed below, met at Yalta to prepare for the end of the war. Seated, left to right, are Winston Churchill of Great Britain, Franklin Roosevelt of the United States, and Joseph Stalin of the Soviet Union. Standing behind them are Anthony Eden (Great Britain), Edward Stettinius (U.S.), Alexander Cadogan (Great Britain), Vyacheslav Molotov (U.S.S.R.), and Averell Harriman (U.S.). The Yalta Conference set a date for the first meeting of the United Nations and was in effect a precursor to its Security Council, with veto power accorded to each of the nations present.

In spring 1942, just months after the United States entered the war raging in Europe, President Franklin Roosevelt informed Soviet Premier Joseph Stalin that he expected the formation of a second front against Germany's Fortress Europe that very year. The assurance proved wishful thinking, but it was the best the United States could offer to the Allied nation confronting the concentrated might of the German Wermacht. Russians were dying by the hundreds of thousands, and Roosevelt knew that a Soviet defeat meant the end of any meaningful resistance to Hitler's juggernaut.

The U.S. military leaders pushed for an attack across the English Channel into occupied France by spring 1943, but that date came and went, as did a second in August. Roosevelt and Churchill tried to appease a furious Stalin by increasing lend-lease and calling for Germany's "unconditional surrender." For Stalin, all this was window dressing. What he needed was a second front to relieve his blood-drained nation from the German onslaught.

It took until November 1943 for the shaky, often bickering alliance to agree on military strategy. After some heated discussions the British and Americans committed to the cross-Channel attack, designated Overlord, and the supreme commander would be General Dwight D. Eisenhower. Stating the plan was simple: find a suitable beach, gather a landing force, isolate the battlefield, and land the men. Once a beachhead was established, pour in the logistical followup, and then break out into the countryside. Executing the plan was not so simple. Crossing the treacherous English Channel with its unexpected storms, enor-

mous tides, and tricky currents would be just the first step of the amphibious assault.

The attack on Fortress Europe from the coast of England required the utmost secrecy. The assembling force was isolated lest the plan leak, and deceptive measures were taken to mislead the Germans about the actual landing site. At best, the Allies could put some five divisions on the beach for an initial assault against a German defender with fifty infantry and eleven armored divisions.

The Allied planners focused on the beaches around Caen and the Cotentin Peninsula in northern France rather than on Calais, even though it meant the force would be crossing at a wider part of the English Channel. That disadvantage was far outweighed by what the site offered: comparatively scanty fortifications and beaches ideally suited for successful exits. The clincher was an isolated battlefield.

The date was set for May 1, 1944, to allow for a dawn invasion at low tide, when beach obstacles that could impede the landing craft would be visible. But it soon became apparent that the May 1 date would find the Allies still short of the landing craft necessary to mount the great invasion. Reluctantly, Eisenhower reset D-Day to the next suitable date—June 5, 1944. The force continued to assemble as British, Canadian, and American youth in uniform flooded into southern England.

A great storm forced postponement to June 6, so it was just before midnight on June 5 that the Allied airborne troops jumped into France. Their mission was to seize and hold the bridges and roads the Germans could use to move to the battlefield once the

great amphibious maneuvers began. The British airborne landed on the left of the invasion area; the Americans on the right. Both drops suffered from scattering, particularly of the U.S. paratroopers, because of enemy ground fire and a lack of navigational aids. The troops had to locate one another and then move and fight in small groups, many unrelated by unit, rather than in organized battle formations as planned. The one advantage of this scattering was to confuse the enemy, who had great difficulty determining the size and scope of the invading force. By the end of D-Day, the exits from the beaches and the entrances to the battle area were held by the Allies.

The assault beaches were named, from right to left, Utah, Omaha, Gold, Juno, and Sword. The Americans attacked Omaha and Utah, the Canadians Juno, and the British Gold and Sword. Shortly after 6 A.M. the invasion rolled ashore. At Sword, Gold, and Utah, enemy resistance was light and the Allied forces had considerable success; on Utah Beach, for example, U.S. soldiers moved rapidly up the causeways to join some of the airborne troops.

At Juno, meanwhile, the invading Canadians faced a beach littered with partially submerged obstacles. When engineers were unable to clear paths, landing craft were forced to feel their way in. The troops waded ashore and zigzagged through the obstacles, but German mines took a heavy toll. In the first hour of the invasion at Juno assault team members faced a fifty-fifty chance of becoming casualties.

The savagery peaked at Omaha Beach, the largest of the Overlord assault areas, where the Germans had built formidable defenses and heavily mined the waters and sand. Their weapons were fixed to cover the beach with grazing enfilade as well as plunging fire. Omaha was designed to be a killing zone.

West of the shale beach, the ominous Pointe du Hoc jutted into the English Channel. The promontory provided an elevated vantage point from which huge German guns could fire upon both Omaha and Utah beaches; intelligence and photo reconnaissance had identified six 155-mm guns in casemates on the point. The Allied command knew Omaha was the key to the fate of the landings.

The task of neutralizing the German guns fell to the U.S. Army Second Ranger Battalion. Three companies landed at Pointe du Hoc at 7:10 A.M. and engaged the Germans on top of the cliffs in a heavy firefight. Within minutes of the landing the first Ranger was up; then the others fought their way in small groups to the casemates, only to find the 155-mm guns removed. The Rangers moved forward, sending a two-man patrol down a narrow road leading south, where they discovered some guns 500 yards from the casemates. The Americans quickly put the guns out of action with thermite grenades. Shortly after 9 A.M. the Army Rangers on Pointe du Hoc had accomplished their mission, the first American unit to do so. The cost was half their fighting force.

At Omaha Beach itself everything went wrong. The tanks launched to support the infantry sank. With few exceptions, units did not land where planned because strong winds and tidal currents had scattered the boats in all directions. Throughout the landing the formidable German defensive positions showered deadly fire upon

Above, a desolate marker indicates the temporary grave of an American soldier who was killed in the shelling at Normandy on D-Day.

the ranks of the invading Americans. Bodies and damaged craft littered the sand. Men seeking refuge behind obstacles pondered the deadly sprint across the beach to the seawall, which offered at least some protection at the base of the cliff.

At 8:30 A.M. all Allied landings ceased at Omaha: the force on the beach was on its own. Slowly, in small groups, the troops scaled the cliffs. Navy destroyers sailed in, scraping bot-

tom in the shallow water and blasting away point-blank at the German fortifications. By noon enemy fire had decreased noticeably as the German defensive positions were taken from the rear and exits opened. By nightfall the Americans—who had suffered 2,400 casualties—held positions nowhere near the planned objectives but they did have a toehold. In eighteen harrowing hours, the walls of Hitler's Fortress Europe had been breached.

begun remolding eastern Europe to its own liking. Under the agreement, however, Poland's boundaries were redrawn to give Russia the eastern half, a move compensated by giving Poland formerly German territory on the west; Marshall Tito's Communist Yugoslav government was recognized, and pending a final settlement Germany and its capital city, Berlin, were divided into four zones respectively controlled by Britain, France, the Soviet Union, and the United States. Finally, Stalin agreed to enter the Pacific war and to conclude a treaty with Chiang Kai-shek's Nationalist Chinese government, thus abandoning Communist leader Mao Zedong.

Apart from producing a signed treaty, Yalta was to World War II what Versailles had been to World War I, a convocation of the victors to decide the peace. The new agreement in fact marked an even higher point of Allied unity, but not for long. Mutual mistrust set in quickly, and in the end Stalin would violate most of the promises he made at Yalta. Even at the time, many American critics complained that Roosevelt had given too much away, while others agreed but excused the president for having done so on the grounds that he was so visibly ill. Reflecting after the war, Henry L. Stimson opined that FDR's policy was "often either unknown or not clear to those who had to execute it"; indeed, major aspects "seemed self-contradictory." Stimson concluded that as a wartime leader the president "proved himself as good as one man could be—but one man was not enough to keep track of so vast an undertaking."

Of course, the war was by no means over after the Yalta conference, as the Japanese threat remained. Although the enormous commitment to the D-Day invasion had rendered the Pacific theater a lower priority, by the end of 1944 Allied forces were in reach of the Japanese homeland. Beginning late in 1942 when the U.S. First Marine Division was replaced by two U.S. Army divisions that cleared the South Pacific island of Guadalcanal of its Japanese occupiers, the forces of flamboyant U.S. Army General Douglas MacArthur and stolid U.S. Navy Admiral Chester Nimitz had been steadily leapfrogging from island to island ever closer to the Japanese mainland, and by July 1944 had reached the Mariana Islands just east of the Philippines. All of the outer island bastions from the Solomons to the Aleutians were under American control.

Under the command of the publicity-mad MacArthur, instantly recognizable by his aviator sunglasses, corncob pipe, and bluster, the Allied campaign to retake the Philippines began in October 1944 and ended in victory that winter. Largely because it gave him a chance to wade ashore on the island of Leyte and proclaim, "People of the Philippines: I have returned," MacArthur had argued for staging the offensive on Japan from the Philippines rather than China, and Nimitz and Roosevelt had gone along. The Japanese responded with ships from three directions that in late October 1944 engaged the Allies in the Battle of Leyte Gulf, the largest naval conflict in history and the one that marked the advent of devastating suicide missions by Japanese kamikaze pilots, named for the "divine wind" that was said to have turned back the Mongol invasion of Japan centuries earlier. The United States had the clear air advantage in the Battle of Leyte Gulf: 1,280 planes to Japan's

716. "With so few planes we can assure success only through suicide attack," Japanese Vice Admiral Takijiro Onishi told his senior commanders. "Each fighter must be armed with a 550-pound bomb and crash-land on a carrier deck." Despite the substantial impact of the selfless kamikazes, much of Japan's sea power was destroyed in the Battle of Leyte Gulf along with its hold on the Philippines. The Japanese lost 56,263 men at Leyte to 2,888 Americans—a truly disproportionate victory for MacArthur.

On February 19, 1945, the U.S. Marines landed on the flyspeck island of Iwo Jima 750 miles from Tokyo, a strategic prize the Allies needed as an air base in the region. The island had been identified as a necessary target of the American advance because it would provide airfields for "short-legged" fighter planes needed to escort the B-29 bombers over the Japanese home islands. The bombers were already raiding Tokyo and other major cities from bases in Guam and Saipan, but were suffering substantial losses because they lacked fighter escorts. To increase the effectiveness of the bomber attacks and thus shorten the war was the rationale and justification for the terrible cost inherent in the plan to capture this island fortress. But Iwo Jima was a formidable fortress—an island formed entirely of black volcanic ash, six miles long, and heavily fortified by hidden concrete bunkers and a labyrinth of underground trenches and tunnels. The U.S. troops took four weeks to

General Douglas MacArthur was photographed below in October 1944 at the moment he made good on his famous promise to return to the Philippines. MacArthur was in command of 130,000 troops in the Philippines when the Japanese initiated an attack the day of Pearl Harbor. MacArthur's force put up a defense, but when it became apparent in March 1942 that most of the remaining troops would be captured, Roosevelt ordered MacArthur himself to leave. The general's words upon departing were "I shall return." He did. When MacArthur accepted Japan's unconditional surrender the following year, though, he was accompanied by one of the real heroes of the Philippines: his successor Jonathan Wainwright, who had been left behind with 15,000 other American troops and survived the conflict in a prisoner-of-war camp.

Above, the death of the commander in chief, Franklin D. Roosevelt, on April 12, 1945, was listed in daily newspapers with the same plain dignity accorded other war deaths. The funeral procession in Washington, opposite page, drew 400,000 people. A young soldier gazing at the White House right after Roosevelt's death said, "I felt as if I knew him." Then he paused and added, "I felt as if he knew me—and I felt as if he liked me."

seize Iwo Jima from the Japanese occupiers, who fought from a subterranean labyrinth effectively enough to kill 7,000 Americans and wound more than 19,000 others in one of the most brutal engagements of the entire war. "We cannot go from Iwo to Iwo," Secretary of the Navy James Forrestal told Rear Admiral Ellis Zacharias. "We must find a formula to sustain peace without this endless, frightful bloodshed." But Forrestal's wish was not to be. On April 1, U.S. troops landed on Okinawa just 360 miles from Japan, and struggled to win an even bloodier battle. After a substantial toll exacted by kamikaze attacks, the fighting ended in late June with almost 12,500 Americans dead and 33,700 wounded—along with 42,000 Okinawan casualties and an appalling Japanese death toll of more than 100,000. With the seizure of Okinawa, U.S. ships were free to cruise the Japanese coast, shelling it at will. Many of Japan's leaders argued that it was time to sue for peace, but the intransigence of others would precipitate the final offensive decision of World War II, which appropriately enough would come from the United States—but not from Franklin Roosevelt.

The Passing of a Leader

In 1944 FDR ran for a fourth term as president with little need to campaign and less doubt as to the outcome. The Democrats did make one crucial decision: to drop Vice President Henry Wallace, whose ties with labor had come to concern both Northern bosses and Southern conservatives, in favor of Senator Harry S. Truman of Missouri, who was pretty much a political cipher at the time. The Republicans, meanwhile, halfheartedly nominated Governor Thomas E. Dewey of New York, who agreed with much of the New Deal as well as the broad outlines of Roosevelt's foreign policies.

With so little reason to change presidents America reelected FDR, although by a smaller margin than in 1940. But less than three months after his fourth inauguration, on April 12, 1945, Roosevelt died of a cerebral hemorrhage in Warm Springs, Georgia. The nation and much of the world went into mourning. Churchill felt as though he had been struck a physical blow. Stalin received the news with apparently genuine distress as well, gripping American Ambassador Averell Harriman's hand for more than thirty seconds before sitting down. Chiang Kai-shek left his breakfast untouched to pray. Nazi propaganda chief Joseph Goebbels told Hitler, "My führer, I congratulate you. Roosevelt is dead. It is written in the stars that the second half of April will be the turning point for us." To a shell-shocked American public, FDR was a martyr, and few believed that the new president—Harry Truman—could ever fill even one of his shoes.

The public was right to be concerned about Truman's qualifications: his background indicated some competence but no special leadership qualities. He had grown up in rural Missouri and after high school worked as a bank clerk in Kansas City, to which he returned after serving as an army captain in France during World War I to open a haberdashery, the failure of which sent him into bankruptcy. The feisty, "show-me" Missourian found his vocation in politics, which he got into through Kansas City boss Tom Prendergast, who

Times Square was jammed on May 7, 1945, with New Yorkers awaiting confirmation of Germany's surrender. The news, however, would not be official until the next day, May 8, which would be celebrated as V-E Day all over the world. The worst of the Nazi nightmare had already ended with Adolf Hitler's suicide on April 30. By the end of his dictatorship, Hitler had come to despise the German people, announcing with peculiar satisfaction in September 1944 that "If the German people was to be conquered in the struggle, then it had been too weak to face the test of history, and was fit only for destruction." His handpicked successor, Admiral Karl Doenitz, was in office only twelve days, long enough to fire all high-ranking Nazis from the government, to urge the German people to begin rebuilding their country, and to authorize an unconditional surrender to the Allies.

helped his friend win a county judgeship in 1922. After that Truman attended the Kansas City School of Law, and in 1934 was elected to the U.S. Senate. Before he was catapulted into the vice presidency at the age of sixty, Truman had seemed destined for a steady but undistinguished Senate career.

But destiny can change quickly for both men and nations. Never before in the history of the United States, not even after Lincoln's assassination, had the nation's leadership changed so suddenly at such a critical juncture. Having been vice president for less than three months, Truman had not been privy to the nation's war and peace plans but nevertheless was being called upon to make important military decisions as well as to deal with the establishment of the United Nations, relations with the Allies, economic conversion after the European war, and a host of other vexing problems. What's more, he was surrounded by FDR's former aides, most of whom considered the new president ill-equipped for the tasks at hand, as did the general public. Truman was in a hopeless position, fully aware that in the minds of Americans he was no substitute for one of the most adored chief executives in U.S. history—and that no matter what policies he presented they would break apart the bipartisan consensus Roosevelt had built up over three full terms in the White House.

In addition to the emotional crater left by Roosevelt's passing, at the time of Truman's accession to the presidency he also had to deal with the Allied bombing of the Japanese mainland. The world's attention had turned to the Far East as the war in Europe drew to a close with Germany's capitulation on May 7, 1945. By then relations between the United States and Great Britain and between both with the Soviet Union had soured. Truman reacted sharply to Stalin's refusal to honor the pledges he had made at Yalta regarding the disposition of eastern Europe as well as to the Soviets' further threats to the independence of Turkey and Iran, also contrary to prior agreements. For his part, Stalin resented the sudden cessation of the Lend-Lease program and the other Allies' refusal to allow his country a role in Italy—plus he feared the development of an Anglo–American alliance against the U.S.S.R.

Truman, Churchill, and Stalin nevertheless agreed to meet in July just outside Berlin at Potsdam to discuss the Pacific war and postwar plans. The conference disappointed all concerned. Truman was still unsure in his new office, and Churchill was out of his midway through the conference, having to resign as prime minister on July 26 upon learning of his defeat in the English election. He was replaced at the global talks by Britain's new premier, Labor Party leader Clement Attlee, who lacked his predecessor's prestige and was content to play a passive role, even though he was better prepared than his American counterpart.

The no-longer-so-big three leaders decided at Potsdam to establish a council of foreign ministers to draft treaties regarding the nations of eastern Europe and to divide Germany and establish reparations schedules. Truman and Stalin clashed over the latter but agreed to refer the matter to the foreign ministers. The Soviets repeated their intention to enter the Pacific war, prompting the Allies to issue a declaration urging Japan to surrender or face "prompt and utter destruction"—an entirely credible threat that gave President Truman an insuperable bargaining advantage at Potsdam, especially after he learned on July 17 that the previous day the U.S Army's top-secret, $2 billion Manhattan Project had successfully tested an atomic bomb in the New Mexico desert, breaking windows 125 miles away in a flash so bright a blind woman reported seeing it. "The war's over," Brigadier General Leslie R. Groves, the administrator in charge of the top-secret Los Alamos project,

From July 17 to August 2, 1945, the three Allied leaders met for talks in the elegant suburb of Potsdam outside Berlin; they are, from left to right, Joseph Stalin, Harry Truman, and Winston Churchill. Midway through the meeting, Churchill's coalition party suffered a stunning defeat in Britain's general elections, and Churchill was replaced both at the meeting and as prime minister by Clement Attlee.

noted upon witnessing the awesome explosion. "One or two of those things, and Japan will be finished." Truman wrote in his diary that "We have discovered the most terrible bomb in the history of the world."

The new president attempted, without success, to use the existence of the bomb to intimidate Stalin into accepting America's wishes at Potsdam. As Churchill put it, the newly confident Truman "told the Russians just where they got on and off and generally bossed the whole meeting," but Stalin still refused to hold free elections in Poland or anywhere else occupied by his Red Army. Meanwhile, J. Robert Oppenheimer and several other Manhattan Project scientists—the only people who really knew what it would do—argued against actually dropping the atomic bomb. But faced with unacceptable estimates of American casualties in a protracted conventional war with Japan as well as the prospect of an expanded Communist presence in Asia should the Soviet Union enter the Pacific war, Truman opted to end the conflict by the quickest, if most devastating, means available.

As the Allies were meeting in Potsdam, Premier Kantaro Suzuki issued a statement rejecting the Potsdam declaration, vowing that Japan would "ignore it entirely and resolutely fight for the successful conclusion of the war." What Suzuki did not admit was that Japan's military forces had been badly crippled.

Truman was convinced that the Japanese would fight to the bitter end, and thus made the momentous decision to authorize the B-29 bomber *Enola Gay* to drop the atomic bomb, which had more power than 20,000 tons of TNT and which all but obliterated the city of Hiroshima on August 6, 1945, killing an estimated 80,000 people. "We turned back to look at Hiroshima," pilot Paul W. Tibbets, Jr., recalled. "The city was hidden by that awful cloud . . . boiling up, mushrooming, terrible and incredibly tall." Nevertheless, as is shown in the minutes of the Japanese conferences held after the first bomb was dropped, Japan's leaders intended to fight on. Two days later, the Soviets entered the Pacific war, and a day after that the United States dropped a second atomic bomb on Nagasaki. The combination forced the Japanese government to offer surrender on the condition that Emperor Hirohito be allowed to remain as a nominal constitutional monarch. "I cannot bear to see my innocent people suffer any longer," the emperor told his war council about his post-Nagasaki decision to surrender. The Allies accepted only if the emperor would be subject to the supreme commander of the Pacific forces. When Hirohito agreed to this, hostilities ceased on August 14, and the Japanese formally surrendered on September 2, aboard the battleship *Missouri* anchored in Tokyo Bay. World War II was over. More people had been killed—over 53 million—than in any other war in history. "The great question is: can war be outlawed?" General Douglas MacArthur would later ask Congress. "If so, it would mark the greatest advance in civilization since the Sermon on the Mount."

Perhaps the most backward, barbarous step civilization has ever taken occurred with Nazi Germany's genocidal acts against an entire race of people. When Allied troops swept into Germany in the spring of 1945, they encountered the Nazi extermination camps, a result of Adolf Hitler's "final solution of the Jewish question," also known as "the Holocaust." Hitler's deranged quest was to render Europe *Judenfrie* (free of Jews). At Nazi death camps like Buchenwald, Dachau, and Auschwitz more than six million Jews were murdered, along with six million other "undesirables," including Poles, Slavs, Gypsies, homosexuals, and the mentally challenged. The Nazis, in Winston Churchill's estimation, had committed "the greatest and most horrible crime ever committed in the whole history of the world." Words can never describe the horrors of these death camps where torture was a routine sport, starvation was the norm, and skeletal corpses were neatly piled up like cords of wood for burning in German ovens. In 1944 at Auschwitz, as many as 10,000 people a day were exterminated.

Preparations for Peace

During the last stages of the conflict the United States and its allies had already begun preparing for the postwar world in economic, political, and humanitarian terms. The Anglo-American passion for spreading democracy and doing good works had intensified during the war, and representatives from forty-four nations had been sent to Virginia in May 1943 to organize the Food and Agricultural Organization with a mandate to combat world hunger. With a similar eye toward international cooperation, in his very last days President Roosevelt had set in motion his plans to create the United Nations, a forum for international cooperation that he and many others hoped would be able to prevent another global conflict. The United Nations was established on June 26, 1945, though one of its bodies, the Relief and Rehabilitation Administration, charged with helping those countries physically ravaged by World War II, had been set up in November 1943. A year earlier, the participants at the Bretton Woods economic conference had organized the International Monetary Fund to stabilize world currencies and set up the International Bank for Reconstruction and Development, better known as the World Bank, to make direct loans to member nations for reconstruction. The Bretton Woods conference also established the U.S. dollar at a value of $35 per ounce of gold, where it had been since early in the New Deal; other nations then fixed their rates according to the dollar, in effect recognizing America's as the world's premier currency.

Thus began, despite Henry Luce's more chronological definition, the real "American Century." Even if it wouldn't last quite that long, for at least the next generation the United States would be the dominant nation on the planet in every sense. "While the rest of the world came out bruised and scarred and nearly destroyed, we came out with the most unbelievable machinery, tools, manpower, money," veteran Paul Edwards bragged to writer Studs Terkel for his 1984 oral history *The Good War*.

America's chief assets were its military and economic strength, but there was something more to call upon, less tangible but potentially more valuable. The United States had provided the tools and the men to save Europe and Russia from Hitler and his Nazis. The Allies had driven the Italians out of their African colonies and soon would throw the Japanese out of China, Indochina, the Netherlands East Indies, the Philippines, Burma, and Korea.

America had asked for nothing in return. After World War I, the Allies had tried to punish Germany through the various punitive clauses in the Versailles Treaty. As a result they got Hitler. After World War II, the United States followed a policy of relative magnanimity toward the losers. In occupied Germany and Japan the United States taught the ways of democracy to the point that Vietnamese nationalist leader Ho Chi Minh hailed America as the true

At left, victims of the atomic attack on Hiroshima gather in search of first aid. On July 26, 1945, the Allies had formally threatened Japan with "utter devastation" unless it surrendered immediately. After Japan issued a defiant response, President Truman authorized use of the atomic bomb. The first one fell on Hiroshima on August 6. Japan still refused to surrender. A second fell on Nagasaki on August 9. The Japanese Army still refused to surrender, but Emperor Hirohito overruled it and capitulated. More than 120,000 people died in the two atomic bomb attacks on Japan, while a conventional invasion would almost certainly have cost millions of lives on both sides. Nonetheless, the misery wrought by a single weapon became one of the most disturbing legacies of World War II. Below, the hands on a watch stopped at the moment the first atomic bomb exploded over Hiroshima, Japan: 8:16 A.M. on August 6, 1945.

friend of the earth's oppressed. So did such dissimilar leaders as Charles de Gaulle, Churchill, and on one occasion even Stalin himself. In a world full of hatred, death, destruction, deception, and double-dealing, the United States at the end of World War II was almost universally regarded as a disinterested champion of justice, freedom, and democracy. American prestige would never be so high again.

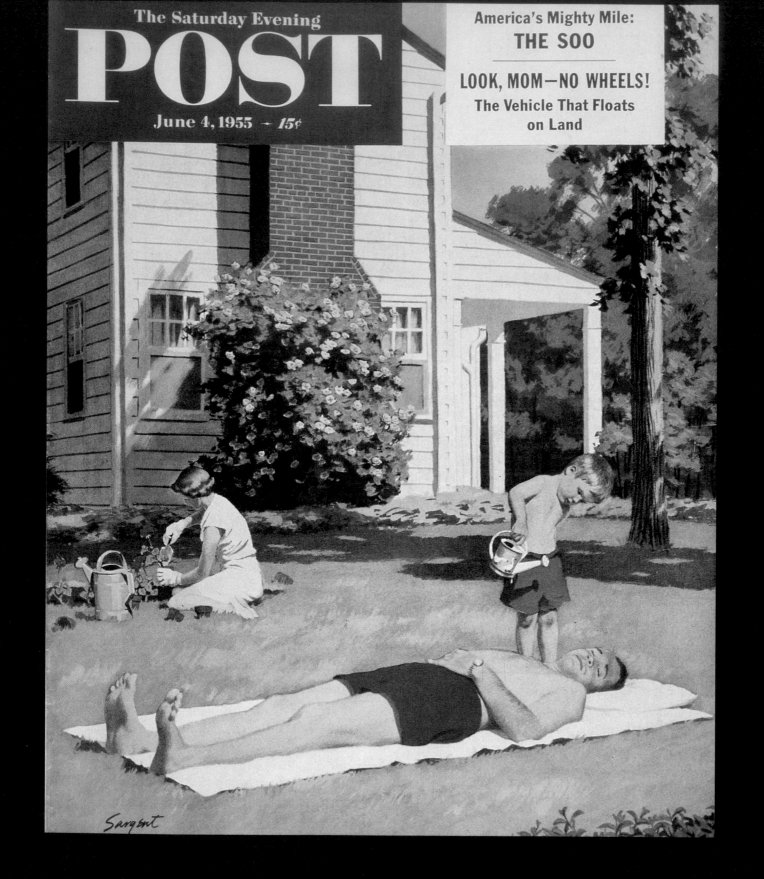

The Saturday Evening

POST

June 4, 1955 – 15¢

America's Mighty Mile:
THE SOO

LOOK, MOM—NO WHEELS!
The Vehicle That Floats
on Land

Sargent

CHAPTER 18

THE COLD WAR

America entered the post-World War II era powerful but uncertain how to use its newfound might. History's most devastating conflict might have ended, but it hardly left the global situation neat and tidy. In fact, the world's power centers were as confused and disorganized as they had ever been, and the new superpower was headed by an unprepossessing former haberdasher who despite having shown tremendous mettle in ending the war was still no Franklin Delano Roosevelt in the eyes of either his nation or the world. But as Truman himself put it: "Well, all the president is, is a glorified public relations man who spends his time flattering, kissing, and kicking people to get them to do what they are supposed to do anyway." As has ever been the case in American history, his leadership grew to fill the perceived void. At the same time, the U.S. economy, driven to new heights by the war, gave no hint of declining any time soon.

For one thing, plenty of reasons remained to keep manufacturing weapons and other war matériel, especially in the nation that had accepted the mantle of Western leadership. Despite the war's end, fighting continued in parts of the Pacific as various European countries tried to regain colonies the Japanese had seized from them amid the chaos resulting from the Axis collapse. In Southeast Asia, for example, in September 1945 nationalist ideologue Ho Chi Minh announced the formation of the Democratic Republic of Vietnam, which France recognized six months later as "a free state within the French Union." Ho went to Paris to sign the accords, but they proved short-lived; as soon as they felt they had the power to do so, French forces in Southeast Asia attacked the nationalist Vietnamese troops and in November 1946 massacred 6,000 civilians in Haiphong. Embittered and far less idealistic, Ho started organizing a new army, the Viet Minh, and the quagmire of the Vietnam War began to form.

The *Saturday Evening Post* cover at left depicts the peaceful world of suburbia in 1955. During the postwar years new tracts outside every American city promised homeowners a bit of extra space and comfort. In the midst of unprecedented prosperity, however, Americans in the 1950s grappled with the deadliest threat ever devised: the specter of mass destruction through atomic warfare. In an attempt to reduce panic while at the same time preparing the public for the possibility of nuclear attack, the Federal Civil Defense Agency issued the above poster in 1950.

During the Chinese Revolution Mao Zedong, right, in a 1944 photograph addressing some of his followers, led the People's Liberation Army, which drew its strongest support from rural districts. China's Nationalist and Communist parties had briefly united against Japan during World War II, but even before it ended, civil war resumed between the two factions. The United States backed the Nationalists under Chiang Kai-shek. Mao's Communist People's Liberation Army fielded a smaller force, but one that proved unshakable even in the face of defeat. In late 1948 the Nationalist army was decimated at the Battle of Hwai-Hai, losing half a million men in two months of fighting. After the British, Americans, and Soviets declined to intervene on behalf of the Nationalists in mid-January 1949, China began its transition to Communist rule.

In the meantime, while the Dutch tried to wrest back control of Southeast Asia from its Japanese puppet government and the British tried to hold sway in India and Malaysia, China roiled as the Soviet-backed Communist forces of Mao Zedong arrayed themselves against those of U.S.-supported Nationalist Chiang Kai-shek. The struggle for the East would simmer until another day, however; immediately after World War II the most important clashes took place in Europe—where Allied armies had replaced the retreating Germans—between the United States and the Soviet Union, and would evolve into what businessman and statesman Bernard Baruch would dub "the Cold War."

Harry Truman would play an even greater role in the Cold War than he had in the hot one just ended—not that even he considered himself qualified for the task, having told reporters upon Roosevelt's death that "I felt like the moon, the stars, and all the planets had fallen on me." For all the doubts about his abilities, Truman developed into the architect of America's position in the world and to some extent determined the course of U.S. presidents for the rest of the century. As he had said in his first message to Congress on April 16, 1945: "The responsibility of the great states is to serve and not to dominate the world."

Early in 1947 Prime Minister Clement Attlee informed Truman that Great Britain, financially weakened by the war, could no longer honor its aid commitments to Greece, Turkey, or the Middle East—just as Yugoslavia–based guerrillas threatened the shaky Greek monarchy while the Soviet Union was challenging Turkey's position as guardian of the Dardanelles strait into the Mediterranean Sea. Truman responded on March 12 by asking Congress for $400 million in aid to Greece and Turkey, arguing, "I believe that it must be the policy of the United States to support free people who are resisting attempted subjugation by armed minorities or by outside pressures. I believe that we must assist free people to work out their own destinies in their own way." The thinking behind this declaration came to be known as the Truman Doctrine, actually a restatement of the previous position that applied in fact rather than theory but coming when and how it did set off a national debate on the nature of U.S. foreign policy heading into the Cold War.

Americans divided among three basic responses to the Truman Doctrine and the president's overall stance on foreign affairs. The first and by far the largest group, Truman's supporters, viewed the U.S.S.R. as a threat comparable to Nazi Germany in the 1930s, whose aggressiveness they believed should have been challenged at the time to prevent World War II. Now this majority of the public looked to their president's strength and firmness to shield the West from Communist advances. A far smaller second group, led by former President Herbert Hoover and Republican Senator Robert Taft of Ohio, agreed that world Communism was now America's greatest enemy but disagreed that the best way to contain Stalin was through alliances with and commitments to other governments. Instead they preferred what some called the "fortress America" approach, in which the United States would develop

The map below shows the Cold War balance of power as it developed in Europe from 1945 to 1955. With the success of the Marshall Plan in the economic sphere, starting in 1948 European nations participated in talks regarding a military pact to be known as the North Atlantic Treaty Organization (NATO). Providing for mutual defense, NATO was to be a fully operational cooperative, not merely a paper commitment as Europe's previous alliances had been. The finished version of the pact was signed in 1949 by the nations shown below as well as Canada, Iceland, and the United States. In 1955 the Soviet Union organized its sphere into a similar organization through the Warsaw Pact.

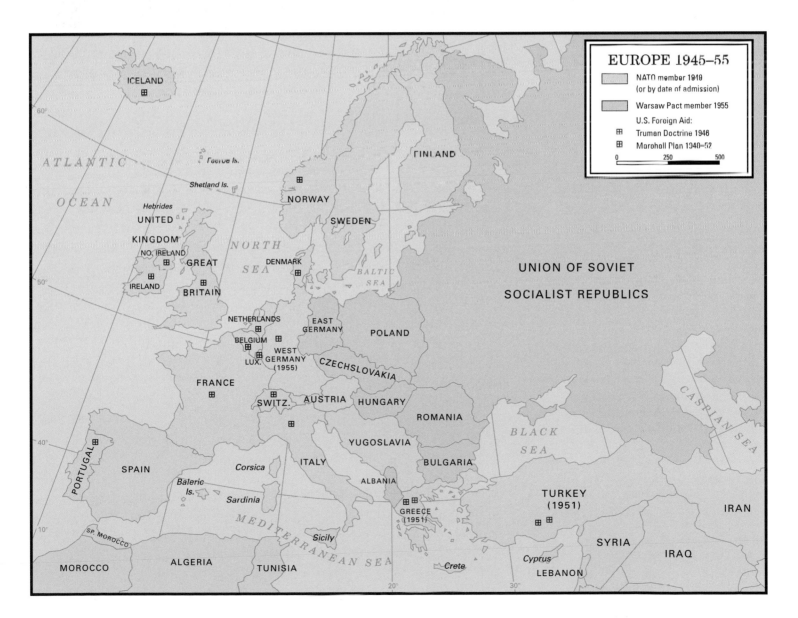

Three of the leading voices of the Truman era emanated from the erudite Dean Acheson, left; the formidable Robert Taft, middle, and George Marshall, right, whom Truman once called "the greatest living American." Their paths crossed during the creation of the Marshall Plan, instigated in 1947 by Acheson, named for Marshall, and strongly opposed by Senator Taft. Under the plan nations struggling in the aftermath of the war were to receive billions of dollars in aid from the United States. "It is necessary for our national security," Acheson asserted in announcing the initiative, "and it is our duty and our privilege as human beings."

massive military retaliation capability and whatever else it took to protect itself from foreign foes, but would not do the same for other nations. FDR's former vice president Henry Wallace and his followers held a third view, that the Truman Doctrine was a front for American imperialism and that the nation should concentrate on domestic reforms rather than a struggle against the Soviet Union, a misunderstood country whose leaders genuinely wanted peace, according to Wallace and his supporters.

Had the Hoover, Taft, and Wallace supporters come together they might have been able to defeat Truman, who instead won out in Congress by fashioning a bipartisan foreign policy with the help of sympathetic Republicans led by Senator Arthur Vandenberg of Michigan. Thus Truman managed to obtain his aid package for Greece and Turkey, the first of several administration efforts to lay down a new framework for U.S. foreign policy.

The next was the grandest of all: the Marshall Plan (although it was more the concept of Undersecretary of State Dean Acheson and State Department Soviet experts Charles Bohlen and George F. Kennan than it was of Secretary of State George C. Marshall). The Marshall Plan called for a large-scale economic assistance program for Europe, including the Soviet Union and its satellites. Marshall estimated that the plan would cost some $17 billion over the first four years, and in December 1947 Truman asked Congress for the initial appropriation. The Soviets promptly attacked what they called "dollar imperialism," while Wallace called it "the martial plan." It was actually the second part of the policy of "containment" that U.S. chargé d'affaires in Moscow George F. Kennan had recommended to President Truman and explained in a seminal article in *Foreign Affairs* magazine under the byline "X": the imposition of "unalterable counterforce at every point where [the Soviets] show signs of encroaching upon the interests of a peaceful and stable world," militarily or economically. With the encouragement of the administration, in 1947 a bipartisan majority in Congress passed the National Security Act creating a national military establishment as well as the Central Intelligence Agency (CIA) to conduct and coordinate intelligence-gathering in foreign countries.

The near-libertarian Robert Taft opposed the Marshall Plan in the belief that it would permanently embroil America in Europe, while Wallace and his followers called the program a betrayal of the World War II alliance with the U.S.S.R. in that it was designed to keep the Soviets from becoming too powerful. The combination of these two forces in Congress might have defeated the measure had it not been for the Soviets' sudden seizure of Czechoslovakia through a Communist coup d'état in February 1948, followed in June by a blockade of Berlin, which obliged the rest of the former Allies to begin an airlift of supplies into the city that would last for 321 days. In the wake of this Communist double whammy Congress quickly passed the Marshall Plan, which would pump $13 billion into Europe's recovery from 1948 to 1951, fueling a 65 percent increase in European industrial production by the end of 1950.

On March 17, 1948, Britain, France, and the Low Countries signed the Brussels Pact, a fifty-year defensive military alliance. Truman applauded the treaty and called for Americans to support it as well as the broader North Atlantic Treaty Organization (NATO) he envisaged binding all the nations of the West into a military alliance against the U.S.S.R. Fueled by growing anti-Soviet sentiment, congressional support grew for the NATO treaty, and it was signed by twelve nations on April 4, 1949, a month before the Berlin blockade ended. The pact declared that any aggressive act against one member of NATO would be considered aggression against every member. The Soviet Union countered in 1955 by ordering its satellites to sign a similar agreement for eastern Europe, the Warsaw Pact. Both superpowers then launched into a nuclear arms race characterized by extensive and mostly unsafe atomic testing that led to the creation of the devastating hydrogen bomb and a rapid buildup of nuclear arms on both sides—as well as public fear that they would soon be used.

The great foreign policy debate that spawned the Cold War was at its height and the Soviet blockade of Berlin still in place when the 1948 American presidential election took place. Truman's popularity was low due not only to the divisions over foreign policy but also to his perceived ineptitude

Above, Harry Truman celebrates his surprising electoral victory on November 2, 1948, by posing with a copy of the *Chicago Tribune* printed before all the results were in. With Henry Wallace running for the liberal Progressive Party and Strom Thurmond heading a ticket for the Southern-based States' Rights Party, the Democratic vote seemed certain to split, leaving the election to Thomas Dewey, the Republican candidate. Most people expected Dewey to win, and the newspaper shown above was hardly the only one that went to press a bit too early on election night. In fact, the issue of *Life* magazine on the stands during election week was just as overconfident, captioning a picture of Thomas Dewey "the next president."

with domestic affairs as well as a series of scandals within his administration involving aides who used their positions for personal profit. Wallace announced that he would run as a third-party candidate, splitting Democratic liberals. What remained of the party's unity further disintegrated at the Democratic convention, where Truman adopted a strong civil rights plank that caused the South to withdraw from the party and nominate Governor Strom Thurmond of South Carolina on the "Dixiecrat" ticket. It appeared that just about any Republican could win, but the GOP chose to nominate Thomas Dewey for the second time.

Truman won in the most stunning upset in presidential election history. When it was all over, analysts reported that by losing Wallace's followers Truman had gained the support of conservative Northern, Western, and Midwestern Democrats who might otherwise have defected to the Republicans but instead supported the incumbent president with the genuine anti-Communist credentials. Likewise, the formation of the Dixiecrats ensured the Democrats the overwhelming allegiance of black and other pro-civil rights voters, while Truman's prompt recognition of the new state of Israel helped him win the Jewish vote, which until then had leaned toward Wallace.

The "Red Menace"

Other than Truman's surprise election, the most important development in postwar American politics was the emergence of anti-Communism as an issue. By 1949 the great debate over foreign policy had all but ended with the Truman Doctrine triumphant, as evidenced by Taft's rejection at the Republican convention and Wallace's at the national polls. American attitudes toward Communism had hardened in the wake of the Soviet Union's takeover of Czechoslovakia and its blockade of Berlin. A wave of "red terror" swept the nation after President Truman announced in September 1949 that "We have evidence that within recent weeks an atomic explosion occurred in the U.S.S.R.," meaning that the United States had lost its monopoly on nuclear weapons. Suspicions arose in some quarters that Soviet agents in America had stolen the atomic information and relayed it back to Moscow. When the Chinese Communists defeated the U.S.-backed Nationalists soon after and forced them to flee to Taiwan, the same sort of suspicions arose among some who wondered how the Communists could have won without help, possibly from American agents. In addition, China was closed off from the West and would remain that way until the early 1970s.

Official suspicion was already afoot at home: the president had created a Temporary Commission on Employee Loyalty authorizing a Loyalty Review Board to investigate federal employees for Bolshevik tendencies. By 1951, some 212 federal employees would be fired for "disloyalty" and another 2,000 would resign rather than submit to investigation. Three years earlier, the Justice Department obtained indictments of eleven Communist Party leaders under the Alien Registration Act, which made advocating revolution a crime. They were found guilty in October 1949 and sentenced to prison.

The executive branch was hardly alone in its paranoia. The notorious House Un-American Activities Committee (HUAC) had also set off on a witch-hunt, and a young Republican congressman from California named Richard Nixon saw in the frenzy a path to national office. In August 1948 an admitted former Communist, Whittaker Chambers, testified that he had had contacts with underground Communist cells in the U.S. State and Agriculture departments, those in the former including the highly respected Alger Hiss, head of the liberal, do-good Carnegie Endowment for International Peace. Hiss denied the charge, but several members of the congressional committee joined the ambitious Nixon in continuing the investigation and turned up enough evidence to charge Hiss with perjury, as the statute of limitations had expired on his liability for espionage. His first trial ended in 1949 in a hung jury; a second lasted from 1949 into 1950 and resulted in Hiss's conviction, sparking a controversy that divided the nation. It would be nearly forty years before evidence came out proving that in fact Hiss had perjured himself and was also a Communist, just as Nixon had charged.

As the nation's anti-Communist hysteria grew on the House committee's regular feedings, other significant issues such as civil rights, farm policies, and housing programs were ignored or cast aside as being various shades of "red" or even just "pink." Truman's proposed health-care program, for example, was labeled "socialistic" by no less than the more profit-minded American Medical Association, while civil rights leaders in general were tarred as "fellow travelers" on the road to Communism. HUAC also went after a number of Hollywood figures, ruining the careers of any number of actors, writers, and others tarred with the pink brush. The committee's actions inspired playwright Arthur Miller to pen *The Crucible*, ostensibly about the

The Cold War began over the German question. By early summer 1948 the West had begun to respond to Stalin's intransigence with what he regarded as threats: The Marshall Plan drew the nations of Western Europe closer together; Britain, France, and the Benelux nations signed a military pact that the United States not only officially welcomed but indicated it intended to join; and the Americans moved to install permanent air and sea bases across Europe. Equally ominous to the Soviets was the West's determination to grant independence to West Germany, which could mean only that the former Allies in the West intended to merge their portion of Germany into the proposed anti-Soviet military alliance that was to become NATO.

Stalin responded to these challenges on March 30, 1948, by clenching his grip on Berlin. The Soviets slowly blocked off all road and rail access to the city and cut electricity to the western sector on June 24, the same day they officially clamped a unilateral blockade on all ground and water traffic to Berlin. The pretext was currency reform, which had just been imposed in the form of a new mark by the other three occupying powers; the real reason, however, was the struggle over whether postwar Germany would be unified and free or divided into a capitalist West and a Communist East. Berlin, after all, was deep inside Soviet-occupied territory. By cutting it off from the outside world, the Soviets hoped to starve into compliance the parts of the city it didn't already control. Within a week the Soviet blockade left West Berliners with just one month's supply of bread and meat. The West responded quickly, with Britain joining the United States in a counterblockade on goods from the East moving into western Germany.

Many in the former Allied nations felt it would be wise to abandon Berlin because it seemed foolish to risk World War III for the sake of the ex-Nazis. President Harry S. Truman and the American military governor in Germany, General Lucius D. Clay, however, scotched such talk. As Clay noted, "We have lost Czechoslovakia. Norway is threatened. We retreat from Berlin. When Berlin falls, western Germany will be next," and all of Europe supposedly would turn Communist after that. The Americans thought they couldn't give an inch. Secretary of State George C. Marshall declared, "We had the alternative of following a firm policy in Berlin or accepting the consequences of failure of the rest of our European policy," which described Stalin's beliefs equally well. Truman had the last word: "We are going to stay—period."

Clay called General Curtis E. LeMay, U.S. Air Force chief in Europe, and asked, "Curt, can you transport coal by air?" The answer was yes, and the Berlin airlift was born. Within days, round-the-clock flights into the city were dropping up to thirteen thousand tons of goods a day. They kept up for 321 days, supplying more than two and a half million Berliners with everything needed to keep a modern city alive: food, medicine, machinery, clothing, and other vital items. Every day the airlift's young children would try to wave down the four-engine C-54s in hopes they would drop candy bars and oranges, twenty-three tons of which were sent wafting down into Berlin in the course of the airlift. "The sound of the engines was like music to our ears," wrote one young victim of the Soviet blockade.

But contrary to popular myth, as Chief of Staff William D. Leahy told the Pentagon shortly after the blockade began, Truman was not committed to Berlin if "that would start a war." As U.S. officials pondered the bleak alternatives in the German question during the first months of the blockade, the airlift barely figured in their thinking. Truman's foreign policy advisers shared Undersecretary of State Robert A. Lovett's view of it as a "temporary expedient" that bought time but offered no solution to the crisis. Even as Clay was ordering the first U.S. flights into the city, he snapped his fingers at a friend and said, "I wouldn't give you that for our chances." Clay predicted that Berliners would start to suffer "in a few days" and advised the White House on June 25 that the deprivation would become "serious in two or three weeks." The newly created National Security Council assumed that bad weather would ground the airlift by October.

The airlift not only survived October but outlasted one of the worst winters Europe was to see in the century, which required landings so low the planes skimmed the rooftops. The credit for the operation's incredible longevity belongs to the heroic American air crews, who endured a relentless flying schedule and difficult living conditions, and the airlift's commander, U.S. Air Force Major General William H. Tuner, who took a chaotic situation and turned it into a model of efficiency, proceeding at a "steady, even rhythm with hundreds of planes doing exactly the same thing, every hour, day and night, at the same persistent beat."

Under Tuner's clockwork precision, as soon as a plane touched down on a crammed West Berlin airfield, it was furiously unloaded and sent back aloft within thirty minutes.

The Americans' dogged efforts succeeded so well that Stalin gave up and lifted the Berlin blockade on May 12, 1949, ten months and eighteen days after it had been imposed. During that nerve-racking time the West delivered an astounding 2,325,809 tons of supplies, two-thirds of it coal, on 277,804 flights—and lost seventy-eight airmen in crashes and accidents. More lastingly, the Berlin airlift transformed the United States from Ger-

many's conqueror to the protector of its people. That humanitarian effort was not forgotten in later German debates about rearmament and membership in NATO. Despite the enormous pressure Stalin's political maneuvering had brought to bear, the Soviets had failed to force the West to yield control over West Berlin. President Truman began using the success of the Berlin airlift as proof that he meant "the buck stops here." Thanks to the airlift, Berlin became the Western symbol of resistance to communism, the rallying point for America's commitment to defend Western Europe against the rot of Soviet expansionism.

Residents of Berlin watch as a U.S. Air Force plane participating in the Berlin airlift lands with food and supplies, below. At the end of the war Berlin was a divided city locked within East Germany. In June 1948 the Soviets blocked all rails and highways leading into the city from the Western democracies. The situation was tense, as almost any overt reaction from the West could have led to war. Truman's policy concentrated on feeding the city without directly provoking the Soviets. The Berlin airlift, operated mainly with U.S. and British planes, began in June and lasted for nearly a year. As a logistical achievement it astonished even the Soviets, especially when the airlift kept operating through a harsh German winter.

Alger Hiss, above, leaves a federal courthouse in 1950 after his conviction on charges of perjury related to his alleged communist affiliations. Hiss, an Ivy Leaguer and former diplomat, had tried his hardest to fight the charges, but found himself pitted against a "red scare" machine operating at full strength. Richard Nixon, then a California congressman, coordinated the case against Hiss. Hiss was convicted on January 21, 1950. Encouraged by the outcry against Hiss, Senator Joseph McCarthy began his own attack against Communists in government in a speech on February 9. McCarthy, a first-term senator from Wisconsin who in large part inspired the anti-Communist hysteria of the early 1950s, was photographed, right, a week before the 1952 election, accusing Democratic candidate Adlai Stevenson of Communist leanings.

Salem witch trials but in fact an excoriation of the anti-Communist menace. Within a year of his unexpected election, Harry Truman and his brand of domestic liberalism were on the defensive.

America's unfortunate foray into paranoid anti-Communism found its spokesman in Republican Senator Joseph McCarthy of Wisconsin, who on February 9, 1950, claimed that, "While I cannot take the time to name all of the men in the State Department who have been named as members of the Communist Party and members of a spy ring, I have here in my hand a list of 205 that were known to the Secretary of State as being members of the Communist Party and who nevertheless are still working and shaping the policy of the State Department," which McCarthy insisted was "thoroughly infested with Communists." His accusations made headlines even if the senator did occasionally fudge the numbers. "McCarthyism" became synonymous with witch-hunting to the senator's critics, but his defenders maintained that he was a bulwark against Soviet penetration into not only America's politics but its culture and economy as well.

The Korean War

The Communist threat suddenly seemed much more immediate on June 25, 1950, when Soviet-backed North Korean troops attacked their former countrymen to the south in the U.S.-supported Republic of Korea, taking Truman's attention away from domestic matters and thus killing any hope of further Fair Deal reforms. The strategically crucial Korean peninsula had been divided along the 38th parallel since the end of World War II, with the North controlled by Communist dictator Kim Il Sung and the South by U.S.-backed dictator Syngman Rhee. Immediately after the North Korean attack Truman asked for a special meeting of the U.N. Security Council, which the Soviet Union was boycotting at the time, to protest the body's refusal to replace its Nationalist Chinese delegates with representatives from Communist China. As a result the Security Council voted 9 to 0 for a resolution branding North

Korea an international aggressor, leading Truman that very evening to order General Douglas MacArthur to begin supplying South Korea with war matériel. When MacArthur reported back that supplies alone would not suffice to stop the North Koreans, he was given the authority to use all the forces at his disposal to assist the South Koreans. The vainglorious general jumped at the chance and sent two U.S. divisions to the region, thereby thrusting the country into the Korean War.

Although at first MacArthur's actions and Truman's support of them enjoyed overwhelming support from the public, before long they began to spur debate. Those who voiced opposition to the engagement argued that no national interest was at stake and that any comparison of the North Koreans to the Germans and Japanese of the 1930s, as Truman would draw later, was more than a little overblown. Supporters of the war, meanwhile, asserted their view that the North Korean attack had been sponsored by the Soviets and the Communist Chinese as part of their plan for world conquest. The president apparently believed the latter, sending U.S. naval units to defend Taiwan and offering support to the French battling Ho Chi Minh in Southeast Asia. Still, Truman hoped to confine the conflict as much as possible to Korea and conduct a "limited war" under his doctrine of helping those who wanted to help themselves to democracy. Thus the U.S. president rejected Chiang Kai-shek's offer of Nationalist troops to help fight the North Koreans, refused to allow the U.S. Air Force to fly over Chinese and Soviet bases in the disputed areas, and rejected suggestions that the United States brand the Soviet Union an aggressor before the United Nations, all the while welcoming the international body to send troops to try to resolve the conflict.

At first the Korean War went badly for the United States and the South

U.S. marines take cover in Seoul's streets. "The entirely new war," as General MacArthur called it, began with China's overwhelming intervention in the Korean War in late November 1950. After MacArthur, supreme commander of the U.N. forces, ignored warnings not to get too close to the Chinese border, half a million Chinese troops swept south, dispersing what had been a workmanlike U.N. advance. "We ran like antelopes," said one American soldier. "We didn't know our officers and they didn't know us. We lost everything we had."

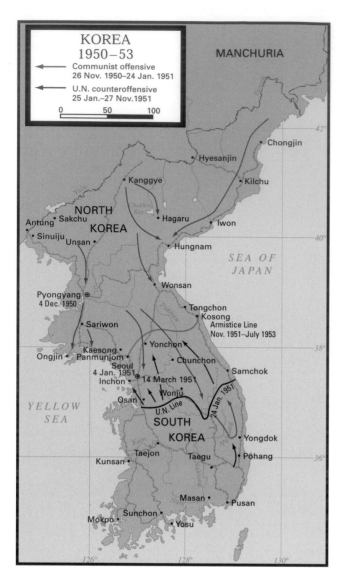

The map above shows the march of armies on the Korean Peninsula from 1950 to 1953. The Korean War began in June 1950 when North Korean Communists invaded South Korea, occupying nearly the whole country. In August 1950, a coalition of United Nations forces began a dogged counteroffensive out of Pusan in the southeast. In September, General MacArthur hastened the counteroffensive with a massive U.N. landing at Inchon, a daring and very successful surprise. U.N. troops (nearly half of them American) made steady progress until November 1950, when they were met by a new wave of enemy soldiers pouring out of Communist China. The remaining years of the war did little but establish a stalemate.

Koreans, but on September 15, 1950, MacArthur launched a brilliantly conceived and executed amphibious landing at Inchon, trapping a large North Korean force after walking ashore several times to ensure a good take for the cameras, his ever-present corncob pipe jutting from his jaw. Although many of the Communist troops slipped away, the multinational U.N. forces went on the offensive, bombing bridges and drawing nearer the Chinese border. On October 7, the world organization's General Assembly adopted a resolution declaring its objective a "unified, independent, democratic Korea," a goal unacceptable to the newly Communist Chinese, who entered the war on November 26. The response precipitated a U.N. retreat all the way back to the 38th parallel, the old border between North and South Korea, where matters remained at a stalemate.

The Korean War intensified America's debate over Communism within the nation and energized those who supported NATO. It also raised the question of whether the United States should consider China a belligerent and widen the war accordingly, a notion MacArthur supported and Chairman of the Joint Chiefs of Staff General Omar Bradley opposed on the grounds that such a conflict would be "the wrong war, at the wrong place, at the wrong time, and with the wrong enemy." General Dwight D. Eisenhower, who would become the first commander of NATO's military forces, was believed to support Bradley's view.

The controversy came to a head on April 11, 1951, when Truman removed MacArthur from command in Korea and ordered him home in a strongly worded letter. The charismatic general responded by taking his case to what he thought was his adoring public, and for a while it looked as though he had a shot at the Republican presidential nomination of 1952 and could go on to challenge Truman via the political route. But the boomlet of support for the volatile MacArthur didn't last, even if the tensions he had created did. Years later, the plain-speaking Truman would explain: "I fired him because he wouldn't respect the authority of the president. . . . I didn't fire him because he was a dumb son of a bitch, although he was, but that's not against the law for generals. If it was, half to three-quarters of them would be in jail."

On March 30, 1952, Truman announced he would not seek another term, dismaying the Republicans who had planned to campaign against the president's record. After all, the Fair Deal had proven a disappointment, Truman's relations with Congress were poor, his administration was plagued by scandals, and McCarthyism was running rampant. The Republicans had been hoping to run against Korea, Communism, and corruption, but without Truman they had lost their whipping boy. Still, it could only benefit the GOP that the Korean War dragged on; although peace negotiations opened at Kaesong on July 10, they quickly bogged down over the issue of returning prisoners of war. Changing the venue for the talks to Panmunjom in October did not improve matters, and as the negotiations went on the public's distaste for the war increased.

The presidential contest kept looking better and better for the Republicans as polls began to show the country turning against the Democrats. Suddenly the Republican nomination seemed worth winning, and several hopefuls jumped into the fray, the most prominent being Robert Taft—until World War II's favorite general, Dwight Eisenhower, announced his candidacy. After a contentious convention, Eisenhower won the nomination and selected the controversial Richard Nixon as his running mate. Because Eisenhower was so popular the Democrats instead opted to attack Nixon, who had been accused of accepting secret contributions from California friends for personal use. Nixon responded to the concerns with his artful "Checkers speech" on national television, vowing that the only payola he'd ever accepted was a "little black-and-white cocker spaniel dog" named Checkers, and "regardless what they say about it, we're going to keep him"; what's more, he pointed out, his wife Pat wore not a mink but a "respectable Republican cloth coat." For once triumphing over the awkwardness that would bedevil the rest of his career, something in Nixon's well-rehearsed candor resonated with the forgiving American people.

Encouraged by Truman's decision not to run again, a number of Democratic aspirants materialized for the party's first contested nomination since 1932. The nod went to erudite and intellectual Governor Adlai Stevenson of Illinois, considered a moderate New Dealer with no connection to Truman, with the vice presidential nomination going to Senator John Sparkman of Alabama in a bid to win back the Dixiecrats. But Eisenhower, the most popular hero to come out of World War II, promised that if elected he would go to Korea, and defeated Stevenson with ease despite the Democrat's campaign slogan that "You never had it so good." The Republicans also won control of the House and the Senate with 48 seats, as opposed to 47 for the Democrats and 1 Independent.

Eisenhower's most important act in his first year in office was ending the Korean War through diplomacy made urgent by the thinly veiled threat of

Richard Nixon delivers his famous "Checkers" speech, September 23, 1952, on national television. He was in the midst of his first national race, running for vice president on Dwight Eisenhower's ticket, when a report that a group of Californians had contributed $18,000 to a slush fund for his personal use nearly derailed his campaign. In his speech, Nixon defended himself with sentimental references to his wife, Pat, their two daughters, and the family pet, a cocker spaniel named Checkers. The overwhelmingly favorable response was an early example of television's power in politics.

U.S. retaliation "under circumstances of our choosing." Some historians would later claim that the Koreans, Chinese, and Soviets feared the new president might use the atomic bomb, which Truman in fact would have found awfully hard after having seen the results in Hiroshima and Nagasaki; others would note that the death of Joseph Stalin on March 5, 1953, changed the situation in the Communist camp and turned support for North Korea into less of a priority for the Soviet Union. Whatever the underlying reasons, the prisoner of war issue was settled in April and an armistice followed in July. It was more a military truce than a peace, but in any event the Korean War was over and Eisenhower got the credit for ending it.

Modern Republicanism

Eager to slap a label on the new administration, the GOP came up with "modern Republicanism," indicating that Eisenhower would accept most of the major New Deal and Fair Deal measures but would go no further in their direction; his would be a presidency of reconciliation and consolidation rather than of bold new ventures. The federal government would no longer seek new areas in which to intervene; in fact, spending would be cut and government would shrink, or at least that was the intention. In any case, popular programs such as farm subsidies were among the first to get the ax.

Throughout his first year in office Eisenhower only hinted as to how he planned to accomplish this federal shrinkage. As great a military strategist as he may have been, "Ike" (as Eisenhower was affectionately known) was among the least experienced politicians ever to inhabit the White House, which ironically may have been the main factor in his becoming one of the most successful chief executives of the twentieth century. Of course, at least some of that success owed to the fact that he staffed his administration with the elite of the business community, including Secretary of State John Foster Dulles and his brother Allen, who was given the helm at the increasingly important CIA.

The year he took office Eisenhower sponsored a tax-reform program, passed twelve months later by Congress, under which businesses and the middle class benefited more than did low-income groups. At the same time, the administration ended most of the economic controls imposed during the Roosevelt and Truman years. Eisenhower did pare the military budget as Secretary of Defense Charles Wilson promised "more bang for a buck," but the falloff in these funds resulted more from the end of the Korean War than from any serious attempt to cut back military spending. In the end, Eisenhower's first budget was unbalanced into a 1953 deficit of $6.5 billion, which prompted Senator Taft to protest that the president was "taking us down the same road that Truman traveled." Nevertheless, Taft continued to lead the Eisenhower forces in Congress until his death on July 31, 1953, when the post of Senate majority leader passed to William Knowland of California, who exercised substantially less clout than Taft had.

Eisenhower also suffered his share of failures. Congress rejected out of hand Agriculture Secretary Ezra Taft Benson's attempt to end many of the

The 1952 Republican convention, above, erupts after the Minnesota delegation changed its vote on the first ballot, ensuring the nomination of Dwight D. Eisenhower for president. Within the party Ike's only competition had come from Senator Robert Taft, an outspoken right-winger and noted isolationist. No one could be quite sure where Eisenhower stood on most issues, yet the nomination, warmly discussed since 1948, was his for the taking in 1952. Most Republicans felt satisfied with the simple sentiment expressed on the button above. Adlai Stevenson, left, was the Democratic presidential nominee in 1952 and again in 1956. The grandson of Grover Cleveland's second-term vice president, Stevenson was wealthy and well-educated, a first-term governor of Illinois running on a moderate platform.

farm support programs of the 1930s and 1940s, after which the administration made few efforts to revamp existing federal programs of any kind. Still, by late 1954 Eisenhower was more popular than ever. After all, the nation was at peace and as prosperous as it had ever been. Troubles remained, but the country seemed convinced that no problem would be too difficult for Ike.

The Demise of McCarthyism

By 1954, Joseph McCarthy and the ugly paranoia he had spawned seemed faded and outworn, more because of his own blunders than because of any direct action on Eisenhower's part. In addition to hinting that the father of the atomic bomb, J. Robert Oppenheimer, might himself be a "pinko," McCarthy had veered even further toward the peculiar by insinuating that the State Department's alleged "fifth columnists" were given to sending one another treasonous notes on perfumed paper. Up to this point Eisenhower had more or less ignored McCarthy and his poisonous suggestions, but early in 1953 the senator had opposed the president's choice for ambassador to the U.S.S.R., launched investigations of the State Department and the Voice of America, and late in the year moved against the military after learning that a U.S. Army dentist had been promoted from captain to major even though he had refused to sign a loyalty oath. The matter escalated into a confrontation between McCarthy and Secretary of the Army Robert Stevens, who traded charges of varying pettiness.

The Army–McCarthy controversy reached its peak in the spring of 1954, when the congressional subcommittee continued its probe of alleged Communist infiltration of the U.S. Army in nationally televised hearings. Soon McCarthy was on the defensive as his opponents rallied to expose what they

Senator Joseph McCarthy, right, on July 9, 1954, uses a map during his testimony at the special hearings called to investigate his 1954 charge that the U.S. Army was controlled by Communist sympathizers. In just two years the senator had created an atmosphere of hysteria based on dramatic, if unfounded, charges against some of the nation's most powerful people. As McCarthyism gripped the country, its instigator turned his attack on the army, charging that it, too, was soft on Communism. The army refuted McCarthy in no uncertain terms, insisting upon open hearings and retaining Boston lawyer Joseph Welch. Before a gigantic television audience Welch dissected McCarthyism, revealing the senator's flawed reasoning and the scandalous conduct of his close associates.

considered his cruel bullying and unfair tactics, such as refusing to divulge the sources of some of his most serious charges and threatening political reprisal against any senators who opposed him. Finally, U.S. Army counsel Joseph Welch forced McCarthy to back down from some of his allegations, whereupon the embattled senator suggested that one of Welch's own aides was a Communist sympathizer. At that point a shocked Welch wondered aloud how far McCarthy would go to destroy someone's reputation and future and asked him, "Have you no sense of decency, sir, at long last? Have you left no sense of decency?" The viewers at home could not help but agree that McCarthy had gone too far.

The Army–McCarthy hearings ended without a clear resolution, but on June 17 conservative Republican Senator Ralph Flanders of Vermont introduced a motion to censure McCarthy for "bringing the Senate into disrepute." A committee headed by Republican Senator Arthur Watkins of Utah was named to investigate the matter, but more significant was the work of a Democratic senator not on the committee—Lyndon Johnson of Texas, at the time Senate minority leader. Sometimes brusque, even vulgar, Johnson was a cautious, conciliatory, and wily backroom politician who knew how to assemble votes. Thus he helped to orchestrate the Watkins hearings and won Republican as well as Democratic votes for the censure measure. Only one Senate Democrat, young John F. Kennedy of Massachusetts, refused to take a stand on the matter. Part of the reason was that he was hospitalized at the time with a chronic back ailment, but Kennedy would later admit that "half my voters in Massachusetts looked upon McCarthy as a hero"—as did his own father, while Kennedy's younger brother Robert had served on McCarthy's staff.

The final vote against McCarthy was 67 to 22, but not for formal censure; instead the senator was "condemned" by his colleagues for "having repeatedly abused the members who were trying to carry out assigned duties." Eisenhower now applauded the Senate's action, leading McCarthy to apologize for having supported the president in 1952. Johnson moved to consolidate his newly enhanced strength in the liberal camp, while McCarthy never came close to regaining his former influence; by the time of his death in 1957 he was an embittered and half-forgotten man as well as a blot on the national conscience.

John Foster Dulles and U.S. Foreign Policy

During the Eisenhower years, Secretary of State John Foster Dulles was such a dominating force in U.S. foreign policy that some journalists thought the president had given him free rein to run it. Indeed, Dulles was brilliant and utterly sure of himself. Once asked whether he had ever been wrong, he replied after some consideration, "Yes, once. Many, many years ago I thought I had made a wrong decision. Of course, it turned out that I had been right all along. But I was wrong to have thought I was wrong." Once the administration's papers were released, however, it became clear that Eisenhower himself was the global strategist, while Dulles took care of tactics in carrying out the president's wishes.

President Eisenhower, above right, confers with Secretary of State John Foster Dulles on national television on May 17, 1955. Intent on using the new broadcast medium effectively, Eisenhower created an office at the White House for actor-producer Robert Montgomery, who developed relaxed studio formats suited to the president's personal style. In Dulles, Eisenhower had a Secretary of State who seemed to be a mass of contradictions. In public appearances Dulles would typically drone on in a slow monotone, yet he had a knack for coining tabloid-style headlines, for example, calling the effort against Communism the "liberation of enslaved peoples." Many people considered Dulles self-righteous, but he enjoyed the complete confidence of President Eisenhower.

Chief among them was Eisenhower's plan to contain the U.S.S.R., blocking its attempts at expansion by building alliances with the nations around its perimeter. But he refused to involve the United States in any more wars in which the nation's vital interests were not at stake, which meant no more Korea-like conflicts; instead he planned to keep the Soviets in line with the threat of the atomic bomb and "massive retaliation." Those threats, especially coming in combination with Joe McCarthy's attempts to incite a red scare, sparked public fear of a Communist nuclear attack upon the United States, prompting Americans to build bomb shelters in their backyards and organize community air-raid drills that sent schoolchildren scurrying to "duck and cover" under their desks. At the same time, however, the president also offered Stalin's successors an olive branch in the form of suggestions for mutual disarmament, while holding out the possibility of rearming Germany in order to create a new military ally. In 1953 Eisenhower offered to start disarmament talks and to help organize an International Atomic Energy Agency within the U.N., but his "Atoms for Peace" program met with no success. More typical of the president's approach was his support for the European Defense Community and the idea of a multinational European army, but French opposition prevented its formation. In part to encourage the French to reconsider, the United States increased aid to France for its struggle in Southeast Asia from about $100 million in 1951 to $800 million in 1953.

France had been fighting in Southeast Asia since the end of World War II in an effort to regain Vietnam. The battles had not gone well for the French, and the Soviet- and Chinese-supported troops led by Ho Chi Minh kept winning more and more important victories. With great optimism in 1954, France adhered to a scheme named for General Henri-Eugene Navarre, who promised to end all Viet Minh resistance by the end of the next year. The Navarre Plan was to draw the Communists into a set battle, for which he chose Dien Bien Phu near the Laotian border, where 15,000 French troops were encamped in what they considered an impregnable position.

Vietnamese General Vo Nguyen Giap was up to the challenge and surrounded the French. The battle for Dien Bien Phu began on March 13, 1954, and the French soon fell back and asked the United States for more aid. France's prime minister wanted still more: a U.S. airstrike at Dien Bien Phu followed by the introduction of U.S. combat troops. The chairman of the U.S. Joint Chiefs of Staff, Admiral Arthur Radford, supported the French request and was backed by both Dulles and Nixon, although the vice president conceded that there was little public backing for any American intervention in Southeast Asia. Powerful Senate Minority Leader Lyndon Johnson, who also was invited to the first meetings regarding Vietnam, was dubious about the proposition and wanted to know whether other countries would join an American effort in Southeast Asia; the answer was no. Yet Eisenhower insisted that Southeast Asia was "of the most transcendent importance to the United States and the free world." As he would explain to the American people on April 7, 1954: "You have a row of dominoes set up, you knock over the first one, and what will happen to the last one is . . . that it will go over very quickly."

Dien Bien Phu fell to the Communists on May 7; shortly thereafter the French government in Vietnam tumbled as well. The new leadership in Paris agreed to meet in Geneva with Viet Minh representatives to discuss peace in Southeast Asia, out of which came an agreement to establish a cease-fire, a buffer zone, and democratic elections to determine the nation's future. Dulles set in motion a plan to create a Southeast Asia Treaty Organization similar to NATO—while it was agreed that the United States would not intervene militarily in the war in Southeast Asia. Vietnam, one of the constituent states of Southeast Asia, was to be divided along the 17th parallel, with Ho Chi Minh in power in the North and Emperor Bao Dai in the South. Countrywide elections were to be held in two years, after which the nation would be unified. The consensus was that Ho would win any election, as the emperor was perceived to be a French puppet. The promised elections, however, were never held.

Realizing that reforms were needed, Bao Dai named as his premier Ngo Dinh Diem, who had been in exile to protest French rule and who promised sweeping changes while still opposing Ho and his Communists. On October 24, Eisenhower pledged $100 million in U.S. aid toward Diem's ends, and in February 1955 the first group

Paratroopers loyal to the French in Vietnam, below, advance gingerly through a forest at Dien Bien Phu, a pivotal area under siege by Communist troops in March 1954. The French effort to stave off Communism in Southeast Asia was a conspicuous failure, ending in total defeat at Dien Bien Phu. The negotiations that followed were a test of the diplomacy that Secretary of State Dulles called "brinksmanship," which meant, as he explained it, "to get to the verge without getting into war." In 1954 America backed away from the brink in Vietnam.

At right, China's Chairman Mao Zedong, left, shares a toast with North Vietnam's victorious Ho Chi Minh, right, after the two signed the Sino-Vietnamese joint communique on July 7, 1955. Mao viewed imperialism as a Western curse and espoused anti-imperialism as a cause that united all of Asia. The United States became "Enemy No. 1" in Beijing's doctrine under Mao. As one of his close associates said in 1962: "The U.S. imperialist aggressors must get out of South Korea, get out of Taiwan, get out of Japan, get out of South Vietnam, get out of Laos, get out of Thailand, and get out of the whole area of Asia."

Below, soldiers mobilize hurriedly after the Suez War broke out between Egypt and Israel in 1956. Within days one-quarter of the Israeli population was in uniform and massed for a bold sweep across the Sinai Peninsula between the two countries. With Britain and France backing Israel and the Soviet Union defending Egypt's position, the Suez War seemed ready to explode into a world war in November of 1956. On election day Eisenhower was compelled to place U.S. armed forces on alert, just hours before the parties agreed to a cease-fire.

of U.S. military advisers arrived in Vietnam. At the time, Diem seemed an attractive alternative to Ho Chi Minh, enjoying the friendship of American liberals such as Senator Mike Mansfield of Montana and Supreme Court Justice William O. Douglas as well as conservatives such as Francis Cardinal Spellman of New York and tycoon Joseph Kennedy. The latter's son, Senator John F. Kennedy, met with the increasingly dictatorial Diem, and in a speech to the Senate warned against any settlement that would leave the country open to Communist control.

By then Dulles was well on his way to completing a circle of treaties around the U.S.S.R. In 1955 he fathered the Baghdad Pact bringing Iran, Iraq, Pakistan, and Turkey into a Western alliance and attempted to foster closer relations with the new Egyptian government under Gamal Abdel Nasser, who had obtained Britain's agreement to withdraw from the Suez Canal by 1956 and who was trying to put together a pan-Arab union. In Iran three years earlier the United States had supported the young shah Mohammed Reza Pahlevi against his nation's pro-Soviet prime minister, Mohammed Mossadegh, and helped overthrow the latter when he seemed to threaten American petroleum interests in the region. Nor did Dulles ignore Latin America; in 1954 a U.S.-sponsored coup in Guatemala put an anti-Communist in control there, in the process establishing the

CIA as the covert operations arm of the U.S. government.

Cuba, however, remained a problem. Fulgencio Batista had ruled the island since 1933, became its president in 1940, been deposed in 1944, and returned to power in 1952 through a second military coup. Batista had originally come to power with Communist support, but by 1952 he had restyled himself a staunch anti-Communist and as such had won U.S. backing. He promised elections in 1953, but few of either his countrymen or his country's clients believed him, and insurrections had broken out early the next year. One of these riots, directed against an army barracks by twenty-seven-year-old intellectual firebrand Fidel Castro, resulted in more than 100 deaths and the capture and imprisonment of the ringleader until he was released under a general presidential amnesty. Castro then left Cuba to organize the resistance against Batista, spending a great deal of time in the United States, some of it trying out for the Washington Senators baseball team—without whose surfeit of starting pitchers history might have been much different. Rejected by the purveyors of the American pastime from the city renowned as "first in war, first in peace, and last in the American League," by the end of 1954 a disappointed Castro was prepared to return to Cuba in the expectation that there he would take command of an insurgency dedicated to overthrowing the Batista regime.

So he did: on January 1, 1959, Batista was forced to flee the country to make room for Castro, who came to power seemingly a young idealist with strong democratic convictions. Before long, however, he took to executing former Batista officials and supporters, while the elections he had promised never materialized. Instead, Castro confiscated and nationalized key industries across Cuba, sending his country's middle class fleeing to the United States.

Eisenhower broke relations with Cuba when Castro proclaimed himself a Communist and his nation a Soviet satellite—within ninety miles of the United States. Although this raised tensions, Eisenhower hoped to lower them through an exchange of visits with Soviet Premier Nikita Khrushchev, who duly came to the United States and agreed with Eisenhower to a summit meeting on the neutral turf of Geneva, Switzerland. The hopes for a thaw in the growing Cold War ended on May 5, 1960, however, when the Soviets announced that four days earlier an American U-2 reconnaissance plane had been shot down over its territory and the pilot captured. The president abandoned efforts to cover up the incident, for which he took full responsibility. The idea of a Geneva summit evaporated and Eisenhower's reciprocal visit

Above, Soviet Premier Nikita Khrushchev has a friendly hug for Fidel Castro, premier of Cuba, at the United Nations in September 1960. The year before, at the age of thirty-two, Castro had wrested control of Cuba from dictatorial president Fulgencio Batista. Castro was not originally committed to Communism, but the Soviet Union made early overtures that swayed him to its doctrine, signing the first of many generous trade agreements in February 1960. Before long the Soviets succeeded in establishing Cuba as a vital front in the Cold War. Even so, Khrushchev's attitude in politics, as in the picture, was to embrace Castro without taking him too seriously.

to the U.S.S.R. was called off. Although he had failed to end the tensions between the world's two superpowers, the gravely disappointed president did succeed in keeping the conflict cold and U.S. military operations low risk.

Eisenhower Embattled

The full consequences of Castro's washing out with the Senators would not become fully manifest for several years. In the autumn of 1956, thanks to a strong economy, President Eisenhower appeared certain of reelection. With realistically scant hopes the Democrats once again nominated Adlai Stevenson, paired this time with Senator Estes Kefauver of Tennessee after a floor fight against his Massachusetts colleague John F. Kennedy. Stevenson gave up attacking the vice president, Richard Nixon, and turned to warning against Secretary of State Dulles—who had sparked concern by saying that the United States would go to "the brink of war" to protect its vital interests—responding for the Democrats that such "brinkmanship" might lead to an accidental atomic confrontation.

War did come during the 1956 presidential campaign, but it wasn't the nuclear kind and it aided Eisenhower rather than Stevenson. Since Stalin's death in 1953, there had been unrest among the Soviet Union's eastern European satellites that would continue through the tenures of Stalin's successor Georgi Malenkov and his 1955 successor Nikolai Bulganin, who would give way to Premier Nikita Khrushchev in March 1958. Shortly after Stalin's demise an anti-Soviet riot had erupted in East Germany followed by rumblings in Poland, where on October 21, 1953, an insurrection had taken place in Warsaw. The unrest continued, growing into widespread rioting in the Polish city of Poznan in the summer of 1956. In October a riot broke out in Budapest, Hungary, and escalated into a major confrontation. In the latter it appeared for a while that the Hungarians had succeeded in repelling the Red Army, leading Eisenhower to hail "the dawning of a new day" and to offer U.S. economic aid to Hungary.

But the Cold War continued its inexorable spread. As the world's attention focused on Hungary, a war broke out in the Middle East rooted in the establishment of Israel in 1948 but sprouting from the rise to power of Egypt's Gamal Abdel Nasser. By playing the Soviets against the Americans Nasser wangled aid from both, including a pledge from Eisenhower to help construct the Aswan Dam on the Nile River in the southeast corner of his country. Domestic opposition led the president to withdraw the pledge, and Britain, France, and the rest of NATO followed suit. Nasser retaliated by seizing the British- and French-controlled Suez Canal on July 26, 1956.

At this point British Prime Minister Anthony Eden entered into secret negotiations with France and Israel aimed at restoring British control of the canal and ending Nasser's threat to Israel. On October 29, as the Soviets remained mired in Hungarian politics and the United States in its own, Israel attacked Egypt and drove toward the Red Sea. According to plan, Britain and France warned both to stop fighting and pledge to keep the Suez Canal open; the United States and the U.S.S.R. called for a cease-fire that neither

side accepted. On October 31, Britain and France launched an airborne invasion of the Suez area, upon which First Secretary of the Soviet Central Committee Khrushchev vowed his country's support for Egypt and the same day sent Red Army troops back into Hungary to crush the nascent democratic government there.

Even Eisenhower's critics at home deemed it unwise to change America's leadership at this perilous moment, and the president won large majorities of both the popular and electoral college votes. Nevertheless, the Democrats solidified their hold on both houses of Congress, although this didn't trouble Eisenhower, as he was on good terms with both Speaker of the House Sam Rayburn and Senate Majority Leader Lyndon Johnson.

The two global crises were resolved as America counted its ballots. No U.S. aid would be forthcoming for the Hungarians despite earlier talk of rolling back what Churchill had dubbed the "Iron Curtain," and the United States joined with the Soviet Union in condemning the attacks on Suez by Britain, France, and Israel, all of which were obliged to withdraw their forces. The series of events had long-lasting repercussions: Britain had to concede that it was no longer a major power, while the Fourth French Republic was so discredited it didn't enjoy even that option and collapsed two years later. Khrushchev, meanwhile, gained an important stronghold in the Middle East

Above, protesters in Hungary wave their nation's flag during a hopeful moment in the country's 1956 revolt. After the nation and its premier shifted abruptly from Communism to establish a new democracy, the Soviet Union made clear its intention to retake the country through military action. Hungary appealed desperately to the United States for help, but received none and the revolt was brutally quashed. "People had been watching from rooftops," said a Budapest resident after Hungary's brief moment of democracy, "hoping to see U.S. planes arriving." For the United States, the Hungarian crisis long loomed as a failed test of its mettle in the Cold War.

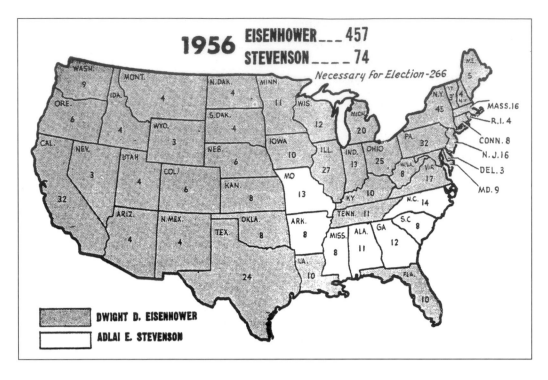

1956 EISENHOWER___457
STEVENSON____74

Necessary For Election-266

WASH. 9
ORE. 6
CAL. 32
NEV. 3
IDA.
MONT. 4
N.DAK. 4
MINN. 11
WIS. 12
WYO. 3
S.DAK. 4
IOWA 10
ILL. 27
IND. 13
UTAH
COL. 6
NEB. 6
KAN. 8
MO. 13
ARIZ. 4
N.MEX. 4
OKLA. 8
ARK. 8
TEX. 24
LA. 10
MISS. 8
ALA. 11
GA. 12
KY. 10
TENN. 11
S.C 8
N.C. 14
OHIO 25
MICH. 20
PA. 32
W.VA. 8
VIR. 17
MD. 9
N.Y. 45
MASS. 16
R.I. 4
CONN. 8
N.J. 16
DEL. 3
ME. 5
FLA. 10

☐ DWIGHT D. EISENHOWER
☐ ADLAI E. STEVENSON

As the map above indicates, Eisenhower enjoyed a sweeping victory in the 1956 election. He was especially proud of wresting Louisiana from the Democrats' "solid South." He claimed he couldn't have been more surprised if he had won Ethiopia for the GOP.

and tightened his grip on power in the U.S.S.R. such that there was no more talk of the collapse of Communism in eastern Europe. Ironically, in the end both Israel and Egypt benefited from the war in the Levant: Israel emerged as the region's major military power, while Soviet support underlined Nasser's key position in the Arab world. In any case, the situation in the Middle East continued to deteriorate throughout the rest of the Eisenhower years and beyond.

The Postwar Generation

To a great extent, World War II had given Americans their fill of global problems, and in the early postwar period the public seemed more interested in domestic affairs. The government responded quickly; in fact, military demobilization began even before the end of the Pacific war, and by June 1946 the U.S. armed forces had shrunk from nearly 12 million to 2.9 million. Although the need for occupation troops in the former Axis powers' conquered territories and for readiness against what was perceived as a growing Soviet threat had led President Truman to ask for an extension of the draft, the military still continued to dwindle, and by the next year America had 1.5 million military personnel.

Some had been so eager to get out of the service that violence had broken out in European port cities as soldiers deserted their posts and tried to stow away on ships bound for home. In the haste to demobilize hundreds of millions of dollars' worth of matériel had been abandoned; guns, tanks, airplanes, and even ships "disappeared," and Allied authorities didn't even bother to look for them. The chaos extended to U.S. industries: many wartime economic controls were lifted immediately after the conflict ended, but because factories had not had time to convert back to the production of peacetime goods their prices rose rapidly. In the first ten months of 1946, consumer prices rose by 30 percent, as much as they had in the years between 1941 and 1945. At the same time, organized labor, which had patriotically accepted wage restraints during the war, demanded pay raises, and when managements refused, many unions struck. Altogether U.S. unions went out on 5,000 strikes that involved an unprecedented 15 percent of the labor force and consumed 116 million workdays, making 1946 the worst year for U.S. labor–management relations in history.

In the midst of these difficulties Truman had attempted to steer a reform program through Congress expanding the New Deal. He succeeded to an extent: among other measures, the legislature passed the Employment Act, pledging the federal government to do whatever it took "to promote maximum employment, production, and purchasing power"; the Atomic Energy Act, establishing a government monopoly on nuclear power and an Atomic Energy Commission to oversee it; and the Legislative Reorganization Act, which streamlined congressional procedures. Beyond that, however, Truman was unable to deal effectively with either Congress or the Roosevelt holdovers in his own cabinet. Late in 1946, then Secretary of Commerce Henry Wallace resigned, taking with him a sizable portion of his fellow old New Dealers who agreed that the new president was not sufficiently in tune with Roosevelt's principles.

Growing inflation, labor unrest, Democratic divisions, the Cold War, and the lingering sense that Truman wasn't up to the job had given the Republicans a new slogan for the 1946 congressional campaigns: "Had enough?" It worked: for the first time since the Great Depression, the GOP had taken control of both houses of Congress as well as twenty-five of the nation's forty-eight governorships. Anti-Truman feeling ran so high in some quarters that Democratic Senator William Fulbright of Arkansas had suggested that the president name Republican Thomas Dewey Secretary of State—next in the line of succession in the absence of a vice president—and then resign in his favor. It wasn't about to happen as long as "Give 'Em Hell Harry" had anything to say about it.

Truman had wasted no time setting his own agenda even before he was elected president in his own right. In his State of the Union address on January 5, 1949, he had set forth a legislative program he called the "Fair Deal," not unconsciously implying an extension of the New Deal. Among his proposals were such civil rights provisions as a federal fair employment practices act, a bill to end segregation in interstate transport, an antilynching law, and the end of the poll tax. The president had also called for repeal of the Taft-Hartley Act curbing union powers, which he had vetoed earlier but Congress had passed despite unions' claims that it was a "slave labor bill"; he also advocated a national health insurance program; passage of the Brannan Plan to thoroughly revamp the outmoded agricultural subsidy program; regional planning boards on the model of the Tennessee Valley Authority; increases in Social Security payments, and a higher minimum wage. Few of these sweeping measures were passed by Congress, but Truman's platform presented a challenge to the next generation of reformers.

More important, however, than any initiative coming out of Washington was the impact the returning veterans made on every town and city—and every aspect of the U.S. economy—in the postwar era. They were a generation born into peace and prosperity in the 1920s, bred in the strife of the Great Depression of the 1930s, and matured during the Second World War that they had done so much to win. The veterans were entitled to the best America could do for them, and a grateful nation agreed. They created the largest middle class in U.S. history with the niftiest new conveniences: in 1944 Congress passed the "GI Bill of Rights," which provided war veterans money while they looked for jobs, low-cost home mortgages, and college tuition and support. The politicians who framed the measure had no idea how

MR. PRESIDENT:
VETO
THE HARTLEY-TAFT
SLAVE LABOR BILL

The International Ladies Garment Workers Union joined the rest of labor in opposing the Taft-Hartley Act in 1947, displaying the banner above at a rally at New York's Madison Square Garden. Harry Truman won friends in labor by vetoing the bill, which was written to give the government new powers over the nation's unions. Congress overrode the veto, as the president knew it would. Less than a year later, though, he did not hesitate to exercise his own new initiative under the Taft-Hartley provisions, requesting a court injunction to end a turbulent strike by the United Mine Workers.

many veterans would make use of the latter two provisions, and were downright stunned by the numbers who flocked to college. In 1940, the last full year of peace, there had been fewer than 1.5 million students in American colleges and universities; in 1946, the first full year of postwar peace, more than 2 million students were in college, close to half of them veterans. Academe expanded rapidly to accommodate them, growing from 106,000 faculty members nationwide in 1944 to 186,000 by 1950. What's more, the students themselves were older, more experienced, and more serious than previous generations of collegians, which transformed the campus culture and boosted the level of American education overall.

The veterans whose lives had been put on hold by the war also returned in droves to start families, causing a boom in new housing construction across a country that had seen little building during the Great Depression and the war. Similarly, the "baby bust" of the 1930s and early 1940s was succeeded by a "baby boom" that started in 1946 and would last until 1964, when the birth rate dropped back below its 1945 level of 20.4 live births per thousand people from its 1952 high of 25.1 per thousand.

From the very beginning, the baby boomers made a huge impact on American society that is only now reaching its apex. As the largest generation in U.S. history grew up, its many members kept requiring more and more goods and services, creating needs no one had anticipated. In the late 1940s and early 1950s these needs became manifest in shortages of housing and nursery schools, followed by an insufficiency of elementary and then secondary schools and teachers throughout the 1950s and early 1960s. In the mid-1960s, the colleges and universities that had expanded to take in the veterans expanded again to accommodate their children. But divorce also became widespread as the American family, despite television shows like "Ozzie and Harriet" and "Leave It to Beaver," felt myriad new pressures. Unforgettable plays such as Tennessee Williams' *A Streetcar Named Desire* and Arthur Miller's *Death of a Salesman* brought family disintegration to America's stages. Socialist C. Wright Mills worried about this "new middle class," which was trapped in large corporate organizations and bland suburban developments where "sameness" was the prevailing doctrine.

The baby boomers also accelerated the rise of suburbia. Having endured the urban blight of the Great Depression and the privations of the war years, young families dreamt of living on their own little pieces of open green spaces, and the suburbs that had begun to spring up before the war offered just that at affordable prices, particularly for veterans. The largest planned community in the mid-1940s, Levittown on New York's Long Island, became the model for suburbs across the nation, offering houses for less than $8,000 with no down payment to those who qualified for Veterans Administration mortgages. By 1960, the U.S. Census would report that more than half the population lived in suburban rather than urban or rural areas.

Because suburbs meant space, they also meant cars, and automobile sales soared. The proliferation of cars created an entire new suburban culture featuring such novelties as drive-in movie theaters and drive-in fast-food chains such as the mighty and soon ubiquitous McDonald's, which began with one burger joint in southern California and by the end of the century would boast sales of "billions and billions" of hamburgers. A nation on wheels also gave birth to safely standardized motels such as the wildly successful Holiday Inns and their many imitators. Road construction picked up across the nation to keep pace with the new American wanderlust, and in 1956 the Interstate Highway Act launched an ambitious effort to build new superhighways and improve existing ones. For those who preferred to stay home, television transformed choices in entertainment and, through advertising, the nation's spending patterns. The spreading use of another new technology, air-conditioning, prompted jobs and people to migrate and expand from the East and Midwest to the suddenly more livable South and Southwest. By 1963 California had surpassed New York as the number one state in population. These and the myriad other changes that met the veterans coming home from World War II combined by the late 1950s to produce

Below, a tract of new houses in suburbia stretches toward the horizon. To writer John Cheever, the suburbs were "a cesspool of conformity." To the people who lived in them, however—people who had grown up during an economic depression and persevered through a world war—they offered stability and a patch of green space.

a nation even more prosperous and progress-minded than it had been in the Roaring Twenties.

Race Relations

America's growing prosperity was not, however, distributed quite equitably, particularly across racial lines. Bigotry still poisoned U.S. society in the late 1940s and early 1950s. "We live here and they live here," African-American novelist Richard Wright complained in *Native Son* (1940). "We black and they white. They got things and we ain't. They do things and we can't. It's like living in jail." Yet the nation appeared to be moving toward more harmonious race relations. President Truman had begun the process of integrating the armed forces, making the Korean War America's first officially integrated armed conflict. More noticeably to the public, in 1947 Jackie Robinson became the first black athlete to break through the color barrier in professional sports as an outstanding infielder for the Brooklyn Dodgers and would later be inducted into the Baseball Hall of Fame. Soon thereafter blacks were admitted in small numbers to several previously all-white Southern universities, and in 1952—for the first time in seventy-one years—there were no reports of lynchings. On the federal front, during his first year in office President Eisenhower established a Government Contract Compliance Committee to ensure that firms with discriminatory hiring practices would be excluded from grants of federal contracts.

As it remains, the liberal hope was for color blindness throughout U.S. society, the belief that a person's race makes no difference to how that person should be treated or expected to act. Several cases aimed at enforcing that position by challenging racial segregation in public facilities, particularly schools, began to wend their ways through the court system. In the 1948 case of *Sipuel v. Board of Regents*, for example, the U.S. Supreme Court had decided that Oklahoma's denying the use of law school facilities to a black student because of his race was a violation of the Fourteenth Amendment. It was a decision that prompted some Southern states to establish separate but clearly inferior law schools for blacks or to instead pay their tuition to law schools up North. Two years later, in the case of *Sweatt v. Painter*, Chief Justice Fred Vinson spoke for the Court in declaring that a separate law school set up for blacks in Texas was inadequate; that same year, in *McLaurin v. Oklahoma State Regents*, Vinson stated that Oklahoma could no longer segregate its law school by obliging its sole black student to sit apart from his white fellows.

Above, new highway systems changed American geography during the postwar years as automobile sales shot up and spending on mass transit atrophied. President Eisenhower signed the Interstate Highway Act into law in 1956, creating a program that would result in 42,000 miles of new high-speed roads. In most American cities, highways were built going through African-American neighborhoods and other urban areas, cutting them off from the mainstream and creating the problematic isolation of the "inner city."

While the Supreme Court began to make progress in the civil rights area under Vinson, its activities accelerated when the chief justice died in 1953 and was replaced by Eisenhower's appointee, Governor Earl Warren of California. In fact, the progressive Warren Court would make possible the civil rights movement of the 1960s through a series of bold and for the time gutsy decisions genuinely meant to enforce the broad-minded tenets of the U.S. Constitution. The Court sent a shudder through the souls of America's racists on May 17, 1954, when it handed down a unanimous decision in *Brown v. Board of Education of Topeka* to the effect that separate facilities for the different races were inherently unequal. Then, in a rehearing of the case a year later, the Court went even further and ordered all local schools to desegregate "with all deliberate speed." Some Southern schools had begun to do so after the first *Brown* decision, but others took the second to mean that delays would be acceptable. Other forms of resistance to the Court's moves surfaced in the deep South, including the formation of the White Citizens' Council in Mississippi, an organization that soon spread across the region. It shortly became clear that to the White Citizens' Council "with all deliberate speed" meant "never," which is where the group's position stood on the eve of the 1956 presidential election.

Perhaps the most important domestic development during Eisenhower's second administration was the acceleration of the civil rights movement; as the president himself wrote, "There must be no second-class citizens in this country." School desegregation under *Brown v. Board of Education* proceeded slowly but nonetheless encountered resistance in the South. The strength of this opposition manifested itself in September 1957, when a small number of black Arkansas students were to enroll in Little Rock Central High School. A local group of white parents opposed the plan and with the help of Governor Orval Faubus tried to prevent the integration, inspiring Faubus to call out the state's National Guard, ostensibly to keep order but in fact to bar the black students from entering the previously all-white schools. The governor's stand against progress drew attention to Little Rock through television cameras that broadcast what was happening across the nation. The U.S. Justice Department obtained an injunction against Faubus, and a riot erupted in the Arkansas capital soon thereafter. President Eisenhower, who had held back to that point, sent federal troops into the city and nationalized the Arkansas National Guard. "Well, if we have to do this, and I don't see any alternative," Eisenhower told Attorney General Herbert Brownell, "then let's apply the best military principles to it and see that the force we send there is strong enough that it will not be challenged, and will not result in any clash." The black students in Little Rock were enabled to attend classes, but the violence sparked similar outbursts in some fifty other Southern school districts that ugly September, including the dynamiting of an integrated school in Nashville, Tennessee.

By that point, however, the burgeoning civil rights movement had found a leader in the twenty-eight-year-old Reverend Martin Luther King, Jr., a Baptist preacher from Montgomery, Alabama, with a voice as rich, pure, and true as the ideas he expressed with it. King had first risen to prominence in

Thurgood Marshall, above, served as a Supreme Court justice from 1967 until 1991. Born to working-class parents in Baltimore, he studied law and later orchestrated a masterful campaign to open educational opportunities to blacks. Marshall won his farthest-reaching victory in *Brown v. Board of Education*. The precedent-setting case, which originated in Topeka, Kansas, ended in a ruling against the segregation of white and black students.

In 1952, Alan Freed hosted a Cleveland radio show aimed at teenagers. Like other disc jockeys, he gave his audience a steady diet of middle-of-the-road music left over from the swing era. One day, someone suggested he go down to a popular record store to see what kind of music teenagers were picking out for themselves. Freed paid the store a visit and was stunned to see the kids skipping over the crooners and the orchestras in favor of records from the rhythm and blues bins.

"Rhythm & blues"—R&B—was the catchall term for music by African-American artists. One style of it—what would come to be called rock and roll—appealed specifically to teenagers, both black and white. The repetitive lyrics dealt with teen problems, primarily young love, and the vocalists used fresh harmonies to bring the most out of simple melodies. Most of all, though, the new sound emphasized a hard-driving beat, and that beat carried the energy that teens liked.

Freed revamped his old show, "The Record Rendezvous," around the vital new teen music. The shift can be heard even in the new title he chose: "Moon Dog Rock 'n' Roll House Party." Freed opted against using the racially specific term "rhythm & blues"; in the 1950s, both the music and his show stood for a better chance without it. Instead, he adopted another term from the realm of black music: "rock and roll."

In the fifties the phenomenon known as pop culture suddenly narrowed to a sharp point: teen culture. Barely heard from in previous generations, postwar teens were in charge of themselves to a greater extent than before, with fewer chores, more free time, and much more spending money. Teens used their new freedom of choice to embrace drive-in restaurants, blue jeans, and hot-rod cars. But it was most noticeably through music that teens left the mainstream behind. A generation before, college kids and voting adults had made jazz music popular; rock and roll was the product of high schoolers.

In some measure, these teenagers were empowered by savvy businesses using ever more sophisticated techniques to define a potent new consumer segment. When record companies, for example, saw that the rock and roll juggernaut had the potential to outsell every other category, they quickly built an industry to churn it out, put it on the air, and make it sell. Freed and some other pioneering disc jockeys were content to promote music made by popular black artists such as the Dominoes, Screamin' Jay Hawkins, and Fats Domino. Other acts, such as the flamboyant piano legend Little Richard of Macon, Georgia, and the duck-walking electric guitar maestro Chuck Berry of St. Louis, Missouri, soon crossed over into pure teen rock and roll. Berry, in particular, had a talent for transforming mundane American realities into tunes that bespoke the frustrations of America's first generation of baby boomers at a time when the Cold War, the lingering McCarthyism, and the threat of atomic destruction played havoc with the nation's social fabric. Early on, however, the search began throughout the music industry for white acts that could replicate the rock and roll sound.

Sam Phillips, owner of Sun Records in Memphis, often lamented, "If I could only find me a white boy with a black sound, I could make a million dollars." For a few months in 1954 he'd been working with a young truck driver named Elvis Presley, who had a rich voice but sang without much distinction in most musical styles. In July 1954, however, Phillips telephoned and finally suggested that Presley try some R&B songs.

"I hung up and ran fifteen blocks to Mr. Phillips's office before he'd gotten off the line," Presley later recalled. He appreciated the R&B sound far more deeply than any other type of music and had been eager to record it. In their own way, fans were barreling just as fast toward Elvis's music: ready for it and waiting. Within a year Elvis was the most popular artist in the country, the undisputed king of rock and roll.

Rock music quickly developed a dimension beyond sound, thanks largely to Presley. Other entertainers had pushed their sexuality before, but none—no males and very few females outside of burlesque theaters—reveled in it the way Elvis did. *Time* magazine may have thought Presley looked like "he had swallowed a jackhammer," but teenagers flocked to what Presley's gyrating pelvis was suggesting. By acting instinctively, absorbing black music and culture because it moved his soul, singing whatever he wished without regard for arbitrary rules governing the proper songs white people were supposed to sing, using his body in a sexy manner because he felt like it, Elvis helped liberate the country from the strictures of its puritanical heritage while blurring the nation's black-white cultural boundaries, making so-called race records popular with white teenagers. Presley's revolutionary message to his generation was: "Ah, just act the way you feel."

Elvis Presley's reign over rock and roll did not last long. Most parents were relieved when he was drafted into the army in 1958 and trundled overseas to Germany. Perhaps he finally grew up during his stint overseas, because when he returned his heart seemed to have gone out of his music. But rock and roll certainly didn't want for other stars, such as teenage Texas phenom Buddy Holly and the piano-banging Jerry Lee Lewis. New acts explored dimensions suited to new times, and so it was that rock and roll matured into the 1960s. But it never died, ultimately becoming the universal language of youth. As sixties folk-rock pioneer and poet Bob Dylan had written in his Hibbing, Minnesota, high school yearbook (class of 1959): "Ambition: To join Little Richard."

Elvis Presley plays the piano as a little girl watches, in a photograph taken during the 1950s. Born in Mississippi, Presley moved to Memphis, Tennessee, as a teenager. He launched his career by paying Sun Records for studio time, so that he could make a record as a birthday present for his mother.

December 1955 when Rosa Parks, a forty-three-year-old black seamstress had refused to move to the segregated back of a public bus in Montgomery and was arrested for her brazenness. As historian Taylor Branch later described her in his magisterial *Parting the Waters: America in the King Years* (1988), Rosa Parks was "one of those rare people of whom everyone agreed that she gave more than she got. Her character represented one of the isolated blips on the graph of human nature, offsetting a dozen or so sociopaths." Early histories of the civil rights movement had stated that Rosa Parks refused to give up her bus seat in December 1, 1955 because she was "too tired to move." Parks took issue with this characterization in her autobiography: "The only tired I was," she wrote, "was tired of giving in." After the now-famous incident, the city's blacks staged a bus boycott in support of Rosa Parks and launched a broader civil rights campaign after selecting King to lead it. King was an undaunted activist, the "complete evangelist," in Branch's words, "who could preach integration to the humble as well as the elite, to the erudite and the ignorant, to the practical and the idealistic." As one Negro Improvement Association leader remarked later about King's ascent: "We wanted a leader and we got Moses." Eisenhower's actions in Little Rock had alienated Southern whites opposed to integration, while his slow and reluctant response to the situation had cost him the goodwill of the civil rights workers; King filled the gap in national leadership. "Nonviolence is a powerful and just weapon," King would write. "It is a sword that heals."

All in all, the decade after World War II proved it really was "the American Century," although its launch was not without glitches. As Dulles carried out Eisenhower's orders to construct a cordon around the Soviet Union, troubles erupted in out-of-the-way corners of the world where none had been expected. Although the administration considered Europe the prime area of contention with the U.S.S.R., more insidious problems had sprung from the seeds of conflict planted in Iran, Egypt, Central America, Cuba, and Vietnam. Similarly, on the home front America faced the dilemmas along with the benefits of suburbanization, while race relations became ever more important and perplexing. At the time, the years immediately following World War II seemed a period of transition to a peacetime economy, in hindsight it is clear that what was happening between 1945 and 1955 was that the agenda for the rest of the century was being laid out. And what a promising future it seemed. As President Eisenhower pointed out as he left office in 1960,

Above, Rosa Parks sits in the front of a bus in Montgomery, Alabama, on December 21, 1956, after a Supreme Court ruling banned segregation on all public transportation. Before this decision, Montgomery and other Southern cities had vigorously enforced Jim Crow laws regarding bus seating: blacks could not sit in the front section, and they could not sit in the middle section if a white person wished to sit there. On December 1, 1955, Mrs. Parks chose to sit in the middle section, tired after a hard day of work. When a white man boarded the bus and wanted a seat, Mrs. Parks was arrested for refusing to give up her seat. A week after Mrs. Parks' arrest, rising civil rights leaders, such as Martin Luther King, Jr., and Ralph Abernathy, called for blacks to boycott Montgomery's buses; the response was overwhelming and proved that the ferment existed to work for even greater change.

"America is today the strongest, the most influential, and most productive nation in the world." By the same token, however, in his memorable farewell address to the American people on January 17, 1961, the outgoing president also echoed the warning George Washington had delivered upon leaving office; Eisenhower said,

> This conjunction of an immense military establishment and a large arms industry is new in the American experience. . . . We recognize the imperative need for this development. Yet we must not fail to comprehend its grave implications. . . . In the councils of government, we must guard against the acquisition of unwarranted influence, whether sought or unsought, by the military-industrial complex. The potential for the disastrous rise of misplaced power exists and will persist.

Elizabeth Eckford ignores the jeers of onlookers as she tries to walk into Central High in Little Rock, Arkansas, on the first day of classes, September 6, 1957. She and eight other African-American students trying to enter the school were blocked not only by the mob but also by state troopers. "When I was able to steady my knees," said Eckford of the day shown above, "I walked up to the guard who had let the white students in. He didn't move. When I tried to squeeze past him, he raised his bayonet and then the other guards closed in and they raised their bayonets." Infuriated, President Eisenhower sent more than 1,000 army paratroopers to escort Eckford and the other students into their school.

CHAPTER 19

THE NEW FRONTIER AND THE GREAT SOCIETY

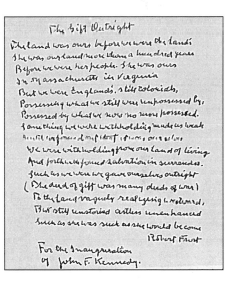

The Gift Outright

[handwritten manuscript of "The Gift Outright" by Robert Frost]

For the Inauguration
of John F. Kennedy.

As Eisenhower served out his second term, both of America's major political parties busied themselves preparing for what would turn out to be the watershed presidential election of 1960, between the Republican ticket of Vice President Richard Nixon and former UN Ambassador and Boston Brahmin Henry Cabot Lodge, and Democratic Senators John F. Kennedy of Massachusetts and Lyndon B. Johnson of Texas. The campaign was the first to feature a nationally televised debate, which pitted a sweaty-lipped Nixon against a handsomely tanned Kennedy with predictable results. Still, the election proved the closest since 1884, and the forty-three-year-old Kennedy became the nation's youngest elected president

John F. Kennedy, left, pointed to a New Frontier on November 8, 1960, the day he was elected to the presidency. In the bright sun at his inauguration ceremony the following January, Robert Frost had trouble reading the poem he had written for the occasion and instead simply recited his 1941 work, "The Gift Outright," above, which he knew by heart. The poem outlined America's history and yet seemed to describe the Kennedy years to come, especially in the line, "Such as we were we gave ourselves outright . . . To the land . . . Such as she was, such as she would become."

Television took its place in American politics when four debates were broadcast during the 1960 campaign. In this photograph of the October 21st debate, Vice President Richard Nixon, at left, listens as Senator John F. Kennedy makes a point. Both men understood the power of television, but only Kennedy used it to his advantage. While Nixon tried to appear statesmanlike, Kennedy—the youngest man ever to run for president to that time—exuded personable intelligence and convinced many voters that he was a natural leader.

only after eking out a controversial victory fraught with charges that dead Democrats had voted for him in Texas and Illinois. The victor would later quip that his wealthy father had sent him a telegram reading, "Don't buy a single vote more than necessary. I'll be damned if I'm going to pay for a landslide."

John F. Kennedy remains the golden boy among American presidents: better looking than Warren Harding, as young and seemingly as vigorous as Theodore Roosevelt, and even richer than FDR. Softening these natural assets with a quick and disarming sense of humor, Kennedy used his vitality and enthusiasm to win the goodwill even of those who had voted against him. The second son of self-aggrandized Irish-American business and political tycoon Joseph Kennedy, "JFK" had been anointed heir apparent to the family's ambitions by his father when his older brother, Joseph Kennedy, Jr., was killed in World War II.

Young John Kennedy had proved more than equal to his father's considerable expectations. After graduating from Harvard he had entered the U.S. Navy and become a war hero when his PT boat was sunk by a Japanese destroyer in 1943, and despite substantial injuries Lieutenant Junior Grade Kennedy had guided his fellow survivors through dangerous waters to safety. After the war he was elected to Congress from the Boston area and in 1953 moved up to the Senate; later that year he married the glamorous Jacqueline Bouvier, and two years later, while convalescing from a back operation, he wrote *Profiles in Courage* (with substantial help from Theodore Sorenson, his future speechwriter), which won the Pulitzer Prize in biography. Kennedy's greatest asset was his large and talented family, which included his younger brother Robert F. Kennedy, whom JFK would name U.S. Attorney General; his brother-in-law Sargent Shriver, who would head the newly formed Peace Corps, and his youngest brother, Edward Kennedy, who would take his place in the Senate. The Kennedy clan came to prominence at a time ripe for change, and their liberalism blew fresh breezes through the halls of power and scattered the musty remnants of the eight-year-old Eisenhower administration. One of the most obvious signs of America's progress was that John F. Kennedy—the first president born in the twentieth century—was also the first Roman Catholic to be elected the United States' highest office, proving just how much things had changed since the days when Al Smith's religion meant his candidacy didn't have a chance. Kennedy had become, in novelist Norman Mailer's opinion, America's "leading man."

Kennedy's inaugural address struck a vigorous and unselfish new tone for the nation, including the memorable plea, "And so, my fellow Americans, ask not what your country can do for you; ask what you can do for your country." Rhetoric aside, the nation soon learned that Kennedy would not ask for many sacrifices, that few of his programs were either bold or strikingly new, and that he would put little energy or imagination into pushing for them in Congress. Although the legislature did approve his Peace Corps initiative and his crash program to put an American on the moon by the end of the decade, Congress rejected most of the new president's requests during his first year in office. After all, among the few factions that Kennedy had not charmed to his way of thinking were the Southern Democrats, who still controlled the House and Senate.

In the end, the new president's greatest successes would come in foreign policy and personal style. Although Kennedy attempted to mold New Deal economic theories into a New Frontier capable of dealing with contemporary problems, within a year he was forced to concede the failure of that approach. Instead he asked Congress for broad discretionary powers to raise or lower taxes when needed to dampen inflation or stimulate the economy, but the legislature was not forthcoming. Undaunted, the president initiated the "Kennedy round" of tariff negotiations to stimulate foreign trade at a time when the national unemployment rate hovered around a disturbing 6 percent. Toward the end of his short administration, JFK managed to push a Trade Expansion Act through Congress that enabled U.S. cooperation with the new European Common Market. Still, his three most significant recommendations to the legislature—tax reform, a new civil rights bill, and a health-care program for the aged to be financed through Social Security— were either bottled up in committee or rejected outright.

Kennedy's stance toward big business, meanwhile, remained downright ambivalent. In 1962 his administration brokered an agreement between the unions and the steel companies under which the former would moderate their wage demands in return for the latter's pledge to hold the line on prices. When U.S. Steel reneged and most of the other steel companies followed suit, Kennedy saw to it that each one's papers were examined, their tax returns scheduled for audits, and federal purchases of their steel halted. In the face of such pressure the steel companies backed down, in the process painting the president as an enemy of big business. Joe Kennedy's son was, of course, nothing of the sort; when Big Steel raised its prices again several months later, Kennedy did nothing.

Civil Rights in the 1960s

The young president was more successful at taking the lead in the struggle for black civil rights. As he explained his views in a message to Congress on June 19, 1963: "No one has been barred on account of his race from fighting or dying for America—there are no 'white' or 'colored' signs on the foxholes or graveyards of battle." It was in the hopeful years of Kennedy's brief administration that the nation's civil rights organizations began to press more aggressively for compliance with court orders against racial discrimination and segregation through such visible new methods as "sit-ins" and "freedom rides" on buses through the Deep South. Among the most instrumental of

The Woolworth's lunch counter in Greensboro, North Carolina, was the scene of a racial confrontation in February 1960, when three African-American students—Ronald Martin, Robert Patterson, and Mark Martin—sat down at a counter reserved for whites. The sit-in had begun the day before when four other students requested service at the restaurant. One of them, Franklin McCain, later recalled that a policeman came by, but was powerless in the face of the nonviolent protest. "There was virtually nothing that could move us," McCain said. "There was virtually nothing probably at that point that could really frighten us off." The sit-in movement quickly spread through the South and helped inspire the civil rights movement of the 1960s.

these groups were the already established National Association for the Advancement of Colored People (NAACP), the Congress for Racial Equality (CORE), and Dr. Martin Luther King, Jr.'s Southern Christian Leadership Conference (SCLC). A newer organization, the Student Nonviolent Coordinating Committee (SNCC), formed during the sit-ins, brought the vigor of youth to spearhead many subsequent demonstrations against the ugliest remaining stain on American society.

The civil rights sit-ins throughout the South garnered enough publicity to mobilize substantial numbers of people across the country to take the same sort of direct action; the famous February 1, 1960, lunch counter sit-in at the Woolworth's in Greensboro, North Carolina, for example, rallied support not only from starry-eyed college students but from older Northern whites of all progressive persuasions. The next spring, when CORE director James Farmer led a group of black and white freedom riders on a bus tour from Washington, D.C., to New Orleans, the deliberately peaceful protesters were assaulted by mobs of angry white thugs in Anniston and Birmingham, Alabama, where one of the buses was set on fire. Bowing to the powerful old-school Southern Democrats, President Kennedy held back from responding to the outrage until his brother, Attorney General Robert F. Kennedy, relayed this report from a Justice Department official at the scene:

Now the passengers are coming off. They're standing on a corner of the platform. Oh, there are fists, punching! A bunch of men led by a guy with a bleeding face are beating them. There are no cops. It's terrible. It's terrible! There's not a cop in sight. People are yelling, "There those niggers are! Get 'em, get 'em!" It's awful.

Indeed it was, and the horrified attorney general immediately got his brother's permission to send in 400 federal marshals to restrain the brutal white mob and protect the freedom riders. As this and other incidents proved, President Kennedy was thoroughly sympathetic to the civil rights movement, but it was through his brother Robert that he acted on his beliefs. In September 1962, for example, it was the younger Kennedy who forced Governor Ross Barnett to allow registered black student James Meredith into his dormitory at the University of Mississippi, which had been ordered to desegregate by a federal court even if it did take several hundred U.S. marshals, two deaths, and 375 injuries to get Meredith into his dorm room. Robert Kennedy also went out of his way to help Martin Luther King, Jr., make his stand against segregation in Birmingham in 1963, for which the black leader was jailed only to issue his eloquent "Letter from Birmingham City Jail" defending civil disobedience in an undeniably just cause. Upon his release that May, King lived up to his word, leading further demonstrations in Birmingham that quickly burst into riots after city police chief Eugene "Bull" Connor set his men upon the protesters with billy clubs, fire hoses, and attack dogs. Black mobs retaliated in kind, and over the next two and a half months more than 750 additional riots broke out in 180 towns and cities across the nation.

The crisis in Birmingham brought the Kennedys into conflict with reactionary but charismatic Governor George Wallace of Alabama, who was well on his way to becoming the leader of America's segregationists. In June, the same year that saw Birmingham set ablaze, Wallace, a Democrat, had tried to prevent two blacks from registering at the University of Alabama, and it took federal marshals to make him back down. But no matter how aggressively Robert Kennedy worked to promote civil rights, John Kennedy always kept one eye on the mighty Southern Democrats whose support he needed in other matters, and limited his civil rights initiatives to implementing laws and court decisions already on the books, introducing new legislation to end segregation and protect black voters only toward the end of his foreshortened presidency.

By that point, however, King had decided to take matters to the streets of the capital and announced a full-scale march on Washington for August 1963. When the president complained that such a mass public demonstration would scare away support for his civil rights bill, King replied much as America's more brazen founding fathers had to the British nearly two centuries earlier, explaining that "I have never engaged in any direct action movement which did not seem ill-timed." Thus on August 28 more than two hundred thousand people assembled around the Lincoln Memorial to hear folk-rock musicians Bob Dylan, Joan Baez, and Peter, Paul, and Mary and to pay attention to the mesmerizingly brilliant Dr. King, who that day delivered a speech explicating the Declaration of Independence in words that would have made Thomas Jefferson proud. "I have a dream," King intoned in his rich Baptist baritone,

U.S. Attorney General Robert F. Kennedy, left, stands with his brother, President John Kennedy, outside the White House. "Bobby," almost nine years younger than the president, had begun his Washington career in 1953 as a congressional aide to Senator Joseph McCarthy, whose methods he soon rejected. Later in the 1950s, Robert F. Kennedy served as chief counsel to the Senate Select Committee investigating organized crime, and by the time his brother was elected president, he had a reputation as a brash antiracketeering zealot. Yet during the Kennedy administration, Bobby exuded a strong sense of compassion, especially toward America's poor and disenfranchised. He was admired for staying true to his promise to preside over the Justice Department, not the "Prosecution Department."

Right, Dr. Martin Luther King, Jr., delivered his landmark "I Have a Dream" speech in Washington on August 28, 1963, to a crowd estimated at a quarter of a million people. It was a deeply patriotic address, placing the African-American quest for civil rights in the context of the entire nation's struggle to fulfill its promise. King said in his speech, "I have a dream that one day this nation will rise up and live out the true meaning of its creed: 'We hold these truths to be self-evident, that all men are created equal.' " Malcolm X, pictured below in 1963 at a Black Muslim rally in New York City, rose to national prominence in the 1950s by expounding the angry view that all whites were devils. He was, however, developing a more humanistic philosophy at the time he was assassinated in 1965. In the early 1960s, Martin Luther King and Malcolm X each claimed a sphere of influence larger than any ever before achieved by a black leader in America.

"that my four little children will one day live in a nation where they will not be judged by the color of their skin, but by the content of their character. . . . And when we allow freedom to ring . . . we will be able to speed up that day when all of God's children, black men and white men, Jews and Gentiles, Protestants and Catholics, will be able to join hands and sing in the words of the old Negro spiritual, 'Free at last! Free at last! Thank God Almighty, we are free at last.' "

His speech at the march on Washington marked the high point of King's career as well as of the traditional civil rights movement he represented. For at the same time that King was elevating America's political discourse to sublime new levels, other, more radical offshoots of the movement were forming behind new black leaders who challenged King's moderation and instead supported separation of the races. The most influential of these leaders was Malcolm Little, better known as Malcolm X, an inspiring firebrand originally from Nebraska who broadened the appeal of the Black Muslim religious sect that had been attracting as many as 100,000 adherents since the 1940s. Brilliant, unabashed, and more than a bit of a hustler, Malcolm X energetically preached the need to separate blacks from white society, to the discomfit of conservatives on both sides, who saw no reason not to leave things as they were. To most whites, in fact, what Malcolm X seemed to be pushing was a variety of separatism closer to the views of George Wallace than of Martin Luther King.

The mutual segregation advocated by Malcolm X and later by political groups such as the Black Panther Party divided America's blacks, whose communities were already racked by more immediate problems, such as the rampant discrimination that drove the booming black population into ghettos where they found a lack of educational opportunities, crime, drugs, and the various other degradations of poverty. It wouldn't be long before segregation would turn into a far more complex economic as well as social issue.

Kennedy's Foreign Policies

In an era in which America's domestic problems seemed too tangled for the government to unravel, President Kennedy's greatest accomplishments came in the realm of foreign affairs—and so did his worst blunders. Among the former, within two months of taking office he created the Peace Corps, a forward-thinking program to train and send young Americans to aid in the development of Third World countries. Similarly, he proposed an "Alliance for Progress" with Latin America under which the United States would fund development programs among its neighbors to the south. These and other such programs suggested that a new era was beginning in America's relations with the world's underdeveloped nations, one in which humanitarian assistance would take precedence over power politics.

The era wouldn't last. Kennedy had inherited Eisenhower's plan to let the CIA overthrow Fidel Castro's Communist regime in Cuba, and was eager to prove his mettle in the Cold War by seeing the scheme carried out. Thus on April 17, 1961, a force of 1,500 U.S.-trained, -armed, and -funded Cuban exiles attempted to attack their homeland, landing ineffectually at the marshy Bay of Pigs. The ineptly planned invasion was executed no better, and within three days Castro's troops had either killed or imprisoned most of the exile forces. The debacle made for so complete a humiliation for the United States that Kennedy's earlier rhetoric about peace through democracy began to ring a little hollow. In fact, when he tried to lead the Organization of American States into a trade embargo of Cuba, Latin American critics charged the U.S. president with trying to control their foreign policies for his own ends.

The Kennedy administration faced troubles in Europe as well. In June 1961, the president held a summit meeting in Vienna with blustery Soviet Premier Nikita Khrushchev, who bullied his young counterpart for two days with demands that the Germanies be reunited and the east and west sectors of Berlin pacified within half a year. Kennedy's misgivings coming out of Vienna proved prescient in August when the Soviet Union and its East German ally erected a heavily fortified stone wall between free West Berlin and the captive rest of the city, in flagrant violation of previous agreements and de-

The Berlin Wall, photographed at right in 1962, halted the passage of people from one side of the German city to the other and tried to stem the flow of ideas as well. The man walking at left in the picture is a West Berliner, while the two men overlooking the wall at right are East German border guards, under standing orders to shoot anyone trying to cross the wall. During the 1950s West Berlin, a capitalist outpost completely surrounded by Communist East German territory, became a magnet for well-trained workers. By the summer of 1961 as many as 25,000 East Germans per day were moving to West Berlin. East Germany abruptly closed the borders on August 13, 1961, and built the wall in a matter of weeks. It remained in place for twenty-eight years.

spite vigorous American protests. Shortly thereafter Khrushchev rattled the sabers a little more, deploying additional troops to East Germany and resuming atomic testing. The immediate threat passed when Kennedy signaled his willingness to risk war to fulfill America's commitments to Europe, but the Berlin Wall would remain an ugly symbol of the Cold War until its joyful destruction marked the standoff's end twenty-eight years later.

Cuba also remained a point of contention that would bring the two superpowers the closest they would ever come to the brink of nuclear war. In October 1962, Kennedy learned from CIA reconnaissance that the U.S.S.R. had been supplying Castro with offensive missiles that could easily be trained upon the United States. The outraged president informed the nation of this on October 22, calling the Soviet action a "deliberately provocative and unjustified change in the status quo which cannot be accepted by this country." He went on to declare that the United States was suffering a "missile gap" with the increasingly better armed Soviet Union, and stressed the strategic importance of Cuba just ninety miles off the American mainland.

In response to the Soviet gambit, Kennedy ordered a blockade of Cuba and demanded that its existing missile sites be dismantled. Khrushchev refused to be intimidated, and Soviet freighters already on their way to the island steamed ahead. For two days the world quaked at the prospect of imminent nuclear war of the massive retaliatory variety, but during that time Kennedy and Khrushchev—who beneath his Communist bluster was a shrewd and solid pragmatist—exchanged a series of messages that resulted in a wise and nonlethal compromise: Khrushchev would withdraw the Soviet missiles from Cuba, Kennedy would lift the blockade and quietly remove the U.S. missiles in Turkey, and both superpowers tacitly agreed to end the threat of nuclear escalation. Although critics charged Kennedy with abandoning Cuba to Communism, supporters noted that he had shown coolness and grit under fire as well as considerable diplomatic skill; as the president himself remarked at the height of the crisis: "I guess this is the week I earn my salary." His handling of the "October missile crisis" not only helped to exonerate Kennedy for the Bay of Pigs fiasco but also marked the start of a new stage in Soviet-American relations marked by both sides' acknowledgment of the need to keep their Cold War tensions from sparking into an atomic confrontation that could blast humanity into oblivion. "We all inhabit this small planet," as Kennedy explained in an address at American University in June 1963. "We all breathe the same air. We all cherish our children's future. And we are all mortal." Along these lines his administration began looking for ways to curb the nuclear arms race, starting with negotiations with the Soviets to ban all above-ground nuclear tests.

While Kennedy's diplomacy with the Communist motherland progressed, his anti-Communist programs floundered in Guatemala, the Dominican Republic, and especially Southeast Asia. Both South Vietnam and Laos were under siege from internal Communists aided by North Vietnam, and Kennedy felt obliged to continue extending Eisenhower's assistance programs to them even while seeking ways to end the conflicts in that part of the world. He succeeded to some extent, hammering out an agreement with the almost always pragmatic Khrushchev in 1962 to create a coalition government for Laos, which quieted matters there even if it didn't put an end to the fighting.

The situation in South Vietnam proved less tractable, but as Kennedy told journalist James Reston: "We have a problem in making our power credible, and Vietnam is the place." Upon taking office Kennedy had learned that the

President Kennedy listens intently to Soviet Foreign Minister Andrei Gromyko, October 18, 1962, during the ongoing negotiations that preceded the Cuban missile crisis. Seated on the sofa before a corps of newsmen were Secretary of State Dean Rusk (left) and special adviser Llewellyn Thompson (right). The conversation between Kennedy and Gromyko proved a futile cat-and-mouse game in which neither man wanted to be the first to mention the U.S.S.R.'s offensive missiles in Cuba. Though Gromyko later characterized the two-hour meeting as "useful, very useful," it accomplished nothing toward avoiding the six-day standoff that began the following week. The Cuban missile crisis brought the world as close as it has ever been to nuclear warfare.

The map at right shows the worldwide scope of U.S. defense systems in 1966. Mutual defense treaties gave America the right to establish military bases throughout the Northern Hemisphere, completely encircling China and the Soviet Union. In addition, the Strategic Air Command, based in Omaha, Nebraska, remained on constant alert, with bombers stationed around the world ready to take off with their payloads. In 1957, however, President Eisenhower had modernized the military not only in structure but in technology. A new industry quickly emerged to develop high-tech defense systems, including over-the-horizon radar and surveillance satellites. Never before had a peacetime military been so active, and never before had any nation established such a complex security system. Nonetheless, the United States would have to accept the fact that, despite its military might, there was a small war in Vietnam it could not "win."

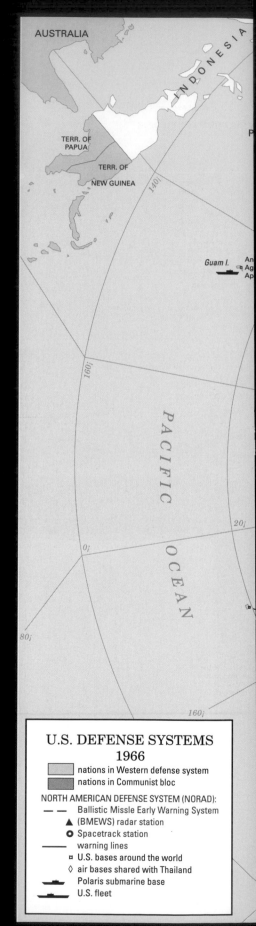

U.S. DEFENSE SYSTEMS
1966

- nations in Western defense system
- nations in Communist bloc

NORTH AMERICAN DEFENSE SYSTEM (NORAD):
- – – Ballistic Missle Early Warning System
- ▲ (BMEWS) radar station
- O Spacetrack station
- —— warning lines
- ¤ U.S. bases around the world
- ◊ air bases shared with Thailand
- ⬳ Polaris submarine base
- ⬳ U.S. fleet

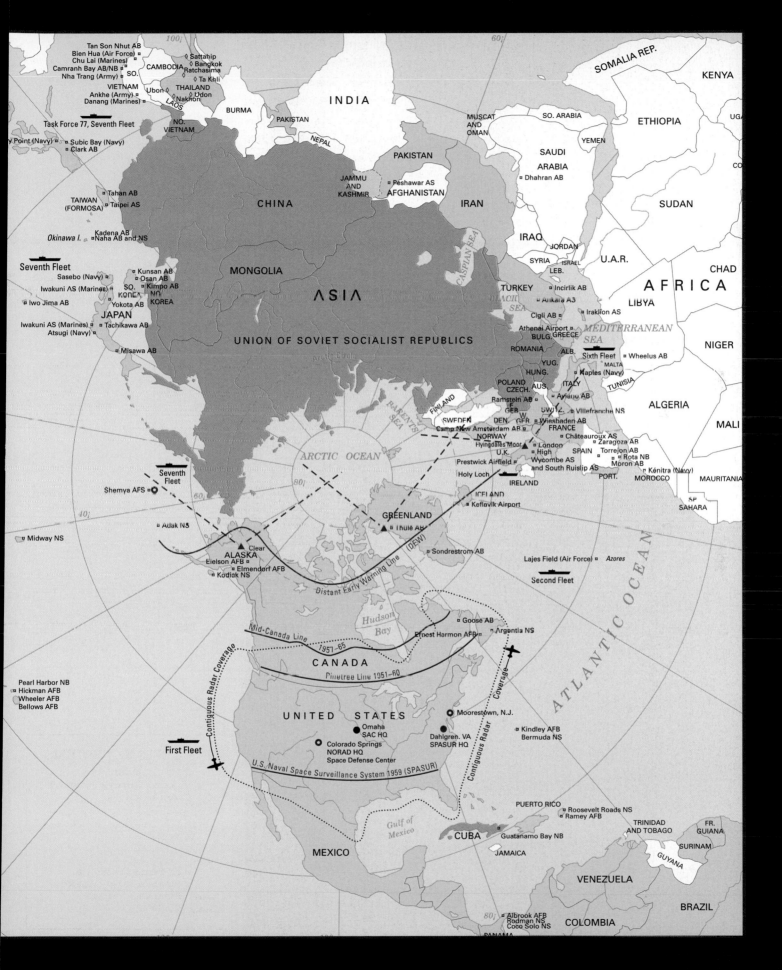

Task Force 77, Seventh Fleet

VIETNAM
Tan Son Nhut AB
Bien Hua (Air Force)
Chu Lai (Marines)
Camranh Bay AB/NB
Nha Trang (Army)
Ankhe (Army)
Danang (Marines)

Sattahip
Bangkok
Ratchasima
Ta Khli
THAILAND
Ubon
Udon
Nakhon
LAOS

CAMBODIA
SO.
NO. VIETNAM

BURMA

INDIA

PAKISTAN

NEPAL

JAMMU
AND
KASHMIR
AFGHANISTAN

Peshawar AS

PAKISTAN

MUSCAT
AND
OMAN

SO. ARABIA

SAUDI
ARABIA

YEMEN

Dhahran AB

SOMALIA REP.

KENYA

ETHIOPIA

UGA

Point (Navy)
Subic Bay (Navy)
Clark AB

TAIWAN
(FORMOSA)

Tahan AB
Taipei AS

CHINA

IRAN

IRAQ

JORDAN

SYRIA
LEB.
ISRAEL

U.A.R.

SUDAN

CHAD

Okinawa I.
Kadena AB
Naha AB and NS

MONGOLIA

ASIA

TURKEY

Incirlik AB

Ankara AS

LIBYA

A F R I C A

Seventh Fleet
Sasebo (Navy)
Iwakuni AS (Marines)
Iwo Jima AB
JAPAN
Iwakuni AS (Marines)
Atsugi (Navy)
Tachikawa AB

Kunsan AB
Osan AB
SO.
KOREA
Kimpo AB
NO.
KOREA
Yokota AB

UNION OF SOVIET SOCIALIST REPUBLICS

Cigli AB

Iraklion AS

Athenai Airport
BULG. GREECE

ROMANIA

YUG.
HUNG.
POLAND
CZECH.
AUS.

ALB.

ITALY

Sixth Fleet

Wheelus AB

Naples (Navy)

MALTA

TUNISIA

ALGERIA

NIGER

MALI

MAURITANIA

Misawa AB

Ramstein AB
GER.
W.
GFR
FRANCE
Aviano AB
Villefranche NS

Châteauroux AS
Zaragoza AB

SWEDEN
DEN.
Camp New Amsterdam AB
NORWAY

FINLAND

Wiesbaden AB

SWITZ.

London
High
Wycombe AB
and South Ruislip AS
U.K.
Prestwick Airfield
Holy Loch

SPAIN
Torrejon AB
Rota NB
Moron AB
Kénitra (Navy)
PORT.
MOROCCO

ARCTIC OCEAN

Hyingdales Moor

IRELAND

SP.
SAHARA

Seventh Fleet

Shemya AFS

ICELAND
Keflavik Airport

BARENTS SEA

CASPIAN SEA

BLACK SEA

MEDITERRANEAN SEA

Adak NS

Midway NS

Clear
ALASKA
Eielson AFB
Elmendorf AFB
Kodiak NS

Thule AB

GREENLAND

Sondrestrom AB

Lajes Field (Air Force)

Azores

ATLANTIC OCEAN

Distant Early Warning Line (DEW)

Second Fleet

Hudson
Bay

Goose AB

Pearl Harbor NB
Hickman AFB
Wheeler AFB
Bellows AFB

Mid-Canada Line
1957–60

CANADA

Ernest Harmon AFB

Argentia NS

Pinetree Line 1951–60

First Fleet

Contiguous Radar Coverage

U.S. Naval Space Surveillance System 1959 (SPASUR)

UNITED STATES

Omaha
SAC HQ

Colorado Springs
NORAD HQ
Space Defense Center

Moorestown, N.J.

Dahlgren, VA
SPASUR HQ

Kindley AFB
Bermuda NS

Contiguous Radar Coverage

MEXICO

Gulf of
Mexico

CUBA
Guatanamo Bay NB

JAMAICA

PUERTO RICO
Roosevelt Roads NS
Ramey AFB

TRINIDAD
AND TOBAGO

FR.
GUIANA

SURINAM

GUYANA

VENEZUELA

Albrook AFB
Rodman NS
Coco Solo NS
PANAMA

COLOMBIA

BRAZIL

increasingly unpopular government of Ngo Dinh Diem was on the verge of collapse after an aborted coup by its own military officers in November 1960. Both the South Vietnamese Communists who supported Ho Chi Minh—the Viet Cong—and the country's non-Communist reformers opposed the Diem regime, disappointed that its early promise had sunk into corruption and ineptitude. Kennedy dispatched Vice President Johnson to Saigon to take stock of the situation; upon his return, Johnson argued for continuing support for Diem and against sending U.S. combat troops to the region. Other envoys came back with the same advice.

Kennedy agreed that aid to the South Vietnamese had not only to continue but to increase; after all, he was as ardent an anti-Communist as Richard Nixon when it came to staving off the "red menace" in developing countries still uncertain whether to swing East or West. On May 5, 1961, therefore, Kennedy announced at a press conference that U.S. military assistance would be forthcoming to the South Vietnamese should it prove necessary, a pledge he repeated several times that year.

On October 11 the president sent General Maxwell Taylor to Saigon to assess the military situation in Indochina. When Taylor reported back that additional aid was needed, Kennedy sent 1,700 more U.S. soldiers to Vietnam, bringing the total to just under 4,000 troops, all restricted to advising the Army of the Republic of Vietnam (ARVN). By July 1962, two of the very "best and brightest" members of Kennedy's cabinet—former Harvard Business School professor, Ford Motors president, and current Secretary of Defense Robert S. McNamara and career diplomat, former Rhodes scholar, and now Secretary of State Dean Rusk—agreed with the commander of U.S. forces in the Pacific that although the conflict was unlikely to end any time soon, it was a foregone conclusion that "the Vietnamese are going to win the war"— the South Vietnamese, that is.

Even the best and brightest can, of course, be wrong, and in the matter of Southeast Asia they certainly were. As domestic dissension stewed in South Vietnam, American training of the ARVN intensified, and by early summer 1963 the two factors combined to slice a sharp breach between Diem's largely Christian supporters and the mostly Buddhist remainder of the nation. This war within a war simmered unnoticed until June 11, when a Buddhist monk set himself fatally and publicly afire in Saigon to protest the policies of the South Vietnamese government. Pictures of this and various other horrors of the war in Indochina began to flicker across the American conscience via the evening TV news and the front pages of newspapers across the nation.

The Kennedy administration, meanwhile, was losing faith in Diem. On September 2, a frustrated president sighed in an interview with CBS News anchorman Walter Cronkite that "In the final analysis it is their war. They are the ones who have to win or lose it. We can help them; we can give them equipment; we can send our men out there as advisers, but they have to win it—the people of Vietnam—against the Communists." By this point some 16,000 U.S. servicemen were stationed in Vietnam, and some of them had begun going out on missions and fighting alongside the ARVN troops. Nevertheless, the next month McNamara told reporters that the United States

would be out of Southeast Asia by the end of 1965, even though the Kennedy administration had no intention of coming to terms with the North Vietnamese.

At around the same time rumors began to be circulated about a U.S.-approved plan to remove the troublesome Diem, whom the ARVN leaders did not trust either. A military coup indeed took place in Saigon on November 1 in which Diem and most of his family were assassinated—a grisly resolution the United States did not sanction even if it had helped instigate the coup that led to the slaughter. In any case, a new government was installed in Saigon that was more to America's liking in that it seemed more capable of winning the war against the Communists.

America's president would not live to see the results. On November 22, while riding in a motorcade in Dallas with Governor John Connally as part of a warmly received politicking trip through Texas, John F. Kennedy was shot and killed by pro-Castro activist Lee Harvey Oswald. Although Kennedy's assassination would set off a flood of controversy and conspiracy theories of varying plausibility that swirl to this day (most involving the president's alleged ties to organized crime figures), the federally appointed Warren Commission that investigated the murder concluded that Oswald in fact acted alone despite the considerable evidence suggesting otherwise; the official report maintained that a single bullet, one of three Oswald fired, had pierced the president's throat, entered Texas Governor John Connally's back,

On June 11, 1963, Buddhist monk Thich Quang Duc settled calmly onto a street in downtown Saigon and set himself on fire. He was in Saigon as part of a contingent of monks from the old city of Huc, protesting the excesses of the South Vietnamese regime. Self-immolation became a horrifyingly common means of protesting the Vietnam War. At least six other Buddhist monks chose to follow Thich's example, while in 1968 an American man set himself on fire in front of the Pentagon.

At 12:30 P.M. on November 22, 1963, President John F. Kennedy was assassinated while riding through Dallas in the back of a limousine. He was shot during the drive downtown from the airport, suffering massive head and neck injuries; in a half hour he was pronounced dead. America itself was paralyzed for days after the trauma of the president's death. As Ted Sorenson, one of Kennedy's top aides, would later write in 1965: "An era had suddenly ended, the world had suddenly changed, and the brightest light of our time had suddenly been snuffed out by mindless, senseless evil."

come out of his chest, and gone through Connally's wrist before lodging in his thigh. In any case, the final bullet shattered Kennedy's skull, brought the New Frontier to an abrupt and heartrending close, and put Lyndon Johnson in the White House.

Such a violent and meaningless end to a dynamic and promising life made America shudder, and the country grew a bit older and sadder that ugly day in November 1963. The sudden disappearance of what administration admirers had dubbed "Camelot" rent the soul of the nation and bound a generation by the remembrance of where each had been when they heard Kennedy had been shot. Within days of his death, John F. Kennedy rose above history into the pantheon of American myth, where he was immediately hailed as one of the nation's greatest presidents—a perspective from which his image lost any resemblance to the inspiring but flawed human being he had been. No one will ever know where Kennedy's presidency should stand. Had he lived to serve out at least one term he could have been judged by his accomplishments or lack thereof; gunned down after just over a thousand days in the White House, he became a martyr whose influence would echo to the end of the century.

Lyndon Johnson, the Great Society, and Vietnam

Few men have ever ascended to the American presidency as thoroughly prepared for the task as Lyndon Baines Johnson, even if he had told *Time* magazine columnist Hugh Sidey in 1960 that "I know I've got a heart big enough to be president. I know I've got guts enough to be president. But I wonder whether I've got intelligence and ability enough to be president. I wonder if any man does." Like the fallen hero he replaced, Johnson believed in the active use of power, but with his political backroom expertise was even better equipped for it and shoved many of JFK's long-sought bills through Congress with ease. For all the differences between them, Kennedy and Johnson shared two overriding goals for the United States: to at least maintain the strength of the U.S. economy and to expand the federal government's assumption of responsibility for the nation's downtrodden.

Universally acknowledged as one of the most skillful and powerful politicians in U.S. history when he was tapped for the Democratic vice presidential nomination in 1960, unlike most of his predecessors in the second chair Johnson had been invited to participate in every major decision Kennedy made. The two men could not have been more different: a suave, lace-curtain New Englander and a rough-hewn, hardscrabble Texas pol who had lucked into marrying a smart heiress whose father owned a number of radio stations and newspapers across the Lone Star State. Kennedy had been a reformer with a profound sense of noblesse oblige rooted in Progressivism and the beliefs of Woodrow Wilson and both Roosevelts; he and his fellow New Frontiersmen considered it no less than their duty to bring the bounties of democracy to those less fortunate and enlightened than themselves. Johnson was every bit as much a reformer as Kennedy, but from a different tradition—the one that ran from Andrew Jackson through the Populists and on to Harry Truman. Raised in rural poverty, Johnson had a far more intimate knowledge of the poor and oppressed than Kennedy, a background that only

Below, Lyndon Baines Johnson took the oath of office at 2:38 P.M. on November 22, 1963, becoming the thirty-sixth president of the United States. Judge Sarah T. Hughes administered the oath aboard Air Force One en route from Dallas to Washington after President Kennedy was assassinated. Some two hours earlier, Jacqueline Kennedy, at right in the picture, had been riding in the car with her husband, cheered by large crowds.

honed the compassion he learned while teaching Mexican students after having put himself through Texas's Southwest State Teachers College and worked with disadvantaged youth as state director of the National Youth Administration, a program in the grimmer reaches of his home state. Soon after he was sworn in as president, Johnson made it clear that he intended to focus his presidency on liberal domestic social programs that would create a "Great Society, a place where the meaning of man's life matches the marvels of man's labor."

In his first year in office Johnson accomplished more in the way of domestic reform than any president since Franklin Roosevelt. The sweep of the advances he ushered in seems unfathomable now, decades after the nation's "discovery" of domestic poverty in the 1950s and 1960s: reduced to its simplest terms, Johnson's Great Society was no less than the boldest attempt in U.S. history to honestly redistribute the nation's wealth. Working swiftly and taking advantage of the draft of social goodwill Kennedy had gone out on, in addition to increasing the minimum wage and Social Security benefits Johnson steered three major pieces of legislation through Congress. The first, the Tax Reduction Act passed in February 1964, lowered tax rates on both corporations and individuals with small incomes. When the measure sparked fears of an unbalanced federal ledger, Johnson responded with substantial cuts in government spending and a 1964 budget under $100 billion.

Riding on the high public esteem his political acumen deserved, Johnson then asked for and got from Congress his cherished Civil Rights Act, under which all races' voting rights would be guaranteed, all racial discrimination in public facilities would be prohibited, and a national Equal Employment Opportunity Commission would be established along with a Community Relations Service to protect the rights of minorities. Finally, Johnson pushed through the Economic Opportunity Act, which among other advances established the Job Corps and Volunteers in Service to America (VISTA) programs, which were designed to provide employment to poor people through what was basically a domestic Peace Corps. Along the same compassionate lines, although the president's proposed program to provide medical care to the elderly was defeated at first, he continued to fight for it until the bill establishing Medicare for those over sixty-five was signed on July 30, 1965, with Harry Truman looking on. Johnson marveled "not simply at the passage of the bill, but that it took so many years to pass it." The following year the Medicaid program was established to provide health care to the poor.

The Great Society was not confined to programs for people. Johnson also got Congress to pass a Wilderness Preservation Act and to establish a Land and Water Conservation Fund to help the states protect and safely develop their natural resources. All in all, Johnson's legislative juggernaut earned him a reputation as a progressive and humanitarian, yet pragmatic reformer, which won him the support not only of Kennedy's admirers but of many of the late president's critics as well. Unfortunately for Johnson's long-term reputation, things did not go so well in the foreign policy realm.

The conflict in Southeast Asia remained America's most pressing international problem when he entered the White House, in part because Kennedy holdovers Robert McNamara and National Security Adviser McGeorge Bundy made Johnson feel obligated to not only continue but extend the aggressive Cold War policies of their beloved predecessor—even if he had to admit that doing so made the politician in him feel like a catfish that had "just grabbed a big juicy worm with a right sharp hook in the middle of it." At the time of Kennedy's assassination American troop levels in Vietnam stood at 16,300; by the end of Johnson's first year in office they had risen to 23,300.

Further alleged justification for America's growing involvement in the war came in early August 1964, when U.S. and North Vietnamese ships were reported to have clashed in the Tonkin Gulf after two U.S. destroyers assigned to intelligence operations had been fired upon in international waters by North Vietnamese PT boats. An outraged Johnson immediately ordered a retaliatory air strike against North Vietnam and asked Congress to allow further military action. The Senate Foreign Relations Committee quickly complied with the Tonkin Gulf Resolution authorizing the president "to take all necessary steps, including the use of armed force," to prevent any further aggression, a measure that passed unanimously in the House and by all but two votes in the Senate. As several Johnson critics suggested at the time and later evidence revealed, the supposed confrontation in the Tonkin Gulf may never have happened and was actually no more than an administration ruse to secure open-ended legal authority for the president to escalate America's involvement in the Vietnam War. Although the U.S. buildup in Indochina continued through the rest of the year, only 147 American soldiers died in Vietnam in 1964, and less than $100 million in war matériel was sent to the region, accounting for less than 0.2 percent of the military budget. It would be the last year President Johnson enjoyed the support of the American people for his Vietnam policies.

The Election of 1964

As the 1964 presidential contest drew near, Johnson remained overwhelmingly popular not only as the political heir to JFK but as one of the most successful presidential reformers in U.S. history. The Democratic nomination thus was not at issue, which left the primary campaign season to the Republicans, who gathered at their national convention in Atlantic City filled with both despair and zeal. The former arose from the party's scant hopes of unseating the incumbent; the latter was spawned by the prospect that for the first time in nearly four decades the party seemed to have a chance to nominate a genuine conservative. And so it did, opting for feisty right-wing Arizona Senator Barry Goldwater, who picked relatively unknown New York Congressman William Miller as his running mate.

The outspoken Goldwater was against virtually all the New Deal and Fair Deal social legislation that Eisenhower and other moderate Republicans had accepted. He had also voted against Kennedy's New Frontier and Johnson's Great Society programs, advocated the pursuit of "total victory" over global Communism, and sworn to rid America of "internal subversives." Although some of his ideas were considered extreme even by conservative Republi-

In late October 1964 Lyndon Johnson, right, waves his hat to a crowd of supporters during his election campaign. Forming a coalition that included rural Americans (see button, inset), city dwellers, and suburbanites, the Lyndon Johnson–Hubert Humphrey ticket gathered runaway momentum as election day approached. Their campaign was defined in large measure by the extremism of the opposition, with the ultraconservative Barry Goldwater of Arizona having taken charge of the Republican Party. Goldwater, seen below dictating a speech aboard his campaign plane, got off to an ugly start at the convention when his followers booed moderate New York Governor Nelson Rockefeller off the stage. Goldwater won only six states, but his candidacy firmly established the right wing within the modern Republican Party.

cans, Goldwater refused to back down or even compromise on any of them; instead he ran on the slogan "a choice, not an echo," which is exactly what the American public was presented with in 1964.

The Democratic convention by constrast was uneventful, as Johnson's nomination was never in doubt. Despite some idle talk that he might select Robert Kennedy for the vice presidency, the two men's bitter rivalry negated that possibility, and Johnson instead tapped Minnesota Senator Hubert H. Humphrey, a leader of the party's liberal wing whose enthusiasm for the social reform battle had earned him the nickname "the Happy Warrior."

The 1964 presidential campaign stayed dull, however, with the outcome never in question; in the end Johnson received 486 electoral-college votes to Goldwater's 52, while the popular tally was 43.1 million to 27.1 million—a margin of 61.05 percent that marked the greatest landslide in U.S. presidential history to that point. The only interesting voting shift appeared in Goldwater's success among normally Democratic Southern whites, many of whom had defected to the Republicans out of distaste for the Civil Rights Act.

Social Tensions

The assassination of John F. Kennedy, the building civil rights dilemma, and the nation's slow descent into the quicksand of Viet-

nam soured America's mood in the mid-1960s to an extent few had anticipated. What happened in Selma, Alabama, is a case in point. The Southern
Christian Leadership Conference headed by Martin Luther King, Jr., had spent
two years trying to add significant numbers of black voters to the registration
lists in Selma. Tensions ran high when the SCLC organized a voting-rights
march from Selma to Montgomery on March 6, 1965. No sooner had the protesters reached the Edmund Pettus Bridge in downtown Selma than the police charged the marchers, beating them with billy clubs and firing tear gas,
sending more than sixty African-American protesters to the hospital that
"Bloody Sunday."

President Johnson immediately addressed the nation on the need for the
police brutality to stop and the Voting Rights Act of 1965 to become law.
"This time, on this issue," Johnson declared, "there must be no delay, no hesitation, and no compromise with our purpose." On August 6, 1965, Congress
passed the Voting Rights Act, which banned literacy tests and other means of
defrauding blacks of their right to vote, and throughout the remainder of his
term spoke often of the need for racial reconciliation and the establishment
of a truly color-blind America.

Yet the nation's long-simmering racial and social strains burst into another large-scale outbreak of violence on August 11, 1965, when a riot

**The Watts section of Los Angeles was nearly
destroyed during race-related rioting on
August 13, 1965. The unrest began on
August 11 after an African-American
suspected of driving while intoxicated
received rough treatment at the hands of a
white police officer. The neighborhood
erupted as tens of thousands of residents
took to the streets over the next five days,
lashing out at white-owned businesses.
Thirty-four people died, and order was
restored only after the governor of
California deployed nearly 12,000 National
Guardsmen.**

erupted in the black ghetto of Watts in Los Angeles. Unlike in the race riots of 1919 and 1943, white mobs did not provoke the mayhem; instead, African-Americans exploded in frustration at their high unemployment and lack of equal opportunity. By the time the Watts riot ended, 34 people had been killed, nearly 4,000 arrested, and nearly $200 million in property damage done in the worst race riot anyone could remember. Dr. Martin Luther King, Jr., denounced the violence as "blind and misguided." The next summer even more violent upheavals broke out in Baltimore, Chicago, Cleveland, and some hundred other cities across the nation where militant blacks clashed with police, followed in 1967 by major riots in Tampa and Cincinnati and still more grisly conflicts in Detroit and Newark. "Get Whitey!" was a popular rant of the bitter blacks who looted white-owned stores, smashing windows and setting fires while chanting "Burn, baby, burn." In most cases these uprisings took place in cities led by liberal mayors and governors who had worked for civil rights; as a consequence, the violence was interpreted as proof that cooperation between the races was a vain hope and polarization between them inevitable. Such responses to the nation's racial tensions had acquired a name—"white backlash"—and its proponents a mantra: "law and order."

Johnson made sure that Martin Luther King, Jr., and other civil rights leaders and workers were protected when they faced threats in the South, and by so doing earned the enmity of many whites in his own home region. This gave a substantial boost to his prime political antagonist in the South, segregationist Governor George Wallace of Alabama. Yet President Johnson stuck to his guns and continued to press for civil rights, making a point of naming blacks to high government posts, including in his cabinet and on the Supreme Court.

Older African-Americans appreciated and supported the president's efforts, but some of their children seemed uninterested in gradual integration as the solution to the nation's racial problems, favoring the more militant approach of Malcolm X over the nonviolent tenets of Martin Luther King, Jr. Unlike King, Malcolm X advocated violence in self-defense. "If someone puts a hand on you," he said, "send him to the cemetery." When Malcolm X was shot to death in Harlem by Black Muslim assassins on February 21, 1965, at the zenith of his popularity, rebellious fervor skyrocketed among young blacks. Malcolm X had come to symbolize defiant black self-respect. Thanks in part to his riveting autobiography he became a martyred hero to thousands of angry "black power" proponents who rejected King's "turn-the-other-cheek" Christian philosophy in favor of militancy. Rejecting their parents' attempts to assimilate into superficial "white culture," many young militants stopped straightening their hair and let it grow into natural "Afros," adopted African garb, and even changed their Anglo names to ones with African roots.

The civil rights movement among blacks in the 1960s arose from routine and glaring injustices against a large section of the American populace; more surprising was the development of the "counterculture" among middle-class white youth, who created a "generation gap" with their elders that first manifested itself on the campuses of colleges and universities across the nation.

OPPOSITE PAGE: Dr. Martin Luther King, Jr., got arrested several times for civil disobedience, as seen in a photograph taken 1967 in a Birmingham, Alabama, jail. Back in 1963, when King was arrested for refusing to comply with an injunction prohibiting him from staging rallies in Birmingham, he responded to a letter from eight white clergymen asking why he did not just wait for the courts to examine the legality of segregation. Compelled to respond, King wrote a reply on any scrap of paper he could find. Published later as "A Letter From Birmingham Jail," the essay was King's reaction to the slow pace of change for blacks in America. It showed that his brand of nonviolent protest lacked neither anguish nor imperative. "When you are forever fighting a degenerating sense of 'nobodiness'—then you will understand why we find it difficult to wait," he wrote.

The equal rights movement of the contentious 1960s and 1970s was hardly confined to the African-American struggle. The women's rights movement, which had languished since the adoption of the Nineteenth Amendment in 1920, was reborn in the 1960s following the creation of the National Organization for Women (NOW) on June 30, 1966, in Washington, D.C., as a civil rights organization for women. Its driving force was Betty Friedan, author of *The Feminine Mystique* (1963), considered the catalyst behind the resurgent women's movement. The forty-two-year-old Friedan, a suburban mother of three originally from Peoria, Illinois, had written that the middle-class American home had turned into a "comfortable concentration camp." She railed against Madison Avenue advertisers' conspiracy to create an image of women "gaily content in a world of bedroom, kitchen, sex, babies and home." Although many women were outraged by the charge that they were willingly living their husbands' lives rather than defining identities of their own, *The Feminine Mystique* sold more than three million copies and generated an outpouring of letters from women relieved to discover that their carefully concealed resentment was shared by others—many others. NOW membership, which climbed from a thousand in 1967 to forty thousand in 1974, was created to attack the source of this resentment by battling for women's "equal rights in partnership with men," mostly by lobbying for new legislation and testing laws in the courts.

Shortly after NOW's formation a new wave of radical feminists emerged: members of the baby boom generation who were making an impact on virtually every aspect of American life. Many of these young women were the daughters of working mothers, raised with some sense of independence into an age of sexual liberation made possible by the introduction of the birth control pill in 1960.

From this new attitude emerged a host of feminist literature that reached a wide audience: Shulamith Firestone's *The Dialectic of Sex*, Kate Millett's *Sexual Politics*, Robin Morgan's *Sisterhood Is Powerful*, and many more such groundbreaking books. "Today is the beginning of a new movement," Millett told a crowd topping ten thousand women at a New York City rally in 1972. "Today is the end of millenniums of oppression." This new generation of feminists challenged everything from women's economic, political, and legal second-class status to sexual double standards. Unlike the more moderate members of NOW, the so-called women's-libbers championed and took direct action, such as picketing the 1968 Miss America Pageant, burning copies of *Playboy*, denouncing male-imposed "standards of beauty," tossing their brassieres into "freedom trash cans," and decrying gender-based discrimination in all its many guises. The fact remained for many women, as it did for Shirley Chisholm, the first African-American woman to serve in the U.S. House of Representatives, that, as she put it, "In the political world, I have been far oftener discriminated against because I am a woman than because I am black."

The primary concerns of the women's movement in the early 1970s were gender discrimination in the workplace and the resultant dearth of professional opportunities, lower pay for equal work, the lack of adequate day care for children, the various states' restrictions on abortion, and, most of all, the male chauvinism captured on Norman Lear's eye-opening series *All in the Family* in the character of Archie Bunker, who in one episode declares to his TV wife, "All right, Edith, you go ahead and do your thing. But just remember that your thing is eggs over easy and crisp bacon." The statistics weren't even grimly amusing: In 1963 women earned on average sixty-three cents for every dollar that men did, and ten years later the ratio had fallen to fifty-seven cents on the dollar. Although the number of women workers in the United States jumped from 23.2 million in 1960 to 31.5 million in 1970 to 34.1 million in 1972, *Ms.* magazine founder Gloria Steinem continued to complain about the workplace "pink-collar ghetto" in which women were "galloping toward tokenism."

Yet the seeds of progress were being planted: Women began to enroll in professional schools in record numbers. In fact, between 1969 and 1973 the number of female law students almost quadrupled and the number of female medical students doubled. Under Title IX of the Higher Education Act of 1972, female college athletes gained the right to the same financial support male athletes received. The same year Congress approved the Equal Rights Amendment and sent it to the states for ratification (it was later defeated). The women's movement soon scored more revolutionary victories: In 1973 two landmark Supreme Court decisions—in the cases of *Roe v. Wade* and *Doe v. Bolton*—struck down state laws that made abortion a crime. Ruling that such laws violated a woman's right to privacy, the Court held that the Constitution protected a woman's decision to end her pregnancy. According to the justices, a state could absolutely ban abortion only in the last three months of pregnancy; during the first trimester state power to regulate abortion was nonexistent, and in the second it was subordinate to the question of the mother's health. The Supreme Court's abortion rulings were considered the most controver-

sial judgment since *Brown v. Board of Education of Topeka* (1954), in which it ruled against "separate but equal" public schools for blacks. Other than the Court's prochoice decisions, perhaps the most vivid proof of the success of the women's movement appeared in politics between 1975 and 1998, when the number of women elected to state legislatures and the U.S. Congress more than doubled, from six hundred to fifteen hundred.

Closer to most homes, by the late 1970s America had seen its first female police officers, airline pilots, railroad engineers, and construction workers. Women had come a long way toward gaining rights equal to those of men, but they still had far to go to attain economic equality. As outspoken New York Congresswoman Bella Abzug told *Time* magazine in 1977, "The issues aren't going to go away and neither are we."

Dr. Kathryn F. Clarenbach, left, of the University of Wisconsin, and author Betty Friedan, right, are photographed at the second annual National Conference of the National Organization for Women (NOW) on November 20, 1987.

At right, Bob Dylan and Joan Baez sit together in London during a visit in 1968. In the early 1960s, Baez had helped to bring folk music into the mainstream of popular taste: Dylan, her protégé (and sometime boyfriend), was often booed when he brought his unique sound to the stage at her concerts. As the sixties progressed, though, Dylan stood out on his own to become one of the most important voices of his generation. "I don't think when I write," he said in 1963, "I just react and put it down on paper. I'm serious about everything I write. I get mad when I see friends of mine sitting in southern jails, getting their heads beat in. What comes out in my music is a call to action."

Like their black compatriots, "antiestablishment" young whites began affecting symbols of rebellion such as long hair and colorful costumes designed to outrage their elders, all the while dancing to the increasingly political and sexual beat of rock and roll music, which had first sounded in America in the 1950s and its black blues roots expanded by "British invasion" groups such as the Beatles and the Rolling Stones. Illicit drug use became popular around the rock music scene in San Francisco, where psychedelic concoctions were pioneered, and quickly spread to the rest of America's disaffected baby boomers now styled as "hippies." The Depression-era parents who had toiled so hard for conventional and financial success found their children uninterested in such things and devoted instead to what they considered social justice—to achieve which many took to the streets and some turned to violence. Draft boards across the nation were bombed and records destroyed, while significant numbers of young American men fled to Canada or Sweden to escape the newly reinstituted military draft. "New Left" leaders rose to hero status, and talk arose of a "second American revolution" uniting militant youth, blacks, and anti-Johnson liberals in a crusade to overthrow "the system" in favor of one based more directly on the U.S. Constitution.

The Quagmire of Vietnam

To most in the counterculture, the main thing to rail against was America's escalating involvement in the Vietnam War. By the time of Kennedy's assassination the government in South Vietnam had sunk into such disarray that the burden of fighting the Viet Cong fell more and more upon the United States. Soon after his election in 1964 Johnson had ordered a massive increase in the U.S. military commitment to Indochina, such that by the end of 1965 there were 185,000 U.S. troops in the region, and more than half a million three years later. During the same period American bombers dropped more ordnance on North Vietnam than had been inflicted upon all of Europe in World War II. U.S. fatalities in Vietnam, meanwhile, climbed from 1,369 in 1965 to 5,008 in 1966 to 9,378 in 1967 and to 14,592 in 1968.

The political situation in Saigon stayed shaky through a procession of governments in 1964 and into 1965, when on June 19 Marshal Nguyen Cao Ky, a flamboyant thirty-four-year-old pilot, seized power and promised to end the war by defeating the North. Favoring a more peaceful alternative in keeping with America's traditional "dollar diplomacy," Johnson offered large-scale financial and development aid to North Vietnam should it agree to end the war, a carrot Ho Chi Minh rejected to take his chances against the military stick. Not quite deterred, Johnson ordered halts to the U.S. bombing of North Vietnam twice in 1965 in hopes of spurring some reciprocal movement toward peace, both times to no avail. Yet he continued to insist, as he did in a March 1965 press conference: "In that region there is nothing that we covet. There is nothing we seek. There is no territory or no military position or no political ambition. Our one desire and our one determination is that the people of Southeast Asia be left in peace to work out their own destinies in their own ways."

Meanwhile, gung-ho General William Westmoreland, who took command of the U.S. Army in Vietnam in June 1964, launched into a hopeless war of attrition against the Viet Cong and then tried to justify it as a pacification program to win the hearts and minds of the Vietnamese people. Westmoreland's scheme, upon which he concocted civilian-relocation policies that proved equally futile in pushing the Viet Cong out of the South failed in every respect. Despite this downward spiral of America's efforts in Southeast Asia, Johnson refused to abandon the effort to prop up the Vietnamese domino in fear of destroying America's international credibility by admitting its first defeat in a foreign war. By the same token, however,

This map of Southeast Asia shows Vietnam in 1966, when a quarter of a million U.S. soldiers served there. At the peak of U.S. involvement in April 1969, the number had more than doubled to 541,000. South Vietnam had been in a state of civil war since 1956, as Communist rebels known as the Viet Cong received continuing aid from North Vietnam to battle the dictatorship in power in the South. In addition to fighting the war in South Vietnam, U.S. forces tried at times to attack the Viet Cong and their allies in North Vietnam and in neighboring Cambodia and Laos. A key target for bombers was the Ho Chi Minh Trail, which brought supplies south from China. However, the fear of provoking China into entering the conflict kept America from prosecuting an all-out war.

VIETNAM 1966
- U.S. base
- 19 main supply route
- U.S.-built highway
0   100   200

Eddie Adams took the photograph at right in Saigon on February 1, 1968, bringing the brutal immediacy of the Vietnam War home to Americans. Adams had been walking through the South Vietnamese capital with an NBC film crew when they noticed the prisoner at right being pulled through the streets. Though dressed as a civilian, he was identified as a Viet Cong officer. As the group made its way through town, Saigon's police commander, Nguyen Ngoc Loan, left, pulled out a pistol and suddenly shot the prisoner point-blank in the head.

the president also refused to bolster the bombings to the point of provoking intervention by China or the U.S.S.R.

By 1967 Johnson's ambivalent Vietnam War policies had sparked open revolt across the nation, including among many congressional Democrats. Reports from the White House and the State and Defense Departments were no longer believed, adding a "credibility gap" to the still-expanding generational one. During that ironically named "Summer of Love," the nation's cities witnessed a sharp increase in protest activities, mostly in the form of street demonstrations, peace marches, and attacks on draft board offices. Satirical songwriter Tom Paxton warbled that "Lyndon Johnson told the Nation/Have no fear of escalation,/I am trying everyone to please./And though it isn't really war,/We're sending 50,000 more/To help save Vietnam from the Vietnamese." "Make love, not war" became the rallying cry of the counterculture. President Johnson, Secretary of State Rusk, Secretary of Defense McNamara, and other administration spokesmen stopped making public appearances outside military bases unless absolutely necessary to avoid the antiwar protesters who had taken to not only jeering and shouting them down but hounding them from platforms.

Such hooliganism was a new twist for America's liberals, who since the days of Thomas Jefferson had agreed with his stance that "I tolerate with the utmost latitude the right of others to differ from me in opinion without imputing to them criminality," insisting that free speech is a basic American right provided by the First Amendment, particularly to those voicing unpopular opinions. In the decades between the founding fathers and the baby boomers, liberals had consistently advocated the right to speak freely in public even if the speaker was a Communist, fascist, or racist. In the mid- to late

Above, antiwar protesters taunt guards during a march at the Pentagon, October 21, 1967. President Johnson tried to ignore such demonstrations, intimating that anyone who spoke against the war had turned "on their leaders and on their country and on our own fighting men." To students and others who campaigned for peace, it was the Vietnam War that was destroying the character of America, as well as the lives of its young men. The photograph below shows members of a U.S. infantry somewhere northeast of Saigon in February 1967. American soldiers fought a nearly impossible war, having dubious allies in the South Vietnamese and an elusive enemy in the Viet Cong. Veteran W. D. Ehrhart wrote a poem about his experience called "A Relative Thing," which included the stanza, "It didn't take us long to realize/The only land we controlled/Was covered by the bottoms of our boots." Approximately 58,000 Americans died in the Vietnam War.

1960s, however, the baby boom's collegiate liberals argued that the Vietnam situation was so heinous that violating its advocates' constitutional rights to free speech was not only justified but necessary and utterly appropriate on the part of any true believer in democracy.

The Haight-Ashbury district of San Francisco became the vortex of the counterculture, attracting dissenting "hippies" and "flower children" from all over America. Because of its denizens' widespread drug usage the area earned the nickname "Hashbury" and became the headquarters for such psychedelia advocates as novelist Ken Kesey, poet Allen Ginsberg, and psychologist Timothy Leary.

The hippies' blurring of ideological tenets and practices spread into the nation's conventional politics as well; such was the nature of the divisive Vietnam War, which cracked rifts between the "my country, right or wrong" World War II generation and its offspring, who were far less inclined to march off to war for vague geopolitical reasons absent any clear call to arms on the order of Hitler's atrocities and Japan's attack on Pearl Harbor. Because of Vietnam, most of President Johnson's political opponents now hailed from his own party. Many Democrats with the same goals for society that the president held dear were not only uneasy with Johnson but longed for a return to the brief shining moment that was Camelot—and saw it glistening in the distance in the person of Senator Robert F. Kennedy of New York. Oddly enough, Johnson gained support from Senate Republicans such as Minority Leader Everett Dirksen of Illinois and even such archconservatives as Barry Goldwater and Richard Nixon while losing the backing of his erstwhile chief allies in the Senate, Democratic leader Mike Mansfield of Montana and William Fulbright of Arkansas (who had pushed the Tonkin Gulf Resolution through Congress). Clearly, America's political tide was taking an unusual turn.

As the antiwar protests made Johnson a virtual prisoner in the White House, rumors abounded of several potential challengers for the 1968 Democratic presidential nomination, the clear front-runner being Robert Kennedy. Although he and Johnson were both from the liberal wing of their party and agreed on civil rights and most other social issues, they had moved to opposite sides on the question of Vietnam. Kennedy, however, held back from the race, so the antiwar Democrats sought and found a more ardent candidate in intellectual yet popular Senator Eugene McCarthy of Minnesota, who took up the challenge in October 1967.

1968

McCarthy's appointment as the New Left's standard-bearer ushered in one of the most eventful years in U.S. history. Like 1776, 1860, 1896, and 1929, 1968 would prove one of those seminal years that somehow felt important from the start, even if the meaning of the events it embraced remained unclear. In some respects 1968 was even more in sync with 1848, the year revolutionary fervor had swept the Western world on the wings of rebellious European youths drawn to the socialist ideas of Marx and Engels in their *Communist*

Manifesto—which 120 years later could again be found on the shelf in many a dorm room.

The litany of issues and controversies that erupted in 1968 redefined America: the Vietnam War, first and foremost, had turned far less promising after the Tet Offensive began on January 30—the Vietnamese Lunar New Year—when North Vietnamese forces attacked Saigon and other major cities in the South, inflicting heavy casualties on U.S. troops. After ferocious and bloody fighting, the Viet Cong and North Vietnamese offensive was quelled. But Tet made a mockery of the Johnson administration's hawkish boast that the United States was winning the war. In fact, Tet demonstrated that the North Vietnamese forces were growing, not dwindling in strength. As if Vietnam wasn't enough, in 1968, America also had to deal with a contentious presidential campaign; the civil rights movement and its fracturing into factions supporting black separatism; the increasingly visible radical feminist movement, some of whose adherents disrupted the symbolic Miss America Contest in September; growing calls for strict "law and order" as antiwar and other demonstrations became more disruptive and menacing; the closing of New York's Columbia University, followed by others, due to student protests; the third-party presidential candidacy of the racist George Wallace; the Democratic convention that descended into violence that shattered the party; and, most significant, the assassinations of Martin Luther King, Jr., and Robert Kennedy, which together marked a tragedy for the United States on a par with the murder of Abraham Lincoln just over a century before.

A combination of circumstances led to those unspeakable losses. America was roiling socially, culturally, and politically, and the Democratic Party led the confusion. The left wing's designated representative, the august but unprepared Eugene McCarthy, had no domestic or civil rights credentials; his only appeal lay in his firm opposition to the Vietnam War and his cachet among intellectuals and the student activists who would do much of the grass-roots political work that year. Their considerable efforts resulted in an impressive showing for the senator in the first primary in New Hampshire—although Johnson won, McCarthy's strong support seemed quite a rebuff to the incumbent. More important, the president's apparent weakness inspired Senator Kennedy to announce his candidacy on March 16, a move that appeared opportunistic and destined to split the anti-Johnson movement. Complicating and simplifying matters at the same time, on March 31, Johnson stunned the nation by appearing on television to announce that "I shall not seek, and I will not accept, the nomination of my party for another term as your president." In fact, he was too smart a politician not to recognize that he had been abandoned by his party, just as Grover Cleveland had been in 1896. Shortly thereafter Vice President Hubert Humphrey entered the race more or less as a surrogate for Johnson—while hinting that if elected he might opt for a different course in Vietnam. Johnson himself would later admit to historian Doris Kearns Goodwin that "I knew from the start if I left a woman I really loved—the Great Society—in order to fight that bitch of a war . . . then I would lose everything at home. My hopes . . . my dreams." So he did, and so did America.

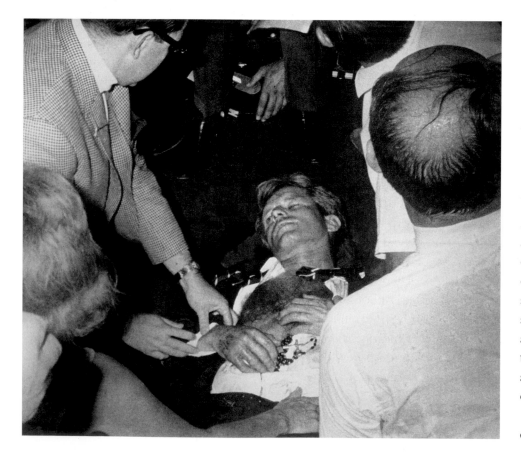

On June 5, 1968, Robert F. Kennedy was shot at close range at the Los Angeles Ambassador Hotel, where he received emergency medical treatment. A kitchen clerk at the hotel pressed rosary beads into Kennedy's hand, while Ethel Kennedy (at bottom left of photograph) asked bystanders not to crowd her husband. It had been a night of triumph for Kennedy, who only moments before had acknowledged his victory in the crucial California primary. He died June 6 and Sirhan Sirhan was charged with his murder the next day. Kennedy had emerged during the spring of 1968 as a source of hope for a country splintered by divisive issues, and his assassination numbed the spirit of many Americans.

McCarthy won the Wisconsin primary, but the nation's attention was jolted from the upcoming contests with Robert Kennedy in the mix by an act as shocking as any in U.S. history: the assassination of Dr. Martin Luther King, Jr., in Memphis on April 4, 1968. The majestic voice of the extraordinary leader whose stirring calls for civil rights had earned him the Nobel Peace Prize four years earlier was silenced by a bullet fired by James Earl Ray of Tennessee, although rumors swirled of a conspiracy to kill other black leaders, and even King's family would later express doubts that Ray had committed the crime at the Lorraine Motel. In any case, blacks and other thoughtful Americans of all descriptions realized the enormity of the loss to the nation, and a pall of grief descended that soon turned into ugly riots in dozens of cities.

Yet the presidential primaries went on. Exactly two months after King's murder Robert Kennedy, who was perceived as an even more ardent advocate for the "underclass" than his martyred brother, won the critical California contest by a slim margin. Minutes after he delivered his victory speech, however, Senator Kennedy was gunned down by Arab nationalist Sirhan Sirhan for reasons that remain murky to this day. The sudden disappearance of the last hope to regain Camelot dealt an even sharper shock to a nation still reeling from the death of King and left many mired in hopelessness for the future. And the senselessness wasn't over yet.

While the Democrats had been battling for their party's presidential nomination, Richard Nixon had won all the Republican primaries and arrived at the GOP's Miami Beach convention confident of victory. His certainty was hardly unjustified; after all, the former near-pariah—who after losing a bid for the California governorship in 1962 had proclaimed to the press that "You won't have Nixon to kick around anymore"—had just fought off liberal New York Governor Nelson Rockefeller and conservative California Governor Ronald Reagan by forming a deft alliance with Southern Republicans led by powerful and politically savvy Senator Strom Thurmond of South Carolina. Nixon was nominated on the first ballot and selected Maryland's less than impressive Governor Spiro Agnew as his running mate—as insurance against assassination, Nixon would later quip to an aide.

As disturbing as Nixon's reascent to political power may have been to many who remembered him as the red-baiting congressman of the 1950s, the relative success of George Wallace's American Independent Party campaign chilled open-minded Americans of all political persuasions with its indication of a mass public swing toward far-right conservatism and racial intolerance. The buzz words of Wallace's campaign were "law and order," which was code for supression of protest. If a civil rights advocate ever lay down in front of his car, Wallace boasted, he would drive over the obstacle. Although Wallace himself would later denounce his own positions of 1968, he attracted considerable support despite considering Kentucky Fried Chicken founder "Colonel" Harland Sanders for his running mate before settling on hawkish, retired Air Force General Curtis LeMay, best known for arguing that the United States should bomb North Vietnam "back to the Stone Age."

It was in this polarized political atmosphere that the Democrats convened in Chicago to select their candidate for president. What happened

In 1968, Richard Nixon, right, was once again the Republican nominee for president, with Maryland's Spiro Agnew, the vice presidential candidate. Merely gaining the nomination was an astonishing political turnaround for Nixon. While his loss to Kennedy in the 1960 presidential election had hurt him, he had been devastated two years later, when he failed to win the California governor's chair. Yet Nixon had rebuilt his reputation by moving to New York from California and finding new sources of support. By 1968 his very familiarity became an asset, as voters turned away from the turmoil surrounding the Democratic Party.

there officially—Humphrey, as expected, won the nomination as McCarthy and equally antiwar South Dakota Senator George McGovern split the disenfranchised Kennedy supporters and their organization—paled in comparison with what went on unofficially in the streets outside the convention hall. Several radical leaders had arrived in Chicago and announced their intentions to disrupt the Democrats' proceedings, leading backroom machine pol and Mayor Richard Daley to counter that he would do whatever it took to prevent any such disruptions. Adding to the chaos was a procession of mule-drawn wagons driven by African-Americans from Reverend Ralph Abernathy's Poor People's Campaign and by the Abbie Hoffman–Terry Rubin-led "yippies," members of the anarchistic Youth International Party, which specialized in disruptive street theater. To cope with the mass protests, Mayor Daley called in army troops and the National Guard to assist his own 12,000-strong police force to maintain order. Tensions mounted, and before long the Chicago police and National Guard clashed with the demonstrators, who through the blows of billy clubs and billows of tear gas meant to quell them kept chanting, "The whole world is watching, the whole world is watching"—which it was via live television. The nation was forced to witness the disintegration of the Roosevelt coalition that had dominated Democratic politics for more than three decades. Inside the convention hall, Senator Abraham Ribicoff of Connecticut tossed aside his prepared remarks to denounce the "Gestapo tactics in the streets of Chicago." Once the eggs, rocks, and nightsticks stopped flying, the established order reasserted itself and unstinting Vietnam War supporter Humphrey won the Democratic presidential nomination, choosing fellow old-guard liberal Senator Edmund Muskie of Maine as his running mate.

The chaos tainting the Democrats sealed the election for Nixon, who had helped his own cause with a skillful campaign exploiting the nation's most incendiary issues and promising stability, law and order, and "peace with honor" in Vietnam. Nixon won the presidency, but with only 43.4 percent of the popular vote, the lowest total for any victor since 1912, most of the Republican ballots coming from the suburbs where a majority of Americans now lived. In fact, Humphrey might well have won had it not been for the defection of so many white Southern Democrats to Wallace, who received 10 million votes, and the desertion of passionate antiwar Democrats who either refused to vote at all or cast throw-away ballots for black comedian Dick Gregory.

To his credit, Nixon seemed to realize that he had not been handed a mandate. The 1968 election produced little of the excitement that usually greeted a change of administrations; instead the nation was subdued by exhaustion and relief that the contentious and costly campaign was over. Never a magnetic or crowd-pleasing figure, the new president seemed just another old face from the politics of the last generation, noted more for his cleverness and caution than for any dramatic qualities that might engender enthusiasm for his ascension to the Oval Office. Of course, that is apparently what a plurality of the 1968 electorate wanted.

Nixon was voted into office by what he astutely dubbed the "Great Silent

Majority" of middle-class Americans sensible enough to have opposed both the police riot in Chicago and the militant antiwar demonstrations that had sparked it, yet socially aware enough to have supported the civil rights movement but not the radical elements that threatened to burn the nation to the ground in the name of the Bill of Rights. This pragmatic majority wanted change without violence, reform without revolution, and generally opposed the Vietnam War not so much because it was immoral as because it was unwinnable. These Nixon voters acknowledged their country's many flaws and problems but loved and took pride in it all the same, railing against the flag-burners who spit upon servicemen returning from Vietnam and called them murderers. The watershed year of 1968 may have belonged to the radical activists, but it ended with the very symbol of the conservative, middlebrow political establishment preparing to move into the White House and take the helm of the United States.

The Chicago police manhandled antiwar demonstrators in the shadow of the 1968 Democratic convention. So much tear gas was used in the streets during convention week that Hubert Humphrey, the eventual nominee, complained that he could feel its effects in his hotel suite on the twenty-third floor. The worst of the clashes occurred August 29 as Humphrey was delivering his acceptance speech inside the convention hall. Alternating between Humphrey's speech and scenes of the violence outside, the live TV coverage had a nightmarish quality that did not reflect well on either the Democratic Party or the well-being of the country.

CHAPTER 20

A SEASON OF DISCONTENT

O ne of the most fascinating and certainly the most flawed of modern U.S. presidents, Richard Nixon relentlessly pursued a Machiavellian political career that to an almost eerie extent mirrored the progress of the American Century, evolving from the anti-Communist hysteria of the late 1940s and 1950s to the swaggering globalism of the 1960s to the mature disillusionment of the 1970s to the self-indulgent capitalism of the 1980s to the hope of cementing marketplace democracy worldwide in the 1990s and into the next millennium. "It has often been said that Richard Nixon was a man without a home, a 'rootless' figure, without a 'stamp of place,'" wrote social commentator Kirkpatrick Sale. "The fact is that Nixon bore very clearly the stamp of place, only the place was Southern California, and *that* was rootless and ill-defined, a mercurial, restless society."

Despite a succession of humiliating, self-created setbacks that would have crushed any other imaginable politician well before they culminated in his forced resignation from the highest office in the land, Nixon continually managed to redefine himself as often as necessary to maintain a major presence on the national scene from the Truman years through the middle of Bill Clinton's first term. In every guise, however, as many observers despised as respected him, and throughout his political career Nixon remained a polariz-

Richard Nixon gives his characteristic double "V for victory" salute while campaigning in Levittown, Pennsylvania, in 1968, left. A candidate for national office in every election but one from 1952 to 1972, Nixon ran his best campaign in 1968, somehow transforming old political battle scars into evidence of experience. At first Nixon seemed above the fray, but his darker emotions later led his administration into the scandals of Watergate. As the button above indicates, many Americans felt there was only one person to blame for Watergate.

ing figure. As Harry Truman put it for many: "He not only doesn't give a damn about the people, he doesn't know how to tell the truth. I don't think the son of a bitch knows the difference between telling the truth and lying."

Born to poor Quaker parents in rural Whittier, California, in 1913, Richard Nixon "wasn't a little boy that you wanted to pick up and hug," as one family friend put it. The already serious and workaholic young Nixon acquired a permanent chip on his shoulder when the obligation to help his widowed mother run the family grocery store kept him from accepting a scholarship to Harvard College and the supposedly easy path to success he thought such an opportunity offered. But the disappointment only made him try harder, and the young Nixon put himself through Whittier College while running his mother's store, earning grades good enough to score a full scholarship to Duke University Law School, where he was so hard up for money he lived in an abandoned toolshed and worked so diligently his classmates gave him the not necessarily affectionate nickname "Iron Pants." When World War II broke out, Nixon joined the U.S. Navy and served as a lieutenant commander in the South Pacific, where he learned to play poker well enough to come home with a substantial bankroll with which to start a political career. By 1946 he had been elected to the U.S. House of Representatives, and after two terms there progressed to the Senate; two years later Dwight Eisenhower tapped him for vice president, to which thankless post he hung on through several political controversies. He lost the presidential election of 1960 to John F. Kennedy and a bid for the California governorship two years after that, but by 1968 it surprised virtually no one that Richard Nixon was back.

Happily for Nixon, who described himself as "an introvert in an extrovert's profession," he came to prominence once again during what novelist Charles Johnson calls in *Dreamer* (1998), a fictional account of Martin Luther King, Jr., "the first truly theatrical decade," the 1960s, a period "so fluid, so polymorphous you could change your identity—reinvent yourself—as easily as you restyled your hair." Richard Nixon did both, and transformed himself from the red-baiting anti-Communist zealot of the 1950s into the "new Nixon" of 1968, a pragmatic yet compassionate spokesman for the "great silent majority" who made up the heartland and soul of America. Oddly enough, once in the White House the supposedly archconservative Nixon would inaugurate and expand domestic social programs so progressive they would inspire some to call him the "last liberal president."

Nixon betrayed a mix of intellectual sophistication and crudity of character that made him one of the most enigmatic figures ever to occupy the White House. His undeniable misdeeds in the complex Watergate scandal would rightly force him to resign from office in disgrace in 1974, but only a very superficial reading of history and of his administration suggests that Nixon's was a failed or even subpar presidency. To the contrary, the bulk of the evidence indicates otherwise—and that, but for Watergate, Nixon likely would be hailed as one of the most effective and forward-thinking men ever to serve as chief executive. In fact he was treated as such by every one of his successors from both parties, all of whom routinely called upon the discredited former president for advice and the trenchant global analyses that informed the influential books he continued to write until his death in April 1994. Still, the utter contempt Nixon showed for certain points of the Constitution as the Watergate morass deepened cannot be explained away, and would end in a pervasive national cynicism that writer Hunter S. Thompson characterized as "The Death of the American Dream." Likewise the impassioned Western essayist and naturalist Edward Abbey spoke for hundreds of 1970s intellectuals when he proclaimed that the moral duty of a writer was to be a "critic of his own country, his own government, his own culture." Taking it one step further, Abbey, a frontline opponent of the federal government's increasing exploitation of wilderness, offered a Thoreau-like aphorism for civil disobedience indicative of the era: "Sentiment without action is the ruin of the soul."

Vietnam and the Counterculture

Like Lyndon Johnson, Richard Nixon inherited the Vietnam War, but was determined not to let it destroy him as it had his predecessor—indicating that Johnson's prescience had referred to something else when the outgoing president predicted before the 1968 election that "Nixon can be beaten. He's like a Spanish horse who runs faster than anyone for the first nine lengths and then turns around and runs backward. He'll do something wrong in the end. He always does."

In most cases Nixon's blunders grew from his near-consuming paranoia, which extended to distrust of even his closest associates. As president he held decision making and even policy implementation as tightly within the White House as he could, freezing out his old associate and now Secretary of State William Rogers in favor of the counsel of longtime rival Nelson Rockefeller's one-time aide Henry Kissinger, a brilliant, German-born and Machiavelli-minded former Harvard professor whom Nixon had made his special assistant for national security affairs and as such his right-hand man in foreign policy. Short, stocky, bespectacled, and given to delivering ponderous policy pronouncements in a heavily accented rumbling monotone, somehow Kissinger became the darling of the social set and took to dating Hollywood starlets. As he would explain in the *New York Times,* "Power is the great aphrodisiac."

With Kissinger's assistance the new president immediately set about finding the means to claim "peace with honor" in Vietnam—a way out of the war that would satisfy both supporters and critics by preserving America's credibility while extricating the United States from the messy conflict. Thus the administration came up with the "Vietnamization" program, whereby

Richard Nixon confers with Henry Kissinger, his special assistant for national security affairs during his first term. President Nixon placed a priority on foreign policy matters and depended heavily on Kissinger, a former professor who had started his government career in the Kennedy administration. Largely bypassing Secretary of State William Rogers to spearhead foreign policy, Kissinger became a specialist in "shuttle diplomacy," flying from one negotiation to another, particularly in the Middle East.

Above, a soldier wounded in action against the North Vietnamese on Dong Ap Bia Mountain is carried to safety, May 19, 1969. While Americans were denied many of the most basic facts about the war, they were inundated with dramatic images from Vietnam on television news broadcasts.

U.S. combat troops would gradually be replaced by ARVN forces. In March 1969, two months after Nixon's inauguration, the United States had 541,000 troops in Vietnam; that June the president announced that 25,000 of them would be withdrawn immediately followed by the rest—and he kept his word, steadily bringing the American boys home until only some 24,200 remained at the end of his first term. In the meantime Kissinger shuttled between secret locations in France and other countries to conduct tortuous peace negotiations with North Vietnam. Although Ho Chi Minh died in September 1969, his successors carried on his demands for the reunification of Vietnam and a complete U.S. withdrawal from the region.

The conflict in Southeast Asia had by that point become even more complicated than it had been in the Johnson years. Throughout the early stages of the Vietnam War, neighboring Cambodia's ruler, Prince Norodom Sihanouk, had succeeded in keeping his country neutral even though North Vietnamese forces had bases in it. To avoid public outcry in the United States—in one of the first of many displays of Nixon's utter disregard for the American people's right to know—in the spring of 1969 the president ordered a series of secret bombings of the Communist supply stations inside Cambodia. A year later a military coup led by General Lon Nol overthrew Sihanouk's government, and the new leader agreed to allow more U.S. strikes against the North Vietnamese in Cambodia. On April 30, 1970, Nixon made it public that American forces would be sent into Cambodia to remove the North Vietnamese bases, a move that energized the antiwar forces at home to mount another wave of demonstrations. Activist Abbie Hoffman spoke for the youth movement when in his Yiddish poem "Nixon Genug" he denounced the president for being a "no-goodnick" who like some "wild beast" enjoyed "screwing the poor and sick." On May 4 the protests turned tragic at Ohio's Kent State University, where National Guard troops opened fire on the mostly student demonstrators, killing four and wounding nine others; shortly thereafter two student protesters at Mississippi's Jackson State College were similarly gunned down. Student shutdown strikes following these campus killings were widespread—more than 400 in all. Toward the end of May more than 100,000 student demonstrators gathered in Washington to stand vigil before the White House and other government buildings. The national outrage after Kent State led Congress to repeal the Tonkin Gulf Resolution, an action Nixon chose to ignore; instead he continued withdrawing troops from Southeast Asia, while the war raged on.

No one hoped for its end more ardently than the young American draftees forced to slog through the bloody jungles of Vietnam to no clear purpose. Increasing numbers of soldiers began to question the point of the war they were fighting, breeding confusion and anger that led some servicemen to desert, many more to turn to the illicit drugs widely available in Southeast Asia, and a disturbing minority to snap and turn savage, committing atroci-

FOLLOWING SPREAD: Nguyen Kong Ut photographed children trying to outrun the horror of a napalm attack in South Vietnam in June 1972. The chemical, dropped from the air, had set fire to the clothes of the girl at center, and she had pulled them off as she ran.

Protests against the Vietnam War reached a tragic climax at Kent State University in Ohio on May 4, 1970, below. Provoked by a spate of rock throwing, Ohio National Guardsmen opened fire, killing four students (two of whom were only walking across campus) and wounding nine. In the aftermath the White House commented rigidly that "when dissent turns to violence it invites tragedy."

KEY TEXTS FROM PENTAGON'S VIETNAM STUDY

The New York Times

The New York Times

The New York Times

MAYOR'S BUDGET OF $8.8-BILLIONS AVOIDS LAYOFFS

COURT SAYS CITIES MAY CLOSE POOLS TO BAR RACIAL MIX

MITCHELL SEEKS TO HALT SERIES ON VIETNAM BUT TIMES REFUSES

On June 13, 1971, the *New York Times* began printing excerpts, above, from the Pentagon's own documented history of the Vietnam War, a report better known as the Pentagon Papers. By that point, more than two years after Richard Nixon entered office promising peace, many Americans were frustrated to the breaking point with misinformation regarding Vietnam. Even though the Pentagon Papers were already outdated, covering only the period up to May 1968, they still offered major background on the buildup of the war.

ties not only against the enemy but against Vietnamese civilians and even one another. The American public was fed up with the war, too; by 1971 polls showed that two-thirds of the population favored immediate withdrawal of the U.S. troops, never mind peace, with or without honor. One survey, for example, reported that 65 percent of respondents thought it "morally wrong" to continue the U.S. role in South Vietnam, although at the same time a clear majority also supported Nixon's position that the North Vietnamese Communists should not be permitted to overrun Southeast Asia. Nixon reacted by sending U.S. troops after the North Vietnamese in Laos in February 1971 and then escalating the aerial bombings of North Vietnam and Cambodia. All the while television kept bringing the horror of war into the living rooms of America, further exacerbating Nixon's Vietnam woes. That March a military court convicted Lieutenant William L. Calley of murder, reminding viewers that Calley's platoon had massacred more than 300 South Vietnamese villagers at My Lai.

As the antiwar protests at home grew more strident and ever more frequently violent, Nixon responded by ordering the Federal Bureau of Investigation (FBI) and even the supposedly overseas-only CIA to beef up their surveillance and in some cases their infiltration of various antiwar and other radical groups, whether doing so was legal or not. The most egregious example to that point of Nixon's abuses of his power in this manner—and the first cog in the twisted Rube Goldberg Watergate machine that would bring the administration down—was spawned in June 1971, when the *New York Times* published what came to be known as the "Pentagon Papers," a top-secret and mostly critical military study of the Vietnam War leaked to the newspaper by disgruntled former Defense Department official Daniel Ellsberg. The Pentagon Papers said nothing whatever about Nixon's policies; the secret documents revealed only that both the Kennedy and Johnson administrations had made dishonest statements to the public about the progress of the Vietnam War. Nevertheless, the White House protested that the documents were stolen federal property that no media outlet had any right to use, a position the U.S. Supreme Court rejected.

Nixon's outrage at the security breach represented by the Pentagon Papers inspired his foolhardy decision to assemble the "plumbers," a covert team of supposed intelligence specialists tasked with preventing any more such leaks. Their first assignment was to find dirt on Ellsberg, which the White House accomplished by authorizing the operatives to break into Ellsberg's psychiatrist's office to search for materials that might discredit the source of the Pentagon Papers.

Détente

As Vietnam continued to dominate and bedevil U.S. foreign policy, Nixon pursued his dreams of an exalted place in history by initiating bold overtures in other parts of the world. With the help of Kissinger's broad if Eurocentric global vision, Nixon took account of the post-World War II recovery and rise back to power not only of Western Europe and Japan but also of China; that, along with the development of a number of Third World countries, inspired his administration's "multipolar" foreign policy of battling Communism simultaneously on many disparate fronts. He and Kissinger responded to the global developments with the "Nixon Doctrine," under which the United States would transfer some of the military responsibilities for containing the Communist threat to appropriate allies such as the apartheid regime in South Africa, Zaire in central Africa, Japan in the Pacific, and the Iranian shah in the Mideast. While such lesser areas of concern were delegated to America's less than superpower allies, the theory went, the United States could focus on the red threat closer to its own backyard, as the administration did in 1970 when elections in Chile—to that point one of South America's few real democracies—ushered in President Salvador Allende Gossens on the votes of a coalition of Communists, Socialists, and other radicals. The CIA reported that Allende's victory was somehow a threat to the United States, and, with Kissinger's blessings, in 1973 a CIA-backed conservative Chilean group succeeded in ousting the leftist government. Then they stormed the presidential palace and assassinated Allende on the grounds that even democratically elected Communists had to be gotten rid of because their very nature posed the threat of dictatorship. On a more positive note, the Nixon Doctrine also freed the administration to pursue geopolitics on the grand scale, including the diplomatic excursions to Beijing that would catch the Soviets' attention and help pave the way to a better relationship with the U.S.S.R. by arousing its concern about a Sino-American rapprochement.

Belying his reputation for staunch anti-Communism, Nixon recognized that the current rift between China and the Soviet Union had created an opening for the United States to chip away at if not break the ice of the cold war. What's more, the shrewd and pragmatic president, so sadly obsessed with his own place in history, understood that his red-baiting background gave credence to what would later become a geopolitical maxim: "Only Nixon could go to China." He therefore launched what would become his greatest foreign policy achievement: the United States' opening to Communist China. After diplomatic discussions that began in 1969, capped by months of secret shuttle diplomacy by Kissinger and others, in 1971 Chairman Mao Zedong finally extended an invitation to the American Ping-Pong team and then allowed a visit to Beijing by President Nixon to engage with him and Premier Zhou Enlai in talks that produced at least the appearance of closer relations between the two countries.

Nixon did even better with the U.S.S.R., proposing "détente" (French for "relaxation") between the two nuclear superpowers through policies and agreements that would set in motion the gradual liberalization of the Soviet

Human beings have been gazing at the stars and dreaming of space exploration since the days of the ancient Greeks, but midway through the twentieth century those dreams began to be realized. With great prescience, French science fiction writer Jules Verne had opined in his 1865 book *From the Earth to the Moon* that "knowing the bold ingenuity of the Anglo-Saxon race," the first men to get to the moon would be American. "The Yankees, the first mechanicians in the world," Verne writes, "are engineers—just as the Italians are musicians and the Germans metaphysicians—by right of birth." In his fictional account the trip to the moon would cost the Americans $4 million, plus funds raised overseas. "Russia paid in as her contingent the enormous sum of 368,733 rubles," he says, not all that surprising considering "the scientific taste of the Russians, and the impetus which they have given to astronomical studies—thanks to their numerous observatories."

This sort of prognostication, however eerily accurate it proved, remained the stuff of dreams until the development of rocketry during World War II offered the real possibility of powering vehicles to leave the Earth's orbit. Several countries, including the United States and the U.S.S.R., experimented with more advanced rockets after the war, and in 1954 both nations revealed that they were exploring ways to go into outer space.

On October 4, 1957, the U.S.S.R. made the first foray by launching the first spacecraft, popularly known as *Sputnik*, a 184-pound man-made satellite that orbited the Earth every 96.1 minutes. The two radios on *Sputnik* sent out signals as the satellite raced through space, and nowhere did those beeps sound louder than in Washington, D.C. Americans were shocked; they had long assumed their country was far in the lead in every technology. They were again proved wrong on November 3, when the Kremlin capped its scientific and political coup by sending *Sputnik II* into orbit carrying a dog named Laika. Earlier in the year, after all, the Soviets had tested their first intercontinental ballistic missile (ICBM). In consequence, talk of a missile gap arose throughout America in the late 1950s, with debate over the perceived failures of American science and education and whether materialism was responsible. When an Eisenhower administration official said that the United States would soon have a satellite in space, Senate Majority Leader Lyndon Johnson, referring to the Ford Motor Company's garish new Edsel, quipped that the satellite too would have a three-tone paint job and windshield washers.

After an initial failure the United States launched its first successful satellite into space on January 31, 1958, atop a Jupiter C rocket, modified from a German V-2. Later that year Eisenhower created the post of Special Assistant to the President for Science and Technology and created the National Aeronautics and Space Administration (NASA) to oversee all U.S. attempts at manned and unmanned flight beyond the Earth's atmosphere. Under NASA's direction, a program was set in motion to create enormous rockets capable of powering larger satellites into space. There was some talk of a manned flight to the moon, but Eisenhower rejected the idea when he was told it would cost between $26 and $38 billion. Even without a moon shot, NASA's budget rose from a third of a billion dollars in 1959 to more than $1 billion in 1961.

Then the effort really took off. During the 1960 presidential campaign Democratic candidate John F. Kennedy promised an active space program, and once elected, he announced: "I believe that this nation should commit itself to achieving a goal, before this decade is out, of landing a man on the moon and returning him safely to the Earth." Kennedy assigned Vice President Johnson to a central and aggressively public role in the space program and didn't flinch when the new head of NASA asked for a supplemental grant of $308 billion to "close the space gap." When the Soviets sent cosmonaut Yuri Gagarin in *Vostok 1* to become the first human being to orbit the Earth on April 12, 1961, and when five days later Kennedy experienced the humiliating failure of the Bay of Pigs invasion of Cuba, the U.S. president turned to the space program to remind Americans of their national pride. On May 5, 1961, Alan B. Shepard, Jr., was rocketed into space aboard the U.S. Mercury program's *Freedom 7* for a three-hundred-mile, fifteen-minute suborbital loop. Further assuaging America's mounting anxieties over the Soviet challenge in space, on February 20, 1962, John Glenn became the first American to orbit the Earth in the Mercury project's *Friendship 7*.

The United States' push toward the final frontier continued under Lyndon Johnson, who was every bit as committed to the space program as his predecessor. In fact, it was under Johnson's leadership that the Apollo program designed to put Americans on the moon was initiated. Unfortunately, the *Apollo 1* mission began and ended in tragedy on January 27, 1967, when fire broke out on the launchpad, killing astronauts Virgil ("Gus") Grissom, Edward White, and Roger Chaffee. The Apollo program continued, nevertheless, with regular takeoffs that year and the next, completing missions that demonstrated the feasibility of docking in space.

Five and a half months before the end of the 1960s three Americans—with the help of thousands more less celebrated—accomplished humankind's greatest feat to date. *Apollo 11*, manned by Neil Armstrong, Michael Collins, and Edwin ("Buzz") Aldrin, Jr., took off from Florida's Cape Kennedy on July 16, 1969, at 1:31 P.M. eastern standard time and landed on the moon 103 hours and 45 minutes later. The crew sent back the message "Houston. Tranquility Base here. The Eagle has landed." Pilot Armstrong was the first person to set foot on the moon. He emerged from the lunar landing vehicle *Eagle* as a television camera mounted on its base beamed the otherwordly images back to the Earth. When his foot first touched the moon's gray surface Armstrong proclaimed, "That's one small step for a man, one giant leap for mankind." The astronauts then planted the American flag, gathered rock samples, spoke with President Richard Nixon, and returned to the Earth on July 24 without a hitch. John F. Kennedy's pledge to land an American on the moon by the end of the decade had been fulfilled.

On July 20, 1969, Neil Armstrong became the first man to walk on the moon. He was followed moments later by Buzz Aldrin, while Michael Collins orbited above in the command module of the Apollo 11 *mission. Among the first things that Armstrong and Aldrin did, once they were used to walking on the moon, was to plant an American flag and set up TV cameras.*

empire and within two decades its collapse and replacement by separate capitalist democracies in its former republics. Three months after his breakthrough to China, Nixon became the first U.S. president to go to Moscow as well. There he met with Soviet Premier Leonid Brezhnev, and the two leaders signed a twelve-point agreement on the basic principles of détente, which amounted to a promise by both countries to respect the other's sphere of influence: the Soviet Union would curb its efforts to spread Communism in Latin America and Africa, and the United States would not press for a rollback of the Iron Curtain in Europe and would stay neutral in the clash between the U.S.S.R. and China. Nixon and Brezhnev also signed the first SALT (Strategic Arms Limitation Talks) treaty under which both countries agreed to limit their development and deployment of intercontinental ballistic missiles and antiballistic missile systems, a small step in the path to eventual disarmament. A year later, in June 1973, Brezhnev demonstrated just how much relations between the superpowers had improved by reciprocating Nixon's gesture and visiting Washington, D.C., for additional talks on extending what was now a limited truce in the Cold War.

"Our Last Liberal President"

During the 1968 presidential campaign, Richard Nixon had presented himself as a conservative devoted to battling the liberal forces of the Great Society, and in some respects he delivered on the image. As president he opposed the further desegregation of public schools through involuntary busing, abolished the Office of Economic Opportunity that had been one of the driving forces behind Lyndon Johnson's social agenda, and tried to block some of Congress's efforts to pass new social legislation by sequestering the funds that would be needed to implement the programs. Nevertheless, the Nixon administration succeeded in starting a host of domestic initiatives that would prod a number of even his customary critics to admit upon Nixon's death in April 1994 that he may in fact have been "our last liberal president," as *Washington Post* columnist Mark Shields put it.

Among his other such "liberal" achievements as president, Nixon sponsored and obtained the legislation to create the Environmental Protection Agency, the most important federal effort to protect the U.S. ecosystem undertaken by any chief executive since Theodore Roosevelt. During Nixon's White House tenure Congress drew up a far-reaching program of environmental legislation. Concern over the environment had been growing since

Above, Richard Nixon and his wife, Pat, visited the Great Wall during their trip to the People's Republic of China in February 1972. The initiative for the landmark visit to China came from Nixon, once one of the staunchest enemies of Communism. When Chairman Mao said at a state dinner that he was glad Nixon had been elected president because he liked right-wing leaders, Nixon responded, "In America, at least at this time, those on the right can do what those on the left can only talk about." In terms of opening relations with China, he was almost certainly correct.

1962, when government biologist Rachel Carson published *Silent Spring*, warning that unrestricted use of chemical pesticides was destroying much of the nation's wildlife. What's more, she wrote, "As crude a weapon as the cave man's club, the chemical barrage has been hurled against the fabric of life." From TV news specials and newspaper editorials, Americans learned that Midwest drinking water was tainted with nitrates from farmers' fertilizers, that fish suffocated by sewage were piling up on the Great Lakes' beaches, that bass and salmon had been wiped out by power plants in some areas, and that even Antarctic penguins carried traces of the pesticide DDT.

The ubiquitous signs of environmental degradation triggered by hyper-industrialism sounded an alarm that planet Earth was dying. America was in danger of losing to extinction the black-footed ferrets of the Great Plains, the bighorn sheep of the Rockies, the whooping cranes of Florida, and the bald eagles of Alaska. Part of the reason was that the United States was gobbling up land resources: every year millions of acres were ravaged by strip mining, broad swaths of national forest laid bare by the clearcutting of timber, and another million acres paved over. Battle lines were drawn between pro- and antidevelopment forces, and conservation groups such as the Sierra Club and the Nature Conservancy adapted a new militancy and swelled with new members. In 1968 protests by environmentalists blocked construction of two U.S. government dams that would have flooded sections of the Grand Canyon. The new president did not ignore environmentalists' concerns. In February 1969, less than a month after his inauguration, Nixon told employees at the Department of the Interior: "I know that we are all working toward the same goal: to see to it that this great and rich land . . . will also retain for the generations to come those great areas of beauty and also an environment, clean air, pure water, which will be one that our children will want to live in."

As evidence of the environmental disaster mounted—such as when the Cuyahoga River in Cleveland caught fire from an oil slick and another caused by a petroleum rig off the California coast turned the pristine beachfront near Santa Barbara into a sticky black wildlife graveyard—citizens demanded action. Many had been stirred by the tocsin Alvin Toffler sounded in his best-selling 1970 book *Future Shock*:

> Industrial vomit . . . fills our skies and seas. Pesticides and herbicides filter into our foods. Twisted automobile carcasses, aluminum cans, non-returnable glass bottles and synthetic plastics from immense kitchen middens in our midst as more and more of our detritus resists decay. We do not even begin to know what to do with our radioactive wastes—whether to pump them into the earth, shoot them into outer space, or pour them into the oceans. Our technological powers increase, but the side effects and potential hazards also escalate.

By the early 1970s, 70 percent of Americans said the environment was *the* most pressing domestic and international problem.

It was in this climate of concern that Earth Day was born on April 22,

1970. Earth Day was the brainchild of Democratic Senator Gaylord Nelson of Wisconsin, who with Republican Congressman Paul McCloskey, Jr., of California organized an environmental "teach-in" in Washington, D.C., an idea that soon grew nationally, with more than 24,000 communities participating. Speaking in Denver, Nelson emphasized that ecological problems were being scanted "by the expenditure of $25 billion a year on the war in Vietnam, instead of on our decaying, crowded, congested, polluted urban areas that are inhuman traps for millions of people." Mass rallies were held in New York, Chicago, and Philadelphia, each drawing 25,000 participants. Tree plantings took place nationwide. All in all, Earth Day inspired an estimated 20 million Americans to turn out for a coast-to-coast ecological pep rally for clean air, pure water, and wholesale environmental improvement. The *New York Times* ran an editorial embracing Earth Day, stating that "no man in public office could be against it."

With the support of the Nixon administration, Congress soon drew up a far-reaching program of landmark environmental legislation. Several amendments to the Clean Air Act of 1963 were passed in 1970 to give the federal government the authority to set clean air standards. Earlier that year the Environmental Protection Agency was established; then came the Water Quality Improvement Act. In 1973, the Endangered Species Act was passed. President Nixon, to the surprise of his detractors, signed into law the most sweeping environmental laws ever enacted.

Also on the so-called "liberal" front, Nixon designed and pressed for a Family Assistance Program providing a federally guaranteed minimum annual income of $5,500 to every family with dependent children. The plan, which also mandated job training for the parents while providing day care for their children, drew charges of unfairness on the grounds that the program would give far less to the nation's richer states than to the poor ones. It was a mean-spirited objection that Nixon dismissed, saying, "We are one country. Consider the name of this nation: the United States of America. We establish minimum national standards because we are united. We encourage local supplements because we are a federation of states. And we care for the unfortunate because this is America."

The president's heartfelt plea notwithstanding, his Family Assistance Program was defeated in Congress by a coalition of conservatives who objected to the very idea of a guaranteed income for the poor and by liberals who feared the initiative spelled the end of welfare, which indeed it did. Nixon was in fact proposing an alternative to the bloated and inefficient New Deal-era Aid to Families with Dependent Children (AFDC) program and, had his Family Assistance Program been implemented, most of the nation's welfare bureaucracy might well have been dismantled and Lyndon Johnson's hopes of eliminating poverty realized. As it turned out, wide-ranging welfare reform would have to wait for another generation, although the Nixon administration did succeed in ensuring that food stamps were guaranteed to all qualified Americans.

Contrary to his reputation, Nixon also supported the "Philadelphia plan" providing for the hiring of minority contractors and workers for federally funded projects. Conservative critics complained that this was a quota system such as they had always opposed, while liberals objected to the administration's claim that the program established not quotas but goals. Nixon brushed both quibbles aside. "The Democrats are token-oriented," he explained. "We're job-oriented." Similarly unremembered is that Nixon made his "number-one domestic priority" the creation of a national health-care plan requiring all employers to offer medical insurance—including dental care, mental-health care, and a choice of doctors and hospitals—to all employees, and to pay three-quarters of the premiums; the plan also provided for the same benefits to be extended to the poor through an expanded Medicaid program. In addition, Nixon insisted that the plan be extended to the offspring of the working as well as the unemployed poor, which meant expanding the coverage from 35 to 100 percent of the nation's impoverished children. To pay for this beneficence Nixon called for the federal budget to boost spending on disadvantaged Americans by nearly a third. Although Congress rejected the most progressive of Nixon's proposals for social reform, his administration did manage to increase federal spending on health and education by more than half and to establish the Occupational Safety and Health Administration (OSHA) to insure safety in every U.S.-based workplace.

Nixon's domestic proposals confounded those who refused to look beyond party labels, even though the Republican president had maintained a "liberal" stance on civil rights dating back to his membership in the NAACP in the 1950s and his voluntary chairmanship of an Eisenhower administration committee set up to seek ways to increase minority employment in federal projects. With the same open mind, President Nixon had appointed liberal if pragmatic Democrat Daniel Patrick Moynihan of New York, a noted champion of federal social welfare initiatives and author of a landmark study of U.S. poverty and federal welfare programs, as his chief adviser on urban affairs. Demonstrating why he had been tapped, early in his tenure Moynihan reminded Nixon that one of their mutual heroes—Victorian-era conservative British Prime Minister Benjamin Disraeli—had succeeded in pushing a number of progressive programs through Parliament for the same reason that only an anti-Communist like Nixon could have gone to China: it took the credibility of "Tory men with liberal policies" to make such advances without looking "soft" in the public eye. It didn't hurt, to Nixon's thinking, that there were also political gains to be won through such programs—for example, by driving a wedge between black and white Democrats and co-opting part of the opposition party's agenda for 1972. But like the similarly reform-minded John F. Kennedy, Nixon never managed to get his comprehensive social agenda through Congress.

While some of his domestic initiatives—such as the Endangered Species Act—baffled those unaware of just how complex a politician Nixon was, others fell more in line with the president's supposed leanings. For example, when many Republicans and even some Democrats argued that the U.S. Supreme Court had become too liberal, Nixon responded by trying to fill the four vacancies that arose during his first term with jurists known for their conservatism, if not for their ability. When controversial but intellectually respected Chief Justice Earl Warren retired at age seventy-eight in 1969, Nixon replaced him with substantially less stellar jurist Warren Burger. Worse, one of the president's later nominees for an associate justice slot had such questionable qualifications that Republican Senator Roman Hruska of Nebraska was inspired to mount the timeless defense that "even if he was mediocre, there are a lot of mediocre judges and people and lawyers. They are entitled to a little representation, aren't they, and a little chance? We can't have all Brandeises and Cardozos and Frankfurters and stuff like that there."

The Demise of the Postwar Economy

Since the end of World War II the United States had justifiably regarded itself as the leader of the free world. After all, in 1945 the country generated nearly half of the planet's gross national product. Such economic dominance couldn't last, however, especially not after the Marshall Plan invested such a large chunk of America's wealth into rebuilding both its erstwhile enemies and the European Allies they had damaged. By the late 1960s, businesses began to notice that the success of the recovery in parts of Western Europe had created new competition for U.S. firms, while among the nation's former adversaries first West Germany and then Japan began to challenge U.S. manufacturers in a number of key industries, including steel, automobiles, and electronics. As a result, by the early 1970s its place in the global industrial order had become a matter of national concern for the United States.

Real panic set in when inflation started to overwhelm both the domestic economy and international oil prices, creating a dire situation that nearly sparked a national crisis. The inflationary virus had been introduced with the Johnson administration's decision to finance the Vietnam War through borrowing rather than tax hikes, and the germ's inevitable spread led to the debasement of the U.S. dollar, the first recession in a decade, and in 1971 to the abandonment of fixed currency rates. The already dire situation was compounded by an "oil shock" created by America's longtime dependence on the products of the Organization of Petroleum Exporting Countries (OPEC), which had been turning increasingly political as the ancient tensions between Arabs and Israelis in the Middle East intensified during the early 1970s. Oil prices finally spiraled out of control in October 1973, when Syria and Egypt attacked Israel on a Jewish holy

In October 1973 the oil-producing nations of the Arab world initiated an embargo on exports to the United States, causing long lines for gasoline, as pictured below. Americans had little choice but to curtail their consumption of fuel, and they adhered to gas rationing rules and rushed to buy compact cars. Although the embargo was lifted the next year, shortages and economic disruptions lasted long enough to show Americans, in a rudely short span of time, that oil-producing nations were another bloc to be reckoned with in the balance of world powers.

day, starting the Yom Kippur War. President Nixon quickly proffered aid to Israel, which ultimately repelled its invaders, but not before OPEC's Arab members imposed an embargo on petroleum sales to countries friendly to Israel and quadrupled prices across the board. The embargo would last five months and sent shudders through the economies of Western Europe and Japan, which imported about nine-tenths of their oil from the Mideast. As the regular importer of some 30 percent of OPEC's total output, the United States was hardly immune to the crisis, and for a while Americans across the country had to get used to waiting for hours in long lines to gas up their cars. In the bargain, the OPEC nations established themselves as major players on the world scene courtesy of the massive wealth recently transferred into their pockets.

By the mid-1970s the oil shock had combined with soaring inflation to send America tumbling into its worst economic crisis since the 1930s. The situation prompted the coining of a new term: "stagflation," the enervating offspring of inflation and recession that would continue to plague the United States for the rest of the decade despite economists' certainty that such conditions simply could not last for long. Yet a modest recovery was quickly followed by more hard times, to which Nixon responded at first with conventional remedies such as tax hikes and spending cuts, while the Federal Reserve instituted a tight new monetary policy and boosted short-term interest rates.

Even before that Nixon had swung the opposite way and borrowed a quick-fix economic tool from the liberal Democrats designed to end inflation and level the nation's negative trade balance. In the summer of 1971, he had declared a national ninety-day freeze on wages and prices, followed by federal controls on increases until the economy began to grow again a year later. As dramatic and un-Republican—and ineffective—as his decision to impose wage and price controls had been, Nixon topped it by taking the United States off the gold standard, effectively ending compliance with the Bretton Woods Agreement of 1945. With one bold stroke of the president's pen, the U.S. dollar that for so long had actually been as good as gold was so no longer. Like his lurches from tight monetary policies to free spending in quest of a way to control inflation, Nixon's seemingly bold move away from gold actually had little effect on the economy.

The Election of 1972

As 1972 progressed and the presidential primaries came to occupy more and more of the public's attention, Nixon and Kissinger stepped up the U.S. pressure on North Vietnam to talk peace. Alternating ever deadlier bombing raids with diplomatic concessions such as abandoning the demand that peace be preceded by the withdrawal of North Vietnamese troops from South Vietnam, the Nixon administration hoped but failed to end the war before the presidential election. Nevertheless, with a clear eye on the contest Kissinger announced at a press conference in late October that "peace is at hand," when in fact it wasn't even in sight.

Senator George McGovern was photographed, above, at a Boston construction site in April 1972, while campaigning for the Democratic presidential nomination. McGovern, who adamantly opposed the Vietnam War, was a popular choice at the party's convention and seemed to have some chance of beating Nixon, who was already answering questions regarding the Watergate break-in. McGovern's campaign, however, never gained enough momentum.

In some ways the 1972 election was as bizarre, if not as sad, as the one before it. The Democratic front-runner in the early primaries was Hubert Humphrey's 1968 running mate, inoffensive Senator Edmund Muskie of Maine, who had made a favorable impression on moderates of both parties until his presidential timber became suspect after he burst into tears in public when confronted with the so-called "Canuck letter" criticizing his wife and alleging that at a Florida campaign rally Muskie had laughed at a mention of the derogatory term for French Canadians. After that supposed breakdown Muskie faded quickly, but neither Humphrey nor any of the party's long-shot hopefuls had the campaign organization to take advantage of the front-runner's plummet. The only exception was Senator George McGovern of South Dakota, whose staunch antiwar views appealed to the Democrats' liberal wing enough to unite the Bobby Kennedy and Eugene McCarthy factions behind him and to attract legions of student volunteers who put together an astonishingly broad grassroots McGovern movement. The Democratic primaries were more than a little complicated, however, by the entry of racist, former third-party nuisance George Wallace, which seriously cut into the strength of the other candidates. On May 15, however, Wallace was shot at a campaign rally in Laurel, Maryland, by deranged twenty-one-year-old Arthur H. Bremer, who left the Alabama governor permanently paralyzed from the waist down and ended his bid for the presidency.

Despite centrist Democrats' distrust of McGovern, the liberal's scruffy but enthusiastic troops, who comprised more women and minority delegates than ever before in national convention history, managed to capture the nomination for their man on the first ballot. Immediately afterward, however, the grassroots campaign's political inexperience began to show. Poor scheduling, for example, put McGovern on the podium to accept the Democratic nomination in the wee hours of the morning, after even the most civic-minded American had turned off the TV and gone to bed. Far worse, McGovern selected Senator Thomas Eagleton of Missouri as his running mate before learning that his choice for vice president had a history of mental-health problems for which he had been hospitalized several times and on at least one occasion received shock treatments. At first McGovern said he still supported Eagleton "a thousand percent," but in very short order he was accused of secretly urging his running mate off the ticket, punching a hole in the Democratic candidate's reputation for broad-mindedness that only got bigger when Eagleton quit within the week. After the election Eagleton dismissed the controversy over him as "one rock in a landslide," but a few years later McGovern would write in a campaign memoir, "Perhaps that is true, but landslides begin with a single rock." In 1972 McGovern tried to forestall the avalanche by quickly replacing Eagleton with popular Camelot cousin Sargent Shriver, whose sterling credentials included marrying one of John and

Bobby Kennedy's sisters, fighting in Lyndon Johnson's war on poverty, and serving as the first director of the Peace Corps.

The Republican Party renominated Richard Nixon and Spiro Agnew and had even less reason to doubt their reelection as McGovern proved an uninspiring candidate and steadily lost support. While it was true that his campaign attracted unprecedented numbers of young people, blacks, women, and the poor, it was also true that far more American voters were white, middle-class, and middle-aged or elderly—and they preferred Nixon. Many of these "average" Americans— disgusted by race riots, antiwar demonstrations and the women's rights movement—began slapping bumper stickers proclaiming "U.S.A.—Love It or Leave It" on their automobiles. The president's "great silent majority" came out in force on Election Day 1972, giving Nixon a landslide of 60.8 percent of the popular vote to McGovern's 37.5 percent, a margin nearly equal to that Lyndon Johnson had enjoyed in 1964. The implications were clear: in the space of only eight years, at least on the national level, the electorate had swung sharply from the Democrats to the Republicans, from the most liberal president of the postwar era to one who was perceived, if incorrectly, as the most conservative. The outcome marked no less a watershed in American politics than the opposite shift in 1932 from Republicanism to the Democratic tenets of Franklin Roosevelt.

Encouraged by his smashing electoral victory, Nixon demonstrated his ambitions for his second administration by asking for the resignations of his entire cabinet and accepting most of them, the most noticeable change being the elevation of Henry Kissinger to Secretary of State. No longer shackled by public opinion, after the election Nixon stepped up the bombing of North Vietnam and then interrupted it to ask Hanoi to resume peace negotiations or face more U.S. ordnance, while Kissinger pressed South Vietnamese leader Nguyen Van Thieu to accept various compromises. The talks recommenced, and on January 27, 1973, both sides signed an agreement to end the fighting under which the North Vietnamese would release their American prisoners of war while keeping their forces in the south. The pact was short-lived, but by the time the fighting resumed Nixon's Vietnamization plan had been largely realized.

Watergate

Although few realized it at the time, President Nixon's downfall began late in the night of June 17, 1972, when five black-clad mercenary intelligence operatives on the payroll of the Committee to Re-Elect the President (CREEP)—and directed from a Howard Johnson's across the street by peculiarly gung-ho CREEP official G. Gordon Liddy—broke into the Democratic National Committee (DNC) headquarters in Washington, D.C.'s posh Watergate office complex for reasons that remain in dispute. Whatever the motive, what White House Press Secretary Ronald Ziegler would call "a third-rate burglary" was born of Nixon's growing paranoia and suspicions about those who challenged his policies, whom he increasingly viewed as a threat to "national security" grave enough to call for effective countermeasures even of dubious legality—an attitude that built upon previous chief executives' progressive efforts to expand the power of their office by whatever means it took.

Nixon, however, got caught, mostly because his abuses of the Constitution rose to a whole new level of egregiousness. Shortly after his overwhelming reelection, his hands already full with the nation's economic troubles and the delicate maneuvers required by his complex foreign policy, Nixon found himself mired in a political scandal that would grow into a constitutional crisis the likes of which the nation had never seen. The tangled web of Watergate (as the scandal became known) would take two years to unravel, mostly through the dogged digging of scruffy young *Washington Post* police-beat reporters Bob Woodward and Carl Bernstein, who first uncovered the DNC burglars' connection to CREEP and reported it in their newspaper—giving the lie to the administration's claim a few months earlier, when the Watergate burglars had gone on trial before federal Judge John Sirica, that it was preposterous for anyone even to suggest that the president had known of the break-in, much less been behind it.

Prompted by Woodward and Bernstein's revelations, however, in 1973 Watergate defendant James McCord wrote a letter to Judge Sirica claiming that others had been involved in the break-in and that there had been a cover-up. A Senate Select Committee on Presidential Campaign Activities was investigating the matter under the chairmanship of deceptively folksy Sam Ervin of North Carolina, a Harvard-educated good old boy whose trenchant approach to the details of Watergate would prove Nixon's undoing. In the months that followed, the situation grew ever more serious as new witnesses kept cropping up before the congressional committee to be grilled on the main point: "What did the president know, and when did he know it?" as Republican Senator Howard H. Baker of Tennessee so memorably posed the question. By then Baker was referring not only to the Watergate break-in but to the more serious matter of the White House attempt to cover up its involvement. The investigation now centered on whether the president himself had committed obstruction of justice, authorized others to do so, or encouraged his staff to perform any other illegal acts. As it turned out, Nixon had done all three in a pattern of illegal conduct dating back to 1969 and including not only break-ins and buggings, but also political dirty tricks, hush-money payments, falsification of records, and the unconstitutional use of the CIA, FBI, and IRS for political purposes. Before long, former White House counsel John Dean offered particularly damning testimony about what he called "a cancer on the presidency," which indeed looked to be metastasizing when presidential aide Alexander Butterfield revealed the existence of a secret taping system that Nixon had used to record his conversations in the

Oval Office. The investigation immediately shifted to the question of whether the White House would make those tapes available to the Senate committee.

The summer and fall of 1973 evolved into one of the most complicated and disturbing periods in U.S. history, and ended by cementing a far greater cynicism into the public's view of its government and the politics that formed it. As the Senate continued its excavation of Watergate the U.S. economy continued to worsen, leading Nixon to order another round of price freezes on June 13 that went virtually unnoticed amid the more scandalous problems of his administration. The situation became even more confused when evidence arose that Vice President Agnew had accepted financial kickbacks for political favors while governor of Maryland. Agnew pleaded no contest to lesser charges of income tax evasion and was permitted to resign from office and escape prosecution. Under the terms of the Constitution, it fell to the president to nominate a new vice president, who would then have to be confirmed for the post by both Houses of Congress. Nixon wisely followed the advice of congressional Republicans and selected well-liked and widely respected Congressman Gerald Ford of Michigan, who had distinguished himself among his colleagues with his compliant behavior as a member of the Warren Commission. As projected, Ford sailed through his Senate confirmation hearings and in December became vice president—and, given that the House of Representatives had begun to prepare for impeachment proceedings against Nixon, potentially the nation's unelected president.

In early 1974 all hell broke loose in political America as the White House came under increasing fire and responded by raising its ramparts. Despite the mounting evidence, Nixon continued to deny any knowledge of any aspect of what was now the far broader Watergate affair as well as of presidential involvement in any sort of cover-up; as he had put it to the American people in a press conference on November 11, 1973, "I welcome this kind of examination because people have got to know whether or not their president is a crook. Well, I'm not a crook." It was neither the first nor the last time Richard Nixon would lie to the American people.

Newly appointed Watergate Special Prosecutor Archibald Cox rejected the administration's attempts to compromise on the issue of handing over the Oval Office tapes—which Nixon had refused to do on the grounds that they were protected by "executive privilege" (a concept he would later explain by saying, "Well, when the president does it, that means it is not illegal"). In response, Nixon ordered Attorney General Elliot Richardson to dismiss the special prosecutor, which Richardson refused to do, instead resigning his own post to become the first casualty in what came to be known as the "Saturday Night Massacre." The ethical bloodletting continued when Richardson's deputy, William Ruckelshaus, was fired after he also refused to dismiss Cox,

This poster, printed during the Watergate investigations, depicts the men involved in Nixon's various scandals—many of whom were ultimately convicted and served jail time. Not included among the mug shots was Nixon's vice president, Spiro Agnew, who was forced to resign in 1973 for committing crimes of his own, including income tax evasion. As the poster indicates, the one man still "wanted" as of early 1974 was President Nixon, who was implicated as an unindicted coconspirator up to the time of his resignation and subsequently pardoned.

On April 11, 1974, the House of
Representatives Committee on the Judiciary
served President Richard Nixon with a
subpoena, above left, for the tapes he had
made of his conversations in the Oval Office.
On April 30, when Nixon finally released
heavily edited transcripts of nearly all the
tapes, he believed—erroneously, it turned
out—that they would vindicate him. After the
Supreme Court ruled that Nixon had to turn
over the actual tapes, their contents proved
"deplorable" and "immoral," in the words of
the Republican Senate minority leader, so
damning that few people in either party
could still argue against Nixon's
impeachment. On the morning of August 9,
1974, Richard Nixon left the White House in a
helicopter, above right, after resigning as
president of the United States the previous
evening. He seemed almost preternaturally
cheerful in his final hours at the White
House, and at peace with his fate. The
complexity of the man echoes in his final
admonishment to his staff: "Always
remember—others may hate you, but those
that hate you don't win unless you hate
them, and then you destroy yourself."

who finally got his walking papers from third-string Acting Attorney General
Robert Bork. After Cox had been replaced, the president's attorneys informed
Judge Sirica that the tapes would be turned over.

So they were in April—in edited transcripts that didn't satisfy the Senate
investigating committee, which led to a unanimous Supreme Court ruling that
Nixon had to provide the complete tapes to new Special Prosecutor Leon Ja-
worski. Shortly thereafter, the House Judiciary Committee got in on the act
and on July 27 voted to recommend the president's impeachment, introducing three articles to do so; the question of whether the full House would have
voted for them became moot, however, when it was revealed that one of the
tapes contained the "smoking gun" Nixon's supporters had been denying all
along. Finally, there was evidence that the president had indeed been involved in the Watergate cover-up: his own statements regarding attempts to
head off an FBI investigation into the matter. With this it appeared that
Nixon's impeachment was inevitable and his conviction on criminal charges
possible. To avoid such consequences the president announced his resignation in a rambling televised address on August 8, 1974, having already withdrawn into a haze from which he had entrusted his administration's foreign
policies to Henry Kissinger and the rest of its responsibilities to White House
Chief of Staff Alexander M. Haig, Jr. The next day Gerald Ford was sworn in
as America's first politically appointed chief executive.

A nation filled with self-doubt after its betrayal by the man it had twice
chosen to lead it was desperate for someone to heal the wounds of Watergate, and quickly found him in Gerald Ford. The congenial new leader of the

free world harbored none of Nixon's grandiose global ambitions or personal demons; in fact, as Lyndon Johnson had once remarked of the former University of Michigan gridiron hero, "Gerry Ford is a nice guy, but he played too much football with his helmet off." The new president was the first to admit he was "not a Lincoln but a Ford"—hardly an inspiring ideologue, but a reliable and unthreatening moderate with a respectable history in Congress. Upon taking office Ford struck exactly the right tone by calmly telling his troubled nation that "Our long national nightmare is over" and supporting his charismatic wife Betty's attempts to soothe the public's concerns through her warm and open discussions of America's social problems. As for policies, Ford announced that a major goal of his administration would be to lower taxes and ease regulations on businesses, stating that the United States had "declared our independence 200 years ago, and we are not about to lose it now to paper shufflers and computers."

The obvious contrasts between the dark and devious Nixon and the unpretentious, apparently uncomplicated Ford automatically made the new president popular and won him a longer than usual settling-in period from an American public eager for its new leader to succeed in wiping away the ugly stains left by the discredited and widely despised Nixon. A month after his swearing-in, however, Ford stumbled badly by granting his predecessor a full pardon for any crimes Nixon may have committed while in office, a controversial move Ford defended as an attempt to salve the wounds of Watergate that a Nixon trial would have kept festering. Many Americans smelled a deal between the two men, however, and Ford's popularity quickly declined, ending his brief honeymoon in the White House. Throughout the mid-1970s the German-born Henry Kissinger remained more popular than either Nixon or Ford, the only member of their administrations to make the "ten most admired" persons list compiled annually based on a national poll.

It is hardly a stretch to say that Gerald Ford joined Lincoln, FDR, and Truman in assuming power at one of the most precarious times in U.S. history, but unlike them he had to face the overwhelming responsibilities of the White House without the cushion of a popular vote into national office. What's more, the blow Watergate had landed on top of the bruise left by Vietnam had begun a bloodletting of presidential power that not even Ford's reserves of goodwill in Congress could stanch. The legislature had become aware of its power when over Nixon's veto it had passed the War Powers Act limiting the president's actions in foreign policy; in late 1974, when it was clear that the public regarded Ford as decent and honorable but dubiously equipped for the nation's highest office, Congress took full advantage of the political opening and went on the offensive, slashing the nation's military budget and cutting aid to Vietnam by half.

The Declining Economy

Adding to Ford's already substantial problems was the grave condition of the U.S. economy, which was in its worst shape since the end of World War II. Inflation was rampant while unemployment was rising; on the day Ford took office the former rate was 12.2 percent and the latter 5.3 percent, and both were climbing while the federal budget deficit had reached a peacetime high of $45 billion. The result was more of the "stagflation" that economists had long argued could only be temporary, as in theory high unemployment was supposed to lead to lower rather than higher prices.

In an address to Congress three days after he took office Ford spoke of the need not only to restore Americans' confidence in their government but also to conquer inflation. The new president vetoed more spending bills during his term than any chief executive since Calvin Coolidge. Ford's fiscal conservatism, however, was instinctive rather than intellectual, and his questionable grasp of economics became apparent when he and his advisers concocted the vague "Whip Inflation Now" program, for which the administration planned to stir up enthusiasm by distributing "WIN" buttons to the American people to display on their lapels in a show of solidarity with the proposed federal spending cuts. The public, of course, scoffed, as did the business and academic communities.

Admitting the failure of the WIN program, Ford called for a nationally televised "economic summit" at which the nation's most prominent economists and business and labor leaders could discuss the nation's financial problems and their potential solutions with the president and his advisers. Thus in September 1974, the country's financial and political gurus convened in Washington. To even Ford's surprise the conservative economists argued that the president should not try to balance the budget through spending cuts that would send unemployment even higher and abandoned their traditional claim that a tight monetary policy was the key to economic stability and growth; their liberal counterparts similarly conceded that the old formulas were not working, which left the floor open to the microeconomists who focused on details rather than on the overall state of global finance. One of these economic miniaturists, Alfred Kahn, suggested that federal deregulation might inspire competition that would in turn lead to lower prices; the appeal of his ideas got Kahn hired as Ford's frontline inflation fighter, while Nixon's holdover Treasury Secretary William E. Simon kept an eye on the bigger picture. A devout believer in free enterprise and open markets, Simon refused to help New York City meet the financial obligations its profligacy had engendered on the grounds that such a bailout would only encourage other cities to keep up their own wasteful ways—a policy that prompted the *New York Post*'s classic banner headline, "Ford to City: Drop Dead." Instead, the Big Apple was bailed out by New York State.

For all the federal and lower government efforts to do something about it, the U.S. economy continued to falter throughout the 1970s as the seemingly unstoppable inflation refused to release its hold. In some ways the decade's "Great Inflation" was an analogue to the Great Depression of the 1930s—just as that economic catastrophe had left what one historian called an "invisible scar" on the national psyche of the 1930s generation, the unremitting inflation of the 1970s did the same to its grandchildren. "I walk to school," noted a conservation-minded eight-year-old Miami boy, "I don't watch much TV. And I try not to take a bath."

Foreign Policy After Nixon

For good or ill, among his predecessor's other potent legacies Ford inherited the Nixon Cabinet over which Henry Kissinger still reigned supreme, largely because he had artfully managed to avoid the slightest taint from Watergate. In addition, the new president had little foreign policy experience, which allowed Kissinger's influence to grow and the Nixon administration's policies to go forward, which actually was not a bad thing for the country. Within months after taking office Ford met with Soviet leader Leonid Brezhnev at Vladivostok, where with Kissinger at his side he and the Soviet premier signed an arms control agreement from which would evolve the second Strategic Arms Limitation Talks (SALT II), which aimed to limit nuclear weapons, long-range missiles, and bombers. The agreement, however, was never ratified by the U.S. Congress. Kissinger would notch a greater success the next year (August 1975) when the United States, Canada, the Soviet Union, and the nations of Western Europe signed the Final Act of the Conference on Security and Cooperation in Europe (or Helsinki Accords, as it is commonly called), which offered formal international recognition of the postwar partition of Europe in 1945. In exchange for this new understanding, the Soviet Union agreed to a set of global human rights standards. In fact, human rights would occupy center stage at the follow-up meetings in Belgrade (1977–78), Madrid (1980–83), Stockholm (1984–86), and Vienna (1986–89). The Helsinki Accords would be Ford's greatest presidential accomplishment, for it introduced the idea of human rights into the official mainstream of East-West relations, laying the groundwork for the revolutions of 1989. The Moscow Helsinki Group became the leading dissident organization in the Soviet Union in the late 1970s, while in Czechoslovakia, 242 people including later president Václav Havel signed the Charter 77 manifesto on human rights.

In Vietnam, meanwhile, the fighting between the North and South had continued despite the peace agreements and the withdrawal of the United States' last combat troops in March 1973. When Hanoi launched a major new offensive in March 1975 Ford asked Congress to vote for aid to South Vietnam, but the legislature refused. Congress, Ford complained, "pulled the plug" on Vietnam. Saigon fell to the Communists a month later and was renamed Ho Chi Minh City, while the North Vietnamese victors turned to the process of reuniting all of Vietnam under the harsh rule of Hanoi. At the same time Lon Nol was ousted in Cambodia by Communist Khmer Rouge forces led by the brutal Pol Pot, who immediately launched a savage reign of terror upon Cambodia that left a third of its residents dead, their corpses stacked in gruesome piles left for all to see in testament to the might of the Khmer Rouge (which would be ousted from power by the Vietnamese after they had invaded Cambodia in 1978). In other words, the Vietnam War did not end when the United States abandoned it completely in 1975, even though the most formidable superpower in the world had sacrificed 57,000 people and spent $140 billion over more than a decade to end it. When it was over, all the United States gained from the Vietnam War was a blow to its self-confidence that on the bright side

The imminent surrender of Saigon to the North Vietnamese in April 1975 led to a desperate struggle for seats on departing American aircraft. After the North Vietnamese successfully took the offensive in 1975, Congress declined to commit further aid to the support of South Vietnam. In the panic that followed several thousand South Vietnamese managed to flee with the Americans, a few by clinging to the runners of helicopters. Within hours of the last American flights on April 30, Saigon fell to the Communists. The two Vietnams would be formally reunited in 1976.

may have justified the entire grim exercise in that it convinced the American people never again to engage in such a foolhardy war.

Elsewhere on the international front, in May 1975 the U.S. merchant ship *Mayaguez* and its crew of thirty-nine were seized by the Khmer Rouge. Ford responded by ordering an air strike and sending in the U.S. Marines, a popular move even if it was technically in violation of the War Powers Act. Daniel Patrick Moynihan, now U.S. ambassador to the U.N., used the event to launch a campaign to restore America's international standing, beginning with a harsh attack on the Third World delegates who had been denouncing the United States. During the same period, Secretary of State Kissinger embarked on a Middle East peace process—based on "shuttle diplomacy" conducted from November 1973 to December 1976—whereby Israel would return a large part of the Sinai region to the Arabs, enabling the Jewish state to move closer to peace with its ancient adversaries than ever before. He also negotiated a disengagement of the Golan Heights between Israel and Syria in May 1974, although relations between the two nations remained hostile. Such diplomatic triumphs earned Kissinger the moniker "Super K," but even his sterling Middle East diplomacy could not offset the U.S. defeat in Southeast Asia.

The Election of 1976

As the presidential election of America's bicentennial year got underway, the only thing that seemed clear was that both parties were in utter disarray, the Republicans split along ideological lines and the Democrats fraught with a field of pallid hopefuls, not one of whom gave any indication that he would be able to unite the party.

Still, the Republicans were in even worse shape in the squalid wake left by Nixon and Watergate. Retooling was clearly called for within the GOP, and its direction seemed determined by the ascendance of conservatism in the party since Barry Goldwater's 1964 campaign, which had shifted the Republicans' traditional dominance in the Northeast and the Midwest to the South and West. Ford had done nothing to take account of his party's growing ideological rift; in fact, by 1976 he had come to be mistrusted by the very factions that had once considered him a model conservative, mostly for appointing the more liberal former governor Nelson Rockefeller of New York as vice president. Although Rockefeller was a smart choice in that most Americans considered him capable of assuming the presidency should the need arise, he was anathema to conservative Republicans—and his selection made Ford even more suspect. The new president had continued the détente policies the right wing distrusted, and although he had tried to prevent the fall of South Vietnam, Ford had been accused of inaction in the region by conservatives, who were angered even more by the president's support for a treaty with Panama that would give it control of the canal. Worse still, Ford had proposed an amnesty program for Vietnam draft dodgers that made conservatives' blood boil, clearing the records of some 22,000 draft evaders and deserters in exchange for their performing community-service work.

It's little wonder, therefore, that the right wing of the Republican Party turned elsewhere for a standard-bearer, and found its hero in Ronald Reagan, the former governor of California. A genial, one-time Hollywood B-movie star with an engaging manner and considerable media skills, Reagan enjoyed the solid support of conservative Republicans who had always distrusted and then been dismayed by Nixon and were now reeling under the suspicion that Ford had also gone over to the liberal side. Encouraged by various disaffected party members, Reagan entered the 1976 Republican presidential primaries and did well enough in them to mount a serious challenge

Gerald Ford campaigns energetically on a stop in New Orleans in 1976; his entourage arrived on the Mississippi riverboat in the background. Ford had been sworn in as president less than half an hour after Richard Nixon resigned from office on August 9, 1974. "Our long national nightmare is over," Ford began his first remarks as president later that day. Ford, who had served on the Warren Commission appointed to investigate the Kennedy assassination, brought integrity to the presidency following Nixon's downfall. Nevertheless, he lost his election bid in 1976.

After many years in which dark limousines created the image of presidential power, Jimmy Carter chose to walk to his inauguration on January 20, 1977 (opposite page, top). The "peanut farmer," as a London tabloid called Carter (opposite page, bottom), had worked his way up in Georgia politics, serving one term as governor before declaring himself a candidate for president in December 1974—almost two years before the election. Amid the cynicism fostered by Watergate, Carter waged a campaign that emphasized honesty and emerged from obscurity to win the election.

to the incumbent president, who responded with an apparent willingness to abandon his more moderate positions in order to win the nomination. Ford agreed to drop Rockefeller from the ticket and allowed far-right North Carolina Senator Jesse Helms, a Reagan ally, to play a major role in writing a largely conservative party platform, but these moves to the right were not enough to satisfy those who saw their new champion in Ronald Reagan. For a while there was talk of a Reagan-Ford ticket that would give the former the dominant role in domestic affairs and the latter, with Kissinger still in the cabinet, the lion's share of responsibility for foreign policy, but this unlikely arrangement never developed beyond idle gossip. In the end the Republican establishment awarded the nomination to Ford, who picked sharp-tongued Senator Robert Dole of Kansas as his running mate.

The Democrats, meanwhile, staged a bruising primary battle that in the end put forth former Governor James Earl Carter of Georgia as the party's presidential nominee. The soft-drawling "Jimmy" Carter was a quintessential political outsider who took pride in having little to nothing to do with Washington, an appealing stance just two years after the Nixon administration's collapse under its own sordidness—especially as it came from a sincere born-again Christian whose campaign emphasized high morals and righteous compassion for the disadvantaged. Carter's rationale for seeking the White House came courtesy of neo-Calvinist theologian Reinhold Niebuhr: "The sad duty of politics is to establish justice in a sinful world." What's more, Carter made it clear that he considered himself neither liberal nor conservative, preferring to be regarded as a pragmatic politician open to looking at every situation with a fresh and politically unjaded eye. Nevertheless, as a sop to the liberal wing of his party, which had acquired substantially more power under new rules adopted at the last Democratic convention, Carter chose as his running mate Minnesota Senator Walter Mondale, a protégé of longtime liberal icon Hubert Humphrey.

Early polls indicated a large lead for Carter in the presidential contest, but it shrank as the campaign wore on and the Democrat looked less and less like an "outsider." Even so, disillusionment with Ford continued to mount, exacerbated by the relentless lampooning of the president not only in the political press but from the entertainment media as well, which even if it was unintentional dealt blows to Ford's standing with the electorate by portraying him as a hopeless bumbler, most memorably in the goofy guise of pratfalling comedian Chevy Chase on the new late-hour TV show "Saturday Night Live." As funny as many of these gibes often were, they did raise the troubling question whether the humor at the president's expense in fact indicated that Watergate had sounded the death knell for public respect for the presidency.

In any case, as has ever been true in American politics, in the final analysis the 1976 presidential election most likely came down to voters' concerns about the nation's ongoing economic problems. But whatever the reasons, Carter received 50.7 percent of the popular vote to Ford's 48 percent, and 297 electoral-college votes against the incumbent's 240, numbers that marked one of the closest presidential elections in U.S. history.

The Carter Presidency

Given how the 1970s had unfolded, one can only speculate why either candidate wanted the office at all. Jimmy Carter was elected into such a sorry state of affairs that it's little wonder his presidency is generally regarded as unsuccessful—although there's little doubt anyone else would have fared much better in the turbulent wake of Watergate. America could not have made a more eccentric choice of presidents than the born-again peanut farmer from Plains, Georgia, who had learned how to do things efficiently from his mentor Admiral Hyman Rickover as a young Naval Academy graduate serving in the nuclear-submarine program. Carter had not, however, mastered the nuances of Washington politics even by the time he was elected president, and before, during, and after his "outsider" presidency establishment critics would charge that Carter offered no grand plan or clear direction for the United States. But his critics perhaps were missing the point that the American people no longer wanted leaders with the kind of hubristic visions that for all their grandeur had in the end brought about the downfall of a president and shame to the entire nation. Humorist Art Buchwald spoke

for many when he said of Carter that "I worship the very quicksand he walks on."

The moralizing Carter in fact had some success in his attempts at reorganizing and reforming the federal government, to which he added the Departments of Education and Energy to address America's failings in those areas. He also proposed genuine reforms to the welfare and tax systems, but they went nowhere due to congressional opposition born of the new president's incompetence at playing the Washington game. Signaling both his often unbending political stance and an unwise aloofness toward his own party, Carter foolishly treated key Democratic leaders in Congress with indifference, including powerful backroom veteran Speaker of the House Thomas P. "Tip" O'Neill of Massachusetts, without whose support no executive initiative had a prayer. "When it came to the politics of Washington, D.C.," O'Neill wrote, "[Carter] never really understood how the system worked." Jimmy Carter ushered a parade of eccentric Georgians into the White House to serve as his closest advisers, and further discomfited the political establishment by seeming to trust his good old boys more than members of his party from elsewhere around the country or even those in his own cabinet.

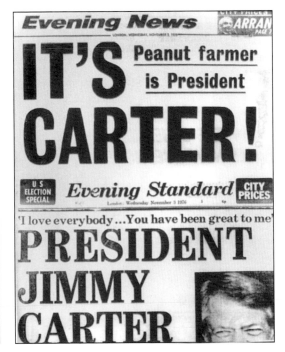

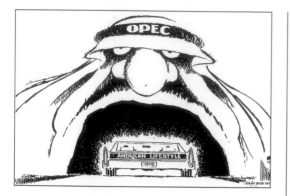

Cartoonist Dan Wright drew the illustration above, showing an oil producer swallowing a big American car—along with the country's carefree, wasteful ways. The world's oil-rich nations cooperated with each other in the late 1970s to raise fuel prices dramatically; in America, the price of gasoline jumped by more than a dollar per gallon in 1978–79.

Carter's problems in office went far beyond his political ineptitude. His proposed solution to the stagflation problem was to cut spending and raise taxes, which didn't work; in fact, as a result of the climbing price of oil inflation actually increased and the consumer price index ballooned to nearly double between 1973 and 1980. The fault did not lie with Carter. In 1979, discord in the Middle East resulted in another oil shock that combined with an OPEC price increase to send inflationary ripples across the world and through the U.S. economy. Again demonstrating a tin ear for politics and public opinion, Carter responded with a speech to the nation in which he averred that a "crisis of confidence" had sapped America's will. Although he never used the soon-to-be-infamous word, Carter's sincere address quickly became known as the "malaise speech" and was derided by some commentators as evidence that the president was blaming the country for his failures to remedy what ailed it.

By 1980 the domestic woes were quite real: inflation in double digits, oil prices triple what they had been under Ford, unemployment above 7 percent, a genuine gasoline shortage, and interest rates topping 20 percent. Having gone four years without projecting a unifying mission or instituting a sweeping program on the order of FDR's New Deal, Truman's Fair Deal, JFK's New Frontier, or LBJ's Great Society, Carter was judged inept and mocked as "Jimmy Hoover"—another well-intentioned engineer president who deserved to be ousted from office for lack of vision. Novelist John Updike captured the mood of the Carter years perfectly in his 1981 novel *Rabbit Is Rich*, set in 1979: "The people are out there getting frantic, they know the great American ride is ending. Gas lines at ninety-nine cents a gallon and ninety percent of the stations to be closed for the weekend. People are going wild, their dollars are going rotten."

No one could argue that Carter's term as president had been smooth, but from the broader perspective time affords, his administration's foreign policy record looks better and better. First among his many notable diplomatic accomplishments was the Camp David Accords he brokered in September 1978 between President Anwar Sadat of Egypt and Israeli Prime Minister Menachem Begin. It is thanks to Carter's tenacity that an unprecedented peace was forged between the two long-adversarial Middle East nations at a retreat in Maryland's Catoctin Mountains. In fact, many Carter supporters felt he should have shared the 1978 Nobel Peace Prize with Begin and Sadat for his dazzling diplomatic efforts at Camp David.

Carter's negotiating skills also brought about the Panama Canal Treaties to defuse a volatile Central American controversy. The first treaty provided for a gradual transition to Panamanian control of the waterway by the year 2000. The second was to provide for "neutrality" in the canal zone, even in wartime, after the Panamanians assumed complete control. By assembling a bipartisan majority to ensure the Panama Canal Treaties' ratification by Congress, Carter scored a major presidential triumph.

In addition, in 1979 Carter normalized diplomatic relations with the People's Republic of China, which President Nixon had jump-started in 1972. Similarly, his support for Nixon's SALT II agreement with the Soviet Union,

although never ratified, demonstrated Carter's very real commitment to détente and arms control. Entirely on his own initiative, Jimmy Carter became
the first American president to visit sub-Saharan Africa, denouncing apartheid
in South Africa and helping to oversee the peaceful transition of white-ruled
Rhodesia into black-controlled Zimbabwe. Carter also restored stable relations with Greece and Turkey on NATO's southwestern flank; pardoned Vietnam War draft resisters; concluded the Tokyo round table trade agreement;
welcomed refugees from Southeast Asia; scrapped the B-1 bomber; and canceled plans to develop a neutron bomb. As historian Gaddis Smith noted, the
Carter administration's "sheer level and range of activity, if not the results,
suggested a foreign policy equivalent of the domestic activity of the first year
of Franklin D. Roosevelt's New Deal."

Carter was the most principled American president since Harry Truman,
and nowhere was his morality on clearer display than in his insistence that
human rights be a cardinal tenet of global governance. "Because we are all
free, we can never be indifferent to the fate of freedom elsewhere. . . . Our
commitment to human rights must be absolute," Carter declared in his inaugural address. They weren't just pretty words; human rights in fact became
the hallmark of his administration, or as he put it, "the soul of our foreign
policy." Although it's true that as president Carter pressed harder for human
rights on the Soviet Union, Argentina, and Chile than he did on such stalwart
American allies as South Korea, the Philippines, and the shah's Iran, his approach to world affairs did focus across the board on international human
rights and the importance of democracy building.

Under Carter, human rights considerations became the litmus test for deciding which governments—left- or right-wing—would receive American financial aid and political support. The State Department was ordered to
document the human rights standards of all foreign governments receiving
American aid and to make its annual assessments public. This meant that
some of the rightist regimes that had grown used to getting substantial economic and military assistance from the United States, including El Salvador,
Ethiopia, Guatemala, Nicaragua, and Uruguay, suffered major cutbacks. The
Carter administration's human rights policy hit hardest in Latin America,
where U.S. military assistance was slashed from $210 million in 1977 to only
$54 million in 1979.

By the end of his term, Carter and his human rights policy had restored
the United States' moral credibility around the world—no small feat after
Vietnam—while putting the Soviet Union on the defensive by calling the
Kremlin "evil" well before Ronald Reagan did. In accord with his Christian
belief in redemption, Carter was prodemocracy, not anti-Communist; he
wanted to wean the Russians away from Communism and toward the Bible.
Among American presidents, only Jimmy Carter peppered his speeches with
the word "love" and earnest Christian entreaties for "tenderness" and "healing." As television commentator Eric Sevareid once quipped, Carter was a
"wheeler-healer" who simply refused to become a "wheeler-dealer." Although this attitude earned him high marks as a humanitarian, it would cost
him dearly as commander in chief during the Iran hostage crisis.

On September 6, 1978, President Carter initiated talks between Egyptian President Anwar Sadat, left, and Israeli Prime Minister Menachem Begin, right, in the seclusion of the Camp David presidential retreat. Egypt and Israel had been enemies for a generation during which bitter fighting had broken out several times. After almost two weeks of negotiations at Camp David, however, the two leaders were ready to sign a "framework" for a peace treaty. It was one of Carter's finest moments as president.

The Iran Hostage Crisis

For more than thirty years the United States had maintained a symbiotic friendship with the shahs of Iran, but by late 1978 Shah Mohammed Reza Pahlevi was growing increasingly unpopular among those in his country who opposed his dictatorial policies as well as with those who resented his attempts to modernize Iran. As a result, in January 1979 the shah was forced to flee his country when power was seized by followers of Ayatollah Ruhollah Khomeini, a strongly anti-Western fundamentalist Muslim leader who deemed the United States the world's "Great Satan." Although Carter at first tried to establish cordial relations with Khomeini's new regime and refused the exiled shah entry into the United States, before long his humanitarian tendencies overtook his geopolitical concerns and led him to the fateful decision that would destroy his presidency.

When the deposed shah arrived in New York that October to be treated for cancer, his admission was taken by Iran and other Muslim states as yet another sign of America's allegiance to the ousted shah and its opposition to the country's new regime. Khomeini encouraged anti-Yankee sentiment to flare into real hatred of the United States, and on November 4, 1979, a mob of angry young Iranians stormed the U.S. embassy in Tehran and seized its personnel, proclaiming that they would be released only after the shah was returned to face his fate in Iran. Fifty-two American hostages would remain in captivity for the remainder of the Carter administration, sparking a sense of national crisis that spawned among other things the late-night TV news show "Nightline."

For nearly a year, the Iran hostage situation handcuffed the Carter administration, which tried everything it could think of to end the standoff: suspending oil imports, freezing Iranian assets, expelling Iranian diplomats, imposing economic sanctions, even conducting clandestine negotiations. Yet the stalemate continued, and Iran looked more and more like an Achilles' heel that would cripple the Democratic ticket if a face-saving remedy was not found—and soon. Carter had made a fatal error by stating at the outset that his primary concern was bringing home the hostages without making concessions—a point Iranians used to blackmail the U.S. administration.

Angry and desperate, Carter finally made the most unfortunate decision of his presidency: on April 24, 1980, he sent a team of army special forces to try to rescue the hostages. Six C-130 transport planes carrying ninety U.S. commandos landed on a remote airstrip in northern Iran's Dasht-e-Kavir region. Eight helicopters were sent to carry out an assault on the embassy, but only six made it to the rendezvous site and one of them had hydraulic problems. The ground commander said the rescue could not succeed with only five helicopters, so Carter agreed to recall the rescue team. As the troops were departing, however, one of the helicopters struck a transport plane that was refueling on the ground, setting off a series of mishaps that would have been comic had the outcome not been so tragic: eight U.S. servicemen died, and four others were badly burned in the fiery explosion that ensued. The surviving commandos did get out of Iran in the remaining planes, but the Iranian militants later put the charred bodies of the eight American soldiers killed on display in the square of the occupied U.S. embassy. Carter went on TV to disclose the attempted rescue and its failure to the public, taking full responsibility for the debacle—which the *The New Republic* dubbed the "Jimmy Carter Desert Classic."

After the secret military attempt to free the hostages failed, Carter was pilloried for having bungled the job and his popularity plummeted to record lows in polls taken as the 1980 election drew nearer. The failed rescue mission continued to bother Carter in the same way Watergate had Nixon and Vietnam had LBJ. "I am still haunted by memories of that day," Carter would state as ex-president. Like Johnson, Nixon, and Ford, Carter appeared destined to leave the White House a failure. Thus he stayed in line with a broader post-Vietnam tendency: the power of Congress grew while that of the White House dwindled. The presidency had become the "fire hydrant of the nation," as Carter's vice president, Walter Mondale, would indelicately phrase during the 1980 campaign.

Below, Iranian students guard one of the hostages seized at the U.S. embassy in Tehran in early November 1979. The effort to resolve the hostage crisis would take more than fifteen months and consumed the remainder of Carter's term in office.

CHAPTER 21

THE REAGAN
REFORMATION

America's two major political parties were in turmoil in 1980, one out of desperation and the other with enthusiasm. As incumbent Jimmy Carter set new lows for presidential popularity he was challenged for the Democratic nomination by Senator Edward Kennedy, an effective and respected legislator with the magic name, looks, and Massachusetts-accented magnetism that couldn't help but conjure up the ghosts of his assassinated older brothers Jack and Bobby. Unfortunately for tough old Joe Kennedy's only remaining son, "Ted" Kennedy was still plagued by memories of his involvement in a July 1969 incident in which a young campaign worker riding with him had died after Kennedy drove off the bridge to Chappaquiddick Island in his home state. Enduring whispers about a drinking problem made voters suspect that Teddy Kennedy might not be made of quite presidential timber. In the end, after a bitter primary struggle the squeaky-clean Carter, who was unpopular for political rather than personal reasons, won the Democratic nomination even though his chances of reelection appeared slim.

Ronald Reagan, left, salutes a cheering crowd during his inaugural parade, January 20, 1981. Promising a return to traditional American values, his conservative administration would ignite a new pride in U.S. freedoms and in "government of, by, and for the people." In 1985, however, Reagan bypassed Congress as well as the people with a secret program to fund support for the Contra rebels in Central America. The inconsistency between his words and his deeds is reflected in the painting above by Robbie Conal.

The Republicans also conducted a lively primary campaign among candidates of wide-ranging GOP visions, all of whom were blown away by the impressive performances in debates and on the stump of the sprightly sixty-nine-year-old former governor of California, Ronald Reagan. The erstwhile Hollywood movie actor and host of TV's "Death Valley Days" certainly knew how to play to an audience with his genial, one-liner persona, his infectiously enthusiastic patriotism, and the sincere, crowd-pleasing belief he had summed up in his gubernatorial inaugural address in January 1967 by saying, "For many years now, you and I have been shushed like children and told there are no simple answers to the complex problems that are beyond our comprehension. Well, the truth is there are simple answers. There are just not easy ones."

Born fairly poor in Illinois in 1911, Reagan had worked his way through Eureka College, near Peoria, where he played football and the lead in school plays and upon graduation put his golden voice to work as a radio sports announcer before his good looks won him a screen test and then a Hollywood contract in 1937. Over the next two decades he appeared in fifty-three movies of varying quality, then gravitated into politics through his presidency of the Screen Actors Guild at the height of its involvement in the McCarthy-era congressional investigations of Communism in the film industry. Reagan would summarize his views on the matter in his 1965 memoir *Where's the Rest of Me?*: "The Communist plan for Hollywood was remarkably simple. It was merely to take over the motion picture business. Not only for its profit, as the hoodlums had tried—but also for a grand worldwide propaganda base." But it was in the 1940 movie *Knute Rockne, All American* that Reagan established the can-do persona that would endear him to the public. In the role of George Gipp, Notre Dame's first All-American football player, Reagan brought tears to millions of eyes with a plaintive yet manly deathbed request: "Someday, when things are tough, maybe you can ask the boys to go in there and win just one for the Gipper."

The ever-personable Reagan attained political prominence in 1964 with a dazzling speech in support of Barry Goldwater's right-wing presidential bid, and remained a favorite among conservatives by maintaining the same uncompromising ideology. "Government is like a baby," as Reagan would explain the next year, "an alimentary canal with a big appetite at one end and no sense of responsibility at the other." In 1976 he made an unsuccessful foray into the Republican presidential primaries, campaigning in favor of balancing the federal budget through spending cuts alone, the idea being to revise the tax structure only once the economy was on a firmer foundation. That approach hadn't worked, however, so in 1980 Reagan came out for tax cuts in addition to slashes in spending, a program that quickly became known as "Reaganomics." It was basic "supply-side" economics based on the "trickle-down" theory that those on the bottom rungs of the financial ladder benefit most when those at the top are free to invest their capital into job-creating enterprises rather than into bureaucracy-absorbed taxes. As an ardent believer in smaller government and free markets, Ronald Reagan hinted that he would roll back many of Lyndon Johnson's Great Society programs and perhaps even some of those dating from FDR's New Deal. But for all his talk that "government is not the solution to our problem; government is the problem," Reagan also supported the repeal of the Supreme Court's ruling in the seminal 1973 *Roe v. Wade* case protecting women's abortion rights. Regarding international matters, Reagan seemed dubious about détente and spoke of the need to confront the U.S.S.R. if and whenever necessary, which meant building stronger armed forces with bigger, better, and just plain more weapons.

In the midst of what was perceived as the wishy-washy Carter years and in the wake of the convoluted prevarications of the Nixon administration, Reagan's plain-spoken refusal to mold his priorities to fit the electorate's whims refreshed American politics—all the more effectively because he was hardly a somber ideologue in the mold of Goldwater on the one side and George McGovern on the other. Instead, Reagan couched his views in deceptively friendly quips such as his explanation of basic economics to *Washington Post* reporter Lou Cannon: "A recession is when your neighbor loses his job. A depression is when you lose yours." The handsome and well-mannered Reagan was so warm and funny that even his political opponents had to admit they liked the guy, just when Americans in general and Republicans in particular were eager for a leader they could feel that way about.

Not the least of Reagan's advantages in conveying that image was his mastery of the use of television, the information and entertainment medium that by 1980 had for a generation been perhaps *the* defining influence on American culture. Ronald Reagan had made his first small-screen appearances during network television's infancy in the early 1950s, when only a few thousand American families owned sets. He had appeared then in mostly serious plays on such popular drama shows as "Medallion Theater" and "Star Time Playhouse." After that he hosted a number of television series, including "The Orchid Award," a musical variety program in 1953 and 1954, and "General Electric Theater," from 1954 to 1962. He enjoyed the highest name recognition of any first-time candidate in California's gubernatorial history mostly thanks to his work as host of the popular TV Western anthology "Death Valley Days" from 1965 to 1966—he left the show after winning the election.

By the mid-1960s the impact of television had ballooned along with the number of U.S. households with sets, which by 1965 exceeded 90 percent. Politicians and their public-affairs consultants were, of course, among the first to recognize the potential of television to affect public opinion. And Ronald Reagan, a professional and practiced old hand at performing on TV, was better equipped than any presidential candidate before or since to make the most of the medium. That he did through artfully produced campaign commercials, in televised debates, and even with his well-spoken "sound bites" on the evening news. It was largely his television appearances that earned Reagan the nickname the "Great Communicator."

Reagan won the nomination and chose as his running mate one of his primary opponents, George Bush of Texas, a former U.N. ambassador and the old-boy-network next in line. John B. Anderson, a moderate Illinois congressman, bolted from the party and ran as an Independent on the grounds that Reagan was too far to the right for centrist Republicans.

Throughout the contest the Carter campaign took a disconcertingly harsh approach to its genial opponent. The president lashed out at Reagan, labeling him an extremist with racist views on civil rights and warning that his statements regarding foreign policy invited armed conflict. Reagan refused to be ruffled and stuck to his script on the issues, scoring the decisive point in a debate a week before the election when he denied Carter's claim that he had once opposed Medicare benefits for Social Security recipients by shaking his head and quipping, "There you go again." That smirk at what looked like Carter's schoolmarmism spelled the end for the Democrat. The ailing U.S. economy, the Iran hostage crisis, and the fact that the American public was sick of dour leaders doomed Carter, who for an incumbent lost not so much by a landslide as under an avalanche. Many voters were so tired of politics that only 53 percent of those eligible even bothered to turn out, most of them from the middle class and above, giving Reagan 44 million popular and 489 electoral votes to Carter's paltry tallies of 35.5 million and 49, with Anderson drawing off 5.7 million popular votes but none in the electoral college. The Sun Belt and Rocky Mountain regions came in so overwhelmingly Republican that newspaper headlines read: WELCOME TO THE REAGAN REVOLUTION. Far worse for Carter, the Southern states, with the exception of Georgia, also went Republican. Millions of anti-Reagan liberals lashed out at Carter for his "vapidity," as novelist E. L. Doctorow later put it, and for allowing "the electorate to bring in the wolves on the right who had all the time been pacing back and forth fitfully, baying in the darkness beyond the campsite."

The voting pattern confirmed that America was turning conservative in a big way. It didn't seem to matter that Reagan made his heartfelt endorsements of "traditional family values" despite being divorced and so alienated from his own children that one of them would write a book about what a rotten father he had been; by the same token, the president's failure to have made regular or even occasional visits to church hardly dimmed his appeal for the resurgent "religious right" led by Virginia's politically minded Baptist Reverend Jerry Falwell and his million-strong Moral Majority organization. The swing from the landslide against Goldwater in 1964 to the even bigger one against McGovern eight years later had tipped many observers to what was happening: America was turning to the right for myriad reasons, including reaction against the anti-Vietnam War protesters; the turn to religious evangelism that ironically

The cartoon below shows the candidates in the 1980 presidential race as they try to break through the nation's preoccupation with President Jimmy Carter and the hostage crisis in Iran. The candidates, from left to right, are Ronald Reagan, Jerry Brown, John Connally, and Edward Kennedy, shown "streaking," a 1970s fad of stripping naked and running through a crowded place, just for the attention. When other Democratic candidates challenged Carter to debates, he refused, pointing to his duty to monitor the hostage crisis from the White House. This "Rose Garden" strategy gave Carter control over the campaign, at least early on.

IF THIS IS THE ONLY SAFE THING WE CAN DO TO GET BACK ON THE FRONT PAGES, THEN I SAY LET'S DO IT!"

had also helped Carter win in 1976; a tax revolt in the states; frustration with the ongoing stagflation; the spreading view that old nostrums no longer applied; a growing conviction that welfare did more harm than good, and a post-Nixon yearning for a simpler kind of patriotism to offset the public cynicism that had been on the rise for so long. In retrospect the pattern is clear that since Johnson had set the high-water mark for New Deal liberalism America's presidents had become progressively more conservative from Nixon to Ford to Carter. But by 1980 the relative failure of every administration in the previous sixteen years had made the public long for a leader in the good-guy mold of Franklin Roosevelt, Dwight Eisenhower, or John F. Kennedy, and it was Ronald Reagan who offered at least an echo of their charisma and convictions. The citizenry accordingly thrilled to their new president's pledge in his first inaugural address to restore "the great confident roar of American progress and growth and optimism."

As if on cue, the day Reagan was inaugurated Iran released its fifty-two American hostages. Although Carter deserved at least part of the credit (in his last act as president he released several billion dollars in Iranian assets frozen by U.S. banks to prompt cash-starved Iran to free the hostages for the money to keep funding its internal war), the details and timing of the hostages' release remain shadowy. At the time, however, the gesture was interpreted not as a sign of any collusion between Reagan's operatives and those of the Ayatollah Khomeini but as proof that the Iranians were afraid of what the cowboyish new U.S. president might do to their country if they didn't release the captives. In any case, the stage was set for Reagan's foreign policy to trade Carter's moralistic approach for a more belligerent and less yielding one.

Whereas Carter had maintained that the United States had not always been a force for good in the world and should work to attain a higher ethical standard than other nations, Reagan instead held to the traditional view that America was already and by definition the standard-bearer of enlightenment around the globe. Reagan's views of international matters may not have been sophisticated, but they were far more forceful and compelling than his predecessor's; where Carter had treated the U.S.S.R. as capable of redemption, Reagan called it an "evil empire."

Reagan's stature only grew on March 30, 1981, when, less than three months after his inauguration, he was shot in the chest while walking to his limousine after addressing a labor convention at the Washington Hilton Hotel. In addition, the would-be assassin's bullets had cut down a policeman, a secret service agent, and White House Press Secretary James Brady. Rea-

A former hostage steps off a U.S. Air Force flight in Frankfurt, West Germany, finally free of Iran and after 444 days in captivity. Deputy Secretary of State Warren Christopher elicited the agreement for the release of the fifty-two American hostages on January 19, the day before the U.S. presidential inauguration. On the following day, the hostages boarded a plane in Teheran and waited on the runway there until a half hour after Ronald Reagan was sworn in as president; only then was the plane allowed to take off. The Iranian government had worked openly for the defeat of Jimmy Carter and soon benefited from Reagan's victory when he authorized secret U.S. arms shipments to Iran.

President Reagan was shot on March 30, 1981, as he walked out of the Hilton Hotel in Washington, D.C. He was hit in the chest, while three men near him were also seriously wounded in a spray of gunfire from a deranged fan of actress Jodie Foster, acting out a scene from the movie *Taxi Driver*. Rushed to the hospital for emergency surgery, Reagan heartened the nation with both his upbeat attitude and his return to the White House after only twelve days. The president was seventy years old at the time of the shooting, and close aides reported later that he suffered more from the attack than he ever let show.

gan was rushed to nearby George Washington University Hospital, where surgeons removed the bullet. While in the operating room Reagan eyed his doctors and joked, "Please tell me you're Republicans." Anxious to reassure his wife Nancy that he was fine, upon seeing her from the gurney carrying him to the ambulance, Reagan quipped, "Honey, I forgot to duck." Such grit endeared Reagan to the American people as never before. In fact, the new president became a folk hero even before his administration accomplished anything of significance. He emerged from the hospital more popular than ever, and few Democrats dared to block his economic proposals.

"Reaganomics"

President Reagan's understanding of finance as of most things was based on a fairly simple interpretation of conventional conservatism: that the wealthy's investments of capital in the economy were the linchpin of prosperity, and as such should be encouraged through tax cuts. Because these cuts would at first further imbalance the federal budget, the effects would have to be stabilized with corresponding cuts in social programs and other forms of government spending.

Upon assuming the presidency Reagan therefore called for massive tax cuts over a three-year period, combined with major decreases in civilian spending, along with equally major increases in the military budget. In 1981 Congress passed much of his tax program, including a 5 percent reduction in federal rates the next year and a 10 percent cut over the following two years, while over his two administrations he boosted defense spending from $132.8 billion in 1980 to $281.9 billion in 1988. "In 1981," Reagan would boast later, "we cut your taxes . . . by nearly 25 percent. And what that helped trigger was falling inflation, falling interest rates, and the strongest economic expansion in thirty years."

By the same token, however, Congress rejected most of the spending cuts that made up the rest of Reagan's economic program. Although along with the presidency the Republicans had won control of the Senate for the first time since 1952 and the Democratic majority in the House of Representatives had as usual taken note of the way the national wind was blowing and turned more conservative, the political split in Congress meant that legislation could be passed only through bipartisan compromise. Nevertheless, Reagan unleashed a blitz of proposals to slash social programs, indicating a rather callous attitude toward America's poor and disadvantaged citizens. Among other actions, he suggested reducing the New Deal's Aid to Families with Dependent Children (AFDC) program no matter how detrimental an impact such a move might have on poor working mothers. He went along with the silly notion of designating ketchup a vegetable for the purposes of the federally funded school lunch program. And he did his best to cut spending on health and housing programs for the poor, although in the offing government expenditures in those areas rose from $104 to $123 billion during Reagan's term in office. The juiciest prospects for cutbacks seemed the entitlement plans such as Social Security and Medicare that accounted for nearly half of the federal budget, but these could not be touched without incurring severe political fallout. When Office of Management and Budget Director David Stockman proposed cutbacks in Social Security payouts, for example, Congress turned such a firm thumb's down that President Reagan himself escorted Stockman to the White House woodshed for a little reeducation. On April 20, 1983, Reagan signed a bipartisan compromise bill rescuing Social Security by raising taxes for it enough to ensure the program's viability into the twenty-first century.

Equally inoffensive to the American people was another revenue-building compromise between the White House and congressional Democrats to boost taxes on alcohol, tobacco, and other vice-related items between 1982 and 1984. Two years after that Democratic Senator Bill Bradley of New Jersey and Congressman Richard Gephardt of Missouri led a movement to simplify the U.S. tax code while eliminating many of its loopholes. After a number of compromises were forged, the new federal income tax brackets were set at 15, 28, and 33 percent, marking the lowest rate levied on the wealthiest Americans since World War II. Less attention was paid to the fact that at the same time virtually all of the nation's tax loopholes were closed, which resulted in most of those in the top bracket paying more taxes than ever before. Critics charged that the new scheme would make the rich richer and the poor poorer, but in reality the share of personal income taxes paid by Americans earning upward of $100,000 a year rose from 29 to nearly 36 percent, while federal taxes on the poor were eliminated. Although federal revenues nearly doubled during the Reagan years, federal spending far exceeded that pace and drove the national debt from $909 billion to $2.6 trillion between 1980 and 1988, by far the highest it had ever been.

Mainstream economists warned that such massive budget deficits would bring back the inflation and high interest rates of the 1970s, but they proved wrong. Instead, the 1980s marked a period of economic stability and growth, evidenced by the statistic that almost 20 million more Americans were employed at the end of the Reagan years than had been when he took office, and not in low-paid, unskilled jobs, either; a full third of the new hires were for professional and managerial posts and another fifth for skilled manufacturing positions. Reagan gibed, "A friend of mine was asked to a costume ball a short time ago. He slapped some egg on his face and went as a liberal economist."

Still, even Reagan's defenders had a hard time finding a response to the charges that America was borrowing from Peter to pay Paul to achieve current prosperity by imposing enormous debts on future generations. By the same token, however, the president's critics found it hard to come up with reasons why a national debt that would climb to 31 percent of the gross national product by the end of the Reagan administration was so unbearable when the United States had done just fine sustaining a debt of around 125

The cartoon above shows President Reagan stepping out of a limousine to chat with a homeless person, telling him, "Oh, me too—why, when we're at the ranch, I just love camping out." The Reagan administration made extensive cuts in funding for programs that supported the indigent and mentally disabled, in the belief that private charities would take care of those in need. The philosophy behind the cuts was explained by early Reagan supporter Henry Salvatori, a California businessman who said, "We don't want to give in to the temptation to help those who are not truly needy and thus destroy the incentive to work."

percent of the GNP in 1945. In any case, everyone could agree that Reagan had remained steadfast in his policies even after the Federal Reserve Board administered some hard-to-swallow medicine to the U.S. economy early in his first term. The Federal Reserve's clampdown on interest rates and the money supply induced the worst recession America had known since the Great Depression of the 1930s. Yet even as the downturn continued until unemployment soared into double digits, Reagan refused to intercede. Although the harsh initial effects of "Reaganomics" seemed bound to make the program unpopular, it would have taken more than that to dim the sheen of the silver-screen hero now leading the free world. Besides, by 1982 inflation had begun to subside, and by the middle of 1983 the U.S. economy had recovered and was once again heading upward, happy trends Reagan ascribed to the Economic Recovery Tax Act he had pushed through Congress in the summer of 1981 to provide an across-the-board 25 percent reduction in federal levies on all American taxpayers.

Reagan's Early Foreign Policy

The new Republican president's views on international matters were as simple and direct as those he held on economic affairs. In sum, Reagan adhered to the fashionable "neoconservative" philosophy of restoring America's resolve to resist radicalism at home and abroad. He apparently really believed that the U.S.S.R. was "the focus of evil in the modern world" as the principal source of godless Communism, and thus justified engaging in an enormous U.S. military buildup that just happened to be a good way to create new jobs in the industrial "rust belt" regions of the country—Midwest industrial manufacturing centers such as Detroit, Flint, Toledo, Akron, and Cleveland—that had been hardest hit by the recent recession.

While spouting a steady stream of bellicose rhetoric toward the U.S.S.R., Reagan's policy toward the Soviets was in fact more pragmatic than Jimmy Carter's. The Democratic former president had stopped sales of grain to the agriculturally bereft Soviet Union to protest its aggressive behavior toward Afghanistan, but Reagan resumed the trade on humanitarian grounds, or at least on the ageless theory that the way to any struggling nation's heart is through its stomach. But to the carrot of aid Reagan applied if not quite a stick then a tight rein. Early in his administration no progress was made in arms control; then the president willingly allowed U.S. relations with Moscow to deteriorate by extending America's sympathy and support to Poland's electrician-turned-activist Lech Walesa and his dissident Solidarity movement after Poland's Soviet-run government imposed martial law throughout the country in response to a wave of Solidarity-led labor strikes. Similarly, Reagan increased American support for the *mujahedeen* rebels in Afghanistan after the Soviet invasion had become mired in what was beginning to look an awful lot like their version of Vietnam.

Toward the end of his first term Reagan began to hear criticism that he was the first U.S. president since the end of World War II not to have met face to face with his Soviet counterpart. But the president simply shook his head and observed that since his inauguration General Secretaries Leonid Brezhnev and Yuri Andropov had passed away in office, while the job's current occupant, Konstantin Chernenko, was reportedly unwell. As he explainded, "I can't help it. They keep dying on me."

America's relations with the Soviet Union took a turn for the worse on September 1, 1983, when a Soviet fighter shot down a Korean Air Lines passenger jet that had inadvertently strayed into the U.S.S.R.'s airspace, killing 269 civilians. Reagan denounced this "act of barbarism" and encouraged the diplomatic situation between the two superpowers to decline; the attack on the airliner certainly seemed to bolster the president's insistence that the United States was justified in boosting its defense spending to ward off the Communists.

Every American president since Franklin Roosevelt has had to wrestle with the unrest caused in the Middle East by the 1948 formation of the nation of Israel, and among them only Jimmy Carter had any success at it. Reagan would not prove another exception; his first secretary of state, former Nixon White House Chief of Staff and NATO Supreme Allied Commander Alexander M. Haig, Jr., attempted to forge an alliance between Israel and the more moderate Arab states to counter Soviet advances in the region, but nothing came of his efforts. In 1982 the Reagan administration refused to criticize an Israeli invasion of Lebanon designed to eliminate the radical Palestine Liberation Organization (PLO) there, but when Israel took matters further and bombed Beirut, a number of Reagan's own top advisers protested, including Haig. After Haig resigned, his successor, former University of Chicago economics professor and Nixon-era Treasury Secretary George Shultz, helped to get the PLO to leave Lebanon.

Soon thereafter a religious war erupted in the already anarchic nation, where the Israelis were siding with the Christians against various Islamic factions. The United States, France, and Italy quickly sent peacekeeping troops to Beirut, but in April 1983 a suicide bomber attacked the U.S. embassy, killing sixty-three officials and bystanders. This prompted an outraged President Reagan to dispatch the battleship *New Jersey* to the coast of Lebanon, from which it lofted heavy bombs onto Muslim positions. In retaliation, six months later, on October 23, 1983, another terrorist on a suicide mission drove a truck full of explosives into the U.S. Marine compound in Beirut and then blew it up, killing himself and 241 Marines. The image of flag-draped coffins returning from Beirut pointed out the grim failure of U.S. peacekeeping efforts in the Mideast. Many Americans questioned why troops had been kept in the area, and Reagan withdrew the rest of the U.S. force the following year. The administration's terrible fumble in Lebanon ended in anger on all sides.

Reagan's policies toward troublesome Libya proved more popular with the American people and their legislators. The president had branded Libyan leader Muammar al-Qaddafi a "mad clown," and for once he wasn't exaggerating. Qaddafi was not only more than a little eccentric, sweeping about in designer mufti outfits surrounded by a cadre of bandoliered young female bodyguards, but more important he was clearly a major sponsor of international terrorism, including against the United States. Relations between the two countries had taken a dive when U.S. and Libyan warplanes had clashed

Above, Secretary of State Alexander Haig (at left) and Israeli Foreign Minister Yitzhak Shamir face reporters after two days of meetings in January 1982. In August of that year the United States sent soldiers into an Arab-Israeli combat zone for the first time, assigning more than 800 marines to an international peacekeeping force in Lebanon. Within weeks the U.S. forces had done their part in restoring peace to the city of Beirut. However, Haig's successor, George Shultz, convinced President Reagan to further America's military role and to take sides in the dispute in Lebanon. After U.S. Navy ships bombarded Muslim villages, partisans viewed the marines stationed in Beirut as combatants, not peacekeepers. In April 1983 the U.S. embassy was bombed, killing 63. At right, President and Mrs. Reagan walk solemnly past a row of caskets containing victims of the attack.

over the Gulf of Sidra off the Libyan coast in August 1981, then simmered until 1986 when a Berlin nightclub frequented by American soldiers was bombed, apparently with the help of Libyan provocateurs. Upon hearing of this latest outrage Reagan ordered an air strike on the Libyan capital of Tripoli targeted on Qaddafi's home. Although the leader emerged unscathed, he claimed to have lost a young daughter in the U.S. assault; in any case, from then on far less was heard from him.

The Reagan administration's deadeye instinct for finding parts that illustrated the whole turned Reagan's foreign policy toward the Caribbean, Central America, and Latin America, which thanks to their proximity to the U.S. mainland had been highlighted by every president since the Russian Revolution as a likely goal of Soviet imperialism. The U.S. government's argument remained, as always, that despotic pro-American regimes had to be better than despotic Communist ones. As a result Reagan continued Carter's policies of propping up the brutal right-wing regime in El Salvador while supporting the Nicaraguan "Contra" rebels' efforts to overthrow their nation's leftist pro-Cuba and pro-Soviet Sandinista dictatorship. To underline his determination to forestall the spread of Communism into America from its closest neighbors, on October 25, 1983—two days after the terrorist attack on the marine barracks in Beirut—Reagan ordered 1,900 U.S. marines and paratroopers to join six much smaller countries in an invasion of the tiny island nation of Grenada to protect and evacuate several hundred Americans enrolled in St. George's University School of Medicine there after the administration determined that Grenada was allowing Cuban workers to build an airfield and had signed military agreements with Communist countries.

The Cuban workers and troops, some 800 altogether, had fought back,

but had no chance of successful resistance and were quickly overwhelmed. A new government was formed under pro-American Governor General Sir Paul Scoon. The Cubans were ordered off the island, the Soviet embassy was closed, and all of their countrymen expelled. Land redistribution policies carried out under the Socialist regime were canceled. Most Grenadans thanked the United States for restoring democracy to their country.

Reagan called the invasion a "rescue mission," an interpretation that got vivid visual support when the evacuated American medical students kissed the ground upon deplaning back in the United States. Latin Americans, fearful as always of the colossus of the north, condemned the invasion as Theodore Roosevelt-like "big stick" tactics. The U.N. General Assembly approved a resolution that "deeply deplored" the American action. Much of the American press was outraged, less by the invasion as by the Pentagon's refusal to let the media into Grenada to cover it. Reagan personally saw the action—in which America had a ten to one superiority over its defenders—as a major triumph. It showed he could be tough and decisive; it enhanced American credibility in the Caribbean; it prevented the Soviets from gaining a strategic airfield; it buried the Lebanon debacle as a news story; it added to the president's popularity; and it served as a warning to Marxist revolutionaries in Central America. As Garry Wills put it in *Reagan's America* (1987), "The war was won because it could not be lost."

By the same token, the Reagan administration was slow to respond to the growing domestic and international pressures to impose economic sanctions against the racist regime in South Africa, whose policies of "apartheid," or separation of whites and blacks, may have been heinous but did not really figure in the Cold War debate. Where there was a choice of anti-Communist leaders, the administration sided with pro-democracy elements, for example, against the repressive dictatorships of Jean-Claude "Baby Doc" Duvalier in Haiti and Ferdinand Marcos in the Philippines, where with American assistance reformer Corazon Aquino was elected the first woman president in the Pacific Rim.

The thinking behind these and other foreign policy decisions came to be known as the Reagan Doctrine. As the president described its main thrust, "We must not break faith with those who are risking their lives on every continent." His objective, therefore, was not just defending against the U.S.S.R.'s expansion but complete liberation of all independent nations from Soviet domination.

Colonel Muammar al-Qaddafi appears at a meeting of Arab nations in February 1991. During Reagan's presidency, Libya was identified as the source of a series of terrorist attacks, including a bombing in April 1986 at a Berlin nightclub frequented by U.S. servicemen. Within the month President Reagan ordered a U.S. Air Force attack on strategic targets in Libya. Qaddafi continued to be associated with terrorism against American installations.

The Election of 1984

As the United States headed toward its 1984 presidential election the nation had plenty of reasons for disgruntlement. The Reagan administration had taken to internal sniping, international time bombs were ticking in Afghanistan and Nicaragua, and détente and arms control with the U.S.S.R. seemed to have become mere memories of the nation's ever more distant diplomatic overtures to its adversaries.

For all the downside, however, an astonishing number of Americans were eager to believe Reagan's warm and gauzy 1984 campaign commercials

This photograph taken in February 1983 shows guerrillas posing before a police station after capturing the city of San Augustin in El Salvador. Reagan continually supported El Salvador's president, José Napoleón Duarte, in his struggle against leftist guerrillas inspired by the Marxist revolution in neighboring Nicaragua. Reagan believed that if Nicaragua succeeded in exporting its style of government to El Salvador the rest of Central America would follow. His pro-Duarte, anti-Sandinista intrigues would eventually jeopardize the balance of powers in the U.S. government.

proclaiming "it's morning again in America" after only four years with a good conservative Republican in the White House. Not only was Reagan's "aw-shucks" personality as popular as ever, but the economy was back in good shape and his tough foreign policies appeared successful as well. Despite some criticism and many late-night TV talk-show jokes that he was lazy and not quite engaged in the details of his job, Reagan's style of management by delegation—which resembled that of Calvin Coolidge, one of his heroes—worked far better for both the administration and the nation than Jimmy Carter's obsessive micromanagement ever had. By the time of his second election it was clear that Reagan had put together a formidable alliance of traditional Republicans, "boll-weevil Democrats" from the Southern Sun Belt region, blue-collar workers, Catholics, and even Democratic moderates drawn to his advocacy of "family values" even if he didn't practice them himself. Whereas twelve years earlier George McGovern had called himself the candidate of the young, the poor, the working class, and the black, in 1984 more young people considered themselves conservative than liberal, good economic times had softened the nation's poverty problem, labor unions were in decline, and the civil rights movement had petered out. Even America's intelligentsia, so long a bastion of liberal Democrats, were now divided as many intellectuals dismayed at what they considered a radical takeover of their party by McGovernites pushing "acid, amnesty, and abortion" restyled themselves as "neoconservatives" who felt more comfortable with Ronald Reagan's happy-faced right-wing philosophy. Yet it still seemed to many that Reagan was insensitive to the poor and homeless and that he failed to understand that two-thirds of American children were spending at least part of their young lives in single-parent households. African-Americans in particular felt victimized by the Reagan administration, which was perceived as allowing Martin Luther King, Jr.'s dream of equality to be eclipsed by stereotypical portrayals in the media. "The true thought police are corporate sponsors and a minority of men who control American public opinion," African-American poet Ishmael Reed would complain of the social climate Reagan engendered. "They are the ones who decide which op-eds are printed or the kind of slant that's to be placed on news involving blacks. Though they pretend that criticism of blacks is prohibited by political correctness, their publications and news and commentaries carry a steady stream of criticism of black behavior." The Reverend Jesse Jackson, a Chicago-based veteran of the civil rights movement, former aide to Martin Luther King, Jr., a rousing orator, and the first serious major-party black presidential candidate in U.S. history, had long complained of the double standard, explaining, "When we're unemployed we're called lazy; when the whites are unemployed it's called a depression, which is the psycholinguistics of racism."

During the Reagan years the racial divide between blacks and whites seemed to widen. In response to this neglect Jackson tried to build a "Rainbow Coalition" of blacks, Hispanics, displaced workers, and other outsiders in Reagan's America. "We must not measure greatness from the mansion down, but from the manager up. My constituency is the desperate, the damned, the disinherited and despised," Jackson exhorted at the Democratic National Convention in July 1984. Years later he would add, on a Sunday-morning political chat show, that "leadership has a harder job to do than just choose sides. It must bring sides together."

But Jackson blew away any chance he had to do so. Sealing the Democrats' doom in 1984, two of the most promising contenders for the party's nomination went down in flames for scandalous carelessness. Jackson ended his chances when he made some anti-Semitic public remarks and then came out in favor of improving U.S. relations with Cuba's Communist leader Fidel Castro. Smart, mediagenic Senator Gary Hart of Colorado did himself in by dallying with a model who was not his wife on the appropriately named yacht *Monkey Business,* adding credence to other evidence of his womanizing. In the end the Democrats nominated Jimmy Carter's rather pallid vice president, former Senator Walter Mondale of Minnesota, who tried to inject a little excitement into his candidacy by naming as his running mate Geraldine Ferraro, a peppery congresswoman from New York, thus offering the first major-party national ticket in U.S. history to include a member of the majority gender. (Of course, in July 1981

Jesse Jackson gives a rousing speech at the 1984 Democratic National Convention in New York City. Jackson waged a vigorous campaign that drew a large number of disenfranchised voters into the process. Jackson's campaign generated momentum at the start, but faltered as the candidate's lack of experience alienated some voters.

Walter Mondale accepts the presidential nomination at the 1984 Democratic Convention, right. Geraldine Ferraro, the vice presidential nominee, is seen applauding at left in the picture. The race between Mondale and Reagan was never close, but Mondale characterized his own attitude in a September 25 speech by saying, "I would rather lose a race about decency than win one about self-interest."

Americans had welcomed Reagan's decision to name Sandra Day O'Connor of Arizona to the United States Supreme Court, making her the first woman ever to wear the august black robes of the nation's highest court.)

If Reagan had an Achilles' heel in 1984, it was his age. During his first debate with Mondale the seventy-three-year-old incumbent appeared listless and confused. Stories circulated that Reagan, who wore contact lenses and hearing aids, would sometimes doze during cabinet meetings. To quell any concerns, during his second television debate with Mondale a more relaxed Reagan deflected the matter artfully. "I will not make age an issue in this campaign," he joked, "I'm not going to exploit for political purposes my opponent's youth and inexperience."

The Democrats were flummoxed. Reagan won in a landslide, taking 59 percent of the popular vote and capturing every state but Mondale's own Minnesota and the always Democratic District of Columbia. Yet it was a victory for the man rather than his party, as was indicated by the Democrats' retaining control of the House of Representatives even though the Republicans held on to their majority in the U.S. Senate. "Reagan is the most popular figure in the history of the United States," admitted Democratic Speaker of the House Thomas "Tip" O'Neill. "No candidate we put up would have been able to beat Reagan this year." Still, Reagan took the opportunity to proclaim in his second inaugural address that "The time has come for a new American emancipation, a great national drive to tear down economic barriers and liberate the spirit of enterprise."

Afternoon in America

Apart from Franklin Roosevelt, few two-term American presidents have enjoyed second terms as successful as their first, and while Reagan's proved better than most his final administration suffered its share of problems. For starters, tensions in the White House led to the unusual move of letting Chief of Staff James A. Baker III and Secretary of the Treasury Donald Regan switch jobs. Unlike the elegant and brilliantly political Baker, a former lawyer from Texas, Regan, a former chairman of the board of the brokerage giant Merrill Lynch, was tough, rough-hewn, and blunt, which hardly afforded him the diplomatic skills needed to run the White House. In very short order he alienated many members of both the cabinet and Congress; worse for him, he also had a falling-out with Nancy Reagan, one of the most powerful first ladies in history by dint of her enormous influence on her husband.

The disarray in the White House soon spread down and throughout the Reagan administration. Deputy Chief of Staff Michael K. Deaver couldn't get along with his new boss Regan and left the White House to open a public relations and lobbying firm, in the process violating several federal statutes against influence peddling; after an attempt at a "whiskey defense" claiming his thinking had been clouded by alcoholism, Deaver was convicted of lying to Congress under oath. Lyn Nofziger, another longtime Reagan crony, also left his position as a White House aide to start a PR firm that was later charged with questionable business practices, although his conviction for violating the Ethics in Government Act was eventually overturned. Even more damaging was what ensued when the president tried to elevate White House Counsel Edwin Meese III to the office of U.S. Attorney General. During his confirmation hearings, Meese faced accusations that he had received special treatment on bank loans in exchange for obtaining federal posts for bank officials and owned stock in companies that did business with the federal government. None of this was proven and in the end Meese was confirmed to head the Department of Justice, but the episode created the perception that the White House was for sale by the president's confidants. After that the administration's troubles turned goofy when it was learned that Nancy Reagan had been routinely consulting an astrologer and using her predictions in planning the president's travel schedule and other appointments.

What was looking like an ever more tangled web of politicking and deceit in the White House got its most disturbing airing in the greatest calamity of Reagan's presidency—the "Iran-Contra" affair, which may well have included worse transgressions against the Constitution than anything the Nixon administration had been guilty of during Watergate. The scandal began to unravel on November 3, 1986, when a Lebanese magazine reported that the United States had secretly sold weapons to Iran. When first issued the allegation was neither confirmed nor believed, but evidence soon materialized that such sales had indeed taken place in the hope they would somehow inspire the release of the handful of American hostages being held at the time by radical Islamic factions in Lebanon. On November 25 the matter widened substantially when Attorney General Meese held a press conference to announce the discovery that some of the money obtained from these alleged sales of arms to Iran might have been diverted to aid the anti-Communist Nicaraguan Contras—after Congress had voted to prohibit any such assistance. At first the Reagan administration denied everything, but over time proof surfaced that funds had indeed been shifted as alleged, indicating the lengths the administration was willing to go to support the guerrillas battling

Reagan is seen above with his chief of staff, James A. Baker III (left), during an appearance in Knoxville, Tennessee, on June 13, 1983. Baker, a polished lawyer from Houston, Texas, first proved his ability during Reagan's 1980 election bid. After serving as campaign manager in 1984 he was named Secretary of the Treasury.

Communism just south of the American border. Reagan, who had always insisted he would never negotiate with terrorists, admitted that the United States had tried to work with Iranian moderates to resolve the hostage situation.

Reports later arose that National Security Advisor Robert McFarlane had been dispatched to Iran open the door to friendlier relations—but the administration denied that there had been any attempt to trade arms for hostages. Reagan later retracted that denial and then conceded that funds had indeed been provided to the Contras, sparking a considerable if short-lived outcry from the American public and the international community. The outrage intensified when subsequent congressional and journalistic investigations revealed that the administration had conducted any number of covert foreign operations evading or breaking U.S. or international laws, including arms deliveries without congressional approval to friendly Central American regimes. These were conducted by the CIA's Southern Air Transport cargo service, which lost its cover when airplane crew member Eugene Hasenfus was shot down during a covert mission in Nicaragua on October 5, 1986, after which he confessed on television what he had been up to.

Nevertheless, Reagan's uncanny talent for detaching himself from blame—for which he had been dubbed "the Teflon president"—again diverted suspicion away from himself and toward those who worked for him. This time, however, the blame fell upon someone with a disarming demeanor and all-American charisma to rival the president's: U.S. Marine Lieutenant Colonel Oliver North, a junior but influential National Security Council aide. Although "Ollie" North charmed the nation in the televised Iran-Contra congressional hearings, the investigation also made it clear that North had not acted on his own but on instructions from the White House. "I assumed that the president was aware of what I was doing and had, through my superiors, approved it," North testified in July 1987. Fortunately for the administration, it appeared that the highest official most deeply involved in the affair had been CIA director and Reagan's first campaign manager William Casey, who had died from brain cancer early in 1987.

Among the revelations as Iran-Contra unraveled was that both Secretary of State George Shultz and Secretary of Defense Caspar Weinberger had known of the arms transactions, although both had strongly opposed all such activities. The central issue, of course, was whether President Reagan himself had approved them or was even aware of what had happened, resurrecting Watergate's notorious question, "What did the president know, and when did he know it?" But two Republican presidents born just two years apart could not have been more disparate in personality and intellect than Richard Nixon and

Nancy and Ronald Reagan enjoy a laugh with Chief of Staff Donald Regan (left) on board Air Force One. In 1986, she initiated a deft campaign to replace Donald Regan, whose official role as chief of staff rivaled her own unofficial one as a power broker in the White House. With President Reagan under fire from the Iran-Contra scandal and ailing from his infirmities, Mrs. Reagan suspected Regan of trying to protect himself even at the expense of his boss. Regan fought long and hard to keep his job, but by February, 1987, he had no choice but to submit his resignation.

Ronald Reagan, and this time the president's denials that he had known of his administration's worst misdeeds at the time they occurred seemed merely implausible rather than impossible. What's more, Reagan continued to maintain that North was "a national hero" and in December 1987 insisted again that "Never at any time did we view this as trading weapons for hostages." Brief talk of impeachment arose, but it couldn't stick to the presidential Teflon.

In 1988, Iran-Contra Special Prosecutor Lawrence Walsh indicted North, former National Security Adviser Admiral John Poindexter, and several lesser administration officials. Less than a week earlier, former National Security Adviser Robert McFarlane pleaded guilty to four counts of withholding information from Congress. The president responded to all the allegations through videotaped testimony in which he appeared confused and unable to remember key events. In the end, all the Iran-Contra defendants were either convicted of or pled guilty to charges of having misused government funds. In 1990 and 1991 federal appeals courts would reverse the convictions of North and Poindexter respectively, on grounds that their own testimony that had been used against them had been privileged and should not have been introduced at their trials.

The Iran-Contra affair cast a pall over Reagan's second term, and its fallout continued after he left office. Although the complicated scandal never attained the notoriety or sense of constitutional crisis of Watergate, it did add to the disrepute into which politics and governance had fallen since the 1950s as well as to the public's overall cynicism and indifference toward civic affairs. The taint left by Iran-Contra would linger even through the great accomplishments of Reagan's last years in office, particularly in foreign affairs.

Three of the leading figures in the Iran-Contra affair were, left to right: Oliver North, listening to a comment from his lawyer during the joint House-Senate Committee hearing in July 1987; CIA Director William Casey, shown in 1984, and National Security Adviser John Poindexter, photographed in 1987. North served as an assistant to Poindexter and his predecessor, Robert McFarlane, and was at the vortex of illegal activities in the executive branch. Combining two directives, he made arrangements to sell arms to Iran secretly in order to raise funds for the Contra forces in Central America. It was Casey, formerly a Wall Street lawyer, who allowed the CIA to be drawn into the scheme. Poindexter, a career naval officer, was an unusually secretive man with a stated disregard for Congressional initiative in foreign policy matters. Encouraged by President Reagan, the three authorized operations antithetical to America's stated policies, as well as to the Constitution.

The Restructuring of America

On Monday, October 19, 1987, Wall Street suffered one of its worst crashes ever as the Dow Jones Industrial Average fell more than 22 percent. The financial system was in such peril that the presidents of the country's major stock exchanges wondered whether they should close early—and whether they would ever reopen if they did. In response the Federal Reserve Board acted quickly to infuse money into the system while investment houses and major financiers bid up contracts based on the future performance of U.S. markets. Such measures stalled the panic the following day, and the system began to recover from the near disaster.

Industrialist Henry Ford could have been predicting the Reagan years in 1945 when he remarked, "We now know that anything which is economically right is also morally right; there can be no conflict between good economics and good morals." Indeed, while the self-absorbed 1970s have been dubbed America's "Me Decade," the 1980s took the trend a step further to earn the moniker the "Greed Decade." A mere twenty years after the antiestablishment, antimaterialistic hippie "Summer of Love," America had returned to the ardent embrace of capitalism and ostentation as epitomized by New York real-estate tycoons and Wall Street wizards such as Donald Trump and Michael Milken. By the late 1980s the almighty dollar again reigned supreme, and the nation's most glorified heroes became the "corporate raiders" who racked up profits for their shareholders, spawning the phenomenon of "yuppies": young, urban professionals who devoted themselves to getting and spending more money. As the 1980s wore on, the frenzy of corporate acquisitions spiraled to new heights and bred an increasingly indebted economy that would suffer quite a shock on the "Black Monday" of October 19, 1987, when the Dow Jones Industrial Average plummeted a record 508 points.

While the Reagan administration had been laboring to curb the government's role in the economy and society, Wall Street investment bankers had been helping gung-ho "takeover artists" carry out the most massive restructuring of the financial and business realm since the turn of the century. As with most such movements, this one had considerable antecedents and had hardly emerged full-blown with the arrival of Ronald Reagan in Washington. In fact, the Ford administration had embraced its own apostle of deregulation, Alfred Kahn, and the Carter administration had continued to act on his teachings.

The twin economic thrusts of deregulation and restructuring that dominated the 1980s grew out of the changes wrought by the great inflation a decade earlier, which had made a severe impact on corporate balance sheets in every industry. The consumer price index, for example, had more than doubled between 1971 and 1983, making inflation to that generation what deflation had been to that of the 1930s: a disturbing economic trend that inspired fears of depression and unemployment. Taking inflation into account, the U.S. stock market as summarized in the Dow Jones Industrial Average had taken a dive between 1969 and 1980 nearly as severe as that between 1929 and 1932, just spread out over a longer period.

No American could stay ignorant of what inflation had done to property values in the post-Nixon era; in some areas houses that had sold for $30,000 in the early 1970s were going for ten times that a decade later. The same ballooning had occurred in America's largest corporations, where, despite depreciation, inflation had driven the value of assets such as plant and equipment to far more than their relatively cheap purchase prices of the early 1970s. In consequence, corporate balance sheets reflected gross exaggerations rather than real values, while simultaneous declines in real securities prices meant that in many cases companies' market values were far below their actual net worth—which naturally inspired purchases of such interests by speculators who sold off their new assets at enormous profits.

Critics of the Reagan administration who decried the president's attempts to dismantle much of both the New Deal and the Great Society regarded the greedy investment bankers and takeover artists as a plague upon U.S. business analogous to what the Reaganites were inflicting upon politics. The powers that were, however, responded with a shrug and a smile that the U.S. economy was performing quite well, large numbers of jobs had been created, and those corporations that had been taken over had merely been transferred into the hands of more competent managers. After all, the argument went, if these entities had been run so well, why had their stocks been selling low enough to allow takeovers. In any event, and as has often been the case after a particularly enthusiastic burst of capitalism, the economy emerged from the Reagan years stronger, leaner, and better prepared than ever for global competition.

Of course, executing such gigantic corporate takeovers required considerable capital, which was generally obtained from investment or commercial banks in the form of short-term loans; once a targeted corporation's shares had been gathered in, the buyer would sell bonds in it through an investment bank and use the revenue to repay the loans. What was left was a company so riddled with debt that no sane investor would buy its "junk bonds" unless they paid high interest. It was a shaky business, but in the 1980s the most prominent player in many of these deals, Michael Milken of the investment banking firm Drexel Burnham Lambert Inc., was deemed the most influential financier America had seen since J. P. Morgan. The only difference was that Milken would wind up in jail.

Many yuppies met the same fate, if only metaphysically. Beginning shortly after Reagan's first inauguration, the yuppie generation began moving into inner cities, bringing with them the coffeehouses and bistros and six-figure condominiums and co-ops where previously there had been family-run delis and affordable rental apartments. Many social activists, including the Reverend Jesse Jackson's Rainbow Coalition, denounced gentrification as being insensitive to the poor, but it could not be denied that the yuppies brought renewal to dying urban areas that politicians and corporations had dismissed as unlivable. The young urban professionals wanted the best consumer products they could afford. "Shopping is a feeling" is the way David Byrne of the band the Talking Heads cynically described the yuppie ethic. Expensive European cars such as the BMW, Porsche, Jaguar, and Mer-

Michael Milken, above, arrives at federal court in New York in 1989, accompanied by his lawyer. Milken had been instrumental in developing the high-yield "junk" bond as a popular investment. Playing the risks, and sometimes underestimating them for others, Milken became a symbol of the rapacious greed on Wall Street in the 1980s. In 1987 he made more than $550 million, but three years later he pleaded guilty to securities fraud and went to jail. Ivan Boesky, below, was a corporate raider, taking companies over only to dismantle them for profit. Here, Boesky leaves federal court after pleading guilty to charges of insider trading.

cedes became status symbols, as did cellular phones, gold credit cards, and posh weekend getaways to exotic resorts. "Through the sheer power of their demand, there are beers and spirits readily available that actually have flavor, and American cities of any size can be expected to have at least a couple of decent restaurants with creative and well-prepared dishes and drinkable wine, not to mention ethnic cuisines ranging from Japanese to Mexican," Mark Rudin, publisher of Library of America wrote in defense of the yuppies.

In the midst of all this gourmet extravaganza, it is not surprising that many Americans began to sense a yawning void in their lives that neither money, career advancement, nor traditional religion could fill. Many of the same baby boomers who had looked for meaning in drugs in the 1960s, stability in the 1970s, and money in the early 1980s now sought spiritual solace in similarly unconventional ways, all of which came to be lumped together under the term "New Age." A broad-based philosophical movement, which started in the 1970s, with many variations but a common set of principles, New Age adherents believed that people consciously or unconsciously choose everything that happens to them.

A wide variety of New Age disciplines appeared: futurist L. Ron Hubbard's Church of Scientology and the Korean tycoon Sun Myung Moon's Unification Church; nominally secular self-improvement programs such as Lifespring and EST; plus the teachings of an odd assortment of gurus who blended psychotherapeutic techniques with Eastern mysticism, the occult, the purported healing powers of pyramids and quartz crystals, theories about reincarnation, pre-Christian paganism, witchcraft, and tarot card readings. Whether expressed in a New Age quest for spiritual growth or in the hilariously arch sarcasm published in the 1980s' trendiest yuppie self-mocking magazine, *Spy*, disenchantment with money grubbing had set in.

Even before the new titans of U.S. finance got their comeuppance there had been a public backlash to the high-rolling excesses of America's new "go-go" years. Tom Wolfe's novel *The Bonfire of the Vanities* pilloried the takeover culture and stayed atop the bestseller list for more than a year; director Oliver Stone's movie *Wall Street,* which also portrayed the corporate raiders of the time as heartless predators unconcerned with the effects of their actions on other people's lives, summed up the zeitgeist in the phrase "Greed is good; greed is healthy," pretty much what real-life stock manipulator Ivan Boesky had said before he too was hauled off to prison for going too far in a quest for wealth in what he claimed was the interest of America's economic growth.

The Beginning of the End of the Cold War

Meanwhile in the halls of the Kremlin where long had dwelt the leaders of America's supposedly greatest enemy—against which the United States never actually had gone to war—a monumental change took place when Mikhail Gorbachev was named general secretary of the Communist Party of the Soviet Union in March 1985. From the first he appeared a far different kind of leader from any of his predecessors. For one thing, he knew something of the world outside the U.S.S.R.; more important, he seemed open to genuine change, including better relations with the West. At home Gorbachev not only recognized but openly admitted his country's economic backwardness, and to reverse it instituted daring new policies of perestroika (economic restructuring) and glasnost (openness). While he stressed that he was still dedicated to the idea of Communism in the abstract, Gorbachev also made it clear that he was willing to undertake substantial reforms in the direction of free enterprise, to the delight of the West. No less staunch a conservative than Britain's Prime Minister Margaret Thatcher reported after an early meeting with the new Soviet premier that Gorbachev was someone "we can do business with."

He would prove even better than that. Immediately upon taking office Gorbachev began a general liberalization of Soviet domestic society while stressing cooperation with the West all over the world, proving his intentions in 1988 by removing the U.S.S.R.'s troops from the hopeless situation in Afghanistan. Stepping out from the long gray line of his drab and geriatric apparatchik predecessors, the fifty-seven-year-old Gorbachev thrust himself upon the world scene with more personality than any Soviet leader since Nikita Khrushchev—and with even bolder and more progressive ideas that indicated the United States might have to rethink its approach to what had for so long been its bitterest enemy.

Faced with this strong new counterpart, Reagan agreed to meet with Gorbachev in Geneva in November 1985, but the momentous encounter was hardly a geopolitical success. Gorbachev had little to say in response to Reagan's criticisms of Soviet violations of existing arms treaties and its record on human rights. With even less cordiality, the U.S. president also made a point of stating America's intention to proceed with its Strategic Defense Initiative (SDI)—dubbed "Star Wars" by the press—a complex, space-based missile defense system designed to tilt the military balance of the Cold War through technology. Despite the points of contention, however, the respective leaders got along well on the personal level, a bond cemented by Gorbachev's admission that he was a fan of Hollywood movies and appeared to enjoy Reagan's yarns about the stars he had known back in his Hollywood days.

In October 1986 the leaders of the two superpower nations held a second meeting in Reykjavik, Iceland, at which Gorbachev proposed that both countries cut their stocks of long-range ballistic missiles in half and limit SDI technology to research without development. Reagan countered with a proposal to eliminate all ballistic missiles, which Gorbachev then topped by suggesting the mutual elimination of all nuclear weapons. Although Reagan refused to enter into such a radical agreement, especially if it meant

In November 1985 President Reagan met with Mikhail Gorbachev, general secretary of the Soviet Union, at a summit in Geneva, Switzerland. "I had to admit," the president would later write, "that there was something likable about Gorbachev. There was warmth in his face and his style, not the coldness bordering on hatred I'd seen in most senior Soviet officials I'd met until then." For his part, Gorbachev found Reagan to be "authentic," and the two men scheduled another meeting even before leaving Geneva.

This artist's conception shows one piece of the apparatus to be developed through the military Strategic Defense Initiative, which was announced in 1983. In the painting, an electromagnetic railgun hovering in space shoots "smart bullets" at nuclear weapons. Known as "Star Wars" after George Lucas's science fiction movie, the SDI program called for exorbitant funding. Although most of it involved ill-conceived technology and never advanced past the drawing board, SDI succeeded in intimidating the Soviet Union, just as Reagan had hoped it would.

giving up his whiz-bang new SDI, the news that such proposals were even being discussed stunned the world; in fact, it appeared that a true breakthrough in the Cold War had finally been achieved. Even when little that could be called concrete came out of the Reykjavik meeting directly, the tenor of U.S.-Soviet relations was changing fast. "We can get along," Reagan said of Gorbachev. "We can cooperate." The following year both sides agreed to remove all of their intermediate-range nuclear missiles from Europe and to allow verification through mutual on-site inspections; as Reagan reminded Gorbachev when the Soviet leader came to Washington to sign the treaty in December 1987: "Trust, but verify." As unimaginable as such a development might have seemed when Reagan had taken office, real progress was being made toward ending the Cold War. Even to Reagan's detractors, it suddenly looked as though the Republican Party might have a point about hanging tough in foreign affairs: if only Nixon could go China, perhaps only Reagan could make peace with the Soviet Union.

Once the Cold War appeared clearly at an end, of course, the pro- and anti-Reagan forces at home took to debating who deserved the credit. The president's supporters argued that Reagan's arms buildup had forced the U.S.S.R. into the harsh realization that their lagging economy could hardly afford to match the United States' military expenditures, which necessitated Soviet acceptance of agreements that both nations cut back their military efforts. To Reagan's supporters, the outcome proved that their man's unwavering anti-Communism had been the right course all along. His opponents instead credited the changes to Gorbachev's fresh approach, making the friendly Soviet premier a global hero to many. Some would even give the nod to Nancy Reagan, who exerted more influence on the president than anyone else and whose astrologer had convinced her to press "Ronnie" not only to meet with but to enter into agreements with Gorbachev—welcome advice considering that it could ensure Reagan's place in history for helping to end the Cold War rather than being buried under the Iran-Contra mess.

Few American presidents have left office popular enough to win another term had they been allowed and inclined to; in the twentieth century only four men left the White House alive and publicly approved: Theodore Roosevelt, Calvin Coolidge, Dwight Eisenhower, and Ronald Reagan. Whether Reagan's presidency was in fact successful is another matter. On the one hand, America's economic accomplishments during the 1980s were undeniably impressive, even if some economists denigrated the administration's "military Keynesianism" and argued that the nation's prosperity had been made possible through government spending on a scale that would have made Franklin Roosevelt blanch. Others, however, countered that the actions of the Reagan-era Federal Reserve had stifled inflation while the government's increased defense spending had created jobs and pumped new wealth into America through newly "globalized" businesses.

It became apparent that Reagan's economic policies left the nation with an enormous federal budget deficit that seemed to bode any number of ills, along with a greatly increased rift between rich and poor Americans. In addition, the president had done little to address the 1980s' particular social ills, such as homelessness, the inadequacy of welfare, and the spread of the AIDS virus, while he had further tainted the credibility of the presidency via the Iran-Contra affair. It was the refurbished na-

Above, Ronald and Nancy Reagan ride horses at Rancho del Cielo, their 688-acre California ranch, in November 1984. Even before leaving office in 1989, Reagan had begun to exhibit mental lapses later diagnosed as symptoms of Alzheimer's disease. At times, control of the government rested with Nancy Reagan.

tionalism that Reagan so energetically promoted that came to define American culture in the 1980s.

Peggy Noonan, the brilliant speechwriter who crafted most of the eloquence for which President Reagan is remembered, offered an elegant explanation of her boss's appeal in an April 1998 essay in *Time* magazine. "It was that he didn't become president to reach some egocentric sense of personal destiny," Noonan wrote. "He didn't need the presidency, and he didn't go for it because of some strange vanity, some weird desire to be loved or a need of power to fill the empty spaces within. He didn't want the presidency in order to be a big man. He wanted the presidency so that he could do big things." He did them, and admist all of his failings, in the eyes of a majority of Americans Ronald Reagan's image—one of folksy charm and unabashed patriotism—as much as anything allowed him to ride off into the sunset as the hero who had saved the range from the poachers. Constantly Reagan would quote Thomas Paine to the effect that it's within us to remake the world—and he believed it in his bones. "In this land of dreams fulfilled where greater dreams may be imagined, nothing is impossible, no victory is beyond our reach, no glory will ever be too great," Reagan proclaimed in a characteristically exuberant 1986 speech. "The world's hopes rest with America's future. . . . Our work will pale before the greatness of America's champions in the twenty-first century."

CHAPTER 22

THE MILLENNIAL NATION

With Ronald Reagan's departure from the White House, politics lost a great deal of its luster in the eyes of the American people, who seemed to become less interested in their nation's governance. Part of this indifference was replaced by enthusiasm for the wondrous possibilities of technology, thanks to whirlwind advances in computers and communications and a host of related marvels including the popular and ubiquitous Internet, which would have a massive impact on the way the world does business. By the end of the millennium, what Henry Luce had dubbed the American Century was giving way to the U.S.-born but internationally reared Information Age.

It would be some of those new electronic gadgets and the impossibility of preventing them from spreading information to every corner of the globe that would quicken the final downfall of world Communism and leave the United States the world's only superpower by the last decade of the twentieth century. What used to be called "underground" political literature now beeped and whirred by fax machine and cellular phone and computer modem to inspire massive student movements in China, the Soviet Union, and throughout Eastern Europe, giving people in every country access to the same uncensored news and information that for so long had fed Western-style democracy.

Governor Bill Clinton, left, reaches out to shake hands with supporters during a stop on his 1992 presidential campaign. The rapport he established with the American people helped to deflect several attacks on his character and carry him to victory over George Bush. The button above from the 1988 campaign links Bush with previous successful Republican presidents.

American democracy, meanwhile, was as vigorous as ever when the first U.S. presidential election campaign without an incumbent in twenty years got underway. The Republicans attempted to portray the 1988 contest as a referendum on the Reagan presidency, and the Democrats obliged during the primaries by sharply attacking the outgoing president's domestic and foreign policies. The opposition party mounted several hopefuls and in the end settled on fifty-four-year-old three-term Governor Michael Dukakis of Massachusetts, considered on the left wing of the Democratic Party, and balanced the ticket geographically, ideologically, and generationally with moderate sixty-seven-year-old Senator Lloyd Bentsen of Texas. On the GOP side, Vice President George Bush was challenged in the Republican primaries by Senate Majority

Above, 1988 Democratic presidential nominee Michael Dukakis, center, clasps hands with his running mate Lloyd Bentsen while Kitty Dukakis, the candidate's wife, looks on at right. The three were photographed at the California State Capitol in Sacramento on October 14, several days after their declining campaign had enjoyed one of its few triumphant moments, during Bentsen's debate with Republican vice presidential nominee Dan Quayle of Indiana. When Quayle compared his leadership experience with that of John F. Kennedy, Bentsen started, "Senator . . . I knew Jack Kennedy, Jack Kennedy was a friend of mine. Senator, you're no Jack Kennedy." Three weeks later, though, the ticket of George Bush and Dan Quayle emerged victorious on election day.

Leader Robert Dole of Kansas in what was a contest more of style and personality than of ideology. The genial Bush won the nomination from Dole, best known as having been Gerald Ford's "hatchet man" in the 1976 presidential contest, but the candidate didn't help his chances by selecting as his running mate conservative Senator J. Danforth Quayle of Indiana, whose giddiness upon being presented as the vice presidential nominee combined with his quickly discovered penchant for gaffes made him seem quite a lightweight.

Bush mounted a slashing attack on the professorial Dukakis, branding him an unregenerate liberal out of step with the conservative turn in the country's mood. The GOP candidate underlined his point by pledging, "Read my lips: no new taxes" and promising to follow much of the rest of the Reagan agenda. At the same time, Bush recognized the need to forge an identity for himself separate from Reagan's, as well as to overcome criticism that he himself was out of touch, having been born into America's upper class, not unlike Franklin D. Roosevelt and John F. Kennedy. Bush responded by making the most of his Texas connections, taking every opportunity to detail how he had left the family estates in Connecticut and Kennebunkport, Maine, to forge his own way in the oil business outside Houston and to build his own political career separate from that of his father, former Senator Prescott Bush of Connecticut. The Republican candidate did have a few major pluses to emphasize, not least among them his heroic exploits as the youngest U.S. Navy fighter pilot in World War II. After that, Bush—who as an adolescent was so imbued with noblesse oblige that his childhood nickname was "Have-Half" for his remarkable eagerness to share his possessions—graduated from Yale and its elite Skull and Bones society before heading to Texas, where he was twice elected to Congress. Upon losing his bid for a Senate seat in 1970, Bush attracted the notice of President Richard Nixon, who put aside his usual disdain for Eastern establishment types and named the young Republican

U.S. ambassador to the U.N. and then America's first liaison officer to Communist China. President Ford later made him director of the Central Intelligence Agency. Although Bush's leadership credentials were impeccable, he suffered from a certain inarticulateness that only underlined his posh beginnings. As salty Democratic Governor Ann Richards of Texas put it, Bush had been "born with a silver foot in his mouth." Meanwhile, Dukakis ran a meandering and sluggish campaign, but nonetheless managed to take an early lead in the polls until Bush put out a series of harshly negative TV ads including one about Willie Horton, a convicted rapist who had been granted a weekend furlough from a Massachusetts prison under a Dukakis program only to commit another rape and a murder. In November, Bush came from behind and won with 426 electoral votes to Dukakis's 111, taking 54 percent of the popular vote. The nation seemed to have stayed as Republican as it had become during the Reagan years, yet the Democrats retained control of both Houses of Congress.

It soon became evident that Bush had grand plans for a strong foreign policy but little interest in showcasing democratic initiatives; having labeled Ronald Reagan's program "voodoo economics" during the 1980 Republican primaries, he was now accused by one commentator of offering "déjà voodoo." Of course, the substantial Democratic majorities in both houses of Congress—combined with Bush's own pledge not to raise taxes and his dedication to reducing the federal budget deficit—meant he could hope for little progress in domestic affairs. Furthermore, because he had not assuaged suspicions on the part of Republican conservatives that he was not wedded to Reagan's programs, Bush could not count on the backing of the right wing in Congress.

For the most part, Bush reacted rather than acted in the domestic arena. Faced with the imminent collapse of the nation's savings-and-loan industry, for example, he prepared a bailout for the distressed financial thrift institutions. In 1990, as part of his deficit-reduction program the president went back on his "read my lips" pledge and accepted a tax increase, confirming what the conservatives had suspected about him all along. The following year he added to the proof, angering the far right again by signing a civil rights law aimed at eliminating discrimination by race and gender. Also in 1990, however, the nation entered what turned out to be a mild recession, for which Bush was blamed by a substantial part of the population.

The End of the Cold War

For all his talk of making America into a "kinder and gentler nation," Bush had both far more experience and far more interest in foreign policy: he had served in a succession of international posts and then traveled abroad extensively during the Reagan years, when as vice president he had once quipped of attending so many state funerals, "You die, I'll fly." But his deep knowledge of geopolitical affairs was no joke, and it would be in this realm that President Bush achieved his most enduring successes.

The greatest of those accomplishments would involve the peaceful disintegration of the Soviet Union in the wake of a cascade of democratic rebellions in Eastern Europe. The Soviet Union had begun to crumble toward the end of

On the afternoon of November 10, 1989, Germans from east and west joined hands on top of the Berlin Wall, below, as their city ended its long period of separation. After twenty-eight years of strict containment, East Germans began to breach the wall in small numbers during early November. Wary soldiers refused to shoot or even try to stop them. The trickle of refugees soon became a flood and by November 11 the Berlin Wall was nothing but a memory of the Cold War.

the Reagan administration, and the pace accelerated after 1988, ushering in what Mikhail Gorbachev himself proclaimed "a new world order" based on the universal desire for life, liberty, and the pursuit of happiness. Freedom became the East's rallying cry as the Soviet monolith unraveled. Poland voted for Lech Welesa's anti-Communist Solidarity movement on June 4, 1989, while on October 7 Hungary denounced communism. On November 9, 1989 the Iron Curtain came tumbling down with the fall of the Berlin Wall, for nearly thirty years the ultimate symbol of the Cold War and Soviet totalitarianism. The unthinkable had become a reality. Summing up the signifigance of the moment, *Time* magazine reported, "It was one of those rare times when the tectonic plates of history shift beneath men's feet and nothing after is quite the same." The tearing down of the Wall was a prelude to the reunification of Germany and a clarion heralding the dawn of a new political age in Eastern and Central Europe. Bulgaria, Romania, and Albania overthrew their respective Communist governments with varying degrees of civil disruption; Gorbachev proved unable to prevent the utterly peaceable secessions from the Soviet Union of the Baltic states of Estonia, Latvia, and Lithuania; Czechoslovakia installed an anti-Communist government and then bloodlessly divided itself into

two countries—the Czech Republic and Slovakia—along ethnic lines, while Yugoslavia split into several, including Croatia, Slovenia, and Bosnia. Ethnic tensions in the former Yugoslav republics unfortunately led almost immediately to armed conflicts between the various new nations' component national and religious factions.

In 1989, even the People's Republic of China was accepting free enterprise within its confines, maintaining its communism more in name only. India also began making strides toward a more open economy, while Southeast Asia demonstrated a greater commitment to free enterprise than was the case in some Western European nations. Of course, democracy did not come smoothly to any of its new adherents; at first, most of the countries that were making the changeover from communism to capitalism had to endure food shortages and other deprivations caused by their long-stagnant economies' unreadiness to compete in the rapacious global marketplace. In April 1989, Chinese students in Beijing's Tiananmen Square began holding mass demonstrations for more freedom and an end to the privileges enjoyed by the elite. In June they were met by tanks and machine guns, leaving hundreds dead. This crackdown forced Bush to suspend military aid to China and temporarily sever diplomatic relations until the Beijing government recognized "the validity of the prodemocracy movement." The killing of the Chinese students sounded an especially dark note of 1989, when global democracy was on the march.

It was Bush's good fortune to take office in what proved to be one of the most momentous years in world history since 1945. So sweeping were the changes around the globe in 1989 that it seemed only appropriate for such critical transformations to occur during the year of the 200th anniversary of the French Revolution. "I felt a tremendous charge as I watched the final break up of the Soviet Union." Bush wrote in his memoir, *A World Transformed* (1998). "I was pleased to watch freedom and self-determination prevail as one republic after the other gained its independence." The United States, however, played almost no role in the worldwide revolution of 1989. Bush was the commander in chief of the leading debtor nation; one of the legacies he received from Reagan was the absence of money in the bank. He could not offer help to emerging democracies desperate for the kind of aid the United States had extended after World War II in the Marshall Plan because the U.S. Treasury had no money to spare. Nor was there much prospect of generating capital to replenish it, because another legacy from Reagan was a pledge from the Republican Party never to raise taxes under any circumstances—a pledge Bush subsequently broke.

Yet the Cold War was finally coming to an end. What caused the demise of Communism in the U.S.S.R., Poland, East Germany, Czechoslovakia, Romania, and Hungary? In part it was the culmination of four decades of patient containment by the NATO alliance and especially NATO's leader, the United States. In part it was the burden of the arms race, which was bankrupting the Soviet Union to the point that the Kremlin could no longer afford to maintain its grip on the satellites. In part it was the people of Eastern Europe themselves and their refusal to ever abandon their high-minded hopes for freedom. Mostly, it was the objective fact that communism was an unworkable system

The photograph above shows a resident of Moscow holding a poster at a rally for Boris Yeltsin, a candidate for president of Russia in 1991. The Soviet Union itself crumbled after it lost control of the Communist states of Eastern Europe in the late 1980s. After a democratic election, Yeltsin took office as the first president of the newly reconstituted nation of Russia. Halfway around the world, General Manuel Noriega of Panama, opposite top, waves his fists in defiance during a rally in October 1989, three months before U.S. forces finally succeeded in arresting him on a long list of drug-dealing charges. The next year, George Bush, opposite below, would find himself in another foreign crisis. Here, he spends Thanksgiving with some U.S. marines deployed in Saudi Arabia on guard against Iraqi aggression. Leading a coalition of nations in a well-defined war the following winter, Bush helped to establish America's global role in the post-Cold War era.

despised by those living under it. Marx and Lenin had predicted that their system would produce a new Socialist man, but it was precisely the young, transfixed by Hollywood and rock and roll, who abhorred it most.

As Gorbachev's international standing grew, his popularity at home plummeted, especially among Communist stalwarts, a group of whom attempted a coup against the Soviet leader in August 1991, setting off a whirlwind of change that would revolutionize the world. When these hard-line plotters kidnapped the general secretary at his vacation home in the Crimea and demanded that he sign his nation's leadership over to them, Gorbachev responded, "Go to hell," which the coup quickly did, in a handbasket. The military old-timers simply hadn't counted on the Soviet people taking to the streets in massive numbers to stand up against the tanks and for democratization. As a result, in June 1991 the freest elections in Russian history were held, and Communist Party defector Boris Yeltsin won the presidency of what had been the largest of the Soviet republics and soon after replaced Mikhail Gorbachev as leader of what remained of the U.S.S.R. With this, republic after republic declared its independence with no opposition from Yeltsin, and within months the Soviet Union was no more. In short order neither was Soviet Communism, as Yeltsin and the new leaders of the other former republics started privatizing their new nations' economies.

Unfortunately, the new Russia would soon learn the hard economic lesson that capitalism is not just about mergers and acquisitions, it is about production as well. For all of Yeltsin's democratic intentions, post-Cold War Russia was dominated by a cabal of Moscow oligarchs who oversaw a reign of high inflation, black marketeering, and questionable export practices that brought the nation to the brink of bankruptcy in a few short years.

Panama and the Persian Gulf War

Of course, the fall of global communism hardly spelled an end to international conflict. For example, Bush took an activist—some critics would say interventionist—approach in Central America, ordering the United States to overthrow the Panamanian government of dictator Manuel Antonio Noriega for his activities in the illicit international drug trade, even if he was a longtime friend and CIA-trained informant of the U.S. government. Despite his considerable earlier usefulness in reporting Communist activities throughout his region, Noriega's continued money laundering, gunrunning, and drug smuggling eventually became too much of an embarrassment for the United States. Matters came to a head when in May 1989 Noriega ran a fraudulent campaign that made a mockery out of democratic elections. Thus Bush had to do something, and on December 20, 1989, he sent 12,000 U.S. troops backed by gunships and fighter bombers into Panama to rendezvous with the 12,000 soldiers already stationed at the American bases around the canal. Dubbed "Operation Just Cause," their mission was to sever Panama's principal lines of communication and capture Noriega. For two weeks American troops circled the papal nunciature where Noriega was hunkered down in a dirty T-shirt, baggy Bermuda shorts, and a baseball cap pulled low over his face while he was force-fed noisy rock songs from giant speakers in an attempt to unnerve him. CNN broadcasted the U.S.

vs. Noriega showdown nonstop as Panama's "Maximum Leader" was transformed into "Hunted Fugitive," a corrupt drug dealer who had thwarted the will of the Panamanian people and was now hiding in a basement. On January 3, 1990, Noriega gave himself up and was held in the United States for more than a year, after which he was tried and convicted of drug-related crimes and imprisoned in Miami. The American people largely approved of the Bush administration's invasion of Panama with 74 percent of those polled calling it "justified." In fact, the Panamanian invasion had liberated Bush from his predecessor's shadow and allowed him to shed his image as a wimp once and for all. Whether intervention in Panama was morally justified could be debated, but it worked for Bush: his overall approval rating skyrocketed to 76 percent. The success also gave Bush's foreign policy team a sense of cohesion and purpose—a post-

Cold War military confidence that would surface again one year later in the Persian Gulf War.

The Bush administration's greatest accomplishment was its conduct of the Persian Gulf War, which originated in megalomaniacal Iraqi dictator Saddam Hussein's ambitions in the region: Hussein had gained free rein when the eight-year war with Iran that had kept him busy to that point came to an inconclusive end. The Iraqi leader quickly began planning to unite all the Arab states under his control and thus achieve sway over the Middle East's vast oil resources; to execute this scheme to become the dominant petroleum power in the region he needed a port on the Persian Gulf, and therefore tried to acquire one by claiming that Kuwait, which bordered both his country and the Persian Gulf, was in fact a province of Iraq. Then, in July, he added to his provocations by asserting that the United States, with the complicity of some of his own fellow gulf powers, had encouraged the overproduction of petroleum to drive prices down. Saddam proved that he was in fact spoiling for a fight on August 2 when 100,000 Iraqi forces attacked Kuwait, which fell in a matter of days, and then turned his focus to an apparent threat against longtime U.S. ally Saudi Arabia.

President Bush responded almost immediately, organizing a multinational coalition to force Iraq from Kuwait and to defend Saudi Arabia against a possible attack. Bush ordered a U.S. naval force to the gulf and asked for a trade embargo against Iraq as a first step in the world's response to Saddam's aggression. On August 6 the U.N. Security Council adopted a comprehensive embargo against Iraq. Then Bush launched a large-scale, U.S.-led multinational arms buildup in Saudi Arabia known as "Operation Desert Shield," in which not only Europe but several Arab countries participated, including Egypt, Morocco, and Syria. Saddam Hussein retaliated by calling for a holy war against both the West and those Arab states supporting the Bush alliance. The Iraqi leader assured Iran's neutrality by returning the lands he had won in the recent war against his neighbor, but except for the relatively small nations of Jordan, Libya, and Yemen, attracted no other overt support from the Arab world. "In the first weeks of the crisis, I happened to be reading a book on World War II by British historian Martin Gilbert," Bush recalled. "I saw a direct analogy between what was occurring in Kuwait and what the Nazis had done, especially Poland."

In November 1990 the U.N. Security Council approved the use of force if necessary to eject Iraq from Kuwait after a January 15, 1991, deadline for its voluntary withdrawal. The prospect of armed conflict this raised set off a debate in Congress and among the American people, as clear memories of Vietnam were evoked; a substantial percentage of the public and their legis-

TO THE HEROES OF
DESERT STORM:

Dear Courageous Soldier:

On August 2nd as everyone Knows,
Our former brothers became our foes.
They invaded our land at night as we slept,
Over our borders by the thousands they crept.
In helicopters and trucks and in tanks they came,
The evil warriors of Saddam Hussein.
But then YOU came and brought hope to us all,
That Kuwait would be free and Saddam would fall.
We'd like to thank you for your courageous stand,
To expel the Iraqis and free our land.
You're in our hearts
this Valentine's Day,
And you're in our prayers
EVERY day.
♥ Sincerely,
The Kuwaiti People

lators opposed military action in favor of an economic boycott and continuing embargo on Iraq. Many of these dissenters from the Bush administration's position believed that the United States was getting ready to fight a war not for humanitarian reasons but for economic ones—oil interests, primarily—and were concerned that the multinational powers sharing those interests had no intention of giving the embargo enough time to work. In fact, the U.S. House of Representatives voted against the president committing U.S. troops to combat in the Persian Gulf without prior congressional approval; Bush responded by asserting his right to act without the legislature's support and asking for another vote on the use of force, which this time went his way by margins of 250 to 183 in the House and 52 to 47 in the Senate.

By January 15 the multinational military strength in Saudi Arabia reached 690,000 troops from twenty-eight nations, who the next day began a massive five-week air bombardment of Iraq that would continue until February 24, 1991, when the allied land armies commanded by U.S. General H. Norman Schwarzkopf launched an offensive of their own. The land war was over within one hundred hours, claiming the lives of only 146 of American troops and forcing Iraq—which had suffered more than 100,000 casualties—to concede defeat on February 28. Although the fighting had been brief, the multinational forces' heavy air bombardments wreaked massive destruction upon Iraq, which itself added to the gulf region's devastation by setting fire to hundreds of Kuwaiti oil wells with appalling consequences for the environment of the entire area.

Bush would later be criticized for not taking the victory a step further and removing Saddam Hussein from power, but would maintain his stance from the beginning of the Persian Gulf War that the multinational alliance had agreed only to limited objectives that did not include the end of the Iraqi regime. To exceed those limits, the U.S. president asserted, would have divided the coalition—which the last superpower's refreshingly cooperative attitude simply would not allow as long as "Have-Half" Bush was in the White House.

The Clinton Years

President Bush's skillful and successful conduct of the Persian Gulf War not only sent his popularity soaring in the polls—to a 91 percent approval rating—but also helped exorcise the ghost of Vietnam from the American consciousness and conscience, making national heroes of commanding generals Schwarzkopf and Colin Powell, the first black to serve as chairman of the U.S. Joint Chiefs of Staff. Oddly enough, it was this very exorcism that would indirectly open the way for Bush's defeat in the 1992 presidential election. The end of global communism took a great deal of their party's purpose away from the Republicans and drew Americans' attention inward—especially in the midst of a recession that had begun in 1990 and that unlike its predecessors was having as great an impact on white-collar workers as on the lower classes. Bush's appeal to educated moderates of both parties took another hit when the confirmation hearings for Clarence Thomas, the questionably qualified nominee to replace revered eighty-three-year-old liberal champion Thurgood Marshall on the Supreme Court, deteriorated into a luridly detailed investi-

The 1992 presidential candidates enjoyed a laugh at the end of their third and final debate. Bill Clinton, left, ran on the Democratic ticket against incumbent Republican George Bush, right. Ross Perot, center, entered the race as a third-party candidate. Despite the respect Bush had garnered during the Gulf War, he failed to give voters a clear picture of his plans for a second term. Perot, a conservative on most issues, ultimately helped Clinton's cause, both by making pointed attacks on Bush and by siphoning support away from the incumbent. On election day voters gave Clinton 43 percent of the popular vote, to Bush's 38 percent.

gation of sexual-harassment charges brought against Thomas by his former aide, University of Oklahoma law professor Anita Hill.

As the 1992 election approached in the wake of Bush's triumph in the Gulf War, the incumbent's reelection seemed so certain that several prominent Democratic hopefuls withdrew from consideration, leaving Governor Bill Clinton of Arkansas a far clearer path to the nomination than he had any right to expect. In fact, with his bland handsomeness, soft Hot Springs accent, and centrist positions, Clinton stormed through the primaries and wound up at the head of the Democratic ticket, then threw geographical, political, and generational balance aside and named fellow baby boomer Senator Albert Gore of Tennessee as his running mate, proudly explaining that "There's a little Bubba in both of us." The contest was complicated by the self-financed third-party candidacy of eccentric billionaire industrialist H. Ross Perot, who ran on a vague platform of balancing the federal budget while opposing government in general.

Clinton was an entirely new kind of national Democrat: a self-described moderate who had founded the utterly middle-of-the-road Democratic Leadership Council with financial aid from party grande dame Pamela Harriman, he also promised to cut the defense budget, provide tax relief for the middle class, and offer a massive economic aid package to the republics of the former Soviet Union. Witty and intelligent, Clinton reminded some Democrats of JFK, although not just in the good sense. During the campaign whispers about Clinton's constant womanizing would be voiced aloud by Gennifer Flowers, who claimed to have had a twelve-year affair with the then-governor of Arkansas. In addition, Clinton earned the nickname "Slick Willie" for his inconsistency on some issues, his pandering to special interest groups, and his carefully constructed responses to reporters' questions about his avoidance of the Vietnam draft and his collegiate marijuana use, which he tried to explain away by saying he "didn't inhale."

Perhaps due to overconfidence, Bush ran a sloppy and surprisingly unprofessional campaign, foolishly relying on his foreign-policy successes when the American people were far more concerned with the economy, the deficit, and the president's apparent lack of a credible domestic program; as colorful Clinton campaign adviser James Carville kept stressing to his own staff, "It's the economy, stupid." Apparently it was: Clinton won the 1992 election with 43 percent of the popular vote to Bush's 38 percent and Perot's 19 percent, and took the electoral college from Bush by 370 to 168 votes with none for Perot. Clinton's victory was clear, but whether he had a mandate was debatable; if anything, the election of such an utter centrist indicated that the nation was evolving beyond partisan politics to an even clearer emphasis on economic concerns.

Nevertheless, President Clinton set out an ambitious agenda for his first administration, the centerpiece of which was a comprehensive overhaul of the nation's health-care system. Early in 1993 he named his influential—some would say too powerful—wife, fellow Yale-educated lawyer Hillary Rodham Clinton, to chair a task force to study the situation and come up with recommendations for improving it. This appointment was a new twist for the American presidency, although the nation's history was full of strong first ladies, from Abigail Adams to Eleanor Roosevelt and more recently even more influential ones such as Rosalynn Carter and Nancy Reagan. None of them, however, had ever exercised real power in as official a fashion as Hillary Rodham Clinton.

After some months of serious investigation and debate, the health-care task force came up with a complicated and confusing set of programs that were immediately opposed by liberals and conservatives alike, upon which the commission released a series of compromise proposals that only muddied the matters further. In the end the Clintons abandoned their attempt to install the most comprehensive national health-care

Hillary Rodham Clinton, below, visits a class of kindergarten students in Philadelphia in 1997. A highly educated lawyer, Mrs. Clinton took an active role early in her husband's presidency through her leadership on the health-care issue. However, there was some controversy regarding the power she assumed over the future of health care, a major industry that accounted for 14 percent of the nation's gross national product. In addition, the health-care task force became mired in its own bureaucracy. One of the hundreds of professionals working with Mrs. Clinton on reform planning said after only two months that, "There's this sense of exhaustion and the real work hasn't begun yet." It never really would, as the prospects for health-care reform faded in Congress in 1994.

WHITEWATER

WHITEWATER INVESTIGATION

$300,000

$30 MILLION

Mike Keefe THE DENVER-POST '97

Question: WHY IS ONLY ONE OF THE ABOVE CALLED A SCANDAL?

Mike Keefe's 1997 cartoon above derided the massive amount of money spent by the special prosecutor during the Clinton administration. The initial investigation related to the financing of a land investment called Whitewater undertaken by the Clintons in 1978, just before Bill Clinton was elected governor of Arkansas. The special prosecutor's investigation eventually strayed away from Whitewater into other aspects of Clinton's governorship and then into allegations of his marital infidelity and perjury while in the White House.

reforms since the Johnson administration, and under a heavy barrage of criticism Mrs. Clinton opted for a lower public profile.

Other initiatives also fell short of success during the early Clinton years. Several of the president's nominees for cabinet posts were either rejected or forced to step down before their confirmation votes. Clinton's efforts to end the ban on gays and lesbians serving in the U.S. armed forces resulted in a compromise policy called "Don't ask, don't tell" that angered those on both sides of the issue. Most damning, congressional investigations were launched into the Clintons' involvement in a complicated Arkansas land-speculation deal, given the umbrella designation "Whitewater," which the Republicans quickly dubbed "Whitewatergate" to add to the whiff of scandal about it. In a nutshell, Whitewater centered on allegations that Bill and Hillary Clinton might have received special treatment and the forgiveness of unsavory loans after the failure of their 1978 investment in a resort project on the White River in northern Arkansas. It didn't help that White House files were found listing Republicans who were being investigated in a systematic way that smacked of Richard Nixon's notorious "enemies list." Still more sordid, at the height of the initial Whitewater investigation key Clinton aide Vincent Foster committed suicide under peculiar circumstances, fueling lurid speculation that he had either been murdered or killed himself over imminent revelations about the administration's activities as well as those of the Clintons back in their days in Little Rock. Bill Clinton, meanwhile, had to dodge new accusations of sexual misconduct while governor, this time voiced by former Arkansas state employee Paula Jones, as well as later accusations that would arise that the White House had sold access to the president for campaign contributions.

All in all, the Clinton administration faced a steady shower of allegations, charges, revelations, explanations, and calls for investigations and special prosecutors. Yet Clinton remained as popular as ever as the economy continued to improve and America's sole superpower status remained secure. The public's lack of outrage at the president's various imbroglios surprised many, but the indifference had several explanations, including that the political depravity of Watergate and the epic sexual peccadilloes of John F. Kennedy had driven down Americans' expectations of presidential character. As Reagan had survived Iran-Contra, Clinton would probably survive the scandals that beset his tenure in the White House, although that remained unclear even halfway through his second term.

Indeed, Clinton would enjoy two major victories during his first administration: congressional approval of his budget, which included a substantial tax increase for the wealthy, and an expansion of the tax-credit system for low-income workers and the poor, among other radical changes from the Reagan-

Bush approach. But Clinton's budget contained a good many spending cuts as well, which to some marked the Democratic president as a pragmatist—if not a conservative—willing to assume centrist positions to stay popular. Still, he also sponsored and pushed the Brady Bill through Congress, establishing a mandatory five-day waiting period for handgun purchases, a measure ardently opposed by conservatives in thrall to the powerful National Rifle Association.

If Clinton deserved credit for any single foreign policy initiative in his first term, it would be for his administration's efforts to dismantle nuclear weapons' stockpiles along with the former Soviet Union, a process begun under President Bush. Clinton's foreign policy team considered the dismantling program as urgent as control of the Soviet tactical arsenal had become scattered among scores of local military commanders rather than centralized in Moscow, as had been the case during the Cold War. The administration's effort culminated in the U.S.-Russia-Ukraine Trilateral Statement and Annex, signed by the presidents of all three countries in Moscow on January 14, 1994, which led to the dismantling of all nuclear weapons in Ukraine. A psychological milestone was reached that same month when Clinton signed a landmark agreement with Boris Yeltsin to detarget U.S. and Russian strategic missiles: for the first time since the early 1950s no Russian missiles would be aimed at targets on U.S. soil. (Of course, the missiles still existed and could be retargeted in a matter of minutes.) Using nuclear disarmament, democracy building, and a joint belief in open markets as their common ground, Clinton and Yeltsin began to forge a fruitful relationship based on cautious trust.

The Clinton-Yeltsin nuclear dismantlement effort was a genuine success. In

On September 13, 1993, Israeli Prime Minister Yitzhak Rabin, above left, shook hands with president of the Palestinian government Yasir Arafat, right, as President Clinton looked on. The gesture stunned those familiar with the bitter past the two men had shared, yet it was symbolic of the peace accord they had signed the same day. The following year Rabin and Arafat were awarded the Nobel Peace Prize in company with Israeli politician Shimon Peres. Rabin's acceptance of Arafat, the former head of the Palestine Liberation Organization, remained controversial in Israel, however, where Rabin was assassinated in 1995.

1990 Russia and the United States each had more than 10,000 strategically deployed warheads. By carrying out the revolutionary START I and II treaties orchestrated by Bush's first secretary of state, James A. Baker, the Clinton administration reduced the total to about 7,000 by the end of 1996 on the way to an eventual goal for each country of just 3,000 warheads—a significant reduction, yet still enough nuclear firepower to incinerate hundreds of millions. By January 1997 Ukraine and Kazakhstan were nuclear-free zones, and Belarus was on its way to nuclear disarmament. And no one could doubt that the Cold War was over once Yeltsin ordered the last Russian troops to evacuate the Baltic States and Germany.

By far the most serious foreign policy problem Clinton inherited, in addition to crises in North Korea, Haiti, and Somalia, was the Balkans. In 1992, the former Yugoslavia had disintegrated into battle zones over which three warring factions lay claim: Serbs (Eastern Orthodox), Croatians (Catholic), and Bosnians (Muslim). During the era of Communist leader Marshal Tito from 1946 to 1980, Yugoslavia had managed to harness its ethnic and religious animosities, but once the hatred was unleashed, the world was shocked by reports of ethnic cleansing, genocidal acts by Serb troops on Bosnia's civilians, and atrocities committed by Serbian forces against Bosnians held in detention camps.

Because the slaughter was covered extensively on television, the domestic political debate over what role Washington should play in ending the war threatened to become a foreign policy crisis for the Clinton administration. While congressional Republicans strongly favored providing arms to the Bosnian Muslims so they could better defend themselves against the Serbs, Clinton steadfastly supported the United Nations' ineffective peacekeeping efforts. While the United Nations made some progress—the sustained artillery shelling of Sarajevo's civilian population was sporadically halted and a war crimes tribunal established—the war continued. A turning point came on February 5, 1994, when sixty-eight civilians died in a mortar attack in Sarajevo. This time the Clinton administration called on NATO to protect the Bosnian Muslim "safe havens," and by April NATO jets were hitting Serb ground targets. Then a Bosnian-Croatian peace agreement was signed under U.S. prodding, ending the "war within a war" and suspending the second front. But a lasting cease-fire proved elusive. Clinton found himself buffeted between the need to maintain NATO and U.N. credibility and an unwillingness to commit U.S. troops.

After months of a temporary cease-fire, Clinton called for a peace summit to be held at Wright-Patterson Air Force Base in Dayton, Ohio, far from war-ravaged Bosnia. With Slobodan Milosevic representing the Bosnian Serbs, Alija Izetbegovic serving as the voice of the Bosnian government, and Franjo Tudjman standing in for the Bosnian Croatians, a tenacious U.S. mediating team brokered a peaceful settlement that solved territorial differences and constitutional questions while forcing everybody involved to lay down their arms. The tenets of the agreement reached at Dayton on November 21, 1995, were officially memorialized in the Paris Peace Accord signed December 14 by the presidents of Bosnia, Serbia, and Croatia. That same month Clinton, despite staunch opposition, committed American troops to Bosnia as part of a NATO-led multinational force deployed to prevent further bloodshed and to support the new peace agreement. Sending in the U.S. troops, Clinton told the nation in a televised address, would signal that America was not shirking its responsibilities as the world's most powerful nation. Clinton went forward with the deployment, and 20,000 U.S. troops joined 40,000 from other NATO and Partnership for Peace countries. The U.S. Congress never officially supported the president's decision to deploy U.S. troops, but did not try to block it. From the start the NATO Implementation Force did an exceptional job of maintaining the cease-fire, stopping the widespread killing of civilians and restoring security to Sarajevo, where people could once again walk the streets in safety. "We stood for peace in Bosnia," Clinton proclaimed in his January 23, 1996, State of the Union address.

Two leading Republicans, Senator Robert Dole, left, and Representative Newt Gingrich present a platform of party goals just before the 1994 midterm elections. It coincided with a strong showing by the Republicans, who gained a majority in the House of Representatives for the first time in forty years. The initiative seemed to wrest leadership of the nation away from President Clinton, while paving the way for Bob Dole's expected presidential run in 1996. By that time, however, Clinton had reasserted his own direction for the country and he easily defeated Dole.

"Remember the skeletal prisoners, the mass graves, the campaign to rape and torture, the endless lines of refugees, the threat of a spreading war. All these threats, all these horrors have now begun to give way to a promise of peace."

Clinton's move to the right in both international and domestic affairs was caused in part by the Republicans' considerable victories in the 1994 midterm elections, which put the GOP back in control of both houses of Congress—a clear indication that for all his popularity, the president had no party coattails at all. For the next year the most compelling figure in U.S. politics was the new Republican Speaker of the House, Newt Gingrich, a forceful and bumptious Georgia conservative intent on transferring power from the federal government to the states by cutting both taxes and spending in what he called the "Contract with America." The Speaker came across as a true Reaganite, and the conservatives who flocked to his cause began to talk of his challenging Clinton in 1996. But then Gingrich misstepped, signing a lucrative book contract that seemed ethically questionably to some, after which his Democratic opponents took aim at his every move. The partisan rancor rose, and when Clinton and the Republican-led Congress were unable to agree on a federal budget the government was forced to shut down, first in November 1995 and again in December lasting until January 1996, to substantial hue and cry if with little effect on the workings of the nation. Still, the public blamed Congress for the impasse, and the ineptitude of Gingrich's responses to it sent his popularity ratings plummeting. By mid-1996 Clinton had recouped his losses and benefited from the Republicans' disarray to increase his standing with the American people.

Among the most significant reasons for Clinton's resurgence was that he had once again shown a remarkable facility for co-opting the most popular parts of the Republican program as his own, including the political hot potato of welfare reform. After the 1994 congressional elections put the GOP back in charge of the legislature, Clinton came out in favor of a program that would transfer much of the welfare system from the federal government to the states. The plan would also put a five-year limit on welfare benefits to any family, require adults receiving welfare to go to work after two years, and deny assistance to noncitizens. With this President Clinton not only helped bring an end to federal welfare programs that had been in place since the New Deal, but also rejected an important symbol of what had been the Democratic Party's long-term commitment to the poor. To mitigate this apparent coldheartedness the president approved a ninety-cent increase in the minimum wage and accepted a measure enabling Americans to continue their employer-sponsored health insurance when they changed jobs. Such gestures to the left were not enough, and overall Clinton's ongoing move to the political right alienated the liberal wing of his party and all but ensured a challenge to Vice President Gore for the Democratic presidential nomination in 2000.

In 1996, however, that economic focus was most of the reason Clinton and Gore had no difficulty winning their party's renomination, apparently protected by a Teflon layer even thicker than Ronald Reagan's. Meanwhile a large field of Republican hopefuls duked it out through the primaries, from which Senate Majority Leader Bob Dole of Kansas emerged with the nomination, in part because he had allowed his natural sense of humor to show through his erstwhile image for meanness. Dole selected as his running mate enthusiastic, conservative former New York congressman, Reagan Cabinet member, and Buffalo Bills quarterback Jack Kemp. Once again, third-party nuisance H. Ross Perot complicated the race and took 7.9 million votes, while Clinton won with 45.6 million popular and 379 electoral-college votes to Dole's tallies of 37.8 million and 159.

Unlike his first term, Clinton's second administration began with international matters on the front burner, where President Bush's old nemesis Saddam Hussein had put them early in 1997 by trying to block U.N. representatives from inspecting Iraq's weapons installations, as had been agreed at the end of the Persian Gulf War. Clinton had no intention of putting up with such intransigence from the world's most troublesome dictator and started assembling a multinational coalition should the need arise to take military action in the region. This proved more difficult than it had been for Bush, as in the absence of an Iraqi attack the Arab states saw little reason to join an alliance against Saddam. Clinton spent much of his second term combating international terrorism and made goodwill trips to South Africa, Russia, and Northern Ireland.

Clinton was happy to immerse himself in foreign affairs, particularly when in early 1998 he was accused of having had sexual relations with a twenty-one-year-old White House intern and then encouraging her to lie about it to a federal grand jury. This delibilitating new scandal drove the Mideast and virtually everything else from the front pages of America's newspapers, but the economy continued to perform well and polls showed that Clinton remained popular even after he was forced to make a televised address to the nation on August 17 admitting that he had indeed had an "inappropriate" relationship with Monica Lewinsky. On September 11, 1998, Independent Counsel Kenneth Starr's scathing report charged Clinton with eleven counts of impeachable offenses that ranged from obstruction of justice to perjury. It looked as if the remainder of Clinton's second term would be an extremely turbulent one.

The Global Economy

While salacious political intrigues dominated the evening news throughout the second half of the 1990s, fewer and fewer Americans cared about national politics. Wall Street was the nation's focus as America experienced its greatest bull market ever. "Where only a quarter of Americans dabbled in stocks before the 1987 plunge," business historian Ron Chernow wrote in a September 1998 *New York Times* op-ed piece, "nearly one half now own stocks, either directly or through mutual funds." According to Chernow, the stock market had become "less a white-collar bastion and more a blue-collar casino." Like Wall Street, society was hurtling ever more rapidly toward the twenty-first century; in fact, the period marked the most significant business restructuring and economic and technological advances in history, particularly in computers, electronics, telecommunications, medicine, genetics, and biotechnology. By the late 1990s it had become evident that in scale and scope these developments ranked alongside if not above the Industrial Revolution of nineteenth century Britain and the swift commercial boom that had accompanied the creation of national markets at the end of that century. In both earlier turn-of-the-century bursts of innovation there had been winners and losers: those who embraced the changes and made themselves useful at the new ways and those who refused or were unable to adapt and lost out by staying wedded to the old ways. Similarly, at the end of the twentieth century there was plenty of opportunity for the computer-literate and technologically educated, while employment prospects dimmed for those without college degrees and facility with the quickly ubiquitous personal computer.

The steel industry provides a perfect case study of what was happening to the U.S. economy and its society heading into the twenty-first century. By the early 1980s, "big steel" had fallen into utter disarray and decline as mills and foundries across the "Rust Belt" closed and dismissed their workers; from a high of more than 450,000 steel employees in 1960 nationwide, by 1990 the figure had sunk to 200,000. Pittsburgh, Pennsylvania, once the center of steel production, now boasted only mile after mile of abandoned facilities, attracting a few curious passersby but few who wanted to redevelop the area or provide jobs for its out-of-work steelmen.

But as the old steel industry deteriorated, a new one emerged in its place. Those companies that survived switched from the old-fashioned methods of making steel to new, foreign-developed continuous casting techniques, which by the mid-1990s accounted for close to 90 percent of all U.S. steel production. Whereas at one time U.S. companies in all industries had scorned borrowing

The gates of a steel mill in Youngstown, Ohio, are locked for good in 1980. As steel production moved overseas, cities such as Buffalo, Pittsburgh, Cleveland, and Youngstown lost companies that had long anchored their economies. They each, in their own way, reinvented themselves. Having experienced a general downsizing of traditional industrial sites during the 1980s, the American economy surged into new directions during the 1990s, especially computers, communication, and information technologies. However, studies of income inequality indicated that during this highly prosperous period the rich were indeed getting richer while the poor were getting even poorer.

ideas and purchasing patents and machinery from other nations, steel and automobile firms began to profit from learning how the Germans, Japanese, and others achieved superior results. In the steel industry that proved to be with "minimills," facilities capable of producing between 100,000 and 500,000 tons of steel per year, as little as a tenth of the output of older, larger steel mills.

Besides radical transformations in industry, much of American community life had become a sterile monoculture of strip malls, subdevelopments, and industrial parks devoted to convenience. Journalist Robert Kaplan in *An Empire Wilderness* (1998) journeyed throughout the American West only to find "standardized corporate fortresses," "privately guarded housing developments," "Disneyfied tourist bubbles," and dozens of self-satisfied cities "influenced by the impersonal, bottom-line values of corporations." In Po Bronson's novel *The First $20 Million Is Always the Hardest* (1997) the main character, an employee at a Silicon Valley microchip company where there is "no view of the marsh" only "the roar of the freeway," complains about his unremarkable Omega Logic office of drab "cord-woven industrial carpet and fluorescent lights, the large open rooms yet unbroken by five foot-high cubicles." The gospel of sameness had taken root across America, lighting up its skies with the logos of national chains of fast-food restaurants, multiplex cinemas, discount stores, and factory outlets. According to author Tom Wolfe, these franchise signs were the "new landmarks of America, the new guideposts, the new way Americans get their bearings."

A Muscovite enjoys a hamburger and a soft drink on January 31, 1990, opening day at the first McDonald's restaurant in Russia. The triumph over communism in Eastern Europe offered prime opportunities for companies from capitalist nations. American cigarettes, soft drinks, and fast-food outlets were among the most prevalent symbols of the Western influx.

As capitalism replaced state-run socialism in much of the world, commercial interests in both mature and developing countries fanned out in search of new markets for their products. American companies strengthened their cultural grip overseas, where McDonald's hamburgers and Levi's jeans soon became omnipresent and where U.S. movies, music, and TV shows grew more popular than homegrown entertainment. Between 1970 and 1994 imports to the United States skyrocketed from $40 billion to $663 billion, while exports soared from $43 billion to $513 billion, creating a clear trade imbalance.

By the mid-1990s no country had a greater share of global trade than the United States, although foreign trade as a percentage of the nation's gross domestic product (GDP) remained quite small, mostly because some 60 percent of the GDP came from the service sector, which unlike agriculture and manufacturing was not greatly affected by foreign competition. In fact, as industrial workers lost their jobs when U.S. businesses moved their operations to countries with lower labor costs, more foreigners began to attend American colleges and universities, check into America's superior hospitals, and visit America's relatively cheap tourist attractions. The result was that these sectors of the economy benefited as much from the increasing globalization of the marketplace as the manufacturing sector suffered from it. From 1993 to 1997 more than 1.6 million new export-related jobs

had been created and the strength of the dollar increased, largely because of the 200 new market agreements the Clinton administration had made.

The most important foreign-trade policy initiative Clinton linked to domestic renewal was the North American Free Trade Agreement (NAFTA). Recognizing that the U.S. economy did not stand on its own but was the hub of an ever-evolving global economy, Clinton had managed to forge a bipartisan congressional coalition to pass NAFTA during his first year in office, despite intense opposition from many Democrats. The trade agreement, which allowed businesses in the United States to form production partnerships with companies in Mexico and Canada, was vehemently opposed by many who perceived NAFTA as undermining the American labor base. Opponents predicted that U.S. companies would send more work overseas, where wages were lower and labor laws less stringent. Not only would the United States lose jobs, but tax dollars as well; in Perot's sound bite, "The sucking sound you hear is all the jobs heading south of the border." Clinton argued the contrary, insisting that NAFTA would not only save jobs but also open new markets for U.S. products by combining 250 million Americans with 90 million Mexicans and 27 million Canadians into a no-tariff trading bloc with a combined GNP of some $7 trillion a year. Despite the frontal assault, the House passed NAFTA by a 234 to 200 vote on November 17, 1993 and the Senate three days later by a vote of 61 to 38.

What Clinton liked best about agreements such as NAFTA was their link to domestic renewal and their emphasis on ensuring that the United States

Above, marchers in San Francisco rally against the North American Free Trade Agreement (NAFTA) in 1993. The rally was sponsored by the AFL-CIO. Most unions opposed NAFTA, a treaty that swept aside tariffs and other protectionist measures among the continent's leading nations—Mexico, the United States, and Canada. The unions feared that the agreement, which took effect on New Year's Day, 1994, would place working-class Americans in direct competition with lower-paid Mexicans.

remained the world's largest exporter. To the Clinton administration, in the post-Cold War era good trade policy was the sine qua non of a sound foreign policy, as a world full of robust, market-based democracies would make the world a safer, richer place. If the Cold War enemy had been communism, the post-Cold War villain was protectionism. Where John Foster Dulles had been accused of "pactomania" for engineering so many security treaties as secretary of state, the Clinton administration seemed to have developed a "pactomania" for free trade. In addition, opposition to NAFTA afforded a new battle cry for Perot in 1996, in which he was joined by conservative commentator Patrick J. Buchanan, who ran a briefly noteworthy populist campaign for the Republican nomination that year.

Clinton's interventionist, anti-isolationist policies countered a far uglier antigovernment movement that was slowly building in pockets of the West. Various antifederalist, antitax, and progun groups began forming their own militias, while other archlibertarians turned to individual terrorism. On April 19, 1995, one such self-proclaimed "patriot," former Army soldier Timothy McVeigh, drove a rental van full of homemade fertilizer bombs to the Alfred P. Murrah Federal Building in Oklahoma City and set them off, demolishing the building, killing 168 people, and wounding 850 more. It was the deadliest terrorist incident in U.S. history, carefully planned for the second anniversary of the day federal agents had raided and burned down the Waco, Texas, compound of the Branch Davidian gun and religious cult, killing eighty members. McVeigh considered himself a defender of individual rights against government intrusion; a federal jury sentenced him to death in 1997.

That the United States had problems to be addressed and flaws to be corrected went without saying, as poverty, homelessness, drug abuse, the deadly and still incurable plague of AIDS, and a host of other troubles remained of grave concern. International terrorism had replaced the Soviet Union as America's greatest national security threat—a fear underlined on August 7, 1998 when the American embassies in Kenya and Tanzania were bombed, leaving more than 250 dead and wounding more than 5,500. Days later, President Clinton retaliated against the Islamic culprits by firing missiles at a suspected terrorist base camp in Afghanistan and a chemical warfare plant in Sudan.

Into the Twenty-first Century

The history of the United States has been marked by several distinct waves of foreign immigration. In the mid-1800s most of the newcomers were German and Irish, followed by Southern and Eastern Europeans from the 1890s until World War I. That trend changed as a result of the Immigration and Nationality Act of 1965, which altered national quotas to eliminate limitations for any one country and brought immigrants flocking to the United States from every part of the world, with the largest numbers coming from Latin America and the Far East. These latest newcomers transformed entire parts of the country. In the Southwest it was as though the boundary with Mexico had vanished, while Chinese, Korean, Filipino, and other ethnic neighborhoods sprouted on both coasts. An astounding 85 percent of the 16.7 million immigrants who entered the United States between the Nixon and Clinton presidencies were from developing countries, nearly half from Latin America. By 1995 total sales of salsa in the United States topped those of ketchup.

The newcomers would have a major impact on the nation's religious makeup as well. In 1900 the vast majority of Americans had been Christians, the largest single denomination being Catholic, although the aggregate of all Protestant sects far outnumbered the Catholics. Although this remained the case in the 1990s, the fastest growth among religious groups took place among the largest evangelical group of Protestants, while the number of Muslims in the United States was growing so fast they were destined to outstrip America's Jewish population early in the twenty-first century. Illegal immigrants from Mexico became a controversial issue in border states such as California, Arizona, New Mexico, and Texas, where they were in high demand for accepting below-market wages in agricultural and construction work.

The new immigration sparked as much opposition as those of earlier eras. Pat Buchanan added to his resistance to NAFTA by calling for an immigration "time-out," without which, he warned, newcomers would not only take American jobs but also wreck traditional American values. Despite the former Nixon speechwriter's attempts to stir up xenophobia, the new immigration continued, and by the end of the twentieth century most Americans seemed to have accepted the idea that a new United States was being fashioned, in part by the lat-

est immigrants, just as had occurred a century before with the last great wave of foreigners.

The United States' embrace of its melting pot—or what Martin Luther King, Jr., called "a single garment of destiny"—has produced a country and a people such as the world has never seen. The nation's lack of ethnic homogeneity can be seen at each Olympic Games, where the U.S. team brings faces of every racial and national origin to the parade of athletes. Whereas other countries' companies must look to natives to staff their overseas branches, U.S. firms can draw upon an extensive pool of Americans with whatever cultural background may help in any given branch office. As a result, no nation on earth has ever assembled a more diverse workforce with a broader range of insights to bring to research, development, manufacturing, marketing, and the rest of what makes for a strong economy and a strong society.

The America that approached the new millennium was a far different nation from the one it had been on the eve of the twentieth century. Then, the United States had just won an exhilarating victory in the Spanish-American War and, if not quite realizing it, had entered upon its imperial age and seen the end of its longstanding isolationism, which would not completely disappear until World War II. But at the beginning of the twentieth century America was merely an emerging power in a multipolar world dominated by Europe; a hundred years later the United States had become the planet's only remaining superpower, with the world's economic focus tilted toward the Pacific Rim. Better yet, democracy was sweeping the globe. In 1974 only thirty-nine countries—one in four of the world's independent nations—were democratic. By the end of 1996, one hundred seventeen countries—nearly half of those with independence—held democratic elections to choose their leaders.

Other changes would prove even more momentous, if not yet played out. In 1900, for example, of the 76 million Americans only 4 percent were over the age of sixty-five; by 2000 there would be some 270 million Americans, with more than 12 percent of them upward of sixty-five years old. By the 1990s, the nation's Social Security system—a New Deal-era program designed to provide modest benefits to those over sixty-five when it was first implemented and sixty-five was the average life expectancy—was paying far more generous benefits to retirees as young as sixty-two who were expected to live another twenty years or more. The strains these changes began to put on the system provided grist for discussion throughout the 1980s and 1990s.

The nation's regional balance had also undergone a substantial shift since the turn of the last century, when the South had been the sleepiest part of the country as well as home to the majority of its blacks, most of whom were employed in agriculture. In 1900 the Southern population numbered 24.5 million; the sparsely populated West comprised just 4.3 million; the industrial heartland of the Midwest contained 26.3 million, and the urban, polyglot East boasted 21 million inhabitants in the smallest geographical quarter. In the course of the twentieth century those numbers would turn all the way around, the South and West becoming the most vigorous regions of the country, with 93 and 58.5 million inhabitants respectively, compared with the Midwest's 43.6 million, although the heartland was starting to experience an industrial renaissance in the 1990s. By then, however, the East's population of 51.5 million made it the second smallest of America's four corners, although its cities remained the centers of finance as well as of telecommunications and the age's other technological growth enterprises. Not that such regional distinctions meant as much as they had a century earlier: heading into the twenty-first century, six of every seven U.S. households had relocated in the previous decade.

Many of these moves followed the migration of jobs and businesses, which in the 1990s generally meant heading for California's Silicon Valley, New York's Silicon Alley, Louisiana's Silicon Bayou, Washington State's Microsoft empire, or myriad other high-tech meccas sprouting up around the country. Whereas the America of 1900 had been transformed by the automobile, the airplane, and the radio, that of 2000 was already well on its way to becoming another society altogether thanks to the incredibly rapid development of the computer, the Internet, and every kind of science.

During the Clinton years telecommunication companies sprang up to take advantage of the new integration of computers, telephones, and other electronic devices by selling rapidly evolving services to an increasingly large public. Meanwhile, by the mid-1990s desktop and briefcase-sized laptop computers tens of thousands of times more powerful than the mainframes that had filled warehouses in the 1960s could be had for $2,000; by the end of the decade the price was half that for machines with twice the speed and storage capacity.

Most computer users by the end of the century made regular use of the Internet, a vast web of worldwide computer networks born in the late 1960s in the work done by the U.S. Department of Defense's Advanced Research Projects Agency and universities it commisioned. Its founders had needed to share information with researchers working on government contracts at various universities. Once computer users at these well-funded institutions realized the possibilities of an electronic network connecting them with colleagues worldwide, word of the wonder spread and the Internet blossomed. By the late 1980s anyone with a computer equipped with a modem hooked up to a regular telephone line could send an "E-mail" message or any other electronic document to anyone similarly equipped anywhere in the world—instantaneously. By 1994, the number of people connected to the World Wide Web of computer networks had swelled to an estimated 15 million. By 1998, some 40 percent of Americans would be communicating regularly over the Internet with some seventy million members of the global electronic village. In a startlingly short time, virtually every large-scale business concern worldwide would establish a presence on and conduct operations over the Internet. Through the free, unregulated, and seemingly limitless reaches of "cyberspace," as science fiction writer William Gibson dubbed it in 1984, Thomas Jefferson's ideal of a truly open marketplace of ideas began to be realized heading into the the year 2000.

America thus entered the third millennium both optimistic and restive, in the time-honored tradition of Manifest Destiny and its relentless push for liberty, equality, and not least, property. The global information highway was bringing commerce to breakneck speeds where business was conducted from anywhere in nanoseconds at the click of a button. Faith in "progress" and "newness" continued to drive the American people, who since the days of Columbus had embraced the redemptive power of movement for its own sake. As John F. Kennedy exhorted, expressing our national dynamism as he so often did: "The United States has to move very fast to even stand still."

ACKNOWLEDGMENTS

Thomas Edison in his 1932 autobiography, *Life,* wrote quite sensibly that "there is no substitute for hard work." But now, having written *American Heritage® History of the United States,* I would take the great inventor one step further by offering that there is no substitute for hard work by a team of dedicated people. The captain of the project was Kathy Huck of Byron Preiss Visual Publications, a dedicated worker who was responsible for directing and editing this opus. She is that rare conscientious spirit who whistles through adversity, laughs at chaos, and never loses her eye for exactitude. This book is a tribute to her editorial savvy and superb judgment. A special thanks is also due to Kathy's A-team of associates responsible for photo research and permissions: Katherine Miller, Karen Cissel, and especially Valerie Cope, who went beyond the call of duty.

There were others at Byron Preiss Visual Publications who made this book possible—not the least being Byron Preiss himself. Over the last several years I've come to appreciate Byron's stunning expertise regarding all aspects of the multimedia world. Other Byron Preiss Visual Publication people include designer Gilda Hannah, who made the book come alive, mapmaker Steve Jablonoski, and copy editor Marianne Cohen. Special thanks are also due Valerie Cope, Nin Chi, Clarice Levin, Dinah Dunn, Kwame Davies, and Mike Asprion, who all helped with additional research, inputting changes, and miscellaneous proofreading.

At American Heritage I had the good fortune to work with the editorial team of Frederick Allen, Richard Snow, and Barbara Strauch. Words cannot express how much I admire this adroit trio of New York intellectuals. They improved the manuscript in innumerable ways, always sharing with me their deep reservoir of knowledge pertaining to our nation's past. Frederick and Richard proved to be my most careful readers; their prodigious knowledge of history is truly astounding. Timothy Forbes—the astute publisher of *American Heritage*—has consistently shown faith in my abilities as a historian, for which I am extremely grateful. Historian Julie M. Fenster, a frequent contributor to *American Heritage,* did a magnificent job of writing captions to the lavish illustrations; it was a joy to collaborate with somebody so competent and creative. Dr. Clayton Laurie at the U.S. Army Center of Military History, Max Epstein of Byron Preiss, Robert Krick of the National Park Service, and Denise McDermott did a marvelous job of fact checking, saving me any number of embarrassing errors.

At Viking Press I had the supreme pleasure of having the indomitable Jane von Mehren as my editor. Jane never failed to be optimistic about this project and offered daily doses of encouragement as deadlines approached. My working colleagues at the publishing house—Susan Petersen, Barbara Grossman, Wendy Wolf, Paul Slovak, Ivan Held, and David Stanford—are all friends whom I cherish greatly. A special salute is owed Roni Axelrod for overseeing the production of this book on a very tight schedule and a special thanks goes to freelancer Susan Johnson for proofreading. My exemplary agent, Lisa Bankoff of International Creative Management, once again offered steadfast counsel and weekly encouragement.

Words will never be able to express my thanks to my first-rate team of consulting editors: Professor Robert Sobel of Hofstra University helped me draft chapters and decide which aspects of American history were essential to include. An unwavering friend and wonderful adviser, Professor Sobel has enriched my life now for ten years. Professor Stephen E. Ambrose, to whom this book is dedicated, offered sound guidance on a regular basis over many meals. The guardian angel of this volume is Shelby Sadler, a dear friend and brilliant essayist, who transformed my often pedestrian prose into something far better. Besides being a gifted editor Shelby is a living storehouse of knowledge and possesses a sense of humor to rival Oscar Wilde.

Individual chapters were read by other consulting editors who deserve special thanks: Robert V. Remini, Ruth Ashby, John Milton Cooper, John Allen Gable, Thomas Fleming, William J. Vanden Heuvel, and David Traxel. Without the support of University of New Orleans (UNO) Chancellor Greg O'Brien, Provost Lou Paradise, and Dean Robert DuPont this book could never have been written. My staff at the Eisenhower Center at UNO—especially Assistant Director Annie Wedekind and Project Coordinator Kevin Willey—always managed my myriad administrative duties when the demands of the book called me away. They also helped me track down valuable secondary sources. Vietnam veteran Ron Drez was a great help in sharing with me his expertise on World War II and Southeast Asia.

A number of good friends provided hearty cheer and happy diversions while writing this tome: Townsend Hoopes, H. S. Thompson, Mark Billnitzer, Robert Pastor, Amy Hanavan, Arthur M. Schlesinger, Jr., David Amram, Greg Smith, Terrance Adamson, Ornette Coleman, Deborah Fuller, Heidi Oppenheim, Lucinda Williams, Tom Beach, Summer Rodman, Doug Whitner, Joe Lee, Susan, Amby and Chevonne Daigre, Oliver Treibeck, William and Dana Kennedy, Nate Brostrum, Mike Snider, Biz Mitchell, and Paul Nitze. My parents, Anne and Edward Brinkley, were a constant source of strength and wisdom.

On a personal note, my fiancée, Tammy Cimalore, helped in so many ways it would be impossible to recount. We are a team and she never lets me down. This book simply could not have been written without her steadfast diligence, tireless commitment, and unconditional love.

SELECTED BIBLIOGRAPHY

Hundreds of books were consulted in writing this single-volume history of the United States. The following are the general texts I found most valuable and were used most frequently. A very special mention is due four comprehensive histories that were indispensable: Samuel Eliot Morison's *The Oxford History of the American People* (NY: Oxford University Press, 1965); Page Smith's eight volumes of *The People's History* (NY: McGraw-Hill, 1976–87); Howard Zinn's *A People's History of the United States: 1492–Present,* revised and updated edition (NY: HarperCollins, 1995); and Mary Beth Norton, David M. Katzman, Paul D. Escott et al.'s *A People and a Nation: A History of the United States* (Boston: Houghton Mifflin, 1986). Relevant novels, newspaper articles, and quotation books are not cited in the bibliography.

Adams, Henry. *The Education of Henry Adams.* ed. Ernest Samuels. Boston: Houghton Mifflin, 1974.

_____. *History of the United States of America During the First Administration of Thomas Jefferson 1801-1805.* NY: The Library of America, 1986

Addams, Jane. *Twenty Years at Hull-House with Autobiographical Notes.* Urbana, IL: University of Illinois Press, 1990.

Agee, James, and Evans Walker. *Let Us Now Praise Famous Men.* Boston: Houghton Mifflin, 1941.

Alger, Horatio. *Ragged Dick and Mark, the Match Boy.* NY: Collier Books, 1962.

Allen, Frederick Lewis. *The Big Change: America Transforms Itself, 1900–1950.* NY: Harper, 1952.

_____. *Only Yesterday: An Informal*

History of the Nineteen Twenties. NY: Harper & Row, 1964.

Ambrose, Stephen E. *Nixon,* 3 vols. NY: Simon & Schuster, 1991.

_____. *D-Day, June 6, 1994: The Climactic Battle of World War II.* NY: Simon & Schuster, 1994.

_____. *Undaunted Courage: Meriwether Lewis, Thomas Jefferson, and the Opening of the American West.* NY: Simon & Schuster, 1996.

_____, and Brinkley, Douglas G. *Rise to Globalism: American Foreign Policy Since 1938,* revised edition. NY: Penguin, 1997.

Aptheker, Herbert. *American Negro Slave Revolts,* 50th anniversary edition. NY: International Publishers, 1993.

Ashe, Arthur, Jr. *A Hard Road to Glory. A History of the African American Athlete 1619–1918.* NY: Warner Books, 1980.

Axelrod, Alan. *Chronicle of the Indian Wars: From Colonial Times to Wounded Knee.* NY: Prentice-Hall, 1993.

Bailyn, Bernard, et al. *The Great Republic: A History of the American People.* Boston: Little, Brown, 1977.

Beisner, Robert L. *Twelve Against Empire: The Anti-Imperialists, 1898–1900.* NY: McGraw-Hill, 1968.

Berlin, Edward A. *King of Ragtime: Scott Joplin and His Era.* NY: Oxford University Press, 1994.

Bernstein, Barton J., ed. *The Atomic Bomb: The Critical Issues.* Boston: Little, Brown, 1976.

Bernstein, Carl, and Woodward, Bob. *All the President's Men.* NY: Simon & Schuster, 1974.

Bernstein, Irving. *Turbulent Years: A History of the American Worker, 1933–1941.* Boston: Houghton Mifflin, 1970.

Beschloss, Michael R., *The Crisis Years: Kennedy and Khrushchev, 1960–1963.* NY: HarperCollins, 1992.

_____, and Talbott, Strobe. *At the Highest Levels: The Inside Story of the End of the Cold War.* Boston: Little, Brown, 1993.

Blockson, Charles L. *The Underground Railroad.* NY: Berkley Publishing Group, 1987.

Bobrick, Benson. *Angel in the Whirlwind: The Triumph of The American Revolution.* NY: Simon & Schuster, 1997.

Boller, Paul F., Jr. *Presidential Anecdotes.* NY: Oxford University Press, 1981.

Boorstin, Daniel J. *The Image: Or, What Happened to the American Dream.* NY: Atheneum, 1962.

_____. *The Americans: The Democratic Experience.* NY: Vintage Books, 1974.

Branch, Taylor. *Parting the Waters: America in the King Years, 1954–1963.* NY: Simon & Schuster, 1998.

_____. *Pillar of Fire: America in the King Years, 1963–65.* NY: Simon & Schuster, 1998.

Brands, H. W. *The Reckless Decade: America in the 1890s.* NY: St. Martin's Press, 1995.

Brinkley, Alan. *Voices of Protest: Huey Long, Father Coughlin, and the Great Depression.* NY: Vintage Books, 1983.

Brinkley, Douglas G. *Dean Acheson: The Cold War Years, 1953–1971.* New Haven: Yale University Press, 1992.

_____. *The Majic Bus: An American Odyssey.* NY: Anchor, 1994.

_____. *The Unfinished Presidency: Jimmy Carter's Journey Beyond the White House.* NY: Viking, 1998.

Brown, Dee. *Bury My Heart at Wounded Knee.* NY: Holt, Rinehart, and Winston, 1970.

Buell, Thomas B. *The Warrior Generals: Combat Leadership in the Civil War.* NY: Crown Publishing, 1997.

Burns, James MacGregor. *Roosevelt: The Lion and the Fox.* NY: Harcourt Brace Jovanovich, 1984.

Cannon, James. *Time and Chance: Gerald Ford's Appointment with History.* NY: HarperCollins, 1994.

Cannon, Lou. *President Reagan: The Role of a Lifetime.* NY: Simon & Schuster, 1991.

Caruth, Gorton, and Ehrlich, Eugene. *The Harper Book of American Quotations.* NY: Harper & Row, 1988.

Cash, W. J. *The Mind of the South.* NY: Alfred A. Knopf, 1957.

Catton, Bruce. *The American Heritage New History of the Civil War.* Ed. James M. McPherson. NY: Viking, 1996.

Chernow, Ron. *The House of Morgan: An American Banking Dynasty and the Rise of Modern Finance.* NY: Simon & Schuster, 1990.

_____. *Titan: The Life of John D. Rockefeller, Sr.* NY: Random House, 1998.

Clanton, Gene. *Populism: The Humane Preference in America, 1890–1900.* Boston: Twayne Publishers, 1991.

Colbert, David, ed. *Eyewitness to the American West: From the Aztec Empire to the Digital Frontier in the Words of Those Who Saw It Happen.* NY: Viking, 1998.

Commager, Henry Steele. *The American Mind: An Interpretation of American Thought and Character Since the 1880s.* New Haven: Yale University Press, 1959.

_____, ed. *Documents of American History.* Englewood Cliffs, NJ: Prentice-Hall, 1973.

Cooper, John Milton, Jr. *The Warrior and the Priest: Woodrow Wilson and Theodore Roosevelt.* Cambridge: Belknap Press, 1983.

Cooper, William, Jr., and Terrill, Thomas E. *The American South: A History.* NY: Alfred A. Knopf, 1990.

Cramer, Richard Ben. *What It Takes: The Way to the White House.* NY: Random House, 1992.

Cray, Ed. *Chief Justice: A Biography of Earl Warren.* NY: Simon & Schuster, 1997.

Crow, Bill. *Jazz Anecdotes.* NY: Oxford University Press, 1990.

Cutright, Paul Russell. *Theodore Roosevelt: The Making of a Conservationist.* Urbana, IL: University of Illinois Press, 1985.

Dallek, Robert. *Franklin D. Roosevelt and American Foreign Policy, 1932–1945.* NY: Oxford University Press, 1979.

Davis, William C. *Three Roads to the Alamo: The Lives and Fortunes of David Crockett, James Bowie, and William Barret Travis.* NY: HarperCollins, 1998.

Deloria, Vine, Jr., ed. *American Indian Policy in the Twentieth Century.* Norman, OK: University of Oklahoma Press, 1970.

Dennis, James. *Grant Wood: A Study in American Art and Culture.* NY: Viking, 1975.

Diggins, John Patrick. *The Proud Decades: America in War and in Peace, 1941–1960.* NY: W. W. Norton, 1988.

Donald, David H. *Lincoln.* NY: Simon & Schuster, 1995.

Dubofsky, Melvyn. *We Shall Be All: A History of the Industrial Workers of the World.* Chicago: Quadrangle Books, 1969.

Du Bois, W. E. B. *The Emerging Thought of W. E. B. Du Bois: Essays and Editorials from the Crisis.* NY: Simon & Schuster, 1972.

_____. *The Souls of Black Folk.* NY: Vintage Books, 1990.

Ehrman, John. *The Rise of Neoconservatism: Intellectuals and Foreign Affairs, 1945–1994.* New Haven, CT: Yale University Press, 1995.

Eisenhower, John S. D. *Intervention!: The United States and the Mexican Revolution, 1913–1917.* NY: W. W. Norton, 1993.

Fehrenbacher, Don E. *Prelude to Greatness: Lincoln in the 1850s.* Stanford, CA: Stanford University Press, 1962.

Felknor, Bruce L. *Dirty Politics.* NY: W. W. Norton, 1966.

Ferris, William, and Wilson, Charles Reagan, eds. *Encyclopedia of Southern Culture.* Chapel Hill, NC: The University of North Carolina Press, 1989.

Fischer, David Hackett. *Paul Revere's Ride.* NY: Oxford University Press, 1994.

Fleming, Thomas. *Liberty: The American Revolution.* NY: Viking, 1997.

Flexner, James Thomas. *George Washington,* 4 vols. Boston: Little, Brown, 1965–72.

Foner, Eric, and Garraty, John A., eds. *The Reader's Companion to American History.* Boston: Houghton Mifflin, 1991.

Franklin, John Hope. *The Emancipation Proclamation.* Garden City, NY: Doubleday, 1963.

Freidel, Frank. *The Presidents of the United States of America,* 11th ed. Washington, D.C. White House Historical Association, 1987.

Fromkin, David. *In the Time of the Americans: FDR, Truman, Eisenhower, Marshall, MacArthur The Generation That Changed America's Role in the World.* NY: Alfred A. Knopf, 1995.

Garraty, John A. *The New Commonwealth, 1877–1890.* NY: Harper & Row, 1968.

_____. *Interpreting American History: Conversations with Historians,* 2 vols. NY: Macmillan, 1970.

_____, ed. *Encyclopedia of American Biography.* NY: Harper & Row, 1974.

_____, and Mcaughey, Robert A. *The American Nation.* NY: Harper & Row, 1987.

Garrow, David J. *Protest at Selma: Martin Luther King, Jr., and the Voting Rights Act of 1965.* New Haven, CT: Yale University Press, 1978.

Garwood, Darrell. *Artist in Iowa: A Life of Grant Wood.* Westport, CT: Greenwood Press Publishers, 1971.

Gates, Robert M. *From the Shadows: The Ultimate Insider's Story of Five Presidents and How They Won the Cold War.* NY: Simon & Schuster, 1996.

Giddins, Gary. *Satchmo.* NY: Doubleday, 1988.

Goldman, Emma. *Living My Life.* NY: Alfred A. Knopf, 1931.

Goodwin, Doris Kearns. *The Fitzgeralds and the Kennedys.* NY: Simon & Schuster, 1987.

_____. *No Ordinary Time: Franklin and Eleanor Roosevelt: The Home Front in World War II.* NY: Simon & Schuster, 1994.

Gould, Lewis, L. *The Presidency of William McKinley.* Lawrence, KS: Regents Press of Kansas, 1980.

Graff, Henry F. *The Presidents: A Reference History.* NY: Scribner, 1996.

Greenspan, Karen. *The Timetable of Women's History.* NY: Simon & Schuster, 1994.

Gridley, Mark C. *Jazz Styles: History and Analysis,* 2nd ed. Englewood Cliffs, NJ: Prentice-Hall, 1985.

Griffin-Pierce, Trudy. *The Encyclopedia of Native America.* NY: Viking, 1995.

Heckscher, August. *Woodrow Wilson.* NY: Collier Books, 1991.

Higginbotham, A. Leon, Jr. *In the Matter of Color: Race and the American Legal Process.* NY: Oxford University Press, 1978.

Hill, Robert A., and Bair, Barbara. *Marcus Garvey: Life and Lessons.* Berkeley, CA: University of California Press, 1987.

Hillerman, Tony, ed. *The Best of the West: An Anthology of Classic Writing from the American West.* NY: Harper Perennial, 1991.

Hobsbawm, E. J. *The Age of Empire, 1875–1914.* NY: Vintage Books, 1989.

_____. *The Age of Extremes: A History of the World, 1914–1991.* NY: Pantheon Books, 1994.

Hobson, Fred. *Mencken: A Life.* NY: Random House, 1994.

Hodgson, Godfrey. *America in Our Time.* NY: Random House, 1978.

Hofstadter, Richard. *The Paranoid Style in American Politics.* NY: Alfred A. Knopf, 1965.

_____. *The American Political Tradition and the Men Who Made It.* NY: Vintage Books, 1989.

_____. *Social Darwinism in American Thought.* Boston: Beacon Press, 1992.

Huggins, Nathan. *Harlem Renaissance.* NY: Oxford University Press, 1971.

Iriye, Akira. *Origins of the Second World War in Asia and the Pacific.* NY: Longman, 1987.

Isaacson, Walter. *Kissinger.* NY: Simon & Schuster, 1992.

_____, and Thomas, Evan. *The Wise Men: Six Friends and the World They Made.* NY: Simon & Schuster, 1986.

James, D. Clayton. *The Years of MacArthur,* 3 vols. Boston: Houghton Mifflin, 1985.

Johannsen, Robert W., ed. *The Lincoln-Douglas Debates of 1858,* by Abraham Lincoln and Stephen Douglas. NY: Oxford University Press, 1965.

Johnson, Paul. *Modern Times: A History of the Modern World from 1917 to the 1980s.* London: Weidenfeld and Nicolson, 1983.

Josephy, Alvin M., Jr., ed. *America in 1492: The World of the Indian Peoples Before the Arrival of Columbus.* NY: First Vintage Books Edition, 1993.

_____. *500 Nations: An Illustrated History of North American Indians.* NY: Alfred A. Knopf, 1994.

Kanigel, Robert. *The One Best Way: Frederick Winslow Taylor and the Enigma of Efficiency.* NY: Viking, 1997.

Karnow, Stanley. *Vietnam: A History.* NY: Viking, 1983.

_____. *In Our Image: America's Empire in the Philippines.* NY: Random House, 1989.

Keane, John. *Tom Paine: A Political Life.* Boston: Little, Brown, 1995.

Kennan, George F. *Russia and the West Under Lenin and Stalin.* NY: Atlantic Monthly Press, 1961.

Kessner, Thomas. *The Golden Door: Italian and Jewish Immigrant Mobility in New York City, 1880–1915.* NY: Oxford University Press, 1977.

Kirkendall, Richard S., ed. *The Harry S. Truman Encyclopedia.* Boston: G. K. Hall & Co., 1989.

Kissinger, Henry. *Diplomacy.* NY: Simon & Schuster, 1994.

Kolko, Gabriel. *Century of War: Politics, Conflicts, and Society Since 1914.* NY: Harper & Row, 1976.

LaFeber, Walter. *The Panama Canal: The Crisis in Historical Perspective.* NY: Oxford University Press, 1978.

_____. *The Clash: A History of U.S.–Japanese Relations Throughout History.* NY: W. W. Norton, 1997.

Lemann, Nicholas. *The Promised Land: The Great Black Migration and How It Changed America.* NY: Vintage Books, 1992.

Leuchtenburg, William E., ed. *The Unfinished Century: America Since 1900.* Boston: Little, Brown, 1973.

_____. *In the Shadow of FDR: From Harry Truman to Bill Clinton.* Ithaca, NY: Cornell University Press, 1993.

Lewis, David Levering. *When Harlem Was in Vogue.* NY: Alfred A. Knopf, 1981.

Lewis, Tom. *Divided Highways: Building the Interstate Highways, Transforming American Life.* NY: Viking, 1997.

Lind, Michael. *The Next American Nation: The Next Nationalism and the Fourth American Revolution.* NY: Free Press, 1995.

Lorant, Stefan. *The Glorious Burden.* NY: Harper & Row, 1968.

McCullough, David. *The Path Between the Seas: The Creation of the Panama Canal 1870–1914.* NY: Simon & Schuster, 1977.

_____. *Truman.* NY: Simon & Schuster, 1992.

McDougall, Walter A. *Let the Sea Make a Noise: A History of the North Pacific from Magellan to MacArthur.* NY: Basic Books, 1993.

McFeely, William S. *Frederick Douglass.* NY: W. W. Norton, 1991.

McPherson, James M. *Battle Cry of Freedom: The Civil War Era.* NY: Oxford University Press, 1988.

Malcolm X. *The Autobiography of Malcolm X.* NY: Grove Press, 1964.

Maraniss, David. *First in His Class: A Biography of Bill Clinton.* NY: Simon & Schuster, 1995.

May, Ernest R. *The World War and American Isolation, 1914–1917.* Cambridge, MA: Harvard University Press, 1959.

Merk, Frederick. *History of the Westward Movement.* NY: Alfred A. Knopf, 1978.

Middlekauff, Robert. *The Glorious Cause: The American Revolution, 1763–1789.* NY: Oxford University Press, 1982.

Milner, Clyde A., II, et al., eds. *The Oxford History of the American West.* NY: Oxford University Press, 1994.

Miner, Margaret, and Rawson, Hugh, eds. *American Heritage Dictionary of American Quotations,* selected and annotated. NY: Penguin, 1997.

Moore, Glover. *The Missouri Compromise, 1819–1821.* Lexington, KY: University of Kentucky Press, 1953.

Morison, Samuel Eliot. *History of United States Naval Operations in World War II,* 15 vols. Boston: Atlantic Monthly Press/Little, Brown, 1962.

_____, Merk, Frederick, and Freidel, Frank. *Dissent in Three American Wars.* Cambridge, MA: Harvard University Press, 1970.

_____. *The Great Explorers: The European Discovery of America.* NY: Oxford University Press, 1978.

Morris, Edmund. *The Rise of Theodore Roosevelt.* NY: Coward, McCann & Geoghegan, 1979.

Morris, Richard B. *The Peacemakers.* NY: Harper & Row, 1965.

Murray, Bruce C. *Journey into Space: The First Three Decades of Space Exploration.* NY: W. W. Norton, 1989.

Nash, George H. *The Conservative Intellectual Movement in America: Since 1945.* NY: Basic Books, 1976.

Neely, Mark E., Jr. *The Last Best Hope of Earth: Abraham Lincoln and the Promise of America.* Cambridge, MA: Harvard University Press, 1993.

Nevins, Allan. *The War for the Union.* NY: Scribner, 1960.

_____. *Grover Cleveland: A Study in Courage.* NY: Dodd, Mead, 1966.

Newman, Richard, and Sawyer, Marcia. *Everybody Say Freedom: Everything You Need to Know About African-American History.* NY: Plume, 1996.

Nies, Judith. *Native American History.* NY: Ballantine Books, 1996.

Novas, Himilce. *Everything You Need to Know About Latino History.* NY: Plume, 1994.

Painter, Nell Irvin. *Standing at Armageddon: The United States, 1877–1919.* NY: W. W. Norton, 1987.

Palmer, Robert. *Rock & Roll: An Unruly History.* NY: Harmony Books, 1995.

Parmet, Herbet S. *George Bush: The Life of a Lone Star Yankee.* NY: Scribner, 1997.

Phillips, Kevin. *Boiling Point: Republicans, Democrats, and the Decline of Middle-Class Prosperity.* NY: Random House, 1993.

Potter, David M. *The Impending Crisis, 1848–1861.* NY: Harper & Row, 1976.

Powers, Richard Gid. *Secrecy and Power: The Life of J. Edgar Hoover.* NY: The Free Press, 1988.

Quarles, Benjamin. *The Negro in the Civil War.* Boston: Little, Brown, 1953.

Reader's Digest. *Our Glorious Century.* Pleasantville, NY: The Reader's Digest Association, 1994.

Reed, Ishmael. *Airing Dirty Laundry.* Reading, MA: Addison-Wesley, 1993.

Reeves, Richard. *President Kennedy: Profile of Power.* NY: Simon & Schuster, 1993.

Reeves, Thomas C. *The Life and Times of Joe McCarthy.* NY: Stein and Day, 1982.

Remini, Robert V. *The Life of Andrew Jackson.* NY: Penguin Books, 1990.

Remnick, David. *Lenin's Tomb: The Last Days of the Soviet Empire.* NY: Vintage Books, 1994.

Rhodes, Richard. *The Making of the Atomic Bomb.* NY: Simon & Schuster, 1986.

Safire, William. *Before the Fall: An Inside View of the Pre-Watergate White House.* NY: Doubleday, 1975.

_____. *Safire's New Political Dictionary.* NY: Random House, 1993.

Salvatore, Nick. *Eugene V. Debs: Citizen and Socialist.* Urbana, IL: University of Illinois Press, 1982.

Schell, Jonathan. *The Time of Illusion*. NY: Vintage Books, 1976.

Schlesinger, Arthur M. Jr. *The Vital Center: The Politics of Freedom*. Boston: Houghton Mifflin, 1962.

_____, ed. *History of American Presidential Elections, 1789–1968*. NY: Chelsea House, 1971.

_____. *The Disuniting of America: Reflections on a Multicultural Society*. NY: W. W. Norton, 1998.

_____. *The Cycles of American History*. Boston: Houghton Mifflin, 1986.

Shannon, William V. *The American Irish*. Toronto: Macmillan, 1963.

Slotkin, Richard. *The Fatal Environment: The Myth of the Frontier in the Age of Industrialism, 1800–1890*. NY: Macmillan, 1992.

_____. *Gunfighter Nation: The Myth of the Frontier in Twentieth-Century America*. NY: Macmillan, 1992.

Smith, Adam. *The Wealth of Nations*. NY: Alfred A. Knopf, 1991.

Smith, Gaddis. *Morality, Reason, and Power: American Diplomacy in the Carter Years*. NY: Hill and Wang, 1986.

Smith, Gene. *When the Cheering Stopped: The Last Years of Woodrow Wilson*. NY: Simon & Schuster, 1968.

Smith, Richard Norton. *An Uncommon Man: The Triumph of Herbert Hoover*. NY: Simon & Schuster, 1984.

Sobel, Robert. *The Great Bull Market: Wall Street in the 1920s*. NY: W. W. Norton, 1968.

_____. *The Manipulators: America in the Media Age*. Garden City, NY: Anchor Press/Doubleday, 1976.

Spector, Ronald H. *Eagle Against the Sun: The American War with Japan*. NY: The Free Press, 1985.

Traxel, David. *1898: The Birth of the American Century*. NY: Alfred A. Knopf, 1998.

Truman, Margaret. *First Ladies*. NY: Random House, 1995.

Turner, Frederick Jackson. *The Frontier in American History*. NY: Harper & Brothers, 1924.

Veblen, Thorstein. *The Theory of the Leisure Class*. NY: A. M. Kelley, 1975.

Ward, Geoffrey C. *Before the Trumpet: Young Franklin Roosevelt 1882–1905*. NY: Harper, 1985.

_____, et al. *The Civil War: An Illustrated History*. NY: Alfred A. Knopf, 1990.

Washington, Booker T. *Up from Slavery: An Autobiography*. NY: Carol Publishing Company, 1989.

Weinstein, Allen. *Perjury: The Hiss-Chambers Case*. NY: Random House, 1997.

Weisberger, Bernard A. *Many People, One Nation*. Boston: Houghton Mifflin, 1987.

Wert, Jeffrey D. *Custer: The Controversial Life of George Armstrong Custer*. NY: Simon & Schuster, 1996.

Wexler, Alice. *Emma Goldman: An Intimate Life*. NY: Pantheon Books, 1984.

White, Theodore H. *America in Search of Itself: The Making of the President, 1956–1980*. NY: Harper & Row, 1982.

Wills, Garry. *Reagan's America: Innocents at Home*. NY: Penguin, 1987.

Winter, Jay and Baggett, Blaine. *The Great War and the Shaping of the 20th Century*. NY: Penguin Studio, 1996.

Woodward, C. Vann. *Origins of the New South, 1877–1913*. Baton Rouge, LA: Louisiana State University Press, 1951.

_____. *The Strange Career of Jim Crow*. NY: Oxford University Press, 1957.

Worster, Donald. *Dust Bowl: The Southern Plains in the 1930s*. NY: Oxford University Press, 1979.

Yergin, Daniel. *The Prize: The Epic Quest for Oil, Money & Power*. NY: Simon & Schuster, 1991.

PICTURE CREDITS

NYHS. **130–131** SJ/AH. **132** Top: NYPL; bottom: GC. **133** GC. **134** Both: LC. **135** Corbis. **136** Top left and right: LC; bottom left and right: CB. **137** CB. **138** Top: The Hermitage: Home of President Andrew Jackson, Nashville, TN; bottom: LC. **139** Courtesy Boston Art Commission 1998. **141** CB. **142** Top: CB; bottom: LC. **144** BA. **145** Broadsides Collection, CN00690, The Center for American History, The University of Texas at Austin. **146** Left: CB; right: BA. **148** The Manoogian Foundation, on loan to the National Gallery of Art, Washington. **150** Top: Courtesy of the Massachusetts Historical Society, Boston; bottom: CB. **151** Photo by L. C. McClure, the Denver Public Library, Western History Collection. **152** The Walters Art Gallery, Baltimore. **153** Top: CB; bottom: LC. **155** SJ/AH. **156** LC. **157** CB.

CHAPTER 7
158–159 The Metropolitan Museum of Art, Gift of Edgar William and Bernice Chrysler Garbisch, 1963. **159** CB. **160–161** The Historic New Orleans Collection, accession no. 1975.93.1, 2, 3, & 4. **163** Missouri Historical Society. **164** LC. **166–167** Chicago Historical Society, neg. #ICHi-07069. **169** CB. **170** Douglas Mudd, National Numismantic Collection, The Smithsonian Institution. **171** Cincinnati Historical Society, 1982.98. **172** CB. **173** CB. **175** Fine Arts Museums of San Francisco, Gift of Mr. and Mrs. John D. Rockefeller 3rd, 1979.7.15. **176–177** BA. **179** CB. **180** SL. **181** CB.

CHAPTER 8
182 The St. Louis Art Museum. **183** NYPL. **184** SJ/AH. **185** Both: CB. **186** Both: CB. **187** Coverdale and Colpitts, a division of URS Greiner. **188–189** SJ/AH. **190** Left: Kansas State Historical Society; right: NYPL. **192** Top: LC; bottom: CB. **193** Both: LC. **196–197** Courtesy of the Illinois State Historical Library. **197** LC. **199** NYPL. **200** Courtesy of the Georgia Historical Society, Savannah. **201** Both: CB. **203** LC. **205** BA. **206** NYPL. **208–209** 7th Regiment Armory, NYC. **209** CB.

CHAPTER 9
210–211 The West Point Museum, U.S. Military Academy. **211** Collection of Don Troiani. **212** Left: Boston Anthenaeum; right: CB. **213** Both: Historic New Orleans Collection. **215** LC. **216** Top: LC; bottom: CB. **217** Left: Wadsworth Atheneum, Hartford, CT; right: LC. **218** LC. **219** Top: Ohio Historical Society; bottom: *Harper's Weekly.* **220** CB. **221** Gettysburg National Military Park. **222** The Museum of the Confederacy, Richmond, VA. **223** LC. **225** LC. **226** NYHS. **227** SJ/AH. **229** LC. **230** Appomattox Court House National Historical Park. **231** Courtesy of the Burton Historic Collection, Detroit Public Library.

232–233 Parks and History Association. **234** CB. **235** Top: CP; bottom: Douglas Mudd, National Numismantic Collection, The Smithsonian Institution. **236** CP. **237** LC. **238** Rutherford B. Hayes Presidential Center. **239** CB.

CHAPTER 10
240–241 LC. **241** NYHS. **243** CB. **244** Top: Christie's Images; bottom: GC. **246** CB. **247** Left: CB; right: White House Historical Association. **248** Top: NYHS; bottom: GC. **250** Union Pacific Museum Collection. **251** Left: CP; right: CB. **252–253** SJ/AH. **254–255** National Museum of American History, Political History Division. **255** Princeton University Library. **257** Courtesy of the Southwest Museum, Los Angeles. Photo #1026.G.1. **258–259** Nebraska State Historical Society. **260** CP. **261** Courtesy of Elisabeth Waldo-Dentzel, Multicultural Arts Northridge.

CHAPTER 11
262–263 Fine Arts Museums of San Francisco, Gift of Mr. and Mrs. John D. Rockefeller 3rd, 1979.7.4. **263** BA. **264** Corbis. **265** CB. **266** Left: Public domain; right: Brown Brothers. **267** LC. **268** GC. **269** LC/Corbis. **270** BA. **271** Top: LC; bottom: SL. **272–273** SJ/AH. **274** SL. **275** BA. **277** Top: CP; bottom: MCNY. **278** CB. **279** NYPL. **280** CB. **281** CB. **282** GC. **284** Top: SL; bottom: MCNY. **285** Top: CB; bottom: SL. **286** GC. **287** LC. **288** SL. **291** CB.

CHAPTER 12
292–293 Chicago Historical Society. **294** LC/Corbis. **296** George Rinhart/CB. **297** CP. **298** Left: GC; right: CB. **299** NYHS. **300** GC. **301** CB. **303** GC. **304** CB. **305** Left: GC; right: Corbis. **306** LC. **307** Public domain. **308** Courtesy of the State of Vermont. **310–311** UPI/CB.

CHAPTER 13
312–313 Brown Brothers. **314** CB. **315** BA. **317** CB. **318** Top: GC; bottom: CP. **319** CB. **320** U.S. Navy Historical Center. **321** Top: UPI/CB; bottom: GC. **324** UPI/CB. **326** Brown Brothers. **327** Top left: UPI/CB; bottom left: CP; right: U.S. Supreme Court. **328** CB. **331** Theodore Roosevelt Collection, Harvard College Library. **332** BA. **333** CB. **335** The Museum of American Political Life, University of Hartford.

CHAPTER 14
336–337 Gift of an anonymous donor © 1998 The Whitney Museum of American Art, New York. **337** LC. **338** BA. **339** CB. **340** LC. **341** CB. **342** NA, neg. #111-SC-26646. **343** Corbis. **345** Corbis. **346** UPI/CB. **347** Top: UPI/CB; bottom: NA. **349** Top: Imperial War Museum, neg. #E(AUS) 1220; bottom: APh. **350–351** SJ/AH. **353** NA, neg. #165-WW-350-5A. **354** Top: NA, neg. #1-SC-31731; bottom: Corbis. **355** UPI/CB. **357** NA, neg. #111-SC-

55456. **358** CB. **359** NA, neg. #165-WW-127-12. **362** UPI/CB. **363** UPI/CB.

CHAPTER 15
364–365 MCNY. **365** CP. **366** CB. **368** APh. **369** © Mazda, General Electric, courtesy of Baker Library, Dartmouth College, Hanover, NH. **371** CP. **372** Corbis. **373** APh. **374** UPI/CB. **375** Top: LC; bottom: The Museum of American Political Life, University of Hartford. **376** CP. **377** Brown Brothers. **378** Top: LC; bottom: Courtesy of American Heritage. **379** LC. **380** Top: APh; bottom left: CB; bottom right: CB. **381** © 1998 The Whitney Museum of American Art, New York. **383** Penguin/Corbis-Bettmann. **384** CB. **385** USDA-Forest Service/Corbis. **386** APh. **387** NYPL. **388** Top: CB; bottom: LC/Corbis. **389** LC. **390** UPI/CB. **391** Underwood and Underwood. **392–393** © The Equitable Life Assurance Society of the U.S.

CHAPTER 16
394–395 National Museum of American Art/Art Resource, NY. **395** FDR. **396** Top: The Museum of American Political Life, University of Hartford; bottom: LC. **397** AP/WW. **399** UPI/CB. **400** LC. **401** FDR. **403** Brown Brothers. **404** LC/Corbis. **405** LC. **406** FDR. **407** FDR. **408** FDR/Corbis. **410** Left: UPI/CB; right: LC/Corbis. **411** Chicago Historical Society, neg. #ICHi-12321. **412** UPI/CB. **413** NA, neg. #69-AG-410. **414** National Museum of American Art/Art Resource, NY. **415** UPI/CB. **416** UPI/CB. **417** UPI/CB. **418** BA. **419** NA. **421** NA, neg. #69-ANP-1-2329-325.

CHAPTER 17
422–423 NA, neg. #111-SC-190968. **423** BA. **425** LC. **426** UPI/CB. **427** GC. **428** Top: LC; bottom: courtesy of Stan Cohen **429** CP. **432** Left: FDR; right: AP/WW. **433** UPI/CB. **434–435** SJ/AH. **436** Imperial War Museum, neg. #A 6872. **437** Left: State Department; right: NA, neg. #208-PU-199R-1. **438** NA/Corbis. **439** Top: NA, neg. #79-AR-82; bottom: NA, neg. #044-PA-191. **440** Public Domain. **441** Public domain. **443** UPI/CB. **444–445** Navy Art Collection, Naval Historical Center. **445** NA. **446** NA. **447** Top: NA, neg. #26-G-2343; bottom: Warren Josephy Collection. **448** NA, neg. #26-G-2517. **449** UPI/CB. **450** NA. **451** NA. **453** NA. **454** LC. **455** U.S. Army. **456** AP/WW. **457** Imperial War Museum, neg. #B.U.9195. **460–461** AP/WW. **461** UN Photo by Yuichiro Sasaki.

CHAPTER 18
462 © The Curtis Publishing Co. **463** Federal Civil Defense Agency. **464** UPI/CB. **465** SJ/AH. **466** Left: CB; center: LC/Corbis; right: UPI/CB. **468** UPI/CB. **471** CB. **472** Both: UPI/CB. **473** UPI/CB. **474** SJ/AH. **475** AP/WW. **476** UPI/CB. **477** Top: AP; bottom

left: UPI/CB; bottom right: APh/Blank Archives. **478** APh. **480** AP/WW. **481** AP/WW. **482** Top: AP/WW; bottom: APh. **483** AP/WW. **485** APh. **486** © 1956, *The Washington Post.* **488** International Ladies' Garment Workers' Union Archives. Kheel Center for Labor-Management Documentation and Archives, Cornell University. **489** Archive/Lambert. **490** UPI/CB. **491** AP/WW. **493** Corbis. **494** UPI/CB. **495** UPI/CB.

CHAPTER 19
496–497 APh. **497** Smithsonian Institution. **498** UPI/CB. **500** Jack Moebes/Corbis. **501** UPI/CB. **502** Top: UPI/CB; bottom: AP/WW. **504** UPI/CB. **505** UPI/CB. **506–507** SJ/AH. **509** AP/WW. **510** AP/WW. **511** NA. **514** Top left: The Museum of American Political Life, University of Hartford; top right: Lyndon Baines Johnson Library/Corbis; bottom: UPI/CB. **515** AP/WW. **516** UPI/CB. **519** UPI/CB. **520** Hulton-Deutsch Collection/Corbis. **521** SJ/AH. **522** AP/WW. **523** Top: UPI/CB; bottom: AP/WW. **525** AP/WW. **526** UPI/CB. **527** BA. **529** UPI/CB.

CHAPTER 20
530–531 AP/WW. **531** Carla Davidson. **533** Nixon Presidential Materials Staff/NA. **534** AP/WW. **535** UPI/CB. **536–537** AP/WW. **538** UPI/CB. **541** NASA. **542** AP/WW. **546** AP/WW. **548** AP/WW. **549** AP/WW. **551** LC. **552** Both: UPI/CB. **556** UPI/CB. **557** Gerald Ford Library. **559** Top: LC; bottom: UPI/CB. **560** Don Wright. **562** AP/WW. **563** AP/WW.

CHAPTER 21
564–565 Courtesy Ronald Reagan Library. **565** *Contra Diction,* October 14, 1987, by Robbie Conal. Photo: Alan Shaffer. **568** LC. **569** AP/WW. **570** AP/WW. **571** Mike Lane/*The Baltimore Sun.* **574** Top: UPI/CB; bottom: Ronald Reagan Library/Corbis. **575** AP/WW. **576** Owen Franken/Corbis. **577** UPI/CB. **578** Owen Franken/Corbis. **579** Courtesy Ronald Reagan Library. **580** Courtesy Ronald Reagan Library. **581** Left: AP/WW; center: UPI/CB; right: UPI/CB. **582** UPI/CB. **583** Top: Reuters/CB; bottom: UPI/CB. **585** Courtesy Ronald Reagan Library. **586** AP/WW. **587** Courtesy Ronald Reagan Library.

CHAPTER 22
588–589 Joseph Sohm; ChromoSohm Inc./Corbis. **589** Forbes Magazine Collection. **590** AP/WW. **592** AP/WW. **594** Reuters/CB. **595** Top: Reuters/CB; bottom: George Bush Presidential Library and Museum **596** Top: UPI/CB; bottom: Reuters/CB. **598** Reuters/CB. **599** Agence France Presse/CB. **600** Mike Keefe, dePIXion studios, inc. **601** Reuters/CB. **603** Reuters/CB. **605** UPI/CB. **606** Reuters/CB. **607** Reuters/CB. **609** Lee Snider/Corbis.

Abernathy, Ralph, 494, 528
Abolitionism
  Dred Scott case and, 193–194
  growth of, 149–151, 188–189,
    190–192
Acheson, Dean, Marshall Plan and,
  466–467
Adams, Abigail, 71, 77, 107
Adams, John, 58, 60, 68, 71, 72,
  76–77, 79–80, 124, 263
  death of, 129
  as first vice president, 111
  on George Washington, 127
  as minister to England, 101
  as second president, 127–129
Adams, John Quincy, 133, 172, 263
  in election of 1828, 138
  presidential election of, 135–137
  as sixth president, 134–135
  on slavery, 207
Adams, Samuel, 56, 58, 60, 63, 67,
  101
Addams, Jane, 281, 324, 325, 355
Advertising
  by General Electric Company, 369
  by McCormick Reaper Company,
    166–167
Africa
  fifteenth-century European
    exploration of, 7–8
  Portuguese trade with, 9–10
African-Americans
  Bush administration and, 597–598
  after Civil War, 228–230, 239
  Constitutional Convention and,
    106–107
  Fugitive Slave Law and, 183–185
  during Great Depression, 403–405
  jazz and, 382–383
  Kennedy administration and,
    499–503
  Lyndon Johnson administration
    and, 514–517
  in late nineteenth century,
    279–282
  1920s lynchings of, 371
  during 1950s, 490–495
  in Old South, 158–164
  in post-Civil War elections,
    237–238
  post-World War I mistreatment of,
    361–363
  Reagan administration and,
    576–577
  rhythm and blues by, 492
  in Union and Confederate armies,
    216–217
  Wilson and, 339–340
  in World War I, 359
African slave trade, 32–33
  origin of, 9–10
  and tobacco plantations, 31
Agnew, Spiro
  in election of 1968, 527
  in election of 1972, 549

resignation of, 551
Agricultural Adjustment Administration
  (AAA), 409, 416
Agriculture
  under Eisenhower administration,
    476–478
  at end of nineteenth century,
    294–295, 302–303
  government price supports in,
    398, 400
  Jefferson's views of, 118–119
  under New Deal, 409–410
  in 1920s America, 370
  in post-Civil War United States,
    243–245
  railroads and, 258–259
  in western United States, 258–261
  See also Cattle; Cotton
Aguinaldo, Emilio, 309, 317–318
Aid to Families with Dependent
    Children (AFDC) program, 544
  Reagan's cutback of, 570–571
AIDS (acquired immunodeficiency
    syndrome), 608–609
Aircraft production, during World War
  II, 440–441
Alabama, racial segregation in,
  491–494, 501
Alamo, Battle of, 144–145
Alaska, 334
  as incorporated territory, 317
  Klondike Gold Rush to, 299, 302
  purchase of, 231
Aldrin, Edward "Buzz," Jr., 541
Alexander VI, Pope, 3
  line of demarcation created by, 14
Alien Registration Act, 469
Alien and Sedition Acts, 129, 131
Allen, Ethan, 68
Allende Gossens, Salvador, 539
Alliance Movement, 295
Alliance for Progress, 503
Allies
  in World War I, 342
  in World War II, 441–444, 445–454
America
  African slave trade and, 30, 31,
    32–33
  discovery and early exploration
    of, 1–23
  See also United States
American Anti-Imperialist League,
  309–311
American Civil Liberties Union, 355
American Civil War. *See* Civil War
American colonies
  declaration of independence by,
    68–77
  rift between Great Britain and,
    50–77
  trade between West Indies and,
    53–54
  War of Independence of, 78–101
  west of Appalachians, 54–56
American Federation of Labor (AFL),

278, 290, 413–414
American Party, 191–192
American Revolution
  beginning of, 66–68
  economic origins of, 42–44, 45–46,
    49
  events leading up to, 50–77
  first blood shed in, 60
  justification of, 71–77
  War of Independence in, 78–101
  See also War of Independence
American Telephone and Telegraph
    Company (AT&T), 265, 368, 384
Anderson, John B., in election of
  1980, 567–568
Andersonville, prison camp at, 229
Andropov, Yuri, 573
Annapolis Convention, 100–101
Anne, Queen, 45–46
Anthony, Susan B., 178, 372, 373
Anti-Communism
  emergence of American, 468–472
  See also McCarthyism
Antietam, Battle of, 214–215
Antietam Creek, Battle of, 217
Anti-Federalist Party, 100, 119
Anti-Masonic Party, 277
Antitrust litigation, 268–269, 291, 420
  See also Clayton Antitrust Act;
    Sherman Antitrust Act
Antiwar protests, 522–524, 534–538
Apollo 11 mission, 541
Appalachian Mountains, American
    colonies west of, 54–56, 95
Appomattox Court House, Confederate
    surrender at, 228, 230–231
Arafat, Yasir, 601
Armstrong, Neil, 541
Army-McCarthy controversy,
  478–479
Army of the Potomac, 211–212, 214
Army of the Republic of Vietnam
    (ARVN), 508–509
Arnold, Benedict, 68, 88
Arthur, Chester Alan, 247, 287
  as twenty-first president, 246
Articles of Confederation
  U.S. Constitution versus, 104, 105,
    108, 110
  United States under, 94–101
Artists
  Federal Art Project and, 420–421
  supported by WPA, 412, 413, 414
Asia, fifteenth-century European trade
    with, 7–8
  See also China; Japan; Vietnam
Atlanta, capture and burning of, 225
Atlantic Charter, 433
Atomic bomb
  construction of, 457–458
  Soviet testing of, 469
  use against Japan of, 458, 460–461
Atomic Energy Commission, 487
Atomic warfare, 463, 505, 601–602
"Atoms for Peace" program, 480

Attlee, Clement, 457, 464
Automobiles
  invention of, 291
  proliferation of, 367, 384–388, 489
Axis powers. *See* Germany; Italy;
    Japan
Aztecs, destruction of civilization of,
    15–17

"Baby boomers," 486–490
Bacon's Rebellion, 41
Baghdad Pact, 482
Balboa, Vasco Nuñez de, 15
Ballistic Missile Early Warning System
    (BMEWS), 506–507
Baltimore, Maryland, in War of 1812,
    132
Baltimore & Ohio Railroad, 176–177
Banking
  at beginning of New Deal, 409
  during Great Depression, 402
  J. P. Morgan and, 269–270
Bank of the United States, 117
  Hamilton's organization of, 116
  Jackson's dissolution of, 142–143
  selling of federal government
    holdings in, 131
Barbed wire, 259, 261
Barker, Wharton, in election of 1900,
    314
Baruch, Bernard, American economy
    during World War I and, 352,
    355
Battle of Long Island, 81
Bay of Pigs invasion, 503
Beauregard, General Pierre G. T., 209
Beer industry, 171
  under Prohibition, 377, 378
Bell, Alexander Graham, 265, 384
Bell, John, 193, 199, 200
Benson, A. L., in election of 1916,
    345
Benson, Ezra Taft, 476–478
Benton, Thomas Hart, 138, 392–393
Bentsen, Lloyd, in election of 1988,
    590
Berlin
  Allied capture of, 448–449
  Soviet blockade of, 467, 470–471
Berlin Airlift, 470–471
Berlin Wall, 503–504
  removal of, 592
Bessemer process, 266
Bethlehem Steel Company, 353
Bidwell, John, 170
  in election of 1892, 296–297
Bigotry, 370–371, 379
Bill of Rights, 113–114
Bingham, George Caleb, 174–175,
    182–183
Birmingham, Alabama, racial
    segregation in, 501, 516–517
Black Hawk War, 186

Black Muslims, 502–503, 517
Blaine, James G., in election of 1884, 246–247
Bland, Richard, in election of 1896, 300
Boesky, Ivan, 583, 584
Bohlen, Charles, 466–467
Bolsheviks, 357
    African-Americans and, 362
    in federal government, 469
    labor agitation of, 372
Bonaparte, Napoleon, 127, 132
    Louisiana Purchase and, 129–131
"Bonus Expeditionary Force," 405
Booth, John Wilkes, assassination of Lincoln by, 231
Bosnia Herzegovina, Clinton administration and, 602–603
Boston, 35, 47
    American colonial unrest in, 59–67
    Battle of Bunker Hill in, 70
    fishing industry and, 43
Boston Massacre, 59–60, 62–63
"Boston Tea Party," 61–63, 64
Bowie, Colonel James, at Alamo, 145
Boycotts, of British imports by American colonists, 59, 65
Braddock, General Edward, 47
Bradley, General Omar, 445, 474
Brady, James, 569–570
Brady, Mathew, 202–203, 204–205
Brandeis, Louis D., 326–328
Brandywine Creek, Pennsylvania, defeat of Washington at, 84–85
Breckinridge, John, 193, 199, 200
Bretton Woods conference, 459, 547
Brezhnev, Leonid
    death of, 573
    Ford's meeting with, 555
    Nixon's meeting with, 542
Bridger, Jim, 256
Brigham Young, 170
Brown, John, 191, 195–196
Brown v. Board of Education of Topeka, 491
Bryan, Charles W., in election of 1924, 390
Bryan, William Jennings, 307, 328, 391
    in election of 1896, 300–301
    in election of 1900, 314
    in election of 1908, 333–334
    as Secretary of State, 340–341, 344
Buchanan, James
    as fifteenth president, 192–193, 201
    at Lincoln's inauguration, 204
    presidential election of, 191–192
Buddhist monks, immolations of, 508–509
Buffalo (bison), importance of, 254
    near extinction of, 330
Buffalo, New York, assassination of McKinley at, 315
Bull Run
    Battle of, 209, 211
    Second Battle of, 214
Bunker Hill, Battle of, 70
Bureau of Labor, creation of, 287

Burgoyne, General John, 83
    American campaign of, 84–85
Burke, Edmund, 59, 63, 65, 92
Burnside, General Ambrose E., at Battle of Fredericksburg, 214–215
Burr, Aaron, 118, 119, 124
    trial for treason of, 131
Bush, George Herbert Walker
    in election of 1980, 567
    as forty-first president, 591–599
    presidential election of, 589–591
Butler, General Benjamin, 216
    in election of 1864, 226
Byzantine Empire, Turkish conquest of, 3–4

Cabinet, creation of, 112–113
Cabot, John, 28
Calhoun, John C., 142, 156–157
    political career of, 134–139
    on southern slavery, 163–164
California
    capture of, 147
    gold discovered in, 150–151
    post-Civil War immigration to, 241
    racial rioting in, 515–517
    settlement of, 170
    statehood of, 153–156
Calvinism, 27
Cambodia, 521, 555–556
    in Vietnam War, 534–535
Camp David peace accords, Carter and, 560, 562
Canada, 47, 63
    British acquisition of, 48–49
    French colonies in, 45
    in Treaty of Paris negotiations, 93
    westward expansion of, 145
Canals, 172–176
Cape Breton Island, 46, 47
Cape of Good Hope, Portuguese discovery of, 10
Capone, Alphonse "Scarface," 377, 399
Carnegie, Andrew, 265–267, 269, 291, 307, 309
    annual income of, 294
    pacifism of, 355
    strikes against, 287
Carnegie Endowment for International Peace, 469
Carnegie Trust, 266
Carolinas, British campaigns in, 87–89
Carpetbaggers, 236
Carranza, Venustiano, 341–342
Carter, James Earl, 228
    in election of 1980, 565
    presidential election of, 557–558
    as thirty-ninth president, 559–563
Casablanca, Allied conference at, 445–446
Casey, William, 580, 581
"Cash and carry" system, 427
Castro, Fidel, 483, 503
Catholic Church
    colonization of Maryland by, 35
    corruption of, 2

Ku Klux Klan versus, 363
    struggle between Protestantism and, 26, 27, 39–40
Catt, Carrie Chapman, 355
Cattle, importance of, 254–258
Central America
    Spanish conquest of, 16–17
    United States occupation of countries in, 319–320
Central Intelligence Agency (CIA), 476
    Chilean coup by, 539
    formation of, 467
    "Iran-Contra" affair and, 579–581
Central Powers, in World War I, 342
Chafin, Eugene
    in election of 1908, 334
    in election of 1912, 338
Chancellorsville, Battle of, 221, 222–223
Charles I, King, 39
Charles II, King, 35
Charles V, King, 17
Charles VIII, King, 2–3
Charleston, South Carolina, capture of, 87
Chase, Salmon P., 156, 207, 226
Chattanooga, capture of, 224
Checks and balances, 109–110
Cherokee, Trail of Tears and, 154
Cherokee Nation v. Georgia, 154
Chiang Kai-shek, 454, 464
Children, as underpaid labor, 277, 284–285, 325, 339
China
    Chiang Kai-shek versus Mao Zedong in, 464, 469
    early European contacts with, 6–7
    Japanese invasion of, 436
    Korean War and, 472–476
    Nixon's trip to, 539–542
    normalization of American relations with, 560–561
    Open Door Policy toward, 318
    relaxation of communism in, 593
Chinese Exclusion Act, 291
Chinese labor
    exclusion of, 291
    in railroads, 250
Christians, struggle between Muslims and, 3–4
Christian Science Church, founding of, 140
Churchill, Sir Winston, 437, 438, 444, 445, 448–449, 454
    meetings with FDR and, 432–433
    on Nazi extermination camps, 459
    at Potsdam, 457–458
    in pre-World War II British-American relations, 429–430
    at Yalta, 449
Church of Jesus Christ of Latter-Day Saints. See Mormonism
Cibola, seven cities of, 17–23
Cincinnati, meatpacking in, 170–171
Civilian Conservation Corps (CCC), 410
Civil Rights Act of 1875, 238
Civil Rights Act of 1964, 512

Civil War, 210–231
    aftermath of, 230–239
    causes of, 182–209
    changes in America following, 240–245
    end of, 227–231
    morality of, 215–220
    onset of, 207–209
    women's suffrage movement following, 373
Clark, George Rogers, 87
Clark, Lieutenant William, 168–169
Clay, Henry, 134, 136, 142, 145, 187
    Compromise of 1850 and, 153–157, 183
    in presidential election of 1824, 137
Clay, General Lucius D., 470
Clayton Antitrust Act, 339, 389
Clean Air Act of 1963, 544
Clemenceau, Georges, 357
Clermont steamboat, 173, 176
Cleveland, Grover, 287, 303
    first presidential election of, 246–247
    second presidential election of, 296–297
    as twenty-second and twenty-fourth president, 246–249, 297–299
Clinton, General Henry, 87–89, 90, 92
Clinton, William Jefferson
    first presidential election of, 588–589, 597–599
    as forty-second president, 599–611
    second presidential election of, 604
"Coercive Acts," 63
Cold War, 462–495
    beginning of end of, 584–586
    détente in, 539–542
    end of, 591–595
Colfax, Schuyler, in election of 1868, 234–235
Collins, Michael, 541
Colombia, Panama Canal and, 319
Colonial trade routes, 41
Columbia Broadcasting System (CBS), 384
Columbus, Christopher, 1, 11–14
Commercial revolution, in Europe, 1–23
Committee to Defend America, 430
Committee to Re-Elect the President (CREEP), 549–550
Committees of Correspondence, 61, 63
Common Sense (Paine), 71
Communism
    collapse of, 591–595
    downfall of, 589
    Gorbachev and, 585–586
    Reagan administration and, 574, 579–581
Communist Manifesto (Marx & Engels), 152–153, 524–525
Communist Party, in election of 1932, 407
Communists

labor agitation of, 372
post-World War II takeover of
China by, 464
in Russia, 356
takeover of Cuba by, 483
takeover of Vietnam by, 480–482
See also Cold War
Compromise of 1850, 153–156, 202
Fugitive Slave Law and, 183–185
U.S. territories after, 188–189
Concord, Battle of, 66–68
Confederate States of America
British recognition of, 209
during Civil War, 210–231
formation of, 201–209
Confederation, Articles of, 94–101
Congress, U.S.
under Articles of Confederation,
94–95
constitutional powers of, 110
initial acts of, 113–114
in post-Civil War years, 245–249
Congress of Industrial Organizations
(CIO), formation of, 414–415
Congress for Racial Equality (CORE),
500
Connally, John, 509–510, 568
Conquistadores, 14, 22
Conservation movement
during New Deal, 410
Theodore Roosevelt's support of,
329, 330–331
See also Environmental legislation
Constantinople
failure of Rome to retake, 8
Turkish conquest of, 3–4
Constitution, U.S.
Bill of Rights added to, 113–114
drafting of, 105–110
implied powers in, 117
as legal document, 103–104
Native American tribes under, 154
ratification of, 110–111
Constitutional Convention of 1787,
78–79, 102–111
events leading up to, 99–101
Constitutional Union Party, in election
of 1860, 200
Consumer goods
1920s proliferation of, 366–367
purchases on credit of, 400–401
Continental Army, 80–84, 87, 88
Continental Congress
first, 63–65
second, 68–77
"Contra" rebels, 574
See also "Iran-Contra" affair
Coolidge, Calvin, 370, 387, 423
in election of 1920, 375
presidential election of, 388–391
rejection of second term by,
395–396
as thirtieth president, 388–393
Copley, John Singleton, 56, 110
"Copperheads," 219
Copyright and patent authority, under
U.S. Constitution, 110
Cornwallis, General Charles, 87–89,
89–92

Coronado, Francisco de, 17–23
Corporations, nineteenth-century
growth of, 267–269, 290–291
Cortés, Hernando, 15–17
Cotton
as major crop in southern states,
158–164, 195, 206
post-Civil War farming of, 244
Cotton gin, 159, 161–162
"Counterculture," 517–520
Vietnam War protests by, 533–538
Cowboys, 255, 261
Cox, James M., 325, 375–376
Coxey, Jacob S., 297, 298
Crash of 1929, 398–400
Crazy Horse, Chief, defeat of Custer
by, 256–257
Credit, for consumers, 400–401
Crimean War, 194–195
Crittenden, John, 201, 202
Croatia, Clinton administration and,
602–603
Crockett, Davy, at Alamo, 144–145
Cromwell, Oliver, 39–40
"Cross of Gold" speech, 300–301
Crucible, The (Miller), 469–472
Cuba, 17. *See also* Castro, Fidel
American annexation of, 309–311
American plans to acquire, 190
Columbus's landing on, 14
Communist takeover of, 483
independence of, 318–319
pressure for independence of,
298–299, 304–307
Reagan administration and,
574–575
sinking of *Maine* in, 292–293
Cuban missile crisis, 504–505
Currency
stability of American, 143
stabilization of post-World War II,
459
Currency Act, 56
Currency devaluations, under Articles
of Confederation, 99
Custer, General George Armstrong,
260
at Battle of Little Bighorn, 256–257
Czolgosz, Leon, assassination of
McKinley by, 315

da Gama, Vasco, 10, 22–23
Darwinism
fundamentalist challenge of, 370
social change and, 264, 303–304
Daugherty, Harry, 375, 387
Davis, Jefferson, 156, 200, 223
at onset of Civil War, 209
as president of Confederate States,
201
Southern Democrats and, 187
Davis, John W., 397
in election of 1924, 389, 390
"D-Day," 446–448, 450–451
Debs, Eugene V., 278, 287, 325, 328
in election of 1896, 301
in election of 1900, 314
in election of 1904, 329

in election of 1908, 333–334
in election of 1912, 338
in election of 1920, 354, 375
on World War I, 354, 355
Declaration of Independence
(Jefferson), 72–77, 104
Declaration of Rights and Resolves,
64
Declaration of Sentiments, 178
Declaratory Act, 57–58, 59
Deere, John, invention of steel plow
by, 165
Defense systems, map of American,
506–507
de Grasse, Admiral François Joseph
Paul, 89–91
Delaware, colonization of, 35
Delaware River, Washington's
crossing of, 81–84
Democracy
in Information Age, 589–590
Wilson's ideas concerning,
340–342
Democratic Party, 143–144, 387
in election of 1852, 186–187
in election of 1860, 196–200
in election of 1864, 225–227
in election of 1868, 234–236
in election of 1876, 238–239
in election of 1884, 287
in election of 1892, 296–297
in election of 1896, 299–302
in election of 1900, 314
in election of 1904, 328–329
in election of 1908, 333–334
in election of 1912, 337–338
in election of 1920, 375–376
in election of 1924, 388–391
in election of 1928, 396–397
in election of 1932, 405–407
in election of 1936, 415–418
in election of 1940, 430–431
in election of 1948, 468
in election of 1952, 475–476, 477
in election of 1956, 484, 486
in election of 1960, 497–499
in election of 1964, 513–514
in election of 1968, 524–529
in election of 1972, 547–549
in election of 1976, 557–558
in election of 1980, 565–569
in election of 1984, 576–578
in election of 1988, 590–591
in election of 1992, 598–599
in election of 1996, 604
at end of New Deal, 420–421
opposition to Civil War by,
219–220
origin of, 142, 144
in post-Civil War years, 245–249
during World War I, 353–354
Democratic Republican Party, 142
de Rochambeau, General Jean-
Baptiste, Comte, at Yorktown,
89–91
Deseret, 151
de Soto, Hernando, 17, 20–21
Détente, in Cold War, 539–542
Detroit

British capture of, 48
War of Independence battle at, 87
World War II race riots in, 442–443
Dewey, Commodore George,
307–309, 311
Dewey, Thomas E., 289
in election of 1944, 454
in election of 1948, 468
Dickinson, John, 57, 58, 63, 68,
70–71
Articles of Confederation and,
94–95
Diem, Ngo Dinh, 481–482, 508–509
Dien Bien Phu, Battle of, 481
Disney, Walt, 379–381
District of Columbia
slave trade ended in, 153–156
slavery abolished in, 216
Dixiecrats, in election of 1948, 468
Dodge, Grenville, 249, 250
Doe v. Bolton, 518–519
Dole, Robert, 603
in election of 1976, 558
in election of 1988, 590
in election of 1996, 604
"Dollar diplomacy," 335
Donner party, 170
Douglas, Stephen A., 151, 183, 190,
193, 202
debates between Lincoln and,
196–197, 198–199
in election of 1856, 192
in election of 1860, 199–200
Douglas, William O., 372, 482
Douglass, Frederick, 190, 215, 216,
237
Draft
during Civil War, 218–219
post–World War II, 486
pre–World War II, 429
Drake, Sir Francis, 22–23
Dred Scott case, 193–194, 198–199
Duarte, José Napoleon, 576
Du Bois, W. E. B., 279–280, 281, 363
Dukakis, Michael, 590–591
Dulles, John Foster, 476, 479–484
Duryea, Charles and Frank, 291
Dutch East India Company, 39
Dutch West India Company, 35, 39

Eagleton, Thomas, in election of
1972, 548
East India Company, 29, 61
Eastman, George, 265
Economic depression
following War of Independence,
99
during late nineteenth century,
283–291
during 1970s, 553–554
preceding Civil War, 194–195
See also Great Depression; Panic
of 1907
Economic growth
at end of nineteenth century,
293–303
during 1920s, 366–367, 367–372

during 1980s, 582–584
during 1990s, 605–608, 608–611
following Civil War, 240–261
See also "Reaganomics"
Economic Opportunity Act, 512
Eden, Sir Anthony, 449, 484–485
Edison, Thomas Alva, 264–265
    motion pictures and, 299, 379
    Progessivism of, 313
Edison General Electric Light
    Company, 265
Edward VI, King, 26, 27
Efficiency studies, 265
Eighteenth Amendment, 372, 376–378
Eisenhower, Dwight David, 405, 418,
    426, 450, 474
    command of Allied forces in
        Africa by, 445–446
    command of Allied forces in
        Europe by, 448–449
    command of D-Day invasion by,
        446–448
    first presidential election of,
        475–476, 477
    second presidential election of,
        484, 486
    as thirty-fourth president, 476–486,
        488–490, 490–495
El Alamein, Battle of, 444–445
Elections, under U.S. Constitution,
    111
    See also Suffrage
Electric lighting, invention of, 265
Elizabeth I, Queen, 26–29
Elizabethtown, New Jersey, George
    Washington at, 112
Ellis Island, 270–271, 273–274
El Salvador, Reagan administration
    and, 576
Emancipation Proclamation, 217–218,
    219–220
Embargo Act, 131
Emergency Banking Relief Act, 409
Emerson, Ralph Waldo, 67–68, 140,
    215
Employers' Liability Act, 329
Employment Act, 486–487
Endangered Species Act of 1973, 544
England. *See* Great Britain
England, Church of, 27
Enlightenment, the, 52, 73
Environmental legislation, 542–544
Environmental Protection Agency
    (EPA), 542–544
Equal Employment Opportunity
    Commission, 512
Equal Rights Amendment, 518
"Era of Good Feelings," 133
Erie Canal, construction of, 174–175
Eriksson, Leif, 11, 22–23
Espionage Act of 1917, 355
*Essay Concerning Human
    Understanding, An* (Locke), 43
Europe
    colonization of America by, 24–49
    early nineteenth-century American
        relations with, 127–131
    exploration of the world by, 1–23
    Hitler's annexations in, 428–430

immigration to America from,
    270–274
map of German conquests in,
    434–435
map of World War I in, 350–351
Marshall Plan for, 466–467
nineteenth-century populist revolts
    in, 152–153
onset of World War II in, 430–436
post-Communist restructuring of,
    592–593
post-World War I depression in,
    402
prelude to World War II in,
    423–428
after World War II, 457, 459–461,
    463–468, 468–472
World War II in, 428–436
World War I in, 340, 342–352,
    352–356, 356–359
Evangelism, 140–141
"Executive privilege"
    Lincoln's interpretation of, 206
    in Watergate scandal, 551
Exploration, age of, 1–23

Fair Deal, 474, 476, 487
Family Assistance Program, 544
Farm Credit Administration, 409–410
Farragut, Admiral David G., 212–214
Federal Art Project, 420–421
Federal Bureau of Investigation (FBI),
    360
Federal Civil Defense Agency, 463
Federal Deposit Insurance
    Corporation, 411
Federal Emergency Relief
    Administration (FERA), 411
Federal Farm Board, 398
Federal government
    assumption of states' debts by,
        116–118
    Bolsheviks in, 469
    in post-Civil War years, 245–249
    states and, 109–110
    Wilson's expansion of, 338–340
Federal Housing Administration, 411
Federalist Papers, The, 100, 114
Federalist Party, 100, 119–120, 124
    early politics of, 127–131
    "Era of Good Feelings" and, 133
    Hamilton and, 117
Federal Reserve System
    establishment of, 339
    under New Deal, 419–420
    during Reagan administration, 572
Federal Trade Commission
    establishment of, 339
    unconstitutionality and, 416
Feminism
    in nineteenth century, 178–179
    in twentieth century, 518–519
Ferraro, Geraldine, in election of
    1984, 577–578
Field, General James G., in election
    of 1892, 296–297
Fifteenth Amendment, 179, 234, 238
Fillmore, Millard

as "Know-Nothing" Party
    nominee, 191–192
as thirteenth president, 153
Fishing industry, 43–44
Florida, 17, 133
Ford, Gerald Rudolph
    in election of 1976, 557–558
    as Nixon's vice president, 551
    as thirty-eighth president, 552–558
Ford, Henry, 313, 407, 440
    mass production of automobiles
        by, 387
    pacifism of, 355
Fordney-McCumber Tariff of 1922,
    398
Forest Service, U.S., formation of, 330
Fort Cumberland, 118–119
Fort Duquesne
    British capture of, 48
    founding of, 47
Fort McHenry, 132
Fort Niagara, 87
"Fortress America," 465–466
Fort Sumter, Confederate attack on,
    201, 206, 207, 209
Fort Ticonderoga, capture of, 68
Foster, William Z., in election of
    1932, 407
"Founding fathers"
    at Constitutional Convention,
        103–111
    in early U.S. government, 111–125
Four Freedoms speech, 431
"Fourteen Points," 356
Fourteenth Amendment, 179, 234,
    490
Fox, Charles James, 63, 92
Frame of Government, of William
    Penn, 35–38
France
    American colonial trade with,
        53–54
    colonial conflicts between England
        and, 45–49
    fifteenth-century political turmoil
        in, 2–3, 26
    formation of Vietnam and, 463
    loss of Vietnam by, 480–482
    Louisiana Purchase from, 129–131
    post-Revolution relations with,
        128–129
    revolution in, 120–121
    siege of Yorktown and, 89–91
    support of American independence
        by, 76–77, 79, 85–87, 92–94
    unification of, 29
    in World War I, 350–351
    World War II conquest by
        Germany of, 431
Franklin, Benjamin, 56, 63, 72, 76–77,
    110
    as ambassador to France, 85, 87,
        91
    as colonial representative in
        London, 58–59, 65
    colonial union and, 47
    Treaty of Paris and, 92–93
Franz Ferdinand, Archduke, 342, 343
Fredericksburg, Battle of, 214–215

Free Soil Party, 153, 187, 191
Frémont, John C., 147, 216
    in election of 1856, 192
    in election of 1864, 226
French and Indian War, 47–49
    aftermath of, 50–52, 53–57
French Indochina
    Japanese occupation of, 436
    See also Vietnam, Democratic
        Republic of
French Republic
    formation of, 120–121
    relations between post-Revolution
        United States and, 122–123
French Revolution, 120–121
Frick, Henry Clay, 287, 296–297
Friedan, Betty, 518–519
Frobisher, Martin, 28
Frontier, 169
    definition of, 168
    disappearance of, 256, 261
Fugitive Slave Law, 183–185, 186, 202
Fulton, Robert, 173, 176
Fundamentalism, spread of, 370
Fur trade, Canadian, 45

Gadsden Purchase, 190
Gage, General Thomas, 66–68
    Battle of Bunker Hill and, 70
Gallatin, Albert, 174
Garfield, James Abram, 318
    assassination of, 246, 247
    as twentieth president, 246
Garner, John Nance "Cactus Jack,"
    430
    in election of 1932, 406
Garrison, William Lloyd, 149–150, 218
Garvey, Marcus, 363
Gates, General Horatio, 83, 88
General Court, 34
General Electric Company, 265, 368,
    369
"Generation gap," 517–520
Genet, Edmond, 122–123
George III, King, 51, 54, 89, 132
    on American intransigence, 63,
        64–65
    ascent and coronation of, 53
    in Declaration of Independence,
        73
    following Yorktown surrender, 92
Georgia, British campaigns in, 87, 88
German-Mexican alliance, 345–346
Germany
    post-World War I depression in,
        401, 402
    post-World War II division of,
        470–471
    rise to power of Hitler in, 424–425
    surrender of, 455–456
    in World War I, 342–344, 350–351,
        356, 358
    World War II campaigns of,
        430–436, 441–444
Gerry, Elbridge, in XYZ Affair, 128
Gettysburg, Battle of, 220–223
Gettysburg Address, 223, 224
Giap, General Vo Nguyen, 481

"GI Bill of Rights," 487–488
Gilded Age, 247, 265–270
  poverty and poor working
    conditions during, 284–285
Glass-Steagall Banking Act, 411
Glenn, John, 540
Global economy, Clinton
    administration and, 605–608
Glorious Revolution of 1688, 41–42
Gold
  American holdings of European,
    194
  backing of American currency
    with, 143, 295–296, 297–299,
    299–301
  discovery in California of,
    150–151, 170
  seven cities of, 17–23
  Spanish hunt for, 14, 15, 17–23
Gold Rush
  to Alaska, 299
  to California, 151
Gold standard, United States off, 547
Goldwater, Barry, 524, 566
  in election of 1964, 513–514
Gompers, Samuel, 278, 283, 290, 309
Gorbachev, Mikhail, 584–586,
  592–594
Gore, Albert
  in election of 1992, 598
  in election of 1996, 604
Grange, the, 295
Grant, Ulysses Simpson, 257
  as commander of Union armies,
    223–224
  Confederate surrender to, 228,
    230–231
  early Civil War victories of,
    212–213
  as eighteenth president, 236–238
  presidential election of, 234–236
Great Britain
  colonial conflicts between France
    and, 45–49
  colonial conflicts between
    Netherlands and, 38–42, 45
  colonial discontent with, 41–44,
    50–77
  colonization of America by, 24–49
  early victories in War of
    Independence by, 79–85
  fifteenth-century political turmoil
    in, 2
  first American settlements of,
    28–29, 29–38
  post-Revolution European
    problems of, 120–122
  post-Revolution relations between
    United States and, 131–133
  pre-World War II relations
    between America and,
    429–430
  War of 1812 with, 132–133
  World War II German assault on,
    431–432
"Great Compromiser, the," 134, 136
Great Depression, 394–421
  New Deal and, 406–421
  onset of, 398–405

World War II as ending, 439–441
Great Northern Railway, 249–254
Great Railroad Strike, 283
Great Society programs, 512–513
  Reagan's reforms of, 566–567
Greeley, Horace
  in election of 1864, 226
  Lincoln's letter to, 205–206, 216
Greenback Party, 242–243
"Greenbacks," 235
Greene, General Nathanael, 87, 88
"Green Mountain Boys," 68
Greensboro, North Carolina, 500
Grenada, Reagan administration and,
  574–575
Grenville, George, 53–56
Grenville, Sir Richard, 28–29
Groves, Brigadier General Leslie R.,
  457–458
Guadalupe Hidalgo, Treaty of,
  147–149
Guiteau, Charles, assassination of
  Garfield by, 246, 247

Haig, Alexander M., Jr., 552, 573, 574
Hale, Captain Nathan, 81
Halleck, General Henry, 214, 221,
  224
Hamilton, Alexander, 91, 124
  drafting of U.S. Constitution and,
    100–101
  in duel with Aaron Burr, 118
  as first Secretary of the Treasury,
    112–113, 114–120
  opposition to Jefferson by,
    120–122
Hamlin, Hannibal, 199
Hancock, John, 59, 61–63, 67, 76–77,
  110
Hanna, Mark, 300, 301, 309, 316
Hanseatic League, 4, 5
Harding, Warren Gamaliel
  death of, 388
  scandals in administration of, 387,
    388
  as twenty-ninth president,
    375–376, 378
Harlem Renaissance, 382–383
Harpers Ferry, West Virginia, John
  Brown's raid on, 195–196
Harriman, E. H., 249, 328–329
Harriman, W. Averell, 449, 454
Harrison, Benjamin, 291
  in election of 1892, 296–297
  as twenty-third president, 246,
    248–249
Harrison, William Henry
  as ninth president, 145
  Tecumseh and, 154
Hart, Gary, in election of 1984, 577
Hawaii
  American annexation of, 303, 309
  as incorporated territory, 317
  Japanese attack on Pearl Harbor
    in, 436–439
Hay, John, 307, 318
Hay-Bunau-Varilla Treaty, Panama
  Canal and, 319

Hayes, Rutherford Birchard
  as nineteenth president, 246
  presidential election of, 238–239
Health-care reforms, Clinton
  administration and, 599–600
Hearst, William Randolph, Spanish-
  American War and, 305–307
Helms, Jesse, in election of 1976, 558
Helsinki Accords, 555
Hemingway, Ernest, 361, 365, 428
Henry, Patrick, 50–51, 56–57, 101
Henry IV, King, 29
Henry VII, King, 2, 28
Henry VIII, King, 26, 27
Henry the Navigator, Prince, 8–10
Hepburn Act of 1906, 329
Hessian mercenaries, 81–84
Hickok, J. B. "Wild Bill," 260
Higher Education Act of 1972, 518
Hill, James, 249–254
"Hippies," 520, 524
Hirohito, Emperor, 437, 458, 461
Hiroshima, atomic bombardment of,
  458, 460–461
Hiss, Alger, 469, 472
Hitler, Adolf, 428, 454
  defeat of, 448–449
  imperialism of, 428–430
  and Nazi extermination camps,
    458–459
  rise to power of, 424–425
  Spanish Civil War and, 427
Hobart, Garret A., 314
  in election of 1896, 300
Ho Chih Minh, 460, 473, 480–482,
  508
  death of, 534
  formation of Vietnam by, 463
  Mao Zedong and, 482
Hollywood
  anti-Communist witch hunts in,
    469–472
  Communists in, 566
Holmes, Oliver Wendell, 213, 241
Holocaust, the, 458–459
Holy Roman Empire, 4–5
Home Owner Refinancing Act, 411
Home Owners' Loan Corporation,
  411
Homestead Act of 1862, 258–261
Homestead Steelworks, 287
Hooker, General Joseph "Fighting
  Joe," 220–221, 224
Hoover, Herbert Clark, 384, 465
  in election of 1932, 405–407
  presidential election of, 396–397
  as thirty-first president, 397–405
Hoover, J. Edgar, 360
"Hooverizing," 396
"Hoovervilles," 402–403
Hopkins, Harry, 411, 412, 413, 419,
  431
House of Burgesses, 50–51
House Un-American Activities
  Committee (HUAC), 469–472
Houston, General Sam, 145
Howe, General William, occupation
  of Philadelphia by, 84–85, 86
How the Other Half Lives (Riis), 284

Huerta, Victoriano, 341–342
Hughes, Charles Evans, 419
  in election of 1916, 344
Hughes, Langston, 382, 383
Hull, Cordell, 339, 436
Hull-House, 324, 325
Human rights legislation, under
  Carter, 561
Human rights manifesto, 555
Humphrey, Hubert Horatio
  in election of 1964, 514
  in election of 1968, 528–529
Hungary, anti-Communist
  insurrection in, 484, 485
Hussein, Saddam, 596–597
Hussey, Obed, 167

Ickes, Harold, 419, 430
"I Have a Dream" speech, 501–502
Immigration
  in demographic map of United
    States, 272–273
  at end of twentieth century,
    608–611
  during late nineteenth century,
    270–274, 274–277, 277–278
Immigration laws, 370–371
Immigration Reform and Control Act
  of 1965, 608–611
Income tax, 372
  initiation of, 339
  See also Taxation
Incorporated territories, 317
Independent Party, in election of
  1968, 527
Independent Treasury Act, 151
India, fifteenth-century European
  trade with, 7–8, 10
Indians. See Native Americans
Indian Wars, 254–258
Indulgences, 27
Industrial Revolution, 183
  cotton and, 161
  effect on midwestern states of,
    170–172
  effect on northern states of,
    164–168
Industrial Workers of the World
  (IWW), 360
  origin of, 290
Industry, rise of American, 262–291
Inflation
  during Carter administration, 560
  during 1970s, 553–554
  during 1980s, 582–583
  "Reaganomics" and, 570–572
Information Age, 589, 606, 610–611
Innocent VIII, Pope, 3
Intellectuals
  among American colonists, 52
  communism and, 407
International Atomic Energy Agency,
  480
International Bank for Reconstruction
  and Development, 459
International Monetary Fund, 459
International relations, Washington's
  views of, 127–128

Internet, 611
Interstate Highway Act, 489, 490
Interstate highways, 489, 490
"Intolerable Acts," 63–64, 65
"Invention factory" at Menlo Park, 264–265
"Iran-Contra" affair, 579–581
Iran hostage crisis, 562–563, 569
Iraq, American war against, 596–597
"Iron Curtain," 485
Ironworkers' Noontime, The (Anshutz), 262–263
Irreconcilables, 357–358
Isabella, Queen, 4
    Columbus and, 12–13, 14
Isolationism
    in post-World War I America, 359–361
    in pre-World War II America, 423–428
Israel, 546–547
    Reagan administration and, 573, 574
    threat of war between Egypt and, 484–486
    Truman's recognition of, 468
Italo-Ethiopian War, 426
Italy
    fifteenth-century political turmoil in, 3
    Mediterranean trade and, 8

Jackson, Andrew, 136
    first presidential election of, 138–139
    on James Buchanan, 192–193
    Native Americans and, 154
    in presidential election of 1824, 137–138
    second presidential election of, 142
    as seventh president, 138–139, 142–144
    victory in Battle of New Orleans by, 133
Jackson, Reverend Jesse, in election of 1984, 577
Jackson, Thomas J. "Stonewall," 207
    at Bull Run, 209
    death of, 221, 222–223
James, William, 307, 309–310
James I, King, 29–30
James II, King, 35, 41–42
Jamestown colony, 30–31
Japan
    Allied campaign against, 452–454
    American relations with, 341
    atomic bombardment of, 458, 460–461
    attack on Pearl Harbor by, 436–439
    declaration of war against United States by, 436–437
    Perry's expedition to, 187
    rising pre-World War II militarism of, 427
    World War II imperialism of, 436–439

Japanese-Americans, "relocation camps" for, 441
Jay, John, 63–64, 100, 119
    anti-French attitude of, 123
    as first Supreme Court Chief Justice, 114
    Treaty of Paris negotiated by, 92–94
Jay's Treaty, 123, 128, 129
Jazz, origins of, 382–383
Jazz Age, 364–393
Jefferson, Thomas, 63, 100, 132, 134
    accomplishments of, 97
    death of, 129
    Declaration of Independence composed by, 72–77
    during era of Confederation, 95–98
    as first Secretary of State, 112–113
    Jay's Treaty and, 123
    Lewis and Clark expedition authorized by, 168–169, 170
    as minister to France, 98, 101
    opposition to Hamilton by, 116–120, 120–122
    on slavery, 196
    as third president, 129–131
    turnpikes approved by, 174
Jews
    American isolationism and, 426
    German genocide of, 458–459
    Ku Klux Klan versus, 363
    persecution of German, 424
Jim Crow laws, 279, 340, 361, 362
Job Corps, 512
John Brown's Body (Benét), 191
John I, King, 8–9
John II, King, 10, 11–12
Johnson, Andrew
    in election of 1864, 226
    impeachment of, 234
    as seventeenth president, 231–235
Johnson, Lyndon Baines, 481, 485
    in election of 1960, 497
    following Kennedy assassination, 511
    in McCarthy censure, 479
    presidential election of, 513–514
    space program and, 540–541
    as thirty-sixth president, 510–526
Johnston, General Joseph E., 207, 209, 225, 228
Jones, Captain John Paul, 91
Jones Act, Philippine independence and, 318
Judicial review, establishment of, 131
Judiciary Act of 1789, 114
Jungle, The (Sinclair), 284–285, 286, 325

Kamikaze pilots, 452–453
Kansas-Nebraska Act, 190–192
    Lincoln on, 198–199
Kefauver, Estes, in election of 1956, 484
Kellogg-Briand Pact, 423
Kemp, Jack, in election of 1996, 604
Kennan, George F., 466–467

Kennedy, Edward, 498, 565, 568
Kennedy, Jacqueline Bouvier, 498, 511
Kennedy, John Fitzgerald, 482
    assassination of, 509–510
    in election of 1956, 484
    lunar landing and, 540
    in McCarthy censure, 479
    presidential election of, 496–499
    as thirty-fifth president, 499–510
Kennedy, Robert Francis, 479, 498, 524
    assassination of, 525–527
    in civil rights movement, 500–501
Kent State University, 535
Kerensky, Aleksandr, 346
Keynes, John Maynard, 412
Khmer Rouge, 555, 556
Khomeini, Ayatollah Ruhollah, 562–563, 569
Khrushchev, Nikita, 483–484, 485–486
    ascent to power of, 484
    Cuban missile crisis precipitated by, 503–505
    Fidel Castro and, 483
King, Martin Luther, Jr., 491–494, 500, 501–502, 515–517
    assassination of, 525–527
King George's War, 46–47
Kings Mountain, Battle of, 87–88
King William's War, 45
Kipling, Rudyard, 340
Kissinger, Henry, 547, 549, 552, 553
    détente and, 539–542
    "shuttle diplomacy" of, 555–556
    Vietnam War and, 533–534
Knights of Labor, 286, 287
"Know-Nothing" Party, 191–192
    in election of 1860, 199–200
Knox, Henry, as first Secretary of War, 112–113
Korean War, 472–476
Ku Klux Klan
    in election of 1924, 389
    open bigotry of, 370–371
    reorganization of, 362–363
    rise of, 237–238
Kuwait, Iraqi invasion of, 596–597

Labor
    immigration as providing, 270–274, 283
    organized, 277–278, 282–291, 413–415
    terrible nineteenth-century working conditions of, 283–291
Labor unrest
    in late nineteenth century, 282–283, 286–291
    during New Deal, 414–415
    in 1920s, 372
La Follette, Robert M. "Fighting Bob," 278, 329–332, 344
    in election of 1912, 335
    in election of 1924, 388, 389
    in election of 1936, 417
    Progressivism of, 325

La Guardia, Fiorello, 378
    during New York racial tensions, 442
Landon, Alfred, in election of 1936, 417
Land Ordinance of 1784, 97–98
Land Ordinance of 1785, 98
Latin America
    Alliance for Progress with, 503
    immigration from, 608–611
    United States in affairs of, 303–311, 319–322, 335, 340–342, 424–425, 482–483, 505, 574–575, 579–581, 595–596
League of Augsburg, 45
League of Nations, 356–359
    American refusal to join, 424
League of Nations Association, 430
Lebanon, Reagan administration and, 573, 574
LeCompton Constitution, 191
Lee, Richard Henry, 56, 71–72
    Articles of Confederation and, 94
Lee, Robert E., 207
    at Battle of Wilderness, 224
    at Chancellorsville, 221
    at Gettysburg, 221–223
    raid on Harpers Ferry and, 195
    at Second Battle of Bull Run, Antietam, and Fredericksburg, 214–215
    surrender of, 228, 230–231
Legislative Reorganization Act, 487
LeMay, General Curtis E.
    Berlin Airlift and, 470
    in election of 1968, 527
Lend-Lease Act of 1941, 427, 431–433
Lenin, Vladimir Ilyich, 356, 357, 360
"Letter from Birmingham City Jail" (King), 501, 516–517
"Letter from a Farmer in Pennsylvania to the Inhabitants of the British Colonies" (Dickinson), 58
Leutze, Emanuel, 82–83, 166–167
Levittown, 488, 530–531
Lewis, John L., 414
Lewis, Captain Meriwether, 168–169
Lewis, Sinclair, 379
Lewis and Clark expedition, 168–169, 170
Lexington, Battle of, 66–67
Liberty Bell, 77
Liberty Bonds, 352
"Liberty League," 153
Liberty Party, 145
Liberty Pole, 73–75
Liberty ships, 440
"Liberty Song, The" (Dickinson), 58
Liberty Tree, 73–75
Libya, Reagan administration and, 573–574
Liliuokalani, Queen, 303
Lincoln, Abraham, 193, 194, 318
    assassination of, 231, 232–233
    emancipation of slaves by, 216–218
    first presidential election of, 196–200

Gettysburg Address by, 223, 224
inauguration of, 202–204
second presidential election of,
    225–227
as sixteenth president, 200–209,
    211–231
Lincoln-Douglas debates, 196–197,
    198–199
Lindbergh, Charles Augustus,
    381–384, 431, 440
    in America First Committee, 428
Line of demarcation, 14
Livingston, Robert, 72, 76–77, 173
Lloyd George, David, 357
Locke, John, 42, 52, 73
Lodge, Henry Cabot, 357–358
Lodge, Henry Cabot, Jr., in election
    of 1960, 497
Log cabins, 169–170
London Company, 30–31
Long, Huey "Kingfish," in election of
    1936, 416–417
Longfellow, Henry Wadsworth, 66,
    196
Longstreet, General James, at Battle
    of Fredericksburg, 214–215
Lon Nol, General, 534, 555
Louisburg, 46–47
Louisiana Purchase, 126–127
    negotiation of, 129–131
Louis IX, King, 7
Louis XVI, King, 85, 86
    execution of, 120–121, 122
Lusitania, sinking of, 344, 345
Luther, Martin, 15, 27

McAdoo, William, in election of 1924,
    388, 389, 390
MacArthur, General Douglas, 405,
    452–453, 458
    in Korean War, 473–474
    removal of, 474
McCarthy, Eugene, in election of
    1968, 524–526
McCarthy, Joseph, anti-Communist
    witch hunts of, 472, 478–479
McCarthyism, 472, 474
    demise of, 478–479
    See also Anti-Communism
McClellan, General George B.
    as commander of Union armies,
        211–212, 214
    in election of 1864, 226
McClure's Magazine, 327, 365
McCormick, Cyrus, 167
    invention of reaper by, 165
McCormick Harvester Company,
    strike against, 287
McCormick Reaper Company,
    166–167
McDonald's, 489, 606
Macdonough, Thomas, War of 1812
    victory by, 132
McDowell, General Irvin, 209, 211
McGovern, George, 576
    in election of 1972, 548–549
McKinley, William, 318
    African-Americans and, 280–281

assassination of, 315
first presidential election of,
    299–302
second presidential election of,
    313–315
as twenty-fifth president, 302–311
McLaurin v. Oklahoma State Regents,
    490
McNamara, Robert S., 508, 522
McNary-Haugen Act, 398
McNary-Haugen Bill, 370, 409
Madison, James, 129
    Bill of Rights created by, 113–114
    drafting of U.S. Constitution and,
        100–101, 105–108
    as fourth president, 131–133
    opposition to Hamilton by,
        116–120
Magna Carta, 114
Maine, statehood of, 134
Maine, sinking of, 292–293, 304–307
"Malaise" speech, 560
Malcolm X, 502–503
    assassination of, 517
Manassas Junction, battle at, 209
Manhattan Project, 457–458
Manifest Destiny, 147
    at end of nineteenth century, 293
    Mexican War as, 149
    politics of, 186–192
    in post Civil War years, 245, 264
Manila, American capture of, 310–311
Manila Bay, Battle of, 307–309
Manufacturing
    during 1990s, 605–607
    in northern states, 135–139,
        164–168
Mao Zedong
    in Communist struggle for China,
        464
    Ho Chih Minh and, 482
    Nixon's meeting with, 539–542
Marbury v. Madison case, 131
"March to the Sea," 225, 227
Marconi, Guglielmo, 384
Marshall, General George C., 445,
    466–467
    Berlin Airlift and, 470
Marshall, John, 128, 154
Marshall, Thurgood, 491, 597
Marshall Plan, 466–467
Marx, Karl, 152–153
Marxism, labor unrest and, 283
Maryland
    Articles of Confederation and, 95
    colonization of, 35
Mason-Dixon Line, 183
Massachusetts Bay Colony
    charter of, 56
    founding of, 34
Massachusetts Government Act, 63
Mayaguez incident, 556
Mayflower, voyage of, 34
Meade, General George G., 224
    at Gettysburg, 221–223
Meat Inspection Act, 286
Meatpacking industry, 170–171,
    284–285
    awful working conditions in, 286

Medicaid
    Clinton administration and,
        599–600
    enactment of, 512
Medicare
    Clinton administration and,
        599–600
    enactment of, 512
    proposed cutbacks in, 570–571
Mediterranean trade, 7–8
"Melting pot," United States as,
    288–289, 609–611
Mencken, H. L., 379, 392
Mercury program, 540
Methodists, 140
Mexican Empire, 144–145
Mexican War, 147–149, 186
    aftermath of, 151–153
Mexico
    alliance between Germany and,
        345–346
    origin of war with, 146
    Spanish conquest of, 15–17
    war between Texas and, 144–145
    Wilson's campaigns in, 340–342
Mexico City, destruction of Aztec
    capital at, 16
Mickey Mouse, 379–381
Midway Island, Battle of, 441–444
Military-industrial complex
    during 1930s, 426
    during 1950s, 476
    defense systems of, 506–507
    Eisenhower's warning against, 495
    World War I origin of, 352–355
Militia Act, 219
Miller, Arthur, 469–472, 488
Miller, William, in election of 1964,
    513
Mint Act, 116
Minutemen, 66–68
"Missile gap," 504, 540
Mississippi River
    discovery of, 17, 20–21
    French exploration of, 46
    Jay's Treaty and, 123
    in Treaty of Paris negotiations, 93
Missouri Compromise, 134, 156, 202
    repeal of, 190–191
    unconstitutionality of, 194
Molasses Act, 54
"Molly Maguires," 282–283
Mondale, Walter, 563
    in election of 1976, 558
    in election of 1984, 577–578
Monopolies, nineteenth-century
    growth of, 268–270
Monroe, James, 154
    as fifth president, 133
Monroe Doctrine, 133, 134
Montezuma, 15
Montgomery, General Bernard, 445,
    446
Moon, landing on, 540–541
Moon, Reverend Sun Myung, 584
Moral Majority, 568
Morgan, John Pierpont "J. P.,"
    328–329, 340
    banking industry and, 269–270

in Panic of 1893, 297
    panic of 1907 and, 332–333
Morison, Samuel Eliot, 18, 339,
    399–400
Mormonism
    founding of, 140
    settlement of Utah and, 151, 170
Morse, Samuel F. B., telegraph
    invented by, 180
Motion pictures
    invention of, 379–381
    sound in, 381
    by Thomas Edison, 299
Mott, Lucretia, 178–179
Moynihan, Daniel Patrick, 289, 545
"Muckraking" journalism, 327
Murfreesboro, Battle of, 214
Muscovy Company, 29
Muskie, Edmund, in election of 1972,
    548
Muslims, struggle between Christians
    and, 3–4
Mussolini, Benito, 424
    imperialism of, 429
    removal of, 446
My Lai massacre, 538

Nagasaki, atomic bombardment of,
    458, 461
Nasser, Gamal Abdel, 482, 484
Nast, Condé, 378–379
Nast, Thomas, 208–209
Nation, Carrie, 373
National Aeronautics and Space
    Administration (NASA), 540
National Association for the
    Advancement of Colored
    People (NAACP), 362, 500
    founding of, 281
National Broadcasting Company
    (NBC), 384
National Credit Corporation, 402
National debt, U.S.
    initial, 116
    massive 1980s increase in,
        571–572
National Farmers' Alliance, 295
National Industrial Recovery Act, 411
National Labor Relations Act of 1935,
    413, 414
National Labor Relations Board
    (NLRB), 413, 414
National Monuments Act, 329,
    330–331
National Negro Business League, 280
National Organization for Women
    (NOW), 518–519
National Progressive Republican
    League, 335
National Recovery Administration
    (NRA), 411
    unconstitutionality of, 416
National Republican Party, 142
National Security Act, 467
National Socialism. See Nazi Party
National Turnpike, 174
National Woman Suffrage Association,
    372, 373

National Women's Party, 373, 374
National Women's Rights Convention, 178–179
Native Americans, 18–19, 51–52
  buffalo and, 254
  Columbus's trade with, 14
  in early nineteenth-century United States, 154–155
  forced migrations of, 154, 155
  at Jamestown colony, 30–31
  Lewis and Clark expedition and, 168–169
  map of, 19
  at Pennsylvania, 38
  at Plymouth colony, 34
  Spanish treatment of, 15–17, 18
  subduing of, 242, 254–258
Nativism, 370–371
Nature Conservancy, 543
Navarre Plan, 480–481
Navigation Acts, 40
  colonial violations of, 42–43, 54–56
Nazi extermination camps, 458–459
Nazi Party
  post-World War I gains of, 402
  rise to power of, 424–425
Netherlands
  African slave trade and, 31, 32
  colonial conflicts between England and, 38–42, 45, 61
  colonization of America and, 25–26, 31–34
  war between England and, 92
Neutrality acts of 1935, 426–427
  effects of, 428–430
New Amsterdam
  colonization of, 35, 39–40
  See also New York City
New Deal, 406–421, 476
  end of, 418–421
  unconstitutionality of, 416
New England
  African slave trade and, 32–33
  colonization of, 31–34
  fishing industry and, 43
  timber industry in, 43
  whaling industry in, 43–44
New England Confederation, 40
"New Freedom," 338–340
New Frontier, 499, 510
New Jersey
  British control of, 81
  colonization of, 35
  War of Independence campaigns around, 86
New Jersey Plan, 105, 108
Newlands Reclamation Act, 330
New Netherlands Company, 39
New Orleans, 126–127
  Battle of, 133
  Farragut's capture of, 212–214
  origins of jazz in, 382–383
New School for Social Research, 392–393
"New South," rise of, 244–245
New York, 46, 77
New York City
  as financial center, 369

French refusal to assault, 87
  as haven for immigrants, 273–274
  War of Independence campaigns around, 85, 86
  See also New Amsterdam
Niagara Movement, 281
Nicaragua, 574, 579–581
Nicholas II, Czar, 346
Nicholas V, Pope, 8
Nimitz, Admiral Chester, 444, 452
Nineteenth Amendment, 355, 372–374
  effect on election of 1920, 375
Nisei, "relocation camps" for, 441
Nixon, Richard Milhous, 481, 524, 590–591
  in Alger Hiss case, 469, 472
  in election of 1952, 475
  in election of 1960, 497–498
  first presidential election of, 524–529, 530–531
  presidential election of, 524–529
  second presidential election of, 547–549
  as thirty-seventh president, 531–552
  Watergate scandal and, 549–553
Nixon Doctrine, 539
NORAD, 506–507
Noriega, Manuel, 595
Normandy, Allied landing at, 446–448, 450–451
North, Lord, 59, 60–63, 64–65, 89
  on British surrender at Yorktown, 92
North American Free Trade Agreement (NAFTA), 607–608, 609
North Atlantic Treaty Organization (NATO), formation of, 465, 467
North Conciliatory Resolution, 65–67
Northern Democrats, 219–220
Northern states
  after Civil War, 240–261
  early nineteenth-century economy of, 134–139, 159–160, 164–168
  Fugitive Slave Law and, 183–185
  post-Revolution financial considerations of, 117–118
  See also Civil War
Northwest Ordinance of 1787, 98–99
Nova Scotia, 45, 46
Nugent, Thomas, in election of 1892, 296–297
"Nullification" doctrine, 138, 139, 142
Nye Committee, 426

Occupational Safety and Health Administration (OSHA), 545
Office of Economic Opportunity, 542
Ohio Valley
  American colonies in, 56
  settlement of, 47, 49, 63
Oil embargo of 1973, 546–547
Old South, the, 160–164
Omaha Beach, 448, 450–451
Omnibus Bill, defeat of, 156–157
O'Neill, Thomas P. "Tip," 559, 578

Open Door Policy, 318
Operation Desert Shield, 596–597
Operation Overlord, 446–448, 450–451
Oppenheimer, J. Robert, 458, 478
"Order of American Knights," 219
Ordinance of Nullification, 142
Oregon Territory, border dispute with Canada over, 145, 146
Oregon Trail, 170
Organization of American States, 503
Organization of Petroleum Exporting Countries (OPEC), 546–547
Orient
  fifteenth-century European trade with, 6–10
  search for passage to, 29
  search for westward passage to, 28
Oswald, Lee Harvey, assassination of John Kennedy by, 509–510
Ottawa League, 54–56
Ottoman Empire, spread of, 3–4

Pacifism, inspired by World War I, 355
Pact of Paris, 423
Pahlevi, Shah Mohammed Reza, 482
Paine, Thomas, 71, 101
  on George Washington, 111–112
Palestine Liberation Organization (PLO), 601
  Reagan administration and, 573
Panama, Bush administration and, 595–596
Panama Canal, construction of, 319–322
Pan-American Exposition of 1901, 315
Panic of 1893, 269, 297–299
Panic of 1907, 332–333
Paris Peace Conference, aftermath of World War I and, 356–359
Parker, Alton B., in election of 1904, 328–329
Parks, Rosa, 494
Parliament, British
  American colonial discontent with, 64–66
  on American intransigence, 63
  support for American colonies in, 57–59
Party politics, Washington's warning against, 127
  See also Communist Party; Democratic Party; Federalist Party; Free Soil Party; "Know-Nothing" Party; Progressive Party; Prohibitionist Party; Republican Party; Socialist Party; Whig Party
Party system, origins of American, 117–118, 124
Patton, General George S., Jr., 405, 445, 446, 448
Paul, Alice, 373, 374
Peace Corps, 498, 499, 503
Pearl Harbor, Japanese attack on,

436–439
Pendleton, George H.
  in election of 1864, 226
  in election of 1868, 235
Penn, William, 35–38
Pennsylvania
  colonization of, 35–38
  War of Independence campaigns in, 86
  Whiskey Rebellion in, 118–119, 120
Pentagon Papers, 538
People's Liberation Army, 464
People's Party
  in election of 1892, 295–296
  end of, 302
Peres, Shimon, 601
Perestroika, 585–586
Perkins, Frances, 397, 415
Perot, H. Ross, 608
  in election of 1992, 598–599
  in election of 1996, 604
Perry, Commodore Matthew, expedition to Japan by, 187
Pershing, General John J. "Black Jack"
  Mexican campaign of, 342
  in World War I, 348–352
Persian Gulf War, 595–597
Philadelphia
  British occupation of, 84–85
  Constitutional Convention at, 100–101, 102–111
  second Continental Congress in, 68–77
  War of Independence campaigns around, 86
"Philadelphia plan," 544–545
Philippines
  Allied campaign to retake, 452–453
  American annexation of, 307–311
  as American territory, 316–318
  American withdrawal from, 425
  MacArthur's departure from, 453
Pierce, Franklin
  as fourteenth president, 187–191
  presidential election of, 186–187
"Pilgrims," colonization of New England by, 31–34
Pinckney, Charles, in XYZ Affair, 128
Pinckney, Thomas, 123, 124
Pinckney's treaty, 123
Pitt, William, the Elder, 48, 57–59
Pitt, William, the Younger, 120
Plantation slavery, 30, 31, 32–33, 158–164
  end of, 236–237
Platt Amendment, Cuban independence and, 318–319
Plattsburgh Bay, Battle of, 132
Plessy v. Ferguson, 279
Plymouth Company. *See* Virginia Company of Plymouth
Pocahontas, 31
Polk, James Knox, 148
  as eleventh president, 145–149, 151–152
  on James Buchanan, 192–193

Polo, Marco, 6, 7
Pol Pot, 555
Pontiac, Chief, 48, 54–56
Poor People's Campaign, 528
Pope, General John, at Second Battle
    of Bull Run, 214
Populist Party
    in election of 1896, 301
    in election of 1900, 314
    silver standard endorsed by, 298
    See also People's Party
Portugal
    African slave trade and, 9–10, 32
    in fifteenth-century exploration,
        8–10
    line of demarcation and, 14
Postal system, founding of, 85
Potsdam, Allied conference at, 457
Poverty, Johnson's programs to
    alleviate, 512–513
Powell, General Colin, 596–597
Powhatan Confederacy, 31
Prester John, 7
Proclamation of 1763, 56
Progressive Party
    in election of 1924, 389
    in election of 1948, 468
    formation of, 335
Progressivism, 313–314, 322–325
    after World War I, 372
Prohibition, 372, 376–378
Prohibition Bureau, 377
Prohibitionist Party
    Eighteenth Amendment and, 376
    in election of 1892, 296–297
    in election of 1900, 314
    in election of 1904, 329
    in election of 1908, 334
    in election of 1912, 338
Promontory Point, Utah, first
    transcontinental railroad
    completed at, 250
Protestantism
    colonization of New England and,
        31–34
    Reformation and, 27
    struggle between Catholicism and,
        26, 27, 39–40
Public Works Administration, 411,
    419
Puerto Rico
    American annexation of, 307–309
    as unincorporated territory, 317
Pulitzer, Joseph, Spanish-American
    War and, 305–307
Pullman Palace Car Company, strike
    against, 287–290
Pure Food and Drug Act, 286
Puritans, 27
    in British government, 39–40
    colonization of Massachusetts and
        New Hampshire by, 34
    economic rivalry between Dutch
        and, 40

Qaddafi, Colonel Muammar al-,
    573–574, 575
Quakers, colonization of

Pennsylvania by, 35–38
Quarantine speech by FDR, 427
Quartering Act, 63
Quayle, J. Danforth "Dan," in election
    of 1988, 590
Quebec, 45
    General Wolfe at, 49
Queen Anne's War, 45–46
Quetzalcoatl, 15
Quotas, immigration, 277–278, 608

Rabin, Yitzhak, 601
Racial rioting, 514–517
Racial segregation
    in late nineteenth century,
        279–282
    during 1950s, 490–495
    in post-World War I America,
        361–363
    under Wilson, 339–340
    during World War II, 442–443
Racism
    in Birth of a Nation, 379
    in 1920s America, 370–371
    in 1950s America, 490–495
    in 1960s America, 499–503
    in sports, 276
Radical Republicans, 231, 234–235
    in election of 1864, 225–227
Radio
    invention of, 384
    national elections broadcast on,
        390
Radio Corporation of America (RCA),
    384
Railroad Administration, U.S., 355
Railroads, 176–181, 187
    failures among, 297
    farmers and, 258–259
    map of growth of, 252–253
    nineteenth-century growth of,
        290–291
    post-Civil War growth of, 242
    rise of transcontinental, 249–254
    strikes against, 283, 287–290
    World War I government control
        of, 355
Randolph, Edmund
    drafting of U.S. Constitution and,
        105–108
    as first Attorney General, 112
Rankin, Jeanette, 374, 437–439
    pacifism of, 355
Ray, James Earl, assassination of
    Martin Luther King, Jr., by, 526
Reagan, Ronald Wilson, 395–396, 527
    assassination attempt on, 569–570
    in election of 1976, 557–558
    first presidential election of,
        564–570
    as fortieth president, 569–587
    second presidential election of,
        575–578
"Reaganomics," 566, 570–572, 587
Reaper, 165, 167
Reconstruction Acts, 234
Reconstruction Era, 230–239
Reconstruction Finance Corporation

(RFC), 402
"Red Menace," 468–472
Reformation, 2, 26, 27
Reid, Whitelaw, in election of 1892,
    296–297
Relief and Rehabilitation
    Adminitration, 459
Religion
    demographic map of United
        States, 272–273
    in founding of America, 27, 31–38
    fundamentalist, 370
    new sects in, 140–141
"Relocation camps," for Japanese-
    Americans, 441
Republican Party, 287, 387
    Clinton administration and,
        603–604
    in election of 1860, 196–200
    in election of 1864, 225–227
    in election of 1876, 238–239
    in election of 1892, 296–297
    in election of 1896, 299–302
    in election of 1900, 313–314
    in election of 1904, 328–329
    in election of 1908, 333–334
    in election of 1912, 337–338
    in election of 1920, 375–376
    in election of 1924, 388–391
    in election of 1928, 396–397
    in election of 1932, 405–407
    in election of 1936, 415–418
    in election of 1940, 430–431
    in election of 1948, 468
    in election of 1952, 475–476, 477
    in election of 1956, 484, 486
    in election of 1960, 497–498
    in election of 1964, 513–514
    in election of 1968, 524–529
    in election of 1972, 547–549
    in election of 1976, 557–558
    in election of 1980, 566–570
    in election of 1984, 575–578
    in election of 1988, 590–591
    in election of 1992, 598–599
    at end of New Deal, 420–421
    gold standard favored by, 297–298
    original, 119–120, 122, 127–131
    origin of modern, 192
    in post-Civil War years, 245–249
    during World War I, 353–354
Reservations, for Native Americans,
    256–257
Revere, Paul, 60–61, 62–63, 66
Richmond, Virginia, Union attack on,
    209
Rights of Man, The (Paine), 111–112
Riis, Jacob, 277, 284–285
Roads, in fifteenth-century Europe, 5
Roanoke colony, 28–29
Roaring Twenties, 365
"Robber barons," transcontinental
    railroads and, 249–254
Rockefeller, John D., 266, 267–268,
    291, 328–329
Rockefeller, Nelson, 514, 527
    in election of 1976, 557–558
    as vice president, 557
Rock and roll, 492–493, 520

Roe v. Wade, 518–519, 567
Rogers, Will, 391, 397, 407
Rommel, General Erwin "Desert Fox,"
    444–445
Roosevelt, Franklin Delano, 391, 393,
    397
    death of, 454–459
    in election of 1920, 375
    first presidential election of,
        405–407
    fourth presidential election of, 454
    1933 inaugural address of,
        407–409
    second presidential election of,
        415–418
    third presidential election of,
        430–431
    as thirty-second president,
        407–421, 422–461
    during World War I, 352–353
    during World War II, 422–461
    at Yalta, 449
Roosevelt, Theodore, 278, 301,
    312–313
    African-Americans and, 280–281
    and conservation movement, 329,
        330–331
    death of, 375
    in election of 1900, 314
    in election of 1904, 328–329
    in election of 1912, 335, 337–338
    in election of 1916, 344–345
    and founding of Progressive Party,
        335
    at premiere of The Melting Pot,
        288–289
    in Spanish-American War, 306–307
    as twenty-sixth president,
        316–333
Root, Elihu, 278, 301, 318, 319
"Rosie the Riveter," 440–441
Rough Riders, in Spanish-American
    War, 306–307
Round ships, 5–6
Royal Africa Company, African slave
    trade and, 32
Rusk, Dean, 505, 508, 522
Russia
    American pre-World War II
        relations with, 424
    beginning of post-World War II
        problems with, 448–452
    Clinton administration and,
        601–602
    collapse of communism in,
        591–595
    Communist takeover of, 356, 357
    Cuban missile crisis and, 504–505
    détente with, 539–542
    Eisenhower's plan to contain, 480
    as "evil empire," 569, 572–573
    in global economy, 606
    and Nixon's China trip, 539–542
    perestroika in, 585–586
    purchase of Alaska from, 231
    space program of, 540
    World War II invasion by
        Germany of, 432
    See also Cold War

Russian Revolution, 346
    African-Americans and, 362

Sacajawea, 168
Sadat, Anwar el-, 560, 562
St. Valentine's Day Massacre, 399
Salt manufacturing, 43–44
San Jacinto, Battle of, 145
San Juan Hill, capture of, 306–307
San Salvador, Columbus's landing on,
    14
Santa Anna, General, 144–145, 147
    capture of, 145
Saratoga, Battle of, 83, 85
Savannah, Georgia, capture of, 87, 88
Scabs, 287
Scalawags, 236
Schwarzkopf, General Norman H.,
    596–597
Scopes "Monkey Trial," 370
Scott, Dred, 193–194
Scott, General Winfield, 147, 186–187,
    207
Secession, of southern states, 200–209
Securities Exchange Act, 411
Securities and Exchange Commission,
    411
Sedition Act of 1918, 355
Selma, Alabama, voting-rights march
    in, 515
Senate, U.S.
    creation of, 108, 109–110
    refusal to ratify Treaty of Versailles
        by, 357–358
Seneca Falls Convention, 178–179
Serbia, Clinton administration and,
    602–603
Seventh Day Adventists, 140
Seven Years' War, 47–49
Sewall, Arthur, in election of 1896,
    301
Seward, William, 156, 199, 200, 201,
    202, 207
    purchase of Alaska by, 231
Shays' Rebellion, 98, 99, 101
Sheppard, Alan B., Jr., 540
Sheridan, General Philip, 154, 211,
    212
Sherman, Roger, 72, 76–77
Sherman, General William Tecumseh,
    212, 224
    and election of 1864, 226
    employment of slaves by, 216
    in Indian Wars, 256
    scorched-earth approach to war
        of, 224–225, 227–228
Sherman Antitrust Act, 268, 328, 332,
    334
Shiloh Church, battle at, 212–213
Shipbuilding, 44
Ships, voyaging to America aboard,
    24–25
Shriver, Sargent, 498
    in election of 1972, 548–549
Shultz, George, 574, 580
"Shuttle diplomacy," 555–556
Sierra Club, 543
"Silent Majority," 528–529

Silver, backing of American currency
    with, 295–296, 297–299,
    299–301
Sinclair, Upton, 284–285, 286, 325
Sioux, defeat of Custer by, 256–257
Sirhan, Sirhan, assassination of Robert
    Kennedy by, 526, 527
Sitting Bull, Chief, 18, 257–258
Sixteenth Amendment, 372
Slave auctions, 162–163
"Slave power," 194
Slaves
    Civil War and, 215–220
    Compromise of 1850 and, 156–157
    as "contraband of war," 216
    cotton and, 159–161
    demands for freedom for, 149–151
    in District of Columbia, 153–156
    Lincoln on, 197–199
    Manifest Destiny and, 147
    in mid-nineteenth-century politics,
        182–209
    on Virginia tobacco plantations,
        30, 31, 32–33
    women's suffrage and, 178–179
    See also Plantation slavery
Slave states, Congressional
    representation of, 108–109
Slave trade, 32–33
    early attempts to abolish, 97–98
    Jefferson and, 77, 97–98
    origin of, 9–10
    western spread of, 188–189
Smallpox, Native Americans and, 18
Smith, Adam, 53
Smith, Alfred E., 406
    in election of 1924, 389–390
    in election of 1928, 396–397
Smith, Captain John, 30–31
Smith, Joseph, 140
Smoot-Hawley Tariff, 401
Smuggling, by American colonists,
    43, 54, 56
Socialism, labor unrest and, 283
Socialist Labor Party, in election of
    1892, 296–297
Socialist Party, 328
    in election of 1900, 314
    in election of 1908, 333–334
    in election of 1912, 338
    in election of 1916, 345
    in election of 1920, 375
    in election of 1924, 389
    in election of 1932, 407
    origins of, 325
    on World War I, 354, 355
Social Security, proposed cutbacks in,
    570–571
Social Security Act of 1935, 415
Sons of Liberty, 56, 57, 60, 73–75
    "Boston Tea Party" and, 61–63, 64
South America, Spanish conquest of,
    16–17
Southeast Asia, countries in, 521
Southeast Asia Treaty Organization
    (SEATO), 481
Southern Alliance, 295
Southern Christian Leadership
    Conference (SCLC), 500, 515

Southern Democratic Party, 187, 241
    in election of 1876, 238–239
    Kennedy and, 499
Southern states
    after Civil War, 240–261
    during Great Depression, 403–405
    post-Revolution financial
        considerations of, 117–118
    secession of, 200–209
    slavery issue and early nineteenth-
        century economy of,
        134–139, 144, 158–164,
        180–181, 182–209
    See also Civil War; Confederate
        States of America;
        Reconstruction Era
Soviet Union. See Russia
Space program, 540–541
Spain
    African slave trade and, 32–33
    annexation of Florida from, 133
    Civil War in, 426–427
    Columbus and, 12
    conflict between Portugal and, 8
    Cuban independence from,
        298–299
    exploration and conquest of the
        Americas by, 14–23
    fifteenth-century political turmoil
        in, 4, 26
    line of demarcation and, 14
    loss of Texas by, 144–145
    Louisiana Purchase and, 129–131
    support of American
        independence by, 85, 92
    trade negotiations between post-
        Revolution United States
        and, 123
    war between United States and,
        303–311
Spanish-American War, 303–311
    aftermath of, 313–315
Spanish Armada, destruction of, 29
Spanish Civil War, American neutrality
    in, 426–427
Spanish Main, the, 14–23
Sparkman, John, in election of 1952,
    475
Speakeasies, 376–377
Speakeasy Era, 365
Spices, Mediterranean trade in, 7–8
Spotsylvania, Battle of, 224
Stalin, Joseph, 424, 446, 448, 450,
    454, 470–471
    death of, 476
    and German invasion of Russia,
        444–445
    at Potsdam, 457–458
    at Yalta, 449
Stalingrad, Battle of, 444–445
Stamp Act
    passage of, 56–57
    propaganda against, 51
    repeal of, 57–58
Stamp Act Congress, 57, 80
Standard Oil Company, 291
    business practices of, 327
    origin of, 267–268
Stanton, Edwin M., 234

Stanton, Elizabeth Cady, 178–179,
    372, 373
"Star Wars" defenses, 585–586
States
    federal government and, 109–110
    War of Independence debts of,
        116–118
States' rights, politics of, 138–139
Steamboats, 172–176
Steel industry, 265–267
    during 1990s, 605–606
Steel plow, invention of, 165
Stephens, Alexander H., 200
    as vice president of Confederate
        States, 202
Stevenson, Adlai E., in election of
    1892, 296–297
Stevenson, Adlai E., III, 472
    in election of 1952, 475, 477
    in election of 1956, 484, 486
Storyville, 382
Stowe, Harriet Beecher, 185
Strategic Air Command, 506
Strategic Arms Limitation Talks (SALT
    II), 555, 560–561
Strategic Defense Initiative (SDI),
    585–586
Strikes, during late nineteenth
    century, 287–290
Stuart, J. E. B.
    death of, 211
    raid on Harpers Ferry and, 195
    at Second Battle of Bull Run and
        Fredericksburg, 214–215
Student Nonviolent Coordinating
    Committee (SNCC), 500
Suburbs
    in post-World War II America,
        462–463, 488–490
    rise of, 368
Suez War, 482, 484–486
Suffrage, women's right of, 178–179,
    355, 372–374
Sugar Act, 56, 57–58
Supply-side economics, 566
Supreme Court, U.S.
    on American territories, 317
    creation of, 109–110
    Dred Scott case and, 193–194
    judicial review by, 131
    Nixon's packing of, 545–546
    Roosevelt's attempts to pack,
        419
    women's rights in 1920s and, 374
Sutter, John, discovery of gold on
    property of, 151

Taft, Robert, 430, 465, 467, 475, 476
Taft, William Howard
    in election of 1912, 335, 337–338
    presidential election of, 332–333
    as Progressive, 325
    as Supreme Court Chief Justice,
        332–333
    as "trustbuster," 328
    as twenty-seventh president,
        333–335
Taft-Hartley Act, 487

Talleyrand, Charles Maurice de, 128–129
Tammany Hall, corruption of, 247, 325
Tammany Society, 119
Taney, Roger Brooke, *Dred Scott* decision by, 193–194
Tarbell, Ida M., 327
"Tariff of Abominations," 137
Tariffs
  affecting southern states, 137, 138, 142
  agricultural, 398
  on American colonies, 53–57, 58–59
  in early twentieth century, 334, 338–339
  to insulate against foreign competition, 401
  "Kennedy round" of, 499
  retaliatory, 401
Taxation
  of American colonies, 53–57, 57–66, 71, 79–80
  under Articles of Confederation, 99
  Bush administration and, 590
  Eisenhower's reforms of, 476
  1980s' reforms of, 571
  Reagan's reforms of, 566
  for Social Security, 415
  under U.S. Constitution, 110
  of whiskey, 118–119, 120
  See also Income tax
Tax Reduction Act of 1964, 512
Taylor, Zachary, 147, 187
  Mexican campaign of, 146
  as twelfth president, 153
Teapot Dome scandal, 388
Tecumseh, 154
Telegraph, 176–181
Telephone, invention of, 265, 384
Television
  in *Apollo 11* mission, 541
  during 1950s, 488
  political uses of, 475, 498, 558, 562–563
Teller, Henry, in election of 1896, 300
Tennessee Valley Authority (TVA), 411–412
Tenochtitlán, 15
Texas
  annexation of, 145–146
  Compromise of 1850 and, 153–156
  recognition of Republic of, 144–145
  war between Mexico and, 144–145
Textile industry
  in northern states, 165–168, 169
  in southern states, 135–139, 144, 158–164
Thirteenth Amendment, 234, 372–373
Thoreau, Henry David, 140–141, 147, 168
Thurmond, Strom
  in election of 1948, 468
  in election of 1968, 527
Tilden, Samuel
  in election of 1876, 238–239
  in election of 1876, 246

Timber industry, 43, 44
Tobacco
  as first American export, 30, 31
  trade with Great Britain in, 53
Tocqueville, Alexis de, 172–173
Tom Thumb locomotive, 176–177
Tonkin Gulf Resolution, 535
Tories, 80, 81
Townshend, Charles, 58–59
Townshend Acts, 58–59, 60–61
Trade
  British discrimination against American, 122–123
  British strangulation of colonial, 42–44
  fifteenth-century increase in, 5
  Jay's Treaty and, 123
  transatlantic routes for, 41
  between United States and Europe in early nineteenth century, 131
Trail of Tears, 154
Transcendentalists, 140–141
Transcontinental railroads, rise of, 249–254
Transportation system, 172–176, 176–181
  See also Canals; Interstate highways; Railroads
Transylvania, 54–55
Treaty of Ghent, War of 1812 ended by, 133
Treaty of Guadalupe Hidalgo, Mexican War ended by, 147–149
Treaty of Paris
  French and Indian War ended by, 48, 53
  Spanish-American War ended by, 309, 316–317
  War of Independence ended by, 92–94
Treaty of Ryswick, 45
Treaty of Tordesillas, 14
Treaty of Utrecht, 46
Treaty of Versailles, 357–358
  Hitler's violation of, 428
Triangle Shirtwaist Company, fire at, 325, 326
Truman, Harry S, 266, 411
  in election of 1944, 454
  on Nixon, 532
  at Potsdam, 457–458
  presidential election of, 467–468
  as thirty-third president, 454–458, 463–476, 486–488
  during World War I, 359
Truman Doctrine, 465–466, 468–469
Trumbull, John, 76–77, 90, 114–115
Trusts, nineteenth-century growth of, 267–269, 291
Tubman, Harriet, 185
Tuner, Major General William H., in Berlin Airlift, 470–471
Turks
  Mediterranean trade and, 8
  wars of conquest by, 3–4
Turner, Nat, rebellion of, 149, 150
Turnpikes, 172–176

Tuskegee Normal and Industrial Institute, 282
Twain, Mark (Samuel Langhorne Clemens), 244, 307
Tweed, William Marcy "Boss," 238
Tydings-McDuffie Act, 425
Tyler, John, 202
  as tenth president, 145–146

U-boats (Unterseebooten), 344, 345
"Uncle Tomism," 237
  of Booker T. Washington, 280
Uncle Tom's Cabin (Stowe), 185
Unconstitutionality, 109
Underground Railroad, 184–185
Underwood-Simmons Tariff, 338–339
Unincorporated territories, 317
Union Party, 231
  in election of 1864, 226
Unions, 282–291
  immigrant labor and, 277–278
  NAFTA and, 607–608
  during New Deal, 413–415
  origins of, 263–264
Union of Soviet Socialist Republics (U.S.S.R.), origin of, 357
  See also Russia
United Mine Workers, 263, 414
  Theodore Roosevelt and strike by, 328
United Nations
  Korean War and, 472–476
  origins of, 459–461
United States
  under Articles of Confederation, 94–101
  British recognition of, 93
  during Civil War, 210–231
  during Cold War, 462–495, 539–542
  declaration of war against Japan by, 437–439
  as emerging global power, 368–370
  emerging western hemisphere leadership of, 133
  at end of nineteenth century, 292–311
  during first half of nineteenth century, 126–157
  foreign immigration to, 270–278
  formation of, 78–101
  during fourth quarter of nineteenth century, 240–261, 262–291
  French recognition of and alliance with, 86–87
  during Great Depression, 394–407
  during Jazz Age, 364–393
  in Korean War, 472–476
  map of defense systems of, 506–507
  mid-nineteenth-century territories of, 188–189
  under New Deal, 406–421
  1950s Vietnam involvement of, 480–482

during 1960s, 496–529
during 1970s, 530–563
during 1980s, 564–587
during 1990s, 588–611
occupation of Latin American countries by, 319–320
post-Civil War reconstruction of, 230–239
post-Revolution financial troubles of, 114–118
prior to Civil War, 182–209
space program of, 540–541
in Spanish-American War, 292–293, 303–311
after Spanish-American War, 312–335
Spanish exploration of southern, 17–23
territories governed by, 317
in twenty-first century, 610–611
war between Mexico and, 147–149
westward expansion of, 97–99, 134–135, 138–139, 144–145, 147–149, 166–167, 168–181
during World War I, 336–363
after World War I, 367–372
during World War II, 422–461
World War I neutrality of, 342–346
See also America; American colonies
U.S. Steel
  antitrust action against, 334
  Kennedy and, 499
  origins of, 266–267, 269
Urbanism, during 1920s, 367–372
U-2 incident, 483–484

Valley Forge, Pennsylvania, Washington at, 84–85
Van Buren, Martin, 137, 139, 142, 153, 156
  as eighth president, 143–145
  Native Americans and, 154
Vandalia, 54–55
Vera Cruz
  Battle of, 147
  Marines in, 341–342
Vergennes, Charles Gravier, Count de
  support of War of Independence by, 85–87
  in Treaty of Paris negotiations, 93–94
Vespucci, Amerigo, 14
Vicksburg, capture of, 223
Viet Cong, 508, 521–522, 525
Viet Minh, 463, 480–482
Vietnam
  Communist takeover of, 480–482
  division into North and South, 481
  Kennedy administration and, 505–508
  Lyndon Johnson administration and, 512–513
Vietnam, Democratic Republic of formation of, 463
"Vietnamization" program, 533–538
Vietnam War, 521–524
  election of 1968 and, 524–529

under Ford, 555–556
under Nixon, 533–538, 539–542
See also Antiwar protests
Vikings, 11
Villa, Francisco "Pancho," 342
Virginia
    African slave trade and, 32–33
    Bacon's rebellion in, 41
    British colonization of, 30–31
Virginia House of Burgesses, 50–51
Virginia Plan, 104, 105–108
Volstead Act, 376–377
Volunteers in Service to America
    (VISTA), 512
Voting Rights Act of 1965, 515
Voyages of exploration, map of,
    22–23

Wade-Davis Bill, 226
Wainwright, General Jonathan, 453
Walden (Thoreau), 140–141, 168
Wallace, George C., 517
    in election of 1968, 525, 527–528
    in election of 1972, 548
    racism of, 501
Wallace, Henry A., 409, 454, 466, 487
    in election of 1940, 430
    in election of 1948, 468
Wall Street, 267–269, 582
War of 1812, 132–133, 165–168, 174,
    186
War of Independence, 78–101
    aftermath of, 94–101
    American victories in, 87–92
    beginning of, 68–77
    early British victories in, 79–85
    French support for, 85–87
    Treaty of Paris ending, 92–94
    See also American Revolution
War Industries Board, 352, 355
Warren, Earl, 491, 546
Warren Commission, 509–510
Warsaw Pact, 467
Wars of the Roses, 2
Washington, Booker T., 279–282, 362,
    363
Washington, D.C.
    British 1812 march on, 132
    compromise on site of, 118

Washington, George
    at Constitutional Convention,
        78–79, 104–108
    death of, 125
    at end of War of Independence,
        94
    farewell address of, 127–128
    as first president, 111–125
    first presidential acts of, 112–113
    at Fort Duquesne, 48
    in French and Indian War, 47
    on government, 98
    inauguration of, 112
    Jay's Treaty and, 123
    leadership qualities of, 105
    neutrality of, 122
    after ratification of Constitution,
        102–103
    reelection of, 119–120
    at second Continental Congress,
        68–71
    turnpikes approved by, 174
    during War of Independence,
        80–84, 88
    during Whiskey Rebellion,
        118–119, 120
    at Yorktown, 90–91
Watergate scandal, 532–533, 549–553
    origins of, 538
"Watermelon Army," 118–119
Water Quality Improvement Act of
    1970, 544
Watling Island, Columbus's landing
    on, 14
Watson, Thomas E., in election of
    1896, 301
Watts, racial rioting in, 515–517
Wealth
    American pursuit of, 159–160,
        265–270
    of American upper classes,
        313–325
Weaver, General James B., in election
    of 1892, 296–297
Webster, Daniel, 134, 136, 138–139,
    142, 153, 156–157, 187
Welfare bureaucracy, 544–545
Westward expansion, 166–167,
    168–181
    annexation of Texas in, 144–145

beginnings of, 97–99
Mexican War as, 147–149
politics of, 134–135, 138–139
Whaling industry, 43–44
Whig Party, 136, 143–144
    in 1840 presidential election, 145
    in election of 1852, 187
    in election of 1856, 192
    in election of 1860, 199
    formation of, 137
    Zachary Taylor in, 153
"Whip Inflation Now" (WIN)
    program, 554
Whiskey Rebellion, 118–119, 120
White, William Allen, 430, 431
Whitman, Walt, 141, 147
Whitney, Eli, 159, 161–162
Wilderness, Battle of, 224
Wild West, 258–261
William and Mary, 41–42, 45
William III, King, 46
Willkie, Wendell, 432
    in election of 1940, 430
Wilmot Proviso, 150–151, 153
Wilson, Woodrow, 278, 375–376
    death of, 360
    disabling stroke of, 358
    on entering America into World
        War I, 346–348
    first presidential election of, 335,
        337–338
    at Paris Peace Conference,
        356–357
    as Progressive, 325
    second presidential election of,
        344–345, 346
    as twenty-eighth president,
        338–360
"Wobblies," 290
Wolfe, General James, 48, 49
Woman's Peace Party, 355
Women
    in Alliance Movement, 295
    Constitutional Convention and,
        106–107
    housework and, 366–367
    peacetime factory work by, 368
    suffrage right of, 178–179, 355,
        372–374
    in textile industry, 169

as underpaid labor, 325
wartime factory work by, 354,
    440–441
Women's Christian Temperance
    Union (WCTU), 373
Woodville, Richard Caton, 148, 152
Woodward, Robert, 550
Woolley, John, in election of 1900,
    314
Works Progress Administration
    (WPA), 412–413
World Transformed, A (Bush), 593
World War I, 336–363
    before American entry into,
        342–346
    American entry into, 346–352,
        352–356, 356–359
    American isolationism following,
        359–361
    events leading up to, 336–342
    initiation of, 342, 343
    map of progress of, 350–351
    race riots following, 361–363
World War II, 422–461
    American entrance into, 436–439
    American isolationism before,
        423–428
    Cold War as aftermath of,
        463–468, 468–472

XYZ Affair, 128–129

Yalta, Allied conference at, 449–452
Yamamoto, Isoroku, 441–444
Yellow fever, 319, 321
Yellow journalism, Spanish-American
    War and, 305–307
Yeltsin, Boris, 594–595, 601–602
Yom Kippur War, 546–547
Yorktown, Virginia, surrender of
    Cornwallis at, 88, 89–92
Young, Brigham, 151
Youth International Party, 528
Yuppies, 583–584

Zhou Enlai, 539
Zimmerman note, 345–346